The Licence Raj
An Economic Comedy of Errors

Amar Maini

Copyright © 2020 Amar Maini

All rights reserved.

ISBN: 978-0-646-81789-7

Cover Image: Prime Minister Nehru with his grandsons, Rajiv and Sanjay, being shown an "improved brick" at Khanpur village near Delhi, October 1958. Courtesy of Public.Resource.Org

VIKSITH

LONDON NEW DELHI CANBERRA

The Licence Raj

CONTENTS

	Introduction	1
1	A Better and Saner Order	11
2	A Scientific Approach	77
3	A Socialistic Picture of Society	123
4	Tillers of the Soil	178
5	The Big Push	241
6	The Right to Live, the Right to Progress	318
7	Actually Existing Socialism	373
8	Indian Exports	442
9	The Bombay Club	486
10	The World Has Changed	541
	Afterword	603
	Notes	612
	Index	638

Introduction

On 6 July 1991 the Reserve Bank of India was given the task of transporting 47 tonnes of gold to the Bank of England. Commercial airlines had excused themselves from the operation due to its excessive risk, which meant that Heavy Lifting Cargo Airlines had to be chartered to take the load to England in four stages. A high security convoy was first needed to transport the gold from the Reserve Bank's vaults in south Bombay to Sahar Airport in the north of the city however, and the length of the journey and the need to involve Indian Customs meant that the operation did not remain secret for long. Details of the gold lift, including a large picture of the plane being loaded with the precious metal, promptly made their way onto the pages of *The Indian Express*.

Indian gold had to be transported to the British reserve bank as the Government of India no longer had the funds to pay for imports of essential items such as oil and fertilisers and faced the serious prospect of defaulting on short term commercial loans. The Bank of England required India's gold in its vaults if it was to advance the government $400 million in order to meet its short term financial obligations and avoid the fate of Mexico which had defaulted on its international debts in 1982. India had in fact been sending its gold abroad as security for cash advances since May. Without a stable government in New Delhi able to present a budget or take economic policy decisions it was simply not possible to raise money, needed urgently, in the usual way.

Whilst the humiliation of pledging gold to pay short term debts was felt by the Indian people throughout the country, the pledging of India's foreign policy in January had caused just as much pain for the elite of Lutyens' Delhi. Along with its commitment to a planned economy, the state had, since Independence, followed a policy of non-alignment with the world's principal powers, the United States and the Soviet Union. Whether in Hungary and Berlin during Jawaharlal Nehru's time, or Vietnam and Afghanistan during Indira Gandhi's tenure, India had always managed to resist American demands to support its cause and denounce its enemies. The ability to maintain an independent foreign policy, often in times of economic, political, and military difficulty had provided India's ruling class with an enduring sense of satisfaction. India would always maintain a studied neutrality, and even its ambiguity, or silence on raging international controversies would irritate the Americans. Yet economic and military aid had flowed with only minor interruptions for 40 years.

When Prime Minister Chandra Shekhar's minority government approached the International Monetary Fund for an emergency loan in January 1991 however, the United States, the chief shareholder in the Fund, decided to drive a harder bargain. In exchange for a loan, the Americans managed to gain landing and refuelling rights at Indian airports for their military aircraft flying from the Philippines to Saudi Arabia for deployment in Iraq. This operation had also been difficult to keep secret; it took just two weeks of landing and refuelling for *The Times of India* to break the story on 28 January. To further the indignity, the Prime Minister of India had to publicly support the American war effort in Iraq.

India's wounded pride and eroded sovereignty were the result of an economic crisis which had arrived at a time of political chaos. A once stable and powerful Congress government had fallen in October 1989; Prime Minister Rajiv Gandhi had to relinquish power to a loose coalition of smaller parties led by his former Finance Minister, Vishwanath Pratap Singh. International Monetary Fund representatives had warned Rajiv earlier in the year of the imminent economic catastrophe of falling foreign exchange reserves and rising short-term debt, and the advice was repeated to the new prime minister, but it had little effect. When V.P. Singh's Finance Minister, Madhu Dandavate presented the Union Budget in March 1990 he added to a fiscal deficit, which was double the amount that had previously been known, by waiving loans to farmers. The prime minister then decided to implement the recommendations of the Mandal Commission which had devised reservations for "Other Backward Classes" in central government institutions, setting off caste violence across northern India and weakening parliamentary support for his already fragile government.

Iraq's invasion of Kuwait in August thus made a bad situation worse. The price of oil rose, Indian exports to the conflict zone ceased, and Indian workers could no longer send money home. International ratings agencies downgraded India's credit rating citing the deteriorating political situation. Indians around the world were just as concerned as ratings agencies and started withdrawing their deposits from Indian banks. The price of borrowing for the Government of India in international financial markets began to rise, and much of the short and medium term debt it had been using to finance its spending over previous years was coming up for repayment.

V.P. Singh's National Front government fell in November 1990, and Rajiv Gandhi used his block of Congress members of parliament to prop up another weak coalition government, this time led by Chandra Shekhar, formerly of the National Front. The new prime minister began to address the economic predicament during the winter, but in the spring of 1991 Rajiv did not allow his government to present a Budget, which might have started the process of stabilising the economy, and shortly thereafter withdrew support, prompting an election in May. The disorder peaked when Rajiv, likely the next Prime Minister of India, was assassinated on the campaign trail in Tamil Nadu. Election results were delayed slightly, but the Congress, after 18 months out of power, returned to government on a wave of sympathy. P.V. Narasimha Rao, a former Chief Minister of Andhra Pradesh and Union Cabinet veteran emerged as a consensus candidate as prime minister. Brought back from the verge of retirement, the old Congressman addressed the nation on 22 June: "There is no time to lose. The government and the country cannot keep living beyond their means and there are no soft options left." He added that his government would work to remove the "cobwebs that come in the way of rapid industrialisation."

P.V. Narasimha Rao's use of the word "cobwebs" carried latent irony. India's first Prime Minister, Jawaharlal Nehru had never intended to create a cobwebbed economy. He was an arch moderniser and socialist, and part of his commitment to socialism came from his judgement that it was the way of the future, just as capitalism was a relic of the past. As his stature grew in the early 1950s and he came to exercise greater control over both his parliamentary party and the Congress organisation, he used India's Second Five Year Plan to fulfil the vision of a modern Indian economy he had nurtured since the late 1920s. He even had the Planning Commission delegate the task of formulating the Second Plan to an old associate from Calcutta, the physicist turned statistician, Prasanta Mahalanobis. Many of the world's finest socialist economists descended on Calcutta and New Delhi in 1954 and 1955 to assist in the enterprise, working on computers which Mahalanobis had collected on his trips abroad. Nehru, Mahalanobis and the visiting economists sought to turn India into a self-reliant industrial economy, ideally within 10 years.

The path to self-reliance was clear: rather than perpetually importing industrial goods and components, they would instead be made in India. Steel mills would be built, factories would be erected to make machine tools, plants would manufacture chemicals and fertilisers, and in keeping with socialist ideals, most of these new industrial units would be owned and operated by big public sector enterprises. Once India had built the capacity to make all the necessities of modern industry within the country it would no longer need to spend foreign exchange on purchasing them abroad and be subject to the vagaries of international trade. The wealth of this modern, technologically adept economy would then be distributed according to a "socialistic pattern of society".

Jawaharlal Nehru had chosen Prasanta Mahalanobis to modernise the Indian economy, yet he was never short of self-appointed advisers. The foreign experts in New Delhi and the districts of India in the 1950s were no longer old British district collectors, officers of the Indian Civil Service, amateur linguists and anthropologists deeply interested in land tenure, Hindu customs, peasant life in Bengal and Punjab, and the workings of the Government of India Act. The British had returned home, both from India and the world, and the task of creating a better tomorrow had been taken up by the Americans. India enthused Americans just as it had British liberals a century earlier. The country was a big, well-armed democracy, and its English speaking political class maintained a deep commitment to Western political institutions even as it began to deal with the daunting challenges of economic development. The United States' principal antagonist in Asia was China, ever on the rampage, supporting Communist insurrections across the continent. The Americans thus saw in India the prospect of another great Asian power which might contain its Cold War opponent and provide an example of democratic development for fragile, newly liberated countries across the world.

Americans arrived in India with bright ideas on the best way to face up to those daunting economic challenges. They had strategies to control the growth of the population, reform land tenure, develop village communities, liberalise the economy, build steel plants, and grow more food. They even knew the best exchange rate for the rupee. Some came as the representatives of American generosity, the Rockefeller Foundation and the Ford Foundation, others came as intellectuals from America's elite universities, some came as emissaries of the State Department or the President himself, whilst others fled from political opponents at home. India in the 1950s was thus a magnet for hundreds of American experts of the sort that Graham Greene wrote about in his 1955 novel *The Quiet American*.

India proved just as frustrating for its resident Quiet Americans as Vietnam did for Alden Pyle in Greene's novel. Young Pyle, an intelligence agent stationed in Vietnam, watched the violent decline of French power and the further descent of the former colony into civil war. He had been influenced by the writing of York Harding, a political scientist who argued that what new nations like Vietnam needed was a "Third Force" which could bind its people together. After some time in the country Pyle thought that General Thế might represent the "Third Force" he was looking for. He began to take sides in the internecine violence, including supporting a car bombing, but in the end his own demise came from his involvement in a love triangle rather than Vietnamese politics.

For the Quiet Americans in India their end was never quite so dramatic, or conclusive. Their ideas often came unstuck when they encountered the realities of Indian life, but the process usually occurred in slow motion, and many years might have passed before anyone realised. Often they were not listened to, and when they were it was because a crisis had erupted, by which time it was too late. The Americans stayed on in India into the 1960s and beyond having abandoned the instinctive optimism which they held when they arrived. They began to mask their inherent dislike of India's politicians and bureaucrats and their frustrations over India's ramshackle economy and its maddening neutrality. India, after all, was too big to fail, and too big to leave to the Russians.

The Americans were not the only ones frustrated with the Indian development project. By the early 1960s Jawaharlal Nehru and his economic planners faced opposition from both within and outside the Congress Party. Chakravarti Rajagopalachari, a long time Congressman, 'lieutenant' of Mohandas Gandhi, Premier of Madras and Governor-General of India, quit the Party and began to rail against Nehru's socialism on the pages of his journal *Swarajya*. When Nehru sought to establish a system of co-operative farming across the country in 1959 Rajagopalachari and Minocher Masani, a onetime Congress socialist, called on Indians to protect their farms and their freedoms and formed the conservative Swatantra Party. Ironically, the socialists within the Congress were equally unhappy with their prime minister's planned economy and felt the need to create a separate forum within the Party to guide the government towards a more authentic socialism. Indian conservatives and socialists were thus in agreement that the greatest impediment to economic progress was Nehruvian socialism. At the same time the Americans were paying many of India's bills for the import of machinery and sending regular shipments of wheat to Indian ports to avert a major food crisis. Thus, when, after almost 17 years in office, India's first prime minister died in May 1964 and a new prime minister took over, it seemed that change was in the air.

Lal Bahadur Shastri had served Jawaharlal Nehru as railways minister and commerce minister, yet he never shared his boss's ideological commitments. He was a homespun Congressman from Uttar Pradesh and his first order of business on becoming prime minister was to reduce the power of the Planning Commission, empower the states' National Development Council and re-orient India's planning effort towards agricultural development. But then, in January 1966, India's second prime minister died of a heart attack in Tashkent, the day after signing a peace treaty which ended a war with Pakistan. Jawaharlal Nehru's daughter Indira, the serving information and broadcasting minister was then elected by Congress parliamentarians as prime minister.

Amidst this political tumult an idea had been circulating within the American Embassy and US AID in New Delhi, and the State Department and World Bank in Washington, for the launch of a "Big Push" on the Indian government to begin a far reaching liberalisation of the economy. Things seemed to be going according to plan when Indira Gandhi visited Washington in March 1966. She said everything that the Americans wanted to hear, and then, conceding to a long standing American demand, devalued the rupee in June. Funds started to flow to assist the liberalisation project, yet by the end of the year the initiative waned as the Americans could not interest other Western donors in the transformation of the Indian economy and were not willing to pay the entire bill themselves. In addition, the Congress suffered serious reverses in national and state elections early in 1967. Indira was leading a Congress which seemed to be in terminal decline, was under attack both from the men who supported her ascent to the prime minister's office, a generally conservative group of Party bosses known as "The Syndicate", and the restless socialists at the fringe of the Party known as the "Young Turks". When the fragile balance broke in the summer of 1969 and Indira went to war with the Party bosses she turned the conflict into an ideological one, became a champion of socialism, split the Party and began to tighten rather than loosen control over the economy. Indian socialism, rather than the quick death that the Americans were hoping for, enjoyed a strange new afterlife.

Indira Gandhi's socialist revival did not last long however. By 1974 students were taking to the streets in cities across the country protesting against hunger and unemployment. They were not motivated by ideology, they were protesting against a system which did not allow them to live their lives in accordance with their modest aspirations. Yet the politicians who took control of their movement did share one specific ideological commitment. They were not just political dissidents, generally former Congressmen, unionists, farmers, ultra socialists and Hindu nationalists, but also principled critics of the economy which Jawaharlal Nehru and Indira Gandhi had built. Their model of big public sector industries and state control of economic life seemed to have betrayed the ideals of Mohandas Gandhi, who envisaged just the opposite; Indians unmolested by the state, largely left to rule themselves, self-sufficient in their villages, working in cottage industries to fulfil their basic needs and spinning khadi in their spare time. What is more, the majority which lived on the land had been neglected, and the sequence of development badly muddled. The government in New Delhi had tried to create an industrial economy before it could even feed its people.

Indira Gandhi imposed a national Emergency in 1975, jailed her political opponents and made the trains run on time, but when her foes defeated her at elections in 1977 and formed a Janata government in New Delhi, they set about making things right. A farmers' leader from western Uttar Pradesh, Charan Singh, long a critic of the Nehruvian economic model, became finance minister in 1979, and true to his word delivered a Budget for the majority which worked the land. The government began to subsidise all manner of agricultural expenses, making the enterprise of farming small and medium sized plots across the country increasingly dependent on government largesse. The Janata government did not last much longer than Charan Singh's Budget, and when Indira came back to power in 1980 and had to deal with one of the government's customary foreign exchange crises, she decided to take a new approach. The government would not curb imports and bring the economy to a halt, but keep it going by other means. Indira's last government would ensure the flow of imports and invest in infrastructure by borrowing, not only from the World Bank and friendly governments, but from commercial banks in international financial markets.

When a debt crisis broke out and Indian gold had to be flown from Bombay to London in July 1991 the flight was symbolic not just of wounded national pride. It was the end of a dream. *The Licence Raj* traces this century long dream of an Indian economic renewal through the writings of the first students of Elphinstone College in 1841, the birth of the swadeshi movement in late 19th century Bengal, Dadabhai Naoroji's publication of *Poverty and Un-British Rule in India* in 1902, Mohandas Gandhi's discovery of the spinning wheel in London in 1908, Jawaharlal Nehru's first glimpse of Soviet Russia in 1927 and Jayaprakash Narayan's attempt to answer the question *Why Socialism?* in 1936. All of India's seminal economic thinkers wanted to rebuild the Indian economy out of the rubble left by long years of British neglect and all agreed that the endeavour could not simply be left to the market forces which had failed the country for so long. India's economy did not suffer from a want of thought, or writing, or, in the end, money; unlike many dreams which remain unfulfilled, India's rulers were able, after Independence, to create the economy they had always wished for.

ONE

A Better and Saner Order

The first Indians to think systematically about the economic effects of British rule were students of Elphinstone College, Bombay. The college was named in honour of Mountstuart Elphinstone, a civil servant and diplomat of the British East India Company who had arrived in India in 1796. He spent most of the following two decades as a resident, or emissary to the courts of Indian rulers in northern and western India, and by 1817, despite not being a military man, found himself in command of the victorious British forces at Khadki, near Pune, effectively ending Maratha rule across India. Elphinstone became Commissioner of the Deccan, then in 1819 Lieutenant-Governor of Bombay, and during the 1820s laid the foundation for a system of English education in the newly consolidated Bombay Presidency. Whilst the town of Bombay had been under British control for 150 years, the countryside now came under British sway, and it was from small towns and villages that students came to study, and think about the dramatic changes which they could see occurring around them.

The influence of Elphinstone College over Indian economic thinking continued throughout the 19th century. Those first, mainly anonymous students of the college described a "drain" of wealth and resources which had occurred as the British tightened their grip on the region. This idea was developed by one of the earliest stars of the college, a poor but bright and determined boy named Dadabhai Naoroji. Dadabhai spread the news of Britain draining India's wealth as far and wide as he could in both India and England, decade after decade as the century wore on. He was joined by another product of Elphinstone, Mahadev Ranade, who initially subscribed to the drain of wealth concept, but gradually began to distance himself from it, preferring to sketch out a theoretical map for a future political economy of India. He lamented the "rustication", or ruralisation of India under British rule and encouraged early attempts to industrialise the Bombay Presidency.

Both these ideas, the drain of wealth, and the rustication of India found a chronicler in Romesh Dutt. He was amongst the first Indians to rank high enough in the Indian Civil Service examination in London to claim a place in the hallowed Service which governed the subcontinent. Unlike some of his Indian colleagues he managed not only to survive, but excel in the Service in the last decades of the 19th century. However, after serving the time required for a full pension he resigned to pursue his interests in literature, economics and politics, and in 1902 completed *The Economic History of British India*. Dutt's work appeared in the same year as Dadabhai's *Poverty and Un-British Rule in India*, and both works went on to influence the nationalists who would eventually see the country to Independence. In the years after the publication of his *Economic History* Romesh Dutt, like Mahadev Ranade, supported efforts to revive Indian industry, becoming an early patron of the swadeshi movement.

If India was being drained of its wealth by predatory British trade policies, its manufacturers destroyed, and once thriving urban centres turned into tattered villages, then the solution might lie in building Indian businesses which would compete with British firms in serving the Indian market, and perhaps even markets abroad. Much of the early theorising of the swadeshi movement came from Bombay, but the most sustained effort to rebuild Indian industry was found in and around the capital, Calcutta. The swadeshi movement as it developed in Bengal in the late 19th century sought to create Indian businesses which would make everything from saris, to medicines, big ships, cigarettes, pig iron, pottery and pencils. The idea, and the word "swadeshi" was so powerful that, for a time, the attempt to boycott British goods in political demonstrations against the partition of Bengal in 1904 came to be known as the "swadeshi movement". Yet, the movement both pre-dated these protests, and continued to live on after they had died down, partially because it accommodated another equally appealing idea for India's economic future.

Rather than building modern industries to compete with the British, some early advocates of the swadeshi ideal saw in industrialism the seeds of India's destruction. Instead they wanted to turn away from large scale production like that found in cotton mills, and encourage traditional village techniques like hand spinning. When they put their ideas to the Anglicised elite of the Congress in the years before the First World War they were laughed off the stage. Yet, when an Indian political mystic long resident in South Africa returned home during the war and began to exercise greater influence over the Congress, and project the spinning wheel as the economic salvation of India, the barristers could no longer laugh at the idea, in public. During the 1920s and 1930s Mohandas Gandhi took the old swadeshi idea, in its revivalist form, and sought to make khadi, or cotton spun on a wheel, into both a symbol of Indian nationalism and a practical programme for India's economic revival. This interpretation of swadeshi; the Indian villager spinning their own cloth in their village, and possibly tinkering with simple tools to manufacture the necessities of life, self-sufficient and self-employed, became a foundational idea of the modern Indian nation for a significant section of the Congress Party.

By the 1930s, another, younger group within the Congress was attracted to a starkly different, and quite foreign ideal. The rising stars of the Party, Jawaharlal Nehru and Subhas Bose, knew that the Congress presidency was largely a ceremonial post, yet they used their presidential speeches to express their admiration for the rising tide of socialism around the world and, tentatively, suggest that the Congress commit itself to socialism and so begin the work of preparing a new economic order for an independent India. Yet even before Nehru and Bose were using the Congress presidency to call for a socialist India, a group of young socialists at the fringe of the Party had created their own 'ginger group', the Congress Socialist Party. These socialists had joined the Congress and accepted its essential role in the struggle against British rule, but also saw the Party for what it was. Young men like Minocher Masani and Jayaprakash Narayan nurtured dreams of turning the bourgeoise gathering into a truly revolutionary organisation, one driven by the new urban working class and the old and boundless peasantry. Less encumbered by high political posts, and the necessities of compromise and conciliation, these ideologues attempted to transform Nehru and Bose's rhetoric into a socialist charter for a free India.

***

The first mention of a 'tribute' which India was paying to England under the rule of the British East India Company came from Ram Mohun Roy in his testimony before a select committee of the House of Lords in 1830. He told the Lords that, by the calculations of English missionaries and the Company's own civil servants, the tribute withdrawn from India between 1765 and 1820 totalled £110 million.[i] The idea of an economic 'drain' of wealth was more forcefully developed in India however, by a small group of Marathi intellectuals. The three who led the way were Bhaskar Tarkhadkar, Ramkrishna Vishwanath, and Govind Kunte, who went by the name Bhau Mahajan. Each was a student of Bal Gangadhar Shastri Jambhakar, the first product of English education in the Bombay Presidency, a relatively moderate social reformer who had started *The Bombay Durpun* newspaper in the 1830s. In the natural order of things, the students were more radical than their teacher, and in the 1840s began to develop a strident critique of both the economic effects of British rule, and the Hindu caste system.

Whilst *The Bombay Durpun* closed down in 1840, the young radicals received an unexpected chance to express their views the following year when the British editor of *The Bombay Gazette* invited readers to come forward with their grievances against the Company's government. Bhaskar Tarkhadkar wrote eight long letters under the pen name "A Hindoo", systematically picking apart the moral and material bases of British rule. He attacked the idea that British rule was based on divine providence, that Britain had a civilising mission in India, criticised Britain's policy of 'divide and rule' in its dealings with Indian princes, questioned its commitment to the rule of law, its education policy, as well as its claims of neutrality between the religions. The British Government, the British Parliament, the Company's Court of Directors, and the Board of Control were all condemned for their callous and cruel actions and policies. Yet the main object of Tarkhadkar's letters was "to show how rigorous the present policy of the British has been in operation in regard to draining India of its wealth and reducing it to poverty".[ii] He and his fellow writers presented the Indian view of the British exploitation of India for the 19th century; heavy taxation of the land, the ruin of traditional Indian industries, the transfer of wealth from India to Britain, the lack of employment of Indians in the higher levels of government, and the needlessly expensive nature of the British administration.

A fellow writer who went by the name 'A Philanthropy' gave a personal account of "the once flourishing inhabitants of the Deccan and Konkan".[iii] They had been reduced to their miserable state due to the destruction of local industry by British imports; "almost all the necessaries and luxuries of life entirely superseding these produced in the country." The weavers of the Konkan had been "reduced to the last ebb of penury, owing to there being no employment left to them for acquiring means of livelihood except cultivation and tillage." A Philanthropy ended his account by bringing together both elements of his generation's critique of the prevailing social and economic order; "It is the priest craft of the Brahmins that have so far lowered the national character of the Hindoos as to be easily governed and even tyrannised over by a handful of foreigners which is greatly to be lamented, but it is the political craft of the later that has now empoverished them, which is still more to be lamented."

Students of Elphinstone College in 1841 nurtured a living, vivid memory of their country prior to British rule. 'A Fairheart' wrote: "...but within so short a period the change in the British policy has wrought in India is wonderfully great...a country very lately glittering in all the splendour of richness and variety would within a few years be reduced to the extremity of poverty, that is be hurled down from the highest pinnacle of affluence to the lowest grade of indigence."[iv] A Fairheart's estimate was around ten times higher than Ram Mohun Roy's: he contended that between the Battle of Plassey in 1757 and the Battle of Waterloo in 1815, the British East India Company's boards had transferred £1 billion from India into English banks.

Bhaskar Tarkhadkar developed the drain theory, addressing the British rulers directly in his letters.[v] He accused them of taking millions of rupees away from India as shareholders of the East India Company, and as civil servants, traders and soldiers. The British were sending India's raw materials to England for manufacture, only to be brought back for sale at a premium; if cotton were manufactured into cloth in India it would be much cheaper, and the country would be relieved from its poverty. In addition, Indian cloth had been subjected to a high duty, whilst English cloth circulated through India duty-free. Tarkhadkar thought that the oft repeated claim that Britain had brought peace and tranquillity to India was a hollow one given that the land had been impoverished in just a couple of generations and Indians now had to live with the worry of how to make ends meet. Towards the end of his letters he worked himself into a state of excitement; "Oh! Unhappy fate, India has been got hold of by a race of demons who would never be satisfied until they have despoiled her of all her precious things and reduced her sons and daughters to total beggary." The publication of the young Indians' letters led to an uproar within the British community of Bombay. The *Gazette's* editor was forced to resign.

In October 1841 Bhau Mahajan started his own Marathi newspaper, *Prabhakar*, and in May 1843 published Ramkrishna Vishwanath's Marathi book through his Prabhakar Press, the title of which translates as *Thoughts on India's Past, It's Present Condition and Their Impact on the Future*. The duo continued the critique of both British rule and Hindu obscurantism. Mahajan's columns in *Prabhakar* advanced the idea that British economic policy in India was crowding out local investment; the Company was issuing bonds at high interest rates to finance its wars of expansion, which encouraged wealthy residents to invest their money with the government rather than lend to local business people.[vi] He predicted that if the Crown took over the administration of India from the Company, it would also inherit its debts and inevitably recover them from the Indian people. Mahajan also published accounts of the British royal family's displays of wealth, including the naming ceremony of Edward VII, future Emperor of India, which were only possible due to the wealth it had drained out of the country. He also wrote stinging criticisms of Marwari money lenders, and graphic eyewitness accounts of peasants and labourers suffering under the rule of the landlords of rural Bombay.

Ramkrishna Vishwanath's book, *Thoughts on India's Past* is a history of India over an 800 year period, starting from the invasion of Mahmud of Ghazni in the early 11th century, up to the year of writing and publication, 1843.

Vishwanath presaged some strands of Marxist historiography in arguing that Mahmud's invasions of India were driven by economic rather than religious motives, yet the lasting value of his book lies in its exploration of India's situation of great poverty, despite its abundant natural and human resources. He argued that "labour is wealth", gave accounts of the sites of mineral deposits in western India, and even tried to visit them. His principal source was the reports of the Bombay Chamber of Commerce, and his criticism largely followed the, even by 1843, standard argument that India's raw materials, particularly its cotton, were being exported to Britain to be manufactured and then imported back at a higher price.

Vishwanath's solution to India's economic problem was simple. India needed to employ the economic tactics which had made Britain great. There were obvious obstacles in the way of such a path; the country lacked both capital and technical knowledge, and the caste system restricted the mobility of labour. Yet the economy did have certain endowments which could make it possible, and industrialisation would begin to transform Hindu society; workers would need to earn wages, they would spend less time on fasts and festivals, and the Brahmins were already losing their influence with economic change. India was a huge market, which meant that modern cotton mills could be established, and given that real wages were much lower than in Britain and other industrialising countries, Indian manufacturers could potentially produce highly competitive exports. The price of cloth would fall for Indian consumers, and India would once again earn foreign exchange from its exports. In Vishwanath's vision capital would be raised through joint stock companies, and backward and forward linkages through the supply chain would create an ever expanding circle of modernity and prosperity.

***

Not long before Bal Gangadhar Shastri Jambhakar's older students were writing their criticisms of Britain's economic policies in *The Bombay Gazette*, the Elphinstone professor had spotted a poor Parsi boy, Dadabhai Naoroji at the school of the Native Education Society and selected him for studies at the college. The professor's choice was an inspired one. As a student Dadabhai was so brilliant that his teachers dubbed him "The Promise of India" and soon after graduating he returned as a professor of mathematics and natural philosophy. But rather than pursue a career in academia or go to the Bar, Dadabhai travelled to England and went into business with some fellow Parsis, the Camas, hoping to earn a profit from the export of British goods to India. His more enduring interest was in politics however, and he established the East India Association in London in 1866, bringing together English officials retired from service in India. Together they produced papers on Indian policy matters and sought to build an Indian library and reading room for members of Parliament. Dadabhai also founded the Bombay branch of the Association, and he would sail between London and Bombay, making the case that Englishmen were just and freedom loving by nature and all that was needed was that they be made aware of their illiberal policies in India, and they would recoil from them and usher in a new, more liberal order. By the early 1870s Professor Jambhakar's scholarship boy had become one of the leading public men of India.

During his time in England Dadabhai had been developing his own "drain of wealth" theory and in 1873 tried to read a paper on the subject before Parliament's Select Committee on Indian Finance. He was not yet familiar with the ways of British parliamentary committees however, and having informed the committee chairman Acton Ayrton in advance of the views he would like to express, found that Ayrton took every measure to stop him from doing so. Dadabhai sought out a more sympathetic figure in the committee member Henry Fawcett, but their efforts to have his views placed before the committee and included in the final report were frustrated by the dissolution of Parliament in 1874. Now, in Bombay in 1876, he dusted off the old paper, gave it the title *Poverty of India,* and presented it before the Bombay branch of the East India Association. *Poverty of India* was the culmination of Dadabhai's intellectual work since his school days at Elphinstone 30 years earlier, and its ideas would drive his political advocacy over the ensuing 30 years. This paper, along with his later speeches and excerpts from Royal Commissions and letters between British officials was eventually published as a book in 1902, *Poverty and Un-British Rule in India.*

Dadabhai's first task was to estimate India's total production. He did this by working backwards from the land revenue collection of 1870-71, which totalled £21 million. Given that the government generally took about one-eighth of the gross produce of the land, India's total produce would come to £168 million. Opium revenue, salt revenue and forest revenue could be added to the sum, making £182 million, which could then be rounded up to £200 million to include coal production, alienation of lands and any other production which may not have been counted. Given that the population of British India was around 150 million, per capita production stood at less than 27 shillings. Total production was then raised to £300 million to include manufactures, excise on alcohol, and a margin of error, which took per capita production up to 40 shillings.

Dadabhai then turned to "necessary consumption", or the bare needs of an Indian which would keep him or her in "good health and decency". The Government Medical Inspector of Emigrants at Calcutta had estimated the nutritional requirements for labourers journeying to colonies in the Caribbean, and from these estimates Dadabhai calculated an annual cost of living of ₹62 based on prices at Ahmadabad. This diet included rice, daal, mutton, vegetables, ghee, mustard oil and salt. He also included another lower figure of ₹48 for agricultural labourers in the Bombay Presidency. Clothing and lodging had to be added to nutritional requirements and his estimate of the cost of living for each family member in the rural parts of Bombay came to ₹45. However, he acknowledged that the figure would be much higher in Poona, and would vary across India. Dadabhai then demonstrated, through an algebraic identity, that it cost more to keep Indian adults in jail than to let them eek out an existence in their villages. The problem of the peasants was that there was simply not enough production to provide for the necessities of life.

Dadabhai began to explain how this situation had come about, and it was at this point that he expanded on his "drain of wealth" theory. The issue centred around India's trading relationship with Britain. Specifically, the excess of exports over imports. He surveyed the trading accounts of Britain, the United States and Canada, as well as Australia and noted that each imported more than it exported annually. Each country's exports allowed it to import more and raise its stock of wealth. The difference which arose when exports allowed for higher imports was a kind of profit margin which each country ran on its trading account that varied from 15% to 30%. During the middle part of the 19th century India had exported £1.43 billion worth of goods, but imported only £943 million, essentially running a loss of half a billion pounds which "...England has kept back as its benefit, chiefly arising from the political position it holds over India." Unlike the Western nations, India was losing 15-30% of its wealth as a result of its trade with Britain. When the opium revenue, Company profits, and interest on railway loans were deducted from the trade gap it still left a drain of wealth of about £144 million. Dadabhai thought of this as a form of economic "exhaustion" which had prevented India from building its own economic infrastructure, such as railways, from its own resources.

It might have been expected that the drain would have subsided with the end of Company rule. Yet Dadabhai demonstrated that it had only increased, from £5 million a year in the 1830s, to close to £30 million each year in the 1870s. This cumulative drain of wealth of over £400 million meant that India had not progressed economically during this time; it was in the same position in 1874 as it had been in 1834. Furthermore, British industry had benefitted from the India trade by supplying the manufactured goods needed by the government in India and all the goods demanded by the British in India in order to maintain a Western mode of living. India only exported so much due to the control which the British Raj and its traders exercised over its economy, and if it was allowed to handle its own exports it would derive its own profits. Even if India did not export at all, material wealth would remain within the country.

According to Dadabhai there were two parts to the drain. The first was made up of the savings which British officials in India sent home, the money they spent in England, the salaries and pensions which the British Government paid to its officers there, as well as government expenditure in both England and India. The second part of the drain came from similar remittances by the British in India who were not in government employment. Furthermore, Indians were prevented from forming capital, whilst the money which the British drained in the first place allowed them to bring capital back to India, monopolise trade and industry, and so only deepen the drain.

By the early 1870s British officials were becoming more sensitive to criticisms from India's new middle class. One such criticism was that Britain imposed a "crushing" burden of taxation on the land. In March 1871 Richard Bourke, the Earl of Mayo and Viceroy of India, tried to show that it was not so, that in fact India was relatively lightly taxed. Dadabhai gathered his own statistics on the topic. The difference between the two men's calculations was one between absolute and relative measures. Viceroy Mayo argued that whilst India only paid 1 shilling 10 pennies per head as tax per year, Turkey paid 7 shillings 9 pennies and in Russia the peasants paid 12 shillings and 2 pennies. Dadabhai pointed out that whilst Turkey and Russia had much higher output per capita, India was stuck at 40 shillings a year, which as he had previously shown, was hardly enough to maintain a subsistence. It was out of this meagre amount that the Indian peasant had to pay his 1 shilling and 10 pennies each year. Dadabhai calculated that rich England was paying 8% a year as tax to its government, whilst poor India paid almost double that figure, 15%. In England they paid £2 10 shillings a head. In India annual per capita production barely touched £2. In addition, the taxation imposed by governments of sovereign nations remained within the country, yet so much of the money raised from India by the British was drained away, further impoverishing the land.

Dadabhai went on to argue that India's trade with Britain was not "true free trade", that price rises were not a sign of prosperity but usually the result of a spike in local demand by railway workers, that the import of bullion was not for payment of Indian goods but the necessities of government expenditure, that the British had broken their solemn pledges on the employment of Indians in the upper reaches of the Raj, and as a result of the enormous waste of money on officials in India the British Government, in constantly trying to find means to pay its way, was increasingly starting to resemble the old oriental despots whom it claimed it had liberated India from.

***

Mahadev Ranade was also a product of Elphinstone College and a public man in Bombay, and he would cross intellectual and political paths with Dadabhai Naoroji during the last decades of the 19th century. Ranade was a lawyer and jurist who served the British state in the districts of the Bombay Presidency and became a leader of good causes in Poona, the region's cultural centre. He never fully embraced Dadabhai's drain of wealth theory however; he thought it largely a waste of time to blame the British for India's impoverishment. India's poverty was older than British rule, "an old, a very old inheritance", only more keenly felt because Indians were waking up from their intellectual slumber.[vii] Instead, Ranade wanted to create a specifically Indian approach to economics.

Mahadev Ranade started his lecture, *Indian Political Economy* at the Deccan College, Poona in 1892 with a contradiction; whilst the historical method was the favoured analytical tool of the late 19th century in almost all fields of intellectual endeavour, Indians were being asked to take an ahistorical approach to economics and accept the tenets of the classical school as universal, applicable to all times and all places.[viii] He looked to the more recent thinking of John Stuart Mill, who conceded that economics was intertwined with other social sciences; although the principles of the production of wealth were universal, the principles of distribution ran into very human, specific institutions and dilemmas. John Cairnes even went so far as to state that economic theory was just that, it could not be verified by empirical evidence.

The more reasonable positions of Mill and Cairnes stood in contrast to the ideas of earlier economic thinkers like Adam Smith, David Ricardo, James Mill, John McColluch, and Thomas Malthus who believed that the assumptions which they made about human beings were actually true. These assumptions were tenfold; that economics is individualistic, an individual's strongest motive is self-interest, the pursuit of individual self-interest serves the collective good, self-interest is served by the largest production of output, economic competition between individuals is the best regulator, regulation by the state is a violation of liberty, every individual knows exactly what is in their economic self-interest, when individuals interact in the market they do so on the basis of freedom and equality, labour and capital can move freely to find the best remuneration or return on investment and so profits and wages find an equilibrium, population grows at a faster rate than the supply of food, and demand and supply always find an equilibrium. Ranade stated that these assumptions were "literally true of no existing community".

Ranade argued that whilst the assumptions of classical economics were distant from reality in the West, they were more the exception than the rule in India. An Indian was the absolute opposite of the "economical man"; family and caste were the dominant bases of Indian life, self-interest in the form of the pursuit of wealth, whilst not completely absent, was just one motivation, there was no desire or aptitude for free economic competition, custom and state shaped economic life, status was more influential than the laws of contract, neither capital nor labour were mobile, wages and profits were fixed, population was controlled by disease and famine, and production was static. He thought that there was as much chance of mountains being washed into the sea, valleys filling up, or the sun going cold as there was of Indians conforming to the assumptions of classical economics.

Ranade then narrated the history of economic thought over the previous two centuries, explaining how the intellectual pendulum had swung from the statism of the mercantilist era in the 18th century, to the laissez faire ideal of the 19th century. Laissez faire was a reaction against the excesses of mercantilism, and it then stimulated its own reaction, principally in Europe among French, Italian and German theorists who began to question the assumptions of classical political economy and argue that it was specifically English, and not suited to the Continent where national survival was more important than individual economic freedom. This reaction took its fullest form in the writings of Friedrich List and the scholars of the German historical school.

Ranade sought to draw on the insights of the Germans and apply a relative and historical approach to Indian political economy, rather than a universal and deductive one.

Ranade examined the 'old legacies' of India, which all amounted to traits of backwardness, and declared that it was providence that the country had come under the rule of Britain, which was, economically, its polar opposite. Yet he questioned the prevailing orthodoxy which consigned the 'torrid' regions of the world to the production of agricultural produce, whilst the temperate climes of Europe were deemed the centres of manufacturing. In this system India would only get poorer, whilst Europe would get richer, and so he made a case for India's transformation into an industrial economy; the country had a long history of manufacturing, which should logically happen close to its supply of raw materials, and it would provide a type of national insurance against the vagaries of rainfall and agriculture. Ranade also argued for urbanisation as a means of providing farmers with access to markets and lamented 'rustication', or the ruralisation of India under British rule and advocated large shifts of population both within rural India and from India to Britain's other colonies which required labour. He further argued for doing away with the land tax, for the protection of peasants, and made a plea for state intervention in economic life, particularly the provision of credit to private businesses and the establishment of state enterprises.

A year after his lecture on political economy at the Deccan College, Mahadev Ranade turned from theory to practice in an address to the Industrial Association of Western India.[ix] The purpose of the Association according to Ranade was to halt the rustication of India. Eighty five percent of India's exports were of agricultural goods, whilst 72% of its imports were manufactures. These agricultural exports did not allow for a highly developed deployment of labour and capital and were simply the result of rudimentary agricultural techniques. The battle against the ruralisation of India was an unequal one, like a struggle between a dwarf and a giant, but Ranade implored his audience to fight it nonetheless.

Ranade did note that there had been a welcome change over the previous 20 years; things were not as bad as they were in the early 1870s. Indian cotton mills had begun to appear across the country, there were jute mills and small-scale manufacturing of silk in Bengal. In addition, there were now wool mills, paper mills, tanneries, breweries, soap and sugar factories, flour mills, factories for tobacco curing and bone crushing, iron and brass foundries, oil mills, salt refineries, saw mills and potteries. British capital had been applied to tea, coffee and indigo plantations, and at least in the case of tea, brought commerce and employment where they had not existed before. Indian coal mines, particularly in Bengal, had also begun to increase production. It was a "humble beginning", but a "hopeful" one. The quiet growth of these industries had checked the rustication which Ranade so abhorred. The challenge before India was now to learn from the British, and through "organised co-operation" take in raw materials from abroad, manufacture them in India, and then send them back to export markets at higher prices. Ranade concluded with his vision of India as a rising economic power, taking advantage of its natural resources, stable government and situation as the 'emporium of all of Asia'.

***

Romesh Dutt was an officer of the Indian Civil Service, which, at the time that he joined in 1870, was the greatest post that a young man of his class and education could aspire to. He spent much of his career dealing with drought in rural Bengal, so when he retired from the Service in 1897 and decided to write an economic history of India in the 19th century, he was able to do so with firsthand knowledge of the government policies which

Dadabhai had spent his career denouncing, and the effects of which Mahadev Ranade had lamented in his essays.

The Economic History of British India begins with a familiar narration of Britain's age of expansion on the Indian subcontinent in the early 19th century culminating with its attempts to march on Afghanistan, the annexation of Punjab and Burma, and the acquisition of myriad small kingdoms. In a few instances these acquisitions were a matter of military superiority, in others the betrayal of the Indian princes by their own men, in some the legalese of the Doctrine of Lapse which allowed for the annexation of kingdoms which did not have a rightful heir, and in yet others it was simple debt trap diplomacy. For an officer of the Indian Civil Service, Dutt looked on this expansion of Company rule with a surprising sense of sorrow; it was unjust, for the British were preying on weak opponents rather than those who were their equals in battle, and he even thought that in many cases princely rule was superior to colonial rule. Mysore and Baroda, ruled by maharajas, were, at the time that he was writing, the best governed states in India.

Romesh Dutt then provided a systematic account of the 'rustication' of India which Mahadev Ranade had railed against in his speeches. Like Dadabhai Naoroji, Dutt based his research on British sources, specifically drawing on testimony given to committees and commissions of the British Parliament investigating various aspects of economic policy in India. When the British East India Company's charter was renewed in 1833, many of its trading privileges had been rescinded. The Company was to focus more on governance than trade, something which led it to petition Parliament to remove British duties on Indian imports which had hampered, and in some cases, even ruined industry in India. A Select Committee of Parliament, chaired by the Whig Edward Seymour, the Lord Seymour, was appointed to examine the petition.

It became evident to the Select Committee that Indian imports of both agricultural commodities and finished goods suffered under heavy import duties into Britain. James Melville, who had served as a financial administrator of the East India Company in London provided the detail. The duty on Indian rum was twice that of Caribbean rum, the duty was higher for Indian tobacco than for Caribbean tobacco, whilst the duties on Indian sugar and coffee had been equalised with their Caribbean competitors. Yet even the fact that the rum duty remained high whilst the sugar duty had been equalised militated against the use of Indian sugar in the manufacture of rum. However, the truly outrageous duties were applied to Indian cotton, silk and woollen textiles. British cottons and silks exported to India were levied with a duty of 3.5%, for British woollens the rate was only 2%. Yet India's exports of cottons into Britain were levied with a duty of 10%, Indian silks were hit with a 20% duty and Indian woollens were subject to a 30% duty. These duties had worked and the import of Indian cloth into Britain had all but died out. Between 1813 and 1838 the amount of raw Indian cotton imported into Britain had multiplied by six times. Melville admitted that the destruction of India's manufactures of cloth had made the Indian people dependent on the import of British manufactures of their own raw cotton.

Sir Charles Trevelyan, who had spent much of his career in connection with economic policy in both India and Britain provided the Select Committee with further information on the displacement of Indian cotton textiles. He explained how in the old days a type of "silky cotton" had been grown in Bengal which was used to make fine Dacca muslins. They could no longer be seen. During the first decades of the 19th century the population of Dacca had declined from 150,000 to less than 40,000, and the jungle and malaria were fast encroaching. Once the 'Manchester of India', Dacca had been reduced from a flourishing town into a poor small one; "the distress there has been very great indeed." The story had been repeated at Surat, and Murshidabad and every other place in India which had previously supported the manufacture of cotton into cloth. The manufactures of cotton which remained in India were of the coarse variety, and were shunned by all but the poorest of the poor. Between 1814 and 1835 Indian cloth exports to Britain had fallen to one-quarter of their former level, whilst imports of British cloth into India had multiplied by 50 times.

The decline of India's shipbuilding industry, was, in Dutt's narration, another example of the rustication of India. In 1795 and 1796 six big ships were built in Calcutta, weighing over 400 tonnes, and five more, each with a tonnage of around 500 tonnes were being constructed. For the remaining years of the 18th century several vessels were launched each year from the dockyards of Calcutta. In Bombay the Parsis had founded a dockyard which they managed for three generations. The *Asia* had been built under the management of Naoroji Jamsetjee, and Parsis regularly travelled to England to study the methods of English shipbuilding. Yet ships manned by Indian lascars, or sailors, docking at ports with which Britain had reciprocity treaties were not treated as British ships. Under the Company's Charter of 1833 Indians were deemed British subjects, however the rule did not extend to merchant ships. As a result, by the 1840s the industry had died out.

Despite the high pay of British officials and the regular expenditure on wars, revenue in India had exceeded spending prior to 1837. Revenue then continued to exceed expenditure during the first 21 years of Queen Victoria's reign until her assumption of responsibility for India in 1858. What had changed was that the 'Home Charges', or the debiting of India for expenses on Indian administration incurred in Britain, had started to add to India's debt. Dutt, like all Congressmen of his generation thought that these Home Charges were unjust and should have been borne by Britain, which had gained so much from its conquest of India. If that was the case then India would have started Crown rule in credit, rather than sunk in debt. Between 1837 and 1858 India's debt had more than doubled, from £33 million to £69 million. Successive viceroys had been at war across the sub-continent: George Eden, the Earl of Auckland had gone to war in Afghanistan, Edward Law, the Earl of Ellenborough had annexed Sind, and Henry Hardinge, the Viscount Hardinge and James Broun-Ramsey, the Marquess of Dalhousie had fought wars with the Sikhs in Punjab. The Indian Army had even been deployed in China. Yet the expenses incurred by the Colonial Office in England on all of Britain's other colonies were incurred by Britain itself. India had even been charged for the cost of shipping out British troops to suppress the Mutiny of 1857. India had thus paid for its own conquest, administration, and re-conquest.

Dadabhai Naoroji's advocacy of the drain of wealth had largely been drawn from textual sources; testimony before parliamentary committees, letters between East India Company officials, and statistical appendices in government fiscal records. But Romesh Dutt, as an officer of the Indian Civil Service, had seen wealth draining out of India, year after year as he went about his work in the districts of the Raj. Dutt's drain had its source in the land revenue which was raised from the peasants of southern India, and the landlords of northern India. The actual cultivators of the land would pay the revenue directly, or pay rent to their landlord, by selling too large a proportion of the produce of their fields, keeping an insufficient amount for their own needs. British merchants had their agents stationed all over India ready to buy what the cultivators were, in effect, forced to sell, and the newly built railways were able to rapidly transport this produce to port cities from where it was exported, principally to Britain;

> *India presents a busy scene to the winter globe trotter when these transactions take place in every large town and market; but under the cheering appearance of a brisk grain trade lies concealed the fact that the homes and villages of a cultivating nation are denuded of their food to a fatal extent, in order to meet that annual tribute which England demands from India.*

Dutt then sought to link the drain of wealth to the prevalence of famines; even in times of famine the export of food continued simply to meet the crushing land revenue demand of the Raj. India, in 1876, on the brink of famine, exported the largest quantity of food that it had ever done and even a famine stricken province would try to keep up with the revenue demand by exporting as much as it could.

Whilst Dadabhai Naoroji had criticised the railways primarily because so much expenditure went towards the employment of British workers, for Romesh Dutt the railways had a more pernicious effect: they contributed to famines. Not the very existence of the railways, but the enormous amounts sunk into them by the government at the expense of irrigation. The railways led to losses, which became a burden on the treasury, whereas irrigation secured crops, led to an increase in production, and averted famines during times of drought. Irrigation works had traditionally been a source of revenue for the government which was why India's old Hindu and Muslim rulers had invested wisely in canals in northern India, tanks in Bengal and reservoirs in southern India. Railways did help in transporting food to districts which were short during famine years, but they did not add to the produce of the land.

Romesh Dutt thought that it should be obvious that the government would prefer investments in irrigation rather than railways, but he blamed the British Raj's peculiar preference on the fact that its officers were more familiar with railways which had expanded across Britain during the 19th century. In addition, British manufacturers thought that railways would open up the interiors of India for their goods much quicker than canals. This led to constant demands on the Company, and then the Crown, which was subject to continuous pressure through Parliament to intensify investment in the Indian Railways despite continuous losses. The Government of India stood as a guarantor of a minimum return on railway investment for private investors; anything below the minimum 5% profit would be paid entirely from the government treasury, whilst for any amount above 5% the government would only get half the excess profit. By March of 1902 the British Raj had spent £226 million on railways and only £24 million on irrigation. The results were there for all to see as famine once again stalked the land. Dutt concluded his *Economic History* with a plea for greater representation for Indians in the legislative councils of the Raj, and reform of economic policy to meet India's needs, rather than Britain's.

Romesh Dutt had been president of the Indian National Congress in 1899 and he was later selected to be president of the Industrial Conference held on the sidelines of the Congress sessions at Banaras in 1905 and Surat in 1907. He contributed not only his time, but his own money to the cause and outlined his views on industrialisation in his presidential speeches.[x] Like Mahadev Ranade more than a decade earlier in Poona, Romesh Dutt made it clear that India had to make a break from its past of cottage and household industries and embrace the modern commercial civilisation of companies, mills and 'combined action'. The main obstacles to the growth of Indian industry were government fiscal policy and a lack of capital for investment, but like Ranade, Dutt was gladdened by the development in industry over the previous 30 years. In fact, he thought that in Asia India was only behind Japan in its industrial revival. Yet Dutt's presidency was taking place in the broader context of a resurgent swadeshi movement, and so he came to comment on it. He saw the purpose of the movement as that of fostering Indian industries and encouraging the use of Indian made goods. Whilst Western countries were adopting something like their own swadeshi policies, they were doing so by erecting protective tariffs. That was not an option available to India, and so the swadeshi movement had to be organic to Indian society. Dutt wanted to see it spread to all of India's towns and villages, for it to remain calm rather than hysterical, and to serve as an example of a nation protecting its industries without the need for government duties and tariffs.

***

Both Mahadev Ranade and Romesh Dutt had, at different times, led elite industrial associations which drew on a movement which had been growing since the middle years of the 19th century in Bombay and Bengal. Both provinces nurtured the idea that a solution to India's economic predicament lay in the creation of Indian businesses which might compete with British firms and so free Indians of their dependence on foreign goods. It was in Bengal that the idea gained full expression however, as middle class Bengalis, and even Bengali landlords attempted to build businesses which served the needs of Bengali consumers, employed educated young Bengalis, and restored a sense of possibility to Indian enterprise.

By the 1850s, the age of wealthy Bengali businessmen either collaborating or competing with British industrial interests had passed and the local business community was made up of small merchants and money lenders. Amongst the earliest efforts to revive industry was Kishorilal Mukherji's Shipbur Iron Works which was established in 1867. Yet consciously swadeshi enterprises only began to develop in the 1870s and 1880s. The ideal of swadeshi, literally 'of one's own country', made demands on both Indian producers and consumers; Indians with access to capital should use it to start businesses even if there were no reasonable prospects of profits in the short term, and Indian consumers should purchase goods and services from these local businesses even if they were more expensive and of lower quality than their foreign competitors.

The Tagores of Jorasankho, who would influence so much of modern Bengali culture, were landlords to begin with. Yet motivated by a spirit of patriotism several members of the clan became involved in swadeshi ventures. Dwijendranath and Gajendranath had helped Nabagopal Mitra start the Hindu Mela, an exhibition of Indian made goods, in 1867. In the mid 1870s Jyotirindranath and Rajnarayan Bose started the Sanjibani Sabha, a secret society, with a teenage Rabindranath, and tried to set up a match workshop and a weaving unit. The matches did not work and the unit produced only one towel. Undeterred, Jyotirindranath tried jute trading at Hatkhola and growing indigo at Shilaidaha. He then launched a bigger venture, the Inland River Steam Navigation Service in 1884. Inland started with high hopes but was ruined by a fierce price war with its more capital endowed British competitor, the Flotilla Company. There was an accident near Howrah Bridge which led to Inland's ruin, and a fellow Bengali, acting as an agent for the Flotilla Company, ended up buying the swadeshi steamer's assets.

Young members of the Hindu reformist Brahmo Samaj were also interested in starting businesses, as were members of the nationalist Indian Association. Anandamohan Bose bought a tea plantation in Tezpur on the banks of the Brahmaputra river in the very eastern part of the Bengal Presidency and even tried to set up a bank with some help from his father-in-law in the 1880s. In 1887 he, along with fellow Indian Association founder

Surendranath Banerjea, became an honorary member of the Bengal Chamber of Commerce.

Pramathanath Bose, Romesh Dutt's son-in-law, published a pamphlet in 1886 pleading for proper scientific education to be included in the university curriculum, and the establishment of a science and technological institute and a society for the development of Indian industries, all of which were needed for the growth of "science industries", or modern manufacturing.[xi] He did set up the Indian Industrial Association five years later, and, as a pioneering geologist and palaeontologist, gave lectures on the coal industry. His fellow Association members experimented with making modern chemicals from the raw materials readily available on their own lands. The Association was largely elitist in its orientation however, and its activities, including its exhibitions of swadeshi products were eventually consumed by the Indian Industrial Conference, which in turn became a feature of the annual Congress sessions.

Ramakanta Roy had travelled to Japan and on his return to Calcutta suggested the formation of a society for scientific education in India, after which the Association for the Advancement of Scientific Education of India was established by Jogendrachandra Ghosh in 1904. The newer Association was a much more popular one; it raised funds through mass collections and donations which provided scholarships for students to train abroad in scientific disciplines, equipped Calcutta schools with science labs, and provided seed capital to entrepreneurs. Committees reached into the districts of Bengal, whilst British officials and Bengali barristers provided support in Calcutta. In its first four years the Association sent over 200 students abroad for technical education, and some went on to establish the Calcutta Pottery Works, Calcutta Chemicals, and the Bengal Waterproof Company.

The swadeshi movement also reached the villages of Bengal with the deshi dhutie hat, or local dhoti stall at

Uttarpara and a mobile exhibition of swadeshi consumer goods at Serempore in 1905. An effort was made to create a more institutionalised sales network for swadeshi goods beyond the irregular swadeshi melas, industrial fairs and exhibitions however, and by 1905 Kunjabihari Sen's shop in Barra Bazaar and Indian Stores on Bowbazaar Street were fixtures in Calcutta. Both dealt exclusively in swadeshi goods.

Bholanath Chandra was one of the early ideologues of the emerging movement. In an essay "A voice for the commerce and manufactures of India", featured in *Mukherjee's Magazine* between 1873 and 1876, he urged readers to think of industrialisation as "the ocean to the river of all their thoughts" and to dethrone "King Cotton" of Manchester.[xii] He thought that one of the last weapons left with Indians was "moral hostility" and that it could be used to "non-consume" English goods. In 1876 the weekly journal *Sadharani* referred to some youths in Dacca who had sworn to not use foreign cloth.[xiii] This idea of a boycott, the swadeshi idea taken to its logical extreme, gained greater support during the 1880s and 1890s as a result of British tariff policies; when the Government of India re-imposed duties on British cloth in 1894 after years of allowing it to be imported duty free in order to replenish its depleted treasury, a countervailing excise was applied on Indian cloth. It was this countervailing excise which provoked Bal Gangadhar Tilak to attempt the first large scale boycott of British cloth in the Bombay Presidency.

A dominant sentiment of the swadeshi movement was that the Indian upper class had taken to foreign goods as a mark of sophistication and that what was required was a return to Indianness. This idea did not just feature in books and newspapers, but seeped into the cultural consciousness through plays and songs. When Sakharam Deuskar wrote *Desher Katha* in Bengali, or *The Story of the Country*, it ran to four editions, selling over 10,000 copies in the first years of the 20th century. Deuskar's book was largely based on the works of Dadabhai Naoroji and Romesh Dutt.

Those who were interested in the constructive element of the swadeshi idea offered it as a solution to the problem of educated unemployment. Prafulla Ray claimed that it was one of his motivations in setting up Bengal Chemicals; he wanted to employ those young men coming out of the colleges who would otherwise be seeking a "soft" government job or a position with a British firm.[xiv] In 1905 Kaliprassana Dasgupta even called for a boycott of examinations, telling students that there were too many lawyers and that what India needed was for its young men to take to industry.[xv] When Dakshinaranjan Ghosh brought out *Industrial Guide* in 1907, he too said that one of his motivations for the publication had come from not knowing what to do with his unemployed younger brother.[xvi]

Yet in addition to these early modernisers, creators of factories and generators of modern industrial employment, others were equally attracted to the swadeshi idea; some wanted India to develop in opposition to this Western model and instead revive handicrafts, handlooms and the spinning wheel. It was there in *Desher Katha*; Sakharam Deuskar thought that if English mill cloth was boycotted, the necessary investment in Indian mills would be prohibitively high, and the much cheaper option would be to invest in handlooms which could produce the cloth to meet Indian demand. Handlooms would also generate employment in smaller towns and villages and provide succour to the traditional weaving castes which had been impoverished by British rule.

Whilst the handloom was still a commercial proposition, and at the start of the 20th century contributed more to India's output than mill made cloth, the charkha, or spinning wheel, was also beginning to be written and talked about in swadeshi circles. It could provide employment to women in the villages, keep widows gainfully employed, and local spinners could provide the yarn for local handlooms which were still dependent on imports from Lancashire for the finer counts. The idea of reviving the spinning wheel did have some popular appeal, but when Motilal Ghosh raised the issue at the Industrial Conference in Madras in 1906 he was laughed off the stage by India's leading industrialists.[xvii] This revivalist strain was captured in the monthly *Swadeshi*, edited by Jogindranath Chattopadhyay. *Swadeshi* attacked western industrialisation and Chattopadhyay did not even think that the newly swadeshi Banga Lakshmi cotton mill project was a singularly good thing- that fact that it was owned by Bengalis was "no doubt a matter of joy", but the less mills there were the better it would be for the country.[xviii] He thought that machines enhanced the suffering of the poor, benefitted only the rich, and produced unemployment, alcoholism and immorality. Handicrafts by contrast produced food for all, freedom and piety.

***

The partition of Bengal was announced by the Viceroy, George Curzon on 19 July 1905. Dividing Bengal and attaching its western, mainly Hindu districts to Orissa and Bihar, and merging the eastern, mainly Muslim districts with Assam would have turned Hindu Bengali speakers, who traditionally dominated the province's economic and cultural life, into a linguistic minority in their new province.

The idea of using an economic boycott as a public protest against the partition of Bengal was first suggested at a meeting in Pabna and started to gain support in public meetings being held across the province. The Chinese had boycotted American goods, something which had received coverage in the Indian papers, whilst the decades old swadeshi movement had gained respectability among the intellectual classes. At public gatherings the assembled leaders were confident that feeling was so strong throughout Bengal that any call for a boycott would succeed. There were concerns about how a boycott would affect their English friends in Calcutta who were sympathetic to their cause though, as well as how it would be received by the British public.

A resolution was passed at a Town Hall meeting in Calcutta on 7 August 1905: British goods would be boycotted as a device to gain the attention of the British public and to put pressure on the Government of India, and once the grievance had been addressed the boycott would be withdrawn. Surendranath Banerjea, the veteran moderate nationalist was among the early leaders of the movement, and he even consulted his English friends before drafting the final resolution.[xix] He was so staunch in his leadership of the movement in its early days that he became known as "Surrender Not". Yet it was when he and his colleagues meekly bowed before British repression of the protests in the later months of 1905 that his regard in Bengal began to diminish somewhat and the movement transformed from one specifically opposed to the partition of Bengal, into a broader anti-British one. It was in this government repression of the movement that the economic objective of the boycott became obscured.

The boycott of British cloth and liquor, shoes, sugar and cigarettes had a limited impact in 1905 and 1906. Yet the movement did quicken a conflict within the Congress. Control of the organisation became the great contest between the older generation of moderates represented by the likes of Surendranath Banerjea, and younger radicals led by Aurobindo Ghosh and Bal Gangadhar Tilak. When the Party split in 1907 the old moderates retained control of the organisation, whilst many of the young firebrands either ended up in jail or in exile.

***

The revivalist stream of the swadeshi movement, the one advocated by Motilal Ghosh and Sakharam Deuskar, survived the protests of 1905. Yet it was lying in slumber in the years between the partition of Bengal and the outbreak of the First World War. The idea had a power of its own; it appealed to a deep sense of nativism, a sentimental attachment to village life, a sense of simpler times in which Hindu spiritualism could be more easily realised, and a fear of the coming industrial age and what it might do to India's ancient civilisation. It is thus difficult to judge whether the idea would have died a natural death without a charismatic political advocate, or whether it would have lingered in some form in the Indian political ether for the remainder of the 20th century. The question need not be answered, of course, as the politician with the charisma to merge swadeshi revivalism, specifically the revival of the spinning wheel, with the mainstream of Indian nationalism returned to India in 1915.

Mohandas Gandhi had discovered the spinning wheel in London in 1908. He was there leading a deputation from South Africa and came into contact with some earnest Indian students. They had a long conversation about the condition of India and it was "in a flash" that he made the connection; there could be no swaraj, or self-rule, without the spinning wheel.[xx] He knew at once that "everyone had to spin". However, he was still new to the subject and did not yet understand the distinction between the spinning wheel, which spun cotton fibre into yarn, and the handloom which wove the yarn into cloth, and so used the term "hand loom" instead of spinning wheel in his dialogue *Hind Swaraj* later in 1908.

It was not long after his return to India from South Africa, at the Missionary Conference in Madras on 14 February 1916 that Gandhi shared his ideas on swadeshi. After much thought he had come to his definition; swadeshi meant restricting oneself to the use and service of one's immediate surroundings, to the exclusion of the more remote.[xxi] In religious matters this meant restricting oneself to one's ancestral religion, if defects were found then those defects should be purged. Likewise, in politics this meant using Indian institutions and serving them by curing them of their defects. In the field of economics, Gandhi suggested that Indians should only use things produced by their "immediate neighbours" and serve those industries by making them efficient and competitive when they were not.

Gandhi soon began to make a connection between swadeshi and swaraj; swaraj, or self-rule, would not be obtainable without swadeshi. It was largely a cultural idea; Indians had to start taking pride in their own languages, dress, religious symbols, food and climate, and if they did not then the attainment of swaraj would be an empty thing. In fact, the adoption of all things foreign necessitated being under foreign rule, or 'tutelage' for a long time to come.[xxii] Nonetheless, swadeshi was in essence an economic idea, and in 1918 Gandhi made it clear that the immediate concern of the country was not how the government was run, but how Indians would feed and clothe themselves.[xxiii] He anticipated that India would spend ₹60 crore on buying imported cloth in that year alone, which meant that Indian weavers were deprived of that amount without giving them any other form of employment. He estimated that 10% of the population was half starved, and most of the other 90% was underfed; even middle class parents could not afford enough milk to feed their babies. The political response of the British Raj, the Montagu-Chelmsford reforms, was not going to fix the problem immediately.

In 1918, after three years of patient practice and effort, Gandhi started to work the spinning wheel. He claimed that swadeshi, which was spinning khadi, would save the "annual drain", restore the honour of Indian womanhood, provide an even distribution of wealth, supplement agriculture, and assist in solving the problem of growing poverty. Swadeshi in the form of khadi spinning was thus the veritable kamadhenu, or the cow which never stops giving milk. It supplied India's wants and solved many of its most pressing problems. Gandhi even raised spinning khadi to the level of a 'religious duty'.[xxiv] He instructed Indians to learn spinning, charging for the labour if they needed the money, or donating an hour of their time each day as a type of national service if they could afford it. They were to make improvements to existing hand looms and spinning wheels, take the swadeshi vow, which was to buy only handspun and handwoven cloth, popularise khadi among their social circle, and clothe their children in khadi. According to this chain of reasoning, the key to swaraj was spinning khadi. The first khadi vow was taken the following year among the "fashionable sisters of Bombay".[xxv]

Gandhi had come under some criticism for his advocacy of spinning, so he made his "incredibly simple" views clear.[xxvi] Each Indian needed about 13 yards of cloth per year, but less than half that amount was produced in India. The problem was not the supply of cotton; it grew in abundance and was exported to Britain and Japan to be received as imports of manufactured calico. India was capable of supplying the entire demand of 13 yards per head simply by hand spinning and hand weaving. Given that the country needed to supplement its main occupation, agriculture, with something else, spinning khadi was the only employment for millions of idle hands. Gandhi did not think that hand spinning was a threat to the Indian mill industry; mills could not meet the present demand for cloth and would not be able to do so for the foreseeable future. That demand could only be met by hand spinning and weaving. The annual drain of ₹60 crore would be saved and distributed among the poor village women of the country who could stay in their cottages and be gainfully employed. Khadi spinning was thus an "automatic, though partial" solution to the problem of Indian poverty.

Indian women were to be the driving force behind the revival of khadi. Gandhi thanked God that "the beautiful women of Punjab have not yet lost the cunning of their fingers".[xxvii] Punjabi women of both low and high class still knew how to spin and had not yet burnt their spinning wheels like the women of his native Gujarat had. It was a "perfect delight" when they threw balls of yarn into his lap. They had the time for it, and were able to produce khadi yarn of a superior quality to machine made yarn. Whilst Punjab was thus proof of what was still possible, there was also cause for concern; each year the amount of handspun yarn was decreasing. Soon poverty would start to rise, and previously industrious Punjabi women would spend their spare time gossiping.

Gandhi thought that the spread of cotton mills posed a menace not only to the women of Punjab, but to women across the land; it was in these factories that they were "exposed to temptations and risks to which they ought not be exposed".[xxviii] Furthermore, those women who were not employed in mills and no longer had work at home were forced into road repair labour and all the risks associated with that life. Given the spinning wheel, no Indian woman would ever need to leave her home in search of employment. Spinning, after all, had traditionally been women's work; it was a slow and silent process and suited to women's nature, which was sacrificial and non-violent. Two hundred years earlier Indian women had spun both for Indian and for foreign markets and so Gandhi urged them to once more form spinning clubs, have spinning competitions and flood the Indian market once again with Indian yarn. Spinning was the widow's companion, supplementary income for the middle class and a means of livelihood for the lower classes. And in the highest appeal of all, it was dharma.

Although he was not an economist Gandhi knew enough, like Mahadev Ranade, to know that "the so-called laws laid down in books on economics are not immutable like the laws of Medes and Persians, nor are they universal."[xxix] Even the economics of England and Germany were different from each other; England had enriched itself by exploiting foreign markets, whilst Germany had grown wealthy by providing bounties, or subsidies to its beet sugar exporters. What was possible in the small countries of Europe was not possible in a huge land like India. The economics of a nation were unique and shaped by its climate, geology, and national temperament; "what is meat for England is in many cases poison for India". Beef tea, fiery whisky and fur coats were all fine in Britain, but would be disastrous in India. Gandhi thought that England's economic model of industrialism, urbanisation, and predatory trade protected by a large navy might be economically sound for it, morally dubious as it was. But free trade had held India in bondage. It had ruined India's peasantry and its cottage industries, and no new Indian industries of any sort were able to compete with foreign goods without protection. Gandhi was thus a confirmed protectionist, even though protection meant tariffs for steel plants and cotton mills, of which he was suspicious.

Gandhi saw the fortunes of the Indian mill owners in direct antagonism with the fate of the Indian masses. He did not think that the capitalists had too much to worry about though. He was trying to wean Indian consumers off foreign cloth, and so until they spent that ₹60 crore a year on khadi rather than foreign cloth, khadi would not eat into their market share.[xxx] But should the Indian mills collapse, it would be the day of India's salvation; the country would be "pulsating with new life". The old relationships of exploitation would be restructured, and peasants and farmers would exchange their produce for things they actually needed. When mill owners pointed out the employment which they generated Gandhi replied that those factory workers had been torn from the soil, and whilst they employed a few thousand, they could never employ the millions still on the land who wanted work. He even gave the mill owners some advice on what they should do; standardise their prices, consult with the leaders of the boycotts of foreign cloth on the requirements of the nation, refrain from manufacturing khadi or those types of cloth which could be made by hand spinners, minimise their profits, and use whatever little money was left on the boycott movement and the welfare of their labourers.

The Department of Industries in Bombay had been making some efforts to encourage handloom weaving, introducing the fly shuttle loom which could improve each handloom weaver's productivity by 40%. There had also been some attempts to train peasants in handloom weaving as a part-time occupation. Orders for hand sizing machines had been placed by weavers' associations and weaving schools had been opened across the province. Gandhi was not enthused by the government's initiatives.[xxxi] He thought that the Department's attempts to introduce the handloom into peasant homes were doomed to failure and betrayed an ignorance of Indian agricultural life. Hand weaving was a long process which required sustained labour, several stages and more than one pair of hands. Such a thing was not possible in a peasant's cottage. Since the days of yore hand weaving had been a separate and independent occupation from which the weaver derived their sole source of income. What the Indian peasants needed was an auxiliary occupation which they could take up or leave as they liked. The only such occupation was hand spinning.

Gandhi estimated that at most 9 million hand weavers would be required to fulfil India's annual demand for cloth, but given that ten spinners supplied one weaver with yarn, encouraging the spinning wheel would give employment to 90 million Indians.[xxxii] Moreover, hand weaving and mill weaving were not complimentary but antagonistic. Mills, like all of machine civilisation, would eventually develop machinery sophisticated enough to make the intricate patterns of the hand weavers redundant. Should the hand weavers rely on mill yarn, they would be squeezed for their last rupee before being abandoned. The hand weaver and hand spinner on the other hand could work together in harmony. One major conundrum however was that in the time that Gandhi had been spinning, the quantity of annual handloom production had almost doubled, but even in the mid 1930s hand spinners were not in a position to supply the yarn to hand weavers. Handspun yarn was weak and uneven and of uncertain supply, and handloom weavers were increasingly specialising in finer counts which hand spinners could not produce.

An All India Spinners' Association had already been established, but the idea of the All India Village Industries Association came to Gandhi when he was on a Harijan tour of the Malabar coast in southern India. He spoke with a khadi worker who impressed upon him the need to have a body which could return to the villagers what had been "cruelly and thoughtlessly snatched away from them by the city dwellers".[xxxiii] The villagers of India were living a hand to mouth existence; small and irregular farm holdings were not paying propositions, their lives were ones of slow starvation and they were in debt to the money lenders. The mill hands who went from the villages to the cities were doing the work that would have previously kept ten of their fellow villagers employed. The true price of this dislocation was not reflected in the price of cloth; in this sense even cheap sturdy mill cloth was expensive, for society.

The goal of the Village Industries Association was to "encourage the existing industries and to revive, where it is possible and desirable, the dying or dead industries of villages according to the village methods, ie the villagers working in their own cottages as they have done from times immemorial." Gandhi thought that these simple processes could be improved just as they had been in hand ginning, carding, spinning and weaving. There was scope for co-operation among villagers, pooling together their produce and profits. They could be supervised and work according to a plan. Raw materials could be drawn from a common stock. Gandhi did however receive criticism from his follower and colleague Joseph

Kumarappa for neglecting village industries and concentrating solely on khadi. Yet he was adamant; khadi was still the sun, other village industries were the planets which would revolve around it. Nonetheless, neither could grow without the other and so both the Spinners' Association and the Village Industries Association would work together to revive rural India.

***

India has a long history of princes who, after a sheltered childhood behind palace walls, move out into the world as young men, and seeing the pain and suffering of the peasantry, become distressed and consumed with guilt. Jawaharlal Nehru was not a prince, but a princeling, the son of one of India's wealthiest barristers. After returning from Cambridge in 1912 he made a brief attempt to practice law at the Allahabad High Court like his father Motilal. Yet the work of a barrister did not sustain his interest, and so he became a politician in the United Provinces, at his father's expense. Even after marriage to Kamala and the arrival of their daughter Indira, it was Motilal who supported the family. Besides any political arguments which they had, it was this financial relationship which would cause strain between father and son. For Jawaharlal had, in an oft quoted passage from his autobiography, met with the farmers of Partabgarh who had come to Allahabad in search of a political patron who might protect them from the ferocity of their landlords. Speaking to them filled him with shame of his own easy going life and sorrow at the degradation of India. He wanted to live a more austere life. He began to accept less money from his father, but was loath to earn any of his own. His wife and daughter would suffer, and Motilal would chide his son for his "false economies".[xxxiv] Jawaharlal was thus a man conflicted. Too Anglicised for India, yet derisive of the Edwardian England of his youth. Equally averse to Hinduism and critical of British imperialism. It was on one of his trips abroad, in 1927, just before he began his rise in the Congress however, that he caught a glimpse of a society which might ease the conflict within.

For Jawaharlal Nehru the fascination for Russia was tinged with self-interest.[xxxv] Russia was a land where vast forces had upset the old order and brought about a new one. Where values had changed and new standards had replaced the old. He thought that Indians were a conservative people, not fond of change, trying to forget their misery and degradation in "vague fancies" of a glorious past and ideas of an immortal civilisation. None of this helped in solving the problems of the day. India had to think in new ways and find new methods to solve its pressing problems and it was for this reason that Russia was of interest. Russia was all the more valuable because it was not dissimilar to India; it was a vast agricultural country with only the beginnings of industrialisation, and it too faced the problems of poverty and illiteracy.

Nehru had been invited by the Soviet Union's Society for Cultural Relations with Foreign Countries to visit Moscow in November 1927 for the celebrations to mark the 10th anniversary of the Revolution. Upon arrival he thought that Moscow could be considered like any other great city, but one which did stand apart from the cities of the West in many respects. He admired its beauty; golden domes, wide squares, broad streets and churches, some of which had been converted into museums. The Soviet Government did not encourage religious worship and carried on intensive propaganda against it. But there were no restrictions on church attendance and many from the countryside still attended; women still visited a chapel dedicated to the Virgin Mary near the Kremlin with the inscription "Religion is the opium of the people" on the wall. The costume and headwear gave a glimpse of Asia. Not the tropical climes of India, but the Asia of the cold steppes. Even the saris of Kamala and his sister Krishna did not attract much attention.

Yet the real difference in Moscow was the atmosphere. The "very air of the place". There were few visible contrasts between luxury and poverty. Or even hierarchies of class. Everyone, including waiters and porters, was addressed as 'comrade', and merit and status were not judged by wealth or the size of one's salary. Nehru thought that the president and his clerk received a similar salary. Though the president would receive accommodation and a car. The peasant or the factory worker would thus meet the president as a member of his own class. Just someone more clever and capable, and would also address him as comrade. When he visited the Soviet President, Mikhail Kalanin, Nehru was pleased to note that he lived in two or three simply furnished rooms with no evidence of luxury.

There were few private cars on the roads. Most vehicles belonged to the state or its associated organisations- soviets, trade unions, co-operatives and factories. There were many shops resembling those of other cities. Yet Moscow's big shops were all owned by the state, only the smaller ones were left to private ownership. Street hawkers also traded petty goods. Nehru was pleased that the goods in the shops were "simple and modest and had no pretensions to fashion or smartness. There were none of the dainties of the Rue de Rivoli or of Bond Street." The people of Moscow did not seem to pay much attention to fashion either. Many of the men were without collars and ties. In many cases because they could not afford them. In some because it was considered bourgeoise to spend too much time or money on clothes. Large squares had loudspeakers broadcasting the news of the day, concerts, political speeches and propaganda to win over those who were still in doubt.

The Nehrus visited the State Opera House, a magnificent building with seven gold tiers built during the Tsar's reign, which would once have been a meeting place for the wealthy and fashionable. But now things were different. The audience was full of people in their working clothes.

In some cases without coats, or even in their shirt sleeves. They were "homely looking folk"; intellectuals, workers and peasants, some of whom brought their children. The performance of dance and song and ballet was a good one, appreciated by the audience which asked for encores. From the perspective of beauty and art it would be difficult to find a better performance anywhere in the world. After the opera they also visited the cinema to watch *The Last Days of Petrograd*. According to Nehru the Russians produced beautiful and artistic films, but Indians did not get a chance to see them and had to be content with the "gorgeous but stupid and inane productions of Hollywood in America". *The Last Days* contrasted the luxury of the elites and the misery of the masses during the days of the Tsar and featured ghastly scenes of war, the Tsar's downfall, the fight between the Bolsheviks and Kerensky, and the victory of Lenin. Nehru thought that it was a powerful and stirring film with immense propaganda value. Outside there were still signs of old Russia in the Drosky, or Russian tonga, a horse drawn rickshaw which could fit one normal sized person and not break 6 miles per hour, and in the ubiquitous beggars, often young women with babies in their arms. He was assured by the Communists that these things were much less prevalent than they used to be.

During his tour Nehru visited the Central Peasants' Home, a large building containing museums, demonstration rooms, lecture rooms and residential accommodation for 350 people. There were displays of agricultural produce which were ticketed with guided tours, and there were halls full of the latest agricultural machinery with models of modern sanitary houses and farms. Health propaganda was featured in another part of the building and pictures, posters and models explained how to avoid disease and keep clean and healthy homes. Another hall was devoted to electricity, full of working models showing its application to lighting and water pumps. Large charts showed the increase in electric power stations all across the land. Peasants were encouraged to stay at the Home for two months to receive agricultural training and Nehru saw it crowded with arrivals fresh from the countryside. There were 350 smaller Homes throughout Russia which he thought would transform the outlook of the peasantry in short time. Lenin, he recalled, had said that Communism was "the Soviet Republic plus electrification". He marvelled at what a stupendous project it was given the vastness of the land.

Nehru saw the power of the peasants in the new state; they could barely eke out a living, and so it was on the richer farmers that the burden of taxation fell- 25% of peasant farms were exempt from the payment of agricultural tax and there was a proposal to exempt another 10%. In theory land belonged to the state, but in practice it was the village soviet which divided it, usually assigning as much as could be tilled by an individual and their family. The extent of land holdings depended on the population density and there were schemes afoot to equalise this density through colonisation. An individual or family holding could be subject to re-distribution at the next soviet. And despite years of war and revolution, Russia had once again started to make strides in agricultural production. It had already exceeded its pre-war level of output.

Amongst the earliest decrees of the Soviet was the nationalisation of land. Land could no longer be bought, sold, rented, provided as security, or expropriated. All had the right to land as long as they were willing and able to work it, and perhaps most importantly, the hiring of labour was prohibited. Despite these early decrees illegal renting had continued however, and those families without horses and other animals to assist in working the land suffered for not being able to hire labour. In 1922 the law was thus changed to allow for renting for a fixed short period and in 1926 renting was once again allowed for an increased duration. Hiring of labour on this rented land was allowed subject to some restrictions such as rental contracts being registered with local authorities.

Those renting labour also had to work on the land with their hired labourers who were entitled to food and lodging.

After the Revolution communes started to spring up. Groups of workers would organise themselves into communities to work the land and live a common life, as did many religious groups. Yet the movement had started to dwindle as conflicts arose over matters of detail. These communes were replaced by 'artels', associations of peasants which pooled their resources to cultivate a common plot of land, and still later came the collectives. Nehru thought that the great advantage of these collectives was in the use of machinery such as tractors, which had previously been out of reach of the peasant. He thought that the tractor was almost a god in contemporary Russia. It was the use of the tractor which had led the peasants towards large scale co-operation. In addition, there were now agricultural banks and credit societies which boasted of 4.2 million members. A redistribution of the population from over-populated to under-populated parts of the country was taking place and cottage industries were also being encouraged in smaller towns and villages.

***

Jawaharlal Nehru had been in jail in the early 1930s. He thought that this was in some way an advantage in observing the Indian and world political scenes; it gave him a sense of detachment. But it is largely a sense of exasperation which pervades the pages of his short tract *Whither India* of 1933. He complained that the nationalist press, subject to censorship as it was, focused on trivia rather than vital matters; whether Gandhi would meet the viceroy, who would be Britain's next prime minister, what the secretary of state for India had said, whether India would get central responsibility in the upcoming round of constitutional reforms. He wanted to view things in the "long range of history". He mocked the "great statesmen" who filled the Round Tables and engaged in "pitiful and interminable talk" which interested few and affected even fewer.

Nehru accused moderate Indian politicians of being stuck in the Victorian age and suggested that they should not wonder why nobody listened to them. Not even the hammer of war or revolution could make a dent in their "hard heads". Some in the Congress hid vested interests under the cover of communalism or nationalism. Others were vague but passionate nationalists who could not envisage precisely what form freedom would take. He dubbed the growing idealism, mysticism, religious revivalism, the feeling of exaltation, the sense of mission of one's own country as middle class phenomena. Given the choice between a nationalism based on magic and religion and one based on science, Nehru chose science.

Understanding Indian nationalism as a middle class phenomenon, Nehru lamented the tendency to gloss over the fundamental divisions within Indian society and imagine that they would all be accommodated once freedom was obtained. He thought that it was an absurd idea that the interests of the landlords, the farmers, the industrialists, the bankers and the workers could all be fitted in without injury to any group. India's nationalists had to face up to the question of exactly which class's freedom they were striving for. When conflicts between groups arose, as they inevitably would, the political class would have to take sides. The refusal to do so just meant the perpetuation of the status quo.

Nehru then turned to the role of economic events in shaping history. He recounted the decline of feudalism in Europe which created a landless and unemployed proletariat in an increasingly global marketplace. Capitalism built on this landless proletariat, employing it as wage labour in factories all over the world. In Europe and North America, the producing countries, it was an active and living capitalism. Yet the colonial countries passively consumed the West's machine made goods. The growth of British capitalism was fuelled by its domination of India, which helped England to industrialise; India provided the raw materials for the factories of England and a market to consume their products. England had become a vast city, and India its hinterland. All of this led to a relationship of exploitation between these two poles and the concentration of capital and wealth.

Amidst this colonial exploitation some of England's newfound wealth had trickled down to its working class. Wages rose, working hours were reduced, insurance and welfare schemes were created, and the standard of living rose. This prosperity took the edge off working class discontent. Something like the opposite took place in India. Cottage industries were destroyed, the burden on the land and unemployment grew, and the country became poorer and more rural. The conditions for industrialisation existed but it was prevented by the British tax machinery. The Indian capitalist class which grew after the First World War was largely controlled by foreign capital and dependent on the foreign banking system.

In Nehru's estimation things had come to a pass. In the West wealth and industrial power were concentrating in fewer hands in the form of cartels and trusts and combines. Advances in technology were leading to greater mechanisation and increased production. But also higher rates of unemployment. Capitalism was producing the greatest amount of goods in history. But the vast majority was too poor to afford them. Such was the crisis of capitalism, or the Great Depression of the early 1930s. At its heart was the ill distribution of wealth, something which was intrinsic to capitalism and would eventually eat it alive. Capitalism had "outlived its day and must now give place to a better and saner ordering of human affairs, which is more in keeping with the progress of science and human knowledge." Capitalism had solved the problem of production, but could not resolve the problem of distribution. Historically it had led to imperialism and conflicts between imperialist powers as they searched for colonies to exploit, seized raw materials and captured markets for their own production. This in turn had led to rising nationalist movements within the colonies and social conflicts with the working classes. It only resulted in political and economic crises and wars. Nehru was certain that communists and socialists were an ever growing power because they had science and logic on their side.

In India the problem was one between the old nationalist ideology and the new economic ideology. That old ideology which Nehru and his colleagues in the Congress had grown up with was no longer adequate. It did not fit with the conditions of India or the world, and so there was a lag. It was 1933, and Congressmen had to move from the 19th century into the 20th. They had to get out of the habit of thinking in terms of "paper constitutions" and their lawyers' mentality which proceeded on the basis of the status quo and precedents. They had to start thinking of vital economic issues; the immediate goal before India was to end the exploitation of the people by ending the connection with Britain as well as all special class privileges and vested interests. Nehru also wanted to drop narrow nationalism in favour of world co-operation and internationalism. India's problems were entwined with those of Asia, and the world. The Indian struggle was part of a world struggle which was in essence economic, driven by hunger and want.

***

The socialism of Nehru's *Whither India* was still one of analysis, and sensibility. He, like most of his fellow socialists in the Congress, was ready to admit that his was an intellectual socialism. Younger men and women in the Party, equally attracted to socialism, but also realistic enough to understand the importance of the Congress to Indian nationalism, came together to form a "ginger group" within the Party in order to turn intellectual musings into specific policies.

The first All India Socialist Conference was held in Patna the day before the All India Congress Committee Conference in May 1934. Narender Dev, one of the Party's leading scholars of Marxism, presided over the session which attracted more than 100 delegates from all over India. He regretted that their leader, Jawaharlal Nehru was still in jail. Nonetheless, he was sure that Nehru would support them in their endeavour to form a new socialist party. The great dilemma for the socialists was whether to form their party within the Congress or establish a new and separate formation. He made his opinion quite clear: the socialists should not break from the nationalist movement and the lower middle class in their effort to overthrow foreign domination. In the end capitalist democracy was preferable to foreign rule.[xxxvi] After all, it was the British Raj which had made the landlords and the Indian capitalists their junior partners. What was needed was an alliance between the urban lower middle class and the rural masses. The intelligentsia had to make it happen. But the Congress as it stood was not helping the movement; the recent strike of workers in Bombay had not received any help from the Party. Most of the urban proletariat came from rural India, and so it was they who would take the revolution back to their villages.

Narender Dev went on to argue that the only solutions to the problems created by capitalism could be provided by socialism and fascism. Given that fascism had not really been established in Italy and in Germany Nazism was an alliance between the lower middle class and capitalists to suppress the socialists, that left socialism as the only hope for the future. Generally, the socialists within the Congress had been of the drawing room variety. But they did have to at least take a stand for scientific socialism rather than the prevailing social reformism (a euphemism for Gandhism) within the Congress. A resolution in favour of the formation of a Party within the Party was then affirmed by two-thirds of the attendees. Narender Dev, Jayaprakash Narayan, C.C. Banerjee and Faridul Haq were given the task of preparing a draft constitution and programme.

Minocher Masani proposed a resolution in which the Congress, having attained Independence, would declare India a socialist state in which all power would be transferred to the producing masses, there would be socialisation of the principle industries, state monopolies on foreign trade and production, the princes and landlords' privileges would be abolished, land redistributed to the peasants, state co-operatives and collective farms would be encouraged to enable the complete collectivisation of agriculture, and the debts of the peasants and workers would be liquidated. The only successful amendment to Masani's resolution was one by Mrs. Rajani Mukherjee which stated that control of economic life should be with the workers so that they could consume the fruits of their labour themselves rather than have them consumed by "capitalist parasites".[xxxvii]

The socialists did not get their way at the All India Congress Committee meeting the following day. Alarmed by their newly organised presence, the conservatives on the Committee prepared a resolution denouncing loose talk of class war and the confiscation of private property. The Congress Socialists had never actually gone as far as that, but the conditions for a split in the Party had emerged.

***

Unusually for an Indian student in the 1920s, Jayaprakash Narayan, having decided to study abroad, travelled to America rather than England. He had momentarily given up studies at his government college under the influence of Mohandas Gandhi and Abul Kalam Azad during the first non-cooperation movement in 1919.

But the nationalist Bihar Vidyapeeth was not able to satisfy his thirst for knowledge. He chose America because he had heard that it was possible for a student to work and earn whilst studying, and so he arrived in California in October 1922 and then enrolled at the University of California, Berkeley in January 1923. He started studying chemistry, but Berkeley soon doubled the course fees, so he headed east to the University of Iowa. He lived an itinerant student life, transferring from university to university, eventually settling down to the study of sociology, attempting to isolate the determinants of cultural change in a thesis titled *Cultural Variation*. He, like Jawaharlal Nehru, developed a sympathy with working people. But unlike Nehru, Jayaprakash's sympathy came from experience as a worker. As he had set out to, he worked whilst he studied: as a mechanic, fruit picker, butcher, salesman and tutor. He was thus in the United States during the roaring 1920s, an era of economic expansion, and some social change, but his experience was of the underbelly of an increasingly affluent society. Rather than an admiration for America's liberal, capitalist order, he largely aligned himself with Leftist academics and eventually discovered the writings of Karl Marx, at the University of Wisconsin.

Jayaprakash returned to India in 1929, and was there at the founding of the Congress Socialist Party in 1934, but his most substantive contribution to Indian socialism came in 1936 with the publication of his polemic *Why Socialism?* The work was amongst the first to apply socialist theory to the contemporary dilemmas of Indian nationalism, and it was directly addressed to Congress workers, in order to help them make "clear cut decisions" when the inevitable clash of ideologies came.

For Jayaprakash it was important to understand that socialism was not a personal code of conduct, but a system of social reconstruction. All political parties irrespective of their colour wanted to capture state power after which they could legislate and use the apparatus of the state for propaganda and education to enforce their own will. Yet a socialist state would be different. It would derive its power from popular support and Jayaprakash wanted to make it clear that he did not believe in violent revolution. In a future scenario in which Jawaharlal Nehru was the 'Premier or President of Socialist India' he did not expect that Nehru would have the potbellied capitalists lined up and shot, or have the landlords blown to bits, seize the treasuries of the princes and the money lenders and distribute them to the people, give the workers ownership of the Tata Iron Works, or divide up the land into little plots. "Socialism is something more sensible, more scientific, more civilized than all that."

The central problem of society was inequality of rank, of culture, of opportunity, and of access to the good things of life. The contrast between the poverty, hunger, filth, disease and ignorance of the many and the comfort, luxury and power of the few were perhaps more evident in India than anywhere else. The socialists wanted to tackle the problem of inequality at its source to check its growth. They did not contest the existence of biological inequality. What they did object to was inequality of opportunity and social inequality, principally the unequal distribution of property. This inequality of wealth was not due to biology. Inheritance of wealth was based on social custom; the idiot son of a millionaire did not receive his wealth due to his abilities, but due to custom. Change that custom and many of the wealthy heirs would be cast into poverty. No doubt it took some ability to become a self-made businessperson. But it seemed odd to Jayaprakash that this one particular ability allowed for the accumulation of wealth whilst other talents, such as those of the scientist, did not bring such great rewards.

Jayaprakash explained to his readers how wealth was accumulated and created. Even the Indian peasant, with his old fashioned tools and methods, could produce more than he needed to live on. Yet millions could not get two square meals a day, whilst others had not only their basic wants satisfied, but lived in comfort. The reason for this was that the people did not work for themselves or have free access to nature. They did not even own their own tools and could not keep their own produce for themselves. Many could not afford access to these means of production and so all they could do was to sell their own labour. The great riches of the rich on the other hand, were not from their own production, but from ownership of the means of production which allowed them to exploit their workers. The whole aim of capitalism was to try to appropriate as large a share of the workers' surplus production as possible. And the bourgeoisie- the lawyers, the doctors, the merchants and bankers- filled up from this bowl of surplus wealth.

Jayaprakash thought that this left two possible solutions. Either return to an Eden in which each man worked for himself and kept and controlled the surplus of his own labour, or embrace the socialist solution- "abolish private ownership of the means of production and to establish over them the ownership of the whole community." In this new form of social ownership people would no longer work for others, but for themselves, collectively producing not for the profits of the owners, but for their own consumption. All wealth would be held in common and shared equitably based on the amount and nature of the work done and the needs of each person. Only a minimum would be held for the needs of national infrastructure like the armed forces, administration, health and education. Such was the basic principle of socialism- socialisation of the means of production.

Opponents of socialism would never tire of pointing out that India's condition was unique. But Jayaprakash insisted that the laws of accumulation worked in India as they worked elsewhere and the way it could be stopped was also the same in India. Although Indian conditions would influence the way that socialism was applied, those first principles were unalterable. He did not think, like some, that the dominant feature of Indian civilisation was individualism, which would make it opposed to socialism. He did agree that the perfection of the individual was an ideal, but this was not the narrow self-seeking individualism found in capitalist societies. Moreover, socialists could prove that the perfection of the individual could only come about by pursuing the common good.

Jayaprakash did not think that the Congress resolutions of the late 1920s and early 1930s went far enough. Could revolutionary changes in the economic structure of society which they spoke of be achieved by the measures proposed- death duties, a graduated income tax, reducing rent for some, whilst abolishing it on uneconomic holdings? He thought that this was all the Karachi Resolution of 1931 offered by way of economic policy. He did not expect the Congress to put in place a programme of "full grown" socialism, but at least one which would free the masses from exploitation and put economic and political power in their hands.

***

The Congress Socialist Party had adopted a 15 point charter in October 1934. It was a statement of principles for an Indian constitution advocating transferring power to the masses, planning of economic life, socialising key industries, encouraging co-operatives for production, distribution and credit, creating a state monopoly over foreign trade, eliminating the privileges of princes and landlords, redistributing land to peasants, encouraging co-operative farming, liquidating the debts of peasants and farmers, providing work to the able bodied and "social insurance" for the unemployed and sick, ensuring adult franchise and the principle of "to everyone his needs", neutrality towards religions, non-recognition of caste and community and non-discrimination between the sexes. It was from these principles that Jayaprakash Narayan attempted to provide a vision of a socialist India of the future.

Economic life in a socialist idyll would be controlled and planned by the state. Much could be learnt from the Russian experiment in socialist planning. All national and international efforts aimed at solving the crisis of the Great Depression had failed, whereas Russia alone was making progress and increasing the standard of living of its people; it was creating more employment than there were ready hands. Production, distribution and savings would all be "properly adjusted" and all three would move along in a way carefully laid out in advance according to the resources, equipment and needs of the people. There would be no private interests separate from social interests. Jayaprakash did not think that excessive centralisation was a concern. Planning had to some extent been decentralised throughout the provinces in Russia. Workers in factories, farms and co-operatives would be taken into confidence to gauge their individual needs when formulating national requirements. The chaotic laws of capitalism dictated what people ate and what they wore but with socialism these things would be under purposive control.

Jayaprakash stated that "all factories, all workshops, all raw material, all trading, all banking and all finance will pass into the hands of the community. There will be no private ownership at all in these spheres." Personal property would be allowed, but only for personal use, not to acquire more property. In addition, banks, transport, plantations, mines, public utilities and insurance would all be brought under social control. He gave the example of cotton; a decree would be issued that the 80 mills of Bombay had become the property of the Indian people. A Cotton Industries Department would then be established to run the mills in conjunction with workers' representatives in accordance with the National Economic Plan. The Department would consult with the planners to decide how much cotton would be bought and what type and quantity of cotton products should be produced to fulfil the community's needs according to available resources. If there was not enough supply then distribution would be rationed. If supply was sufficient it would be made available in the market at fixed prices. Rationing would only be an inconvenience to the rich.

With the socialisation of the mills the workers, previously wage slaves, would become masters of the factories in which they had toiled and sweated. Their unions would have a greater say in the running of their mills, wages would rise, and working hours would fall. There would be schools for their children, maternity houses, parks and libraries and museums: "The workers would be transplanted to a new world- a world of freedom, of initiative, of power, of opportunities for cultural advancement." The owners would have to become workers- those with ability would be kept on as managers and experts. And owners would not receive any compensation; it would be an ideological breach, given that their ownership was based on exploitation. Their fate would be largely dependent on their own behaviour in the tense new atmosphere. But Jayaprakash thought the noble among them would throw their lot in with the workers in creating a new order.

The state would also monopolise foreign trade as part of its planning process. It would be difficult, if not impossible, to engage in economic planning were trade left to the private profiteers. It was big business which would be socialised at first. The small-scale sector would thus need co-operatives for production, distribution and credit. Small stores would come into a co-operative of consumer stores, and those who did not join would be driven out of business by the new co-operatives. The privileges of the princes would be abolished without compensation, as would those of the landlords.

Although common ownership was the goal, it would not come about immediately, and so the socialists would have to start with peasant proprietorship. The aim initially was to remove inequalities in the size of holdings. The solution to the ills of Indian agriculture was to remove the vested interests exploiting the tiller of the soil, clear all agrarian debts, pool holdings of land and establish co-operative and collective farming, state co-operative credit and marketing systems, and co-operative subsidiary industries. Jayaprakash agreed that no advance in Indian agriculture was possible until each Indian village was converted from a collection of small isolated holdings into a single co-operative farm. The individual farmer or peasant would be more secure in co-operatives, besides which economic planning would not be possible with small fragmented individual holdings. Each village would become a unit of agricultural production, working in unison with other villages.

In Russia three types of socialised agriculture had emerged. The first was co-operative farming in which individual land and instruments remained individual property but the holdings were pooled and the crop harvested with joint labour. The produce would then be distributed according to the size of the holding and the amount of labour contributed. These co-operatives led to a community of spirit. More socialist than mere co-operatives were collective farms; there were no individual plots and distribution took place solely according to the labour put in, but there was still some individual ownership of tools and animals. These collectives were an advance in communal living, yet much of life was still lived apart. The highest form of socialist agriculture was the commune. Jayaprakash thought that if communes could work in Russia, there was no reason that they would not work in India. But he did admit that the pace should be slower in India, and socialisation of agriculture would need to be encouraged rather than forced.

Under socialism cities would be planned and there would be no concentration because industries would be diffused. There would be geographical planning as much as statistical planning, and villages would no longer be isolated, they would be transformed into progressive communities connected to the world by radios, phones, roads and buses. There would be industries in the villages just as in the cities, and recreation centres, schools and museums. Jayaprakash was particularly enthused by the vision of socialist cities and villages sketched in Mikhail Ilin's *Moscow Has A Plan*.

Ilin thought that the new cities would not be built around fortresses as in days gone by, but around factories and electric power stations. The residential areas of the city would be separated by a "green wall" of parks to protect workers from the pollution of the factories. There would be flower beds, dwellings facing the sun, trees at every entrance, and the happy singing of birds. Cities would be smaller, ideally with less than 100,000 residents. Factories would not be lumped together, but distributed across the land according to a rational plan. There would be no more villages, instead agricultural cities, based on agricultural processing factories which would come up around government and collective farms. The distinction between city and village and peasant and worker would disappear. Jayaprakash thought that Ilin's was "A superb vision! And so practicable, and so much within the reach of your arm. This is the great thing about socialist visions- they are translatable into fact."

***

Jayaprakash Narayan began to work through the alternatives to socialism and inevitably came to an examination of Gandhism. His association with Gandhi dated back to 1920 when, as a young, newly married man, he dropped his wife off at Gandhi's Sabarmati Ashram whilst he worked in Patna. But since that time he had been to America, discovered Marx, become a committed socialist and arrived at a different perspective on Gandhi's philosophy. Jayaprakash took an interview Gandhi had given to some landlords in the United Provinces, which had been published in *The Leader* on 3 August 1934, as a precis of his approach to the problems of economic exploitation and inequality. Until this point

Why Socialism? had been an analytical work, calm in tone, in keeping with the academic bent of most young Indian socialists of the time.

Given that Gandhi had not fully explained his concept of swaraj, Jayaprakash thought that he had not provided an alternative to socialism, although some of his followers claimed that the sum total of his philosophy amounted to an Indian socialism. He referred to Gandhi's often repeated theory of trusteeship as a "curious philosophy". He claimed that Gandhi's idea was not particularly Indian and that it was essentially reformist, interested in maintaining the established order of society. All Gandhi was telling the landlords was that they should improve their relations with their tenants and labourers and there would be no discontent, revolt or class war. This type of reformism was not interested in social justice but "covering up the ugly fissures in society".

In the interview in *The Leader* Gandhi had said that his Ram Rajya, or Kingdom of Lord Ram, would ensure the rights of the prince and the pauper. Jayaprakash thought that this well illustrated Gandhi's social philosophy. He found it breathtaking that in Gandhi's utopia there would still be paupers. Jayaprakash argued that the difference between Gandhism and socialism was not one between spirituality and materialism as often claimed, but one of curiosity and enquiry. Socialism started with the question of why there were princes and paupers, found the reasons, and then suggested a remedy. Gandhism never even asked that question. It simply accepted the established order and only sought to improve the behaviour of the higher to the lower classes. This was a form of self-deception. In the socialist analysis the landlord's wealth came from theft. Gandhi let it go unquestioned, or even sanctified it in his deceptive philosophy of trusteeship. What is more, there was violence behind the landlords' domination.

Gandhian trusteeship was also quite vague. If the

landlord was holding his wealth in trust, exactly what portion of it? If his tenants held an equal share, what did that mean exactly? Were the landlord and tenant equal partners? What did Gandhi mean by "family"? Could the tenants have the run of the palace? If the tenants were equal owners because of their production, why should they not keep that production? Why should the landlords act as trustees if their wealth was earned because of their ability? It was really either of the two: the landlords' wealth was ill-gotten and should be appropriated, or it was rightfully earned and they should be left alone. Pious concepts like trusteeship did not provide any clarity. Jayaprakash went on to mock Gandhi's appeal to the landlords' sense of morality and his attempt to reach their hearts. This type of thing was common to all the great religious teachers, including Jesus Christ. It was evident how much success he had. Gandhi had come along "wielding his wand, claiming to perform the old magic."

Jayaprakash also thought that Gandhi's comments on nationalisation were quite fuzzy or "arrant nonsense". Gandhi had claimed that talk of nationalisation, particularly coming from Jawaharlal Nehru, should not alarm the landlords given that Nehru shared his commitment to non-violence, and that "The nation cannot own property except by vesting it in individuals." Jayaprakash pointed out that this was bringing Nehru to a position which he did not hold and asked Gandhi who owned the state railways, and the nationalised mines, banks, and factories of Soviet Russia? He thought that Gandhi was confusing property for individual use, like houses, clothes and cycles, with ownership of the means of production like land, mines, and factories. What is more Gandhi's advocacy of khadi had at its core a disdain for machines and modern industrial civilisation. He thought that when Gandhi criticised machinery he was confusing it with capitalism and all the dislocation and violence inherent in it. The problem of unemployment was intrinsic to capitalism, not to the advance of machinery; if the same machinery was put to use in a socialist way then the problem would not arise. For Jayaprakash, Gandhism was "a dangerous doctrine", hushing up real issues, and instead trying to remove the evils of society by pious wishes.

***

Jawaharlal Nehru had been in jail for most of 1935, but was released in October and travelled to Europe to be with Kamala who was being treated for tuberculosis in Lausanne. She died in February 1936. He then returned to India and Congress politics, taking up the presidency with Gandhi's blessings. It was a time of relative calm; the civil disobedience movement had petered out and a new Government of India Act had been passed. The big dilemma was whether the Congress would co-operate with the Raj in its plans to hold elections in the provinces in 1937. This issue would have been enough to keep most Congress presidents busy, but Nehru was in a more expansive mood.

In his presidential address at Lucknow in April Nehru built on his Marxist interpretation of history from *Whither India* and presented the world as he saw it; a decaying capitalism latching on to imperialism and fascism in the West and the nationalism and socialism evident in Soviet Russia marching from "progress to progress". India had to make a choice which side it was on. He went on to make the case that India's national problem was but a part of the wider world problem, that of "capitalist imperialism". He admitted that he was going "a little beyond the beat of the usual Congress President", but did not want to hold the office under false pretences. Besides which his views were well known, yet he had still been elected to lead the Party. Although all Congressmen did not support his ideas, they would at least indulge his expression of them.

Nehru saw no way to end India's poverty, unemployment, degradation and subject status except through socialism.

This would entail revolutionary changes, including the ending of vested interests in land and industry as well as the system of princely states. Private property would be abolished, except in a "restricted sense", and the profit system would be replaced by co-operative services. He envisioned the birth of a new civilisation, of the type which he had caught a glimpse of in the Soviet Union. If there was hope for the future, it was because of the achievements of Soviet Russia, and barring a "world catastrophe" he saw this civilisation spreading across the world and putting an end to the wars stoked by capitalism. Nehru was working for Indian independence not just as a nationalist wanting to overthrow foreign domination, but also because political freedom would be a step towards social and economic change. He therefore wanted "the Congress to become a socialist organisation and to join hands with the other forces in the world which are working for the new civilisation."

The thought of the Congress president supporting communist world domination was enough to alarm Bombay's capitalists, usually generous donors to the Party. Ardeshir Shroff of the Indian Merchants' Chamber told his colleagues at the end of April that Nehru's comments "were more likely to injure the best interests of this country if they result in checking industrial enterprise and encouraging flight of capital from India."[xxxviii] Shroff was trying to gather support for a public letter on behalf of Bombay's businessmen denouncing Nehru's ideas, just as he arrived in the city.

Nehru did not mind the attacks; Shroff was representative of the very vested interests he wanted to do away with in his socialist state and the avoidance of conflict over interests and ideologies was something which he had been lamenting for years. And so in a public meeting Nehru did lambast Shroff for raising the "bogey of socialism" to cast a veil over the real issues facing the country, for teaming up with the Congress's opponents, and for not even being representative of the Indian merchant class.[xxxix] Shroff's letter denouncing Nehru's socialism appeared on 20 May, signed by 21 Bombay businessmen. Yet Nehru claimed that big business was veering towards fascism. He was able to derive some satisfaction when a delegation from the Merchants' Chamber visited and assured him of their support to the Congress and the nationalist cause.[xl]

Trouble in the Congress only started brewing after the announcement of provincial elections for 1937 at the end of May. Many of the conservative Congressmen, influential in their provincial Congress units and responsible for the Party's performance in the upcoming elections, began to reassure their Party workers and landed interests that the Congress president's radical utterances did not herald the immediate dawn of socialism in India. And then, on 29 June 1936, seven members of the Congress Working Committee led by Vallabhbhai Patel, Chakravarti Rajagopalachari, Jivatram Bhagwandas Kripalani and Rajendra Prasad wrote to Nehru insisting that despite their best efforts to work together they found that they could not do so and that the preaching of socialism by both himself and his socialist appointees to the Committee was prejudicial to the nationalist movement and left them with no option but to resign.

On 1 July Rajendra Prasad wrote personally to Nehru, arguing that in propagating socialism he was acting as the mouthpiece of a minority group. The conservatives felt hurt, and marginalised; "There is a regular and continuous campaign against treating us as persons whose time is over, who represent and stand for ideas that are worn out and have no present value, and who are only obstructing the progress of the country and who deserve to be cast out of the position which they unreservedly hold."[xli] Nehru then complained to Gandhi who tried to play peacemaker. He suggested that the conservatives should have been more frank with Nehru, whilst Nehru should be a bit less superior in his dealings with them.[xlii] Eventually Nehru moderated his rhetoric and the conservatives also backed down.

Jawaharlal Nehru was succeeded as Congress president by Subhas Bose, another young star of the Left wing of the Party. Bose's adherence to socialist doctrine was questionable, and his call for a fusion of socialism and fascism made him dubious in the eyes of many of the more doctrinal socialists in the Party. Nonetheless, he was supported by the Left wing during his initial election as Congress President in 1937. Conflict within the Party quickened however when Bose stood for re-election. He saw his Gandhian opponent Pattabhi Sitaramayya enjoying Right wing support and so explicitly cast the presidential election as one between opposing ideologies. He won, narrowly, with Left wing support, but his endorsement of contest rather than consensus in presidential politics alarmed conservative members of the Working Committee who then began to make his job difficult. When one had a resolution passed that Bose should appoint a Working Committee of Gandhi's choosing, his Left wing supporters absented themselves. Both the Congress Socialist Party and the Communist Party of India, which had supported his election as president failed to support him in his dispute with Gandhi and his followers. Given a choice between Bose and Gandhi, they chose Gandhi as the "greatest mobilising power" of the nationalist movement.[xliii]

Bose did make some efforts to seek Gandhi's advice in forming a new Working Committee, but by April 1939 his position had become untenable and he submitted his resignation. In May he created a Forward Bloc which brought together the Leftist groups within the Congress. Yet Bose's new bloc was attacked not just by conservatives, but by the Congress Socialist Party and Communist Party of India. The Leftist groups did come together briefly in June under a Left Consolidation Committee, but the Congress Socialist Party soon withdrew from the arrangement. Bose was administered disciplinary action by the Congress, and the Communist Party of India started denouncing him as a "Left Demagogue" and his Forward Bloc as a "counter-revolutionary organisation".[xliv] Yet with Gandhi back in control of the Congress and insisting on adherence to his constructive programme of village improvement and mandatory khadi spinning both the Socialists and Communists reverted to their customary criticism- Gandhi's policies showed the "helplessness of the national leadership".[xlv]

***

Mohandas Gandhi had studied the works of both Dadabhai Naoroji and Romesh Dutt closely. It was said that he even shed tears when he read Dutt's *An Economic History of British India*. Yet having read Dadabhai and Dutt's books, he took both men's work to his own conclusions. The modernising Congressmen of the Victorian age envisioned a post-British future based upon industrial renewal. But Gandhi's solution to India's economic calamity was to turn back to a pre-British idyll of self-sufficient village life. When he began to espouse the case for khadi spinning as India's economic salvation after the First World War many Congressmen indulged him. They thought that spinning khadi was symbolic. For Gandhi the spinning wheel was not a symbol. It would be the bedrock of the Indian economy in the 20th century. Yet his ideal of self-sufficient villagers at work in their fields, spinning khadi in their spare time, did live on with a little help from Joseph Kumarappa. He led a movement for village industries, taking his advocacy to all the high tables of the Congress in the years before and after Independence, making it as difficult as possible for Party elites to forget Gandhi and his ideas as they made their plans to modernise the Indian economy.

Whilst Mohandas Gandhi read Dadabhai Naoroji and Romesh Dutt's works, Jawaharlal Nehru's abiding influence was Karl Marx. Nehru's understanding of world history and capitalism was essentially Marxist; he relished Marx's analytical, materialist explanation of the world. He saw capitalism as intertwined with, and fuelling imperialism. It was a part of his objection to British colonialism. Yet Nehru was not a Communist. He did not take Marx's analysis to its logical conclusion- class war and the triumph of the proletariat. Nehru's fascination for Soviet Russia was thus not based on its mere enaction of Communism, but that Russia bore some resemblance to India; it was large and agricultural, and until recently pre-modern and feudal. Soviet Communism also appealed to his aesthetic sense, both for simple, unpretentious living; the opera goers in shirt sleeves, and scale; the sheer size of the projects to electrify the Russian countryside. Nehru thus settled into the sensibility of the Fabian socialism of his day. That of the Labour Party in Britain, with its admiration for the Soviet economic transformation, and unease over its inherent violence.

Indian socialism on the eve of Independence had largely come to be embodied in the figure of the soon to be prime minister, Jawaharlal Nehru and the small band of young socialists who reposed their hopes in him. These Congress Socialists were universalists. They saw India as being part of a world capitalist system, subject to the remedies of socialism. Whilst Nehru called for India to join the new socialist civilisation as it spread across the world, and then learnt to moderate his rhetoric, it was Jayaprakash Narayan who provided the first detailed charter for socialism in India in *Why Socialism?* He wanted to nationalise the cotton mills, socialise the factories with worker control, implement land reform, and establish co-operative farms. Incredibly for a young man familiar with Bihar in the 1930s, he thought that co-operative farms of the Soviet variety could be created there without much difficulty. Jayaprakash, like Nehru, did not oppose machinery. He thought that the solution to the ills of mechanisation was to socialise ownership. But unlike Nehru, he did not have to temper his criticism of Gandhi's obsession with khadi, and his sanctification of capitalism and feudalism in his theory of trusteeship. This tension, between the socialists of the Congress and the Gandhians, who sometimes called themselves socialists, or Gandhian socialists, or democratic socialists, which would eventually manifest itself on the streets of cities across India in the 1970s was thus cast as early as the 1930s.

Despite the tensions between the Gandhians and the socialists within the Congress Party in the 1930s, most educated Indians had come to a common understanding that India's poverty had been caused by equal measures of British malice and apathy. Dadabhai Naoroji had created a picture of India as a vast marketplace being looted by British traders year after year as they sold India's produce abroad, taking their profits and investing them in England rather than India. He was not against trade, but protested that what was happening in India was "not true free trade". Romesh Dutt lamented the British Government's failure to invest in irrigation and made it the chief cause of the famines which swept the land every few years during the late 19th century. India, in Mahadev Ranade's reckoning, would never be able to develop without government involvement in the creation of heavy industry and without state credit to private enterprise. Even Karl Marx, predating all the Indian thinkers, writing in *The New York Daily Tribune* in 1853, detailed the British neglect of public works in India, the deterioration of agriculture and the breakdown of textile manufacturing communities across the land under a system of laissez faire trade. Marx however, did not think that this was an entirely bad thing; it might usher in the social revolution needed to breakdown India's archaic social structure.

That intellectual backdrop, of a British Raj which had left India open to be looted and failed to invest in its infrastructure, made an idea just coming into vogue in Europe and Soviet Russia in the 1920s particularly attractive. India's civil servants, its engineers, capitalists, socialists, communists, and even Gandhians thought that the idea of economic planning, the state taking responsibility for the process of economic development and directing scarce resources to accelerate the growth of the economy, was just the tonic which India needed.

TWO

A Scientific Approach

When the Bolsheviks enacted the world's first successful communist revolution in 1917 they did not yet have well formed ideas on how they might run a communist economy; Karl Marx had left them with some abstractions, rather than the mechanics of a post-capitalist economy. It was in 1920 that the Bolshevik leader Nikolai Bukharin came to the conclusion that a "consciously implemented plan" would be the antidote to the "blind market forces" he and his comrades had been fighting to overthrow.[xlvi] The Bolsheviks had already begun the process of implementing state control over industry, nationalising land, outlawing private enterprise and forcefully acquiring the peasant's agricultural surpluses, but the creation of a planned economy in Soviet Russia was not an easy one. Vladimir Lenin announced a New Economic Policy in 1921 and a State Planning Committee came into existence but by the mid 1920s there was still no integrated plan for the production and allocation of resources and many of the early state efforts to take control of trade and agriculture had waned. As the tenth anniversary of the Revolution approached the debate over the future of planning intensified and two schools of thought emerged. One advocated 'genetic' planning based on the existing economic structure and reasonable future projections of trends within the economy. 'Teleological' planners wanted to take more dramatic measures to accelerate industrialisation by appropriating agricultural surpluses for investment in heavy industry. Joseph Stalin supported the teleological planners and their First Five Year Plan began in 1928.

The first known attempts to institute economic planning in India were not, however, inspired by Soviet Russia. Ramsay McDonald's newly elected Labour government had established an Economic Advisory Council in Britain in 1930, which was in turn stimulated by the publication in 1928 of a "Yellow Book" authored by John Keynes and his colleagues which advocated state involvement in rationalising increasingly uncompetitive British industries. It was in fact the Viceroy's Finance Member, Sir George Schuster who circulated "Notes on Economic Policy" in New Delhi which advocated the creation of India's own Economic Advisory Council. The first Indians to chart out economic plans for the country in 1934 were, again, not socialists but engineers, advisers to princely courts, and proto capitalists. Satish Mitter wrote a plan specifically for Bengal. He thought that India was just too big for a single plan. Sir Mokshagundam Visvesvaraya, deeply influenced by Mahadev Ranade, wanted the government to exercise agency in turning the economy into a modern industrial one. Ghanshyamdas Birla put his plan for the Indian economy to a meeting of the Federation of Indian Chambers of Commerce and Industry in New Delhi. None of these early Indian planners were particularly inspired by Soviet Russia's First Five Year Plan; a planned economy need not be a controlled one. India's businessmen and technocrats took the word "planning" in its commonly understood sense rather than for its specifically communist associations. Economic planning simply meant better government management of scarce resources and their direction towards industrialisation of the Indian economy. They were more likely to draw inspiration from the massive government spending taking place in the United States under Franklin Roosevelt's New Deal than Joseph Stalin's Second Five Year Plan.

Nonetheless, the specifically Soviet ideal of economic planning did make its way into the Congress Party through its socialists. By 1936 enough information on the Soviet planning experiment had made its way back to India for Jayaprakash Narayan to present a detailed picture of what Indian socialist planning might look like in *Why Socialism?* Jawaharlal Nehru and Subhas Bose alternatively held the Congress presidency in the late 1930s and both advocated socialist planning in their presidential speeches. These annual calls for planning contained more passion than detail however. Both Nehru and Bose were aware of the concerns over socialist rhetoric among their colleagues and so to address both the want of detail and potential for division, Subhas Bose, in keeping with Congress custom, instituted a National Planning Committee, one which would bring diverse elements within the Party and the country's leading technical experts into the planning process. Jawaharlal Nehru was appointed chairman, and so the process of bringing planning into the national political mainstream began.

But the word "committee" was indicative. Planning by committee was a difficult task because despite the socialist commitments of the National Planning Committee's founders, it brought together a wide spectrum of Indian economic opinion. There were Gandhians and Gandhian industrialists, and trade unionists, and Bombay capitalists, scientists, engineers and doctors, and Soviet inspired socialists all working, eventually in 27 sub-committees, to forge a plan for an independent Indian economy. Those subcommittees and the National Planning Committee itself could not come to many specific agreements for either the subsectors of the Indian economy, or the Indian economy as a whole. When the Second World War broke out and the committee members went their separate ways, some decided to do away with planning by committee and instead resolved to write their own plans.

J.R.D. Tata of the house of Tatas decided to bring some of India's leading industrialists together to forge their own plan. It was not quite the strident advocacy of a capitalist future that one might have expected of Bombay and Calcutta businessmen. They knew that their position politically and economically and in public opinion was tenuous and so their *Memorandum Outlining a Plan of Economic Development for India*, or the 'Bombay Plan' as it came to be popularly known, was a rather spare, tentative document, but one which did outline some key ideas, notably that of industrialisation led by import substitution. A few lapsed communists in the labour union movement were also commissioned, indirectly by the Government of India, to write their own plan. It arrived shortly after the Bombay Plan and was self-consciously a rebuttal to it. Despite its suitably communist sounding title, *The People's Plan*, and the antecedents of its authors, it did diverge from the communist and socialist orthodoxy of its time in one important respect; it thought that Indian prosperity would be led by the agricultural sector, rather than industry, at least initially. Planning was an idea associated at the very least with state action, and given that Mohandas Gandhi had long been opposed to statism and the centralisation of economic and political life, a Gandhian Plan might have seemed incongruous. But given the power of the idea, and the word 'planning' in India in the 1940s, a college economics professor resident near Gandhi's Wardha ashram published *The Gandhian Plan for the Economic Development of India*, one which stretched the meaning of the word 'planning' to its very limits.

***

What made the need for economic planning seem so urgent in India was that there had been so little of it during the previous hundred years of British rule. The principle of laissez faire, or a free market economy, had been an enduring ideal of the British Raj, much like that of the British as a ruling race and the nobility of Britain's mission in India. The British Government had held so fast to laissez faire both at home and abroad throughout the 19th century that it had, over time, come to be associated with the British sense of self.

Such was the British commitment to laissez faire that until 1854 India did not have a Public Works Department. Each presidency's Military Board was responsible for the construction and maintenance of public works, which were sporadic and largely devoted to the development of an infrastructure for defence. It was only after Viceroy Dalhousie established a separate Public Works Department that more attention was given to civil public works; during the later years of the 1850s the budget for public works quadrupled as more money was spent on roads, civic buildings, canals, embankments and irrigation.

It was also during the 1850s that a mercantile association of Manchester sent a memorial to the directors of the East India Company for 'facilities', a euphemism for a guaranteed rate of return, for the extension of irrigation and canals in southern India.[xlvii] As a result a Madras Irrigation Company was formed, with the requested guarantee, and another, an East India Irrigation Company, without it. And whilst both companies did build large irrigation works, the rate of return was so low that each relied on the government for loans and East India Irrigation eventually handed its operations over to the state in the 1860s.

During the early 1860s India experienced a 'cotton boom', which prompted the Public Works Department to spend money on 'cotton roads' into and out of the cotton producing districts. In fact, James Wilson, Finance Member of the Viceroy's Council and founder of *The Economist* thought that the building of public works and roads for increased production of cotton, flax, wool and other raw materials was the highest duty of the government, particularly given that the textile industry in Lancashire was being starved of supply due to the American Civil War.[xlviii] The Cotton Supply Association of Manchester, the Manchester Chamber of Commerce and the 'cotton MPs' all lobbied the Government of India to expand the supply of cotton.

The British cotton lobby argued that the Indian people were unambitious, and generally opposed to innovation and change, which made it essential that roads and transport facilities be built to provide them with an incentive to produce more.[xlix] It wanted roads, harbours, railways and canals built, whether by the Government of India or private British capital. Both Manchester associations were champions of laissez faire in England, yet wanted the state to play a greater role in India. To complete the circle of irony, when they lobbied the Government of India for greater state intervention they were met with the same laissez faire arguments which they would themselves have made in England- that it was not the government's place to interfere, and where there was a demand there would be a supply. Nonetheless, the merchants of Manchester replied that what held true in England did not in India. The Government of India remained firm however, and would restrict itself to providing aid to private enterprises to build the roads and railways which would open up the Indian hinterland.

It was the Railways in which this state aid to private enterprise was most evident. The Government of India provided the land and guaranteed a minimum rate of interest, usually 5%, on paid up capital for 99 years. This guaranteed rate was actually higher than the rate paid on government bonds. The government also suffered losses on foreign exchange transactions, had no means to control expenditure, and the railway companies would overdraw their accounts and fail to keep up on payments in England for advances in India. The private railway companies also had the privilege of handing over railway lines to the government and receiving full compensation for all capital expenditure at any point prior to the lapse of the 99 year agreement. At the end of the 99 years the railway lines and works became the property of the Government of India.

In the late 1860s the government did however start to

build railways under the tutelage of the Viceroy, Sir John Lawrence, who had widespread support for his position that state railways would be cheaper and more efficient than private companies. He faced some resistance at home from the Secretary of State Sir Stafford Northcote, who only conceded that "political lines", those built for security purposes, should be built by the state.[i] Yet Sir John gained the support of a new Secretary of State, George Campbell, the Duke of Argyll during his last months in office, who pointed out that these guaranteed railway companies did not represent the highest ideals of private enterprise.[ii] Richard Bourke, the Earl of Mayo succeeded Sir John as Viceroy and Argyll was, together with the new viceroy, able to convince the government to construct two new railway lines. It would be cheaper to raise funds; the government could borrow at 4% rather than the 5% guaranteed to the companies, it could involve Indian capital rather than rely exclusively on British capital, do away with private management, and also bring construction costs down.

By 1869 and 1870 the forces in favour of, and against laissez faire clashed once more, this time over the issue of the establishment of a Department of Agriculture, Industry and Commerce. Viceroy Mayo and the members of his Council were largely in favour of the Department. Mayo thought that the duties which were performed by a good landlord in England fell to the government in India, or to put it another way, the only Indian landlord who could command the requisite knowledge for improvement of the land was the state.[iii] However back in England, Major-General Sir Henry Durand argued that the government had no special aptitude for the task, and that the education of private enterprise was not the function of the government.[iiii] He would rather trust the slow growth of private enterprise. Viceroy Mayo and his Council retorted that it was sometimes necessary for the government to be the pioneer of private enterprise; as in the case of the tea industry in India for which the state made the outlay and assumed the initial risk and then private planters took over at a later stage.[liv] Even back in the days of the East India Company, the state encouraged the cotton trade by improving local varieties of raw cotton.

Yet despite Viceroy Mayo's advocacy, the government stuck to its principle of laissez faire in most aspects of economic life in India; it refused to interfere with the flow of food grains during famines, refrained from spending on social overheads, played little role in promoting industry, and made no effort to create a system of progressive taxation.

***

Indian objections to the laissez faire policies of the British Raj were quite different to those made by British merchants. Indian politicians and journalists were less concerned with the Government of India's approach to building infrastructure like railways, and more concerned about the tariffs it levied on the import of British goods into India. Educated Indians could become quite emotional when import duties on British textiles were reduced or repealed, or excises, nominal or countervailing, were applied to the cloth produced in Indian mills.

In 1858 British cotton twist and yarns were levied with a 3.5% duty and other British goods such as cotton pieces had to pay a 5% duty on arrival in India. The rates of duty on imports from other countries were double those on these British goods. But the Government of India was facing financial difficulties after the Mutiny and so it was forced to raise the import duty to 5% on cotton twist and yarns and to 10% on other British goods. By 1860 it also had to raise the import duty on cotton twist and yarns to 10%. Cotton manufacturers in Britain began lobbying the British Government and the Government of India to reduce the tariff once more, and by 1861 it was back down to 5% and the following year to the original 3.5%.

The duty on cotton piece goods was also brought down to 5% by 1862. General import duties were reduced from 10% to 7.5% by 1864 and to 5% by 1875.

In 1874 the already low cotton duties, which made up half of the Government of India's revenue from import duties, came under attack from the cotton manufacturers of Lancashire. The Manchester Chamber of Commerce addressed a memorial to the secretary of state seeking the abolition of duties on cotton manufactures. In reply, a committee of the Government of India rejected the idea that the duties were protective in nature. Nonetheless the new Secretary of State, Robert Gascoyne-Cecil, the Marquess of Salisbury lobbied the Government of India to eliminate the tariffs. He argued that they were opposed to Britain's general policy of free trade, and also harmed British manufacturers by restricting their exports to India.[lv] In addition, with protection from the Government of India, prices would rise for the Indian consumer and the Indian textile industry would only grow under artificial stimulation and thus become dependent on the state. Salisbury issued a directive, but the Viceroy, Thomas Baring, the Lord Northbrook put up resistance, arguing that the tariffs were not protective and even placed a 5% duty on the import of long staple cotton.[lvi]

But then in 1875 Northbrook departed as viceroy and was replaced by the arch conservative Robert Bulwer-Lytton, and so resistance from the Government of India waned. In 1877 the House of Commons passed a resolution that the duties should be repealed. Despite the financial demands of a war in Afghanistan, famines, and the depreciation of the value of silver, import duties on coarse cotton goods were abolished in 1878 as were those with a count lower than 30 the following year. After 1882, with the budget in surplus, duties on cotton imports were abolished. Only the duties on salt, arms and wine remained. For the following 12 years India was without tariff protection and, at least in the realm of international trade, was one of the most laissez faire economies in the world.

As early as 1874 *Sahachar* was remonstrating against the repeal of duties on cotton imports. By 1879 the leading public men and journals were condemning the repeal of duties on coarse cotton goods and the further exemption from duty of grey cotton goods. Surendranath Banerjea referred to these policies as a "wanton sacrifice" of India's interests, whilst *Sadharani* expressed its disgust with Viceroy Lytton's character and referred to the "imbecility" of his policies.[lvii] When the complete abolition of cotton duties was announced in 1882 the *Anand Bazaar Patrika* called it a "crime".[lviii] British officials argued that import duties were providing artificial protection for Indian cotton mills, but the nationalists retorted that the duties had relatively little impact on Indian industry, which had natural advantages in the production of coarse cotton, whilst it did not produce many of the finer cotton counts made in England. Most nationalists argued that it was better for the Government of India to raise revenue from tariffs rather than go into debt to finance its spending.

It became apparent to Indian nationalists that the Government of India's tariff policies were not being maintained as a matter of principle. Neither did they benefit the Indian people, or the government itself. They were instead being driven by the influence of Lancashire's cotton manufacturers on British parliamentarians. This idea was captured in the title to the *Bodha Sudharak's* 15 December 1875 editorial: "The Selfish Merchants of Manchester and their Bounden Servant the Secretary of State for India."[lix] In Bombay moderate nationalists like Mahadev Ranade and Rao Bahadur Khrishnaji Nulkar of the Poona Sarvajanik Samaj shared the sentiment. Ranade thought that British officials in India had "sacrificed the interests of India in the name of free trade" and surrendered vital revenue to "gratify Manchester".[lx] Nulkar even accused the same officials of "prostituting their power...in order to gain favour with Manchester."[lxi]

At a more profound level British tariff policy was betraying the idea that Britain ruled for the welfare of the Indian people. Bholonath Chandra made the point in *Mukherjee's Magazine* in 1876. He thought that the tariff issue was indicative rather than substantive. Indian cotton mills would grow irrespective of the government's policies due to their natural advantages. Instead he asserted that "the real point struggled for by our nation was to know whether India was being governed in Indian interests or in the interests of England."[lxii]

During the 1880s imports into India surged, the construction of the railways accelerated, military expenditure rose, and the value of the rupee fell. The finances of the Government of India were put under pressure once again, but a resort to fresh taxation did not bring the budget back into balance. In 1894 the Government of India was faced with a deficit of ₹3.5 crore, and so it took the advice of the Indian Currency Committee of 1893 which had recommended the imposition of import duties as the best way to raise funds without exciting political opposition. A new Tariff Act was thus passed in 1894, imposing a general 5% duty on all imports. Yet cotton fabrics, yarns and threads were all exempt from the new Act, something which unleashed the anticipated protests from Indian nationalists. So in December 1894 the government passed a new Act which subjected imports of cotton fabrics and yarns to a duty of 5%. But, a countervailing excise duty of 5% was imposed on higher quality cloth coming out of Indian mills.[lxiii]

It was the Secretary of State, Henry Fowler who insisted on the countervailing excise duty in opposition to his officials in India, something which brought 20% of the total production of Indian mills under what amounted to a new tax on production. But the mill owners of Lancashire were still dissatisfied, and so in February 1896 the Government of India enacted two new pieces of legislation which abolished both import duties and excise

A Scientific Approach

on cotton yarns and also reduced the import duty on woven goods from 5% to 3.5% whilst imposing an excise on woven goods coming out of Indian mills. This meant that the Government of India's revenues on imported goods declined by 37%, whilst revenues on Indian products rose by 300%.[lxiv]

Not only did the new tariff and excise rates set off expected newspaper headlines and editorials, but also the first boycott movement in Bombay under Bal Gangadhar Tilak's leadership. It was also at this time that redress for tariff policy came into the mainstream of Congress politics. Even the most moderate of Indian political leaders were stirred to sharp language on account of the duty. In 1902 and 1904 the Congress passed strongly worded resolutions against the countervailing duty. Gopal Krishna Gokhale, the leader of the moderate Indian nationalists in the Indian Legislative Council, argued for repeal of the duty in his speeches in the chamber, whilst Congress Presidents Narayan Chandavarkar and Surendranath Banerjea continued to demand the abolition of the duty. Romesh Dutt wrote of the duty in his *Economic History of British India* as a case of "fiscal injustice...unexampled in modern times".

***

Tariff policy, like much of the British Raj, was largely static between the Mutiny of 1857 and the outbreak of the First World War in 1914. Small adjustments were made, and they were fiercely debated, but the basic pattern remained. Yet just as political power was increasingly devolved to Indian politicians in the provinces and the elite services of the state were opened to Indian officers with the outbreak of the war, long held British positions on trade and industry also began to change.

The Government of India established an Industrial Commission chaired by Sir Thomas Holland of the Munitions Board in 1916. The Commission was influenced by the need to increase wartime industrial production as well as the idea that nations which were self-reliant in industrial production would be at an advantage after the war. Sir Thomas produced a report in 1918 which outlined a plan for industrial development and advocated a large role for the Government of India in industrialisation by investment in social overhead capital, the promotion of technical education and research, the establishment of industrial banks, and the direct supply of financial and entrepreneurial assistance to private industry.[lxv]

In 1920 the Munitions Board was converted into a Board of Industries and Munitions. The new Board was to frame more detailed proposals for a Department of Industries, to be inaugurated the following year under Sir Thomas's direction. The Government of India and the British Government wanted industrial policy to be made a central subject under the Government of India Act 1919, knowing that the provinces would not be able to handle it, however Indian politicians wanted the subject devolved to the provincial level where they would be able to exercise greater control.[lxvi]

The government responded to Indian opinion however, and industrial development was made a provincial subject under the 1919 Act. There were still plans for central cadres of technical advisers to the provinces, but these were abandoned in 1922. Sir Thomas left the Executive Council in 1921 and the Department of Industries was stripped of its responsibilities, except for the protection of labour. The only roles which the Industrial Commission had recommended which remained were the supply of industrial intelligence and the creation of state factories. Provincial governments did not want the intelligence and the money made available for state factories achieved little.[lxvii] After the pressures of the war, the case for a bold new industrial policy for India gradually started to weaken.

There was however a growing sense of a self-contained,

self-reliant British Empire, and so the idea of 'imperial preference' began to gain ground over the long held laissez faire ideal. Tariff policy was largely devolved by London to Delhi, with the secretary of state only intervening in matters of security. An Imperial Preference Committee was established within the Government of India's Secretariat which recommended considering a policy of protection for India. The recommendation was accepted and the protectionists within the government packed a new Fiscal Commission with members who favoured protection rather than preference. The Commission reported in 1922 and found a middle ground between the two ideas; 'discriminating protection' would be provided for industries which could serve an import substituting role.[lxviii] The measure would be 'dynamic comparative advantage'; if given a period of protection, local firms would need to be able to achieve the economies of scale which would eventually allow them to compete with foreign competitors without assistance. They would also have to show that there was sufficient demand for their products in the Indian market and enough supply of labour and materials.

A Tariff Board was then established to hear cases and make non-binding recommendations to the Government of India. The Board conducted 51 enquiries and granted protection to 11 industries: iron and steel, cotton textiles, sugar, paper, matches, slate, heavy chemicals, plywood and tea chests, sericulture, magnesium chloride and gold thread. Some protection was also provided to growers of wheat and rice. Until 1914 the customs duties on imports had been low: there was a 5% ad valorem duty and 3.5% on cotton goods. In 1916 both rates were raised to 7.5% and in 1921 to 11%. Duties on sugar were raised to 15% and on luxury goods to 20%. The general ad valorem rate was raised to 15% in 1922. The tariffs on sugar went up to 25%, and on luxury goods to 30%. The ad valorem rate went as high as 25% by 1931. The rate on motor cars was 37.5% and on wireless instruments it was 50%. In 1930 a rate of 20% was fixed for low quality cotton goods (15% for British goods) which was increased to 50% for non-British goods in 1932 and to 75% in 1933. There was a tariff on imported sugar of 190% by 1931. Indian mills producing paper, matches, rubber and sugar all grew after the war behind a wall of protection.[lxix]

It might have seemed that the British Raj's embrace of the idea of "discriminating protection" and the subsequent creation of tariff walls for the protection of Indian industries would have largely met the demands of the Indian nationalists of the pre-war era. Yet the criticisms of Dadabhai Naoroji and Romesh Dutt and Bal Gangadhar Tilak lamenting the inequity of laissez faire economics found new life in the 1930s and 1940s. Laissez faire was no longer identified with specific British trade policies as in the 19th century. In Jawaharlal Nehru's writing laissez faire was capitalism, which fuelled imperialism, and both were destructive, outmoded forces which needed to be remedied with a modern, scientific and humane socialism. The term "laissez faire" was held in such low esteem that even India's capitalists thought that there was little point in talking about it.[lxx] Laissez faire thus remained synonymous with predatory British capitalism in India, which is why the word, and the idea of "planning" came to hold such appeal for so many within the Indian elite. Planning was the antonym of laissez faire; Indian ingenuity would finally replace British negligence.

***

The first Indians to advocate economic planning saw it as a means to forge a purposeful Indian industrial capitalism which would replace Britain's exploitative colonial capitalism. Specifically, they wanted to end the pillage of India's raw materials, modernise agriculture, and move Indians off the land and into a growing industrial sector. For Indian industry to truly develop however, it would need to acquire the capacity to make the machines and industrial components which were imported from Europe and Japan.

Sir Mokshagundam Visvesvaraya had worked for the Bombay Government and the Nizam of Hyderabad overseeing sanitation, irrigation and dam projects before becoming chief engineer of the princely state of Mysore. He became dewan in 1913 and had also been a director of Tata Steel. He knew that Sir George Schuster, the finance member had since 1930 been trying to convince the government to establish an Economic Advisory Council which might lead to an economic plan for India. Sir Arthur Salter, an officer of the Home Civil Service had visited India in 1931 and had similarly tried to persuade the government, but, by 1934 the British Raj had not been stirred to action. Sir Visvesvaraya's book *Planned Economy for India* thus sought to stimulate government action. Satish Mitter had served in the Department of Industries of the Bengal Government, and like Sir Visvesvaraya knew of Sir George and Sir Arthur's attempts to start a movement towards economic planning. But unlike Sir Visvesvaraya's Indian plan, Mitter's was *A Recovery Plan for Bengal*; he thought that India was just too vast a land for a single economic plan and instead wanted to steer young Bengalis who had taken to political violence back towards the more useful task of economic reconstruction.

The aim of Sir Visvesvaraya's plan was to double India's national income within ten years. He thought that there was limited demand for agricultural products, which meant that the "money value" of industries was more important. During the Depression in America the prices of agricultural products had fallen by 69%, whereas those of industry had fallen by only 24%. He thus wanted to triple investment in industry and quadruple production. He did not think that his proposed investment of ₹700 crore over 10 years was too ambitious; it paled in comparison to the almost ₹2,000 crore invested in the Soviet Union in one year alone. The initial investment would be in factories which would produce the machinery for the Armed Forces and Railways and after that industries connected with electrical machinery, metals, chemicals, tractors and automobiles. There would be even regional distribution of these industries; two or three would be located in each province. Emphasis needed to be placed on steel as it was the basis of industries such as transport, mining, agriculture and textiles, besides its obvious importance for metals and machine industries.

Importantly, Sir Visvesvaraya did not think that these industries would make very much progress were they left to the private sector. The government needed to take the lead, "as every progressive government is now doing". There needed to be an official organisation for the purpose with better reporting and statistics. Without this data there would be uncertain production, tariff protection might be insufficient, foreign competitors may be let loose and public support for the planning project may wane. The most important support which the government could provide to new industries would be easy access to capital and tariff protection from foreign competitors.

Sir Visvesvaraya's plan for agriculture was quite modest. He wanted to reduce employment in agriculture by 20%. He thought that Indian agriculture was in a primitive state. Some of his remedies included preventing fragmentation of land holdings and encouraging their consolidation, employment in cottage industries, a reduction in rural indebtedness, the establishment of co-operative credit societies, land mortgage banks to provide the capital for improvement of the land, a proliferation of agricultural education in schools and colleges, modern tools and machinery, and farmers acting in co-operation in the spirit of collective self-help.

Sir Visvesvaraya wanted to double road mileage and electric power and increase the railway network by a third. Shipping would be vastly expanded and all automobiles would be manufactured within the country. He thought that the general aim of trade should be to export as many manufactured goods as possible whilst minimising their import. He did not think that there should be any objection to importing machinery or other products which could not yet be made in India or supplies needed for local manufacturers. But given India's vast supply of underemployed and unemployed labour it was humiliating to be sending commodities to the world and importing manufactures. Nonetheless, he did recognise that foreign trade supported business activity and a high standard of living. He also foresaw that the Indian central and provincial governments would have to go into debt during the first half of his plan. He did not think that this would pose a problem given that economic growth in the second half of the plan would generate higher tax returns.

It was during the First World War that Ghanshyamdas Birla, still a young man in his early 20s, began to transform his family's trading house into a modern industrial business. His grandfather, father and uncles had been banias, or traders, in Bombay and Calcutta dealing in opium, silver, sugar and cotton. Yet Ghanshyamdas used the wartime boom in demand for raw jute to open an office in London, quickly quadrupling the family's net worth.[lxxi] The Indian trading community had traditionally functioned in a relationship of co-operation with the government and big British businesses, happy to take its cut on the distribution of British goods in India. Likewise, British businessmen had been content to leave the work of trading in raw materials to their banias, as long as they were able to monopolise their manufacture in their Calcutta mills. When he established the Birla Jute Mill in Calcutta in 1918 Ghanshyamdas was thus both breaking away from his own socially and economically conservative Marwari community, and acting in defiance of Calcutta's Scottish jute barons. During the early 1920s he would lead a more progressive section of his Calcutta based Marwari community and, in 1927, collaborate with Purushottmadas Thakurdas of Bombay to form the Federation of Indian Chambers of Commerce and Industry. Ghanshyamdas was, among Indian businessmen, an ardent nationalist known for his proximity to the Congress leadership, particularly Mohandas Gandhi. He sat in the Imperial Legislative Assembly in Delhi, attended Round Table Conferences in London and thus acted as an intermediary between the Raj and the nationalist movement.

G.D. Birla placed his thoughts on economic planning before the Federation of Indian Chambers of Commerce and Industry at its Annual General Meeting in April 1934.[lxxii] He did not think that planning was an intrinsically good concept, it generally benefitted from its good associations. He wanted to specify the aims of planning so that the idea not be misused and the country be led astray: the object of planning should be to bring about maximum prosperity with reasonable effort. Birla thought that there was a limit beyond which the Indian standard of living could be raised without adopting "unjust means". An idea prevalent among the Indian elite was that the high standards of living enjoyed in the West could only come about through colonial exploitation. Birla maintained that India had been at the receiving end of such exploitation and did not wish to inflict it on others. Those who thought that the country could attain the Western standard of living "without any colony to feed or slave for her" were under a "gross illusion".

India had not yet "infringed the natural law" like England and Japan had done in building up their industries along "artificial lines". This had made them dependent on their colonies for the supply of raw material and the sale of manufactures. India's problem was different, it had as a colony, even when it had both the supply of raw materials and a ready domestic market, been relying on the import of manufactured goods. This situation had to stop. Production had to be increased so that local demand could be met by the supply of local goods. The balance would have to be imported, and then exports would have to be encouraged for goods which could not be consumed in the Indian market but for which a market existed abroad.

One of the founding principles of planning, according to Birla, would be that self-sufficiency should not be attempted "except where the conditions are decidedly in favour of it". He did not think that there was much point in trying to produce a product for which the country did not enjoy any natural advantages or a ready market. Products like tea, jute, paper, cement, steel, cloth and sugar did not fall into this category however. Birla did not aim for complete self-sufficiency but saw a time under a planned economy when imports would actually exceed existing levels as the standard of living rose and Indians began to demand consumer goods which they were not yet familiar with. He did not think that there would be a need for self-sufficiency in machinery or motor cars, apparatuses and appliances, wool, silk, cotton fabrics, dyes and chemicals, or mill stores and mineral oil. When India's international trade was brought under planning there would be no need to enter into iniquitous trade pacts. Trade would only occur when India could not produce a product or when it produced too much for the home market.

Industry would not need too much direct encouragement in Birla's plan. Protective tariffs combined with a burgeoning home market would suffice. However, agriculture would require "some big concentrated effort" and it would take direct subsidies in order to get the farmer to produce more. Sufficiency in food was crucial for national health and no cost was too much to attain it. There would need to be a change in the land laws, a reduction in rents, direct subsidies to dairy and fruit producers, and the regulation and organisation of cattle breeding.

Birla argued that it was outmoded to think in terms of gold and silver and paper currency. But even if financial resources were to be counted in such terms, India did not suffer any shortage. There were ₹53 crores stored in the Gold Standard Reserve. If the paper currency was revalued at the current price of gold then there would be no shortage of money to spend on economic development. India's real wealth lay in its labour; in this sense India was one of the wealthiest countries in the world. Yet nobody complained of the unutilised labour as they did of the practice of hoarding wealth in the form of gold. The question of financing the plan was thus not a cause for concern. Like Sir Visvesvaraya, Birla thought that if spent properly, money would flow back into the government's coffers. He cited the examples of both Hitler's Germany and Roosevelt's America which had undertaken massive spending on public works and infrastructure. He was clearly a Keynesian, stating that sometimes a cottage needed to balance its books, but a national exchequer did not. India's challenge was to utilise idle labour and capital and produce goods to meet demand.

Birla did express some concern over centralisation of production and creating too large a gap between the upper and lower stratas of society. He was speaking mainly of geographical centralisation of industry; it would disturb rural life, cause a waste of labour and lead to industrial unrest. The sugar industry in which mills were located close to the fields could provide a model. Workers would ideally be able to work close to their own homes rather than having to travel to distant cities. Industrial expansion would take place in rural areas and might be brought about by zonal planning. Given that India would industrialise on the basis of its home market however, he did not see Indian industry being more than "a tiny little spot on the map of India" for some time to come. In order to increase production it was necessary to increase the purchasing power of the masses. Without such an increase in purchasing power India's new production would simply decorate its warehouses. The extra wealth created would have to find its way into the "cottages", or rural India, and not form a "stagnant pool".

***

A Scientific Approach

When Jawaharlal Nehru and Subhas Bose began to advocate economic planning in their presidential speeches in the late 1930s it was not India's capitalists or their friends in the Congress whom they had to convince. The biggest sceptics of planning were the Gandhians.

Jawaharlal Nehru's presidential speech at the Congress session at Faizpur in December 1936 dealt with the gamut of issues facing the Party. He acknowledged comrades in and out of prison, spoke of the rise of fascism in Italy, the civil war in Spain, the fragility of peace in Europe, the need for internationalism, the constitutional problems arising out of the Government of India Act 1935, and the prospects of broadening the membership of the Party. Mention of planning thus came as a rhetorical flourish at the end of a long speech. There were so many problems facing India, and the land was so vast and complex that the solutions could not come from "petty tinkering and patchwork" in which vested interests would stand in the way: "Only a great planned system for the whole land and dealing with all these various national activities, co-ordinating them, making each serve the larger whole and the interests of the mass of our people, only such a planned system with a vision and courage to back it, can find a solution." Such a planned system would not come about in the midst of monopolies and imperialist exploitation however. Political independence was first needed to bring it about.

After victories in the 1937 provincial elections the Congress adopted a resolution at Wardha in August 1937 on national reconstruction and social planning. It was the first time that planning had found mention in an official Congress document and it recommended the appointment of a committee of experts to examine river valley projects, the sugar industry, a debt moratorium and explore the possibility of an All India Industrial Plan.

Subhas Bose outlined some of the principles on which

India's future reconstruction would take place in his presidential speech at Haripura in February 1938. Bose thought that the national problems of poverty, illiteracy, disease, and the challenge of establishing scientific production and distribution could only be tackled along socialistic lines. It was in this context that he proposed that a future national government establish a commission which would "draw up a comprehensive plan for reconstruction". There would be a short term and a long term component to the plan. This commission however, and indeed the proposed plan, were not purely economic but would seek to balance national unification with regional autonomy. Bose also addressed the population issue: with so much poverty and misery India could not afford to have its population increasing by 30 million each decade. If it did, he feared, "our plans are likely to fall through".

Bose went on to argue for the abolition of both landlordism and peasant indebtedness and for greater availability of cheap credit on the land. Co-operatives needed to be established and agriculture would have to be put on a scientific basis. But agricultural revival would not be enough. State control and state ownership would be necessary for industrial revival, and so the proposed planning commission would have to assess which of the "home industries", or cottage industries, could be revived and in which industries large-scale production would be encouraged. Bose made it clear that despite a dislike of modern industrial civilisation amongst some in the Congress there was no turning back to an earlier era. He was making a pitch for the advance of industrialism whilst also calming the nerves of the Gandhians in his audience; there would be plenty of room for cottage industries "like handspinning and weaving". He ended with a call for the state to completely socialise the agricultural and industrial system in both production and appropriation.

Subhas Bose called industry ministers from the Congress provinces to New Delhi in October 1938 to report on existing industries and discuss the possibilities of further industrialisation. In addition to Sir Visvesvaraya and G.D. Birla who had already written their own plans, Meghnad Saha, an astrophysicist at the University of Calcutta, and Lala Shri Ram and Lala Shankar Lal of Delhi Cotton & General Mills were also invited to attend the meeting. The socialist ideal had been put aside and national autonomy, development of mother industries, technical education and research, and an economic survey of the country were discussed. The conference also directed the provinces to start manufacturing units. It was at this conference that the National Planning Committee was initiated. Bose was to select the committee members and V.V. Giri, the industry minister from Madras was given the task of setting up an All India Planning Commission.

Soon after the conference Subhas Bose made his appointments to the National Planning Committee. Jawaharlal Nehru was appointed chairman and Sir Visvesvaraya, Meghnad Saha, and Ardeshir Shroff also accepted invitations. Cotton magnates, Purshottomdas Thakurdas of Bombay, and Ambalal Sarabhai of Ahmadabad were also brought on board, as were the scientists A.K. Saha, Dr. Nazir Ahmad, Dr. V.S. Dubey, and Dr. J.C. Ghosh. At this time the only economist on the committee was Khushal Talaksi Shah, a professor of economics at the University of Mysore and committed socialist who shared Nehru's admiration for Soviet Russia.

***

And so, by 1938, an attempt to chart a course for a planned economy for India had finally begun. Significantly, the meeting of minds was called the National Planning Committee, rather than the Congress Planning Committee; every effort had been made to bring as broad a cross section of Indian political opinion and professional competence onto the committee as possible.

The first session of the committee was held in Bombay in

December 1938. Subhas Bose inaugurated the meeting and had to reassure the Gandhians that there was no inherent conflict between large-scale and cottage industries.[lxxiii] He suggested that an All India Village Industries Association representative be brought onto the committee, and so Joseph Kumarappa was appointed. Narayan Malhar Joshi of the All India Trade Union Congress was also inducted to represent the labour movement at Nehru's behest.[lxxiv]

The committee's first task was to draw up a questionnaire for government departments. Three major issues were debated. Sir Visvesvaraya wanted the committee to direct the provinces to set up industries, but most committee members thought that such a directive could not be imposed upon the provincial governments which held jurisdiction over industrial policy. Nehru maintained that it was not the committee's role to issue such specific directives but to evolve a general plan for economic development.[lxxv] The discussion then turned to the relationship between cottage and large-scale industries. Joseph Kumarappa questioned whether the committee should be discussing large-scale industrialisation at all.[lxxvi] Nehru once again assured all members that there was no conflict between the two. The majority of the committee members disagreed with Kumarappa and the questions on large-scale industries were included.[lxxvii] Ambalal Sarabhai, who was both an industrialist and a Gandhian, wanted to know what stand the committee would take on the land question.[lxxviii] The initial response was that land issues were beyond the committee's purview. It was subsequently decided that agrarian issues were essential to the idea of planning and so they were included in the questionnaire.

The second session of the National Planning Committee was held six months later in Bombay in June 1939. Jawaharlal Nehru had to emphasise that the Congress agenda of encouraging cottage industries did not preclude a focus on industrialisation, and in fact industrialisation was the reason for the formation of the committee.[lxxix] Ambalal Sarabhai also submitted his own note that no large-scale industry be allowed to grow which might compete with cottage industries.[lxxx] He also wanted more government involvement in agriculture, specifically, a government corporation which would purchase produce directly from farmers, and for industries to be licensed, prices controlled, and the renting of land banned. Purushottamdas Thakurdas wanted the scope of the committee restricted but Nehru maintained that what they were really doing was just a beginning, some preliminary work for the planning process which would develop later.[lxxxi] Joseph Kumarappa then tried a new argument; he was not opposed to large-scale public utilities, but they should be owned by the government. Yet as the Congress did not have control over the government the committee should limit itself to the development of cottage and village industries.[lxxxii] Nehru however maintained that whilst the Congress had always encouraged village industries, it was the development of heavy industry which was most urgent, the two had to be co-ordinated and this was the purpose of planning. Kumarappa was not content with Nehru's attempts at conciliation and wrote to Congress President Rajendra Prasad asking him to intervene. Prasad refused to do so. But he did suggest that foreign or Indian cloth which might compete with khadi would be discouraged, whilst similar protection would be provided to cottage industries once the Congress was sure that they could function independently of their mechanised competitors. The Congress President's reassurances were not sufficient for Kumarappa. He began a period of non-cooperation with the committee.

The main accomplishment of the second session of the National Planning Committee was the formation of 27 subcommittees. They would analyse the replies to the questionnaires and submit reports within three months. The committee also issued a resolution calling on the provincial governments to stop foreign companies from

"Indianising" their factories to confuse Indians who wanted to boycott foreign goods, and to prohibit the establishment of new factories or the transfer of ownership without prior permission. The committee also wanted the government census of 1941 to collect economic data and for Prasanta Mahalanobis at the Indian Statistical Institute, Calcutta and John Mathai at Tata & Sons in Bombay to provide suggestions to the government on the type of economic data it should collect in the future.

The Second World War broke out and both Sir Visvesvaraya and Joseph Kumarappa resigned from the committee. Nehru then called a meeting of the chairmen and secretaries of the subcommittees in February 1940 in order to give them some collective direction. It was decided that defence industries would be state owned, yet the committee could not agree over whether "key industries" should be owned or controlled by the state. The majority favoured ownership, whilst a substantial minority preferred control. It was agreed however that control of key industries would be rigid.[lxxxiii] The third session of the National Planning Committee was held in May 1940 and two more were held in June and August. With the antagonists gone the meetings proceeded in a more orderly manner. Of the 27 subcommittees, 19 had submitted their reports by the time of the fifth session in September 1940.

The National Planning Committee resolved in favour of the establishment of heavy engineering industries, and that key industries would be "owned or controlled" by the state. But the state would also initially encourage private enterprise by offering guarantees and protection from foreign competition for a transitional period. The committee was opposed to monopolies and would acquire those which were injurious to the public interest. Foreign companies would be tightly controlled and foreign countries would be treated in a reciprocal manner in trade matters. The committee also wanted a limitation in working hours, a minimum wage, safety and sanitation, social insurance, a standardisation of measures and better statistics. Further, private enterprise would come under a system of licensing. There were also three resolutions on land ownership: all forms of national wealth would be vested in the people, collective or co-operative farms would be established, initially on waste land which would be acquired by the state, and intermediaries and subletting would be prohibited.[lxxxiv] Nehru was sending subcommittee reports to Prasanta Mahalanobis in Calcutta before they were considered by the committee.[lxxxv]

That September session was the last for many years. The enterprise fell into disarray. The committee was dependent on the funds of the monied men like Ardeshir Shroff and Purshottomdas Thakurdas who had lost interest in the endeavour, Mohandas Gandhi did not want the reports published, Jawaharlal Nehru was in jail and so it was left to K.T. Shah to keep the Congress's planning effort alive. He published more subcommittee reports and managed to produce his own treatise, *Principles of Planning* in March 1943.

Whilst the efforts of British civil servants in the early 1930s to institute some form of economic planning had been unsuccessful, the need to plan for India's industrial future did lead the government to establish a Post-War Interdepartmental Reconstruction Committee in 1941. The committee was even to "prepare developmental plans for India".[lxxxvi] Four subcommittees were formed and late in 1943 the Viceroy, Victor Hope, the Marquess of Linlithgow replaced the Interdepartmental Committee with a Reconstruction Committee of his Viceroy's Council with its own policy committees. As of early 1944 however the only firm decision to emerge from the work of these committees and subcommittees was "to appoint Development Officers responsible to the appropriate department of the Central Government for the preparation of an all-India plan as the basis for discussion by the appropriate Committee concerned."[lxxxvii]

***

Jehangir Ratanji Dadabhoy Tata, Chairman of Tata & Sons had only returned to India in 1924 at the age of 21. He had been born and raised in France, his father Ratanji Tata was a cousin of Jamsetji, the founder of the group. J.R.D. Tata's position in the Indian political milieu was quite different to that of G.D. Birla. The Tatas had been much closer to the British, both economically and culturally, and had, since the arrival of Mohandas Gandhi and his calls for non-cooperation and civil disobedience, largely opposed the Congress. Their business, by the 1920s, was already a modern industrial concern, and the largest, and in some cases only customer for their products such as steel and railway sleepers was the government. In addition, the Tata Board of Directors was usually well staffed with retired Indian officers of the Indian Civil Service.

It took 10 years for the Tatas to join the Federation of Indian Chambers of Commerce and Industry but the association did not last long. Tata & Sons resigned from the Chamber in 1939. The Second World War had broken out and it was likely that Tata Steel would benefit from a surge in demand from the government. J.R.D. did make some halting efforts to establish better relations with Jawaharlal Nehru, but he was not invited to be a member of the National Planning Committee.[lxxxviii] So in November 1942 he wrote to Purshottamdas Thakurdas to inform him that the first informal meeting of his own 'Post War Economic Development Committee' would take place in the Tata boardroom the following month.[lxxxix] Given that most of the invitees owned cotton mills, it was timed to coincide with a Standard Cloth Conference being held in Bombay so as not to raise suspicions. Lala Shri Ram, Ghanshyamdas Birla, Kasturbhai Lalbhai, Ardeshir Shroff and John Mathai joined J.R.D. and Purshottamdas Thakurdas at Bombay House on 11 December 1942.

John Mathai prepared a note on planning in June 1943 and it was considered by the Committee in August. By December Mathai had drafted an outline in conjunction with P.S. Lokanathan, an economist from the University of Madras.[xc] It envisaged a 55% increase in industrial production and a 60% increase in agricultural production. But Thakurdas and Birla thought that this would expose the committee to the charge of industrial bias and so recommended a 100% increase in agricultural production over 15 years.[xci] The outline was then revised incorporating these suggestions and *A Brief Memorandum Outlining a Plan of Development of India* was presented at a press conference at Bombay House on 19 January 1944.

The principal object of the Bombay Plan was to double India's per capita income within 15 years. The Bombay planners had factored in an increase of 5 million new Indians each year over the period, and so in order to achieve the goal, national income would have to be tripled. For that to happen net output of agriculture would have to double and the output of industry, both small and large, would have to multiply by five times.

The main initial thrust of the Bombay Plan would be to create power and capital goods. The lack of both had hindered India's economic development. Not only would power and capital goods industries accelerate economic growth, but the ability to produce both in India would reduce the dependence on imports of plant and machinery and the need to rely on external finance. Yet the Bombay planners also wanted to make provision for the manufacture of essential consumer goods so as not to impose hardships on Indian consumers. This would provide an opportunity for small and cottage industries. Besides creating employment, this emphasis on small industries would ease the demand for expensive foreign machinery.

The Bombay planners also wanted to create a more 'balanced economy', moving beyond the traditional dominance of agriculture. In 1931 industry contributed 17%, agriculture 53% and services 22% to national income. By the end of their plan industry would contribute 35%, agriculture 40% and services 20%. This would mean that net income of industry would rise by 500%, agriculture by 130% and services by 200%. The planners explained the extravagant rise in industry by the low base which it was working off and the long way it had to go to reach the levels of the advanced economies. Nonetheless, India would remain an agricultural country and agriculture would continue to employ a large section of the population just as it had in Russia despite its rapid industrialisation.

The Bombay planners wanted to increase the production of crops which fed the population rather than cash crops like jute, tea and cotton which were exported. They noted that average land holdings were small, usually not more than three acres scattered across a village. Yet consolidating holdings was necessary for intensive agriculture and so they advocated co-operative farming, which seemed to offer "less difficulties" than other methods; the size of the holding was increased without depriving farmers of their ownership of their existing holdings. In addition, measures had to be taken to mitigate soil erosion by terracing arable lands and launching schemes of afforestation. Production could then be increased by bringing more land under cultivation, or by increasing the production of existing farms, or a combination of the two. Larger investments in irrigation were needed, as well as new canals and large dams. Rural indebtedness had to be wiped out, finance co-operatives established and 65,000 model farms created across the country.

Basic industries, including power, mining and metallurgy, engineering, chemicals, armaments, transport and cement were to be given priority in the early years of the

Bombay Plan. They were the basis on which the economic superstructure would be erected. Industry could not function without inputs like power, machinery and chemicals, and neither could agriculture progress without fertilisers. Without transport and shipping the economy would remain stagnant. If these building blocks of economic growth had not been neglected under British rule, India would not have remained so far behind other colonies like Australia and Canada. Amongst the basic industries to get priority, power was at the top of the list. Of the 27 million kilowatts of hydroelectric energy available in India only 500,000 had been developed.

The Bombay planners foresaw India being almost completely dependent on the import of machinery and technical personnel for the establishment of basic industries, something which would initially require a large amount of external finance. This external finance consisted of the hoarded wealth of the country, mainly held in gold, sterling securities held by the Reserve Bank of India, a favourable balance of trade, and foreign borrowing. India's internal finance consisted of domestic savings and new money created against government securities. The Bombay planners thought that if a national government came to power it would instil sufficient confidence in Indians to invest their hoarded wealth, totalling about £750 million, into productive enterprises. Throughout the war the British Government had been selling bonds and making purchases of war supplies from India and the accumulated debt came to be known as the "sterling balances". India's credit rating in foreign capital markets was high and so it could borrow large amounts, particularly in the United States. Even were the Reserve Bank of India to create money it would be doing so to stimulate the economy, something which would not affect India's credit standing abroad. This commercial borrowing and drawing down of the sterling balances would pay for the import of capital goods which would be used to build the basic industries in India which would eventually produce the machinery and inputs for Indian capital goods, so saving on foreign exchange towards the end of the plan.

***

The Indian Federation of Labour broke away from the All India Trade Union Congress in 1941 under the leadership of Manabendra Nath Roy, who was both an ex-Communist and an ex-Congressman. It was the attitude of both the Communists and the Congress to the Second World War which had precipitated the formation of the IFL. The Congress had only supported the British in their war effort on the condition that India be granted independence after the war, whilst the Communists had opposed it, denouncing it as an 'imperialist war'. However, M.N. Roy and his new Party, the Radical Humanists and the IFL offered the British unconditional support, co-operating with the government in delivering war propaganda. The Government of India thus made a request to Roy when it required a paper on labour and post-war reconstruction for submission to the Pacific Relations Conference. Roy wrote his paper and the IFL then established a committee in December 1943 to formulate a plan for the economic development of India. The committee was led by Vithal Tarkunde, a young barrister from Poona who had been active in the Congress Socialist Party in the 1930s and had temporarily given up legal practice to devote himself to the Radical Humanist Party. The result of the committee's work, *The People's Plan*, was published in April 1944.

The People's planners identified poverty as the central problem of the Indian economy. Indian poverty was caused by labour on the land using primitive tools and methods resulting in low productivity. This low productivity led to underemployment, and in some cases unemployment. The key to removing poverty was, therefore, to increase the productivity of labour, something which would take place through the mechanisation of both agriculture and industry. The idea that the solution to poverty would come through the development of large-scale industries had been prevalent in Indian planning circles, yet the People's planners were sceptical. The reason for the lack of development of large-scale industries in India, they argued, was the lack of purchasing power of the vast swathe of the population, rather than a lack of capital.

In *The People's Plan* agriculture formed the basis of Indian economic renewal. By increasing the purchasing power of rural Indians industries would also grow and absorb labour from agriculture, relieving pressure on the land. The process would be slow, and could be stopped altogether should production be allowed to pursue profit. The history of capitalism both abroad and in India was proof of that. Hence a change in the motive of production was required. The new objective of industrialisation would be the productive employment of labour and natural resources for increasing national income, something which would not be possible with unrestricted private ownership. Consumer goods had to be sold at prices within reach of the common people and production had to be reoriented to human demand rather than effective demand. Given that there would be little profit to be earned, it would be the state which would have to finance the mechanisation of agriculture and industrialisation.

The first order of business for a plan focusing on agriculture would be to provide the tillers with both the incentive and the means to improve their productivity. Both rack renting by landlords and usury by money lenders would therefore have to be wiped out. In addition, mines and banks would have to be nationalised, foreign trade and financial transactions with foreign countries controlled, agricultural co-operatives created and private traders in agriculture subjected to regulation keeping in mind the artificial shortages and profiteering that were taking place during the war.

It was not necessary that feudal rights be "confiscated",

but land needed to be nationalised to abolish intermediaries between the state and the cultivator. This would entail the payment of compensation to the larger landholders, yet not be so extravagant that future generations would be burdened. Compensation would have to be paid to the landlords on their rent receiving lands as well as those lands devoted to public and charitable purposes, and to non-cultivating land owners in southern and western India. It was this reform of land tenure which would enable an increase in the productivity of agricultural labour. The rights to mineral deposits and fisheries would have to be acquired and arrears in rent cleared. In addition, rural debts would have to be scaled down to 25% before being taken over by the state. And so, like the landlords, the moneylenders would also receive some compensation. The compensation mechanism would work through the issue of 40 year bonds paying 3% per annum.

Individualistic small-scale cultivation would not be able to provide a sound basis for the development of agriculture, and so the People's planners advocated voluntary "collectivisation" of tiny holdings. They wanted to introduce modern machinery through the establishment of state farms, about 8,000 to 10,000 acres in size, equipped with mechanical means of cultivation which could be lent out to peasants in the neighbouring areas. There would be about 25,000 of these farms across India initially. It was the forecast surplus from agriculture which would allow the government to invest in the other sectors of the economy. In *The People's Plan* the domestic market would expand allowing it to absorb greater consumption.

Increasing incomes of the cultivators would create the demand for consumer goods: textiles, leather goods, sugar, paper, drugs and chemicals, tobacco, oil, furniture and glass. The People's planners did not want to neglect the heavy industries which were also needed for the development of agriculture and consumer goods industries. Yet the sequence needed to be correct;

> *But it is indeed a little pathetic, and may even prove to be considerably harmful, to start with half filled bellies and half clad bodies, thinking in terms of automobiles and aeroplanes.*

The People's planners were the only advocates of planning in India to completely dismiss the idea of encouraging cottage industries. However, even they understood the influence of the Gandhians and noted that the issue would have to be "very delicately and carefully handled". Their reasoning was clear: an improvement in the standard of living was dependent on an increase in the productivity of labour, which was in turn dependent on an improvement in the application of machinery. They did not think that greater mechanisation would lead to unemployment, but to increased leisure time and a foundation for cultural development. A vast amount of labour would be released from agriculture as the process of collectivisation developed, some of which might be absorbed onto new land, irrigation works, health, education and housing services, industries and communication services. The remainder of this labour coming from country to town would be absorbed by the private sector in small and medium sized industries.

The People's planners wanted to organise the flow of commodities through both producers' and consumers' co-operatives. Collective farms would be wholesale co-operatives in rural areas, whilst state owned industrial units would perform this function in urban areas. A national network of co-operatives controlled by consumers would be provided with commodities at prices fixed by the state and would then have to sell them at regulated prices. This would remove all the problems of a system which worked according to the profit motive and the laws of supply and demand. It would be impossible to end the "anarchy" of production without ending the anarchy in the circulation of goods.

The People's Plan's finances were dependent on the initial generation of an agricultural surplus. The first two years would focus on the re-organisation of agriculture after which the plan could begin to progress. *The People's Plan* would thus become self-financing after three years. Money would initially be spent on agriculture and so the first five year plan would essentially be an agricultural plan, whilst the second would focus on industry.

***

If the unionists rejected the capitalists' plan for being excessively bourgeoisie, then the Gandhians rejected both, for being un-Indian. The thought of a Gandhian plan would have seemed incongruous to both the man himself, and his more doctrinaire followers. After all Gandhi had rejected statism and centralisation of political and economic life. But so pervasive was the planning idea in India in the 1940s, that one of his followers, Shriman Narayan Agarwal, an economist and principal of Seksaria College of Commerce, Wardha decided to write an economic plan for India based on Gandhian principles. Gandhi had not had time to read the document, *The Gandhian Plan of Economic Development for India* closely, but he did write a short forward nonetheless. From his brief perusal of Agarwal's work he could state that, despite his opposition to planning, it had at least not misrepresented his ideas.

The Gandhian Plan sought to reconstruct India on the basis of self-governing village communities or gram panchayats. They would be autonomous in their administrative functions and self-sufficient in their basic needs such as food, clothing and building materials. These communities would not be isolated little village republics however; they would be linked to the taluk, district, division, provincial and national levels of government in keeping with common interests and policies. Gram panchayats would collect the land revenue, maintain peace and order in co-operation with the police, resolve local disputes through arbitration and amicable settlement, organise both basic and adult education, provide medical care through dispensaries, cottage hospitals, and maternity wards, be responsible for the sanitation of public places, improve agriculture through co-operation, regulate the village economy by organising credit co-operatives, make purchases of raw materials and consumer goods and also sell their farm produce and village handicrafts through co-operatives. Agarwal thought that up until 1944 the co-operative movement had not been much of a success in India. The reason was that "it did not have its roots in Indian soil". It was in the revival of the panchayats that "lies the hope and prosperity of the Indian nation".

In order to raise the productivity of agricultural labour land needed to be nationalised and a system of village land tenure established. Agarwal advocated a mauzawari settlement to replace the old zamindari and ryotwari settlement; the whole village community would be responsible to the state for the payment of revenue and the allocation of rent among the cultivators would again be decided by the entire village, rather than a single all powerful official, the patwari. The panchayat would lease out land to farmers on long term leases which would continue as long as the rent was paid. Existing rates of rent and revenue would have to be reduced. Arrears of debt would be recovered through the court system rather than arbitrary ejectment and rent would be payable in kind rather than in cash. The state would lose cash flow, however the tiller would not be ruined by a bad harvest. In this scenario there were no landlords, whether present or absentee. Agarwal even wanted to end private property in land within two generations by levying steep inheritance, death and succession taxes.

Agarwal recognised, like all his fellow planners, that the

greatest impediment to increased productivity in agriculture was the subdivision and fragmentation of land holdings in the villages. And just as in the other plans, holdings in Agarwal's *Gandhian Plan* would be consolidated through co-operatives. Adjacent plots of land would become one by removing the boundaries, whilst maintaining distinct ownership. Land would not be able to be subdivided upon inheritance below a certain minimum and those uneconomic small holdings which remained would be rent free.

Agarwal envisioned workshops and cottage factories operating nearby the fields. He called this the "integration" of labour. As would be expected in a Gandhian plan, khadi occupied pride of place among cottage industries. The khadi plan was quite precise: there would be 375 spinners in each village to meet its cloth needs. They would only work part time, 320 hours a year, or about 5 hours per week, or one hour a day. Agarwal's list of potential cottage industries was a long one: paper making, paddy husking, gur, date palm and vegetable oil processing, bee keeping, soap making, flour grinding, poultry farming, carpentry, smithy, match making, pottery, toy making, cutlery making, bamboo and cane work, rope, tile, brick, bangles and glass making. The state could play a role by providing cheap credit to cottage industries through co-operatives, provide the villagers with technical training, set up research establishments which could disseminate their work through the panchayats, collectively purchase necessary supplies for the artisans, and assist the co-operatives with the sale of products at good prices in the towns and cities. In addition, the state should protect cottage industries from competition with large-scale industries.

The sort of public distribution which the socialists advocated would not be necessary in a Gandhian system. Self-sufficiency would prevail within distinct regional economic zones as far as possible, with exports to other zones only in the case of surplus or to make up for deficiencies elsewhere. There would be no further large towns. Those which existed would be better planned and large-scale industries would be decentralised and located in the villages. Towns would not be able to produce those goods which could be made in villages, and they would draw their supplies from the neighbouring villages, rather than distant villages or towns. The Gandhian ideal would be a barter system within the rural economy.

***

Viceroy Linlithgow departed India in October 1943. He was replaced by Archibald Wavell who created a Department for Planning and Development. The new viceroy appointed Sir Ardeshir Dalal, a retired Indian Civil Service officer who had been a director of Tata & Sons and worked on the formulation of the Bombay Plan, as a special Member for Planning and Development on the Viceroy's Council in May 1944.

The Government of India had written to the provincial governments for the submission of provincial economic plans, yet only the Bombay Government had prepared a draft plan. Sir Ardeshir then sent his own circulars from the new department to the provincial governments instructing them to create both 5 and 15 year plans using the Bombay Government's draft plan as a model. The submissions from the provincial governments would allow the Government of India to draft a plan for all of India. Yet the provincial governments wanted explicit assurances that any plans which they created would be funded by the central government and not deplete their own treasuries. The Government of India wanted submissions from the provinces so that it could address the larger problem of unemployment, but the issue became stuck in a maze of federalism and when Sir Ardeshir resigned from his post in December 1945 both provincial and all India plans remained elusive.

An informal meeting of the National Planning Committee

was held in September 1945. The meeting called on all those subcommittees which had not yet submitted their reports to resume work and do so by March 1946. Another subcommittee was formed to take the changes of the previous years into account. This subcommittee met in October and once again committed to a strong role for the state; heavy and defence industries would be under state control and the state would fix prices of industrial and agricultural produce. The first full session of the committee was held in November 1945 in Bombay, but by October of 1946 Jawaharlal Nehru, who had joined the Interim government awaiting Independence, had already established the Advisory Planning Board within the Government of India. In December 1946 the National Planning Committee was finally disbanded.

The Advisory Planning Board was formed to review previous efforts at planning, including that of the National Planning Committee, the Bombay Plan, the People's Plan and the Gandhian Plan and make appropriate recommendations for future objectives, priorities and a machinery for planning. The Board was chaired by Kshitish Chandra Neogy, a conservative Congressman from Bengal, and included K.T. Shah and Meghnad Saha from the National Planning Committee. However, most of the Board's members were Indian civil servants, advisers and secretaries to key departments. The Board's report would thus give an insight into the thinking of the bureaucrats who would administer the Indian planning effort in the years immediately after Independence.

The Advisory Planning Board did not think that the development of large-scale industries would be possible were planning to be left to the provinces. All provinces needed to work together under a common plan and for this to be successful central planning and control would be required. Capital resources would be conserved, and wasteful competition and undue concentration of industries in particular regions would be avoided. The board then recommended central planning over 21 industries, ranging from defence and heavy industries, to cotton, sugar and vegetable oil. Although the common plan would come about by voluntary agreement from the provincial governments, there needed to be a way to enforce it. The obvious way was by legislation, and the board recommended bringing industrial policy back under the control of the central government. The proposed legislation would ensure that "no new factory should be started or an existing one continued without a licence".

Whilst the railways, munitions factories and some public utilities were already state owned and the government had resolved to bring aviation under state ownership, the Industrial Policy of 1945 had left the question of nationalisation unresolved. It had called for the nationalisation of heavy industries of national importance provided that private capital was not forthcoming. The Advisory Planning Board continued with this ambiguity, but did suggest that the nationalisation of coal, mineral oils, iron and steel, motor, air and river transport should be "considered", and that state enterprise should be conducted through public corporations. The board was quite emphatic in stating however, that "the intrusion of foreign firms in the field of Indian industry should not be allowed." If foreign firms were allowed in the Indian market in sectors in which Indian firms were not yet established, there would be little chance of their growth in the future.

One of the Advisory Planning Board's clearer recommendations was for the establishment of a planning commission. It would be a "single, compact, authoritative organisation" which would be responsible directly to the Cabinet. The new commission would be a non-political body, ministers would not be allowed to join so that its status would not fluctuate with changing political fortunes. The five members of the commission would include a chairman with "general experience in public affairs", two members from outside the government who would have knowledge of industry, labour or agriculture, a government official with experience of finance, and an eminent scientist. The board envisioned the planning commission as an advisory body; it would make its recommendations and the decision to implement them would rest with the government. Yet in cases of the allocation of scarce resources the commission would act as a "priorities Board" and take final decisions, subject only to an appeal to the government. In addition, the commission would be authorised to initiate action on matters relating to planning and development and call for reports and memoranda from the departments of the Government of India. A much larger consultative body of 25 to 30 members representing the states and economic interest groups would meet twice a year to which the planning commission would present its reports and discuss policies which might require co-operation from the state governments, farmers, industry and labour.

***

Britain's laissez faire trade policies in 19th century India became conflated in the Indian mind with capitalism generally. Laissez faire was variously associated with government apathy, neglect, and malevolence. The appeal of planning on the other hand was that it was associated with purpose, action, and foresight. The nation's best minds and leading experts would come together to intelligently organise and distribute scarce resources to raise living standards and modernise the Indian economy. The inherent problem with the idea of planning however, was just how broad its appeal was. Planning was equally appealing to diverse sections of the Indian economic community because they each interpreted the word according to their own ideological and sectional interests. And so, even after a capitalist plan, a communist plan, a Gandhian plan, a Congress Plan, and, almost, a British Raj plan for India, by the time the Advisory Planning Board submitted its recommendations to the government on the eve of Independence in 1947, very little could actually be agreed upon.

Whilst there was no shortage of conflict and notes of dissent in the National Planning Committee, and later the Advisory Planning Board, the most fundamental divergence of ideas was that between the Bombay planners and the People's planners. Both India's capitalists and socialists agreed that the biggest impediment to the development of the Indian economy was a lack of capital. They were referring to physical capital: tools and machinery and factories which could power India's industrialisation. The People's planners however, thought that rather than a lack of capital, India's problem was a lack of purchasing power, particularly on the land. Without rising incomes in rural India the country could not hope to have any sustainable industrialisation, and so India's planners needed to create rural prosperity before they thought of machines, tools and factories. The People's planners were thus in fundamental disagreement not only with their antagonists, the Bombay planners, but also their fellow Leftists who tended to associate too great a focus on agriculture with economic backwardness.

Ghanshyamdas Birla was not a member of the National Planning Committee, but the influence of his ideas is found in the Bombay Plan. The core ideas of the Bombay Plan of 1944 largely resemble those which he had placed before the Annual General Meeting of the Federation of Indian Chambers of Commerce and Industry ten years earlier in 1934. Civil servants within the Government of India even referred to the Bombay Plan in their correspondence as "the Birla scheme".[xcii] The most enduring of these ideas was that of industrialisation by import substitution. The government would have to facilitate the import of the tools and machinery to create the capacity for manufacturing industrial goods. The process would cost foreign exchange initially, but over the medium term India would be able to make its own sophisticated manufactured goods and so save foreign exchange in the long run. This would help with a transition from an agricultural to an industrial economy, and more specifically propel India towards self-reliance. In a sense it was a continuation, in a new form, of the old and deeply appealing swadeshi idea.

Neither the National Planning Committee, nor the Advisory Planning Board, nor the Bombay planners were willing to make any decisive statements on reform of the pattern of land ownership in rural India. It was just too divisive an issue, and so rather than stoke controversy, they thought it better to focus on less contentious but equally important economic issues. The People's planners and the Gandhian planner were less shy. The People's planners were most Russian in their outlook; huge state run farms would be formed to take advantage of modern machinery which would be applied to boost agricultural output. Yet one idea which was amenable to all the planners irrespective of their ideological commitments was co-operative farming. It was seemingly a middle way between large-scale capitalist or communist farming and tiny uneconomic plots scattered in villages across the land. Farmers would still keep ownership of their land, but they would pool it with fellow cultivators to create larger holdings more amenable to investment and economies of scale.

All of the Indian economic plans of the 1930s and 1940s contained elements of fantasy. The Bombay Plan was produced by India's leading capitalists, yet there was little concern for where the money to pay for the plan might come from. Ghanshyamdas Birla, a Marwari businessman from Calcutta, had absorbed early Keynesian thinking and seen the example of Franklin Roosevelt's New Deal and came to the understanding that a national economy was different to a private business. Given India's good credit standing and ample reserves of pounds sterling, ambitious investment programmes would therefore not be difficult to fund. *The People's Plan* was equally fantastic in its approach to both time and Indian government capacity. It thought that land reform would take just two years, and having been swiftly and thoroughly implemented, the fetters on Indian agricultural production would be removed. In the third year of the plan agricultural surpluses would be available to fund industrialisation. These plans could be forgiven their other worldliness, they were ideologically driven policy proposals, the products of eager, earnest minds. Yet, disturbingly, much of the drift to fantasy, and lack of concern for both money and state capacity would endure within the government as it set about creating its first five year plans after Independence in 1947.

THREE

A Socialistic Picture of Society

Given how pervasive the idea of planning had been in India in the 1930s and 1940s it might be surprising that in the first years after Independence a planned economy seemed far from certain. The Indian National Congress of 1947 was not one riven by faction. Rather than two factions, there were really two parties within the Party, divided by ideology but united by a common purpose. Jawaharlal Nehru's first government after Independence thus resembled a government of national unity, in which socialists and conservatives came together to provide the young nation with a stable government and begin the basic tasks of national reconstruction. The socialists took the prime minister as their leader whilst the conservatives looked to the home minister and deputy prime minister, Vallabhbhai Patel as their guide and patron. Nehru could thus no longer promote the idea of economic planning within elite bodies like the National Planning Committee or the Advisory Planning Board, but had to convince the conservatives within the Congress who had always been sceptical of his socialist ideals. A mark of just how difficult the task would be came in January 1948, when Vallabhbhai Patel, the man who exercised day to day control of the Congress Party machinery, addressed a meeting in Shillong and compared the socialists to a bunch of parrots.[xciii]

Parallel to this tussle between Nehru and Patel over socialism and economic planning another conflict emerged over a draft of a law which sought to control private enterprise through a system of licensing. The

Advisory Planning Board had recommended legislation which would license all new private industrial units. This idea had not found a place in the Industrial Policy Resolution of 1948, so bureaucrats in the Ministry of Commerce and Industry set about drafting an Industries Bill which would create an apparatus for the control of Indian enterprise. Whilst the contest between Nehru and Patel over planning was intensely political, it was the businessmen of the Federation of Indian Chambers of Commerce and Industry who tried to stifle the Industries Bill as it made its way through the Lok Sabha's committees and subcommittees. The Commerce Ministry's bureaucrats were the Bill's staunchest defenders, whilst successive commerce ministers were largely ambivalent, content to play mediator between the bureaucrats and businessmen.

Despite opposition from Vallabhbhai Patel and the Congress conservatives a powerful Planning Commission was created in 1950, and then in 1951, despite the best efforts of India's leading businessmen to prevent its passage through Parliament, an Industries (Development and Regulation) Act became law. India's First Five Year Plan grew out of the need to present a paper to a Commonwealth Conference which was working on what came to be known as the Colombo Plan. The subsequent Draft First Five Year Plan and the Final Plan document largely resembled that first paper and so it remained unclear just how much of a plan India's First Plan really was. Some pointed out that it was merely a cobbling together of projects carried over from the last years of the British Raj. It failed to enthuse the man who had done the most to bring it about. Jawaharlal Nehru did not think that it was much of a plan at all, it bore little resemblance to the Soviet planning he had been so inspired by 20 years earlier. If anything the First Plan had carried something of the spirit of *The People's Plan* and invested relatively large amounts in agriculture and irrigation. Irrespective of just how much of a plan the First Plan actually was, when successive good monsoons led to plentiful harvests and relief from the scarcity conditions of the first years of Independence, it seemed that the idea of planning had been vindicated.

The man to truly radicalise and transform Indian Planning was an old associate of Jawaharlal Nehru, Prasanta Mahalanobis, a physicist turned statistician from Calcutta. He shared Nehru's admiration for the economic transformation of Soviet Russia, and once Nehru took control of the Congress after Vallabhbhai Patel's death in December 1950 and gradually steered it towards an embrace of socialism, it seemed that the time was ripe for a more ambitious form of planning. Mahalanobis had come to economics late, yet he gathered around him at his Indian Statistical Institute in Calcutta some of the world's leading Leftist economists to help draft a Second Five Year Plan, a task which had been delegated to him by the Planning Commission at Nehru's behest. Surprisingly, Mahalanobis's Draft Plan Frame shared much of the Bombay planners' vision from the 1940s. The Draft Plan Frame identified a lack of capital as the main impediment to economic growth, called for the immediate establishment of heavy industries and outlined a policy of import substitution led industrialisation, diverging significantly only in its provision for a vastly expanded public sector.

Yet the halcyon days of Nehru and Mahalanobis's socialist dream lasted only as long as the monsoon of 1956. A foreign exchange crisis loomed, one that could not be directly attributed to the Second Plan, it had hardly had time to get started, but was most likely caused by the Commerce Ministry's liberal provisions for imports as well as tepid export performance. India's reserves of foreign currency were at dangerously low levels by the end of 1957 and it seemed as if large parts of the ambitious Second Plan might have to be abandoned. If India was to continue on its experiment with planning it would have to approach foreign donors, both to tide over the foreign exchange shortage, and fund the part of the Plan it could not do so itself. And so, India's quest for self-reliance was, from the start, dependent on aid from foreign governments. And, in a further irony, India's principal donor during the 1950s and 1960s would be not the Soviet Union, which had inspired the socialist project, but the United States and its arm of economic diplomacy, the World Bank.

***

The Government of India had been ignoring the Advisory Planning Board's recommendation from 1947 that it establish a national planning agency "responsible to Cabinet...which should devote its attention continuously to the whole field of development." Even when the All India Congress Committee's Economic Programme Committee recommended the immediate establishment of a planning commission in January 1948 little was done. In July Jawaharlal Nehru, by now prime minister, suggested setting up "a Board or Council of expert advisors whose sole function should be to watch every aspect of the economic situation and advise on it."[xciv] Vallabhbhai Patel, by now home minister, countered with a suggestion for the establishment of a committee of experts made up of industrialists, economists and civil servants which would work to implement the economic policies already decided upon by the government.[xcv]

As the prime minister and home minister clashed over the establishment of a planning commission, a small group of Leftist Indian diplomats were working as intermediaries for the American engineer Solomon Trone in New Delhi, suggesting that he act as a consultant to the Government of India on economic planning. Trone was in fact a naturalised American, having emigrated from his native Russia as recently as 1931. He had been a member of the Russian Communist Party and worked at Soviet power plants in the 1920s before becoming disillusioned with the state after its show trials of dissident engineers. Trone tried to get Nehru's ear, and when he did he knew just what to say. He warned the new prime minister that "powerful influential industrial groups" were plotting to "deepen the existing economic crisis" in order to promote "their laissez faire policy".[xcvi] Heavy industry was the key to economic growth, and the process of industrialisation would need to be managed by a strong planning body.

Jawaharlal Nehru needed little convincing on the issue of course, and referred to Solomon Trone's statements and reports as he made his own case for a planning commission again towards the end of 1949.[xcvii] Vallabhbhai Patel was unreceptive towards the idea, but on 19 January 1950 the Congress Working Committee, after much debate, finally resolved in favour of the creation of a planning commission. It was a significant, but not yet emphatic victory for Nehru and the socialists; Patel had a key socialist sounding passage from the draft resolution deleted. It had defined the objective of planning as "the progressive elimination of social, political and economic exploitation and inequality, the motive of private gain in economic activity or organisation of society and the antisocial concentration of wealth and means of production."[xcviii] Instead the planners would work according to the Directive Principles of State Policy in the new constitution. The Cabinet resolution on the establishment of the Planning Commission which was passed on 15 March did have a slightly more socialist tenor however; the Commission had terms of reference which stated that ownership and control of resources would serve the common good, economic policy would not result in the concentration of wealth and the means of production to the detriment of the common good, and citizens would be ensured a right to livelihood.[xcix]

Whilst the conservatives of the Congress put up resistance to the establishment of a planning commission and the adoption of socialist resolutions, the businessmen of the Federation of Indian Chambers of Commerce and Industry came together to attempt to prevent the passage of an Act which would place production and distribution in the private sector under government control. The Advisory Planning Board had, in 1947, recommended legislation which would ensure that no new factories could be started or existing ones continue without a licence, and although the Industrial Policy Resolution of 1948 had not made any explicit mention of licensing Indian private enterprises, S. Bhoothalingam in the Industry Ministry set about drafting an Industries Bill in June 1948.[c]

In March 1949 the Industries (Development and Control) Bill was submitted to the Constituent Assembly for approval. The Bill stipulated that every new industrial venture and every expansion of industrial capacity above a certain size would require a licence from the government. The state would have the power to regulate the operations and investments of private firms and any contravention of the new regulation would be a punishable offence. The state could intervene not just in instances of gross mismanagement, but also when the firm's managers were engaging in practices which reduced its production capacity or economic value. However, the Bill did make provision for a Central Advisory Council for Industry, one which had been mentioned in the Industrial Policy Resolution and would include representatives from industry. The Council would have to be consulted whenever a decision was being taken to revoke a licence or takeover the operations of a non-compliant firm. Yet the Advisory Council was just that, and ultimate authority remained with the government.

A Central Advisory Council had in fact already been formed and a draft of the Bill had been submitted for its approval earlier in 1949. Some of India's leading industrialists, including Ghanshyamdas Birla, Ardeshir Shroff and Lala Shri Ram were members of the council and had given their assent to the Bill. Yet it soon became apparent that these leaders of industry did not speak for the whole of the Indian business community and their signatures could not prevent a growing tide of criticism from many of their peers. The only part of the Bill which received support from the business community was the provision to take responsibility for industrial policy away from the state governments and return it to the Centre. The main point of contention was that the state would approve, monitor and guide private investment.

As soon as the Bill appeared in the Constituent Assembly it received criticism in the newspapers and industrialists began their efforts to lobby against it. The aim was to stall its passing so that alternative legislation or suitable modifications could be proposed. Their efforts did elicit the desired result; the Constituent Assembly immediately referred the Bill to a select committee to review and submit it for reconsideration.

Even India's industry associations, usually divided by faction and region, managed to work together to lobby against the Bill. The Federation of Indian Chambers of Commerce and Industry, the Indian Merchants' Chamber, the Bengal Chamber of Commerce, and the Associated Chambers of Commerce all sought to influence the government. Civil servants tried to make it clear to the industrial associations that they were willing to make significant changes to the Bill as long as it did not appear that they were "yielding to outside pressure".[ci] The Select Committee was similarly accommodative during its work in April and May of 1949. However, the growing sentiment among business leaders was not for alterations to the Bill, but its scrapping. Braj Mohan Birla, Ghanshyamdas's brother called the Bill "fundamentally objectionable".[cii]

When FICCI members appeared before the Select Committee they expressed the mood of the business community when they demanded the withdrawal of the Bill from the Constituent Assembly.[ciii] Shyamaprasad Mookerjee, the Minister for Industry and Supply pointed out that it was pointless for FICCI to appear before the

Select Committee only to say that it was against the very existence of the Bill.[civ] Yet the minister was hardly a staunch defender of it; he thought that the Bill could be changed as much as they all liked so long as it retained its title and preamble. FICCI members responded to Mookerjee's minimalist position, suggesting an alternative Bill which retained the Central Advisory Council and Central control over industry policy, but that authority to license be withdrawn, and industrial policy be formulated by industrial committees made up of businesspeople in each industry.[cv]

Lala Shri Ram of Delhi Cotton Mills was realistic enough to know that the government was not going to withdraw the Bill and suggested to his colleagues that they put their efforts into alterations which might "take the stink out of it".[cvi] Six weeks after its appearance before the Select Committee FICCI sent through its amendments, including a complete removal of all clauses dealing with licensing. It further wanted the Bill to apply to just six industries, and even wanted the Central Advisory Council disbanded. In its place FICCI suggested a Central Industries Development Board which would be mainly made up of industrialists nominated by the government with its approval. The board would hold executive power for industrial policy rather than the state.

The Select Committee submitted a revised bill, taking FICCI's proposals into account, to the Constituent Assembly in February 1950. It was again rejected and sent back to another committee by which time the Planning Commission had been established. In the version passed in October 1951 the number of industries covered by the Act had actually increased, however, going some way to meet FICCI's concerns, provision was made for Development Councils, sectoral bodies which would connect the Planning Commission with industry. The Development Councils would be made up of technical specialists and representatives from industry, collecting information, distributing inputs, relaying standards of efficiency, and influencing whether the state would take punitive action against a firm. A Central Advisory Council for Industries was also created in order to give government the ability to gauge industry, consumer and labour opinion when formulating industrial policy. The new Industries Minister, Harekrushna Mahtab thought that the introduction of the Development Councils was the most important feature of the new bill and they would "keep in close touch" and "try to help" industries in all possible ways.[cvii]

***

Part of the reason that the First Five Year Plan was a modest and conservative document was that the first members of the Planning Commission were modest and conservative people. Jawaharlal Nehru chaired the Commission, but closer direction was given by the Deputy Chairman, Gulzarilal Nanda, a leader of Ahmadabad mill workers and founder of the Indian National Trade Union Congress. Sir Chintaman Dwarkanath Deshmukh, Rao Bahadur Sir Vangal Thiruvenkatachari Krishnamachari, and Ramrao Krishnarao Patil were all former officers of the Indian Civil Service. Sir Chintaman had more recently served as Governor of the Reserve Bank of India, whilst Sir Krishnamachari had served as Diwan of Baroda and Prime Minister of Jaipur. R.K. Patil had resigned from the Service during the Quit India movement of 1942 and held the post of food commissioner in New Delhi. Gaganvihari Lallubhai Mehta had not served in the Indian Civil Service but spent his career as a manager of the Scindia Steam Navigation Company before being appointed president of the Tariff Board. Midway through the Plan period Kshitish Chandra Neogy, who had represented Bengal in the Central Legislative Assembly after the First World War, chaired the Advisory Planning Board and had been appointed minister of commerce, replaced Mehta after he was sent to Washington as ambassador.

Prime Minister Nehru announced to Parliament on 1

August 1950 that the new Planning Commission was at work on a five year plan which would be divided into two stages, the first covering two years, from 1951 to 1953, and the second the ensuing three years to 1956. By the end of August the Commission had put together a plan which would be submitted to the Commonwealth Consultative Conference which was working on what came to be known as the Columbo Plan for the economic development of South and South-east Asia. From September 1950 the Commission engaged in consultations with central and state ministries, and industry on the shape that the Plan would take. The central ministries and state governments submitted their detailed proposals by February 1951, and the states were directed to make sure that they had sufficient financial resources to meet their development programmes. The Draft First Five Year Plan which was published in July 1951 was not very different from the document which had been submitted to the Commonwealth Consultative Conference the previous year. The Draft Plan did however allocate significantly more resources to agriculture, particularly irrigation, and fewer resources to transport and communications. By August 1951 Nehru could state that there was "general agreement" on the First Five Year Plan.[cviii]

The final First Five Year Plan was published on 7 December 1952. One major change from the Draft Plan was that the allocation for agriculture and Community Development had increased from 12.8% to 17.4% of total outlay.[cix] Almost half of this increase was accounted for in funding the new Community Development Programme whilst substantial allocations went to minor irrigation works. There were also modest rises in the outlays for public sector industry as well as cottage and small-scale industries. The largest part of the increase in expenditure on public industry went to the development of a new iron and steel works. A resources gap, albeit a relatively small one of ₹655 crore emerged.[cx] Deficit financing would total ₹290 crores, largely drawn from the sterling balances, whilst the remainder would be met from external resources, or increased taxation and borrowing and further deficit financing. A foreign exchange gap of ₹180-200 crore was forecast for each remaining year of the Plan of which ₹50 crores would be covered by the sterling balances, whilst the remainder would have to come from external assistance.

The Planning Commission identified India's low stock of capital as the main impediment to higher economic growth. The speed of development would be based upon two key variables; the rate of population growth, and the amount of output which would be generated from a given stock of capital. The population was expected to grow at 1.25% per year, based on figures from the previous census, and the capital-output ratio was assumed to be 3:1- one unit of increased output would require three units of capital.[cxi] The rate of capital formation needed to be raised from 5% to 20% of national income to achieve the required rates of growth, and much of the increase would need to be drawn from a higher rate of saving.[cxii] The Planning Commission sought to encourage capital formation through higher saving over the medium to long term rather than force it through taxes, credit and monetary policy.

Using these figures, the Planning Commission forecast that India's national income would grow by 160% by the early 1970s, and per capita income would double if two-thirds of the additional national income generated each year went toward capital formation.[cxiii] However, this would lower rates of consumption and so such an ambitious target would need to be scaled back. Instead, during the First Five Year Plan period just 20% of the increase in national income would be diverted to capital formation, and so by the end of the period national income would rise by 11-12%.[cxiv] But in the ensuing Plan period the rate might rise to 50%, and the rate of savings might rise to 20% in the 1960s by which time capital investments would continue to grow, yet plateau as a percentage of national income.[cxv] India would have reached economic take-off, needing to devote decreasing shares of national income to capital formation. By the end of the 1970s per capita income would double and consumption levels rise by 70%.[cxvi] The Commission also wanted the public sector to "take over progressively the promotional and managerial functions necessary for development".[cxvii] This was the Planning Commission's first attempt at 'perspective planning'.

The government treasury was in a healthy state due to the plentiful harvests of 1953, which had already exceeded Plan targets by 150%, and the balance of payments and inflation were under control. The Finance Minister, Sir Chintaman Deshmukh did not think it right that a government of an economy at India's level of development should run budget surpluses, and instead in November 1953 announced a relatively small increase in the size of the Plan expenditure of ₹175 crores.[cxviii] More funds would be spent on rehabilitation, roads, repairs of tanks, flood control projects, improvements to the railways, loans to shipping companies, unemployment benefits, water supply, sanitation and power projects. Much of this outlay was however, to make up for previously allocated expenditure which had yet to be spent.

By 1956 the First Plan had managed to achieve, and even exceed many of its key production targets. The production of food grains rose by 143% and exceeded its target by 3.3 million tonnes.[cxix] National income had risen by 18.4% in the Plan period, per capita income had risen by 10.8% and per capita consumption had risen by 8%, whilst 4.5 million new jobs had been created.[cxx] Yet it was unclear whether the success of the Plan was due to the wisdom of the planners, or the good monsoons. The data could not demonstrate any clear causation between spending on irrigation, the use of the Japanese method of paddy cultivation, land reclamation and distribution of improved seeds, and buoyant agricultural production.

Only the increased use of fertilisers seemed to produce an empirically verifiable result.[cxxi] Sir Chintaman's predecessor John Mathai thought that most of the Plan outlays preceded both the creation of the Plan, and Independence; they were mainly a repackaging of projects which had been formulated in the last years of the British Raj.[cxxii] Even Sir Chintaman did not think it was "completely integrated".[cxxiii] One of India's leading economists, Professor Dhananjay Gadgil went so far as to argue that the achievements of the First Plan "were not planned at all".[cxxiv]

***

Jawaharlal Nehru did not think much of the First Plan; it was "not planning in the real sense of the word".[cxxv] Prasanta Mahalanobis thought that the First Plan was merely an "anthology". He wanted the Second Plan to be a "drama".[cxxvi] The two men had known each other socially for decades. Mahalanobis would meet Nehru when he came to Calcutta to see Rabindranath Tagore in the 1920s and 1930s. Yet their professional association dated to 1940 when Mahalanobis visited Allahabad on committee work and at the end of the day had dinner with Nehru at Anand Bhavan. They stayed up talking until past two in the morning and Nehru confided in Mahalanobis that the planning effort was still a fragile one in the Congress and he felt as though the National Planning Committee might have been setup just to humour him.[cxxvii] It was after this meeting that Nehru began to send minutes of the National Planning Committee's meetings to Mahalanobis in Calcutta.

Prasanta Mahalanobis was not an economist, but a physicist who founded the Indian Statistical Institute in the Physics Department at Presidency College, Calcutta. Yet he had a sense of mission, and the role he might play after Independence, and so he went out from India to the leading centres of economic research in order to overcome his "inferiority complex" in the field.[cxxviii] He visited both the United States and the United Kingdom in 1946 in order to study the application of statistics to economic planning and even met mathematicians at the American telecommunications conglomerate AT&T. His travels in England and America had stimulated his interest in the applications of statistics to economic planning, but it was his trip to the Soviet Union, some 20 years after Nehru's, which convinced him of the need for planning in India.

Mahalanobis was clear that he wanted planning to move beyond just medium term plans for government spending and begin to exercise control over private sector production and consumer spending. On his trips to Moscow he had been convinced of the merits of this "physical" planning, the need for the nationalisation of industry, and even accepted Soviet assurances that agricultural co-operatives like those which had been established in China could be established in India without any government compulsion.

Naturally, when word of Mahalanobis's possible role in the formulation of the Second Five Year Plan spread, the Russians were among the first foreign economists to arrive. Mahalanobis sensed that the civil servants in the Ministry of Finance were going to resist any radical change of direction and thought it would be better to keep his Soviet guests at the ISI in Calcutta when they arrived in November 1954; they would only get lost in the bureaucratic maze of New Delhi and end up writing "background papers".[cxxix] The Soviets had slightly different ideas about their role in India however. They tried to use the Indian Communist Party to further their agenda and also met with the Finance Minister, Sir Chintaman Deshmukh, Secretary to the Planning Commission Tarlok Singh, and Prime Minister Jawaharlal Nehru when he visited the ISI campus on Christmas Day. Ilia Mikhailovich Rubinshtein, a veteran of Soviet planning, encouraged Indian officials to think big and not be discouraged by a shortage of funds. He even hinted that the Soviet Union might provide financial assistance should the need arise.[cxxx]

Ragnar Frisch, a pioneering mathematical economist from Norway was also on the ISI campus at the time. He spent most of his first months in India stricken with illness, but he continued formulating his vision for India's future from his bed in Calcutta. He wanted to use "deep ploughing scientific procedures", save "millions and millions" of lives, and avoid "unnecessary political friction" in attaining the economic optimum.[cxxxi] He too was in favour of physical planning and shared the prevailing Indian desire for economic self-reliance. Like Mahalanobis and the Russians, he wanted a large public sector, tight regulation of the private sector, and brought the techniques of input-output matrices and linear programming to the ISI's planning effort.

It was Frisch who came up with the term "Plan Frame" and outlined the sequence which Indian planning would have to take.[cxxxii] First, political commitment would be required; the political organs would have to formulate the goals of planning, and then take responsibility for their achievement. The Plan Frame would then be created by the economists and technicians who would use scientific methods to determine the best policies and investments. Nehru visited Frisch at his bedside on his December trip to the ISI and was won over; there were now techniques which could solve all of the problems thrown up in the process of economic planning. Soon after, the Planning Commission delegated the task of creating the Plan Frame to the Indian Statistical Institute.

The foreign economists would continue to arrive at the ISI throughout 1955. Oscar Lange, a Polish proponent of "market socialism" recommended radical land reform, co-operative farming, and the transfer of the "basic" means of production to the state. Joan Robinson from Cambridge, who had lived in India as a young woman 30 years earlier, thought that the real challenge was not to solve input-output matrices but to change them by encouraging capital accumulation, regulating prices and investing funds back into the expansion of the public sector. Nicholas Kaldor, also from Cambridge, proposed a tax system which could raise the resources required for the proposed public sector expansion, whilst Charles Bettleheim, a French Marxist, advocated a round of nationalisation.

***

Ragnar Frisch had spoken of the need for political commitment for the planning process. It was an issue which Jawaharlal Nehru had struggled with since Independence. When Purushottamdas Tandon was projected as Congress President in September 1950 by conservatives claiming the support of Vallabhbhai Patel, the socialists who had remained within the Party put up their own candidate, Jivatram Bhagwandas Kripalani. Tandon won the day in the All India Congress Committee by 250 votes, and he seemed to continue a purge of the socialists started by Patel two and a half years earlier, bringing his own state Congressmen onto the Congress Working Committee. Tandon's faction was more socially than economically conservative; his Congressmen were motivated by a dormant sense of Hindu nationalism, which, naturally, predisposed them to some scepticism of Nehru's rhetoric on international socialism. Nehru had not taken sides in the presidential contest, but it was generally accepted that his sympathies lay with Kripalani.

Purushottamdas Tandon's election as Congress president precipitated months of splitting and joining. The socialists, led by Kripalani, were increasingly frustrated by their marginalisation both in the state units and the central decision making bodies of the Congress, and so formed a Congress Democratic Front. The Front was drawn from dissatisfied socialists and Gandhians from Uttar Pradesh, West Bengal, Andhra and the Malabar coast. In November 100 Congress members from West

Bengal left the Party. Tandon directed Kripalani, still within the Party, to dissolve the Democratic Front, however he refused. But then, on 15 December 1950, Vallabhbhai Patel died, after which Nehru attempted to exert some authority and had a unity resolution passed at the All India Congress Committee in January 1951.

Nehru's unity resolution was only partially effective. Kripalani could not gather support for his candidates for the Central Election Committee, and so in April the dissidents from Andhra also left the Party. Nehru tried to assure Kripalani that he would use his office to have some of Kripalani's men placed on the Central Election Committee at the All India Congress Committee meeting in May. But he was powerless to effect much change; it was, by this stage, Tandon's committee. And so Kripalani also left the Party and joined ex-Congress members from West Bengal and Andhra to form a Kisan Majdoor Praja Party, or Farmers Labourers People's Party in June 1951. Nehru lost two of his ministers in the process, including Rafi Ahmed Kidwai, who joined the new KMPP. This galvanised the prime minister; he also decided to resign from the Working Committee and the Election Committee, and encouraged suggestions that he take over the Congress presidency. By September 1951 Tandon's resignation had been accepted and Nehru had been elected Congress president by a large majority. Yet he did not launch a counter purge of conservatives, which in turn did not convince the dissident socialists that he was serious, and so few of them returned.

The country went to the polls just a month after the change of Congress president, completing its first general election since becoming a republic, and the largest in world history. When the results were released in February 1952 the Congress, despite suffering some losses in the states, gained an absolute majority in the Lok Sabha, winning 364 of 489 seats. The biggest opposition party was the Communist Party of India, which held 16 seats, followed by two splinter parties from the Congress, the

A Socialistic Picture of Society

Socialist Party which had won 12 seats and the Kisan Mazdoor Praja Party which secured 9 seats. Jawaharlal Nehru was now in control of both his parliamentary party and the Congress organisation.

Yet even with a resounding majority in the Lok Sabha, Nehru still did not seek to purge the Congress Working Committee of his antagonists. It was a 20 member body which had to be appointed according to the Congress constitution, and so a balance of regional and ideological representation needed to be maintained. Throughout 1952, 1953 and 1954 as Nehru continued as president of the Party only minor changes to the Working Committee were made when the need arose. It was also a time of relative ideological quiet, there was little socialist rhetoric, relatively mild factional squabbles, general consensus around Nehru as the keeper of Party unity, and even as late as July 1954 when the All India Congress Committee, the larger 500 member body, gathered at Ajmer, there was a sense of disappointment. The rank and file were expecting something big, a major statement on economic policy which they might take back to their districts, yet little could be agreed upon.

The stasis started to break with Nehru's speech before the National Development Council in November 1954. He told the chief ministers and members of the Planning Commission that "The picture I have in mind is absolutely and definitely a socialistic picture of society. I am not using the word in a dogmatic sense at all. I mean that the means of production should be socially owned and controlled for the benefit of society as a whole."[cxxxiii] It was in the same speech that he put forth his vision of import substitution, capital formation and heavy industry: "the basic things" would be built in India, whilst consumer needs, instead of being met by imports or made with imported machinery, would increasingly be made by small-scale units in India. On 18 December 1954 the Lok Sabha for the first time passed a resolution affirming a commitment to a "socialistic pattern of society". Weeks later at Avadi, near Madras the Congress also endorsed a resolution calling for a socialistic pattern of society.

Much was made of the new commitment to the socialistic pattern of society. Four hundred thousand people gathered at Avadi as Nehru spoke of his dreams coming true, and his guest, the Yugoslavian Communist dictator, Marshall Josip Tito expressed his approval at India's leaders taking their people towards "socialist directional planning". However, the Avadi resolution was not quite as epoch making as it was understood either at the time, or in retrospect:

> *...planning should take place with a view to the establishment of a socialistic pattern of society, where the principal means of production are under social ownership or control, production is progressively speeded up, and there is equitable distribution of national wealth.*

Jawaharlal Nehru had a resounding majority in the Lok Sabha, and the principal opposition parties were Communist and Socialist, so the parliamentary resolution endorsing the socialistic pattern of society had not been a difficult one to pass. Yet he had not purged the Congress Working Committee and packed it with fellow socialists. So to have a Congress Select Committee endorse a socialistic pattern of society, until recently so controversial within the Party, at the annual session with its full diversity of Congress members might have seemed a triumph for Nehru's powers of persuasion. Yet the most important words in the resolution were not "socialistic pattern of society", but "social ownership or control".

Most Congressmen, even if they were opposed to the statism and socialism which Nehru stood for, considered themselves socialists. Even Gandhians were comfortable with the word- they called themselves "Gandhian socialists". Those not averse to private enterprise would refer to themselves as "democratic socialists". What made the Avadi Resolution acceptable to all was the use of the term "social control". It was a nebulous term, one which seemingly fell short of state ownership or nationalisation of private enterprises and entailed mere government direction of private enterprise for social purposes when the need arose. In the Congress Party, therefore, the spectacle at Avadi had resolved very little at all.

***

Prasanta Mahalanobis did not attend the Congress session at Avadi in January 1955, he had been preparing for meetings with the Planning Commission's Panel of Economists which had been formed to provide an impartial and technical appraisal of his *Draft Plan Frame*. Mahalanobis's document made the case for a bold plan in the context of providing employment for India's burgeoning population; 4.5 million people were added to the population each year, 1.8 million were entering the labour force, whilst there were both unemployment in the cities and underemployment in the villages. Planning thus had to be bold enough to create jobs for those 1.8 million new workers each year, besides creating employment for the unemployed and underemployed.

The Second Five Year Plan would thus be formulated with a view to expand the public sector in order to attain rapid growth and a socialistic pattern of society, develop heavy industries, increase the production of consumer goods through household or hand industries and provide an adequate market for these products, develop factory production of these consumer goods in a way which did not impinge on household producers, increase the productivity of agriculture and implement land reforms to raise the purchasing power of the peasantry, provide better housing, health services and education, "liquidate unemployment" within 10 years and increase national income by 25% within 5 years whilst providing for more equitable distribution.

According to Mahalanobis, increasing the production of coal, steel, electricity, iron, heavy machinery, heavy chemicals and heavy industries would increase the capacity for capital formation and hence the rate of industrialisation and the rate of growth of the national economy. India was to overcome, as quickly as possible, its dependence on imports of producer goods which were holding up capital accumulation. Rather than importing the machinery to erect a steel plant, investment would be made in large engineering workshops which would manufacture the machinery needed to build the big plants. The aim would be to make the machines needed to build a one million tonne capacity steel plant each year. Producer goods industries would be developed "mainly" in the public sector, with the continued involvement of the private sector in the production of cement and chemicals.

Mahalanobis did recognise that heavy industries, being capital intensive, would not provide much scope for meeting the employment goals of the Plan. They would generate a large demand for consumer goods however, which they would not be able to supply themselves which is where household and hand industries came into the equation. They would supply the consumer goods for the demand created by heavy industries whilst generating employment all over the country. Idle labour would also be put to work on construction projects, roads, housing, irrigation and flood control projects which would in themselves generate employment and also boost demand for consumer goods. The more that household and hand industries took up the function of producing consumer goods, the more investment could take place in heavy industries without the fear of inflation. National income would rise and a greater proportion of it would go to the poor in these household industries.

A part of the argument against factory production of consumer goods was that these factories would require a high rate of capital investment per worker and would compete with household industries. Until unemployment was eliminated or brought under control, factories had to be restricted from producing those goods which could be made by households. This would leave them for the supply of essential goods like medicines as well as goods for export. Given that household and hand made goods would in many cases be more expensive than factory made goods, an excise would have to be levied on factory goods in order to increase their price and make them less attractive to consumers. Once the unemployment problem was solved, the household sector would be mechanised to improve its productivity, whilst factory production would also be allowed to grow.

The public sector had to be expanded at a greater pace than the private sector specifically for the fulfilment of the principles of socialism; the government would have to be prepared to enter banking, insurance, foreign trade and internal trade in order to make capital resources available for the Plan. There would be some allowance for public-private collaborations, however the government would hold the controlling share. The private sector would thus have to produce in consonance with the Plan, but it would be assisted in doing so by the government and enjoy the benefits of a growing market.

Mahalanobis then proceeded to set the targets for production, something which would distinguish the new physical planning from the old financial planning. Electrification held highest priority- it was the main link in the economic development of India. The hydroelectric projects from the First Plan needed to be continued and expanded. Regional grid systems needed to be planned with a view to an all-India super grid system in the future. Small power stations could be built for small towns and villages, whilst the use of electricity by small and household industries needed to be increased as they had been for tube wells. The aim was to more than double electric capacity from the 1953/54 figure of 2.8 million kilowatt-hours to 6 million in 1960/61. The target was almost as ambitious for coal; production was to rise from 37 million tonnes to 60 million tonnes during the Second Plan period.

Given India's vast resources of iron ore, it had to increase production of steel, with the aim to add one million tonnes beginning in 1960. This would secure the foundation for the building of plants and machinery and allow for the expansion of construction work on railways and transport. Steel might also be exported to neighbouring countries which needed it. India could also draw on its reserves of bauxite to manufacture aluminium which could replace the use of copper which was in short supply and needed to be imported. Public sector aluminium plants needed to be established to raise production from 5,000 to 40,000 tonnes. The production of manganese ore and cement needed to be increased as did fertiliser production by establishing three more plants like the one at Sindri in Bihar. The production of heavy chemicals was to be increased by four times. India relied on imports for most of its petrol, and so there was a need for more oil prospecting and the establishment of a state plant to produce 300,000 tonnes of petrol which could then be used for the development of associated chemical industries.

Mahalanobis planned net investment in both the public and private sectors totalling ₹5,600 crores which would require raising the rate of net investment as a proportion of national income from 7% to 11%. The total expenditure of both the central and state governments would come to ₹8,800 crores. However, taxes would only raise ₹5,200 crores, borrowing from the public ₹1,000 crores and the railways ₹200 crores, which meant that the government would only take in ₹6,400 crores. This would leave a resources gap of ₹2,400 crores for government spending alone. Mahalanobis thought that external assistance might provide ₹400 crores, which would still leave a gap of ₹2,000 crore, which would have to be partially funded by more taxation and profits from the public sector. Given that the deficit needed to be kept to around ₹1,000 crores, taxation would have to rise from 7% to 10% of national income.

Mahalanobis knew that the public sector would take some time to become profitable, foreign assistance might not materialise, and lower income earners would not be taxed. He thus urged that government spending outside the Plan be controlled, price and subsidy policies be adjusted, new savers be reached, and changes to the tax structure be made. He did not think that credit to the private sector would be a problem, but larger imports of capital goods would be required throughout the Second Plan period. The bill would come to ₹1,600 crore. Mahalanobis saw this being paid for by three principal means: the increased production of food, sugar, cotton and petrol, which would mean lower spending on imports of these goods, foreign aid and withdrawal from the sterling balances, and curtailment of non-essential imports and the promotion of exports.

In meetings in February and March of 1955 Mahalanobis made his case to the Panel of Economists not as a matter of ideology, but on the basis of linear programming techniques which would optimise planned investments. Ragnar Frisch also travelled to New Delhi to try to win over the Indian Panel, as did members of the Soviet delegation. The Russians repeated their dictum to the Planning Commission; it should not "allow financial resources to impede economic development".[cxxxiv] The Finance Minister, Sir Chintaman Deshmukh chaired the Panel of 21 economists, mainly professors of economics drawn from universities across the country. The Panel was representative of a broad spectrum of ideological commitments, ranging from sceptics of the planning process like Professor Bellikoth Raghunath Shenoy from the University of Gujarat and Professor Dhananjay Gadgil of the Gokhale School of Economics and Politics, to committed socialists like V.K.R.V Rao and K.N. Raj, both of the Delhi School of Economics.

The Panel largely subscribed to the thinking of the Draft Plan Frame and agreed that a bolder Plan was needed. The panellists endorsed the goal of raising national income by 25% by the end of the Second Plan, however to do so investment would have to be increased from 7 to 11% which was "not too high a target" but was "fairly ambitious". This would mean doubling the rate of investment from the First Plan period. To do so would "strain the economy a very great deal".

The Panel foresaw a problem with taxation. Given the aims of the Draft Plan Frame it would be likely that 9% of national income would have to be taxed if deficit financing was to be kept within safe limits. Yet it would take considerable fresh taxation just to be able to maintain the current share of taxation of national income of 7%. India's existing tax structure was inadequate to deliver a proportionate increase in tax receipts to the government as national income rose. Furthermore, most of the production envisaged in the Draft Plan Frame was to take place in large-scale public sector projects, and small-scale and cottage industries, neither of which were likely to expand the direct or indirect tax base. Increases in incomes were likely to be experienced by farmers, peasants, and workers on public works projects, none of whom were likely to be taxed.

The Panel did not think that there was any inflationary pressure in the economy, and so deficits of around ₹200 crore a year for the first two years of the Second Plan would be within safe limits. It cautioned against "undue optimism" over the use of deficit financing to raise money in the absence of increased taxes or savings just because deficits had been run in previous years without giving rise to inflation. Part of the reason that inflation had remained moderate was that the weather had been favourable and harvests plentiful. It was difficult to predict whether this good fortune would continue. The Panel also foresaw the increase in the import of capital equipment which would be necessary for industrialisation and the heavy strain on the balance of payments that this would create. It would be likely that foreign assistance of around ₹600 crore over the Second Plan period would be required to avoid a draft on foreign exchange reserves.

More broadly the Panel was in full agreement with the investment pattern of the Draft Plan Frame, particularly the greater weight given to industry and mining. It did not want to underestimate the importance of agriculture to the Indian economy, yet agriculture had done well during the First Plan period, both due to good weather and increased productive capacity. But beyond a certain point the agricultural sector required an expanding industrial sector, which would provide a bigger market for agricultural output and produce the industrial consumer goods which would provide an incentive for greater agricultural production. Moreover, it was industry which could produce the modern equipment and fertilisers which would increase agricultural productivity. Agriculture and industry were thus not in competition but were complimentary. In conclusion the Panel thought that behind the Draft Plan Frame were "major assumptions" regarding the capacity of the country and the government to implement the proposed programme: "For these assumptions to materialise a big organisational effort will be called for."

Professor Shenoy was the only one of the 21 economists on the Panel to write a formal note of dissent. His first doubts were about the size of the Plan. If the 25% increase in national income was to be achieved over the Plan period, there would need to be a 50% increase in net investment. He felt that his colleagues had not adequately indicated the risk that this type of increase might involve. To force the pace of development beyond the real resources of the economy would likely give rise to inflation, and social instability. Rather than the ₹200 crore annual deficit recommended by his fellow panellists, Shenoy argued that ₹40 crores would be more appropriate.

Shenoy thought that the planners, in a democracy like India, first needed to assess the real resources of the economy and then formulate their Plan. In this case they were behaving more like communists who could formulate their Plan and then look for the resources to make it work. Ultimately India had to rely on its savings to fund its Plan and over the previous four years net domestic capital formation had been stagnant at around 6% of national income. Yet the Draft Plan Frame was aiming at a rate of 10%, or an increase of 60%. The Draft Plan Frame was similarly over ambitious in its goal for an increase in national income. Even with the favourable monsoons of the First Plan period, national income rose by about 12%, whilst the figure aimed at during the Second Plan period was 25%. It was unlikely that savings in India would rise dramatically. If income was distributed more equitably as the government aimed to do, the poor would most likely spend their money on food rather than save it. Shenoy warned that good monsoons, "in conformity with traditional experience", would be followed by bad ones, which when they came would further strain the capacity to save. The size of the Plan thus needed to be revised to match India's real resources.

The Panel of Economists' endorsement of the Draft Plan Frame only stretched to 18 pages, and Professor Shenoy's dissent covered 11 pages. Yet attached to these two papers were over 500 pages of technical articles, some of which had been prepared by government ministries, statistical institutes, and the Reserve Bank of India, and some of which were written by the panellists themselves. Read together they showed, in great detail, exactly how and why the Draft Plan Frame would not work; there was too little emphasis on agriculture and land reform, and too much on heavy industry and the public sector, consumer goods were not provided for, and the Plan was only likely to generate inflation.

Bal Krishna Madan of the Reserve Bank of India wrote a paper titled *The Second Five Year Plan: Problems of Resource Mobilisation* in which he criticised the short-term approach being taken to the unemployment problem and the expectation that the small-scale sector could perform its function without mechanization. He argued that more consumer goods were needed, the quest for self-reliance in capital goods was futile, capital-output ratios were unrealistic and too few resources were being allocated to the development of transport infrastructure. Nonetheless, he signed off on the Panel's support for the Draft Plan Frame. Likewise, Professor Dhananjay Gadgil of the Gokhale School of Economics and Politics gave his assent only to express his reservations at an annual meeting of Indian economists in Pune in January 1956.[cxxxv] At the same meeting another panel member, who had also formally supported the Draft Plan, Kakkadan Nandanath Raj of the Delhi School of Economics, expressed his apprehensions of what might occur were the monsoon to fail and food production decline. Fellow panellist Professor Chandulal Nagindas Vakil of the University of Bombay also gave his support to the Draft Plan only to set about writing his own plan with his colleague Palahalli Ramaiya Brahmananda which gave precedence to agriculture rather than heavy industry. The criticisms of Mahalanobis's Draft Plan Frame thus seemed to appear everywhere and in all forms other than the 18 page endorsement which made its way through New Delhi's decision making bodies- so much so that when it was presented for review by the National Development Council Jawaharlal Nehru could state that there had been "broad agreement about the targets proposed in the draft plan frame".[cxxxvi]

***

Milton Friedman had been teaching at the University of

Chicago since the end of the Second World War and had been a visiting Fulbright Fellow at Cambridge in 1954 and 1955. By 1957 he would publish *A Theory of the Consumption Function* which detailed his "permanent income hypothesis" and then in 1962 his collection of essays, *Capitalism and Freedom*, became an international bestseller. He was thus just on the cusp of fame when he arrived in India in the summer of 1955.

Friedman's formal invitation had come from the head of American Aid in India and the Indian finance minister, yet he was, in essence, an emissary of the Eisenhower administration sent to counter the pervasive Leftist influence on Indian economic policy making. However, upon getting to work he thought that his patrons in the American aid organisations had become fellow travellers, sympathisers with the socialist planning experiment. At the end of his stay he wrote *A Memorandum to the Government of India* which he submitted to his superiors at the United States International Co-operation Administration and Sir Chintaman Deshmukh.[cxxxvii] The *Memorandum* was circulated within the Government of India and parts of it found their way into the press.

Friedman thought that there was a tendency to regard the ratio of investment to national income as the key to development and take it for granted that there was a mechanical ratio between the amount of investment and an increase in output. The form and distribution of investment, after all, were as important as its sheer magnitude in increasing productivity. Investment in capital was only part of the expenditure needed to increase the productivity of the economy. He thought that the major source of productive power in an economy was not machinery and other physical capital, but human beings. In the United States, of the total national income only 20% was returned from physical capital, 80% was a return on human capital. He thought that even if all the physical capital, the plants and factories of the United States, was destroyed but the human capital remained,

Americans would only take a few years to rebuild the physical infrastructure needed for production. Yet in India in 1955 it was only investment in machinery which was being talked about.

In addition, Friedman thought that the problem with Indian policies was that they concentrated investment in heavy industry at one extreme of industrial formation and on handicrafts at the other. Small and medium sized industries were left out. Thus, capital was used inefficiently by combining it with too little labour in heavy industry, and labour was being used inefficiently by combining it with too little capital in handicrafts. The optimal use of capital was somewhere between these two extremes. Heavy industry could best develop upon a base of diversified and expanded light industry. The attempt to protect small-scale industry by excise taxes on factory made shoes and cloth was actually doing more harm than good. The main problem in India was the inefficient use of labour. Such policies were only protecting this inefficiency. The high prices paid by consumers and direct subsidies from the government could have been channelled into investment. Investment was actually declining as shoe factory capacity remained idle. These policies just increased the number of people being employed inefficiently, whilst reducing the numbers in factories working efficiently, and reducing the disposable income of factory workers which would boost demand. The net result was likely to be lower employment.

Friedman noted the tendency in India to want to do too much in the public sector. This had been tried by countries in Europe after the Second World War and to his knowledge the results had been disappointing, every single time. The enterprises in India which could only be undertaken by the government were so large and complex, requiring such large investments and placing such a huge burden on civil servants, that wherever possible business needed to be left to businesspeople.

There was also an attempt to control private investment too rigidly and in too detailed a manner. Denying the private sector the ability to invest in particular projects may not make capital available for other uses, but private firms and households may direct their investment into consumption and the purchase of gold. It was impossible to predict which businesses would be successful. What was needed was a system of flexibility. Detailed direction wasted the time of civil servants in producing and enforcing regulations, and individuals in trying to avoid or change them. Given that the public sector had first claim on resources, should the market not decide how the remaining capital was allocated? To not allow this was to reduce freedom of choice for consumers and reduce the value of the goods produced. The government had to keep inflation under control, but should do so through monetary and fiscal policy rather than detailed regulation. Private industry was being coddled in selected sectors, whilst being subject to stifling regulation in others. Giving these selected firms special favours like loan guarantees, refusing licensing to competitors, permitting price fixing and market sharing encouraged inefficiency and wasted scarce resources. The energies of businesspeople were then directed to carving up existing markets, rather than opening up new ones.

Milton Friedman saw a looming financial gap of between ₹1,000 crores and ₹1,200 crores even after allowing for substantial foreign aid. Government efforts to raise tax revenues or any other methods of revenue raising were severely limited. It would even be preferable to cut the size of the Plan rather than have to raise taxes and depress private sector activity. Yet beyond the finance and resources gap, there was, more specifically, a foreign exchange gap; elements of the Second Plan, particularly the need to import machinery were likely to lead to an excess of demand for foreign exchange. Friedman thought that the existing regime of exchange controls and import and export licences and discrimination between sources of purchases were a major obstacle to the growth and progress of the Indian economy. They wasted and inefficiently used foreign exchange, brought delays, uncertainty and arbitrariness to the process of doing business, and imposed an impossible task on civil servants who allocated foreign exchange. Those businesses which were granted import licences were essentially receiving a subsidy whilst inefficient and monopolistic Indian producers were protected from foreign competition.

***

The Planning Commission produced a Draft Memorandum of the Second Plan by the end of 1955 which was considered by the National Development Council in January 1956. The question of resources inevitably arose, and Sir Chintaman Deshmukh forecast that the fiscal position would be "very difficult indeed". The states were likely to fall short of the projected tax revenue by ₹70-80 crores. Sir Chintaman was projecting an overall resource gap of ₹400 crores, yet even this figure factored in ₹800 crores of foreign aid, none of which had yet been committed.[cxxxviii] Chief ministers were both opposing a reduction in the size of the Plan, whilst being sceptical about their own ability to raise tax revenue for a large Plan. There was no shortage of suggestions for raising money at the meeting: the appointment of a panel of financial experts, bold government policies, earmarked taxes, compulsory saving and even raising money by raffles. The meeting of the National Development Council was not however, able to come to any conclusions on the issue of finance for the Second Plan.

The Draft Memorandum was approved by the National Development Council and the Planning Commission issued a Draft Plan in February 1956. The relative outlays shifted to industry, but the absolute level of outlays to all sectors increased and the planners thought that the agricultural problem was on its way to a solution. The issue of the ₹400 crore gap still lingered however. The foreign exchange situation was thought to be manageable, but the estimated net deficit on the current account was based on some unrealistic assumptions- that steel imports would not be needed by the end of the Second Plan, the terms of trade would remain favourable, agricultural imports would be constant, and imports of industrial supplies would not rise.

In May 1956 the Commerce and Industry Minister, K.C. Neogy and the Deputy Chairman of the Planning Commission, Sir V.T. Krishnamachari clashed over the looming resources gap. Neogy largely repeated Professor Shenoy's concerns over the inflationary tendency within the Plan and the Panel of Economist's note on the lack of technical personnel and organisational capacity within the government. However, he also spent some time expanding on the futility of such an ambitious Plan in the absence of the transport infrastructure, both rail and shipping, which could move industrial supplies around the country. Neogy argued for a more modest plan but the chief ministers, particularly Morarji Desai of Bombay, Ramakrishna Rao of Hyderabad and Chidambaram Subramaniam, the finance minister of Madras were all in favour of a more ambitious Plan.[cxxxix] Sir Krishnamachari suggested that the resource problem would be largely solved by an increase in agricultural production of 40% by the third year of the Plan. This 40% figure was less an emphatic statement however, and more of a suggestion to the state governments that they formulate programmes to achieve the target.[cxl] Sir Krishnamachari's astounding 40% received support from Jawaharlal Nehru, Morarji Desai, C. Subramaniam and Sir Chintaman Deshmukh. The only member to completely dismiss it was the Chief Minister of West Bengal, Dr. Bidhan Chandra Roy. Nehru then deferred the matter of target setting to the Planning Commission and the states, and a resolution approving the Draft Second Five Year Plan was passed.

The Draft Second Five Year Plan then made its way through the Lok Sabha and its committees during May

1956. It had only been days since the National Development Council meeting, and Prime Minister Nehru remained committed to Sir Krishnamachari's target of a 40% increase in agricultural production. On 23 May he addressed the Lok Sabha and put the ambitious target in the context not only of domestic consumption but the need to export; some of the anticipated bumper harvest could be exported, which would help to solve the anticipated foreign exchange gap. Nehru did not address the issue of transport however, getting it slightly confused with an associated concern on the equitable regional distribution of development. When three ministers addressed the Council for Industries in June 1956 the confusion seemed to continue. Tiruvellore Thattai Krishnamachari, the new finance minister announced higher targets for the production of consumer goods and expressed confidence that Plan targets would be met, whilst the Commerce and Industry Minister, K.C. Neogy forecast "stresses and strains everywhere", and the Railways Minister, Lal Bahadur Shastri complained of a lack of funds for the railways when targets for industry and agriculture were being raised.[cxli]

The Planning Commission published the final Second Five Year Plan in August 1956, and it was debated in the Lok Sabha between 17 and 22 September. The most penetrating speech was given by the prime minister's son-in-law, Feroze Gandhi who marshalled facts and figures to show that transport was being dangerously neglected. Gulzarilal Nanda, the minister for planning endorsed the call for a 40% increase in agricultural production, whilst the Deputy Minister for Planning, Shyam Nandan Mishra suggested that the anticipated shortages of transport might be filled by stimuli from other spheres of the economy. Mishra betrayed his lack of understanding; railways were not stimulated by the production of coal, the production of coal would only be stimulated if there were enough railway wagons to transport it across the country. T.T. Krishnamachari forecast that total Plan allocations might rise, whilst also informing the House of deteriorating foreign exchange reserves and pressure on vital points of the economy. Prime Minister Nehru invited members with constructive criticisms, like Feroze, to take them up with the Planning Commission, but he maintained the position he had held since May: "...the difference of ₹800 crores or whatever the gap is supposed to be in our foreign exchange and other matters, all these gaps can be very largely covered if we can increase our agricultural production."

***

The Second Plan had been in operation for just four months before the question of money arose. India's reserves of foreign exchange had been relatively stable at the time that the Draft Plan Frame and the final Second Five Year Plan documents were being formulated. However, almost as soon as the Second Plan period began in April 1956, those reserves started to deplete by ₹6.5 crores a week. The statutory minimum for the Reserve Bank of India at the time was ₹400 crores, a level which would be breached within a year if the trend continued.

Officials in New Delhi started to become concerned in August and Jawaharlal Nehru instructed his bureaucrats to brief him on the issue. The briefing did not come from the Planning Commission however, but from his cousin's son, Braj Kumar Nehru, who was a civil servant in the Ministry of Finance. He warned his prime minister, and distant uncle, that the Government of India might default on its international obligations unless urgent action was taken. Nehru then wrote to his chief ministers warning them that the situation was grave, and encouraging them to increase agricultural production to reduce the need to spend scarce foreign exchange on imports of food.[cxlii] He did not allocate any further funds to the states to do this, but did reinstate foreign exchange regulations, tightened import licensing, and imposed a "virtual embargo" on new foreign exchange commitments through the later part of

1956.[cxliii] At this point he was still insistent that Plan expenditure would rise, and the states took to raising more taxes.[cxliv]

From early 1957 the private sector was prohibited from entering into new foreign exchange commitments unless they were covered by foreign aid or deferred payments or were in core or foreign exchange earning sectors. The measures had a limited effect. By May 1957 it was envisaged that the foreign exchange gap would be much more than originally planned for. T.T. Krishnamachari said as much in his budget speech and it became a matter of whether the core of the Plan could be saved. Agricultural production slumped whilst prices rose. Deficit financing doubled and foreign exchange assets fell by one-third. Central and state taxes did not yield as much as expected.

The Planning Commission blamed the crisis on the private sector for exceeding its allocations of foreign exchange. Prasanta Mahalanobis did not think that there was anything to worry about. He did not understand the crisis in purely economic terms, but as "the inevitable difficulties of adjustments to the requirements of a new policy...it will take some time for things to settle down."[cxlv] Nehru had to deal with the practical fallout of the crisis, but was, as always, of one mind with Mahalanobis; he thought that such problems "were bound to crop up in an underdeveloped country's economy."[cxlvi] T.T. Krishnamachari also shared the sentiment; he thought it was a "crisis of development, and not a crisis of stagnation or confidence."[cxlvii] He thought that the crisis was brought on by a boom in the private sector, one which he might have caused himself whilst at the Commerce Ministry. The Reserve Bank endorsed this idea, largely blaming the foreign exchange crisis on a surge of imports by the private sector after the liberalisation of licensing in 1955 and 1956.[cxlviii] After reading a report he had commissioned from the Planning Commission, Nehru came to the conclusion that "not much thought appears to have been given at the time as to how to raise the necessary finance."[cxlix]

***

The quest for industrial self-reliance had, within a year, made India dependent on the generosity of foreign donors. Given that the Second Five Year Plan had been inspired by the Soviet example of rapid expansion of heavy industry and public sector enterprises, it might have seemed natural that the Russians would be approached for aid. They had been active in India in the 1950s supporting the creation of a steel mill at Bhilai in central India and a model large scale mechanised farm at Suratgarh in Rajasthan and were always ready to assist in projects for oil exploration. Yet the Russian capacity to assist in India's economic development was confined to this project based aid. The Soviet Union was itself short of foreign exchange and had limited opportunities to earn more. It was undertaking the task of integrating the economies of Eastern Europe and did not have any hard currency to spare. The Government of India would thus have to look elsewhere in its time of crisis.

The National Security Council's statement of United States policy for South Asia, NSC 5701, was approved by President Dwight Eisenhower on 10 January 1957. NSC 5701 maintained continuity with previous policy statements in prioritising the need to prevent the region's fall to Communism and maintain Pakistan as a military ally. However, the new element in the resolution was the recognition of the importance of India's economic development to American interests in Asia. India had emerged as the leader of the non-aligned group and the Soviet Union's diplomatic initiatives in New Delhi were causing some concern. The resolution clearly stated that the United States "should provide economic and technical assistance to India, placing emphasis on projects and programs having the maximum potential of support of the goals and aspirations of India's second five year plan."

Economic development in India would also have "international ramifications"; "The outcome of competition between Communist China and India will have a profound effect throughout Africa and Asia."

There was, however, some unease in the American foreign policy establishment over this change of orientation. If economic, and possibly military aid was provided to a non-aligned nation like India, what incentive would there be for nations actually aligned to the United States to remain loyal? Yet the Secretary of State John Foster Dulles, who had previously been a staunch critic of neutrality, argued that national interest was more important than principle and he would rather keep India and lose Thailand.[cl] Months later in May, the administration requested the establishment of a Development Loan Fund to provide economic assistance to Asian and African nations in order to facilitate this new element of economic diplomacy. India's foreign exchange crisis thus came at just the right time for the Eisenhower administration.

State Department officials were aware of the magnitude of the problem by May 1957. They forecast the worsening of the crisis and suggested that the president use Development Loan Fund and Export-Import Bank resources to address the problem.[cli] But it was only in September that Jawaharlal Nehru announced that he would be willing to accept a $500 million loan from the United States and sent T.T. Krishnamachari to Washington to discuss terms. The Eisenhower administration was fully aware of India's strategic importance and the importance of the success of the Second Plan, however it did have to take into account the mood of the Congress, as well as the fact that the American economy was technically in a recession. Another fortuitous event for India was the victory of Communists in state elections in Kerala in the middle of 1957. This just served to raise the spectre of a Communist takeover of India within the State

Department.

By November 1957 President Eisenhower had approved assistance of $250 million a year to India for the remainder of the Second Plan. Given the size of India's foreign exchange requirements there was some discussion in the White House over the need to go to Congress for funding. Eisenhower managed to avoid doing so, and by January he was able to announce that the United States would provide India with $225 million a year in loans from the Development Loan Fund and Import-Export Bank.

B.K. Nehru was commissioner general for economic affairs and by May 1958 he persuaded Morarji Desai, the new finance minister, that what India needed was not aid for capital goods for Indian industry but "free money" to finance current imports for the maintenance of the economy.[clii] He was arguing for a shift from project to non-project aid. He wanted to internationalise India's quest for foreign money and suggested bringing current and potential lenders together under the auspices of the World Bank. He wanted a "combined operation" of the World Bank, the International Monetary Fund, friendly foreign governments and money markets.[cliii] Nehru thought that the World Bank President, Eugene Black was sympathetic to India's cause; he had been tying the success of the Bank's development lending programme to the success of India's planning effort. Nehru thought that having the World Bank on India's side would help in any arrangements to be made with the International Monetary Fund and that Black's influence with the American president and the Congress would also help to loosen purse strings in Washington.[cliv]

B.K. Nehru's idea won support within the Indian and American governments and so they got to work creating a consortium, or lenders' group which would meet at the World Bank in Washington and discuss an assessment of the Indian economy prepared by the Bank's staff. In this arrangement India would not have to ask any foreign government for aid directly or even have a representative present at the meetings. The State Department responded positively- it was one less thing for them to have to worry about. The World Bank sent its team to India during the monsoon of 1958 and a meeting was convened in late August in Washington to discuss "India's foreign exchange situation". Besides the United States, representatives from the United Kingdom, Canada, West Germany and Japan were invited, as were observers from the International Monetary Fund.

The reports of the World Bank staff which informed the meeting were not flattering for the Government of India.[clv] The perennial criticisms were all there; spending on the public sector needed to be cut, whilst agriculture had been neglected and the private sector too tightly controlled. Future World Bank lending would thus be dependent on Indian economic and financial policies. Eugene Black only seemed to emphasise his frustration with the obstinacy of Indian government policy. The invited representatives all agreed that they wanted to influence the remainder of the Second Plan, without actually issuing a list of actions which the Government of India needed to take. West Germany was the most staunch in its conditions; the Government of India needed to understand that it had to slow down investment in the public sector, increase it in agriculture, and loosen controls on the private sector if it wanted ongoing support. But B.K. Nehru's judgement of Eugene Black was good in the end. As the meetings went on it was the World Bank President who did most of the work in raising the donors' initially tepid financial commitments. He worked the back rooms, applied peer pressure and made commitments for World Bank matching grants. By the end of the third day of meetings he was able to say that the donors could reach their target of $350 million in immediate assistance.

The creation of the Consortium also realised B.K. Nehru's

vision of a change from project to non-project aid; the totals that were being discussed were for direct transfers to the Government of India rather than funding for individual projects. Yet Nehru would still have to go to each donor individually and come to bilateral agreements, and each donor would administer its aid in its own way. It was when Morarji Desai went on a tour of Western capitals that he learnt that it was not the "free money" that B.K. Nehru thought it would be. Wrangling the money out of the United States, generally the most willing and able donor, was always tough, despite the favourable press coverage which India was receiving as a model of non-communist development in Asia and the warm welcome that Desai received as a staunch anti-communist.

In addition to the foreign exchange crisis the anticipated resources gap, the government's inability to finance the Plan from its own funds, had also materialised and during 1958 there was much debate over whether the initial projected outlay of ₹4,800 crores could be maintained. Aid from the United States was not yet certain and the gap was variously estimated to be about ₹300 crore. Cuts were anticipated in key sectors such as industry, minerals, transport and communication and the pace of investment in public sector enterprises was likely to be slowed. The Planning Commission had accepted the need for cuts, and Morarji Desai argued its case at the National Development Council, whilst Jawaharlal Nehru tried to broker a compromise and divide the plan outlay into core and non-core spending. However, by the beginning of 1959 aid from the United States had started to arrive and the economy showed signs of improvement. The slowdown in industrial growth had brought inflation under control, foreign exchange reserves began to stabilise, both as a result of the tighter import licensing policy and the receipt of American aid, and the central government was raising more money from bonds and taxes. State governments were also able to increase their revenue and the rate of small savings rose. After a plentiful harvest in the spring of 1959 most of the anticipated cuts were avoided and the total plan outlay came to ₹4,600 crore.

The first documents for a Third Plan appeared just before this turn of events in December 1958. Prasanta Mahalanobis would not author another plan, but one of his proteges from the Second Plan, Pitambar Pant was head of the Planning Commission's Perspective Planning Division. Pant produced a paper, *Dimensional Hypotheses Concerning the Third Five Year Plan*, which aimed to double the size of the Second Plan, taking net investment up to ₹10,000 crore. The Third Plan would continue the government's existing policy of industrial development and its emphasis on the public sector in keeping with its objective of achieving a socialistic pattern of society. The balance of investment would be largely the same as that of the Second Plan with industry alone receiving one-third of total investment. When industry, mining, power, transport and commerce were taken together they would account for half of all investment.

Pitamber Pant thought that the foreign exchange crisis of the Second Plan only intensified the need to continue the heavy industry import substitution strategy; the quicker that heavy industry was built in India and capital goods imports were substituted with Indian goods, the quicker India would become a "self-generating economy".[clvi] When the Planning Commission produced a *Main Issues* paper for the National Development Council in April 1959 it repeated Pant's aim of achieving "self-sustaining" growth as quickly as possible, but, for the first time, the Commission acknowledged that this strategy would be dependent on the availability of foreign exchange, which would increase the need for "external assistance".

Another fortunate turn for India came when Walt Rostow published his *Stages of Economic Growth* in 1959. Rostow and Max Millikan of the Massachusetts Institute of Technology had, throughout the 1950s been advocating a liberal diffusionist model of economic growth for the Third

World. That is, economic growth occurred with the diffusion of capital, technology and education from the First World to the Third. Rostow had outlined five stages of development: the "traditional stage" in which a country would be provided with economic and technical assistance to prepare it for the "preconditions of takeoff stage" after which it would move to the "takeoff stage", "the drive for maturity", and then finally reach "self-sustained economic growth".

Walt Rostow and Max Millikan had been at work on India for years, and tried, without much success, to get American economists involved in the planning process in New Delhi. Their advocacy had more success in Washington however. They started advising the young senator from Massachusetts, John Kennedy and his colleague John Cooper as they proposed a congressional resolution providing India with an open ended commitment of funds for its Second Plan. The duo also reported to the Draper Committee, a presidential commission examining foreign aid, arguing that India had all the resources needed for sustained growth. India seemed a perfect model of diffusionist development: it had a basic network of transport, communications and power, a skilled labour force, and a stable, democratic government run by well trained administrators. Rostow insisted that India was "the big urgent test case" for his principles of economic growth.[clvii]

It seemed then that the intellectual climate in Washington was remarkably receptive to the financial needs of New Delhi. However, some concerns over India's "socialistic pattern" and particularly its commitment to public sector heavy industry did remain. Yet both Rostow and Millikan maintained that India was pursuing a mixed economy and given its state of underdevelopment Indian planners were justified in their large scale public sector investments.[clviii] Millikan saw India's private economy stagnating without large investments in economic infrastructure, or what he called "social overheads".[clix] American assistance was needed for the creation of such infrastructure so that Indian savings could be directed into private enterprise. Both Rostow and Millikan accepted the explanation that the 1957 foreign exchange crisis had been caused by a buoyant private sector's demand for imports. Thus, if the United States supported India with foreign exchange its private sector would be able to expand without restraint and achieve self-sustained growth faster. Even the Republican President, Dwight Eisenhower took a relaxed approach to India's commitment to the public sector. He also recognised the need for government involvement in a country as poor as India and even thought the American commitment to rugged individualism was best left on its frontier in the earlier part of the century.[clx] When Senators Kennedy and Cooper sent a World Bank study team to India in 1959 to report back to the Consortium on the likely requirements for India's Third Five Year Plan it too recommended large scale, long term aid. When another World Bank team visited India in 1960 it "accepted the basic theory of Indian plans".[clxi]

Third World nations were presented to Congress as "islands of development" in requests for approval for assistance and it seemed that India was potentially the biggest such island. By 1960 most of the $700 million in DLF funds was flowing to India. India had been receiving around $200 million a year and there was some talk of raising that sum to $1 billion a year over the ensuing five years. John Kennedy was elected president at the end of 1960 and he made reference to India in his first State of the Union address in January 1961; he referred to Jawaharlal Nehru's "soaring idealism" and made the point that the Communist Chinese menace reached all the way to the Indian border.

In June 1961 the Consortium met and, faced with a likely requirement of $5.5 billion for the Third Plan, it agreed to provide over $2 billion in assistance for the first two years. The United States alone contributed $1 billion with Germany, France, Britain and Canada contributing $780 million and the World Bank pledging another $400 million. Of the United States' $900 million foreign aid budget in 1962 $500 million went to India. Most of the money was flowing into industrial projects: large scale dams, the purchase of steel, machinery parts and the technology needed to sustain industrialisation. This was the "non-project aid" which B.K. Nehru had been seeking. It was not tied to particular projects under the auspices of the Government of India or United States Government, but was money transferred directly to the Indian treasury which used it to import machinery and tools which might otherwise have sapped its meagre reserves of foreign exchange. The first such loan came in October 1961 from the Development Loan Fund totalling $20 million for the import of non-ferrous metals. There were two more loans in 1962 and 1963 totalling $400 million to pay for imports of steel, automobile parts and machine tools. Electrical power was also a priority- between 1961 and 1963 the Kennedy administration provided $250 million for the construction of hydroelectric and thermal power projects. In 1963 it also provided $72 million for the construction of the Tarapur nuclear power station near Bombay.

***

With American aid pouring in the prospect of the Planning Commission launching India onto a path of self-sustaining growth might have seemed imminent. Yet during the summer of 1960, just prior to the start of the Third Plan, the Indian economy endured what came to be known in the press as the "steel-coal-transport crisis". It was difficult to isolate the precise origin of the crisis however. Each element seemed to be caused by another.

The power shortage in the summer of 1961 was most calamitous in Calcutta and its hinterland. It was blamed on generators breaking down due to a lack of maintenance, as well as the imbalance between supply and demand. There were similar woes on the other side of the country in Ahmadabad where industrial units had to reduce production and work fewer days and shorter hours. In the south, in Andhra Pradesh the supply of power to industries had to be cut by 20%.[clxii] By the summer of 1962, the Minister of State for Irrigation and Power, Ozhalur Viswanatha Mudaliar Alegasan, took the power shortage to be inevitable and stated in the Lok Sabha that even if all the power generation projects of the Third Plan were completed on schedule there would still be a shortage of 500,000 kw at the end of the Plan period.[clxiii] The government even had to import six small 10,000 kw generating plants to relieve some of the distress in Andhra and Bengal.[clxiv]

Things had not improved by the monsoon of 1962 in Calcutta when two units of the Damodar Valley Corporation broke down. Despite these breakdowns generating capacity remained constant. The problem was the spike in household consumption which meant that supply to industry had to be curtailed; over 100 applications for industrial licences in West Bengal had to be rejected for want of adequate power supply.[clxv] Production had fallen 30% and jute mills, among India's biggest export earners, were running idle for 10 hours a day due to a lack of electricity.[clxvi] The local power crisis was being blamed on the failure of the Durgapur thermal power station and the fourth unit of the Bokaro thermal power plant. Even government owned units like Hindustan Machine Tools, Indian Telephone Industries and Bharat Electronics in Bangalore had machinery left idle due to a shortage of power. In the summer of 1963 Kanpur textile and jute mills, leather units, woollen and rayon mills had all closed down due to the persistent power shortage.

Only 5% of the Third Plan outlay for power generation was allocated to the private sector, whilst the Electricity Act discouraged the establishment of small private sector plants which might have reduced the need to build huge public sector units.[clxvii] This brought into question the purpose of planning. Was there any point in bringing new industrial plants into existence if they were left idle due to a lack of power? A basic tenet of planning around the world was the expansion of transport and power capacity ahead of industrialisation, rather than behind it.

Blame was being heaped on the Railways for not doing enough to alleviate the coal shortage in the country. Although production had been lagging behind Plan targets, there were large accumulations of stocks at colliery pitheads and large dumps of coal near railway sidings at the collieries, and so the immediate bottleneck was not of supply, but of transport. The Railways could not keep up with its minimum guaranteed number of wagons and had also missed its Second Plan target for the movement of coal by 1.5 million tonnes.[clxviii] The shortfall of wagons was running at 1,000 a day.[clxix] In January and February of 1961 the movement of coal had fallen behind by 500,000 tonnes.[clxx] Some collieries were having to restrict their output due to the accumulation of stocks. At Gidi colliery in Bihar 200,000 tonnes of coal had accumulated without a wagon arriving to move any of it.[clxxi] As of the start of 1961 the National Coal Development Corporation held a stockpile of 1 million tonnes of coal just waiting to be moved.[clxxii] These stocks would deteriorate in the sun and rain, and there was always the risk that a fire might break out. Part of the problem was with planning. The planners were trying to do away with a dependence on the Bihar and Bengal coal fields but despite their best laid plans the dependence just kept increasing and outlying coal fields remained neglected. This meant that coal from eastern India had to be transported via Uttar Pradesh to northern and western India, and via Calcutta to southern India when coal fields nearer these consumers could have been developed.

India had invested a relatively large amount in thermal rather than hydro-electric power plants. Thermal power plants like those of Durgapur and Bokaro were fuelled by coal which was found in deposits mainly in the eastern part of the country. And so the more miniature crisis of coal and transport was also circular. Coal had to be transported. It was transported by rail. Railway wagons had to be manufactured. They were made in four private sector units in Calcutta. But these units could not build the wagons to transport coal around the country if they did not have electricity, which was supposed to come from coal fired thermal plants like Durgapur and Bokaro.

Industries like steel, cement, textiles, glass, ceramics and engineering all suffered for a lack of coal. These industries mainly made intermediate products, components or materials which were necessary for the manufacture of finished products. A chain reaction was thus started which upset production schedules throughout the economy.

Bombay builders faced a shortage of cement. Production of cement was increasing but it was unable to keep up with demand. A black market in cement had thus opened up because the market rate was almost double the controlled rate. Black market cement was often adulterated. Building activity was thus paralysed. Part of the reason for the difficulty in producing cement was the delay which cement producers faced in procuring plant and equipment. Maharashtra had to ask for an increase in its cement quota from the Centre. However, even with the increase it would only meet half the state's total demand.[clxxiii] At the state level the allotment then had to go through the Controller of Iron Steel and Cement and in rural areas through the District Collector.

Engineering industries suffered on account of a lack of steel, pig iron and non-ferrous metals. The Bokaro steel plant was experiencing protracted delays and the Plan production target of 10 million tonnes was unlikely to be reached. Foundries had to close down in eastern and western India for lack of pig iron and industries which depended on virgin copper, lead and zinc had to cut down on production due to the 50% cut in imports precipitated by another foreign exchange crisis.[clxxiv] Commercial foundries only received 10% of their requirements as most of the available supply was allocated to steel works maintenance, railway sleepers, spun pipes, industries focusing on exports, and government and defence contracts.[clxxv] Pig iron would thus either have to be imported or the production of steel would have to be curtailed. And so despite massive investments in steel production during the Second Plan period, the country would still have to import 1.5 million tonnes of steel costing ₹135 crores and non-ferrous metals costing ₹40-50 crores.[clxxvi]

The Third Plan was only likely to widen the gap between domestic production and demand for these metals, yet production targets could not be jeopardised. This meant that the only way to afford these imports was to ask for foreign aid; most likely Development Loan Fund transfers from the United States, or imports on the rupee account from the Soviet Union. Even with foreign assistance, only 900,000 tonnes of steel could be imported, leaving a gap of some 600,000 tonnes. The result was a shortage of plates and sheets.[clxxvii]

Foreign exchange reserves had reached just ₹98.02 crores in the early months of 1961.[clxxviii] The trade imbalance, the excess of imports over exports, had doubled. The increasing demands on foreign exchange were largely coming from the rapid expansion of public sector projects. The demands from the private sector were decreasing.[clxxix] In the private sector the largest allocations were going to the synthetic fibre, automobile parts and paper industries. In 1961 India had to take a loan from the International Monetary Fund to tide over the crisis and by 1962 the government was eagerly awaiting Consortium meetings and announcements on untied credits, rather than aid for capital goods and maintenance imports. Travellers had to take permission from the Reserve Bank before booking flights out of the country. So dire was the situation that Indian ministers had to curtail their trips abroad.

It did not take long for the "coal-steel-transport crisis" to make its way to the Lok Sabha. On 22 June 1962 Nath Pai, the Praja Socialist Party member from Rajapur in Maharashtra tabled a motion: "This House takes note of the serious shortfalls in the targets of the Third Five Year Plan and the growing misapprehensions in the country about the implementation of the Third Five Year Plan." Nath Pai was a supporter of the planning process and so his motion was tabled both as an opportunity to be able to hold forth on some of the ongoing difficulties of the Plan and suggest some remedies, and allow the Planning Minister, Gulzarilal Nanda to inform the House of the government's thinking on the ongoing crisis. Nanda came to address the concerns raised in the motion two months later on 25 August and he admitted that demands for transport "tend to rise faster than our estimates allow for". The government was investing more in the Railways which would gradually ease the transport component of the crisis but the power component had been foreseen years earlier. After the foreign exchange crisis of 1957 the bulk of foreign exchange allocation cuts had fallen on investment in power generation and the planners had foreseen that "this would bring problems in the future". Power generation in the Third Plan period was already falling behind and it was only likely that it would accelerate in 1964 and 1965. The planning minister struck a note of optimism however; "We shall not be found wanting in effort and determination to overcome whatever difficulty may confront us today and in the future."

By August of 1963 the mood had turned against Prime Minister Nehru and his government, principally over his handling of the border war with China in the last months of 1962. The Socialists in the opposition were no longer content to table motions in the Lok Sabha to "take note" of the problems of planning, but, for the first time since Independence, tabled a motion of no-confidence in the government. The no-confidence motion was proposed by

J.B. Kripalani, the old Congress stalwart who had left the Party during the fallout from the Tandon presidency back in 1950. He was supported by his fellow Socialist, Ram Manohar Lohia, and an old socialist turned capitalist, Minocher Masani. They had all recently been elected to Parliament in by-elections and between them could count on a not insignificant minority, 72 members of the Lok Sabha, to support the motion.

Given the diversity within the opposition the criticisms of the government came from all sides, perspectives and ideologies. Kripalani attacked Nehru's policy of non-alignment and claimed that people in the villages were telling him that they preferred life under British rule. Lohia was most personal in his attacks against Nehru and his alleged preference for family members in high government posts and lambasted the endemic corruption within the Congress. Masani criticised Nehru's preference for heavy industry at the expense of agriculture and light industry. Nehru was, by now, an old man, nearing the end of his life, and his response after four days of debate on 22 August was considered so "rambling" that the press preferred to cover the more spirited jousting between the former Defence Minister, Krishna Menon and his critics in the opposition.[clxxx] Nonetheless, the prime minister did address some of the criticisms of his heavy industry policy. He insisted, till the end, that he had the sequence correct; it was only once India had built an industrial base that it could progress and be truly free and independent, and once heavy industries were established smaller industries would flow from them.

Whilst there were shortages of coal, steel, transport and foreign exchange, the most important shortage of all was that of food. Harvests had not been disastrous in the early 1960s, but overall production had been stagnant, whilst the population had been rising rapidly. The government felt confident that it had buffer stocks to manage the crisis, however during 1964 as the months passed and stocks were released and prices did not fall and rationing had to be resorted to in some states, the government took to blaming traders, and sometimes even farmers for hoarding and black marketing. The traders did not appreciate being the villains of the piece and so insisted that the problem was one of production rather than distribution; they were not hoarding stocks, and if they were given supplies they would distribute them immediately. This anti-trader atmosphere was stoked by the new Agriculture Minister, C. Subramaniam. His fellow ministers periodically talked of cracking down on the traders, but by September, when Prime Minister Lal Bahadur Shastri addressed the Lok Sabha, he had to rest on a familiar crutch.[clxxxi] He was confident that the crisis would be averted. Imports of wheat from the United States were on their way.

***

Prasanta Mahalanobis's Draft Plan Frame shared some of the fantastic thinking of the capitalist and communist and Gandhian plans of the 1940s. Much like the People's planners more than a decade earlier, Mahalanobis thought that land reform could be completed within two years and millions of peasants could be put to work on public works projects on the land. The financial and logistical problems of the Second Plan were foreseen. First by Mahalanobis himself, and then by Milton Friedman, the Panel of Economists, Bellikoth Raghunath Shenoy, World Bank economists, members of the National Development Council, Kshitish Neogy, and Feroze Gandhi. Yet these concerns never stopped the passage of the plan from its draft form to its final publication, largely due to assurances from the prime minister and deputy chairman of the Planning Commission. Jawaharlal Nehru, Sir V.T. Krishnamachari and a few chief ministers all thought that increased agricultural production would cover any gaps in the plan. No sooner did they speak than the monsoon failed, as it always did after a few plentiful years, and a decade long agricultural crisis began.

When a foreign exchange crisis emerged in 1957 few of India's leading policy makers saw it as a structural problem. The Prime Minister, Jawaharlal Nehru, the Finance Minister, T.T. Krishnamachari, and the author of the Second Five Year Plan, Prasanta Mahalanobis all thought that it was in the natural order of things; when something as grand as physical planning was being attempted, minor problems like foreign exchange shortages were bound to occur. Yet as aid began to flow from the United States from the beginning of 1958 and India's planners had the money not only to salvage most of the Second Plan, but to redouble their efforts at import substitution and the creation of a dominant public sector, the same problems began to recur.

The various economic crises of the early 1960s were thus revealing of more fundamental problems. The failure to move coal was generally blamed on the railways and the shortage of wagons. However, production of wagons was hampered by a lack of power and steel. Steel production and power generation were running below target in the public sector plants. When factories could not get coal to power their units, capacity went unutilised. During 1961 and 1962 India experienced another shortage of foreign exchange, which had by this time come to be recognised to be the result of weak export performance. However, exporters would be hit by power cuts and shortages of component parts, some of which had to be imported and were subject to strict import licensing in order to conserve foreign exchange and advance the programme of import substitution. Power generation was also hampered by a lack of foreign exchange, as well as shortages of steel and cement. When socialists were being generous they would admit that whilst capitalism had solved the problem of production, it was incapable of solving the problem of the equitable distribution of wealth. Yet by the summer of 1960 it was clear that socialism in India struggled with the problem of production. The question of the distribution of wealth would never arise.

Part of the problem with the Indian economy of the early 1960s lay in one of its foundational ideas. Jawaharlal Nehru, when addressing the National Development Council in November 1954, just as he began his quest for a "socialistic pattern of society", expressed his irritation at bureaucrats in his own government departments "who have a peculiar way of calculating things, [they] try to show that it is cheaper to get things from abroad than to order them from here." He called it "a perverted approach". He insisted that "Anything that comes from abroad is more expensive than the one produced by Indian labour, even though it may cost ten times as much."[clxxxii] He did not refer to it by name, but his understanding was shaped by Karl Marx's labour theory of value; that a good's true value could be calculated by the socially necessary labour which went into its production. It was an idea also present in much of Mohandas Gandhi's thinking on the benefits of village industries. The bureaucrats whose calculations Nehru thought of as "peculiar" and "perverted" arrived at their sums based upon the principles of classical economics, those of supply and demand determining price, and the theory of comparative advantage. It was thus inevitable that when an economy being constructed on the principle of Marx's labour theory of value met a world based on money, crises would ensue.

The Americans were in the unenviable position of funding the Indian experiment with economic planning, without really believing in it, simply because of India's strategic importance in Asia and potential as a beacon of democracy for the Third World. Year after year Congress and the World Bank kept transferring resources to the Government of India in the form of project and non-project aid, loans and technical personnel, and it was only by the mid 1960s, with the death of Nehru, the ascent of Shastri and another looming food crisis that their patience began to run out. Almost two decades after Independence the problem of food persisted and it seemed that the foreboding of *The People's Plan* had come to pass; India could not industrialise with such an abjectly poor and unproductive agricultural sector. The peasantry simply did not have the purchasing power to provide the demand for India's manufactures or consumer goods. Both Nehru and Mahalanobis were certain that a base of heavy industry would spur consumer demand and so put scarce resources into aeroplanes and automobiles, or more accurately, steel mills and machine tools, before filling half-filled bellies or clothing half-clad bodies. And so, in 1965, India's ability to feed itself was still largely dependent on the kindness of the rain gods, and the President of the United States.

FOUR
Tillers of the Soil

As wider tracts of the subcontinent came under the rule of the British East India Company after 1830, the production of cereal and pulses began to decline and per capita output actually fell by 1%.[clxxxiii] The new land brought under cultivation was increasingly used for the production of "cash crops" bound for export markets, such as tea, cotton, sugar cane and nuts. The productivity of these cash crops grew by 50% during the later part of the 19th century and when combined with a rapacious system of land taxation and regular monsoon failures a series of famines ensued.[clxxxiv] Two million people died in northern India in 1860, 4 million died in the Deccan in 1876, and another 5 million died across the land in 1897. The first decades of the 20th century were not quite as catastrophic; irrigation systems were built, rail and road transportation spread over a wider area and each province instituted a Famine Code. Nonetheless Bengal did experience famine as late as 1942, a situation caused largely by the Japanese invasion of Burma, India's neighbouring rice bowl, as well as subsequent government maladministration. The experience of the Bengal famine did stir the Raj to start a "Grow More Food" campaign in 1943, encouraging farmers to grow food rather than cash crops, but when the British departed in 1947, the government of newly independent India inherited a precarious food situation.

A complex system of food rationing had been established at the Centre and in the provinces after the Second World War. There were six types of procurement by which the government would buy produce from farmers for distribution to the rationed population. There were then three types of rationing. Towards the end of 1947 54 million Indians were served by statutory rationing and another 90 million by other channels of public distribution. Yet during these years the Government of India's attempts at internal procurement had always proved inadequate. Its need to import food kept growing. In 1947 the figure stood at 2.74 million tonnes. These imports had to be paid for in foreign exchange. Yet because this foreign food was more expensive than Indian, the government then had to subsidise it for distribution to the wider population, which cost over ₹26 crore each year. It was thought that this policy of controls and imports and subsidies would not solve India's food shortage however, and so a move to decontrol the food market began in December 1947. Floods then followed in Uttar Pradesh and Bihar, and droughts in Gujarat and Rajasthan. During the summer and monsoon of 1948 food prices rose by 15%, and by September in West Bengal and Bombay, where the vestiges of rationing were still in force, the quantity of rations had to be reduced. [clxxxv] In the same month the government had to announce new controls over prices, procurement and distribution of major food grains. By March 1949, 126 million Indians were again under some form of controlled food distribution.

In addition to a food problem, independent India had also inherited a land problem. Contrary to the hopes of the British rulers in Calcutta in the early 19th century the system they devised did not create a dynamic class of landlords interested in the improvement of their holdings. Throughout eastern and northern India the British entrusted the delivery of land revenue to zamindars for whom the proposition was a simple one- they had to raise as much revenue from their own tenants or tillers as they could, above the amount required by the government in order to maximise their profits. At the start of British rule in Bengal this profit was only supposed to be about 10% of the revenue required by the state, but by the end it had swelled to 500% in many cases.[clxxxvi] In Bihar it exceeded 700%. During the 1930s and 1940s the tillers would pay somewhere between 40% and 80% of their crop as rent to their landlords whilst also being subject to a range of illegal extractions. These extractions of cash or produce or labour were given different names across the country. They were called 'begar' in the north.

Among the first American scholars to take up work on the Indian economy was Daniel Thorner, a graduate student at Columbia University in the 1930s. He had served on the India desks of the American bureaucracy during the Second World War and went on to write a doctoral thesis on investment in Indian transport in the 19th century. Thorner had visited India during the war in connection with his government service, but received an unexpected opportunity for a longer stay when he refused to inform on his Leftist colleagues or renounce his own Left wing beliefs before a Congressional committee headed by Senator Patrick McCarran. His prospects of a comfortable academic position at the University of Pennsylvania disappeared, and so he returned to India with his wife Alice in 1952, spending the next years travelling across the country watching the state governments' first attempts at land reform. It was in 1955 that he came to deliver a lecture on the subject at the Delhi School of Economics.[clxxxvii]

According to Thorner there were three principal groups on the land; the proprietors, the working peasants, and the labourers, or the maliks, the kisans, and the mazdurs. The maliks derived their income from property rights in the soil. They took a share of the produce of their land, most often in the form of rent, but it could also be taken in kind from those who worked for them as crop sharers. The kisans also held some recognised property rights in their land, albeit inferior to those of the maliks. They could be owners or tenants, but they held smaller holdings, and unlike the maliks, their holding would be just enough to support their family so long as they worked the land themselves. They would generally not hire labour and would not receive rent. The mazdurs on the other hand earned their living from working on other people's lands. Some may have had tenancy rights or even own some bit of land but these were 'uneconomic' and so either cultivating it themselves or hiring labour to do so would not sustain a livelihood and they were forced to labour for cash wages or a share of the crop.

Daniel Thorner made the point that the largest proportion of agricultural income went to those who did not perform any agricultural labour. Even after the superior rights holders had taken their share, those who worked the land may still have had to hand over a portion of their meagre earnings to the village moneylender to pay off their debts. The kisan thus had little surplus income to invest in better implements, seeds, or fertiliser, and no incentive to increase his productivity. With tenancy rights so insecure, he had little incentive to think of the future. If this was the case for the kisan with a bit of land, the situation for the mazdur without any was even more hopeless. The mazdur probably had a rational disincentive to work harder and more efficiently. The maliks, with superior rights, might have been thought to have some incentive towards improvement of their lands, but generally they were only interested in immediate returns and found it more profitable to rent out their lands rather than invest in improvements. The dynamic on the land was not therefore to invest in physical improvements or increase productivity but to seek status by abstaining from agricultural work to the extent possible. This was what Thorner called the "built-in depressor" in the Indian countryside.

Elections had taken place in the provinces the year before Independence, and the first order of business for most of the new provincial governments was to pass legislation abolishing the system of landlordism, or zamindari and its variants, bringing the farmer into a direct relationship with the state. Land and agriculture remained a state subject under the new constitution of 1950, which meant that the government at the Centre had relatively little to do with this first wave of land reform legislation. Yet this early dose of land reform being directed from the state capitals was a mild one. In most states the old zamindars were allowed to keep the largest part of their estates in the form of "home farms" and were provided with compensation for what little land they lost. In addition, it was difficult for tenants to acquire ownership of the land they were working and sharecroppers were not recognised as tenants. It was more a case of land rearrangement than land reform, with most people in rural India left where they had always been. The first attempt to truly transform rural India thus came from an unlikely source. An American engineer who had been stationed with United States forces in northern India during the Second World War had been putting his spare time to good use.

***

Albert Mayer was a New Yorker who studied engineering at Columbia University and the Massachusetts Institute of Technology. He practiced civil engineering for some years after the First World War, yet he was increasingly drawn to design and urban planning and eventually decided to register as an architect. He designed many of New York City's new large scale apartment blocks in the late 1920s and early 1930s and by 1935 he had established a firm with two partners, Mayer, Whittlesay & Glass. When he arrived in India during the Second World War however, it was in his original professional capacity- he was an officer of the United States Army Engineers.[clxxxviii] Mayer knew that it would be possible to lead a colonial life, keeping aloof in the foreigners' clubs, but he chose to look around, and tried to mingle and learn about Indian society. Neither the British authorities nor the United States Army encouraged this endeavour, but he found it was possible to meet friendly, eager Indians, keen on explaining themselves as much as learning about the

American engineer in their midst. Towards the end of the war, in 1945, just a few weeks before he was to return home, an Indian friend suggested that he meet Jawaharlal Nehru.

Nehru had just been released from jail, and his days were busy with meetings, but he suggested that Mayer stay as his guest at the family home, Anand Bhavan in Allahabad, and that they talk in the evenings. When the time came Mayer got straight to the point, offering suggestions as to what he would do in rural India if given the chance. The discussions went well into the night, and he told Nehru that he would try out pilot projects, which would be experimental, to see what would work and what would not, before attempting a later, bigger project. They discussed establishing some model villages which would be exemplars of good housing, sanitation, and community structure.

Albert Mayer returned to the United States, met his family after three years, and settled down into his normal work routine. But then, after six months, a letter arrived from Jawaharlal Nehru. He had often thought of their talks at Anand Bhavan and suggested that Mayer return to India and try out some of his ideas in the field. Mayer accepted the invitation. Nehru then wrote to Govind Pant, the Premier of the United Provinces to enlist the provincial government's support for Mayer's pilot project. It was June 1946 however, the start of the monsoon, and so work would have to wait a few months until the rain subsided. Mayer arrived in India towards the end of September, and as the weather cooled down he went out wandering through the villages of the northern India.

Mayer quickly abandoned his original idea for "model villages". He did not think that they would have any real roots if they were artificially encouraged and built up separate to the national development effort. He saw much evidence of what he called "single lobe" development which had fallen into disuse. Villages had been given brick roads which had fallen to pieces due to a lack of maintenance, there were public latrines which had never been used, and house ventilators had been installed under official pressure and then filled up as soon as the officer left the village. He came to the conclusion that "the single lobe, the outside gift, the unprepared general atmosphere" were a "fatal combination". Mayer thought that the problem with regular government work was in the aloofness of government workers, who had little interest or understanding of the people's requirements and little practical experience or willingness to work in the field. Orders were handed down from above by senior officers who had never done the work in question and whose estimates of the time needed for such work were unrealistic. The government workers in the villages were not consulted in the decision making process and would just make a show, seen through by the villagers, for the senior officer when he came visiting.

After three months wandering through the villages, Mayer returned to New Delhi and Lucknow in December 1946 for discussions with Nehru and Pant. He revised his earlier proposal for a programme of architectural and physical planning; rural socioeconomic development would have to precede such planning. Instead Mayer outlined one basic rural pilot project. The objective of this project was "the physical and social reconstruction of the village, so planned and carried out that its results will be sought and valued and retained by the villager." This objective would be realised in three steps; increasing production and income in agriculture, which, having gained the confidence of the villagers would lead to the acceptance of, and demand for "allround benefits" which might be less easily understood, which in turn would lead to general improvements in the quality of life of the village. In the end the work would become self-perpetuating and continue even when the "main pressure" of the pilot project was removed. The essence of the method would be that the project's representative at the village level would become the funnel through which all the development departments would be available to the villager. And unlike the government's workers, the project's village level workers would be constantly available and at work in the villages. Two tehsils, or revenue subdivisions of a district would be chosen in two or three districts, which would mean that work would start in 700 or 800 villages in the first year. It was hoped that the objective of village reconstruction would be achieved in three to four years.

In February 1947 the United Provinces legislature approved the budget for the pilot project which Albert Mayer had submitted to Govind Pant. The Premier then invited Mayer to carry out the programme. With official approval, and a budget, Mayer started consulting as many people as he could, began the search for personnel, and started reading on the subject of rural development. He read standard Western texts such as Loomis's *Studies of Rural Social Organisation in Europe, the United States and Latin America*, Ensminger, Bruner and Sanders' *Farmers of the World: The Development of Agricultural Extension*. But he was also keen for a deeper understanding of Indian village life, and so consulted Wisers's *Behind Mud Walls* and *The Hindu Jajmani System* as well as the works of Gandhians like Joseph Kumarappa and British officers like Malcolm Darling.

At the end of his reading and consulting Mayer created the role of the rural life analyst, a trained sociologist who would act as a "participant observer". He would analyse the "human relations structure" prior to the launch of the project and the changes which occurred as the work progressed. The rural life analyst had thus to study the villagers, understand their way of doing things, liaise with the technical specialists in order to enhance the timing, pace and content of programmes, as well as educate local leaders on the benefits of village improvement activities. He would also provide materials to the state and central governments which they could use to foster interest in the work of village improvement by reporting on the progress of the project as it unfolded.

Albert Mayer began recruiting his team for the pilot project. By March of 1948 three Americans had arrived. Horace Holmes took up the work of agricultural extension, Eldon Collins worked as an agricultural engineer and R.D. Trudgett was the town and village planner. Of the three only Horace Holmes, a veteran of the agricultural extension movement in the United States, who had also worked as an agricultural officer in China, stayed throughout the first two years of the project. At this time the Americans were joined by Dhyan Pal Singh, an officer of the Indian Administrative Service, who became the district development officer, and Rudra Dutt Singh, who became Mayer's rural life analyst.

During the monsoon of 1948 the Americans and Indians went touring through the United Provinces and narrowed their choice for the pilot project to three districts: Etawah, Pratabgarh, and Azamgarh. Azamgarh was just too overpopulated and prone to flooding for a project of limited scope to be effective, whilst Pratabgarh had a wide range of problems, but none of them were desperate enough to warrant urgent attention. Etawah was thus chosen because it, like Pratabgarh, had a wide range of problems, but one, that of soil erosion, was desperately urgent and thus required immediate attention. The team was joined by Harish Seth, who had run his family farm and would work on agriculture, and Baij Nath Singh, a young Gandhian, who would encourage village participation.

Mayer sought to democratise the development process, both within his pilot project team, and in its interactions with the villagers of Etawah. He called the first element in this approach "inner democratisation", and the second the search for "felt needs". Mayer wanted the highest officer in the project team to regularly invite all those below him to offer their experience and advice, and the lowest worker to feel free to express their opinions freely and without fear. Breaking the traditional hierarchy of government work in India would release energy and initiative and improve planning and performance at all levels.

The first step in choosing development works in the villages would be to ask, "What are the felt needs in this place?" Every development activity thus had to answer some felt need of the villagers, but the initial problem for Mayer and his team was that the villagers of Etawah saw them as representatives of the government and thought that they could do all that the government could, like remit tax and annul a marriage. The rural life analyst had to draw up a list entitled "What the Pilot Project Organization in Etawah Cannot Do." It could not, for example, construct roads or houses for the villagers or decide in cases of conflict in the villages. The progress in democratising pilot project meetings was slow at first. When Mayer visited meetings of village level workers he noted that the district level workers did 90% of the talking, mainly giving out instructions and then arguing among themselves and the meetings would drag on, sometimes for six or seven hours. Often the district level workers would sit with their backs to the village level workers. What Mayer really wanted was a good old "bull session"- a free for all discussion.

***

Chester Bowles had been a successful New York advertising executive in the 1920s and 1930s. He had established a partnership, Benton & Bowles, with William Benton and counted some of America's biggest companies among his clients. His heart was never entirely in his business however. He had since his youth been drawn to public service, and so, in 1941, he sold his share of the firm for several million dollars and joined the Roosevelt administration as a wartime price control administrator. After the war he ran for governor of Connecticut, at first unsuccessfully in 1946, and then successfully in 1948, but lasted only two years in the governor's mansion. He was considered too liberal for the job by Connecticut's voters. Bowles then went to Washington, from where he was sent to India by President Harry Truman in 1951. When he accepted the ambassadorship he thought that one of the most important things he could do was to put together a "practical joint programme" through which American aid could contribute to Indian economic development.[clxxxix]

Bowles had welcomed President Truman's Point Four programme which had, since 1949, provided technical assistance, rather than aid payments, in an effort to win "hearts and minds" in Asia, Africa and Latin America. He was also familiar with the work of Y.C. James Yen, a graduate of Yale University who had returned to China after the First World War. Yen rose to become minister of education in Chiang Kai Shek's Nationalist government and had sought to create an effective programme of village development which would change the face of China. He found that literacy teachers, doctors, and agricultural workers each made some progress when working on their own, but would be far more effective when working together on a broad and co-ordinated development programme. Further, permanent progress could only be made once villagers controlled their own local government, and so a fourth worker was added who would encourage democratic local government. Yen had brought 20 million Chinese villagers into his programme before the Second World War and the Chinese Civil War put an end to it. Bowles thought that the Chinese Nationalists might have defeated the Communists had Yen's development programme been allowed to continue and they were able to retain the support of the villagers.

Just two or three weeks after arriving in India in October 1951 Bowles visited the Etawah pilot project and saw something like Y.C. James Yen's vision coming to life in the Uttar Pradesh countryside. Albert Mayer's pilot project had been in operation for three and a half years by the time Bowles visited. He saw it in full flight: work was being carried out in 97 villages and 60,000 villagers were involved in its activities. The village workers had been carefully trained first to win the confidence of the villagers and then introduce improved seeds, fertilisers, public health measures, education and sanitation. Bowles was most impressed by the 50% increase in food production, as well as the sight of clean, healthy villages, and villagers learning to read and write. The main difference with Yen's programme was that a new generalist, the village level worker was trained with some knowledge of agriculture, medicine and education, and so three workers were present in one. The village level worker would get work started in three or four villages and could consult the technical specialists, who would cover 10 to 20 villages when necessary. In Etawah Bowles saw "the key to the future of India and Asia".

That night Bowles went to work with his pencil and paper trying to calculate how many village level workers it would take to cover every village in India, how many public health specialists, agricultural engineers, soil conservation specialists, irrigation specialists and literacy teachers would be required, and how long it would take to train them all. Once the news arrived that India's share of the technical assistance programme for 1952 would be $54 million, he prepared a proposal for the Government of India and sought an appointment with the prime minister. Bowles secured a meeting with Nehru for the next afternoon, 22 November.

The Embassy was closed for Thanksgiving which meant that Bowles stayed at home all morning preparing for the meeting. He thought through the conversation ahead, marshalling the facts and preparing to be as persuasive as possible. He had learnt from experience that important men were poor listeners and so put all his ideas into a single, brief memorandum. Later that afternoon, on his way to meet the prime minister, Bowles did feel a sense of reservation; he had heard that Indians were "very proud and sensitive" and "unwilling to ask for foreign aid". What if the Indians refused the offer of assistance? How would it look back home?

Bowles began by asking Nehru whether Asian democracy could compete with Asian communism unless it too organised its villages on a large scale and substituted persuasion and co-operation for violence and concentration camps. He emphasised his lack of first-hand experience and conveyed a sense of humility when dealing with the problems which all Asian leaders were well aware of. Bowles then asked Nehru to read his memorandum. After he finished reading it, Bowles told him that he had been authorised to offer $54 million in economic assistance for "some such village campaign or other program". There would be no strings attached. The American desire was only to help Indian democracy succeed. Nehru engaged with Bowles's idea. He accepted that India was one of democracy's testing grounds and welcomed the challenge. The Communists claimed that poor, newly independent countries could not combine democracy with economic development, but India disagreed. The prime minister and ambassador then spoke for two hours about the "exciting possibilities" which lay ahead. Bowles's account of the conversation makes no mention of Albert Mayer, or Etawah, but it could only be assumed that Nehru would have asked after his old acquaintance and the progress of the pilot project which Bowles had visited just weeks before and been so inspired by.

An agreement between the governments of India and the United States was signed three weeks later and put before the media. It was "simple, direct and free of any language by which any nefarious implication could be read." For Bowles it was a triumph of diplomacy; he understood the Indian mistrust of white men bearing gifts, as well as the impatience among Americans for favours to be returned. Soon afterward, Surendra Dey, a young engineer who had studied in the United States and overseen a township, Nilokheri, for the rehabilitation of refugees from Pakistan, was appointed director of what had become the "Community Development Programme". Clifford Wilson of the Colorado Development Authority arrived during the winter, as did Bernard Loshbough, one of America's leading development and housing administrators.

Two competing schools emerged within the Government of India over how to proceed. One group wanted each development to be "a model utopia", as Bowles put it, with impressive schools, hospitals, roads, industries and improved agricultural and health services. The other argued that quality would have to be sacrificed if the programme were to be extended to every village across the country. Both Bowles and Nehru accepted the second school of thought and sought to expand the programme as quickly as possible whilst sacrificing some quality in delivery. The money which the two governments were putting into the programme would only scratch the surface of rural development- the more important objective was to serve as a "catalytic agent", to release "popular energy and enthusiasm" which would then lead the villagers to generate their own capital and regenerate their villages with their own labour as had occurred in Nilokheri. The aim was to utilise the labour of the Indian farmer who for several months a year had little to do.

On Mohandas Gandhi's birth anniversary, 2 October 1952, Ambassador Bowles travelled with his family to Alipore near Delhi to take part in the official launch of the Community Development Programme. He attended the opening of one of the 55 projects which were being launched that day. In all these initial projects would cover 16,000 villages and more than 11 million people. He remembered Prime Minister Nehru addressing a crowd of peasants under the "scorching sun": "The work which has started here today spells the revolution about which some people have been shouting for so long. This is not a revolution based on chaos and the breaking of heads, but on a sustained effort to eradicate poverty. This is no time for speeches. We must make India great by our toil."

***

A vast national Community Development bureaucracy had been under development from the start of 1952. A community projects administrator directed the programme from New Delhi, development commissioners were in charge in the state capitals and there were both Central and state committees to oversee their work. The district collector was responsible for the programme at the local level and was assisted by a district development officer. Each project had a project executive officer who worked with technical experts and a project advisory committee. The last man in the chain however, and the one upon whom the success of the Community Development Programme would depend, was Albert Mayer's village level worker. One such worker was followed and observed by a team of researchers in "Rajput village", somewhere in northern India, during the sowing of the rabi crop towards the end of 1954.[cxc]

The village level worker, Ashok woke up at 5:30 am on Monday 1 November 1954 and went to the co-operative seed store to pick up dibblers. Along with the manager of the seed store he walked to Bhamula Singh's fields. He had met him the previous night and arranged for a dibbling demonstration that morning. But when they met Bhamula told Ashok that he had to go to another field, which meant he could not have the demonstration that morning. They agreed to defer it until Wednesday. Ashok went to visit Kabul Singh with whom he had earlier spoken and agreed to have a demonstration on Tuesday. He was able to convince him to have it immediately instead.

Kabul Singh, his three sons, Ashok, the seed store manager and two servants all went out into the fields for the dibbling demonstration on half a bigha of land. Other farmers also came along, including Bhamula Singh, who had apparently found the time. Most stayed a few minutes and then returned to their work. They did not seem very impressed and asked Ashok whether he used the technique himself- it seemed awfully slow. They thought they would need 20 times the labour and time they normally used for sowing and their agriculture would be ruined as a result. Ashok had heard the objection before. He agreed that using the technique for all of their sowing would be time consuming. What he was demonstrating was not a technique for wheat cultivation for domestic consumption or for sale, but for seed improvement for the following year's sowing. He asked them to come back and see the seed from the demonstration plot after it was harvested as proof of what he was saying.

After lunch Ashok and the cotton supervisor went to see Malkhan Singh, who had sown the improved variety of cotton seed the previous year, and explained that they wanted to buy some of it. Malkhan initially refused, saying that he needed it for making cloth, besides which the womenfolk would never agree to sell it. After some negotiations he did eventually agree to sell the improved cotton on the condition that he would be supplied with an equal amount of the local cotton variety. Ashok had a similar experience later that afternoon at a nearby village where he had been trying to persuade the villagers over the previous days to sell him the improved cotton seed. Some relented based on Ashok's "personal influence and pressure" but one, Krishan Singh, refused. He also offered the excuse that the women of his family would not part with it as they needed it for making cloth, and also for feeding the cattle. Later in the afternoon Ashok returned to vaccinate the adults. Small children under six months were still a rarity for vaccination. Afterwards he went to the college nursery and gave instructions on watering the beds.

Ashok then returned home to a depressing note from the Assistant Project Officer (Agriculture), Om Prakash. He was addressed without "shree" before his name, and in the lower register of politeness in Hindi, as "tum", even though "aap" was required in government correspondence. He was being reprimanded for not being at headquarters to meet Om Prakash on his visit. He thought that he would have been scolded had he been there with some comment like "Have you no work to do? Field staff are supposed to be out most of the time." Ashok did not know in advance about the visit and was being scolded for going out with the cotton supervisor rather than doing his own work. Om Prakash's letter also contained instructions to give fertiliser demonstrations which would require seven bags of super phosphate and twelve bags of mixture. Ashok saw it as an order from above, he had not been consulted, and this being the first he had learnt of it he had not been able to speak with the villagers to arrange for the demonstrations. He was also rebuked for not arranging seed drill demonstrations. The village was three and a half miles away and he had no means to transport the seed and so would now have to put some pressure on one of the villagers to lend him some bullocks. Om Prakash's letter ended with a warning that severe action would be taken against him if he did not comply with the orders. Later that evening Ashok met with Mulhad Singh to arrange for a half field demonstration of the improved seeds, Panjab 591 and NP 710 the following morning.

Mulhad Singh was good on his word and he and Ashok went to his village about a mile away. There were to be three demonstrations. The first was a half field demonstration to contrast Panjab 591 with the local variety. The second was a manure demonstration- five bighas were divided into three, and in the first section super phosphate was applied, leaving the other two empty for the time being. They were still waiting on a further supply of fertiliser which would include the manure needed for the demonstration. The third demonstration was a varietal one- four bighas were divided into four plots. In the first was sown Punjab 591, in another NP 710, in the third the local variety, and the fourth was reserved for a dibbling demonstration. The three demonstrations took three hours. No other farmers turned up to watch. After this it was Ashok who was late. He eventually reached Budh Singh's fields for a dibbling demonstration. They rounded up five boys from the village to do the dibbling work and this time there were five other farmers present.

After lunch Ashok had to carry out Om Prakash's most urgent orders and managed to get a bullock on loan from Shyam, a local student. He met the Assistant Project Officer (Social Education and Public Participation), Rakesh on the way, who told him to get going. It took about two hours to reach the village four miles away. When he arrived the local village level worker was not present and the seed drill was in the possession of a farmer who would not hand it over without a letter of authority. Ashok showed him Om Prakash's letter. The farmer wanted to keep the letter. Ashok refused to let him. A compromise was reached. The farmer handed over the seed drill in exchange for a receipt. It then took two hours to return to the village. He went to meet Yogesh, the agricultural extension teacher to ask him to come along for the demonstration the following day.

Ashok rose the next morning at 5 and met with Yogesh to go to Tikka Singh's field about a mile from the village. Along with Tikka Singh and his two sons and two servants they went out and tried to start the drill. But the drill did not work- it was releasing more seed than was required. They then had to go back to the college building to arrange for a bullock cart to bring the defective drill machine back. Along with Tara Chand and six students Ashok went out into Mulhad Singh's fields for another dibbling demonstration. He came back before lunch to meet the extension teacher, but he was out. Ashok then advised the village midwife, Shanti Devi, that Rakesh wanted to see her. Ashok went to meet Rakesh about the possibility of visiting a nearby hamlet, but this would not be possible- he would be busy meeting with Shanti Devi.

Instead, after lunch Ashok went to the seed store to get 27 seers of superphosphate for Isam Singh. Isam had come to the store and they then proceeded to his fields and divided it into three equal parts. In one part they applied superphosphate, whilst the other two parts were left unmanured. In the second part they would apply another fertiliser when the field was to be irrigated, and the third would go without any chemical fertiliser. Two other farmers in attendance assured Ashok that they would follow this method. Ashok then went to the tube well and requested the operator to speed up work on the construction of pucca channels and plant some papaya trees around the well. He then went to see Gaje Singh's vegetable plots, which seemed to be very close together, and suggested that he do some thinning, which was agreed upon. Ashok then went back to Isam Singh's fields to take a look at the nursery and found that the leaves of the plants had fallen off and only bare stems were left. It would be no point in keeping the plants any longer in the field. Later that evening Ashok went with Rakesh to the village head's house in order to find suitable accommodation for Shanti Devi. But the head of the village was not in, so the task had to be postponed.

Ashok made his usual 5:00 am rise and met Isam Singh. They had arranged for a dibbling demonstration the previous day. But Isam told him that as he had to go out to another field in the morning the demonstration would not be possible and should be shifted to the evening. Ashok suggested the following morning, for the soil would be at its most humid. Instead they would give a varietal demonstration in the evening. Ashok then went to the seed store with Rakesh. It had earlier been decided that they would go together to headquarters to inform Om Prakash that the seed drill was out of order. But Rakesh assured him that he would send Om Prakash to the village to have the machine repaired. Instead Ashok went to the field of Kabul Singh. He gave the usual superphosphate demonstration. Along with Yogesh he went to the college, inspected the seed drill and found that its chain was out of order. They waited for Om Prakash, but he did not arrive and so Yogesh suggested that Ashok get the chain repaired at headquarters. On the way Ashok went to Om Prakash's house to inform him about the repairs and take instructions but found that he had left for a tour the previous day. He then went to Natthu Mistry's shop and had six joints on the chain repaired and headed back to the village. On the way he passed the social education teacher, Deepak a note to give to Om Prakash regarding the chain and its repair. When he reached the village he handed the repaired chain to Yogesh for fitting on the machine.

Later in the afternoon Ashok went to visit the Jatia Chamars, formerly the village's "untouchables", who lived in their own part of the village. On his way Ashok met Kanhaiyya Julaha who asked him what the Community Development Programme could do for his caste of weavers. Ashok told him that they could get improved machines for weaving and a better supply of raw materials and suggested that they form their own co-operative society. He soon arrived at the Jatia Chamars' quarters and convened a meeting of about 25 people and explained the benefits of the Community Development Programme. He told them that if they were willing to undertake village improvements like paving lanes, constructing houses, digging new wells or repairing old ones, the government would pay half the cost. He was distributing medicines for free and could be approached at any time. Shanti Devi's services could also be availed of free of charge. Ashok made a point of telling Baru, a farmer, that he could get loans for agricultural improvements and irrigation works. Those in attendance informed Ashok that they had already applied for funds for repairs to their wells, but also wanted to be able to acquire the premises near the community well. They had traditionally used the place for meetings of their caste panchayat, but it had been taken over by the village's

Rajput landlords. They wanted to construct a building for their community meetings. Some wanted credit facilities. Ashok repeated his suggestion that they form a co-operative society of their own.

That night Ashok went to a community building of the Rajputs and took some agregene with him for Kabul Singh. He gave it to Bharat Singh to hand over to Kabul and explained its benefits to all present. It was agreed that a demonstration would be given in the fields of Isam Singh and agregene mixed seed would be sown in Shyam Singh's part of the field. A varietal demonstration was also fixed for Tikka Singh's fields.

Ashok woke up at 4 the next morning and walked to Shyam Singh's fields in the company of several farmers. Four bighas were divided into four and one part was sown with the agregene mixed seed. He then gave the varietal demonstration in Tikka Singh's field and tried to persuade some of the onlooking farmers to have a free trial of the chemical fertiliser in their fields. The response was not encouraging. One-third of one of Isam Singh's fields was then prepared for a dibbling demonstration. The farmers offered a new objection to dibbling; it might be better to have an iron dibbler rather than a wooden one. Ashok explained that the wooden dibbler was cheap and effective and had been devised after much work by the state's director of research. He then went back to the village to speak to the tube well operator about providing water to fields above the channel level but was told that it would have to wait until the following year.

After lunch the Rajputs arrived with their bullock carts in order to get fertiliser from the seed store. But along the way Ashok was taken aside by a Jatia Chamar to complain that one of them had manhandled his brother. Ashok consoled him and "asked him to suggest politely to Malkhan Singh not to repeat this thing in the future." Ashok did not want the Jatia Chamar to let anyone know that he had been brought into the matter. He then spoke to Bharat Singh and suggested he have a word with Malkhan. In the afternoon he went to see the extension teacher about the chain for the machine but was told that after the initial repair it had broken again, which meant that the machine would be out of use for the time being. He later did another demonstration, this time explaining to the farmers the method of preparing good dung manure. He explained the advantages of good green manuring and advised them to grow sanai, moong, and dhencha.

Waking up at 5 the next morning Ashok went with Tirath Singh and Kabul Singh to the seed store to get strains of barley, K12 and C251. The fields were then divided up into three equal parts in order to give a varietal demonstration of the improved barley seeds with the local variety. Six other farmers were in attendance for the demonstration. Afterwards Ashok explained the benefits of sowing berseem which made for an excellent fodder crop. He also suggested planting papaya and banana.

Later in the afternoon Ashok had another meeting with the Jatia Chamars. About the same number were in attendance as at the earlier meeting and he made a similar pitch to them about the aims of Community Development and his role in the programme. However, this time he told them that they could get financial assistance for purchasing improved looms and implements. The weavers made their own demands for a cheap supply of yarn. Ashok repeated his appeal to form a co-operative society. They replied by pointing out the troubles they were having from an overflowing pond near their living quarters. They promised to contribute to the construction of proper drains but wanted help in this regard. Ashok assured them that he would try to persuade the Rajputs to make their own contribution which would reduce the burden on the weavers. He told them that he would try to get a one-third subsidy for the improvements. The weavers then raised the difficulties they were having because the Rajputs would not allow them to use the nearby well whilst the water in their own well was brackish. Ashok suggested two possible solutions; either they get a community handpump installed in their own part of the village, or he would try to persuade the Rajputs to let the weavers use their well. The Rajput well needed some repairs anyway, and Ashok received an assurance from the weavers that they would contribute to the repairs if the Rajputs allowed them to use it.

Ashok also had to play village veterinarian. Latour Singh met him at Fattu Singh's meeting house, told him that his bullock was ill and asked him to come and see it. The bullock did look weak. It had lost its appetite and was having loose motions, which Ashok thought were symptoms of indigestion. He wrote out a prescription based on a home remedy made with local ingredients. He took the time to explain to Latour, as well as Fattu and Amar Singh who were also present, the symptoms of various cattle diseases and how they should be treated. Ashok also went to see the Co-operative Society doctor to ask him to come along and examine Kanhaiya Julaha's son who had an enlarged spleen. The boy seemed alright upon examination. Fattu Julaha's daughter was also examined for the same condition and the doctor requested some medicines for her from the village dispensary. The next day Ashok had to turn village pharmacist cum doctor, taking a medicine chest to the locality of the Jatia Chamars. On the way he asked the Julahas if they needed any medicine. Fifteen took medicines for cough, two for ringworm, two for boils and one each for fever and constipation.

Ashok continued his fertiliser demonstrations and advocacy for the planting of papaya and sowing of berseem and it was during his field demonstrations that he noticed three or four heaps of cattle dung lying on the open ground. He explained to the villagers that the dung should be covered with earth to prevent the valuable nitrogen content evaporating or being washed or swept away. The villagers were instructed to dig pits and further warned of the possibilities of open manure spreading crop diseases.

The tenth day of November was the day of the fortnightly meeting of Community Development staff. Ashok collected his records and reports and left for the project headquarters on his bicycle. The meeting started on time at 11:00 am. The new deputy project executive officer started the meeting with some good news. He had recognised that the workload on the village level workers had been great and so he was redistributing some of it to other staff such as panchayat secretaries and cane supervisors. One of the hamlets Ashok had been looking after would be transferred to a panchayat secretary and he would now only have to focus on Rajput village. A cash prize of ₹100 was announced for the village which showed the most enthusiasm and achievement. The responsible village level worker would be recognised by a special entry on his service roll. A refresher training camp was being organised for the village level workers, and it was suggested that they provide some feedback on their fertiliser demonstration at the meeting. However, they pointed out that collecting these thoughts would take time, and so this was deferred for a future meeting. New allocations and terms for the provision of fertiliser were announced and the village level workers were asked to prepare statements assessing the results of kharif crop demonstrations. The best farmers were nominated for the rabi crop competitions. The village level workers were further asked to get started on planting community orchards and focus more on the college nursery. Reports on kitchen gardens were required within a week. Statements were also required on the land under cultivation and under irrigation from tube wells. New credit schemes for the purchase of equipment and animals were announced. Village level workers were instructed to get one footbath for cattle constructed in each village. The water would contain disinfectant and protect the cattle from hoof and mouth disease. Village level workers were to actively promote model sanitary repairs in the village wells and give priority to their paving. The meeting was a long one, ending at 7 in the evening.

***

The Community Development Programme was trying to bring about revolutionary changes in rural India without actually starting a revolution. The much more profound issue however, not touched for so long because of its potentially flammable properties, was whether the iniquitous pattern of land holdings in the Indian countryside would be allowed to continue. Both the central government in New Delhi and the Americans were, to a large extent, spectators to the first wave of land reform. The real action was taking place in the 28 state capitals.

At its first meeting after Independence in November 1947, the All India Congress Committee appointed a high level committee with Prime Minister Jawaharlal Nehru in the chair in order to draw up an economic programme. The Economic Programme Committee stated that "All the intermediaries between the tiller and the state should be eliminated and all middlemen should be replaced by non-profit making agencies, such as co-operatives."[cxci] When the Congress met in Jaipur in December it approved the Economic Programme Committee's recommendations. State revenue ministers had been called to New Delhi by the Congress President, J.B. Kripalani in December. Whilst they insisted that the diversity of land and legislation meant that land reform efforts should be left to the states, they did agree that once the zamindars had been eliminated there would be more scope for direction from the Centre.[cxcii] Kripalani appointed an Agrarian Reforms Committee, headed by Joseph Kumarappa, in order to provide greater clarity about the path ahead after the abolition of zamindari. Kumarappa submitted his report to the Congress President 18 months later in July

1949. Its recommendations for tenancy reform and ceilings on agricultural holdings were not formally endorsed by the Congress.

As the state revenue ministers had suggested in New Delhi, the abolition of zamindari was left to their governments. The process had started prior to Independence after the provincial elections of 1946. When the Congress came to power in the United Provinces the Premier, Govind Pant formed a Zamindari Abolition Committee. The United Provinces became Uttar Pradesh, the largest state in the new union, and its zamindari abolition legislation was held up as a model. The Uttar Pradesh Zamindari Abolition Bill was introduced into the state legislature in June 1949. The Bill was passed by the state legislature and then with the president's assent became law in early 1951.

The aim of the law was to abolish the rights of intermediaries and bring the tillers of the land into a direct relationship with the state. At the time of the enaction of the law these tillers were of two types: principal tenants who held stable, substantial rights in land, and insecure tenants with a more tenuous hold on the land which they worked. The principal tenants were hereditary tenants and ex-proprietary tenants. The more insecure tenants generally worked on the zamindar's home farms, which were known as "sir" or "khudkasht" lands.

The Uttar Pradesh Act created four categories of rights in land: bhumidars, sirdars, asamis, and adhivasis. The word "bhumidar" was just a Hindi translation of the old Urdu "zamindar", and these new landlords were given absolute rights in land: they could sell, mortgage or dispose of it as they wished and also use it for non-agricultural purposes. All that they had to do was to pay land revenue to the government. All the former zamindars were given bhumidar rights in their home farms which they had not let out. Smaller zamindars were even given bhumidar rights for the home farms which they had let out.

The former occupancy tenants, tenants at fixed rates, hereditary tenants, ex-proprietary tenants and rent free grantees were given sirdari rights in their land. Tenants on the leased out home farms were given sirdari status. Sirdars were granted permanent and heritable rights in the land, largely a recognition of the rights they already enjoyed. But they did not own their land, so could not sell or mortgage it, could only use it for agricultural purposes and in certain circumstances even be ejected from the land. Now, a sirdar, a tenant, could become a bhumidar, a landowner, by paying the Uttar Pradesh Government a lump sum of ten times the rent he had been paying to the former zamindar. If he did not acquire the land in this way, he would continue paying the same amount to the state as he had been paying to the former zamindar. If he did acquire the land, he would then pay the state half the rent he had been paying to the zamindar. The rent these tenants paid to their zamindars was usually twice the amount which the zamindars paid to the government. Thus, the tenants would have to pay ten times the already doubled rate of rent, just to have it halved. Meanwhile, the former zamindars would continue paying rent at the old rate on their home farms, which was half what the tenants used to have to pay them.

The third tier of rights was that of asamis who were tenants or sub-tenants of grove lands, tenants' mortgagees, non-occupancy tenants of pasture lands, or lands covered by water, set apart for aforrestation, in the bed of a river, or used for casual or occasional cultivation.[cxciii] Asami rights would be granted to future leasees of bhumdars and sirdars. Adhivasis were the fourth tier. They were tenants at will on the home farms of the small bhumidars and tenants. They could hold their land for five years from the commencement of the Act. If they continued beyond five years they could acquire bhumidar status by paying 15 times the hereditary rate on bhumidar land or 15 times the rent of the superior tenant in the case of sub-tenants. The Act was later amended in 1954 to convert all adhivasis into sirdars. The Act prohibited more leasing out of land by all the new rights holders. The only exceptions were children, spinsters, the physically disabled or mentally handicapped, members of the armed forces, or prisoners. Importantly, share cropping arrangements were not considered leases.

The Uttar Pradesh Act also provided for compensation for the old zamindars equivalent to eight times their net assets. In Uttar Pradesh there were 2 million former zamindars. Eighty five percent of them paid less than ₹25 in land revenue. Only 1.5% paid more than ₹250. The Act provided for graded rehabilitation grants to these smaller zamindars who paid less than ₹10,000 in land revenue. In India's largest state only 390 zamindars paid more than this amount. The other 1,999,610 all qualified for rehabilitation grants. The very smallest zamindars would qualify for grants equivalent to 20 times their net assets. Those paying closer to the upper limit of ₹10,000 would receive a grant equivalent to their net assets. The compensation payable under the law came to ₹93.43 crore. Rehabilitation grants cost almost as much, ₹70 crores.[cxciv]

Part of the problem with the Uttar Pradesh land reform legislation, and the legislation being passed in most state capitals in the early 1950s, arose from the definition of the word "cultivator". Land was supposed to be returning to the cultivators, and so the committee which drafted the Uttar Pradesh Zamindari Abolition Act specified four criteria for inclusion in the category of cultivator: performing some or all of the manual tasks of cultivation, providing capital and credit for cultivation, managing or supervising agricultural operations, and running the risk of loss on an agricultural operation.[cxcv] Only the first of these criteria would describe cultivators as they were commonly understood. The committee did not think that it was necessary or indispensable for being included as a cultivator. A cultivator in the Uttar Pradesh sense of the term did not have to do manual labour. The justification for this provision was that upper caste men like the Brahmins and Rajputs were prohibited by caste customs from doing certain types of manual work and ploughing the land, yet they had been treated as cultivators since time immemorial.

The only state which defined a cultivator or tiller in its commonly understood sense was Kashmir. The Kashmir Big Landed Estates Abolition Act of 1950 defined a tiller as "a person who tills the land with his own hand". Perhaps in reference to developments in the rest of the country the Act was framed as one "to provide for the abolition of big landed estates and their transfer to the actual tillers".[cxcvi]

***

Something of the charade that was the abolition of zamindari found its way onto the cinematic screen during the monsoon of 1953. Bimal Roy had himself been kicked off a zamindari estate in eastern Bengal as a young man upon his father's death. He journeyed to Calcutta in the 1930s where he became a cameraman and publicity photographer for documentaries and films before making his directorial debut with *Udayer Pathey* in 1944. With the collapse of Calcutta's New Theatres after the Second World War Roy made a second migration to Bombay, to the new world of the Hindi film industry. He directed *Maa* in 1952 and then started his own Bimal Roy Productions, the first release of which was *Do Bigha Zameen*, or *Two Acres of Land* in June 1953. *Do Bigha Zameen* chronicled the travails of a hapless north Indian peasant and his attempts to save his land from a rapacious landlord. What made *Do Bigha Zameen* unique among the Indian cinematic epics of the era set on the land was that it was set in the present. Mehboob Khan's *Mother India*, Satyajit Ray's *Jalsaghar*, Guru Dutt's *Sahib Bibi Aur Ghulam*, and later, Shyam Benegal's *Ankur* were all set in the distant past. Bimal Roy's film thus retains a documentary quality, providing a picture of the Uttar Pradesh countryside as the spectre of land reform loomed.

In one of *Do Bigha Zameen's* first scenes, in a stark shot, the peasants emerge from across the horizon like little worker ants, tools in hand ready to work the land. Each then goes to work their little parcel of land, engaging in banter, and the women arrive with lunch. Shambhu's wish is for a good harvest after which he will be able to buy some anklets for his wife Paro from the village jeweller. And then, in drives a big, likely American car, the only sign up to this point that the film might be set in the 20th century. Out comes the Thakur sahib, big, burly, dressed in silk, with his advisers in tow. The peasants stop work and speculate on what his visit could mean. There had been talk of a mill coming up. But the Thakur sahib does not own all the land. Amidst his holdings Shambhu owns two bighas.

Word gets back to Thakur sahib, who holds a little durbar to discuss the issue. A businessman from the city shows the Thakur sahib a prospectus for "The Great Janata Mills Ltd". The chairman of the new mill will be none other than Rais-e-azam Thakur Harnam Singh ji. The only problem would be getting those two parcels of land. Thakur sahib is not too worried about the land issue. He thinks he has Shambhu in his grip. He is more concerned about the money he is going to spend with his new associates. This type of business is new to him. His partners assure him that he would have to spend money to make money and that the results will be dazzling; the village will become like a city, the townspeople will arrive, the place will be electrified. Thakur sahib, reclining on his cushion, smoking a hookah, calls for the naib and asks how much Shambhu owes. The naib will check the accounts and call for Shambhu the following day.

Shambhu arrives at the appointed time. Thakur sahib is

reclining once again, smoking his hookah, this time having his feet pressed by an attendant. The Thakur has some good news for Shambhu. He has decided to change the face of the village. A mill will come up, roads will be paved, houses electrified, and everyone will benefit. Shambhu assures the Thakur that he has no problem with any of this. Thakur sahib, after all, knows what is best for his people. The trouble starts when Thakur sahib pushes some paper in front of Shambhu and wants him to affix his thumbprint in lieu of a signature. The Thakur explains that he needs Shambhu's two bighas of land for the mill to come up. He will even forgive all of Shambhu's debts if he signs. Shambhu says that he will pay his debts, all he needs is a bit of time. The Thakur sahib will now not only forgive Shambhu's debts but also provide some compensation. Shambhu replies that the land is like a farmer's mother. Could he sell his mother? Shambhu insists he won't sell his land and the Thakur's patience runs out. Shambhu has until the following day to repay all his debts.

Shambhu's son Kanhaiya has learnt calculations at school and so they deduce that they owe ₹65, a huge amount for a peasant. Shambhu resolves to sell off whatever household goods and possessions he has. He starts with the pots and pans. He arrives at the mansion with his ₹65. This time the Thakur is playing cards. He asks the naib to total up the account. The naib counts the debt to be ₹235 and 8 annas. They are counting the debts from Shambhu's father's day. An argument ensues. Shambhu insists that his father had wiped the debt clean with his free labour, or 'begar'. He then falls at the Thakur's feet. The Thakur tells him to take the matter to court.

Shambhu appears in the witness box at the local court, but the same problem recurs. He claims that his father worked off his debts through begar, but he does not have the required receipts because the naib did not give him any. Ultimately he does not have any legally permissible proof or witnesses. He claims, earnestly, that God is his witness. The advocate suggests that he call God to the stand. The courtroom erupts into laughter. The court's order is then read out: the Thakur's claim to take Shambhu's land is rejected, however given that Shambhu cannot produce any proof for his contention of a smaller debt, he will be given three months to raise the full amount of ₹235 8 annas in order to prevent his land from being put up for auction.

Shambhu wanders the village when a chacha, or village uncle beckons him to share a hookah under the shade of a tree. Shambhu narrates his tale of woe. He went to the village money lender, but he demanded some security for a loan. The pots and pans which he had sold went to pay his court costs. He had nothing to provide as security. Chacha then tells him about his son-in-law who had returned from Calcutta. He wears a coat, and pants with a belt, and the place where he works in Calcutta even provides food. He works in a Calcutta hotel. He isn't sure exactly what it is he does though. Shambhu's attention only really perks up when Chacha begins to explain how money floats around in the air in Calcutta- all a man needs to do is pluck it out of the air and put it in his pocket. Chacha suggests that Shambhu should try his luck in Calcutta. Shambhu is not averse to the idea. But he does not know anyone in the city. Chacha points out that he would only know people by actually going there. Besides, how would he raise the money in three months by just sitting around in the village?

Shambhu is on the train to the city when little Kanhaiya pops up in the carriage. He has snuck away, but protests that he told a friend at the station that he was going and to pass the word back to his mother. Father and son, in their dhotis and tattered shirts, rush across a busy street in the film's first glimpse of Calcutta. Kanhaiya points to Howrah Bridge. Like country bumpkins they stand in the middle of the road staring at the bridge before a car starts honking to get out of the way. They make their way over the bridge and into the city. Shambhu starts his search for work at the first shop he sees, a sweet shop, and is promptly told to go away. He approaches a babu in a suit lighting a cigarette and is given the same response. He and Kanhaiya decide to take rest by a bronze statue of a British soldier near the Glorious Dead Cenotaph.

Father and son have to fulfil their first requirement, satiating their hunger. Kanhaiya is told to stay where he is whilst father goes to find some food. But, like children everywhere, he decides to explore his new surroundings. He walks over to another child shining shoes. He wants to know where Lalu the shoe shine boy stays. Lalu tells him that he stays at Grant Hotel. Specifically, the footpath outside the hotel. Shambhu comes back with food. They decide to rest by the Cenotaph but get robbed of their possessions as they sleep. Kanhaiya suggests that they go to Grant Hotel. He wakes Lalu up, who, still half asleep, tells him that all this "zameen", this land, the footpath, is theirs and they should find a place and go to sleep. A man startles them with a sudden movement. Lalu explains that the man lost his leg in an accident at a mill and continues to have nightmares and spasms in the middle of the night. To add to the woe Kanhaiya catches a fever before the night is out.

They have been robbed, but Kanhaiya still has a bit of money tucked away, enough for a couple of cups of tea. Shambhu then asks the tea vendor about accommodation. The tea vendor stays at Lala Babu's tenement, and so they make their way there. Shambhu, carrying Kanhaiya on his shoulders walks into a fight over water. The women are clashing with their rival buckets, trying to fill up for the day. The malkin, or landlady is an obese, loud Bengali woman who first insists that she has no place to spare. But a young woman, Rani reminds her of a spare room. She lays down her stipulations. Shambhu does not have money for an advance of course, and so the landlady tells him to go away. But the loud landlady has a heart. As Shambhu is walking away she calls him back. What were you going to do? Where will you go? Are you just going to kill your sick child by wandering around the city? She will give him a place to stay. She marches father and son to their new room and even gives them a bed and blanket free of charge. But she wants her first rent by the end of the day.

Shambhu does manage to return with the rent from some coolie work which he picked up wandering the streets. Kanhaiya's fever has started to lift, but Shambhu is woken by loud coughing. He rushes into the next room to find an old man who also has a terrible fever. The old man asks Shambhu to do him a favour. Could he return his foot rickshaw to the owner for him? If it is not returned on time, the owner will charge him another day's rent whilst he is sick in bed. All he has to do is ask anyone the way to Nandi Babu's cycle shed. Shambhu takes the rickshaw, but without a licence he has to be careful. A babu in a dhoti carrying a briefcase hails him down and wants a ride. He won't accept no for an answer. He has to go to the railway station and threatens to call the police if Shambhu refuses. And so, quite accidently, Shambhu has a job.

Shambhu does not even know how to lower the rickshaw so that his passenger can get down, but after a bit of confusion he earns 8 annas for his first ride. He looks amazed, and relieved. He is an honest Indian peasant, and so does not think of pocketing the 8 annas but goes and returns it to the old man. The old man accepts the money, but Shambhu has an idea. Whilst the old man is ill, he will run his rickshaw for him and cover his daily expenses. All he needs is to be taught how to control the rickshaw properly. He will make his ₹235 and 8 annas as a Calcutta rickshaw puller. He will also need a licence, which won't be easy. The old man teaches him to pull the rickshaw and on his first day he manages to make one and a half rupees which he uses to buy Kanhaiya a new shirt. Kanhaiya is told to keep the remaining money. The daily grind towards ₹235 and 8 annas begins.

Shambhu starts a daily job taking two schoolgirls to the Sarojini Girls' School. The elder girl, perhaps six or seven years old, bosses the peasant around like a memsahib, telling him sternly to come on time. Meanwhile Kanhaiya has a chance meeting with Lalu, his first friend in Calcutta. Lalu is on his way to the Baghdad Cinema. Kanhaiya is amazed to learn that he had earnt ₹2 just by polishing shoes on Park Street. An English speaking sahib had been generous. He shook the boy's hand and told him "very good, first class". Kanhaiya then wanders back to the tenement and approaches the old man. Could he make him a "baksa", or box for shining shoes on the street? That way he could also earn whilst they are in Calcutta. The old man should not tell his father though. He wants to surprise him by earning and bringing home a good amount of money.

Kanhaiya turns up for work the next day on Park Street to find Lalu sitting in a row with two other shoe shine boys. None of the boys resent the new arrival. Lalu welcomes Kanhaiya to sit down in their row. A customer arrives and is about to put his foot down on Kanhaiya's box but Lalu plucks the foot away for himself and in the process of shining the shoes he takes some of Kanhaiya's polish. Lalu then shares the money with Kanhaiya and even gives him a bigger share, 4 paise, whilst he keeps 2 paise. Lalu explains that he hadn't stolen Kanhaiya's customer, but that Kanhaiya being new at the job might have got polish on the customer's trousers and received a kick in the head for it. The next customer arrives wearing a dhoti and Lalu excuses himself. He doesn't have black polish. He sends him next door to Kanhaiya.

There follows a manic scene in which Kanhaiya returns to the tenement at the end of the day with his earnings of 12 annas. He meets his father in their room. Shambhu pulls the money out of his pocket and accuses him of theft. I go out and work honestly and you have become a little thief! The old man intervenes and tells Shambhu to apologise to his son who had also been out working and shows him the shoe shine box. Shambhu had struck the boy, but then draws him close and implores him to strike his father back. They embrace and Shambhu thinks that all their problems are solved. They will send the money back to the village and he will write proudly to Paro that their son is now working.

After a few days of success however, earnings begin to fall. The job ferrying the schoolgirls is gone, Kanhaiya is not earning as much, and he is hungry. Shambhu feigns an illness; he can't eat much anyway and so tells Kanhaiya to go and get something for himself to eat. But Kanhaiya understands what is happening and does not go past the door. He comes back and deposits the food money in the savings tin. He also has a sudden stomach ache. He too won't eat today. Shambhu gives him a knowing smile and they embrace. Time is running out and they need to earn ₹4 a day. Could Kanhaiya earn ₹1 a day? Shambhu could earn ₹3, but he would also need to do some labouring work. There are some quick cuts of Shambhu pulling the rickshaw, Kanhaiya polishing shoes, and Paro counting down the days in the village. Shambhu sets down a customer, who possibly underpays him, but he is too tired to argue. This opens up the most startling scene in the film.

A fashionable young lady hires the rickshaw next to Shambhu's and tells the puller to get going. Then in comes the young lady's suitor who tells Shambhu to do the same. A chase ensues down the broad avenues in front of the Victoria Memorial. The scene is difficult to watch. The rickshaw pullers are put into a race, like horses, both the youngsters telling them to go faster. There is a horse drawn carriage in the scene to reinforce the point. Strangely, Shambhu seems to enjoy the contest. The suitor keeps increasing the rate, if Shambhu will only go faster: 2, 3, 4, 5, then 6 rupees. But just as Shambhu catches up to the young lady's rickshaw disaster strikes. The wheel on his rickshaw comes loose. He loses control and the rickshaw topples over.

But then, back at the tenement Kanhaiya finds the mangled rickshaw. In their room a wounded Shambhu is surrounded by Rani, the landlady and the old man. Kanhaiya is about to take some money for his father's hospital expenses but Shambhu suddenly awakes. He will do no such thing. Time is running out. He will get better and keep earning. There are still a couple of days to go. Shambhu insists he will keep working despite his injuries but can't make it one step out of bed. The landlady suggests that Kanhaiya bring some nourishing food like fruits back for his father. Kanhaiya then goes to his regular shoe shine spot and Lalu asks after his father. They will share their earnings with Kanhaiya. When a boy objects, Lalu calls it "income tax". The boys scatter due to the arrival of the police. Kanhaiya drops his box and it is run over by a vehicle on the road.

A pickpocket Kanhaiya had met earlier at the paan shop appears. He tells Kanhaiya not to worry about his stupid box. Today there is a horse race. There will be easy pickings. The duo then proceed to work together. The pickpocket poses as a tout whilst doing his work and then gives the pocketed items to Kanhaiya standing at a distance. But after some time Kanhaiya gets spooked and runs away. The pickpocket runs after him. What were you thinking? There was great earning going on. You ruined it by your cowardice. They start to go through the looted items. There is not much of value. But then the pickpocket examines a watch. It is real gold. It could be worth ₹300.

Kanhaiya gives up his aversion to a thief's earnings and asks the pickpocket to give him ₹50 out of the likely ₹300. It will be the first and last time. The pickpocket tells him to go away. Kanhaiya then falls at his feet. The pickpocket isn't moved. After a few seconds Kanhaiya's mood turns. He tries to wrestle the pickpocket to the ground and grab the watch. After a few seconds he has a crisis of conscience and lets the pickpocket go. He doesn't want the watch anymore. But the pickpocket now feels pity for him. They go to the paan vendor to exchange the watch for cash and Kanhaiya receives his share. He then returns to the tenement with fruit and medicines and enough money to save the land. But Shambhu is suspicious and it only takes a firm clutch of his left ear for the boy to reveal the truth. Enraged, Shambhu picks a piece of wood off the end of his bed and starts beating the boy. How could you do this? You are a son of a farmer! He quickly tires of beating the child. Kanhaiya then picks up the stick and tells his father to keep beating him, but at least eat the fruit otherwise he will die. Shambhu responds that he would be better off dead. Both tearful, Shambhu tells his son to go and return the money.

Kanhaiya writes to his mother that if she does not come to the city father will likely die. There are only five days to go with ₹50 to make. Kanhaiya has a conversation with a picture of the Goddess Kali on the wall: he will take to stealing again, but it will just be this once to save his father and their land, and the goddess should forgive him. He does manage to snatch a lady's purse and finds an envelope with ₹100. Meanwhile Paro has arrived in the city and been accosted by a local ruffian whilst asking for directions to the tenement. She manages to escape, only to be hit on the road. A crowd gathers and one bystander tries to hail a rickshaw to transport her to hospital. It is Shambhu's rickshaw, of course. He finds his wife bleeding from the mouth, lying on the road. Kanhaiya gets information about his mother's accident and rushes to the hospital. He thinks it is all karmic retribution for his theft of the purse.

The drums beat back in the village. The 90 days are up. An announcement is made. Shambhu, Paro and Kanhaiya's whereabouts are unknown and father Gango has gone mad. The land will be put up for auction. Work on the mill starts. The trucks roll in. The scaffolding goes up. Brick walls are erected. Smoke starts to blow from a stack. Shambhu, Paro and Kanhaiya return only to view the scene from behind barbed wire. Their old home was where the smoke is now blowing from. Paro used to cook their meals there. Shambhu kneels to pick up a fistful of their old soil, only to be accosted by a guard. What has he stolen? Shambhu opens his fist and the soil spills out. For the last time, he is told to go away. And then, in one of the long shots which Bimal Roy was so fond of, the three walk up a hill, into the horizon. Where they might be going or what their future might hold is unclear, but they do take one last look back at their old home.

***

Whilst the abolition of zamindari had not, in most of India, ushered in a new era of equity and opportunity on the land, it had at least put an end to the worst excesses of the colonial system of land tenure. Although most peasants could not raise the money required to become landowners, they were at least spared the rack renting and forced labour which they used to suffer under the zamindars. Putting an end to zamindari was largely a matter of bringing peasants into a direct relationship with the state. They would now be able to pay their revenue to their state government rather than their local feudal lord, yet these local powers were left with the largest parts of their old estates. The next phase of land reform legislation, addressing tenancy and land ceilings however, would be even less successful, largely marking a limit which the Indian state would never be able to cross.

In the First Five Year Plan the Planning Commission divided tenants into two categories; those who were cultivating the fields of large landowners, and those working on plots of small landowners. The Commission directed that all landowners, big and small, be allowed to retake possession of land being let out to tenants for 'personal cultivation'. It recommended that owners be given five years to resume personal cultivation of their lands, rents for tenants be reduced to one-quarter or one-fifth of the produce, and the smaller and medium landowners be encouraged into more organised agriculture. For larger holders the Planning Commission recommended an upper limit of three times the size of a 'family holding' for resumption of personal cultivation. It was this right of resumption, and the loose definition of 'personal cultivation', besides the lack of clarity on upper limits, which created an environment in the 1950s in which many tenants were even more insecure than they were prior to the start of land reforms. Landowners big and small had five years to kick them off the lands which they may have been working for generations.

By the time the planners came to write the Second Five Year Plan 'voluntary surrenders', which were usually the involuntary ejectment of tillers from the fields, had become a widespread practice across India. The planners wanted to tighten the definition of 'personal cultivation' and also require all voluntary surrenders to be ratified by the district authorities. They did not go so far as to recommend that personal cultivation require working in the fields, but that the entire risk of the agricultural operation lie with the owner, that they be in residence for the greater part of the agricultural season, and exercise direct supervision of the work. None of the state governments incorporated this recommendation into their land laws. In addition, the Planning Commission recommended that in future the ability to lease land be restricted to serving defence forces personnel, widows, children, the mentally ill and the physically disabled. With tenants being ejected upon the landowners' resumption of personal cultivation, the Planning Commission thought the solution might lie with the government redistributing land when land ceiling legislation came into place.

Fair rents were fixed in most of the state laws by the end of the 1950s. It was not rent that was the problem for tenants, but security of tenure. Were they to insist on fair rent they would be threatened with eviction and a lack of land records usually meant that their tenancy agreements were oral and unenforceable. Tenancy laws were strengthened, yet they suffered from the old defects- novel definitions of commonly understood words such as 'tenant' and 'personal cultivation', poor land records, and plenty of comfort clauses for the landowners. One major problem was that sharecroppers, the sajhis of Uttar Pradesh and the bagardaars of West Bengal were not included in the definition of 'tenant' in their state legislation.

Whilst the Congress Committees on Agrarian Reform and Economic Programme had both been reasonably clear in calling for a ceiling on land holdings, the Congress had never accepted their recommendations in their entirety. The Draft First Plan, concerned that land ceilings might lead to the breakup of large, potentially productive farms, ruled the matter out. Then, the final First Plan Document ruled it back in. The Congress continued to vacillate on the issue in the early 1950s, and then in May 1955 the Planning Commission, by now the director of land reforms at the Centre, formed a Panel on Land Reforms in order to review the implementation of land policy and recommend new measures for the Second Plan. The Panel oversaw four committees, one of which was to examine the size of land holdings. It did decide in favour of land ceilings, primarily on the basis of social justice.

The Panel on Land Reforms recommendations were taken up by the planners during the Second Plan period. Neither did they think that attempts at redistribution would prove successful, but it had to be done, as a start, in order to bring the peasantry into the process of economic development and give it some feeling of status. The only economic argument they made was that more equitable land holdings may be more suitable to the development of co-operative farms in the future. The Planning Commission delegated the task of determining the nature and size of land ceilings to the states. The main point at issue was the size of a 'family holding' and the multiple of such a holding which might be permitted under new land ceiling laws. The Planning Commission had tentatively endorsed land ceiling and left the matter to the states, but it was the National Development Council, the states' consultative body in New Delhi, which decided to force the issue and directed all states which had not already done so to pass land ceiling legislation by March 1959 and implement the law within three years. The Congress then endorsed the National Development Council's directive at its Nagpur session in 1959. By the end of 1961 all states of the Union had complied.

Kashmir and West Bengal had already passed their own land ceiling legislation earlier in the 1950s, however the directives coming from the Centre set off a wide array of state legislation. Each state had its own definitions of 'families', 'family holdings', and 'standard acres'. The main problem was the sudden spate of transfers, some of which were legal. There were partitions and transfers within families, and orchards and co-operatives sprang up overnight. Trusts, religious and educational, suddenly came into vogue. Landowners went to the courts, land records were unreliable, and the patwaris, the village land clerks, corrupt and in the pocket of the local powers. The result of it all was that as late as 1970, only 1 million of India's 300 million acres of agricultural land had come into the possession of the state as result of land ceiling legislation.[cxcvii] Only half of that land had been redistributed. After 20 years of land reform, and the creation of the world's largest and most intricate corpus of land legislation, the percentage of India's agricultural land which had been returned to the tiller thus stood at 0.17%.

***

An oppressed peasantry, suffering under rapacious landlords and state governments content to pass legislation which rationalised the payment of revenue but did little to redistribute land, might have seemed ripe for a Communist insurrection. And so it was, on the Deccan plateau, in the districts of Telangana, ruled by the Nizam of Hyderabad, widely considered the richest man in the world in the 1940s. The insurrection was in 1946 first directed against the Nizam's landlords, and then, with the independence of India, against the Nizam himself and his personal militia, and then, with the merger of the princely state with India in 1948, against the Government of India and the Indian Army. During these years Communist Party of India workers had formed guerrilla groups to seize property, establish village republics, and redistribute land to landless labourers and evicted tenants. The Indian Army's actions to put down the movement had been largely successful however, and by the start of 1951 the Communists could not agree on whether to lay down arms or continue the fight.

Although he had not been directly involved in the ongoing Communist agitation in Telangana, a loyal disciple of Mohandas Gandhi, Vinoba Bhave, had been keeping track of developments.[cxcviii] He did not think it was necessary to panic; new cultures were always born from bloodshed, but what they needed to do was keep cool heads and find a peaceful way to resolve the conflict. He did not think that the police or the government would be of much use; they could be counted on to clear the jungle of tigers, but here they had to deal with human beings, who had a new idea, one which would have to be dealt with in a new way. He had decided to undertake a tour of the region, but rather than do so by train or car or plane, he would do so in the way of the old saints of India. He would proceed on foot, for walking helped thought to become clear, mature and remodelled.

Vinoba began his walk from Wardha, in the centre of India, due south to Shivarampalli near Hyderabad city for the third annual conference of the Sarvodaya Samaj in April 1951. The Sarvodaya Samaj, or Upliftment of All Society, was a forum for followers of Gandhi to gather and continue their teacher's work outside the Congress Party and the government. On his way to meet his fellow

Gandhians Vinoba tried to come up with a solution to the problem which the Communists had attempted to solve by their own means. Deep in thought he had a vision of Vaman, the figure from Hindu tradition who begged for three steps of land from the demon king Bali as a ruse to banish him. He immediately thought of applying the story to the problem in Telangana. After the end of the Sarvodaya conference on 15 April Vinoba continued walking. He began begging for small parcels of land. He was not confident of success initially; how could such small parcels of land solve such a big problem? But he felt that the landowners knew what was coming: a revolution which even the Government of India would not be able to protect them from. The land donations started to come through in larger orders than even he had anticipated.

Vinoba wanted the rich to look upon the poor as members of their own family. They should think of the poor as an additional son; should another son be born to them, would they not provide for him with a share of the land? Following this logic, the rich landowners should think of Vinoba as another son and give him land, which he would then distribute to the poor. And if the rich should think of themselves as a benevolent father to the poor, they should equally be a self-sacrificing mother and tend to the needs of their child before their own. This sort of psychological change could not be brought about by war or violent revolution, but only in the way of the great teachers; Buddha, Christ and Ramanuja. The Communists retorted that these land gifts were an attempt by the rich to deceive the old Gandhian and that such a change of heart was bogus. But Vinoba thought that anything was possible, given that God resided in the hearts of all beings and controlled their actions and thoughts. If He willed it, that change of heart would come. Besides which, times were changing, and this wind of change would also help blow hearts in the right direction.

Vinoba saw himself as the instrument through which God was sprinkling his love in the Indian countryside. He went into some detail on the mechanics of this change of heart; when rich landowners donated a parcel of land God blessed them and assured them that they would not have to flee to the cities to save their lives. Vinoba was thus generating a good thought which would defeat the evil thoughts in the landlords' minds. Eventually they would come to repent for amassing such large amounts of land, which could have only come from historic cruelty and injustice. God would then grant them wisdom and they would give up all wrongdoing. Giving was a divine weapon, daivi sampatti, which would ultimately defeat the more base weapons, asuri sampatti, which were centred upon selfishness. Gift giving would thus generate purity of mind, brotherly and motherly love, and feelings of friendship with the poor. This sense of empathy then manifested feelings of equality. The old feelings of hatred were unable to survive. Virtue was like light. It had power. Whereas sin was like darkness. It had no power of its own. It was negative, the absence of substance.

The virtue of land donations would wipe away the sin of feudalism. It was an application of non-violence, an experiment in the transformation of life. Vinoba told the Communists that they should either prepare for a total large scale world war or test their ideology at the ballot box, but they should definitely give up their guerrilla tactics. The landholders obviously had to give up their attachment to their land or be faced with the prospect of prolonged violence. Modern science meant that the only solution was one based on pure universal love.

After touring for three days Vinoba reached Pochampalli on 18 April 1951. When in the village the Harijans came to ask him to help them with the acquisition of some land. Vinoba replied that there was no use asking for government help until they could help themselves. He then started to make enquiries as to whether the landlords might give some land to the landless. One Ram Chandra Reddy, a landowner, replied that he was willing to give as much as was needed. He then signed away 100 acres. Vinoba thought that there was a social force behind Ram Chandra's individual donation.

At his next halt Vinoba named his programme the Bhoodan Yajna, or land gift sacrifice. His Telangana tour lasted 51 days and took in 200 villages and received over 12,000 acres for redistribution. He then returned to his ashram at Panaur, but set out on 12 September 1951, vowing not to return until the problem of land distribution was solved in India. On his way from Paunar to Delhi to meet Prime Minister Nehru and the Planning Commission he collected over 200 acres a day, higher than the Telangana average. On 2 October 1951 he announced at Sagour that he wanted 50 million acres of land for redistribution by 1957. Vinoba spent almost a month in Madhya Pradesh and collected another 6,000 acres. By the time he reached Delhi on 13 November he had received almost 20,000 acres at an average of around 300 a day. On 24 November 1951 he left for Uttar Pradesh. Baba Raghavdas, a state legislator, joined the movement and they set the target of 10 million acres. Half a million acres was to be collected in the first year alone. Raghavdas left the Uttar Pradesh Assembly and devoted himself to the movement. He went on a two year walk across Uttar Pradesh and received 38,000 acres.

Whilst on the road in Banda, Uttar Pradesh Vinoba Bhave met the old socialist, Jayaprakash Narayan on 30 May 1952 and formally converted him from Marxism to Gandhism. For those who had read Jayaprakash's polemic *Why Socialism?* of 1936 the conversion might have seemed stunning. Yet it had been many years in the making. Of late Jayaprakash, a stalwart of the Congress Socialist Party, had come to spend much of his time arguing with his fellow socialists over their doctrinaire approach and would recount his disillusionment with the totalitarian ways of Russian Communism. He even came to ridicule those like his younger self who dismissed Mohandas Gandhi and his teachings. He had come to admire much of Gandhi's philosophy, particularly its basis in moral values, its emphasis on non-violent social change, and the decentralisation of political and economic life. He had even called for a joining of forces with the Sarvodaya workers and thought that much of the Sarvodaya manifesto, based as it was on Gandhian thought, was thoroughly compatible with socialism.[cxcix] And then, in June, although still nominally a Socialist, he shocked his colleagues by using a distinctly un-socialist tool of protest in support of postmen and their strike for higher wages. He went on a three week long fast.

Another Sarvodaya conference was held on the banks of a river in Chandil, Bihar in March 1953 and Vinoba tried to broaden the Bhoodan movement to include the Gandhian constructive programme of village works and khadi spinning, donations of wealth, and shramdaan, or voluntary labour. In April 1954 the next Sarvodaya meeting was held at Bodh Gaya and Jayaprakash Narayan devoted his life to the movement. He called on the youth for jeevandaan, or devoting their lives to rural reconstruction. After Bihar Vinoba walked to Orissa where entire villages were donated. And then to Andhra and Tamil Nadu. He then walked to Kerala, up to Bombay, Rajasthan, Punjab and then Kashmir, back down to Punjab and then to Indore in central India. He then walked all the way to Assam. By April of 1965 Vinoba and his colleagues had collected 4.2 million acres of land.[cc] About one-third of this collection was of bad land, unfit for cultivation, which brought the figure down to 2.8 million acres of which 1.1 million acres had been distributed.

***

Whilst much effort had been made since the start of the 1950s to bring peasants into a more direct financial relationship with the state and develop their village communities, agricultural production was still largely dependent on the monsoon rains. Grain production had, by the summer of 1957, fallen below the high point reached in 1954 and the price of food had begun to rise. The monsoon then failed, leading to a 10%, or 6 million tonne drop in food grain production.[cci] The Food Minister, Ajit Prasad Jain, addressing the Lok Sabha, called it "a year of scarcity the like of which did not occur in living memory".[ccii]

The government could only import 4 million tonnes of food grain which meant that scarcity conditions prevailed in most parts of the country. When the National Development Council met in November 1958 and had to grapple with the prospect of reducing the size of the ongoing Second Plan, the Finance Minister, Morarji Desai argued against further deficit finance without an assurance that food production could be stepped up and food prices lowered.[cciii] Prime Minister Jawaharlal Nehru seized this opportunity to introduce an old idea, which had seemingly been amenable to all, that of co-operative farming, as the solution to India's ongoing food production problem.[cciv]

Nehru argued that the Second Five Year Plan could be maintained at the existing size if the states implemented co-operative farming on a large scale and the state took control over trading in food grains. The National Development Council largely accepted the prime minister's suggestion, and set the end of the Third Plan period as the target for the re-organisation of Indian agriculture on co-operative lines.[ccv] State trading in food grains, rice and wheat would start immediately. A month earlier at a meeting of the All India Congress Committee Nehru had appointed an agricultural production subcommittee which then reported to the Congress Working Committee at Nagpur in January 1959.

The subcommittee's recommendations were incorporated into a Resolution on Agrarian Organisational Pattern, which came to be known as the Nagpur Resolution, edited by Nehru and then approved by the Working Committee, Subjects Committee and an open session of the Congress.

Legislation on land ceilings would be completed by the states within one year and the land above the ceilings which came into the state's possession would vest in the village panchayats and be managed by landless labourers as co-operative farms. The Nagpur Resolution accelerated the drive towards co-operative farming: it would be implemented within three years, by the end of 1962, rather than 1965 as envisaged by the National Development Council. Nehru noted the uneasiness and emerging dissent in the Subjects Committee, Working Committee and the open session, but thought that his colleagues would eventually come around to the idea.[ccvi]

In February, after a rather meek reference to agricultural reforms by President Rajendra Prasad in Parliament and an emotional and ideological attack on the proposal for co-operative farming by Minocher Masani, the Independent member for Ranchi, Nehru had to rise to assure the House that there was no plan to enforce co-operative farming through legislation.[ccvii] He did not want to be seen to be withdrawing from his stated position however; he was as committed to the idea of co-operative farming as ever, and should the need arise he would go from field to field and village to village in an effort to persuade the farmers of India of the rightness of the idea. But, if, having done this, he could still not convince them, then he would have to admit defeat, as he was not about to force anyone into anything. Yet by March Nehru was in retreat and started to temper his commitment to co-operative farming by placing greater emphasis on the establishment of co-operatives for services such as credit and marketing, which could then lay the foundations for co-operative farms to be formed voluntarily in the future.

Minocher Masani had made the lines of his attack on the Nagpur Resolution clear: it was an "insidious attempt to bring in Collective Farming of the Communist pattern by the back door."[ccviii] During early 1959 the Forum for Free Enterprise organised meetings to denounce the Nagpur

Resolution. Other groups were doing the same, particularly in the south where Chakravarti Rajagopalachari presided over meetings in Bangalore. And so, the two forces came together to call a meeting in Bangalore for 29 May. The meeting was sponsored by the Forum for Free Enterprise, Rajagopalachari was the chairman, and Minocher Masani was the first speaker. Masani recalled that the atmosphere was "electric". When he stood down after delivering a fierce denunciation of the Congress and its Nagpur Resolution, the aged Rajagopalachari rose, to suggest that he had been too restrained.[ccix] Together they resolved to form a new political party, but decided to defer it for another occasion; they did not want the new formation to be too closely identified with the Forum for Free Enterprise, a group sponsored by Bombay capitalists.

Instead Rajagopalachari and Masani, and many in attendance at the Bangalore meeting, were heading to Madras the following week for a meeting of the All India Agriculturalists' Federation which had also been denouncing the Nagpur Resolution. They would form the party there and instead have it associated with relatively prosperous middle caste farmers across India. This also brought the peasant leader and Congressman N.G. Ranga into the emerging movement. As well as his role with the Agriculturalists' Federation, he was secretary of the Congress Parliamentary Party and had been organising his own meetings to denounce the Nagpur Resolution since shortly after it had been announced in January. He had even managed to attract 100 Congressmen to one of these meetings in New Delhi.[ccx] Minocher Masani saw his opening; the Nagpur Resolution had succeeded in uniting a disparate Right wing across the country and would give a new Swatantra, or Freedom Party the opportunity to unite the landed peasants of India, 53% of the population, with the urban middle class by explaining to them the common peril which the Congress's statist policies were posing.[ccxi]

***

Given that co-operative farming would not be required by legislation, it was to be a party political movement; Prime Minister Jawaharlal Nehru might not have been able to do it himself, but his Congress workers would go out into the villages across the country and educate the villagers on the benefits of co-operative farming. Whilst the task of forming co-operative farms had been postponed, even forming service co-operatives across India was a formidable task; 6,000 co-operatives would have to be setup each month for three years, requiring the labour of about 70,000 workers each year.[ccxii] When Nehru's daughter, Indira Gandhi, by now Congress President, attempted to recruit Congress workers for the task only 600 volunteered.[ccxiii] When the All India Congress Committee directed state units to organise their own training programmes it was largely ignored. And when the AICC announced its intention in April to hold its own training camp on co-operative farming for its workers in Madras in June, it could not be held due to a lack of grass roots support.

Daniel Thorner was still in India in 1959. He would leave the country in 1960, not to return to the United States, but to take up an academic post at the Sorbonne in Paris. His last big tour of the country took place during the first half of 1959, just after the passing of the Nagpur Resolution. He went out in search of India's best agricultural co-operatives.[ccxiv] As agriculture was a state subject under the Indian constitution, the states had, in some cases since prior to Independence, passed legislation encouraging co-operative farming. Thorner toured all the states of the country barring West Bengal and Assam, but it was only in the Niligiri hills of Madras that he "heard" of some joint farming societies. One of them was located on forest land given by the government but it was so deep in the forest that the farmers did not dare stay there overnight. The road was so bad that Thorner was told not to waste his new jeep on the journey and instead take an old jeep. When he heard however, that the officers of the "co-operative" were the district collector, district agricultural officer and deputy registrar, he decided to leave the journey to someone else.

Similarly, just a few years earlier, in 1956, a team of researchers from the University of Delhi, H. Laxminarayan and Kissen Kanungo, had toured Punjab and western Uttar Pradesh, amongst the most fertile and dynamic agricultural regions in India, to investigate the results of the state governments' long standing attempts to encourage co-operative farming.[ccxv] When Laxminarayan and Kanungo made personal visits they discovered "paper co-operatives" which turned out to be cultivated and managed by an individual. Only one-quarter of the societies in Punjab and one-third in western Uttar Pradesh had their co-operative societies consolidated into a single block and it was generally the smaller societies which had their lands scattered, which militated against economies of scale.

There were three main reasons for the growth in co-operatives in Punjab in the mid 1950s- refugees having come in from Pakistan, an attempt to evade land reform laws, and the appeal of benefits being offered by the government for co-operative farming. There was a much smaller growth of co-operatives in Uttar Pradesh- there were only 15 in the entire state by 1955. In Uttar Pradesh legislative provisions were mainly being used to encourage colonisation of the difficult Terai region near Nepal. Many co-operatives belonged to a single family, or relatives, or outsiders who had some economic or social interest with the family. Servants were brought in as co-operative members to do the work that the real owners did not want to do. There were also non-resident members who were paid dividends. In Punjab most of the co-operatives were essentially family farms. The women members did not work on the farms. The situation was the same in western Uttar Pradesh, particularly among

Punjabi refugee families from Pakistan; they would reside in Punjab with a few members remaining to supervise the work. Even when co-operatives were formed by local initiatives the owners did not reside on the farms and the labour was carried on by others, who were also nominally members of the co-operatives. The committees were in name only, usually dominated by one or two members, and cultivation was done on an individual basis.

Amongst the many dozens of co-operative farms which the Delhi University team visited, one they called "Semri", located in Bareilly district of Uttar Pradesh, came very close to fulfilling the ideals of co-operative farming. Semri's founders were Punjabi refugees of the same Bhatia sub-caste. Their joint family had scattered in Punjab but they wanted to live together. A zamindar was selling off his land fearing land ceilings. And so in 1949 the Punjabis purchased 542 acres and organised as a co-operative to take advantage of government concessions. All 22 members of the co-operative were Bhatias and were related to one another. They did engage in co-operative management however; the members would meet together in the evenings and it was initially obligatory for members to put in a minimum amount of labour on the farm. The labour requirement had to be given up with time however, and they came to hire a lot of labour from the eastern part of the state. The Bhatias grew a mix of crops and practiced both mechanical and manual cultivation. By the mid 1950s they experienced a huge increase in total output due to their more intensive utilisation of land. They were shifting to cash crops like sugar cane and were able to reduce output costs. The produce was sold at a nearby market through commission agents who secured higher prices. Semri also became rapidly more mechanised with investment in tractors and seed drills. The farm was profitable as of the winter of 1956/57 and the owners were able to hire out their tractors. Most of the society's resources had been raised internally and 80% of gross profits went back to members as dividends. The remaining 20% went to a school and dispensary.

***

With declining stocks of food in 1957 and 1958, the Government of India had commissioned the Ford Foundation to prepare a report on food production. A group of experts, led by the agricultural economist Sherman Johnson, arrived from the United States, and after two months in the country filed its report, *India's Food Crisis and Steps to Meet It*, in April 1959. The report recommended a minimum guaranteed price for farmers, a public works program, increased use of fertilisers, improved irrigation and drainage, the allocation of scarce resources to more receptive parts of the countryside, a final settlement on the land ceiling issue, strengthening of service co-operatives, a reduction in the cattle population and greater responsibility and clarity from the Government of India on agricultural policy.

The Ford Foundation's recommendations led to the creation of the Intensive Agricultural Districts Programme in June 1960. The Intensive Programme aimed to demonstrate through pilot projects in selected districts the best way to increase food production, increase family incomes, grow the economic resources of villages and create a base for further social and economic development. The aims were distilled into a ten point programme of providing adequate credit and supplies, assured prices, improved marketing services, planning at the level of individual farms and villages, a public works programme, analysis of the effectiveness of the rural administration, and a willingness to change those procedures if needed. Expanded irrigation had to be dropped from the ten points however. Neither the Government of India nor the Ford Foundation was willing to pay the bill.

Fifteen districts, one in each state, were selected for the Intensive Programme. It was a small experiment, considering India had over 300 districts at the time. The chosen districts were supposed to be the most receptive to the aims of the programme; they had successful Community Development Programmes, functioning service co-operatives for credit, marketing and supply, reasonably assured rainfall and irrigation facilities, no major problems with land ceilings, farm consolidation or drainage, and a local leadership which was receptive to change. Eleven of the fifteen districts were paddy growing districts, only two grew wheat. One district grew millet and another grew sorghum. Nonetheless, the 15 districts contained 20 million acres of agricultural land which was worked by almost 3 million cultivators. The Intensive Programme as it was practiced during the Third Plan period diverged in some important ways from its stated principles however; minimum support prices for the selected districts could not be agreed upon, there was little extra technical assistance for irrigation and water management, and the project officer held little administrative control. In addition, whole farm plans were rarely implemented.

Whilst a start had been made in changing Indian agriculture, the results were disappointing. Only 3 of the 15 districts exhibited any improvement in their output and yield of food during the Intensive Programme years. Only two of the selected districts performed better than their neighbouring districts which were not a part of the Intensive Programme experiment. Some improvement in the output of cash crops occurred, however there was no great increase in the use of fertilisers and pesticides in their production. Most of the differences in results within the Intensive Programme group of districts and between Intensive Programme and non-Intensive Programme districts could be attributed to the profitability of crop production, which was in turn determined by changes in prices and availability of technology and their adaptability to the land. The technologies provided by the Intensive Agricultural Development Programme were not very different from those provided by the Community

Development Programme during the 1950s- fertilisers, improved seeds and pesticides. The Intensive Programme was thus not able to produce remarkably different results.[ccxvi]

***

Chidambaram Subramaniam came to New Delhi from Madras and had been given the Steel, Heavy Industries and Mines portfolio.[ccxvii] It was after the death of Jawaharlal Nehru in 1964 that he was offered the Agriculture portfolio. The new Prime Minister, Lal Bahadur Shastri was frank enough to admit that no other minister wanted the job. It was considered something of a "Waterloo" by most senior politicians, but Shastri thought it was a challenging job and that Subramaniam should take it. Put that way, he could not refuse. Soon after accepting the post, Subramaniam told Shastri that he would like some time to study the situation and prepare a paper for the Cabinet. If the Cabinet accepted his proposals he would continue, otherwise he could be dropped.

From his experience with steel and heavy industry Subramaniam understood that no industrial unit could continue unless it became profitable. After much study he came to the conclusion that Indian agriculture was ill because it was a losing proposition for the farmer. He did not receive a return commensurate with any labour he may apply or any investment which he may make. Subramaniam blamed this lack of profitability on the price policy pursued since Independence. Compulsory government procurement and controlled prices started back during the Second World War were continued intermittently throughout the 1950s. This meant that private sector investment in the agricultural sector had all but dried up and any investments being made were those by the government. The low levels of investment explained the stagnation in production.

Subramaniam took his analysis to the Cabinet with the recommendation that food prices needed to rise in order to provide farmers with incentives for investment and production. He did receive some opposition, mainly from T.T. Krishnamachari, who had returned as finance minister, and argued that rising food prices would only stoke urban unrest. But Subramaniam let the prime minister decide, and his position prevailed. A small committee was established under the chairmanship of the civil servant Lakshmi Kant Jha. In October 1964 the committee announced an increase of 15% in the procurement price for the following crop season. In January 1965 an Agricultural Prices Commission was established. A Food Commission of India was also established with the aim of reducing the dependence of farmers on traders who might use their financial strength and geographical reach to depress the price paid before the government could procure at its stipulated minimum price.

Subramaniam was also keen to revamp India's approach to agricultural science. He did not think that agriculture was attracting the best scientists and so revised pay scales to make work in the field more attractive for young scientists. He wanted to make the Indian Council of Agricultural Research less of a bureaucratic organisation and so replaced the serving civil servant with an eminent agricultural scientist as director-general.

The other major factor deflating food prices was PL480 imports of wheat from the United States. It had been about 10 years since these imports, payable in rupees rather than dollars, started in earnest, and rather than being used for humanitarian relief in years of shortage, successive agriculture ministers had used them to avoid facing up to the structural problems of Indian agriculture and simply wanted to keep the flow of food relatively constant and affordable. Subramaniam wanted to stop the supply of PL480 wheat upon becoming agriculture minister, but his first year in the job coincided with scarcity conditions, which only worsened in 1965 and 1966. From 1 million tonnes year in the mid 1950s, to 4 million tonnes in the early 1960s, PL480 imports rose to 10 million tonnes during the mid 1960s. Thus none of Subramaniam's big ideas would be able to address the immediate problem of scarcity; his proposals for price increases and any revamp of agricultural science would take years to bear fruit. Rather than do away with PL480 imports he had to suffer the indignity of doubling them.

Subramaniam's openness to new scientific approaches to agriculture became known shortly after becoming minister, and he was approached by Ralph Cummings, the India representative of the Rockefeller Foundation. The Foundation had been working towards the development of high yielding wheat seeds in India by importing small quantities of new Mexican varieties. They had supplied them to the Indian Agricultural Research Institute, Delhi and the Agricultural University, Ludhiana for testing in local soil and climatic conditions. Cummings informed Subramaniam that the results had been encouraging; on research farms yields of 5,000 to 6,000 kilograms per hectare, about double the usual amount, had been common. But the seeds had not yet been distributed to farmers for pilot experiments. Two years had lapsed since the start of testing, but local scientists were still apprehensive about spreading the area for testing given that they could not predict whether any new pests or diseases might develop. Cummings was not happy about the delay and suggested that given Subramaniam's keenness on science and technology he might accelerate the programme.

Subramaniam garnered relatively little support for the introduction of the new varieties to start with. Senior scientists were sceptical. There was too much uncertainty about the seeds, besides which Indian scientists had been at work on high yielding seeds and so it was thought better to allow them to continue their work. Some thought that the impressive results which occurred under controlled conditions might not continue when the seeds were put into the hands of illiterate and uneducated Indian farmers. Economists were concerned over the foreign exchange costs which would be incurred by the need to use so much fertiliser on the improved seeds. Others thought that with land reform incomplete, the new seeds would be of disproportionate benefit to larger landowners. Communists suspected that the new seeds would allow America to exercise greater control over Indian agriculture. Perhaps the only firm support came from junior scientists. Rather than taking the matter to Cabinet, Subramaniam took it to the prime minister. Nonetheless, he could not introduce the new seeds on a large scale for the 1964/65 sowing season and so decided to delay sowing by a year.

***

Much hope had been pinned on the Community Development Programme when it was launched on 2 October 1952. It largely followed the ideas of Albert Mayer and the model of his pilot project in Etawah. Whilst much good work was done, it did not usher in the new dawn that Jawaharlal Nehru and Chester Bowles had hoped for. As the programme moved out of its home in Etawah and became fully merged with the Government of India machinery across the country, it came into the Indian system of bureaucracy. Furthermore, the Community Development Programme was predicated on the idea that an Indian village was made up of one community, rather than four or five antagonistic ones. The problems thus started when the village level worker encountered the Indian village. Ashok had to do his work in an unreformed Indian village; he demonstrated new seed varieties to the Rajput farmers, whilst urging the Jatia Chamar weavers to form a co-operative. He studiously avoided getting involved in any caste conflicts. Ashok was at the bottom of a vast bureaucracy stretching back to the state and national capitals but his main concern was with the man directly above him, the

Assistant Project Officer (Agriculture), and his attempt to make his job as difficult as possible. Ashok, the bearer of Community Development, was thus stuck between an unreformed Indian village and an unreformed Indian bureaucracy. His work was slow going, quite literally: he often did not have the transport to get from one village to the other. It might have taken longer than the envisaged three years to transform the village. It might have taken thirty.

Ashok was doing his work in 1954 just after the first flush of land reform. At least in his village nothing much seemed to have changed. The Rajputs were still farming, the Julahas were still weaving, and they lived in an uneasy peace. Part of the reason for this was that the state governments were ambivalent about returning land to the tiller. Zamindars have traditionally evoked images from cinema of variously villainous, rapacious, or indolent local rulers lording over vast estates of thousands of acres, terrifying their peasants, sending out armed thugs to extract money, forcing them to work for nothing, and sometimes raping their wives and daughters. Yet in India's largest state, Uttar Pradesh, there were only about 390 landlords of this cinematic variety. Behind them stood close to 2 million smaller, real life zamindars. They controlled hundreds of acres, rather than thousands, and whilst the bigger zamindars were universally despised and lost their only political patron when the British left, these smaller zamindars had entered the Congress Party and filled up its kisan sabhas, or farmers' units. The Congress chief ministers thus balked, there were just too many small zamindars, and so rather than returning land to the tiller, they just redefined the word "tiller". A tiller need not actually till the fields, someone supervising a person tilling the fields could now also qualify. It was this lack of political will and refuge in legalese that caused problems for the next stage of land reform, that of tenancy. If the person who owned the fields, but did not work on them himself, was dubbed a tiller and allowed to continue his ownership, then there would be no prospect of land returning to the real tillers of the soil. Landowners would always need to be allowed to rent their land out to those who were willing to work. And so despite the initial urge to abolish, or at least vastly reduce tenancy across India on the principle that land should be worked by its owner, land reform never progressed very much further.

The question remains of why there was no great pressure from the Indian peasantry, particularly landless peasants, for land reform. The answer might be gleaned from *Do Bigha Zameen*. Shambhu's greatest ambition, prior to the start of the dramatic loss of his land, was simply to earn enough to be able to buy his wife Paro some silver anklets. This would conform to the general observation that he, as the owner of an "uneconomic" two bigha plot had little incentive to invest in any improvements in his land. The picture was confirmed by the journalist Kusum Nair in her book *Blossoms in the Dust*. She went travelling the country in 1962 and found, contrary to the general perception among the intellectual class that the peasants were hungry for land, that they were, in most cases, content with their lot and had very little ambition. This stasis would only be disturbed by the arrival of some Communists to stir things up, as happened in Telangana in the late 1940s. It was what sparked the arrival of Vinoba Bhave and his Gandhian approach to land reform. In some ways his approach was just as paternalistic as that of the government; he would go out begging for more land on behalf of the peasants and then distribute it to them. He was often ridiculed, some thought it was a sham, that only waste land was given, but when the Congress Party's statist approach to land reform and Vinoba's spiritual approach were compared, Vinoba came out well ahead.

As the 1950s closed and another food crisis loomed, land reform and Community Development seemed to have borne little fruit. The 50% increase in food production which Chester Bowles saw when he visited Etawah in 1951 was the result of an improved wheat seed, Punjab

591, which had taken well to the local soil. It was the same seed which Ashok tried to get the farmers of Rajput village to sow in 1954. Yet after an initial burst yields began to plateau. The available seed technology had been used and there were no significant improvements for the remainder of the 1950s. Prime Minister Jawaharlal Nehru thus dusted off an old and seemingly universally popular idea, that of co-operative farming. In the pre-Independence days it had been a part of everyone's plan- the socialists, communists, capitalists and Gandhians all thought it was a good idea. Despite their divergent ideological perspectives they all accepted the idea of "economies of scale"; that larger, consolidated land holdings would provide an incentive for increased investment and more productive use of supplies and labour than small fragmented holdings. In the co-operative system, landowners could keep ownership of their land whilst pooling it with others. The idea was appealing for its middle wayness; it could improve productivity without disturbing ownership patterns. Thus, when the time came in 1959 to roll co-operative farming out across India, it might have been surprising that the only thing it seemed to achieve was to organise a new pole of opposition to the government in the form of the Swatantra Party. Not only was it an unpopular idea amongst the newly powerful middle caste farmers across India, but, it might have been noticed that it had been tried before in the states. State governments had been offering incentives towards co-operative farming since the 1940s, yet even in some of the most prosperous and relatively progressive farming communities of Punjab and western Uttar Pradesh not a single example of a genuine co-operative, amongst people unrelated to each other, could be found. Co-operative farming, like Community Development was a good idea until it met the realities of Indian society.

Do Bigha Zameen was, unfortunately, as prophetic as it was illuminating. Its tale of peasants moving off the land, in this case involuntarily, into the city in search of jobs, and taking to shining shoes and pulling rickshaws was as relevant in 1993 as it was when it was released in 1953. Harnam Singh was transforming from an old style zamindar into a new style capitalist of sorts; a mill was coming up on his land. It might have been expected that Shambhu and his fellow peasants would find work in the mill, steady wages, education for their children and relief from the hardships of the land. But in Bimal Roy's story Shambhu is quite literally locked out from the new mill and walks into the distance. It is uncertain where he is going and what he will do. He might have become a landless labourer somewhere else in Uttar Pradesh, or returned to Calcutta's slums, peddling his rickshaw. Given the model that Mahalanobis and Nehru were building it is unlikely that he would have found sustainable employment. They thought that they would put people like Shambhu to work on public works projects, or possibly in cottage or small-scale industries. Yet village industries never appeared. The result of this unbalanced equation of economic development was the slum life of India's biggest cities. By the mid 1960s, everyone sensed that something had to give.

FIVE

The Big Push

Prime Minister Jawaharlal Nehru's call for co-operative farming had only served to form a new, more organised pole of opposition to his government. Men like Chakravarti Rajagopalachari and Minocher Masani had been increasingly sceptical of the course the prime minister had been taking the country on. The issue of co-operatives was therefore a useful one for Masani. It is unlikely that he felt an instinctive alarm over the prospect of pooling farm land in rural India. But he did see opposition to co-operative farming as a way to relate to the vast majority of Indians on the land, particularly the newly empowered small and medium sized landowners, the perils of excessive state control of economic life; farmers should not be forced into anything, it would ruin individual incentive, it was but one step towards collectivisation of farming, and Communism in India. The rise of the Swatantra Party in the early 1960s meant that there was a voice, principally Masani's, in Parliament, permanently critical of the Nehruvian planning project. The Party also served as an intellectual hub around which otherwise lonely figures like Professor Bellikoth Raghunath Shenoy could gather.

Although criticism of the planned economy by free marketers, libertarians and conservatives might have been expected, the socialism of the Second Plan period was also quite disappointing for the socialists of the Congress. They did not view it as an authentic socialism, and did not think that the ideology had really taken hold in the Congress Party. Socialism was really just embodied in one man, Jawaharlal Nehru, rather than seeping down through the organisation to the grass roots. The results of the 1957 election, whilst not disastrous, had been disappointing for the Congress, and so these socialists, initially Gandhian socialists, decided to form a Socialist Study Group, a policy think tank which might promote the ideology within the Party. They were soon joined by younger scientific socialists, which then led to a disagreement over the meaning of socialism. The Study Group had been defunct until Gulzarilal Nanda decided to revive it in the form of a new Forum for Labour, Planning and Socialist Action. He was a Gandhian socialist, but more tellingly, a stalwart of the Planning Commission.

Whilst those on both the Left and the Right of Indian politics were dissatisfied with the planned economy, the Americans sensed an opportunity. Despite their reservations over the Indian economic model, they had gone along with it primarily due to India's geopolitical importance. It was a huge Asian country pursuing economic development within a democratic framework and could be both an example for other newly independent countries and a counterweight to Communist China. The type of socialism being pursued was quite mild compared to what the Americans had to deal with in Eastern Europe and Latin America and Africa. It was more irritating than alarming. Given that India was officially pursuing a mixed economy with some scope for the private sector Americans would take solace in India's democracy rather than despair at its socialism. They had always had reservations that not enough attention was being paid to agriculture and that there was an excessive emphasis on the public sector. By the early 1960s their patience was starting to wane. India was not quite the beacon that American policy makers thought that it would be; it was stubbornly Non-aligned, the economy was not producing results, and American farmers were keeping Indians from starvation with their shipments of wheat. After Nehru's death in May 1964, and the ascent of Shastri, the Americans decided to make their move. They felt that the government was more sensible, and that they might start to use their aid money to nudge the Indian economy in the direction they wanted.

But then Indian politics took a series of strange turns. After Shastri's death in January 1966 a new and uncertain prime minister, who had largely complied with American requests and suggestions, went to the polls and suffered a serious setback. Both Indira Gandhi's own authority and the appeal of the Congress Party seemed to be in decline, the effort at economic reform had halted, the country was on the brink of famine, and so the socialists of the Congress sensed their own opportunity. Shortly after the election debacle of 1967 they pushed for a 10 point programme for the implementation of socialism. It became an ideological axe, revealing a profound division within the Party. Indira was initially willing to negotiate the power politics of the upper echelons of the Congress, and strode a relatively centrist path until she felt her position threatened. The Party's power brokers were ready to oust her, and so, she clutched at one of the few ready sources of support available to her- the members of the old Socialist Forum.

Indira won the split in the Congress, and so would have to make good on her socialist rhetoric. Power became personalised in her coterie, a spate of socialist legislation followed- the Monopolies and Restrictive Trade Practices Act, the Foreign Exchange Regulation Act- and industrial licensing, which had been liberalised, was tightened again. She went to the polls in 1971 and won on the 'Garibi Hatao', or 'Get Rid of Poverty' slogan. Yet two old problems remained- food and jobs. Although there were some encouraging harvests after the application of high yielding seeds in the northern wheat belt in the late 1960s, they were not enough to guarantee food security. One of Indira's socialist initiatives in 1973 was an attempt to nationalise the grain trade, something which led to disastrous results. Youths in cities across India had very little hope of finding secure employment commensurate with their education, and so when the food shortage of 1973 hit a university campus in Gujarat, the tinder box was lit. Throughout 1974 protests spread, principally to Bihar, and an old warhorse, the first Congress Socialist, and later convert to Gandhism, Jayaprakash Narayan also saw an opportunity; he would co-opt the movement and launch a revolt against Indira and her regime.

***

Although conservatives had been putting up resistance to the advance of socialism in India since the 1930s, they had been "reactionaries" in the true sense of the word. Most books and polemics and movements and rallies had been thought up by India's socialists, inspired as they were by Marx and Russian Communism and its potential application to India. In each case conservatives had been content to frustrate Indian socialism, rather than make the case for Indian capitalism. It was only when Indian socialism began to take fuller form in the mid 1950s, and ideologues on both the Left and Right began to leave the Congress, that Indian conservatism found a philosopher in the person of Chakravarti Rajagopalachari, better known as "Rajaji".

Rajaji was almost of Mohandas Gandhi's generation and had been active in elite politics before the start of the First World War. Like most Congressmen of his time, he was a lawyer, however he was a product of Madras rather than London. His instinctive conservatism receded somewhat when he came under Gandhi's spell after the war and he became a staunch non-cooperator during the 1920s. He changed his mind in the 1930s though, and worked with Vallabhbhai Patel to begin the process of turning the Congress into a parliamentary party. Rajaji became Premier of Madras after the 1937 elections. It was from this time that he seemed a man perpetually out of place.

Rajaji was a Brahmin in a province gripped with a fervent

anti-Brahminism. His decision to make Hindi, a symbol for Tamils of northern Brahminical culture, compulsory in Madras schools set off widespread protests. When his Congress Ministry fell at the start of the Second World War he opposed the official Congress line and supported the British war effort. He then opposed the Quit India movement of 1942. He insisted on a dialogue with Mohammad Ali Jinnah and the Muslim League. After Independence he was sent to West Bengal as governor, only to encounter opposition to his presence because of his earlier criticism of the Bengali hero Subhas Bose. Rajaji then acted as governor-general in New Delhi until the establishment of the republic in January 1950. After Vallabhbhai Patel's death he served briefly as home minister. However, differences with Jawaharlal Nehru over foreign policy, the demand for linguistic states, and the government's attitude to Indian Communists led to his resignation. He then returned to Madras citing "ill health", but got to work forming a Congress led government, installing himself as chief minister. The horse trading that took place in the process of government formation irritated Nehru further. It was under Rajaji's tenure that Madras was split between its Tamil and Telegu speaking regions. He came under further attack from the state's Dravidian parties for his institution of a system of vocational education. They thought that the old Brahmin was trying to deny their children a proper modern education. Rajaji took a break from active politics and devoted himself to literature for some time. In August 1956 he began writing for his journal *Swarajya*. By January of 1957 he had formally resigned from the Congress and in 1959 he helped found the Swatantra Party. It was Rajaji who coined the term "Licence-Permit-Quota Raj".

The philosophical bases for an Indian conservatism began to take shape on the pages of *Swarajya* each week as Rajaji applied his mind to the perils of Nehruvian socialism and the degeneration of the Congress Party. He warned that once the state took control of society's body, its soul would also be swallowed up.[ccxviii] If the economic life of society and all its individuals were to be completely regulated, the rulers would feel the need to obtain a "willing obedience" to the regime which would only come through moulding its young minds from childhood. Given that action came from thought, were action to be regulated, thought would have to be shaped to it. Statutory compulsion would result in corruption and evasion and regulation would be met by disobedience and fraud to which the bureaucracy would soon adjust itself. If this comprehensive economic regulation were to succeed, it must necessarily bring the mind of the people under complete subjugation. Thus, a state working toward complete control of economic life could not tolerate freedom of thought, despite having a few statutes on the books claiming to ensure it in some form. Freedom of thought and culture were incompatible with socialism. Wealth could not be produced by equalisation, but only by more rapid production. Redistribution could only take place after the wealth had been produced. But in India socialism was preceding prosperity.

For an adherent of Gandhism like Rajaji, perhaps the greater sin of socialism was in its inherent violence.[ccxix] It was not lathis and rifles which were necessary for violence, legislative compulsion also qualified; it could be even more effective, and even more harmful. It was the state which could exercise this violence without making it apparent. It was all the worse in a welfare state in which people's private lives and their professions were dependent on the state; the processes of coercion were worse. The Gandhian dream was of the whittling away of the state, but India was going in the opposite direction; industrialisation, centralisation, more state control of everything, all in the name of "democratic socialism". Rather than training in self-reliance, the training going on in India's remotest villages was to expect the government in New Delhi to provide public money and subsidies for every purpose, and then give grateful homage to the Congress. The governments of independent India had undermined this spirit of self-reliance and thus produced a tamer people. The people, as a result, were more self-reliant in the days of the British Raj when the government confined itself to law and order. The Gandhian way was to achieve social justice by a spiritual reformation of the people. In its absence, mere legislative coercion amounted to a violent state socialism.

It was self-evident to Rajaji that socialism could not produce wealth but only distribute that which was produced.[ccxx] Given India's situation, its main task was not how to distribute, but how to make wealth in the first place. This need to produce more should inform all policy making, and when it came to the matter of distribution, it was Gandhi's theory of trusteeship which would serve best rather than high taxes, confiscation of land and property or an enforced egalitarianism. He thought that this idea of trusteeship of wealth was actually practiced in the United States- the wealthy in America believed in it and practiced it; they used their wealth to help others without being forced to do so by the state. In fact, it had been practiced to such an extent there, without the practice being given the name, that America could claim better and more equitable social conditions than many countries which had declared themselves to be egalitarian. The lesson to be drawn from the United States was thus: produce before you try to distribute, increase your own wealth by treating yourself as a trustee of your superfluous wealth for those for whom you have compassion, be the master of your possessions, but express that mastery altruistically.

Rajaji had to mount a defence of profit, which was under attack both from nationalisation and excessive taxation.[ccxxi] He thought that people were ready to talk of the sinful nature of profits, but spoke nothing of losses. Whenever a person produced and distributed at their own risk there would be profits and losses, and the losses would be met out of the gain from profits. The government levied its taxes on profits, but if profits were eliminated by nationalisation or legislation or taxation, then all that would remain would be losses. When industry was driven to loss it would be the nation which would suffer. The profit system was thus "the only machinery for ensuring economy and good management in production or in distribution." The only way to ensure economy in the production and distribution of any commodity was to apply the consumer's check; the producers and distributors had to compete among themselves to make a profit and bear the losses if they could not. The profit based system of private enterprise was thus the one which worked to the consumer's advantage.

If the profit based system of private enterprise was replaced by the public sector, then Rajaji thought that the fear of losses would go with it, and so would economy; expenses would increase and vigilance decrease. The results were already there for all to see in government managed enterprises. Attacking profits was to attack capital formation; without profits wear and tear could not be repaired. New machinery could not be purchased. Trying to bring everyone back to the mean in a poor country would result in no new capital formation, a little like peasants eating up their harvest without planting any seeds. "Profits are the source of inspiration and the resource fund for all new adventures in human effort." The benefits of modernity were the product of this system, and no matter how "eminent and technologically well-equipped governments, cabinets and officials may be...they cannot do what the manufacturer would be able to do if he be given a free field and fair chance to make profit or lose at his own risk."

Rajaji gave an account of the *Etiology of Controls*, or, the cause of the disease.[ccxxii] It all went back to the Second World War when controls were instituted to cope with the emergencies of the time. Yet once the war had ended, instead of doing away with the controls, civil servants with an appetite for exercising them kept them up. They enjoyed exercising supreme authority over wealthy people, and so maintained their regime of regulations, found reasons to justify it and most importantly, indoctrinated the politicians who made policy. They convinced the ministers in the interim government, who were new to administration, that without controls there would be a shortage of commodities which would result in terrible public distress. The new government accepted this advice and so the regime of wartime controls and regulations continued, despite the absence of a war. The Congress's ambitious Plans were then formed and a "conspiracy of action" ensued between the government and civil servants to stiffen the regime of controls. An appetite for power motivated the civil servants, whilst an ambition to produce spectacular progress and the vanity for international appreciation drove the Congress rulers. When Jawaharlal Nehru declared the goal of the Congress to be the establishment of a socialistic pattern of society civil servants welcomed it; controls could now be heaped upon controls. Party men now found a good business in these controls.

Things had come to such a pass that Rajaji wanted to implement a rule that, barring the veterans of the original non-cooperation movement, nobody should be allowed to hold office within the Congress or be fielded as a Congress candidate in state or national elections unless they had an occupation or some other known means by which they supported themselves and their family.[ccxxiii] He wanted an end to fulltime Congressmen "parasiting" on the organisation. He thought that the Congress had come to resemble a mutt, or monastery in which people with no known calling of their own moved in and started to take control over the affairs of the mutt itself. The "revolutionary passion" of the Congress had died out, there was no effective opposition, and "paternal threats" from within the Party could be easily soothed by assurances of dependence and obedience. During the days of the independence movement it was desirable to have Congressmen devoted full time to the cause, and for that they would have to give up their occupations. But in independent India it was an anomaly to have a Party of jobless people who did not follow an occupation or do "honest work" laying down the law and controlling the activities of those who did.[ccxxiv]

Rajaji chronicled the Congress's internal feuds.[ccxxv] Newspapers daily carried stories of quarrels, compromises, and attempts at arbitration made in the state units of the Party. The disease was openly admitted, but Congress officials were reluctant to make their own diagnosis for fear of tarnishing the prestige of the Party. Part of the problem was that little real power, be it economic or political, was vested with the state governments. Power had accumulated at the Centre, which meant that state Congress ministers had to fly to New Delhi for a decision on any matter of substance. All that was left with the state Congress ministers and Party bosses was petty patronage; largely bureaucratic, the work of the departments and their ability to influence the industrial, transport and commercial life of the state. These opportunities to favour friends still counted at the local level and passed for "power". The sum total of the quarrels and feuds over such influence went by the name of "power politics". This was the root of all "schismatic movements" within the Congress. The question was not that of redistribution of power between the Centre and the states, but really whether governments at any level should be exercising such power over trade and industry. Such was the power of officials, ministers and Party bosses that anyone trying to do business was at their mercy in their daily lives.

The people were supposed to feel elated when they read of government spending in "selected pockets of development".[ccxxvi] The residents in these areas were supposed to think of this spending as a gift from the Congress bosses and a result of Congress policy, but in reality it all came from the national till, and would only result in the need for more taxation in the future. The increasing controls and regulation of the economy were opening up a "big market for politicians to secure monopolies for their chosen beneficiaries". Congress bosses were coming to depend for their own personal expenses on their ability to influence government controls and distribute licences.

The Congress had started mining the welfare state for its riches, its Party members wielding official influence without taking official responsibility.[ccxxvii] When a crisis broke, the government official was thrown to the wolves, whilst the Congress Party man evaded attack or investigation. The veterans of the non-cooperation movement would be astonished at the "voluntary" contributions which the Party was now able to command. Much of this fund raising was taking place in the name of "stability"; business people would be given a friendly budget without the burden of new taxes and, over tea with ministers asked to contribute to the Party purse in order to ensure the continuance of a stable government, which was largely being financed by high excise duties and loans from foreign countries.

How long would the civil servants be able to maintain standards of probity when their political bosses in the Congress had turned "rotten"? They too were losing the respect which they had once enjoyed. It was Nehru's socialism which was absorbing the nation's resources into the state and entrusting its spending to government officials. They in turn had to exercise their responsibilities under the "interested supervision" of Party men subject to "palace influence". They were not very competent to start with, and had little interest in the results of their spending. Even in the best of circumstances production would suffer when entrusted to government officials rather than private entrepreneurs driven by personal interest. It was thus the rot in the Congress Party which meant that most public expenditure in the country went to waste. Rajaji opened his article *Moral Bankruptcy of the Congress*: "Here is a party that sits in office and spends all the time at its disposal this year in selling or promising, or indirectly binding itself to sell to individuals favours and monopolies, large or small, according to capacity, under the deceptive name of a controlled economy."ccxxviii

***

Minocher Masani, better known as "Minoo", had been a man at the fringe of Indian politics since the 1930s. He was well aware that he had one flaw which prevented him from becoming a great political leader. He was just too Westernised. Indian leaders, after all, were expected to wear dhotis, be strict vegetarians, abstain from alcohol and write dense literature in Indian languages. Minoo did not do any of those things. He was a Parsi from Bombay whose father, Sir Rustom, had been a municipal commissioner of the city and vice chancellor of Bombay University. Minoo had been sent to England in the 1920s and studied economics at the London School of Economics and law at London University before being called to the Bar at Lincoln's Inn. He became a student leader and member of the Labour Party during his London days and upon returning to Bombay to practice law became a socialist activist. Having been arrested during the civil disobedience movement of 1932 he met Jayaprakash Narayan in jail and the duo formed the Congress Socialist Party two years later.

There were a few young Parsis of the time who were drawn to socialism and its sensibility, however they could only have been described as rebellious sons. The Parsis were India's most quintessentially bourgeoisie people, who, through an easy relationship with the British, a great passion for English education and culture, and an unceasing spirit of entrepreneurship, had amassed wealth and influence far in excess of their small numbers. When Minoo became disillusioned with socialism generally, and Russian Communism in particular, towards the end of the 1930s and took up a position with Tata & Sons, he was, thus, returning home.

Whilst increasingly fierce in his denunciation of Communism, Minoo was, at the time of Independence, still relatively mild in his advocacy of capitalism. What he wanted, like many others, was a "mixed economy". He still maintained an amicable relationship with Jawaharlal Nehru, and so was sent to the United Nations, and then made India's ambassador to Brazil. The two men disagreed over whether India should denounce the Soviet Union's treatment of its minorities however, and when Minoo returned to India he retreated from public office for a time. During this time he founded a new journal, *Freedom First* in which he made the case for classical liberalism in India. It was in 1957, with a little help from a local raja, that he was elected to the Lok Sabha as an Independent candidate from Ranchi, deep in Bihar, possibly the place in India most culturally distant from his own south Bombay milieu.

Now, in the Lok Sabha, Minoo Masani could speak directly to power, which, at the time, meant Jawaharlal Nehru. The prime minister had declared the aim of his economic programme to be maximum production and the prevention of the concentration of power, that is, economic power, in private hands.[ccxxix] In August of 1960 Masani rose to inform the House that he and his Swatantra Party colleagues felt that the bigger danger was the concentration of economic power in government hands. No matter how big an industrialist became, there would always be the power of society and the state to keep him in line and bring him to justice should the need arise, but when the state held police power and economic power, or the policeman, judge and factory owner were the one entity, there was no one to appeal to. That was a true concentration of power.

Masani maintained that he was not against heavy industry and rapid industrialisation, but that it had to be balanced by the development of an agricultural base and light industries to supply the needs of the people. He gave the contemporary example of a proposed fourth steel plant. There would come a time when India needed more steel plants, but the money allocated in the Third Plan for such a plant could have been better spent on "a hundred other purposes", most notably agriculture. Steel plants had the poorest ratio of output and employment to capital invested; ₹180 crores would be sunk in a steel plant which would only turn out ₹45 crores worth of steel each year and employ 8,000 people. A similar investment in light engineering industries would produce goods worth ₹200 crores and employ 100,000 people. If similar examples were cited in fertiliser production, insecticides and agriculture, the employment and output benefits would multiply.

The proposed Third Plan was putting two-thirds of the nation's resources into the public sector, of which three-quarters was invested in sectors other than agriculture. This, when 70% of Indians were making their living in rural India. Masani thought that this showed a lack of balance. The problem was in trying to reconcile a Soviet command economy with parliamentary democracy. They were contradictory and sooner or later one would have to go. The Soviet model asked the present generation to starve for the benefit of generations yet unborn, but Masani pointed out that Indians wanted to see the fruits of their labours for themselves and their children, "whilst they are still alive". He mocked the Planning Commission's projections on national income, asking, "is it planning or astrology?".

In August 1963, during the no-confidence motion against Prime Minister Nehru's government, Masani rose once again to express the people's feeling of exasperation; he felt that they had reached the limits of their endurance.[ccxxx] The lot of landless labourers had not improved, nor had that of small landholders. There had been no rise in the standard of living of the working class, whilst the middle class was being ground between two millstones, rising prices and rising taxes. Industry was faced with endless regulations and a super profits tax. The only class which was better off in 1963 than in 1947 was that of politicians, civil servants and a few businessmen who worked hand in glove with them. Far from being more free and equal, the people were "tied up in a mass of red tape". Whilst businessmen had to make trips to New Delhi in aeroplanes to get their work done, peasants had to walk or catch a bus to the district headquarters "to get some wretched form filled or completed".

Part of the reason for all this was a dependence on the state, a continuation of the colonial 'ma-baap sarkar' mentality. The people had not been given the feeling of freedom to go out and do things for themselves as had been the case in West Germany after the war. There men and money had been let loose in order to make the country strong. In India neither men nor money were trusted, only the government. The result was an agricultural sector with amongst the lowest productivity in the world. The reason was the diversion of resources into heavy industry and away from productivity improving infrastructure and supplies for agriculture. Instead of producing more food there was endless discussion on distribution, controls, zones and cordons. After all the resources which had been poured into the public sector, the Finance Minister, Morarji Desai, in the budget of 1962 had announced an average return from public sector enterprises of 0.3%. Masani thought that if any businessperson tried to go to the market promising 0.3% return "he would be considered insane". He criticised Nehru's oft repeated refrain that Indian Planning was good, it was just the implementation which went wrong. Masani likened that to an army general ordering his troops up a steep hill with heavy equipment in order to surprise the enemy. When the troops could not climb the hill the general blamed them rather than his planning.

With the death of Nehru, Masani maintained his criticism,

but now had to direct it against the bearers of the Nehruvian ideology in the Congress and the Planning Commission.[ccxxxi] The finance minister had started his 1965 Budget by invoking Nehru's legacy, hoping that he and his colleagues might be worthy of maintaining it. Masani wanted none of it. It was to oppose Nehruvian polices that the Swatantra Party had been formed in 1959. And now, in 1965, the Party would oppose such a "disastrous legacy". Masani thought that the Finance Minister, T.T. Krishnamachari's invocation was telling; he and his colleagues were not free men, able to meet the challenges of the present with clear thinking- "they are prisoners of their past and they are unable in spite of their intelligence to free themselves from that legacy." He thought that the upcoming Fourth Plan was "the nigger in the woodpile", or the thing of crucial importance which was being concealed. The Planners had learnt nothing and forgotten nothing, and would only bring about organised chaos in the country. "Who are these Planners?" he asked, "Let me say quite frankly that they are a group of bookish intellectuals, completely divorced from economic realities, none of whom has any experience in even producing a thousand rupees of goods and services in this country." They were incapable of producing anything but words, barely measured up as socialists, and were really just Communists, like Prasanta Mahalanobis and V.K.R.V. Rao, who made little effort to hide their admiration for Communist regimes. Masani thought that Asoka Mehta, now deputy chairman at the Planning Commission was going the same way with his calls for greater economic and planning co-operation between New Delhi and Moscow.

***

Bellikoth Raghunath Shenoy, originally from Mangalore, had studied at the London School of Economics, but unlike many of his Indian peers he did not come under the influence of Harold Laski, the charismatic professor and leading light of the Fabian socialist movement, but was instead inspired by a young Austrian classicist, Friedrich Hayek, and his defence of the market price mechanism. Shenoy was perhaps India's first economist of international repute, having his papers published in leading scholarly journals as early as 1931. He returned to India, and after the Second World War wrote incisive papers on the sterling balances, and maintained his links with the Austrian School, becoming a member of the libertarian Mont Pelerin Society. After his note of dissent to the Second Five Year Plan Shenoy found that his opinions were much less keenly sought in government circles. He did have a couple of friends like Rajaji and Minoo Masani, who would quote from his work, but he was largely a loner in the Indian economics community. What was particularly irritating for Indian planners was that Shenoy did not confine his opinions to *The Times of India* and *Swarajya*, but would write for papers like *The Wall Street Journal* and regularly make them look silly before an international readership.

In an article in *The Wall Street Journal* in 1962 titled "Social Injustice in India", Shenoy, with co-author Patrick Boardman of Bucknell University argued that Indian planners, rather than eliminating social injustice, were actually increasing it.[ccxxxii] The authors wanted to make it clear that a "mere piling up of output", particularly when it did not meet consumers' needs, as was occurring in India, could not abolish poverty. They likened India's river valley and power projects, steel plants, heavy engineering and heavy chemicals units to the pyramids, forts and palaces of earlier civilisations. In both cases it was possible to have full employment whilst the majority of the population remained abjectly poor. Abolition of poverty meant raising living standards, and for living standards to be raised economic activity had to be directed to meeting the people's need for consumer goods. In India economic activity needed to be directed towards the production of food and clothing. Shenoy and Boardman thought that history had shown that the best way to overcome poverty was to give the consumer "unfettered sovereignty over production". The consumer's daily purchases would then guide production towards meeting his needs. On the other hand, it was the consumer's needs which were the first to be sacrificed in statist economies. With the rise of statism during the Second Plan period consumption of both food and clothing in India had declined on a per capita basis. The authors explained this by the fact that investment was being guided by the needs of the state, rather than the needs of Indian consumers.

Investment in the public sector had more than doubled during the Second Plan, and quadrupled during the Third Plan, and it seemed that the trend would continue. Yet Shenoy and Boardman pointed out that even after 45 years of planning in Russia there were scarcities of meat, clothing, shoes and housing, whilst investment continued to be directed into huge power and irrigation projects, heavy industries, "rocketry systems", nuclear weapons and space science. An example of the social injustice of the planned economy in India lay in the indexes of output from the 1950s. Output of machine tools, commercial vehicles, coal and caustic soda all multiplied many fold whilst production of the goods used by the lower middle class like matches, cotton and cloth remained constant. The goods consumed by the wealthy, which were largely curios to the lower classes, like electric lamps and fans, radios, sewing machines and rayon also multiplied by many times. In addition, the prices of food, grains and clothing had all risen steeply, reflecting a forced transfer from consumer to non-consumer industries, whilst luxury goods had remained constant in price. Both the real and nominal incomes of the wealthy were rising at a faster rate than the working class, as the workers had to spend a higher proportion of their income on relatively expensive necessities. Furthermore, the neglect of agriculture was really the neglect of employment, which was reflected in the fact that the number of unemployed had actually risen by 3 million during the Second Plan period. Shenoy and Boardman argued that the best protection for the weak was the price system and competition. When the state interfered with them, it was really protecting the forces of exploitation.

In *Anti-Progress Planning* in 1963 Shenoy pointed out some of the distortions in India's trading economy for his American readers.[ccxxxiii] He suggested that a drain was taking place due to the difference in price between relatively expensive Indian goods and their much cheaper foreign competitors. The cost of imported penicillin was one-tenth that of the product made in India, the cost of an imported refrigerator was one-third that of the Indian product, and an imported diesel engine for irrigation was about two-thirds the price of an Indian made engine. In addition, Indian made goods were usually inferior in quality to their foreign competitors. Producing goods in India which could be bought more cheaply abroad was thus essentially a waste of resources. In addition, when there was surplus production of a good in India it would be sold abroad at a vastly reduced price. Indian diesel engines were being sold in the Middle East at a price which reflected less than two-thirds of their cost, which was the highest price they could be sold for given competition in the international market. Indian exporters did not have to worry about the loss as they were compensated by various government schemes for export promotion. In the end the loss was incurred by the Government of India. Shenoy ended his article by suggesting that economic growth would become truly "self-sustaining" if the sequence was made right: consumer goods industries needed to be developed, after which heavy industries would grow. With higher income would come higher savings, and so greater resources would be available for industrialisation.

The article which really irritated India's planners was *Aid For India* and its subtitle *Why It Does So Little For Nation's Economic Growth*.[ccxxxiv] In May of 1964 Shenoy noted that whilst during the First Plan period grants and loans had averaged about $84 million a year, towards the end of the Third Plan period the figure had grown to $800 million. In 1961 aid accounted for almost one-third of scheduled investments in the Indian economy. Almost two-thirds of the aid flows of the early 1960s were coming from the United States. India's next biggest donor was West Germany which accounted for 12% of total aid, whilst Britain and the Soviet Union each contributed around 7%. Shenoy saw the American objective in providing aid as that of accelerating economic development and keeping India in the free world. Yet he noted that these huge aid flows had done little to ease Indian poverty and unemployment. The obvious question was: where had all the money gone?

Part of the flow of foreign aid had been used for foreign exchange to build production facilities which were standing idle, in some cases because they were uneconomic projects from their inception. In many industries production capacity was working at only 50-60%. Generally their output was of high cost and low quality. Foreign aid was being used to cover the operating costs of these "industrial white elephants". Foreign aid allowed for the purchase of imported supplies, accessories and spare parts which plants might not otherwise have been able to procure under normal competitive conditions. These plants were an enormous drain on the Indian economy as it would in most cases be cheaper to import the required products. Shenoy estimated the drain to be 45% of the cost of domestic output at these plants. Foreign aid was thus doing a disservice by keeping industries alive which should really have been giving way to ones which were better suited to India.

Given that foreign aid was supporting India's balance of payments deficit, it was indirectly supporting all sorts of strange economic activities like providing foreign exchange for the illegal export of capital and illegal import of gold and consumer goods, for the construction of urban property as a hedge against inflation, and the consumption of luxury items among the wealthy. Part of the ruse originated from traders going to the Reserve Bank of India for foreign exchange, understating the value of their exports, and hence the amount of foreign exchange which they would hand over to the Bank, and overstating the value of their imports, hence increasing their requirements of foreign exchange. As long as India continued with its planned economy foreign aid would make little difference. What India needed was sound fiscal and monetary policies and less government intervention. Only then, Shenoy thought, might foreign aid make any difference.

***

Given the opposition to the Licence Raj from the Right, it might be surprising that it stirred almost equal dissatisfaction from those in the Congress on the Left. Shyam Nandan Mishra, the deputy minister for planning led a group of Gandhians and Leftist intellectuals inside the Congress in the late 1950s which was increasingly dissatisfied with the slow pace of implementation of social and economic reforms both in rural and urban India. The ideals of the Avadi Resolution of 1955 were not being fulfilled and Congress sessions were becoming less democratic, with measures dictated by the High Command and then rubber stamped. It seemed as though most of the Congress's socialism came from one man, the prime minister, rather than grass roots doctrinal commitment. Both the Jana Sangh on the Right, and the Communists on the Left had fared well in the 1957 general election. There was a feeling that if the Congress was to survive and prosper it would have to move to the Left and become more serious about the implementation of its fine sounding resolutions. The Congress Socialist Forum was thus formed in December 1957.

Forty Congress workers attended the first convention and signed a document titled *Keeping The Flame Alive*. A committee was formed with S.N. Mishra as convenor in order to implement the Forum's objectives of studying socialism, sharing the results with the Party and society, and educating the Party workers in the tenets of the ideology. The group would seek to influence policy at the level of the Congress Parliamentary Party and the All India Congress Committee. The Socialists also had the tacit support of Prime Minister Jawaharlal Nehru and Labour Minister Gulzarilal Nanda. Indira Gandhi, who acted as Congress President in 1959 and 1960, also read the group's thesis and signed it, but neither did she join. The Forum advocated organisational reform within the Congress, published papers on the Third Five Year Plan and organised seminars which Nehru attended, but its suggestions advocating a greater emphasis on agriculture were rejected. The Forum had advocated co-operative farming, panchayati raj, or village government, land reform and a coalition between the Congress and the Praja Socialist Party.

One major problem facing the Socialist Forum was a fundamental division over the meaning of the word 'socialist'. In the Congress of the 1950s there were essentially two types of socialists- Gandhian socialists and Nehruvian socialists. The Nehruvians, who dubbed themselves 'scientific' socialists, often had little common cause with the traditional, socially conservative agenda of the Gandhian socialists. This became apparent when the Socialist Forum, already a small gathering of interested Congressmen, began to split in the early 1960s. Keshav Dev Malaviya, one of the younger scientific socialists, complained that S.N. Mishra, a Gandhian socialist, was trying to turn the Forum into his own fiefdom and they started to argue over the round of land ceiling legislation being implemented by state governments.[ccxxxv] S.N. Mishra and his Gandhian colleagues were suspicious of K.D. Malaviya and his smaller group within the Forum, and thought that they were trying to bring Communism in through the back door.[ccxxxvi] By the early 1960s the Forum's units at the state and district level were defunct. It could attract barely a dozen members of Parliament.

The situation in 1962 was even more crisis laden than in 1957. The Congress vote share had decreased in the 1962 elections and four cabinet ministers had lost their seats in Parliament. It seemed that the Rightist forces within the Party were again in the ascendant. The political opponents of the Congress were gathering strength, economic stagnation and inflation prevailed, and a sense that the system might be upturned without some radical and intensive action grew. The Congress needed a clearer idea of its ideology in order to attract fresh talent to the Party and so it was Gulzarilal Nanda who floated the idea of a new Forum for Labour, Planning and Socialist Action with some parliamentary colleagues associated with the labour movement in May 1962.

The Forum made the expected statements about avoiding factionalism and groupism and studying and disseminating socialist thought. Interestingly, it spoke of members adopting socialism in their personal lives, something which piqued Nehru's curiosity as he gave his customary tacit approval to the formation of the new Forum, which by the following month had come to be called the Congress Forum for Socialist Action.[ccxxxvii] Most of Nanda's first notes seemed to repeat the concerns of Mishra and his original Forum; the need to reform the Party structure, improve lines of communication between workers and leaders and the need to educate the Congress workers and the masses in socialism.[ccxxxviii] The first meeting was attended by 17 members. This time Nehru came to inaugurate it himself.

The Forum started its work as a pressure group within the Congress at the Bhubaneshwar session in January 1964. Bibhuti Mishra proposed a change to Article I of the Congress constitution to include the goal of achieving "a complete socialist state within 10 years based on parliamentary democracy". Other members of the Forum suggested that the Congress change its name from the Indian National Congress to the Indian Socialist Congress. The suggestion was partially accepted, and the goal of a socialist state by parliamentary means was incorporated into the Congress constitution, although no time frame was specified. The Forum also managed to influence the Congress leadership under Kumaraswami Kamaraj to call all socialists to join the Party, something which led to the arrival of Asoka Mehta, Chandra Shekhar and Mohan Dharia, as well as hundreds of other members of the Praja Socialist Party.

The Congress Socialists seemed to be gathering momentum at the start of 1964, however Prime Minister Nehru's death in May 1964 proved to be a great setback. Lal Bahadur Shastri was not a bitter opponent of socialism and planning, but neither was he a great supporter, and when he became prime minister began to bring many of the Congress's conservative critics of planning back into government. Morarji Desai refused a Cabinet position, but Sadashiv Kanoji Patil was given railways, Sanjeeva Reddy was given mines, and K. Kamraj acted in an advisory role. Indira Gandhi was however brought into Cabinet as information and broadcasting minister. Shastri appealed for a "common man's plan" and wanted a shift in economic policy towards agriculture.[ccxxxix] During Nehru's time the Planning Commission's power and autonomy stemmed from the prime minister's ability to override the objections of his state and Party leaders. Shastri proceeded to put Planning Commission members on fixed term contracts, whilst a separate secretary would now work with the Commission rather than the cabinet secretary. Shastri then created his own prime minister's secretariat as a new centre of economic policy decision making. L.K. Jha was appointed head of the new secretariat, but he was not a member of the Planning Commission, which meant that the Deputy Chairman of the Planning Commission, Asoka Mehta, would have to come to Cabinet and mutually agreeable policy solutions be found. Prime Minister Shastri then started to challenge the Planning Commission's Plans through the National Development Council. He wanted greater emphasis on agriculture and formed a separate National Planning

Council with the deputy chairman of the Planning Commission as head, but without other members of the Commission. The new Council was primarily made up of technical experts and advisers. Responding to the chief ministers' complaints over the planning process Shastri then created five committees of the National Development Council to look into the details for the Fourth Plan.

***

By 1964 the Licence Raj seemed hemmed in from both the Left and Right of Indian politics. The Americans were also increasingly dissatisfied with the performance of the Indian economy and where their aid money had been going. Congressional opposition to aid to developing countries had been rising, yet aid to India continued to flow through the Consortium. A group of American officials sensed an opening. The Embassy and US AID in New Delhi, and the State Department and World Bank in Washington all seemed to coalesce around the idea of a Big Push on the Government of India to get the economy moving in the right direction. The idea originated with John Lewis, a professor at Indiana University and veteran of the American economic bureaucracy. By American standards, he was an old India hand. He had written a book in 1962 titled *Quiet Crisis in India* in which he argued that non-project aid would allow the United States Government to "weigh in" on India's overall economic policy. When he arrived in India at the end of 1964 as the new head of US AID he sought to turn his academic theories into a major diplomatic initiative.

In *Betting on India*, a memorandum sent back to Washington in January 1965, John Lewis tried, as the title suggests, to make the case for a larger American commitment to India.[ccxl] The United States had, he argued, since 1947, maintained a great interest in India's "constitutional style development effort", something which had only become more intense by 1964 due to a sense of a rising China. India's commitment to constitutionalism only seemed to be reinforced by the orderly transfer of power from Nehru to Shastri. Lewis thus thought that India's importance to United States foreign policy was based on rationality, but that some in Washington still harboured doubts; they saw India as inefficient, committed to a misguided ideology, with contention over basic issues of foreign policy. Matters were not helped by India's slowness in reforming its economy and in taking up non-project aid. There were some in Washington who thought America's mission in India was without focus. Lewis had arrived in the country and things were not as bad as they had seemed from back home.

Lewis argued that the record of production for the Third Plan period had been quite good, given the need for the military build-up on the border with China. Industrial capacity had been expanding at a greater rate than output. Agriculture had not been doing well, but it was on an upward trend from the 1950s, the political leadership was the best ever, the weather was improving and the new policy of price supports, fertiliser imports and production expansion was starting to show results. Farm output had grown 6% and food distribution policy was moving in "a sensible direction". Taxes had been raised, exports were doing better than expected, and some foreign investments were shaping up. Lewis knew that "in a vast country committed to evolutionary process, breakthroughs are seldom going to be clean, sharp and dramatic enough to be fully recognized until after the fact." The Government of India was spending a greater part of its non-project aid as the United States would like, on fertiliser imports, and the Ministry of Finance was going to request more loans to bust bottlenecks in the system in the coming months.

Lewis foresaw a rapid rise in Indian obligations for debt repayments which would mean lower net aid receipts. For this reason it was imperative to maintain the level of gross assistance. Maintaining the same net aid level would mean raising aid by $1.5 billion from the Consortium over the coming five years. If gross aid per capita was to match that of Pakistan, the total aid bill for India would need to be doubled. Lewis wanted the Consortium to bet on India as "a major island of orderly development promise and achievement in a sea of considerable confusion". Of course, he recognised that selling a "Big Push" both in Washington, and to the other Consortium members would require improved performance from India. In some cases this would entail quid pro quo bargaining, but in others better policy directions from the Government of India would come naturally if it was given greater foreign exchange resources.

Lewis did not think that the Government of India would have any trouble in absorbing the extra aid inflow. The aid pouring in would buy imported fertiliser, pesticides and small tractors, establish more domestic fertiliser, pump and tractor factories, accelerate rural electrification, increase the availability of consumer goods and would provide greater productive incentive. The result would be a 5% increase in farm and food output. The more liberal availability of imports and stronger rural demand would stimulate small modern private sector factories to manufacture the consumer goods which would lead to a more viable pattern of industry. The growth rate would increase to 6 or 7%, or more. An expansion of supply and ample imports would encourage greater employment and it would help to remove the inflationary constraints on public works. Taxes had already been raised in the Third Plan, and so the dilemma before the Government of India was how to raise more without stifling private enterprise. With greater aid flowing in and the economy growing, tax takes would increase as incomes rose. Such economic growth would also raise living standards, the best deterrent to larger families, and the best incentive to smaller ones. A greater push for aid in the near term would also bring the date of true Indian self-reliance forward; the day when India could form its own capital in sufficient amounts to propel its own growth. It would also mean a bigger cadre of managerial and technical professionals for the Indian economy. In conclusion, Lewis termed this prospect "exciting speculation" and wanted the policy institutions to get together and discuss the idea over the first half of 1965.

In March Chester Bowles, who had returned to New Delhi as ambassador after 10 years away, wrote back to the State Department, keeping up the note of optimism about India and the United States' ability to influence the course of events.[ccxli] He saw the United States' role as establishing India as a major force for economic and political stability, and that project was reaching a "very sensitive stage". On the plus side was India's antagonism to Communist China and the consequent awareness of how important it was to stop China overrunning south-east Asia, something which would only leave India vulnerable on its eastern flank. In addition, there was a disillusionment with various leaders of the Non-aligned Movement, a breaking away from the romanticism of the Nehru years and a move towards economic pragmatism under Shastri and competent young leaders were coming through in the states. The Shastri government was facing up to the food problem and had some real accomplishments to its credit in its first months in power.

Bowles also listed the negatives; the legacy of Nehru and its associated idea of democratic socialism, which was often mistaken for a serious set of policies, the tilt to the Soviet Union just to spite China, the overindulgence of Left wingers due to "traditional Indian political tolerance", the presence in the Cabinet of T.T. Krishnamachari, and the tolerance rather than acceptance of the private sector. Bowles continued to complain about T.T. Krishnamachari and his contempt for the private sector and American fertiliser projects but related that Asoka Mehta had assured him that the Indian Cabinet and prime minister also saw Krishnamachari as a problem and most of them would welcome American aid and fertilisers. At a more fundamental level Bowles did think that political and economic forces were moving in a favourable direction for American interests. All that was needed was a "keen sense of proportion and timing". He thought that with the help of friendly foreign governments and the World Bank the Indian economy could make a major breakthrough. But before that could happen they would have to face up to "a major showdown" with the Government of India. The pressure could not be overt however; it would be better to let the World Bank and International Monetary Fund make the running with the support of other Consortium partners like Japan. The showdown would only likely occur once discussion on the Fourth Plan started in October.

Robert Komer, one of the first recruits to the Central Intelligence Agency and a long standing member of the National Security Council briefed President Lyndon Johnson in April.[ccxlii] He got straight to the point; the massive investment that the United States had made in India, about $6 billion, had not been because of India's foreign policy, but in spite of it. India could not be allowed to go the way of China, and it, along with Japan, was a valuable counterweight to China. The containment of China's spread through South-east Asia would be up to India to preserve and so it played its role, albeit indirect, in containing communism in Asia. The previous four United States administrations had been committed to India, which was taking in 43% of the America's food surplus, which had led Washington to tolerate its neutralist policies and the problems of its emergence as an independent nation. Komer did not think that either India's position on Pakistan, or its tendency towards isolationism were unreasonable; this posture was similar to that of the United States at an earlier stage of its development. India realised its own importance and its ability to command aid from both the United States and the Soviet Union and given its status as a newly independent nation with its Gandhian heritage it often expressed itself in anti-Western and pacifist terms. Americans had swallowed their "distaste for the dogmatic and inefficient Indian brand of quasi socialism" and supported the Planning process from the start.

Komer noted that despite the help that the United States had given, due to its inefficiencies India had just about been moving ahead slowly. Despite increases in industrial and agricultural output, the population explosion had meant that per capita income was rising at about 1% a year, and the surplus food that the United States was sending acted as an "indispensable cushion". India had belatedly woken up to the Chinese military threat and was re-arming itself, but American military aid had been outstripped by Soviet aid. He posited that if a free and independent India was of great long term interest to the United States then even greater investment might be required. He repeated John Lewis's point that whilst the absolute amount of aid given each year to India may have seemed high, in per capita terms it was still a relatively small amount.

Komer informed the president that experts were starting to argue that stepping up aid would pay greater dividends if linked to "several key things we want". Like Lewis, he argued that this would get India to self-reliant status quicker and save future United States administrations in the long run. It did not look like the advocated increase was likely to appear instantly, but the time to move might be in 1966 at the time of the Fourth Plan. They wanted major economic changes, something supported by Consortium members, but the Indian position that they could not decontrol the economy without a major run on foreign exchange was a reasonable one. They also wanted a nuclear non-proliferation pledge from New Delhi, an even stronger anti-Chinese stance and some détente with Pakistan, perhaps starting with greater economic co-operation rather than Kashmir. And they could not let the India-Pakistan relationship dictate their stance towards either nation. Likewise, the sooner both India and

Pakistan realised that they could not "jockey" the United States, the sooner, Komer thought, they might resolve their problems.

One of the experts that Komer was referring to was Bernard Bell, who had been chief economist at the Export-Import Bank and was commissioned by George Woods in September 1964 to lead a study of the Indian economy and report back to him personally. The report would help Woods in making decisions as the leader of the World Bank, Consortium and International Development Association. Bell made an initial draft report in May 1965. It was a personal report to the President of the World Bank, and so he made no effort to present his opinions in a way which would be "least bruising" and "most persuasive" to Indian politicians and bureaucrats.[ccxliii] The inference that Indian politicians and bureaucrats needed to be coddled might have come from frustration; during his time in India just about everyone he met in the Indian Planning establishment had some complaint about him.[ccxliv] He had, in his short time in the country, managed to conform to every Indian stereotype about brash, abrasive and tactless Americans.

In his report Bell cited the most critical limiting factor on the rate of growth as the lack of foreign exchange. It fell most heavily on the import of maintenance goods, that is, materials for current production. This was limiting output in all sectors and the expansion of productive capacity, exports, and consumption. One major problem was the overvaluation of the rupee combined with the system of administrative controls over imports. It was working against import substitution and export promotion attempts by the Government of India and led to loss of foreign exchange. It also operated against the economically efficient use of imports and capital equipment. Bell argued that the system of import controls had been an inefficient allocator of scarce imports and reduced the efficiency of enterprises. The Government of India tried to counter the overvaluation of the rupee by applying import duties, but even these, generally pegged at about 10%, did not go far enough to meeting the disparity between import and internal prices, which could be between 50% and 100%, and import licences were known to sell for 75% to 500% of their face value. At the overvalued rate of the rupee, the demand for imports exceeded the supply of foreign exchange which put pressure on the system of controls. Those lucky enough to receive import licences were thus being heavily subsidised by the Government of India. A high rupee gave an incentive to import rather than buy in the domestic market.

Bell went on to show that both public and private sector companies had been started which were not efficient users of the capital which they employed. The Government of India had provided a number of incentives: for the newer manufacturing industries there was an import entitlement scheme. However, generally, the import entitlement allowed to exporters was about double the amount of imports which actually ended up in their exports, and so there was a premium at work. There were also cases of tax rebates and concessions. However, jute and tea, which accounted for 75% of exports did not receive a premium. This premium system for exports was a difficult one; the Government of India was essentially saying that it could successfully calculate the price elasticity of foreign demand for each commodity, each year, and then devise a premium for each, and maximise foreign exchange returns, whilst also regulating the profits of Indian exporters. Bell expressed his "profound scepticism".

Bell explained that instead of its stated aim of promoting exports, the system tended to be for disposing of some pre-determined amount of exports in foreign markets each year. It did not allow for short term reactions of Indian suppliers to foreign demand, mainly because it underestimated the price elasticity of foreign demand, or even Indian producers taking market share from foreign competitors. There was no stable basis on which Indian producers could plan export drives, and so there were few who did so. A more appropriate exchange rate would get Indian producers to respond. The Indian authorities had not anticipated the enduring hunger for imports on the part of Indian manufacturers, or even their capacity to react to increasing supply of imports, which had resulted in unutilised industrial capacity. A devalued rupee would provide stability to Indian exporters in their planning, whilst the government could intervene in special circumstances when warranted for individual industries.

Imports of all materials for all producers were administratively determined. The system had not served as an efficient allocator of scarce imports, or maximised the output of domestic production using these imports. It had not even been able to maximise production in key sectors as the judgements of import requirements could not be accurately made. It was commonplace that domestic output was lost due to a shortage of imports. There was also an incentive to holding back excess stocks of imports and selling them on the grey or black markets. The system was dividing the market between the licensed producers, stifling competition and leaving profits to all but the most inefficient producers. It had created a stimulus towards expanding production inefficiently in order to get import licences, discriminated against small-scale producers, threatened corruption, and imposed a heavy administrative burden. Bell wanted to replace the existing system of administrative controls with one of indirect controls layering the price mechanism.

The term "liberalisation" was already being used. Bell argued that a devalued rupee would allow supply and demand for imports to equilibrate. Indian authorities were having to make a choice between maintenance and project imports and were choosing the latter, which meant underutilised capacity. He wanted a devaluation of the rupee and a freeing of maintenance imports from controls, but recommended a continuation of controls on capital goods. In order to make this work in the short term greater aid for foreign exchange would be required. In the long term higher exports from a more appropriate exchange rate would increasingly provide for maintenance imports.

India-Pakistan tensions and their associated defence expenditures and lack of economic co-operation were another obstacle to development. Family Planning had not been vigorously pursued and only 2% of Indian couples in the reproductive age group were using some form of contraceptive. During the Third Plan period the incremental output went to sustaining the increased population at the existing standard of living. In agriculture Bell suggested that there needed to be strong and stable price incentives, and better supplies of physical inputs- fertiliser, irrigation water, improved seeds and pesticides. Industrial production needed to be geared towards providing inputs for agriculture even if that required changes in the existing pattern. There needed to be more farm credit, better directed research, better extension work, irrigation planning, tenancy security and consolidation of fragmented holdings. Bell repeated the familiar American complaints about impediments to private foreign investment, particularly the requirement of limiting such investors to minority equity shareholdings in partnerships with both private and public Indian enterprises. He also included the old criticisms of overinvestment in public enterprises and underinvestment in rural works.

Even with the proposed reforms, Bell knew that there would not be nearly enough foreign exchange to make the Indian economy viable in the near term. The foreign exchange estimates for the Fourth Plan were not yet available, however it was obvious that increasing the utilisation of capacity of industry would require an increase of foreign exchange. The amount required for maintenance imports would be $300 million to $500 million higher each year. During the Fourth Plan period about $2 billion in additional foreign exchange would thus be required. This could only come from aid. India's debt servicing obligations at the end of the Third Plan would come to $2.2 billion which meant that an additional $1 billion to $1.5 billion in aid would be needed just to help service existing debt. Aid for project imports would need to be maintained, and so if aid for foreign exchange was not forthcoming then the desired results would not materialise. On the other hand, unless the desired policy changes were made, increased aid would not see the desired results. Bell argued that there would be a multiplier effect for the increased imports; if put to maintenance use they may add to production by a factor of four- net output of industry would rise by 12% and Gross National Product would grow by 2% per year. Even before the Fourth Plan estimates were in Bell was willing to project a need for 40-60% more aid besides PL480 shipments. To the extent that India's debt could be rescheduled, the need for more future aid would be reduced and increased private foreign investment could also help.

Bell's report to the World Bank President ended with the action to be taken by the Government of India, and the United States and the Consortium. India's list was longer: devalue the rupee, remove controls over imports of production supplies, energise the population control program, double the rate of agricultural production through a combination of supplies, prices, land reform, infrastructure, research and extension work, restrain defence expenditure, organise rural works, develop transport, simplify controls and abandon the industrial licensing system, improve planning and management of the public sector, research and financial policy, attract private foreign investment, allocate foreign exchange to domestic producers, and abandon import substitution "at any cost". The United States and the Consortium had to increase aid levels and reschedule debt, establish a contingency fund for devaluation of the rupee, provide aid on easy terms and better liaise with the Government of

India.

***

The Americans had all been enthused by Prime Minister Lal Bahadur Shastri and his "sensible" policies. However, India's second prime minister died in Tashkent in January 1966 the day after signing a peace treaty to end a war with Pakistan. He was not very old, and had only been in office for 19 months, and so the question of succession recurred much sooner than power brokers in the Congress had expected. These power brokers were known in the media as "The Syndicate" and had installed Shastri primarily to block Morarji Desai's ascent to the prime ministership. It is an old pattern in power politics; a group of roughly equally powerful and capable leaders cannot agree amongst themselves on a leader, but they all despise the one among them who is slightly less equal and more able, and so they combine to elect a relative novice whom they think they will be able to control. The pattern repeated after Shastri's death; the Syndicate once again combined to block Desai's claim to the top position and this time installed an even more inexperienced, but fabulously pedigreed replacement. Indira Gandhi became Prime Minister of India in January 1966. A new era in Indian politics began.

Relatively little was known of Indira's ideological predilections. She had not been a prolific writer like her father and was not given to philosophising in long and winding speeches. She had studied at Oxford in the 1930s, and whilst she did not complete her degree, she did come into a social circle full of young Indian socialists and communists. One among them was her future husband, Feroze Gandhi. She imbibed, both through her friends and her father's influence, a socialist sensibility, but understood little of economics. Her abiding interest was in international relations and her most deeply felt commitment was to India's standing in the community of nations. She was particularly sensitive to being slighted or condescended to by Western powers, be they former imperialists or neo-imperialists, and so when she arrived in Washington in March 1966, just two months after becoming prime minister, and facing the spectre of famine at home, her summit with President Lyndon Johnson was considered to have gone surprisingly well. Indira even largely followed the script which had been written out by diplomats in the United States Embassy just a few weeks earlier.[ccxlv] In fact, the summit was so successful that President Johnson began to move on a backlog of requests made by the India lobby in Washington. Within days he began to make personal appeals to Congress to provide as much aid as possible to India to avert a great tragedy.

The Indian official who had the task of negotiating the details of increased American assistance was Asoka Mehta, the minister for planning, who was quickly dispatched to Washington. In a sense Mehta was the one who bore the full weight of the Big Push. Once he arrived he was bombarded by interested American officials who wanted their long standing demands met. Bernard Bell wanted the Government of India to allow the World Bank's New Delhi office a greater role in Indian economic policy making.[ccxlvi] Dean Rusk, the secretary of state wanted India to make peace with Pakistan and express support for United States policies in Vietnam.[ccxlvii] At one point Mehta had to ask Walt Rostow, the economic growth theorist, and by now national security advisor, whether continuing American assistance would be dependent on India's foreign policy positions in South and South-east Asia.[ccxlviii] Mehta was mainly negotiating with World Bank officials, with the State Department trying to maintain the fiction that it knew little of what was being discussed between the two sides.[ccxlix]

Out of the meetings with the World Bank came a summary of 60 policy recommendations divided into eleven broad policy areas.[ccl] Most echoed those that the Bank had been making over the previous decade;

increased imports of fertilisers, capacity to manufacture fertilisers in India, deregulation and population control, but also included suggestions to boost tourism and improve transport infrastructure. Mehta insisted that the list was not an imposition on the Government of India, but largely made up of policies which it wanted to pursue if it could.[ccli] Oddly, the most pressing demand from the American foreign policy establishment, devaluation of the rupee, was not among the 60 points outlined in the summary. Mehta made it clear that measures like import liberalisation would be dependent on increased amounts of aid being made available.[cclii] This was well understood by the other side, it had been factored in from the start. The Consortium put together $900 million in non-project aid for the following year. But there was little detail or agreement about what would happen beyond that.

Indira consulted her Cabinet and then moved to devalue the rupee on 6 June. The political reactions were adverse, with most politicians and the public at large taking it as an affront to India's international prestige. The devaluation of the rupee was accompanied by short lived policies to reduce export subsidies and ease the flow of imports through lower duties and more liberal licensing. With the new lower level of the rupee the Government of India would need greater foreign assistance in the coming months, particularly as national elections were due in February 1967. Official commitments of aid from the United States, the Consortium and the World Bank had not yet come through. The Ministry of Finance had to dispatch its officials to Western capitals to try and shore up these commitments. Initially Lyndon Johnson, convinced by his advisers that Indira was living up to her part of the deal by the act of devaluation, approved increased aid for India. But German and Japanese representatives at the Consortium stated that they would not meet the new goals, and so the World Bank President, George Wood asked US AID to make up the shortfall, but was rebuffed.[ccliii] When the Consortium met in November 1966, Bernard Bell warned that India's nascent reform process would stall without adequate and early support.[ccliv] The Germans were arguing that India's economic performance, with or without aid, did not merit increased assistance.[cclv]

The Congress suffered serious losses in the 1967 election and Indira Gandhi was forced to bring Morarji Desai back into Cabinet as finance minister. The Consortium met again in March 1967, but there was little discussion on new commitments and instead a focus on rescheduling existing debt. The following month the Consortium met again and once more agreed in principle to provide another $900 million. But practice diverged from principle and even with fiddling over food relief and debt rescheduling only $600 million materialised. However, not even the World Bank president's stern words could produce better results. The Germans again demurred whilst others said they would only increase commitments if the Germans did.[cclvi] The group would meet in another six weeks' time. About half the agreed figure would come in the form of debt rescheduling which would at least ease India's foreign exchange commitments, albeit indirectly.

Another Consortium meeting was delayed until September 1967. But then at the next meeting a new criterion was introduced: performance. The Government of India's performance would be measured rather than policy reform and encouraging statements. It was not able to meet the required standards. The Americans were still defending India, but most other Consortium members expressed their dismay and disappointment.[cclvii] The focus of their criticism was on the weakness of Indian exports and restrictive import policies. This time commitments came to only $350 million. The downward slide in aid continued in March 1968. John Lewis, the head of US AID who had started the Big Push, then fell out with Morarji Desai and the senior finance civil servant, Indra Gordhan Patel.[cclviii] Morarji Desai also wrote to the new World Bank President, Robert McNamara in early 1968 complaining about the lopsided bargain which had taken place.[cclix] To add another dimension to the acrimony, when McNamara visited India at the end of the year, Asoka Mehta at the Planning Commission told his assistant that he "would not lend a cent" to the Indian political leadership.[cclx]

***

A conclusive end to the American project to liberalise the Indian economy came not from disputes over aid commitments from Western donors, but from the dramatic split in the Congress Party during the monsoon of 1969. India's grand old party, the bearer of Indian nationalism since 1885, had in fact split once before, in 1907, when moderates expelled extremists who wanted to secede from the British Empire. Nonetheless, since then, the Party had only splintered, first due to disagreements over whether to participate in provincial elections in the 1920s, and then over the question of socialism from the 1930s. Various socialist splinter Parties, and the conservative Swatantra Party had been established, yet the Congress had, with much difficulty, maintained its essential character as a Party of national unity providing a home for Indian nationalists of all ideological colours.

The immediate origins of the Congress split lay in the results of the 1967 national election. The Congress suffered its worst performance in the Lok Sabha since Independence, retaining only a slim working majority and was unable to form governments in key states in both the north and south of the country. Morarji Desai, the former finance minister and arch conservative, who had been denied twice before by his peers in the Syndicate, made preparations to challenge Indira Gandhi for the prime minister's post. He was persuaded against a bid for power by the Party President K. Kamaraj. He was instead compensated with the post of deputy prime minister, besides being given his old finance portfolio.

With the issue of the parliamentary leadership settled, the first shots in an ideological conflict were fired by K.D. Malaviya at a Congress Working Committee meeting held in New Delhi on 7 May 1967. He argued that the Party should cease to be an umbrella organisation for Indian nationalism and instead become an ideological Party with precise programmes and policies.^{cclxi} He wanted the Congress to become a progressive Party with clear policies favouring the peasants and workers and the urban lower middle class. He did not garner much support, with the usual formulations about national and Party unity ensuing. Nonetheless, Malaviya and the Left did score a significant victory at the meeting when the Congress Working Committee passed their 10 point programme as an official resolution for the first time. The socialist programme called for banks to be brought under "social control", for general insurance to be brought into the public sector, and for the state to take over the import and export trade as well as the trade in food grains. There would be an expansion of consumer co-operatives, monopolies would be curbed, there would be better child nutrition, restrictions on individual ownership of private land would be enforced, rural works and land reform implemented and the princes' privy purses abolished. Despite the inclusion of the term "social control" in their 10 point programme, which made it more palatable to the Working Committee, what the socialists really wanted was the nationalisation of the banks.

When the All India Congress Committee met in July it did not accept a lack of ideological clarity as a reason for electoral decline, but it did accept the Working Committee's resolution on the 10 point programme. Mohan Dharia had an amendment moved that the government take steps to remove the princes' privy purses. K.D. Malaviya kept up his advocacy for greater ideological clarity and the acceptance of socialism. He thought that either he, or the conservative S.K. Patil would have to go, the Party could not hold them both.^{cclxii} Socialists in the Congress like Dharia and Malaviya had come to be known in the media as "Young Turks", who were pitted against the older and generally conservative members of the Syndicate like K. Kamaraj, Sanjeeva Reddy, S.K. Patil, Atulya Ghosh and S. Nijalingappa. At the close of the meeting Indira suggested that it was the older members of the Party who had to bear the responsibility for the debacle at the 1967 elections.[cclxiii] The two sides clashed once again at the AICC session at Jabalpur at the end of October.

The principal issues within the Congress in 1967 were social control of banking and the abolition of the privy purses. S.N. Mishra, the old Gandhian socialist and deputy leader of the Congress Parliamentary Party, argued that social control of the credit system could be achieved without nationalising the banks and that abolition of the privy purses should be done in negotiation with the princes.[cclxiv] Mishra called the type of socialism being pushed by adhoc measures "lollypop socialism". But Bhagwat Jha Azad argued that the Congress had already committed to both measures and need not keep arguing over it.[cclxv] Indira was non-committal on the bank issue, whilst Morarji Desai preferred social control to nationalisation. S.K. Patil was conniving with Kamaraj to get the 10 point programme shelved. He thought that the Party should focus on major economic and communal issues, but agreed with his opponent K.D. Malaviya; if the focus on the 10 point programme continued he and other senior leaders would have to oppose it openly which would create the situation for a split.[cclxvi] Kamaraj was Party President and so insisted that the meeting was called specifically for the 10 point programme and it could not be so easily sidelined.[cclxvii] Just to up the ante the Congress Forum for Socialist Action issued a statement that the Congress needed to implement the 10 point programme "or perish".[cclxviii] The Forum now wanted a timetable for the implementation of the programme. The Working Committee took the conservative position on social control of banking rather than nationalisation and preferred a negotiated settlement of the privy purse issue with the princes. Morarji Desai made a presentation on the virtues of social control of banking and he was supported by the prime minister. Yet Indira assured the socialists that if social control was avoided or bypassed, then the government would not hesitate to move towards nationalisation.[cclxix]

And then, on 7 December 1967, Siddavanahalli Nijalingappa, the Chief Minister of Mysore and yet another Syndicate member, was elected Congress President unopposed. Relative calm prevailed within the Congress during 1968. The usual tension occurred over appointments to the Working Committee and the socialists maintained their call for the implementation of the 10 point programme, but Indira gave no indication of favouring them or their agenda. As late as April 1969 she was calling for a programme of action largely devoid of ideology; socialism in India she insisted, had "nothing to do with the left or the right".[cclxx]

The 72nd session of the Congress began at Faridabad on 25 April 1969. An electrical short circuit ignited a fire which consumed the stage. Tempers also became heated on the panel chaired by Morarji Desai on economic and social problems. He was symbolic of the "reactionary Right" for the Young Turks, and had previously come under personal attack from the young socialist Chandra Shekhar. The following day Mohan Dharia told Desai "You have failed the country. You have failed the people and also failed the youth." He exceeded his allotted time for speaking and Desai asked him to resume his seat, but he shouted "You can choke my voice but you cannot choke the voice of the people." To which Desai retorted "You are not my boss", to which Dharia replied "Nor are you my boss. It is not individuals but people who will decide the fate of this country."[cclxxi] Desai then tried to read out a document prepared by the Planning Commission on the implementation of the 10 point programme. Chandra Shekar said the document was "vague and evasive" and asked "Who are you bluffing- yourself, the country or the party?"[cclxxii] Bhagwat Jha Azad, Mohan Dharia and Chandra Shekhar all came together to attack Desai's explanation. S.N. Mishra rose to attack the young socialists. Indira largely supported Desai and said that the Party had to take responsibility for government performance, and had to take a realistic view of nationalisation; she was not opposed to it in principle, but it was doubtful whether they had the personnel to undertake the task, besides which nationalised undertakings had not all been performing well.[cclxxiii]

What really turned the drama was the Congress President Nijalingappa's speech:

> *"While we should encourage the development of industries we must see that big industries are not established in the public sector without due regard to demand and the capacity to produce. I am told that some industries in the public sector are so badly managed that the full capacity is not utilised and that they are run on very unscientific methods. I believe that industries, by whomsoever established, should be encouraged. If private industries misbehaved or made undue profits they can both be punished and controlled through fiscal measures."*
> *"If production of articles in the private sector can be achieved more economically we can even encourage the private sector. There is a case for reviewing this public sector attempt at establishing large scale industries."*[cclxxiv]

Indira offered a spirited reply by citing the performance of the armed forces in the most recent war with Pakistan as a justification for the huge outlays on the public sector.[cclxxv] She insisted that the private sector was not interested in establishing steel plants or investing in heavy industrial projects which were not immediately profitable and had gestation periods of 15 years or more. The defects of the public sector came out because of their accountability to Parliament. The private sector, she insisted, would not survive similar scrutiny. The Young Turks then sought to censure the Congress president's address. And then, just to confuse the issue, Nijalingappa closed the session by claiming to be the leading proponent of "democratic socialism".[cclxxvi]

On the eve of the All India Congress Committee session at Bangalore the Young Turks resolved to reopen the bank nationalisation issue. On 7 July they submitted a memorandum to the Congress High Command in which they expressed their disappointment over the policies to implement the 10 point programme over the previous two years and demanded an "outline of national economic policies".[cclxxvii] S.K. Patil thought that bank nationalisation would be harmful to the economy and had been trying to get Kamaraj to exclude it from any resolution.[cclxxviii] In addition to the ideological conflict over economic policy, the issue of the presidency of India was ever present. President Zakir Hussain had died in May, only two years into his five year term, and so the need to elect a new head of state had unexpectedly arisen. The Syndicate preferred the name of one of its own, Sanjeeva Reddy from Andhra Pradesh.

On the first day of the Bangalore session, Indira claimed to be indisposed, and sent Fakhruddin Ali Ahmed to the Working Committee with a note titled "Stray Thoughts on Economic Policy".[cclxxix] She wrote that she had only "glanced" at the Young Turks' memorandum, yet her note did seem to take its cue from their call for "an outline of national economic policy" and went very close to meeting all of their long standing demands.

Indira thought that it would be possible to take "full or partial action" on imposing ceilings on consumption and expenditure by corporate bodies, changing the credit worthiness criteria employed by government financial institutions, encouraging new entrepreneurs in backward regions, appointing a Monopolies Commission, giving greater autonomy to public sector projects and building a cadre for the public sector, reserving most consumer industries for the small-scale sector, imposing heavy penalties for restricted trade practices, excluding foreign capital from fields in which local capacity existed, and developing service co-operatives and minor irrigation works in rural areas. She was still uncertain on the big issue of bank nationalisation however, noting that the All India Congress Committee had already taken a decision, "but we may review it". She stated that they could "consider" nationalising the top five or six banks or, returning to the social control idea, "issue directions that the resources of banks should be reserved to a larger extent for public purposes." Indira further suggested raising the amount which banks had to invest in government securities, preventing industrialists from becoming chairmen of banks, nationalising the import trade in industrial supplies and reviewing the licensing system to prevent big houses dominating import licences and requiring the government to purchase its supplies from the public sector. She ended her note by making the case for rural employment schemes, minimum wages for agricultural labourers, and an implementation of land ceiling legislation and tenancy reform.

And then, on 10 July, Indira and S.K. Patil clashed over economic policy after which Yashwantrao Balwantrao Chavan drafted a resolution asking the government to implement the contents of Indira's note. Morarji Desai had already made it clear that if the decision was made to nationalise the banks, he would not continue as finance minister and undertake the task. Yet, strangely, he was put up to propose Chavan's resolution. However, it seemed that the Syndicate might go along with another radical economic policy resolution which may never be implemented, in exchange for support for its candidate for president. On 12 July the Congress Parliamentary Board met and confirmed Sanjeeva Reddy as its candidate, voting down Indira's choice of Jagjivan Ram. But then on 13 July Varahagiri Venkata Giri, the previous vice-president entered the contest. Giri, an old time Congressman, would contest as an Independent. On 16 July Indira relieved Morarji Desai of the finance portfolio, but did not name a replacement. Desai immediately resigned from the Cabinet. At this stage Indira claimed to support the Congress Parliamentary Board's nomination for president, Sanjeeva Reddy. [cclxxx] Yet it was becoming clear that the contest for the presidency of India was the new and most pressing front in the developing war between Indira and the Syndicate.

Indira nationalised India's 14 leading banks through an ordinance on 19 July. She received backing from the Congress Parliamentary Party, but the Young Turks were restrained in their support. There was no parliamentary revolt against her, only the suggestion that she take Morarji Desai back as finance minister. The prime minister addressed the Lok Sabha, telling it that it was important to have public control of national savings and channel it towards productive purposes. She had taken over the finance portfolio to make good on "declared socialist objectives".[cclxxxi] The Lok Sabha expressed its support for bank nationalisation. Meanwhile, whilst demurring from making a public appeal for the support of Sanjeeva Reddy for president, Indira did not do anything to undermine his candidacy. V.V. Giri called for a conscience vote. The Rightist parties, the Swatantra Party and the Jana Sangh, supported Sir Chintaman Deshmukh for the presidency. The Leftist opposition parties were gathering around Indira, and on 11 August her supporters within the Congress Parliamentary Party launched a signature campaign for a conscience vote.

S. Nijalingappa made one more appeal to Indira to

publicly endorse Sanjeeva Reddy. Two of Indira's supporters, Jagjivan Ram and Fakhruddin Ali Ahmed, wrote to Nijalingappa detailing their concern that he had been reaching out to Right wing parties and that some sort of constitutional coup might be in the air.[cclxxxii] The rumour had been circulating that, having installed its own candidate as president, the Syndicate might use him to dismiss the prime minister. Nijalingappa claimed that he was just seeking as broad support as possible.[cclxxxiii] He was against a conscience vote and wanted Indira to issue a whip to force parliamentarians and state legislators to vote for the Congress Parliamentary Board's candidate.

Three days before the polling the prime minister continued to keep everyone guessing. Indira was not replying to Nijalingappa's letters and had instead convened her own kitchen Cabinet. Ram and Ahmed wrote back, and Nijalingappa stated that if the letter was written at her residence, with her knowing, then she was working against the Congress candidate.[cclxxxiv] Indira's supporters were trying to equate a conscience vote for the presidency with the proper implementation of a socialist programme. Nijalingappa's supporters wanted a mandate from the High Command for the preservation of Party unity. There was chaos in the states, with collections of signatures for a conscience vote, but whips also issued to vote for Sanjeeva Reddy. On 14 August Indira wrote to Nijalingappa stating that she did not think it would be appropriate to issue whips.[cclxxxv] She tacitly agreed with the letters of her supporters and their concerns about Nijalingappa's appeal to the Right wing Parties for support. She argued that this had altered the basis on which the Party had endorsed Sanjeeva Reddy. But she did not expressly call for a conscience vote either. The Jana Sangh and Swatantra Party had shifted their support to Sanjeeva Reddy. The signature campaign for a conscience vote seemed to gather ground and started showing impressive numbers. Nijanlingappa once again refuted the charges against him and appealed to Indira to issue a whip.[cclxxxvi] As if to return the barbs about fraternising with the Right wing parties, Desai and Nijalingappa accused those around Indira of fraternising with the Communists.[cclxxxvii]

By 15 August, the eve of the election, Indira finally officially called for a conscience vote.[cclxxxviii] V.V. Giri became President of India the following day on the second count. There was an attempt at reconciliation between Indira and her opponents which had equal elements of routine and farce, but it was clear that support for the Syndicate leaders was waning. Nonetheless, the sniping went on with Nijalingappa deploring the growing personality cult around the prime minister, and Indira pointing out that those who opposed bank nationalisation had only quietened down as a tactical move rather than from a change of heart.[cclxxxix] Amidst all this the Young Turks and the Communists were still critical of her selling out to the reactionaries.[ccxc] Indira then called for disillusioned socialists to return to the Party fold.[ccxci]

There were essentially two All India Congress Committee meetings in November. Indira's camp wanted to requisition the 700 member AICC to endorse the moves made at Bangalore and the nationalisation of the banks and continue on the road towards socialism, and hence came to be known as the Congress (R), for requisition. On 12 November the Working Committee expelled Indira from the Congress and directed the parliamentary party to elect a new leader. The Syndicate then boycotted a meeting of the Congress Parliamentary Party called by Indira the following day and their segment of the Party came to be known as the Congress (O), for organisation. The parliamentary party was thus split, a three-quarters majority supporting Indira, and the remaining one-quarter meeting at Morarji Desai's house to elect a new leader. Indira was thus forced into the position of running a minority government. Morarji Desai's Congress claimed that rather than democratic socialism, Indira was promoting authoritarian socialism.[ccxcii] The requisitioned meeting of Indira's group began on 22 November. They voted to remove Nijalingappa as Congress President and replace him with the former Agriculture Minister, C. Subramaniam and then removed Nijalingappa and his supporters from the Working Committee and restored their own members. Addressing her new Congress, Indira noted that many resolutions of socialist tenor had been passed- at Avadi, Bhubhaneswar, Bangalore and elsewhere across the country. She told her loyalists: "I wish to assure you that everything stated therein would be carried out."[ccxciii]

***

Whilst Amitabh Bachchan rose to stardom playing the "angry young man"- Vijay Khanna, Vijay Verma, Vijay Kumar, Vijay Pal Singh, Inspector Vijay, or just Vijay, in film after film from 1973 onward, there was a young man who was even angrier who preceded him. Satyajit Ray's *Pratidwandi*, or *The Adversary* was set in February and March of 1970 and released later that year in October. *Pratidwandi* was the first in Ray's Calcutta trilogy in which he explored youth unemployment and corporate fraud in the city, and it was this film which introduced the original angry young man, Siddhartha Chaudhuri, to the Indian cinema screen.

Pratidwandi opens in a negative print, black is white and white is black. A corpse is being carried into a room and down the stairs and there is religious chanting. Women try to comfort a distraught widow. Siddhartha Chaudhuri watches his father's burning funeral pyre. In the next scene a tram travels down a Calcutta street, Siddhartha is now holding onto a rail, half his body hanging out of the crowded carriage. There are hands clasping rails, blank faces, white shirts, street traffic. The bus is even more crowded. The pace through the streets becomes more frenetic. Siddhartha approaches the Government of India's Botanical Survey of India (Central Office) on Madan Street.

Siddhartha sits down with the other job candidates, but has time to duck out and get his trousers repaired whilst he waits. He is eventually welcomed into the interview room. The interview begins. It is in English, and like all characters in the film, when speaking in English, or dropping an English word in a Bengali sentence, the interviewers and the candidate speak with accents which could pass in the home counties of southern England. The candidate is asked his name. He is asked for his papers and hands them over. Each of the three interviewers take a look. He had graduated as a B.Sc. in 1966 and then studied medicine for two years, but with his father's death he had to drop out of medical college. "What is your aim in life?" one of the interviewers asks. "Right now it is to find a job" Siddhartha replies. He had studied botany in his science degree. He is a little flippant with the interviewers. When asked whether he likes flowers he replies: "not unconditionally, some I like, some I don't." He is able to answer the technical question on mitochondria. He is then asked who the prime minister of England was in 1947, which he gets correct- it was Clement Atlee. Siddhartha seems to be doing well but then comes unstuck when asked what he thought was the most outstanding and significant event of the previous decade. There is awkward silence. He replies: "The revolution in Vietnam." The strength and resilience of the Vietnamese people were amazing. His interviewers do not seem impressed. "More significant than the moon landing?"- "Well we were all prepared for the moon landing, the spirit of the Vietnamese was surprising. It was plain human courage which takes your breath away." The interviewer rocks back in his seat, scratches his chin, looks at the young man, somewhat disturbed, and asks "Are you a communist?" Siddhartha insists that he does not need to be one to admire the people of Vietnam. The interviewer notes that this does not answer his question. He pushes a buzzer under the table calling for the next candidate.

Siddhartha then takes tea in a tea house and is approached by a Communist who tries to recruit him. He insists that no problem would be solved until he got a job. The Communist does not push the point. He even offers to set Siddhartha up with a job. It is outside of Calcutta though. As a medical representative with Dr. Soren Das of National Pharmaceuticals. But first Siddhartha needs to pop a pill himself, and after that sits down at a cinema. There is an announcement on the 1970-71 Union Budget. The narration is in English. There will be proposals to stimulate growth, and a drive for export promotion and import substitution. There will be taxes on luxury items and consumer goods and an increased wealth tax and higher income tax rates for upper income groups. Incomes will be tax free up to ₹5,000 and "a greater sense of security" will be provided "to low income groups through revised pension proposals". These taxes will raise ₹1,700 million in new revenue. Siddhartha is dozing off when he is woken by a bomb blast. He rushes out of the cinema hall and begins to wander through the streets. He gets his watch fixed. He sits and smokes a cigarette. He overhears some Western hippies who are in love with India, and Calcutta, and the cows.

Siddhartha then heads to his friend Adinath's place. He is reclining on a bed narrating his tale of woe when he notices that Adinath is trying to pick open a Red Cross donation box. He tries to wrestle the box away. How can he do such a thing? Adinath snatches it back and gives the somewhat tenuous excuse that he too had been walking all day in the sun. Doesn't he deserve a share? Siddhartha came to relax and instead had to watch his friend stealing from the sick and needy. Adinath then offers him some drugs to relax, "The whole country is going down brother." Adinath is still in medical school, two of his textbooks have been stolen, so he was stealing from the Red Cross to buy new ones so that he could pass his exams.

A new strand in the story begins with the visit of

Siddharth's sister's boss's wife to their home. Mrs. Sanyal is angry and tearful that Sutopa is ruining her marriage, her home. She admonishes Mrs. Chaudhuri- "I don't know how you have brought her up". Mrs. Chaudhuri simply has to sit and listen. Mrs. Sanyal leaves it to the older lady to find a solution, otherwise she will have to do something herself. Siddhartha arrives home as Mrs. Sanyal walks out wiping away her tears. Siddhartha does not believe the innuendo about his sister and the boss. He thinks Mrs. Sanyal is "a neurotic woman". But it is past 10 and his sister is still not home. Sutopa does walk in, and Siddhartha questions her. It is not clear whether she is actually having an affair with Mr. Sanyal, but she does have to do his bidding and can't refuse his invitations. She is coming up for a promotion to personal assistant with an increment of ₹200. Siddhartha starts to stew in anger. He approaches his brother Tunu for money. He wants to finish the bastard off. He even visualises himself as a revolutionary. His skin darkens, he is emaciated, bearded. He resembles a Bengali Che Guevara.

Siddhartha decides to go and see Mr. Sanyal at his Alipore residence. The two men sit opposite each other in a bright drawing room. Siddhartha claims that Sutopa is feeling the strain of work. Mr. Sanyal hasn't noticed. He is not phased by the boy's innuendo and suggests he just say what he wants to say. The conversation then turns to Siddhartha's employment status. He doesn't have a job, does he? Instead of his sister leaving her job, wouldn't it be better that he find one? Siddhartha senses an opportunity. In your company? No, but he could make a recommendation elsewhere. However, Mr. Sanyal gets a trunk call and has to leave the room. Siddhartha does not wait for him to return and walks out onto the street. He is about to join a melee in which a crowd is attacking a car which has hit a poor child. He notices that the car is a Mercedes and tries to get in on the action, but can't, and slinks off.

Siddhartha decides to take up the Communist's offer to

setup an interview with Dr. Das of National Pharmaceuticals. The recommendation is for a medical representative, but when Siddhartha arrives there are no vacancies, only one for a sales representative. Siddhartha seems downcast, but the doctor assures him that he had started as a salesman himself. Does he think he would have to carry medicines in a bag and move around like a hawker? The job entails going to hospital dispensaries and noting their requirements down in a book. It would require a lot of travel and the post is based in Balurghat in West Dinajpur, from where he would travel in a radius of 70-80 miles. Siddhartha imagines himself on a dusty road, trying to hail down a bus, which would just speed passed. He replies that he does not want to leave Calcutta. Dr. Das gives him 10 days to make up his mind.

Siddhartha goes to visit Adinath and muses that the only way out is revolution. He would not start one, but if it did start, he would definitely join the fight. Adinath laughs at him- Siddhartha is the thinking type, he won't actually do anything. Adinath then drags him along on one of his evening escapades. He visits a nurse who is moonlighting as a lady of the night. But Siddhartha is disgusted by the whole thing and storms out onto the street. Then, walking down a desolate Calcutta street in the early evening, he gets beckoned from the dark by a small sari clad young lady. The fuse has gone out and she can't fix it. The servants have gone off to the cinema. Can he help? He manages to fix the fuse, get the light going, and goes to wash his hands. By the time he returns the young lady has a soft drink prepared for him. She wouldn't have beckoned just any stranger off the street. She prods his memory. Does he not remember her? They had met before at his cousin Aruna's place. Her name is Keya Mukherjee. She had seen him walking down the street many times, always with a serious face, looking very intent. Siddhartha finishes his drink and then excuses himself. Keya suggests that he should drop in again- if he came the following day she would serve him tea.

Siddhartha returns home to talk to his sister. He tells her that he had been to Mr. Sanyal's and the two men agreed that it was better that she stop work before she has a breakdown. Sutopa laughs at her brother. No one could force her to stop work. To make matters worse, as she checks herself in the mirror, she asks him whether it might be a good idea if she starts modelling. She throws him a magazine. Plenty of girls are doing it these days, and the money is good. Siddhartha is sceptical. What if they require her to wear a revealing outfit? What would be wrong in that? Is her figure so bad? To add to the distress, Sutopa is learning ballroom dancing after work, and shows her brother her newly learnt dance moves on the terrace. Siddhartha then checks in on his brother Tunu, who would not say so, but is giving up a promising academic career to join the revolution in the villages. And so he starts to have nightmares; his interviewers, a landscape strewn with corpses, waves lapping at the shore, aborted foetuses, his sister modelling a swimsuit, a mob attacking a Mercedes in the background, his brother being lined up to be shot by Indian Army soldiers. His brother is shot on a beach and the nurse comes to attend to him, but the nurse is not his friend's prostitute, but his sister Sutopa, and then becomes Keya, of the blown fuse and soft drink and polite conversation.

A couple of days later Siddhartha goes to see Keya. It is a good thing he didn't go the previous day on which he was invited, she had gone out with some friends. Her father and his lady friend walk in on them, and then Keya makes an excuse to leave and asks Siddhartha to join her. They take a bus, and see a bright shining tower hotel. Siddhartha has a friend who works there. They will go for a meal. Keya feels bad that he has to spend so much on a meal in such an expensive place. Siddhartha protests that he is not so poor. Besides, just let him get a job and he will take her to even better places. He has the medical salesman job but doesn't want to take it, and has another interview coming up on Tuesday. Keya does not know how long she will be in Calcutta. Her father works in the

Income Tax department which means that his job is transferable. Her mother had died when she was seven. She muses out aloud; it would have been great if Siddhartha had become a doctor.

Keya and Siddhartha meet on Monday on a terrace of an empty floor of an office tower overlooking the city. There is a demonstration in the park and they discuss their plans. Siddhartha has his interview the following day. Hopefully he will get the job, but if he doesn't then he will have to leave Calcutta. If that happens Keya will also leave the city, go to Delhi, stay with a friend there and enrol in a course. She would leave her father in Calcutta, who is getting married to the lady friend. They take the elevator down. Will she write him letters? She would, but he should write first.

It is the day of the big interview. Siddhartha combs his hair and puts on a fresh shirt. His mother sends him off with the appropriate rituals. Sutopa sticks her head out, gentling teasing him that he will get a job, just like she had got one. He is told to keep his temper in check. He walks down the road and Keya waves to him from her window. He arrives at the office, gets his name checked off, and joins the other hopefuls outside the interview chamber.

But the heat is oppressive. There is the usual chatter amongst the candidates. How long will it take for my number to come? There are just four vacancies and so many candidates have been called. Chanchal Mukherjee emerges from the interview and is mobbed by the other candidates. Can he tell them some of the questions? The questions were on history, geography and politics. Like, where is Bonn? The attendant emerges and shouts at the young men in Hindi to keep the noise down or all the interviews will be cancelled. There is Communist graffiti on the walls: "Striker, non-striker. Discrimination should go." One of the fans is not working. There are not enough chairs for everyone. One of the candidates faints. The young man is carried aside. Siddhartha asks whether he should go and see the interviewers. After all they should take some responsibility. They called so many candidates; they should at least provide some chairs.

Siddhartha leads the way with some fellow candidates in tow. He walks in on an interview and is initially quite meek in his request. Could they possibly provide some chairs? He is told by the interviewers that they should all just adjust: they could not provide 75 chairs. He informs them that it is hot and one of the fans is not working. One person has even fainted. Another interviewer says the young man should not have applied for the job if he had such a "weak constitution". He would have to work harder on the job. That is one thing, but Siddhartha insists that he should at least get a chair at the interview whilst waiting. He is told to leave the room. He does so. He goes and stands in a corner resting against the wall. His mind starts to wander. The final straw comes when it is announced that the interviewers will be breaking for lunch. He marches back down the hall and into the office. He goes berserk. Are they animals? Are they servants? He throws one of the interviewers, who is trying to push him, across the room. I want an answer! He throws ink on the wall and upturns a desk and smashes a chair. He then storms back out of the room.

The next scenes are of the Bengal countryside. Siddhartha is leaving the city. He has taken the job in Balurghat and so writes back to Keya. He is in a hotel for the time being, though it is more like a boarding house. He will send her his address once he moves into a proper house. A frame zooms in on him behind the window bars of his bedroom. The birds whistle. He emerges and from the terrace sees a funeral procession with religious chanting- "Ram Naam Sat Hai", Ram's Name is Truth.

***

For Siddhartha Chaudhuri the prospect of life in Belurghat

was a form of dying. After his father's death and the abandonment of his medical studies, he had, for about a year, joined the ranks of India's young, educated unemployed. His ideal job was a government post, like the one at the Botanical Survey of India. It would have provided a secure, if modest income, the likelihood of promotion, and some social standing. It would have allowed him to get married. It would also have allowed him to stay in Calcutta. Instead, after his rampage at his last interview in the city, he had to accept defeat and move out into the countryside to work as a wandering sales representative. The type of anger, and then sorrow that he felt was shared by millions of young men in towns and cities across India.

Siddhartha had watched, or rather slept through an announcement on the Union Budget of 1970 during a cinema screening. It was Indira Gandhi's first budget after the split in the Congress just months earlier. After she had sacked Morarji Desai the previous July she had not named a replacement, and so presented the Budget herself, acting as her own finance minister. The narrator at the cinema announced that taxes would be increased on the rich in order to raise resources for the government and the poor would benefit from revised pension proposals and a higher threshold at which they would not have to pay any tax. The reason that Siddhartha had fallen asleep during the announcement was that none of this would have affected him. He was unemployed, and so the question of tax was not especially pressing. What he desperately wanted was a job. The success of Indira Gandhi's new socialist government would depend therefore on its ability to create employment for the millions of angry young men like Siddhartha Chaudhuri across the country.

A spate of socialist inspired legislation and policy changes took form in the early months of 1970. The government moved to implement the recommendations of the Industrial Licensing Policy Enquiry Committee. A new licensing policy was announced in February 1970 which reversed the trend towards decontrol which had been taking place over the previous five years. The earlier exemptions of 41 industries were withdrawn, which meant that the applications for expansion or new undertakings by bigger businesses would be subjected to special scrutiny. Legislation was passed which came into effect from April 1970 which abolished the managing agency system, a relic of the British Raj in which owners devolved the management of their business interests to a firm of professional managers. The Company Law Department also prohibited anyone from acting as managing director of more than one company. The Company Law Board would have to approve future appointments of paid directors. Orders reduced maximum salaries, allowances and other perks which could be paid to company executives. From August 1970 the government would also take over voting rights and directorships in lieu of loans provided by public sector banks.

New measures ensured that all companies with assets above ₹20 crores would have to register with the Ministry of Company Affairs and also conform to the new Monopolies and Restrictive Trade Practices Act. The Act established the Monopolies and Restrictive Trade Practices Commission which would advise the Ministry of Industrial Development, potentially affecting 1,200 companies. The inter-ministerial licensing committee would need to be satisfied before the application for a licence could move to the Ministry of Industrial Development for final approval. Applications could also be referred to the Monopolies Commission or the Economic Affairs Committee of the Cabinet. This would essentially mean getting approval from the prime minister through her advisers. Dozens of former Communists had joined the Congress in the late 1960s and become active in the Party's Socialist Forum and it was these new Congressmen that Indira Gandhi rewarded with committee appointments and Cabinet berths. They were staunch in their support for her, whereas the Young Turks, non-communist socialists and long time Congressmen, were just too doctrinaire, and principled, to restrain their criticism or profess their complete support. Soon she would force the old Socialist Forum to disband and replace it with a new Nehru Study Forum. After an eventful year, at the end of 1970, on 27 December, Indira announced that the country would hold an early election.

Indira Gandhi began her election campaign in Haryana in the middle of January 1971 and hit the note she would maintain throughout: she did not care whether she would remain prime minister or not, but she would always fight for the landless, the jobless and the poor.[ccxciv] She developed the message a few days later in Gujarat, Morarji Desai's home state and the hub of the old Congress he had taken with him.[ccxcv] This election would be unique as it would focus on national issues of development rather than personalities and local and regional issues. She said that her opponents were mistaken if they thought that by removing her they could crush the "upsurge". Even if she went there would be millions to carry forward the struggle. She wanted her party workers to spread the message of socialism from door to door. She was even more dramatic the following day in Bombay when she said that "you can kill a person but an ideology could not be killed".[ccxcvi] She claimed that several people had threatened to kill her. She also told the crowds that she was determined to abolish poverty. Prior to the start of the election there had been some talk in the opposition parties of "Indira hatao" or getting rid of Indira. However, as she famously put it, "Kuch log kehte hain Indira hatao, main kehti hu garibi hatao". Some people say get rid of Indira, I say get rid of poverty.

Indira was appealing to the most enduring ideal of Hindu culture, that of selflessness. She was not fighting for herself but for others, and a higher cause. If she won she would carry on her selfless service as prime minister. If she lost she would be a martyr, or renunciant for socialism and the poor of India. In addition to the fight to eradicate poverty and establish socialism, the other key theme of Indira's campaign was the election of a stable government. Only her Congress, united, could provide that stability. Her opponents had come together in a four party alliance- the Congress (O), the Jana Sangh, the Swatantra Party and the Socialist Party. And then, logically, she merged the two themes: only a strong Centre could bring about socialism. She even framed her campaign as a quest for a mandate for ushering in this socialism, which she dubbed the second phase of the freedom struggle.[ccxcvii] She insisted that she was not about taking anything away from anybody, she just wanted to put some curbs on those who had large amounts of land and wealth and wanted to implement the programme of the undivided Congress, which was the 10 point programme.[ccxcviii]

Indira claimed that it was because her opponents had opposed her first measures to reduce inequality that she had to seek a mandate from the people.[ccxcix] She asked for support for her non-violent revolution and was seeking support so that she could take practical steps for the poor rather than the usual slogans.[ccc] Amidst the campaign she gave an interview to the editor of *Blitz*, R.K Karanjia, in which she accepted the need for drastic changes to economic planning.[ccci] She felt planning had been "lopsided" and foresaw a more decentralised planning process in the future, one which would be less wasteful and make more use of local talents. On the question of unemployment she liked the idea of creating a "land army" of unemployed youth from both rural and urban India. Among the few specific policies she was willing to announce on the campaign trail was higher taxes on the rich to prevent the further accumulation of wealth in their hands.

The results of the 1971 election were emphatic. Indira Gandhi was returned to power with a commanding majority in the Lok Sabha. Her Congress (R) held 352 seats in the lower house, whilst Morarji Desai's Congress (O) was reduced to 16. The Swatantra Party, like most of the opposition parties suffered serious losses. From its high of 44 members in the Lok Sabha in 1967, it was reduced to just 8. Rajaji died the following year, at the age of 94, whilst Minoo Masani continued to play a minor role in opposition politics throughout the 1970s. The Swatantra Party was dissolved in 1974.

With a clear mandate Indira Gandhi's socialist rhetoric and policies continued at pace throughout 1971 and 1972. At the All India Congress Committee meeting in October 1972 at Gandhinagar, the Congress made it clear that it was committed to the creation of a public distribution system to provide essential commodities at fair prices. It was thought that this system would only be successful if the government could control the distribution of grain and so the committee reaffirmed its commitment to nationalising the wholesale trade in food grains. It was the fulfilment of a longstanding demand of the Congress socialists dating back to the 10 point programme of 1967. Under the new system the government would have a monopoly over procurement which it would use for an effective system of retail distribution, the holding of buffer stocks and the management of prices. In December the annual Congress session urged the immediate implementation of the policy for rice and wheat procurement. The states accepted the decision and it was endorsed by the chief ministers in March 1973. There were some dissident chief ministers however, and even Indira Gandhi's Leftist adviser Parmeshwar Narayan Haksar and the Steel Minister, S. Mohan Kumaramangalam, an ex-Communist, were against it. Yet the Minister for Planning, Durga Prasad Dhar was a strong supporter of the policy and it came into effect in April.

The government's decision to nationalise the wheat trade grew out of the euphoria, and relief, which prevailed across the country as food stocks began to grow dramatically after 1967. C. Subrahmaniam's efforts to distribute high yielding wheat seeds during his time as agriculture minister in 1966 had borne great harvests. The seeds, Lerma Rojo 64 and Sonora 64, were Japanese in origin, and had been worked on by American scientists and then sown in Mexico as part of a Rockefeller Foundation project in the late 1950s. The results were astounding; Mexico had been transformed from a wheat importer to a wheat exporter in just a few years. The Indian scientist Mankombu Sambasivan Swaminathan sought samples of the seeds from the Mexican project's American director, Norman Borlaug, and the Rockefeller Foundation provided the financial support for early testing in India. Subrahmaniam had to face some opposition from the Planning Commission but was supported by Indira Gandhi in his efforts to import huge quantities of the new seeds in 1966. The initial results were encouraging; the high yielding varieties were sown in the irrigated wheat belt of northern India, and despite drought conditions, the state of Haryana saw an increase in its wheat yield.[cccii] The Government of India then got to work expanding distribution of the new seeds; between 1966 and 1972 the area being planted with the high yielding varieties expanded from 504,000 hectares to over 10 million.[ccciii] This huge rise in yields, not just in India, but around the world, was dubbed the "Green Revolution" by the US AID administrator William Gaud in 1968. It would turn the world's peasants away from the red revolutions of Communism.

Indira Gandhi's socialist agenda also had its influence on India's international relations. An Indo-Soviet Treaty of Peace, Friendship and Co-operation was signed in August 1971 and relations with the United States reached a low when the American Navy entered the Bay of Bengal in December in a move to thwart the Indian Army's support for separatists in East Pakistan. The American naval operation never went further. The Indian Army defeated the Pakistani Army and a new nation, Bangladesh was born. Indira was at the height of her popularity, increasingly being likened to the Goddess Durga, and it was amidst the elation over a successful war and growing anti-American feeling in New Delhi that the decision was taken to end imports of wheat from the United States. Yet despite the initial success of the Green Revolution food grain production began to decline, first by 3 million tonnes in 1971/72 and then by 8 million tonnes in 1972/73.[ccciv] The utility of the new seeds had started to reach its limit. The quality of the seeds had been deteriorating; a farmer could use the high yielding seeds for four or five years after which they would require a change, yet such replacements, or new high yielding varieties were not yet available for widespread distribution. The stagnating wheat yields when combined with a return to drought conditions, low procurement prices and widespread resistance from wholesale wheat traders meant that the government could only procure about half its targeted amount. By the end of 1973 the government had run out of food and had to revert to importing wheat, initially from the Soviet Union, and then from the United States. The Government of India withdrew from the wheat trade in January 1974.

By the end of 1973, Gujarat, a food deficit area, had suffered a cut of two-thirds to government ration shops, whilst there had been 100% price rises in cooking oil and food grains over the previous year.[cccv] There was a bumper crop of rice and millet, but the government did not make up for the shortfall in other grains by any procurement drive. Price rigging by politicians and traders was blamed. The situation exploded in January 1974 at the Lalbhai Dalpatbhai Engineering College in Ahmedabad. Students, protesting rising charges for mess bills set fire to the college canteen and then attacked the college rector's house. The chief minister ordered riot police onto the campus. About one-third of the student body was arrested.

A students' council, the Vidyarthi Lagni Parishad was formed to formalise demands and call for a bigger shutdown on 7 January. They linked their demands to popular grievances, calling on the state government to arrest the hoarders and profiteers. The strike was agreed for 10 January and looting and riots ensued. The Parishad then became the Navnirman Yuvak Samiti, or the Youth Group for Regeneration. They wanted to wage a non-violent struggle to purify society. They wanted the Chief Minister of Gujarat, Chimanbhai Patel to resign. The Indian Army had to be called in on 26 January. By February, on orders from New Delhi, Chimanbhai did resign and President's Rule was imposed on the state. The students started to get broader support over the following weeks, importantly from Jayaprakash Narayan, who by this time had become widely known as JP. Indira Gandhi thought that arresting 200 of the Samiti leaders would break the movement, but then her old antagonist, Morarji Desai announced on 11 March that he was going on a fast unto death. On 15 March Indira dissolved the Gujarat state assembly.

Similar unrest broke out in Bihar in March. Student agitators protested against soaring prices, shortages of essential commodities, mounting unemployment and outmoded education. They planned to surround the state assembly and demand the resignation of the government. The movement was dominated by the Hindu nationalist Jana Sangh's student front, the Vidyarthi Parishad. The action took place on 18 March and looting and violence was so widespread that the army had to be called in once again. JP volunteered to lead the movement, and began to orient it towards rooting out corruption from public life. Indira and JP traded barbs in the press: Indira suggested that the student movement might have "wealthy friends" and be influenced by American capitalists, and JP accused her of leading India towards a Soviet backed dictatorship.[cccvi] A "Paralyse the Government Agitation" was started in April, and even as the movement was gathering momentum in Bihar, a national railway workers' strike was scheduled for 8 May. Indira put the strike down under the Defence of India rules. A march of half a million people on Patna took place in June, a three day strike occurred in October, and another massive demonstration took place in November. The Bihar Government undertook mass arrests and disrupted transport services to prevent more people gathering to protest.

By December of 1974 JP was drawn into defining the objects of the movement which he had come to lead in the journal *Everyman's*.[cccvii] He started off by refuting the charge of the Congress that the movement was one of the opposition trying to rest power by "taking to the streets". The opposition parties were relatively marginal to the movement, it was jan shakti, people's power, and chhatra shakti, students' power on the one side, up against rajya shakti, or state power on the other. Furthermore, the movement did not just want to capture power, in the sense of replacing the Congress government, but wanted to purify politics and government and create a system which would tame and control power irrespective of which Party was ruling on any given day. The movement was also for the removal of corruption from business, industry and education, and most importantly for social, economic, political, cultural and educational change. The movement was a continuation of revolutionary change, and so rather than governments and political parties it was direct action of the youths and people which would be the main driving force. It had to be peaceful and constructive whilst also maintaining a combative quality. JP acknowledged that whilst he and some of the opposition parties might have helped, the movement had grown from the grass roots, and was a product of the frustration which people felt with "all sorts of conditions which they find irksome or intolerable". He felt that they were fighting against all-round corruption and that the remedy lay in addressing its roots in political and economic corruption.

JP was increasingly being asked to define the movement's socio-economic aims, or its 'frame'. He did not think that a detailed programme like that of political parties, particularly Leftist parties, was what this movement needed. But he did think that he and his colleagues had a reasonable sense that theirs was a "Gandhian frame". Such an outlook would lay emphasis on the development of agriculture, equity in land ownership, "appropriate technology" for agriculture such as labour intensive tools and gobar, or cow dung gas plants, developing domestic and rural industries, spreading small industries as wide as possible, planning and development on a regional basis, maximum decentralisation, reform of the elitist education system, and dismantling the caste system and the economic hierarchy. JP did not think that nationalisation of private sector businesses had actually achieved anything in India; it had just replaced private ownership with state ownership and actually worked against socialist aims. But, in the old lament, he said that what was lacking was not such socio-economic programmes, but a willingness to actually implement them. He looked forward to the students doing so.

JP then began to elaborate on how the people's movement was related to the Sarvodaya movement which he had been a part of over the previous 20 years. The Sarvodaya movement had been led by Vinoba Bhave and was aimed at achieving social change through peaceful people's power. Both the movements wanted radical social change, which was why they were now using the term 'total revolution', one which Vinoba had used in the past. They also wanted social change through legal and administrative action. He reminded readers that Gandhi wanted self-rule in the villages. The Sarvodaya leaders had spoken of Gram Swaraj, or village autonomy, and the work of the Bhoodan and Gramdan, or land-gift and village-gift movements, had been working to achieve this. But after years of effort they had not been able to awaken people's power in the way it was now being awakened.

The Bihar movement started with the objective of addressing four main issues: unemployment, high prices, educational reform and corruption. If any of them were to be addressed however, it would take radical reform of society. JP was already being accused of advocating a parallel government but insisted that what he wanted was a people's government, and one which would be formed in the villages, the long cherished desire of the Sarvodaya workers. The Bihar movement was thus an opportunity for the Sarvodaya workers to establish village government, and this outburst of discontent was in fact also their movement, just in a different form and with a different background to their own. It was not, as yet, a movement to oust Indira Gandhi and the Central Government, just the state government of Bihar.

JP had not been successful in getting the Bihar government to resign, and so he took his movement national by daring Indira to call early elections and let the people decide. He got the main opposition parties to endorse his call for "Total Revolution" and started travelling around the country and calling people to non-violent action. The Congress was divided. The ex-Communists saw the hand of America's Central Intelligence Agency in JP's movement and urged Indira to launch a crackdown. The socialists Mohan Dharia and Chandra Shekhar acknowledged his patriotism and advised her to begin a dialogue.[cccviii] Morarji Desai went on another fast in New Delhi in April 1975 for the restoration of democracy in Gujarat.

By May of 1975 JP was expounding on his theme of the neglect of rural Bihar in *The Economic Times*.[cccix] He thought that India's approach to agriculture since Independence had suffered from Jawaharlal Nehru's "giganticism"; building the largest dam, the "largest this, largest that", when in an economy at India's stage of development it would have been wiser to have projects of a more modest type which would have had wider "spread effect" than the dam at Kosi in Bihar. As a result, agricultural development had been slow and the area under cropping was not much more than at the time of Independence. Tenants and sharecroppers were not secure. The irony was that Bihar was a state which hosted many of India's heavy industries. JP thought that what was needed was the spread of small-scale industries and rural industries, resource and need based industries, and schools in which students could be taught practical skills which could service the agricultural economy. This would have led to more employment and production. The mechanics of Bihar did not even know how to repair an agricultural pump set, and so it would have to be transported 30 miles on a bullock cart for a simple repair.

When asked what his vision of industrial development was, JP returned to Gandhian themes. He was not opposed to industry of the modern sort, automated as much as possible in steel mills and the like, but the rest of industry should be small, medium and rural. The smaller industries could be co-operative and could also be private. In Bihar the co-operative movement and the state co-operative department were in bad shape, and so he had been advising small groups of farmers to pool their land without going to the department and having to go through the form filling and bribe giving. He wanted the private sector, as long as it was not able to manipulate political power, to be left to run as "responsible companies". He was not going to use the term "trusteeship", as it was out of vogue, but he would not be opposed to private firms which were responsible to their stakeholders and which would not sell overpriced or shoddy products. JP wanted workers to exercise some sort of control over management and wanted firms to be responsible to the community, perhaps with a ceiling on profits. Similar principles should apply to the public sector, which would be responsible not just to Parliament, but to the people more generally.

Morarji Desai's April fast was successful; Indira Gandhi reversed her course and provided assurances that elections would be held in Gujarat in June. Her authority had been eroding through May and by the time the Allahabad High Court announced its decision in a four year old electoral malpractice case against her on 12 June her position became officially untenable. The Court exonerated her on the more serious charges but held her guilty on relatively minor ones and so invalidated her election from the Rae Bareli seat in 1971. She would be further barred from holding elected office for six years. That same evening election results came through from Gujarat. The Congress had lost power in the state. On 25 June JP called for the launch of a nationwide satyagraha for Indira's resignation. That very day she announced a national state of Emergency. Opposition politicians were arrested and without its senior leaders the Bihar and Gujarat and Students' and JP movement disintegrated, for the time being.

***

Prior to the start of the Emergency, Indira Gandhi's younger son Sanjay had not been a central figure in Indian politics. Several urban legends had grown about his hard drinking, womanising and youthful, possibly criminal pranks. In public life he was best known for his involvement in a project to manufacture a "people's car". The car was called "Maruti" and Sanjay had figured in parliamentary exchanges over the legality of land allotments to the factory in Haryana, near Delhi. Despite having seemingly been favoured with generous amounts of land, by 1975, after about seven years of trying, his company could still not produce a car in sizable numbers for the Indian market. Curiosity about Sanjay was high during the monsoon of 1975 and so it seemed that the Delhi journalist Uma Vasudevan had landed a scoop in August when he agreed to be interviewed in her magazine *Surge*. The interview was titled "Sanjay Gandhi: Man, Myth and Maruti". [cccx] Uma first had to clean up the text due to some of Sanjay's bad language, and then released a pre-publication text to Indian and international wire services. From the long and comprehensive interview the journalists immediately picked up on Sanjay's broadside at India's Communists, many of whom were supporters of his mother's government. Circulation was stopped in India but continued in international papers.

The interview started with the myths surrounding Sanjay- his drinking, his fast living. He denied all the charges. Uma even put it to him that some people thought that he had a "file" on his mother, something which might explain his seeming hold over her. The questioning soon shifted to the "Maruti" element of Sanjay's persona. He thought that one of the problems with the business was having to buy supplies in the open market, and that he had in fact been too honest in selling surplus steel and cement in the name of the factory rather than on his or the manager's personal account. He was confident that the car would be able to sell for a low, competitive price because he was not pocketing anything from the production process unlike others who put aside money for themselves whilst showing a higher cost of production. He was having a problem with petrol and had not been able to meet his initial production target of 50,000 cars. Instead he had used the excess factory space to diversify into making road rollers and bus bodies. The company was making just 7 or 8 cars a month, but he was confident of increasing the number to 15, and then to 200 a month. He thought that might still be some way off however.

When Uma asked Sanjay what might be hampering production he replied that the enterprise was a capital intensive one, and the money market was tight- banks were not willing to lend. Uma was a bit sceptical: "Even to you?". He insisted that this was the case and the government- that would mean his mother's- had put the small car in a low priority sector which also affected his competitors like the Ambassador and Fiat. "The government is not bothered whether they run or not." He also thought part of the problem lay with weak consumer demand in India. The people as yet could only afford to catch a bus or ride a cycle, the thought of spending ₹10,000 or even ₹5,000 on a car was out of the question for most.

Sanjay was given an opportunity to elaborate on his car. He insisted that it was not a superior car to its competitors as such, but it was cheaper. For a lower price the consumer got more seating space and lower fuel costs and better cornering. Uma put it to him that it might overturn given how light it was. He insisted that its centre of gravity was much lower and its suspension much more modern. He claimed that its lower cost lay in its light weight; it was about half the weight of an Ambassador, which meant much lower costs of materials even though they were using aluminium which was relatively expensive. He was aware of the small increases in the price of aluminium and steel, the differences between the controlled and market rates, and the effect of the Emergency on prices. It looked like the car would cost ₹25,000 due to the hike in the prices of supplies, but it was still ₹10,000 cheaper than its competitor. He valued the total capital of the company at ₹2 crores and maintained that it had no major shareholders; no big businessmen had invested in the company and instead he had a large number of small investors, many of whom were being singled out for tax raids because of their association with him. He even thought that the bureaucracy, under pressure from the opposition, was targeting the company.

In the third part of the interview Uma came to the man and his political and economic convictions. She asked him, as a businessman, whether he thought that big business houses should be curtailed and whether he was in favour of a controlled economy. He stated that the controlled economy actually favoured big business houses because they had the resources to navigate the system of controls whereas the smaller businessmen did not. He thought that if all the controls were removed it would "virtually finish off the big businessmen". They were the ones who were lobbying to keep them. He also blamed the bureaucracy, it was they, after all, who received money and patronage.

Sanjay felt that encouragement to private enterprise would be the quickest way to grow. He thought that money kept pouring into the controlled sector just to keep it going somehow or the other. He wanted to use the efficiency of the private sector: "the expertise and the hard work that they have you'll never get in the public sector." He thought that the private sector would gladly invest in welfare projects rather than hand over an equivalent amount to the government which would only be sunk in the inefficiency of the public sector. He cited the situation in Uttar Pradesh in which power generation was not over 36% of capacity, whereas the private Birla power plant was running at 90%. Further, he did not think nationalisation was a good idea. It had happened to coal: prior to nationalisation coal was selling at a lower price whilst the owners were making profits, whereas since nationalisation prices had risen and the public sector was making a loss. Again, he thought that only the bureaucracy benefited. He came out as an economic classicist; the best way to ensure growth was to lower taxes. Excessively high taxes only reduced incentives to earn and increased incentives for tax evasion. He even claimed that where the public sector could not compete with the private sector it should be "allowed to die a natural death". He was also an advocate for a participatory capitalism in which workers were given shares in the companies in which they worked which would provide them with an incentive for harder work. The best way to bring down hoarding and the black market was to lift restrictions on production. And then, in the line which caused alarm, and got the interviewed withdrawn in India, he stated, "people in the Communist Party, the big wigs- even the not so big wigs- I don't think you'd find a richer or more corrupt people anywhere."

***

India had been on a roller coaster from 1965 to 1975. The movement against the government, when it came, united the disparate opposition parties against the figure of the prime minister and found a leader in Jayaprakash Narayan. For over 20 years he had been working quietly amongst the Sarvodaya movement, the Gandhians who objected to the prevailing centralisation and statism of the regime in New Delhi. In fact, the Sarvodaya group was, by the 1970s, just one of at least three variants of Gandhians; they were the "pure Gandhians", largely spiritualists and agrarians, but there were also Gandhian socialists in the Congress Party who advocated village industries, and even Gandhian capitalists like Rajaji of the Swatantra Party. JP used the student movement which had spread from Gujarat to Bihar as a vehicle for this latent Gandhism and launched what amounted to a Gandhian revolt against the Nehruvian state. He thought that everything had gone terribly wrong after Independence, and the results were there for all to see. The events of early 1975 thus made it clear just how opposed the Gandhian and Nehruvian visions of the state and the economy were. Nehru's "giganticism" had led to massive waste and concentration of development JP reminded Indians, whereas a more decentralised, small-scale and modest approach would have served India better.

Despite the persistent criticism that Mohandas Gandhi had sanctified poverty, he understood the dynamics of wealth creation as well as anyone else. It was for this reason that the entrepreneur was to be left alone to do business, his area of expertise. To disallow him from doing so would be to stifle the means through which society prospered. This idea was central to his "theory of trusteeship". Businesspeople, particularly the Indian cotton barons of his day were to be left to grow their businesses and then share their profits through welfare measures for their employees and society at large. A businessman like Ghanshyamdas Birla largely conformed to this ideal. A retrospective explanation for Jawaharlal

Nehru's hostility towards commerce suggests that it might lie in his Brahminism. However, this notion is flawed in two ways. Although he was given the title "pandit" out of respect and affection, it was in many ways ironic. Nehru absorbed very little of Brahmanism, or even Hinduism in his youth and was a lifelong rationalist. If at all, his disdain for money making might have come from the aristocratic English culture imbibed during his school and university days. Furthermore, it is not self-evident that Brahmanism is necessarily opposed to commercial life. Rajaji was an authentic southern Brahmin whose caste sensibility had led him in an opposite direction. When he advocated Gandhi's theory of trusteeship on the pages of *Swarajya* he was really drawing on an older, dharmic conception of wealth. He was a Brahmin, a scholar and a public man. He would not lower himself to money making. It was not his dharma. But it was the dharma of others, without whom society could not progress.

Back in 1965 just about everyone in the Indian political milieu sensed an opportunity for change. The Swatantrists knew that they were not about to come to power any time soon, but they could at least make their intellectual case and act as a pressure group on the ruling Congress Party. The Congress socialists were growing increasingly impatient and saw the cure for the ails of Indian socialism as more, or a more authentic socialism. The Americans were enthused by a new prime minister who seemed to take a more pragmatic approach to the economic challenges facing India, and thought that they could use their aid money, both in the form of direct transfers to the Government of India, and food aid, which was essentially propping up the Indian economy, to guide the regime towards liberalisation. News of the Congress president lambasting the public sector and advocating a greater role for the private sector in the summer of 1969 might have rekindled some of their hopes. Yet, by 1975, all the political actors in New Delhi had been flummoxed by the intricate twists and turns of Indian politics. Rather than a more liberal economy, India found itself under a dictatorship which had taken to cracking down on restive labour unions and making the trains run on time.

It seemed that Indira Gandhi was just as bewildered by the course of events as everyone else. During her initial days as prime minister she had been content to go along with the United States and straddle a middle path in Congress politics. But then, in a seemingly adroit move, she used the latent division in the Congress, and the socialists' need for political patronage, to split the Party on ideological lines. The division was old and deep, it dated back to 1955 and the unresolved issue of what "social control", and what in fact socialism in India, actually meant to the members of the Congress. Upon splitting the Party and reinventing herself as the bearer of socialism Indira passed a series of socialistic laws, cracking down on big business and personalising power in her coterie. She rode the wave of both socialist rhetoric and policy, until it came unstuck due to mismanagement of the food supply and an inability to create jobs for young people. She had, by 1975, largely discarded the Congress socialists who supported her through the split of 1969. She seemed now to be facing a split in her own family.

Sanjay Gandhi's ideological bent represented a split within the first family of the Congress Party. Although a son of privilege, not in desperate need of a job, he shared many of the frustrations of young men of his generation. He wanted to get things done and had little patience for the type of abstruse planning and bureaucracy that so enthused his grandfather. He had no time for dimensional hypotheses and perspective planning and saw the planners and their socialistic approach as largely responsible for the perpetual crises of India in the late 1960s and early 1970s. He wanted action rather than endless talk, and he was a businessman, of sorts. He had been working on the people's car project since 1968, and although it had been mired in accusations of cronyism, and had not produced many cars, he had, at least, been trying to get something done. He also shared the growing terror felt by Indians of his class over the uncontrollable growth of the country's population. He thought it would be futile to keep pursuing economic development if the expanding population negated whatever gains were made. It was, in essence, a sense of exasperation with 25 years of failed policies both to develop the Indian economy and control the growth of the Indian population.

SIX

The Right to Live, the Right to Progress

The British Raj was reaching the height of its power when it decided to conduct the first Census of India in 1871. The population was estimated to be 206 million. There were some nominal increases as more areas and peoples were counted each decade, however the late 19th century was a time of diseases and famines, and so the censuses of the era did not record any large real increase in the population. There were famines in the late 1870s, and again in the 1890s, and the influenza epidemic of 1918 and 1919 killed more than 12 million. The only periods of large population growth therefore were during the few years between the famines and epidemics, between 1881 and 1891 and the period prior to the First World War. The first big surge in the population was recorded in the Census of 1931. The birth rate had remained constant, but the death rate had fallen dramatically, leading to an increase of 34 million. It was this figure which alarmed Subhas Bose as he addressed his fellow Congressmen at Haripura in 1938:

> *I simply want to point out that where poverty, starvation and disease are stalking the land, we cannot afford to have our population mounting up by thirty millions during a single decade. If the population goes up by leaps and bounds, as it has done in the recent past, our plans are likely to fall through. It will therefore be desirable to restrict our*

population until we can feed, clothe and educate those who already exist.

The Indians who took an interest in the population issue during the last years of British rule were all members of the colonial elite. Indian population theorists were, even prior to the publication of the 1931 Census, concerned about the quality rather than the quantity of the population. They thought that Indians were leading short, miserable lives, and even those who did live to an old age were weighed down by the burden of having to support large families. Most early population activists were enthusiastic proponents of eugenics, and equally forceful in advocating the use of artificial contraceptives. Most were iconoclasts however, dismissive of the social and religious mores which were dearly held by most in a conservative, intensely religious society. Thus, birth control advocates, both male and female, would run into opposition from a wide spectrum of religious conservatives during the 1930s, most often Catholic priests and nuns, Muslim clerics, and Hindu Gandhians. By the late 1930s a standard Hindu objection to birth control was that Muslims were unlikely to practice it which would mean that they would soon be outnumbered. Even the National Planning Committee, otherwise a hub of modernism, did not betray any sense of alarm over the issue in 1939. The Government of India's Health Survey struggled to come to many firm conclusions on the issue in 1946.

As in most areas of public policy at the dawn of Independence an uneasy co-existence prevailed in family planning between Gandhians and modernists. And as in most areas of contention, the Gandhians were content to let the modernists go ahead so long as their methods were also tried. This first attempt at population control in independent India thus did not involve artificial contraception, but a technique of selective abstinence known as the "rhythm method". It was tried and it failed, and so the modernists' methods grew up alongside it, albeit slowly at first. The health bureaucracy established clinics to which couples were supposed to come on their own initiative. There they would be able to avail of family planning services, including artificial contraceptives. This clinic based approach did not work very well either. The assumption was that family planning would be demanded by the people, yet it was soon apparent that there was no great rush for the services being provided. By the late 1950s a new health minister, without Gandhian scruples, assumed office and decided to take family planning to the people. This was known as the "extension approach", one based on education and cultivating thought leaders at the village level. A sense of urgency in government only arrived by the mid 1960s with the publication of the 1961 Census and mounting international pressure to do something. Population was just one of many crises of the day, but it was so ominous that the government decided to attack it on a war footing.

At around the same time that high yielding wheat seeds were beginning to transform Indian agriculture, a technological solution to the population problem also presented itself. The intrauterine contraceptive device, or the loop, began to be imported into the country in large quantities. The loop had been tested both in India and abroad and seemed to offer the prospect of a quick end to the population problem. The United Nations, the World Bank, and the American President had all been putting pressure on the Government of India to control its population and so it decided not just to deliver the loop in massive numbers, but to set specific yearly targets for the states to meet.

Within two years it became apparent that the loop would not put an early end to India's population problem; the technology was faulty, the delivery system inadequate and Indian women were unwilling. Instead some of the states took to encouraging male sterilisations. Vasectomies had been tried on a limited basis in the states since the late 1950s, principally in Madras and Bombay, yet with the crisis only growing a few district collectors in Kerala and Gujarat took the initiative in starting their own sterilisation programmes. These sterilisation "camps" were relatively successful, yet before they could be institutionalised family planning budgets were cut and a new health minister arrived. He announced that development would be the best contraceptive. It was an old argument, that between whether population could only be controlled if the people experienced the benefits of development, or whether development would not even be possible were the population to be allowed to grow unchecked. Not long after the health minister spoke however, Sanjay Gandhi began his rise to become an unofficial, but effective boss of population control in India.

***

The Census of 1921, the results of which were released in 1923, did not show an appreciable rise in the Indian population. The population had been stable over the previous decade at around 318 million. The birth rate, 36.6 per 1,000 of the population was roughly in balance with the death rate of 33.9 per 1,000. A global influenza epidemic had spread to India in 1918 and 1919, however the Census Commissioner, John Marten did not think that it was part of "Nature's ordinary programme" for controlling the population in India. This might mean that the 1921 Census was not the best material with which to study the population problem. The natural checks to population in India were famine, malaria, cholera and plague, however influenza had thrust itself into India. It was equally lethal in town and country, its origin was uncertain, and so it was something of an unknown quantity. Marten calculated the rate of increase in the population over the previous 50 years, since the start of census taking, to be 20%, which would mean that it would take almost 200 years for the population to double.

The argument had been made that an improvement in the standard of living would work to bring the birth rate down, however Marten did not think that this would be the case in India. He thought that the main determinants of both the birth rate and death rate in India were diseases, which were determined by climate and the environment, and the ability of the people to resist them, rather than economic circumstances. Most Indians lived in "economic simplicity", married early and had as many children as possible, which determined the high birth rate. The high death rate was the result of the climate and physical conditions and unhygienic practices from infancy to adulthood. There had been development of economic resources in rural communities across India over the previous 50 years yet it had not been accompanied by a similar cultural advance. Old customs and attitudes had remained unchanged and until there was greater care for infant life, or science could improve the surrounding conditions in villages to help develop resistance to epidemic diseases, little was likely to change. Progress, according to Marten, could thus only come with education, change in the social culture and improvement in the physical environment.

Pyare Kishen Wattal, Assistant Accountant-General in the Indian Finance Department, had written *The Population Problem in India: A Census Study* in 1916. There was no data to suggest that the Indian population might be growing at a rapid rate, nonetheless it was already huge. Wattal's main concern was that India had both a high birth rate and a high death rate which meant that Indians were living short and hard lives. He had a particular sympathy for Indian men, many of whose ambitions in life had to be sacrificed in the interests of supporting their large families. Wattal also showed that there might come a time when India would struggle to feed its population and made a tentative case for birth control.

During the 1920s two social reformers from Bombay joined Wattal in his advocacy. Raghunath Dhondo Karve took things one step further and, after returning from a study tour to Europe in 1921, tried to provide the people of Bombay with information and appliances to practice birth control. He lost his job as a professor of mathematics at Wilson College as a result, and so began to devote himself full time to the cause. He wrote *Morality and Birth Control* in the same year. His book was more specifically a defence of artificial means of contraception that Wattal's *The Population Problem in India*. Karve largely took it for granted that India had a population problem, and instead sought to refute the suggestion that couples practice abstinence in order to control the population. His criticism was not of Mohandas Gandhi, whose opinions on the topic were not yet well known, but the 19th century population theorist, Thomas Malthus.

Narayan Sitaram Phadke was a professor of philosophy and writer of Marathi novels who, in the early 1920s, began to correspond with Margaret Sanger, the American birth control activist. It was at this time that he started to write for her journal *Birth Control Review*. He argued that India had to keep its population proportionate to its resources so that in the future there were no "unwanted" children.[cccxi] Phadke was inspired by eugenics, or the attempt to breed a better race, an idea also prevalent in American birth control circles. He went on to establish the Bombay Birth Control League, yet it never gained widespread support and he too lost his academic post. Being forced out of Bombay city, first to Nagpur, and then to Kolhapur, he was able to take his message of birth control to the smaller towns of the province. In 1927 the Sholapur Eugenics Education Society was formed with the aim of educating the public on the "responsibilities of parenthood" as well as opening Mothers' Clinics in order to prevent the birth of the lower orders and encourage those of the "superior types".[cccxii] Sharing this eugenics orientation was the Madras Neo-Malthusian League. The League was dominated by the province's Brahmins and aimed to give medical assistance and hygienic contraceptives to married couples who wanted to limit the size of their families or were unfit for parenthood. The League sold contraceptives and had its own journal, *The Madras Birth Control Bulletin*. The means of artificial contraception available to men in the 1920s included condoms and vasectomies. For women the options were limited to sponges and pessaries, or small soluble blocks, and tubal ligation, or sealing the fallopian tubes. Whilst Karve preferred sterilisation for both men and women, Phadke was a proponent of pessaries.[cccxiii] The leading pessaries on the market towards the end of the 1920s were the Pro Race Cap and the Dutch Cap.

The All India Women's Conference had been formed in 1927 to suggest an appropriate curriculum and system of education for girls. It was intended to be a one-off meeting in Poona, but those who gathered decided that they could not reform female education in India without discussing the social and economic issues facing Indian women. They thus resolved to meet annually, and in order not to alienate any section of Indian womanhood eschewed discussion of political issues. When the Women's Conference met at Madras in December 1931, Dr. Rani Lakshmi Rajwade tried to have a resolution passed which would create a committee to devise ways to educate the public on means to limit the size of families. The reasons offered for encouraging smaller families were the "immense increase in the population of the country" as well as the "poverty and low physical standard of the people".[cccxiv] Dr. Rajwade's resolution was defeated. It received only seven votes in its favour. Most of the opposition came from religiously orthodox Muslim and Catholic women, as well as those who accepted Mohandas Gandhi's ideal of self-restraint as the best means of birth control.

Dr. Rajwade's resolution was defeated at Madras, but during 1932 she did her work through the regional constituents of the All India Women's Association, and at the session held at Lucknow had Vimala Deshpande introduce a similar resolution. This time there was a specific call on municipalities and local councils to open centres to provide instruction on birth control. She received support from Rameshwari Nehru, Jawaharlal's cousin's wife, who argued that it was the poor who were being "crushed" under the weight of uncontrolled procreation and needed the advice and guidance of elite women like themselves.[cccxv] This time the resolution passed with only seven votes cast against it. Whilst the annual sessions of the Women's Association continued passing similar resolutions throughout the 1930s, opposition to birth control did remain at the regional level. Such resolutions were defeated in Andhra and Lahore, whilst the Central Provinces group could not hire a place to meet in Nagpur due to opposition to their activities.

The 1931 Census, the results of which were released in 1933, was the first to show a dramatic increase in the Indian population. In the decade since 1921, the population had risen from 318 million to 352 million, an increase of close to 34 million, or just over 10%. The birth rate was steady at 34.2, yet the death rate had declined sharply to 26.1. The new Census Commissioner, John Hutton did not think that there was an immediate danger of population pressure creating a situation in which India could not feed itself. The real problem was that most of the population increase was taking place on the land, and so there was an excess of labour for the needs of economical agricultural production. Indian agriculture simply did not need so many hands for production. The real danger was that the increase in population might lead to subdivision of land holdings which would make agricultural production more uneconomic. Any surplus labour from the land could be directed to industrial production, but this would only work if food production was able to keep up and it did not exceed industry's demand for labour. Hutton knew that for most of India's small farmers life on the land was not just a means to produce food but a way of life, an end in itself, and a rapidly expanding population would make such a life gradually more difficult.

The population problem in India in 1931, according to Hutton, was thus not simply a rise in the population, but a rise in the population of the peasantry. Indian farmers had little access to capital to increase production, mechanisation would do little for peasants who were idle much of the year, and there was no market for many of the products which kept small farmers in Europe employed like poultry, pigs and potatoes. Hutton did welcome the efforts towards birth control, particularly the Madras Neo-Malthusian League, and the establishment of birth control clinics in Mysore, but he, like his predecessor, saw the culture of the Indian peasantry as the main impediment to progress; education and cultural and psychological change were all needed- a changed outlook which valued this world rather than the next. Hutton was pessimistic however: "it seems doubtful that a materialistic standpoint would commend itself to Indian culture."

In 1934 Dr. Alyappin Padmanabbha Pillay founded *Marriage Hygiene*. It quickly became a journal of international note, drawing praise from H.G. Wells and contributions from American scholars like Norman Hines and Joseph Spengler. The following year Dr. Pillay also established the Society for the Study and Promotion of Family Hygiene. Family hygiene in this case meant sex education and contraceptive advice to married women who needed it. Sir Vepa Ramesam, a justice of the Madras High Court was the Society's first president, whilst Margaret Sanger acted as vice president. Dr. Pillay served as the Society's organising secretary. The Managing Committee included P.K. Wattal, Gyan Chand, Professor of Economics at Patna University and Dr. Ruth Young, Director of the Maternity & Child Welfare Bureau of the Indian Red Cross Society.

Dhunbai Jehangir, wife of the philanthropist Sir Cowasji Jehangir, was also involved with the work of the Family

Hygiene Society and oversaw the opening of two clinics in Bombay. One amidst the cotton mills of Parel, and another at Parakh Hospital on Sandhurst Road. Lady Jehangir appealed to the mill owners and local doctors to make the female mill workers aware of the services offered by the Parel clinic, for if they did not appropriately space their pregnancies their efficiency and productivity as workers would suffer.[cccxvi] The effort was a small one however. After a year in operation, opening each afternoon, the clinic had only advised 107 women, most of whom already had four, or five or six children.[cccxvii]

There were similar efforts to start clinics in Calcutta. Owen Berkeley-Hill, a former officer of the Indian Medical Service and army doctor who had retired with the rank of lieutenant-colonel was a regular contributor to *Marriage Hygiene*. Dr. Berkeley-Hill formed a Women's Welfare Society and established a birth control clinic at Dufferin Hospital in June 1935. The hospital did not allow the clinic to advertise however, and it attracted few clients. The following year the Society changed its name and location. It became the Marriage Welfare and Child Guidance Association and started an independent clinic in rented premises under the direction of Dr. Margaret Neal. The new Association broadened its offerings to contraception, vocational advice, child guidance and sex hygiene. The Association's clinic only saw poor women and operated until 1942 when it had to close down as the Japanese invaded Burma and seemed to be nearing Calcutta.

In May 1935 the Delhi Municipal Council debated a proposal to open a birth control clinic. It received little support. Muslims argued that birth control was against the tenets of the Quran, whilst Hindus argued that if Muslims did not accept birth control and they did, they would be reduced to a minority.[cccxviii] One Hindu member quipped that in that case Hindus would at least be able to avail of minority rights and privileges.[cccxix] A similar scene played out in Bombay in February 1937. The Bombay Municipality rejected a proposal to establish birth control clinics, although the margin was much closer than in Delhi. Similar arguments were offered against the proposal; it was medically dangerous, would foster immorality, and soon Muslims would outnumber Hindus.[cccxx]

Margaret Sanger arrived in Bombay in November 1935. She had been active in Leftist bohemian circles in New York prior to the First World War and had become an untiring advocate for birth control, specifically, artificial contraception, during the war years. Sanger faced constant legal impediments to her work in establishing birth control clinics and importing artificial contraceptive devices into the United States and would often provoke police action and criminal and civil charges in order to get the courts to adjudicate on contentious points of law. By the 1920s she had become a household name across America as a founder of the American Birth Control League. Her books, *Woman and the New Race* and *The Pivot of Civilization* sold over half a million copies. Sanger had secured an invitation to speak before the All India Women's Association through Margaret Cousins, an Irish feminist long resident in India. Cousins had been instrumental in the formation of the Association and was close to Dr. Rani Lakshmi Rajwade. During her first days in India Sanger met Dr. Pillay, her old associate, the suffragette Edith How-Martyn, and also tried to lobby Michael Knatchbull, the Baron Brabourne and Governor of Bombay in an attempt to get the government interested in the issue of birth control. She did not have much success with Brabourne who maintained that the government could not involve itself in such an issue for fear of stoking religious conflict.[cccxxi] Sanger did not have a better time at the annual All India Women's Association conference in Trivandrum in December.

Both Edith How-Martyn and Margaret Cousins had assured Sanger that Maharani Sethu Parvathibai of Travancore was sympathetic to her cause.[cccxxii] However, when the time came, the Maharani, who presided over the session, suggested that Sanger not speak in favour of birth control, but instead confine her advocacy to the suppression of brothels.[cccxxiii] The Maharani's change of stance may have been influenced by the strength of the Catholic Church in Travancore. The Church was organising the accommodation for delegates to the Conference, was a force in the local educational system and the nuns were distributing pamphlets against birth control to delegates. The Maharani even excused herself on the day that discussion was due and instructed her replacement to only allow two delegates to speak in favour of birth control.[cccxxiv] Despite the concerted opposition from the Catholic lobby and its supporters, and their arguments that birth control led to the annihilation of the race and encouraged immorality, they lost the vote by 82 votes to 25 and eventually withdrew from the Conference.[cccxxv]

Margaret Sanger then proceeded to Wardha to meet Mohandas Gandhi.[cccxxvi] Their meeting was well covered by newspapers and magazines in both India and America. Both, after all, were international celebrities. Sanger spent two days at the ashram. The dialogue could only begin on the second day however. When she arrived Gandhi was observing a day of silence.

Gandhi thought that there would be no birth control problem in India if he could only drive it into women's minds that they were free; all they had to do was say 'no' to their husbands when they were approached for sex. The real problem was that Indian women did not want to resist. He thought that the women of India, the masses, already had too many things to think about to pay attention to Sanger's message on birth control. Sanger disagreed, she had been to the chawls, or tenements of Bombay, seen the women sitting around with 3 or 4 or more children, grieving for others who had died in childbirth, and all but one were adamant that they did not want any more and asked her what could be done to prevent bringing more children into the world. She wanted to go to the villages and speak with village women; it was important first to know their concerns and desires and then worry about the methods. For Gandhi the solution was to get women to say no to their husbands. He did not think it would cause any trouble in 99% of marriages. Sanger thought it would not be practical. It would be a revolution in the home, and most likely lead to more divorces. Gandhi insisted that Indian women just needed to learn "the art of resistance". His was the necessary "primary education" which attention to birth control would only obscure.

Margaret Sanger argued that the two things, education and birth control, could go together. The experience in England and America had shown that instruction in birth control among poorer women meant that they could prevent having five or more children and the further slide into poverty and degradation and alcoholism. In America cases were closed on the welfare books once women had been given birth control information and couples were living more productive lives. Sanger asked Gandhi whether he saw the difference between sex love and sex lust, and whether it was not in fact sex lust which he was opposed to. Gandhi thought that if it really was love then it would transcend carnal instincts and regulate itself. Sex without the consequence of children could not be love. Sanger argued that even if a couple only had sex once a year, the wife would likely have 10 or 12 children by the end of her child bearing years, and what she called sex love should not be restricted to three or four times in an entire marriage. Gandhi thought that it would be a good idea for husband and wife to sleep apart after three or four children.

Sanger pointed to medical evidence showing the physiological problems associated with abstinence, but Gandhi dismissed it. He thought that the sample patients were all imbeciles rather than healthy minded people to start with. He even suggested that separation and divorce were preferable in instances when couples could not practice self-restraint and it led to mental illness. Gandhi thought that a big difference between he and Sanger was not the difference between East and West or man and woman but their generation gap; he felt that his generation was committed to self-restraint whereas Sanger's was committed to the multiplication of wants and desires. He did not think that high fertility was a problem of the poor in India, but of the middle class where indulgence was running riot. The starving could not be fertile after all.

***

When the National Planning Committee was formed in 1938, one amongst its 27 subcommittees was devoted to the population issue. The subcommittee was chaired by Radhakamal Mukherjee, an economist from Lucknow University and was primarily made up of subject matter experts. The subcommittee presented its report in 1940, and whilst expressing some concern over India's rising population, it did not betray a sense of alarm. The effort was to examine how economic planning could be used to serve a large and growing population.

A focus of the subcommittee's report was on the creation of a planned food policy which would necessitate reforms of the agricultural sector. The subcommittee noted the deteriorating food supply situation and recommended an agricultural pattern which would increase the production of heavy yielding and energy producing crops. Besides reform of Indian agriculture the subcommittee recommended a range of social reforms including improvements in diet and food preparation, reform of marriage customs, the dissemination of birth control information among the masses "to prevent the deterioration of the racial makeup" and even a programme of eugenics to encourage inter-caste marriages. The subcommittee recommended including courses on contraception in all medical colleges and establishing birth control clinics which would be attached to maternity welfare centres, health units and hospitals in which contraceptives would be provided for free. Encouragement was also to be given to the local manufacture of artificial contraceptives to bring their cost within the reach of the masses and a programme of propaganda was to be launched by the municipalities, district boards and village councils in favour of spacing the birth of children to limit the size of families to six.

The Health Survey and Development Committee, which came to be known as the Bhore Committee after its chairman, Sir Joseph Bhore, a retired Indian Civil Service officer, issued its report in 1946. The National Planning Committee was made up of nationalists, whereas the members of the Bhore Committee were largely loyalists, mainly titled Indians, Rai Bahadurs and Khan Bahadurs, and Indian officers of government hospitals and health departments. The Health Survey was just that, long and thorough, and its treatment of the population issue came in a small section in the second volume of its report. The Bhore Committee's recommendations betrayed its social composition. The committee was reluctant to too emphatically call for an increase in the age of marriage due to the inherent social conservatism of its members. Yet they had few links to the Congress or any pressing political need to assuage the feelings of Gandhi and his followers and so were able to be more forthright in dismissing self-control as a means of limiting family size.

Whilst most members of the Bhore Committee agreed that contraception should be practiced in the interests of women's health, some saw any state programme for birth control as only being likely to succeed with support from public opinion. The committee doubted the existence of this public opinion; women were not sufficiently educated to effectively practice contraception, the people were poor, and so the cost of the state placing contraceptives in their hands would be enormous, birth control would have to be imparted to the women of India by female doctors and nurses of whom there were only about 2,000 in the whole country, and "certain communities" looked on contraception with disfavour for religious reasons. It did not seem therefore that a birth control movement would be successful in applying a check to population growth in the immediate future. Any such programme would need to be preceded by widespread educational work to convince the people of its desirability for health and social reasons. The committee was aware that the population would continue to rise, but besides an education programme, the only the thing the government could do was to work to raise the standard of living to bring the birth rate down.

India's population had been rising since the end of the First World War as a result of a rapidly declining death rate and a buoyant birth rate. The trend was still new in 1931 and so it did not receive a great deal of attention from John Hatton in his Census report. Hatton thought that the declining death rate was the result of improved methods of fighting epidemics such as cholera, plague and kala azar. He thought that the case of kala azar, or black fever was particularly illustrative. A treatment had been discovered as early as 1913 but at that time it took three months to apply and so did little to prevent an epidemic, but by 1917 the treatment had been reduced to one month and by the 1920s it was only ten days or fewer.

Between the censuses of 1931 and 1941 the Indian population grew by another 37 million. The total population now stood at 389 million. The birth rate was once again stable at 34.6, and the death rate once again declined to 23.3. The Commissioner of the 1941 Census, William Yeatts was able to note a 20 year trend of declining mortality for mothers and infants as well as mortality for the main epidemic diseases such as cholera and the plague. The Public Health Commissioner's figures showed that half a million fewer Indians died of cholera in the 1920s than they did in the previous decade and the mortality rate continued to decline. A million lives were also saved due to the diminution of plague. Yeatts saw the effect of protective health measures and the potential of preventative measures. Satya Swaroop, a statistician with the Indian Medical Service attempted to project India's population for the decades ahead assuming a continued decline in infant mortality. He assumed that the birth rate and the death rate would continue on their trend line from 1921 and projected that by 1961 the decline in infant mortality alone would have added another 13 million people to the Indian population.

On the eve of Independence it was apparent that India had a population problem. One of the books most widely read by college students during the 1940s was *India's Teeming Millions: A Contribution to the Study of the Indian Population Problem* by Gyan Chand. The source of the problem was not difficult to isolate; a stationary birth rate combined with a steadily declining death rate meant that India was adding 30 or 40 or 50 million people to its population each decade. The reason for the declining birth rate was not so clear however. Hatton and Yeatts had not spent a lot of time on the topic but their assertions that the declining death rate had been the result of better treatment and prevention of epidemic diseases was partially true. Although it was not apparent at the time, decades later demographers were able to deduce that the dramatic fall in the death rate in India was in fact due to the lower lethality of epidemic diseases, but that this had occurred largely due to the development of natural immunity rather than the administration of vaccines, or preventative measures such as better sanitation.[cccxxvii]

From the period of the first census in 1871 until the end of the First World War and the taking of the Census in 1921 India had sustained a high death rate to balance its high birth rate and population growth had been moderate. It was this high birth rate and high death rate, indicative of short, hard lives that first concerned P.K. Wattal. In 1921 John Marten attributed the high death rate to famines, plagues and diseases like influenza. However, most of the deaths occurring in India between 1871 and

1921 came not from these sensational diseases, but from more regular ones; malaria killed a million Indians annually, whilst pneumonia and respiratory illnesses were the leading causes of death. Tuberculosis, typhoid, cholera, measles, puerperal fever and smallpox were other major killers. Other diseases killed fewer yet still had a significant impact on mortality: diphtheria, tetanus, black fever, hepatitis, scarlet fever, syphilis, encephalitis, enteric fever, typhus and blackwater fever.

Until the First World War India was an ideal spreading ground for these diseases. The land was modernising, transport was improving, ports were being opened up and labour was more mobile. But this modernisation coexisted with poverty, lack of sanitation, overcrowding in towns and cities and inadequate medical care, all of which worked on a poorly immune population. Government health and sanitation programmes after the First World War only covered a tiny proportion of the population and could only have limited impact on diseases such as malaria and cholera. However, from around the time of the First World War malaria was becoming much less lethal, immunities had been developed over a century or more and the disease was becoming increasingly benign in places where it had previously wiped out entire villages. Indians were even developing immunity to plague. Mothers were passing immunity on to their newborns resulting in lower infant mortality. These natural immunities were impacting the declining death rate eight times more intensively than the government's limited measures for sanitation or the provision of medical treatments.

***

After Independence the Planning Commission created a Health Panel which was chaired by the Health Minister, Amrit Kaur, a member of the royal family of the erstwhile princely state of Kapurthala in Punjab. Dhanvanthi Rama Rau, founder and President of the Family Planning

Association of India and wife of Sir Benegal Rama Rau, Governor of the Reserve Bank of India, suggested including family planning in the panel's ambit, but was firmly opposed by the health minister.[cccxxviii] Lady Rama Rau received support from some of the non-government members on the panel, and the minister eventually relented. Family planning was included in the Health Panel on the condition that "no contraceptives should be used".[cccxxix] The panel then appointed a Subcommittee on Population Growth and Family Planning in April 1951. The subcommittee was convened by the Census Commissioner, Ramaswami Ayyangar Gopalaswami and included Gyan Chand, the mathematician Amiya Charan Banerjee, the writer Nripendra Kumar Basu, the demographer Chidambara Chandrasekharan, Dr. Sushila Nayyar, and Lady Rama Rau.

The subcommittee recommend lowering the birth rate in order to ensure the success of programmes for health and economic development, and also advocated proper spacing and limitation of births to enhance family welfare, the health and welfare of mothers and children, and ensure adequate resources to raise each child, as well as investment in a research centre for birth control techniques based on knowledge available abroad.[cccxxx] Importantly, the subcommittee did favour government support for sterilisation and the provision of advice on contraception. This was to be practiced to the extent that staff in clinics and hospitals could provide such advice whilst not impacting their existing responsibilities. Lady Rama Rau thought that this clause was overly restrictive and in her supplementary note argued for a separate birth control department in all existing and future government medical facilities, as well as for free birth control information and literature being made available all over the country.[cccxxxi] Dr. Sushila Nayyar, a physician to Mohandas Gandhi during his last years who had recently returned to India after postgraduate training in the United States, firmly disagreed with Lady Rama Rau.[cccxxxii] She thought that the priorities for the state were the promotion of education and economic development, which, if achieved, would create the right incentives for parents to limit the size of their families. The most that the state should do was to not interfere with any non-government organisations which wanted to promote family planning. Any efforts by the state were doomed to failure; success could only come from education and economic development. Dr. Nayyar advocated self-control and increasing the marriage age as better alternatives to artificial contraception.

The population policy of the First Five Year Plan largely conformed to Dr. Sushila Nayyar's thinking. It was as yet a tentative policy statement, with many injunctions for further research and study of demographics and family planning techniques. Yet one of the firm proposals which it did make was that government clinics and hospitals should give family planning advice, primarily for the health of mothers and children, whilst providing education for a reduction of the birth rate. The principal technique for birth control was to be the rhythm method in which sex was avoided in the days close to a woman's menstruation when she was most fertile. Forms of contraception, whether biological or mechanical could be advised to women whose health might be endangered by pregnancy.

A Family Planning Research and Programme Committee was appointed in May 1953. Cheruvari Krishnan Lakshmanan, Director Health Services, a former Olympic athlete and major-general of the Indian Army was chairman. Much of the research on the rhythm method during the First Plan period centred around the "coloured beads" experiment. Dr. Abraham Stone, an American family planning expert had devised a "rosary" with 28 beads, each representing one day. The first four beads represented the menstrual days. The "safe period" which started five days after menstruation was signified by green beads whilst the "danger period" leading up to menstruation was signalled by red beads.

The committee found that there were 165 family planning centres in the country run by the government and voluntary organisations, and in addition to these there were also centres run by people not qualified for the job and other centres run for profit.[cccxxxiii] The committee thus recommended the provision of a minimum staff for family planning centres which would include one qualified doctor, a public health nurse and a social worker. The committee also wanted clinical trials of contraceptives, field studies on social attitudes and motivations affecting family planning, and long range studies on host factors, environmental factors and agent factors.

The 1951 Census report was released towards the end of 1953. India had lost about one-fifth of its population to the partition of the land which meant that there were some discontinuities and anomalies with the censuses of the previous decades. The population was now estimated at 360 million. This meant that despite losing 20% of its people, the population of independent India had only declined by less than 10%. The reason was the persistent imbalance between the birth and death rates. The birth rate had increased to 40 per 1,000 of the population, whereas the death rate was still much lower at 27 per 1,000.

In February 1954, the Ministry of Health announced that it had accepted the recommendations of the Family Planning Research and Programme Committee and offered the states assistance for the delivery of family planning services on a sliding scale: the ministry would cover the full amount of the programme expenses for the first six months, and then for the following year it would cover one-third.[cccxxxiv] Funding was provided to 15 states, 8 local councils and 35 voluntary organisations. New centres were started- 147 in total, including 27 in rural areas. Financial assistance was also provided for the Contraceptive Testing Unit in the Indian Cancer Research Centre which had been established in collaboration by the

Government of India and the Sir Dorabji Tata Trust in Bombay. A clinic for field trials was established in Naigaum, north of Bombay in September 1956.

After one of its early meetings the Family Planning Research and Programme Committee visited the Godfrey Clinic in Bombay. The clinic provided family planning, maternity and paediatric services to the shipyard workers of the Indian Navy and their families.[cccxxxv] Dr. Sushila Gore, who had travelled to Scandanavia to study family planning techniques managed the clinic. The Godfrey Clinic had been providing courses of instruction with the support of the non-government Family Planning Association of India. The committee then recommended that Dr. Gore be appointed to run a Family Planning Training Centre. She was made Officer on Special Duty in the Directorate General of Health Services in June 1955 and the Centre began operations in March 1957 in the old Parakh Hospital building on Sandhurst Road. The building was acquired by the Ministry of Health and courses of instruction were provided in birth control, sex education, marriage counselling and human behaviour. A baby clinic and a day care centre were also established. The education programme was still limited however. There was a lack of clarity over the precise message to be conveyed as well as some concern that providing education about birth control without adequate availability of services and devices might affect the credibility of the programme.

Sir V.T. Krishnamachari, Deputy Chairman of the Planning Commission had been concerned at the slow progress being made by the family planning programme and had been in touch with Douglas Ensminger, Head of the Ford Foundation in India.[cccxxxvi] He had suggested the creation of an autonomous Family Planning Institute in India which might receive initial funding from the Foundation. Prime Minister Jawaharlal Nehru was said to be supportive of the idea, but Ensminger could not get the required approval from his head office in New York. The Ford

Foundation was as yet hesitant to provide direct support to family planning programs, whether at home or abroad due to the possibility of a backlash from conservative religious groups in America. Sir Krishnamachari then suggested that Ensminger approach the Health Minister, Amrit Kaur with the idea of an informal mission of the New York based Population Council. She agreed, and Leona Baumgarnter, New York City Health Commissioner, and Frank Notestein, Head of Princeton University's Demographic Centre arrived in India. Leona Baumgartner was also hesitant to be associated with a "Family Planning Mission", informal as it was.[cccxxxvii] John D. Rockefeller III provided a solution. He funded the visit, and also suggested that she travel to India as a member of a "Maternity and Child Welfare Project".[cccxxxviii]

Leona Baumgartner and Frank Notestein submitted their report to Amrit Kaur in December 1955.[cccxxxix] They recommended the establishment of a semi-autonomous institution, a board which would draw officials from the ministries of health and finance and the Community Development Programme and eminent persons and experts in the field which would devise the broad policies to be implemented by the government departments. Baumgartner and Notestein also advocated the creation of a fuller research structure and provided a detailed proposal for a Centre for Demographic Training and Research. For birth control they recommended focusing on three methods- rhythm, coitus interruption, and foam tablets. Foam tablets were supposed to be much cheaper than jelly and diaphragms.

The Government of India acted on Leona Baumgartner and Frank Notestein's recommendations. A Demographic Training and Research Centre was established in July 1956, a Central Family Planning Board was created in September and foam tablets were distributed on a wider scale. Colonel Bishen Lal Raina, a former army doctor, took charge as Director of the Family Planning Cell in September 1956. In 1957 Amrit Kaur retired as health minister and was replaced by Dattatraya Parasuram Karmarkar. The new health minister did not share his predecessor's reservations about artificial methods of birth control. He supported adding sterilisation onto the list of officially approved methods. Karmarkar also encouraged a shift from publicity to education and more schemes to collect information on the disposition of couples to family planning. During Karmarkar's tenure facilities were created for mass communication, community education and imparting technical knowledge and skills. Mobile teams were formed which included a health educator, a doctor, and a volunteer family planning educator. During the Second Plan the number of centres delivering family planning services rose from 147 to 4,165.[cccxl] D.P. Karmarkar was also a proponent of identifying natural groups and group leaders in villages who might be used to communicate the family planning message, which by now was that two or three children were enough. The staff of these centres were urged to work in the field and organise groups and mothers' clubs with the assistance of village leaders, who were known as parivar kalyan sahayaks and sahayakas, or family welfare helpers.

Whilst the proliferation of clinics seemed impressive on paper, in reality the opening of a clinic in rural India generally involved adding just one more worker to an already overburdened primary health clinic. On average each clinic had to serve a population of 66,000.[cccxli] These new family planning workers were given at most two months training, and sometimes none at all whilst being expected to motivate, educate and screen their clients and supply them with contraceptives. Recruiting such a large number to work in rural India which had sufficient qualifications in health care or social work was a difficult task and so in some cases personal qualities were substituted for educational qualifications.[cccxlii]

By 1959 bureaucrats in the states were taking their own measures to control the population. R. A. Gopalaswami, the former census commissioner had become chief secretary of Madras and decided to initiate a ₹30 rupee payment to anyone undergoing sterilisation and ₹15 to the motivator who delivered them to the clinic. Gopalaswami had come to the conclusion that sterilisation was the only solution for the "large mass of the people" who would not space pregnancies or limit their family size except under government duress.[cccxliii] The Central Family Planning Board also made sure that sterilisations would be performed free of charge at 3,000 hospitals across the country and those undergoing the operations would be compensated for their travel and lost work expenses.[cccxliv] Sterilisations were undertaken during a 5 week intensive family planning campaign in Maharashtra in 1960 in which 10,000 men were sterilised. In 1962 158,000 Indians, three quarters of them men, were sterilised.[cccxlv]

The Health Survey and Planning Committee, better known as the Mudaliar Committee, reported in 1961 and found that the family planning programme had proved largely inadequate and wanted it transformed into a mass movement. In order for this to happen non-government organisations such as the Indian Family Planning Association needed to be supported with government aid. The committee emphasised that there needed to be more supplies of contraceptives, either from Indian production or from imports, more information, and better co-ordination with other government programmes such as the Community Development Programme.

The Central Family Planning Board endorsed what came to be known as the "reorganised programme" in April 1963. Until this point the clinic had been the primary hub of family planning to which clients came for a medical examination and provision of contraceptives. The board thought that an extension approach would reach the masses quicker.[cccxlvi] Extension education would be provided, there would be greater availability of contraceptives, and less dependence on the clinic approach. The stated aim was to reduce the birth rate from 40 to 25 per 1,000 by 1973. This was to occur by getting 90% of married couples to accept the smaller family norm, provide them with knowledge of family planning methods and make supplies and services more easily available. The new blueprint provided for one auxiliary nurse-midwife for every 10,000 of the population. These nurse-midwives were supposed to educate women on family planning, manage supplies of contraceptives and refer cases for sterilisation, in addition to their regular workload of providing maternal and child health services. There would also be one male worker per 20,000-30,000 of the population who would perform similar duties. The rural family planning unit would cover one development block and the family planning unit would be attached to the block health unit. Each block unit would need a female medical officer as well as a full time family planning extension officer. There would be a Family Planning Bureau at the district level which would have the staff and supplies to support the programme in all blocks in the district. The Government of India accepted the blueprint for a reorganised family planning programme and in October 1963 issued a circular to the states outlining the financial and organisation structure of the new programme.

The 1961 Census report was released at the end of 1963. The Indian population had, over the previous decade, which coincided with the government's first serious attempts to control the growth of the population, risen by 80 million. The population of India now stood at almost 440 million. Furthermore, family planning initiatives had no discernible impact on the fertility rate. The birth rate had actually increased to 41.7, whilst the death rate had once again declined to 22.8.

The Planning Commission's Programme Evaluation Organisation examined the family planning programmes in the states in 1964 and early 1965 and reported back in the summer of 1965.[cccxlvii] Their aim was to examine the "current and emerging problems" in the Reorganised

Family Planning Programme. The evaluators reported that there were 3,195 family planning units at the district and block levels and 80% were managed by state governments. In Kerala there was one unit for 48,000 people. In Bihar one unit serviced 715,000 people. Each unit had only one full time worker. Workers were not aware of what precisely they were supposed to do and with whom, job descriptions and supervisory methods were unknown, and the local leaders had not been properly trained in ways to promote family planning in their areas. There were usually not enough supervisors and support from district family planning committees was weak, often because full time district staff was not available to guide the committees. Those at work in the field were not getting the salary, service benefits and allowances that other workers with similar qualifications in the health services received. The staff shortages were being attributed to the lack of appeal of working conditions. The states did not think that they had long term support for funding their programmes. Only a little over half the funds were being spent. The Reorganised Programme had been launched in the middle of the Third Plan period so the states would not allocate budgets for beyond the end of the Plan. In the state capitals the officer in charge of family planning was usually an assistant director when, in order to get resources and co-operation he needed to be a deputy director of health services. State family planning boards were often moribund.

***

Whilst metal devices had been inserted into wombs as early as the 18th century it was only in the late 1950s that a device made of a new type of plastic, polyethylene, allowed for the manufacture of various types of intrauterine contraceptive devices such as spirals, loops and coils. These new devices were trialled around the world and the national conference of the Population Council, New York evaluated the results in May 1962.

Shortly thereafter trials were initiated in India under the auspices of the Indian Council of Medical Research.

Fifty clinical studies were undertaken between August 1962 and October 1964 according to a uniform pattern across the country using both the loop and the spiral. The Indian Council of Medical Research's Advisory Committee on Scientific Aspects of Family Planning assessed the results of the trials in January 1965 and found that the loop was preferable to the spiral: it had to be removed due to discomfort in 5.27% of women, whilst it was naturally expelled from the body in 4.89% of the sample.[cccxlviii] The loop had resulted in pregnancy in only 0.46% of cases. When it was naturally expelled from the body it was successfully reinserted in almost three-quarters of all cases. The committee thus endorsed the loop as safe and effective and recommended its manufacture in India.[cccxlix] The committee did however recommend that only trained physicians be allowed to insert the device. The Government of India accepted the committee's recommendations.

By July of 1965 Dr. Sushila Nayyar, now the health minister, began to promote the use of the loop. She claimed that it was simple and efficacious and would soon become the most popular method of family planning.[cccl] The loop had the added benefit that it could be removed whenever a woman wanted to have a child, whereas the reversal of a sterilisation was a much more complex procedure. Dr. Nayyar claimed that trials had shown that there were no physical injuries to women as a result of the insertion of the device. There was some pain and bleeding for a few days after insertion, but this was not unbearable. The Population Council of New York had already sent 600,000 loops, whilst another 600,000 were on the way. The Government of India intended to distribute one million over the coming year, however that figure could well be exceeded. In addition, a factory had been established at Kanpur to manufacture the device.

Distribution of the loop had already started and over the previous two months 20,000 had been inserted, 4,000 in Delhi alone, and demand was increasing rapidly. Dr. Nayyar claimed that the device was not just popular among urban women; she quoted a health officer at Hoshangabad in rural Madhya Pradesh who maintained that women there were coming forward in greater numbers asking for the new device. By the time of the Fourth Plan, due to start the following year, it would be possible to take the loop to all the villages of the country and the sterilisation programme would gradually diminish as people seemed to prefer the loop. A few days later Dr. Nayyar announced a "crash programme" to popularise the loop among the masses.[cccli] She envisaged mobile units carrying out the programme in rural areas. The loops would be provided free of charge and supplied to private doctors and other social organisations which could help with distribution.

The loop had been in use in India for almost a year before the inventor of the device visited the country in May 1966 at the invitation of the Government of India. Dr. Jack Lippes, a gynaecologist from Buffalo, New York spent the summer travelling to the states where the loop had been incorporated into the family planning programme and visited the factory at Kanpur. He claimed that his invention had a 99% success rate.[ccclii] He promoted its inexpensiveness; it cost only 10 paise, took only 6 minutes to insert, lasted indefinitely, and was ideal for Indian conditions. Addressing a press conference in Bombay, he told reporters that 2 million loops had already been used by women in Asia, the Middle East and North America and he was pleased to know that 130,000 had already been administered in Maharashtra alone over the previous year.[cccliii] He had heard that the loop was popular in West Bengal and Punjab, but also that the response in Bihar and Uttar Pradesh had been disappointing. Some concerns had been raised that the device might cause cancer and he took the opportunity to refute them: no foreign body could ever cause cancer;

the human body had been hosting foreign matter ever since horse hair had been used to stitch up cuts.[ccclvi] Later in Madras Dr. Lippes advocated making the loop a "routine appliance", one made available at all hospitals and dispensaries across the country.[ccclv] He made several recommendations to the Government of India before ending his tour, mainly focusing on education and training for medical staff and making family planning work more attractive. He also recommended offering incentives for doctors, canvassers and volunteering women.[ccclvi]

By the end of June Dr. Sushila Nayyar announced a target of 6 million insertions for the coming year.[ccclvii] This was based on the figure of 20 insertions per 1,000 of the population in urban areas, and 10 per 1,000 in rural areas. Thirty highly populated districts were being taken up for intensive work. These districts would be subject to higher targets which would make it possible to bring the birth rate down within a year or two. Dr. Nayyar noted that the Planning Commission was concerned about how much this accelerated programme would cost but she urged state governments to start training centres straight away. Two hundred doctors were being recruited by the Government of India and their services would be made available to the state governments. Dr. Nayyar was heartened that the loop had been accepted by the people: until March 1966, roughly the first year of the programme, 804,504 women had accepted the device.

The first sounds of discontent came in September when the governments of Maharashtra, Mysore, Punjab, Uttar Pradesh and West Bengal all refused to accept the targets set by the Government of India.[ccclviii] They fixed their own targets, which were between half and a quarter of the Centre's figures. A stalemate ensued as the Centre refused to revise its overall national target of 6 million insertions and instead advised the states to "endeavour to work towards the achievement of the targets already suggested." The dissident states, barring Uttar Pradesh, had all achieved their targets for the previous year but all thought that the new targets were unrealistic.

It was also in September that the first reports of women requesting "de-looping" began to surface.[ccclix] Women were complaining of constant bleeding after insertion of the loop and were lamenting that they were being made to suffer. Many of these complaints were being made in Delhi which had been an early adopter of the programme. In West Bengal there was even a political campaign against the loop in rural areas; opponents of the government were claiming that it was enforcing family planning as a ruse because it was reluctant to enforce fair distribution of food supplies.[ccclx] Some private doctors were even working against the programme in the state, refusing to treat women unless they had the loop removed and bureaucrats were also partial to sterilisation for couples with three or more children. By December these concerns were being reported from states across the country. There were "exaggerated statements" and "false rumours" about the after effects of loop insertions as well as opposition from private doctors and midwives.[ccclxi] The Centre had lowered its target somewhat, from 6 million to 4 million, but as of September only 382,000 insertions had been recorded nationwide, or 9% of the revised target.[ccclxii] The reasons cited for the deteriorating progress of the programme were a lack of follow up medical attention and pain relieving medicines for women and their inadequate preparation and education. The vilification campaign against the loop was being blamed on vested interests- mainly manufacturers of the contraceptive pill.[ccclxiii]

Uttar Pradesh, the largest state in the Union, was reaching just a quarter of its relatively modest pre-revised targets and it was becoming evident that the success or failure of the programme would depend on health infrastructure and staffing in the states.[ccclxiv] Little had changed since the Planning Commission's report in 1965. There was only one training centre of any note in all of Uttar Pradesh and that was in the capital

Lucknow.[ccclxv] Shortages of doctors, particularly female doctors as well as midwives were being reported in Kashmir.[ccclxvi] A similar story emerged from Mysore where the family planning administration was well staffed at the higher levels in the capital with a band of enthusiastic officials and their clerks, drivers, storekeepers and peons, but suffered a shortage of doctors, nurses and midwives in the districts.[ccclxvii] It was becoming evident that the problem was not a shortage of money or supplies but of trained workers who were willing to work where they had been posted.

By January of 1967 the New Delhi Municipal Corporation was reporting a "de-looping" rate of 25%.[ccclxviii] The Corporation had administered 1,000 loops during 1966 and 250 of them had to be removed. This rejection rate was close to the national average. By the end of 1967 it was reported that 30% of women who had received the loop could not retain it or complained of bleeding or backaches.[ccclxix] Field tests worldwide were starting show that, much like in India, about a quarter of women experienced minor complications, usually within the first three months of receiving the loop. Dr. Lippes's claim of 99% success might have been in reference to the rate of pregnancy prevention, whilst the Indian field trials' rate of rejection of 5-10% may have reflected strict standards, laboratory controls and the provision of vitamin supplements. Some of the blame may have laid with medical staff who did not select a loop of the correct size for each patient. Follow up care was also required which was largely absent, and so it seemed that the loop was just not suitable for the mobile clinic method of mass distribution. The Family Planning Department in New Delhi had directed the Small Industries Service Institute in April to make a die for an improved loop which would be made at the Kanpur factory.[ccclxx] It was thought that a "loop in loop" design would reduce the abrasion from the pointed end of the loop which was responsible for the bleeding and pain.

The Kanpur factory did not have time to start manufacturing an improved loop. By March of 1968 it was facing closure.[ccclxxi] Half the loops the factory had produced were piling up. There was a stockpile of 1 million loops for which there was no demand. The factory had been exporting loops, however even international demand was falling. Studies were showing that across the world only half of the women who received the device were still using it after two years.[ccclxxii] Dr. Lippes had earlier estimated that 10 million loops would have to be inserted each year to have any appreciable effect on the birth rate.[ccclxxiii] The Government of India had aimed for 6 million, and then 4 million. By early 1969 it seemed unlikely that the number of insertions would touch half a million.

***

The problems with the Government of India's ambitious targets for loop insertions lay partly in the technology and partly in its delivery. Dr. Jack Lippes's loop was not quite the simple and effective technology it had been claimed to be. Field trials both in India and across the world in the early 1960s had been conducted under ideal conditions. When the loop began to be delivered in greater numbers after 1965 it had to encounter the real world. Women complained of pain and bleeding and so the rejection rate came to 25% or 50% rather than the 5% or 10% anticipated from the field trials. In addition, the loop had to be delivered by India's underfunded and understaffed public health system.

Reports by Government of India committees, the Planning Commission, the Indian media and international agencies had all documented the problems of staffing and infrastructure faced by the public health system across the country. A more intimate and illuminating account however was left by a young American Peace Corps volunteer. Carl Pope had graduated from Harvard College in the spring of 1967 and landed in India at the end of the year with his wife Judy. They were members of the Peace Corps' India 51 programme. Carl and Judy had received some training in Lexington, Kentucky prior to departure, and then a bit more at Rajgir, Bihar once they arrived "in-country". The couple were to work for two years on the family planning programme in a cluster of villages in southern Bihar. They came at the wrong time. The loop, the centrepiece of family planning over the previous couple of years was falling into disrepute. In addition, Bihar, the poorest state in India, had just been on the verge of famine. Nonetheless, Carl Pope left an account of his time promoting family planning in Bihar in his book *Sahib: An American Misadventure in India*.

Carl and Judy met Dr. Usha Narayan, who would be working with Judy in supervising the female family planning staff, as well as Mr. Kumar, the block development officer, as they were drinking tea. Both emphasised that the main problem was that the staff did not work. They were unmotivated and lazy. But despite its staff, the programme had been going well until the chief doctor, Dr. Agarwal, who had performed the most male sterilisations in Bihar over the previous year, had to leave for Calcutta to be with his ill son. That left Dr. Narayan in charge. But only for a week, before she was to take up an appointment at another hospital. The extension educator who was to be Carl's co-worker had recently resigned. Yet the extension educator's resignation had not been accepted, which meant that no one could be sent to replace him. Carl and Judy then met B.P. Katriar, the mukhia, or chief of Barhi. He owned a food storage plant, the town's only industry, and had contacts in the state government and the Congress Party. Kumar had told Katriar of the Americans' arrival and thought he might be able to arrange some accommodation for them.

Carl and Judy were to be the catalysts of an educational programme in family planning. Carl decided to check out the heavy register which held the names and addresses of the 2,000 men who had undergone sterilisations over the previous year. He wanted to do a rough census of the areas in which progress had been made, and those where the work was just beginning. Several villages had the same name, Tiliya, whilst some places mentioned in the register did not appear on the map. After filling out a map with dots and stars he came to the conclusion that about 10% of eligible men in the block had either had vasectomies themselves, or their wives had received the loop. Judy had seen more action than Carl during Dr. Narayan's last week in Barhi. Women had been coming in to get the loop inserted. Judy assisted both the doctor and the nurse with the insertions, observing the arguments between the doctors and the patients, attempts to keep the women in line, and the need for endless book-keeping. At the end of it, 70 women had been fitted with the loop. Family planning did not seem so difficult after all.

The government was offering ₹6 to any woman who had the loop inserted and ₹1 to the person who 'persuaded' her. Men who were sterilised received ₹25. The women thronging Dr. Narayan's house were all poor. In the first two days alone 160 loops had been inserted. The following day the local pharmacist explained what was really happening. He showed Carl a mass of dirty strings. They then found 32 loops from the first day's insertions behind the dispensary. These 32 women had collected their ₹6. The village midwife had been the real winner. She received a total of ₹64: ₹1 each for persuading the women to have them inserted and ₹1 each for the removals. "A very good business, isn't it?" He tossed Carl the plastic snakes and threads, bits of dirt, flesh and blood on some of them. Carl knew that all he had to do was search around for the other 128 loops. He would find them all. He now had to ask himself: "What did the little dots on my map really mean?"

Carl and Judy cycled to the Kariatpur Family Planning Centre and met the Family Planning Worker, Priog

Mandel. Carl was at the same level as an extension educator, and in the absence of the doctor and the extension educator, was something like Priog's boss. On their visit to Bersot, Carl introduced himself in his halting Hindi and explained the purpose of his visit and the family planning programme. The villagers agreed on the necessity for family planning and assured him that Bersot was one of the leaders among local villages; over 50 of its men had undergone a vasectomy. But they were more concerned with irrigation. Carl pleaded that he could not help with irrigation, but tried to make a connection between the government's inability to provide more irrigation and India's large population; the government had to spend so much on schools and famine relief that there was not enough left over for development work.

Carl and Priog then went out to Dulmaha. If he been doing his job Priog should have known the leaders of the village well, but he had to ask for their names in Kariatpur before leaving, something which alarmed Carl. Priog did not even know how to get to the village. Upon arrival they spoke with a group of Muslims who evinced no interest in family planning at all. Whilst there was no Koranic injunction against family planning, there was no sura in its favour, and so until the time came when they might be desperate enough for ₹25 there was really no need to make life any tougher than it already was. Priog later emphasised the point that the Muslims were all "dead against" family planning. Carl thought that Priog was quite defeatist; he would be engaging and lively off the job, but then leave the task of explaining family planning to the American when actually faced with villagers. Priog thought that the villagers were all ignorant, barely a high school graduate among them; "No wonder I can't get anywhere." Carl felt that what he really wanted was life in an office or a school. He was supposed to be the government's instrument for the family planning programme, but he was an unwilling one at best. When Dr. Agarwal returned from Calcutta after his son's death he largely echoed Priog's sentiments; the staff have no real idea what the work means or how to do it, and we can make no progress until we do something about the Muslims.

Carl and Judy decided that they had to shake the villagers' faith in the idea that children were a gift from God and also convey a seemingly foreign idea- 'planning'. They made a series of simple diagrams, and with a box of condoms headed to the monthly meeting. Yet when Dr. Agarwal arrived he was more interested in correcting the registers and setting a target for each of the staff for the month. Each of the male workers would have to bring in 20 men for vasectomies, whilst each female worker would have to bring in 20 women for loop insertions. This would help the block to reach the targets set by the Hazaribagh District Office. The Popes had other ideas, specifically, slow education, and given that Dr. Agarwal himself recognised that the targets were unrealistic, and that the staff would not be penalised for not meeting them, they seemed largely pointless. When Judy pointed out that the targets for loop insertions were unrealistic given that there was no lady doctor, Dr. Agarwal thought it was not a bad thing; the village women were not suited to the loop which had too many complications:

> *It will be better if we can't insert them. But we must give the nurses targets anyway. If we don't they won't know what is expected and won't work. If we prepare the case and cannot do the insertion for lack of a Lady Doctor, we can always indicate in our quarterly report, 'so many cases prepared but not inserted due to absence of assigned Lady Doctor.' So no problem there.*

The Popes then a gave a little presentation on condom use. The workers seemed receptive and Dr. Agarwal gave

The Licence Raj

an instruction that supplies of condoms be carried by the staff: "Enter that in the record". More orders were given, and minutes taken, but not distributed to staff. Dr. Agarwal explained: "If we didn't write the orders down, then we wouldn't have a record. And next month when the staff comes in and hasn't followed them, we wouldn't be able to prove we gave them." Distributing the minutes to staff however would discourage them from listening at meetings.

Whilst Dr. Agarwal was not too worried about the absence of a lady doctor, Dr. Gope, the civil surgeon at Hazaribagh had too many of them, and so decided to send one to Barhi each week to oversee the loop insertions. On the following Friday, the midwives brought the village women in an hour before the stipulated time of eleven in the morning. They waited until twelve when they would have to return and prepare lunch. The lady doctor arrived at two to find no patients. Judy intervened and explained the situation which saved the nurse from a scolding. The lady doctor came early the following Friday and they sent a jeep out to collect the women. It returned empty; it was a feast day, and so considered unclean to have the loop inserted. A week later the women did arrive to find no jeep and no lady doctor. Carl got on the phone to the civil surgeon at Hazaribagh. The sahib was out to lunch. It turned out that the jeep had not left for Barhi because he had been busy and had not had the time to give the lady doctor the keys and money for petrol.

Dr. Agarwal's drift into English at the monthly meetings tended to cause some problems. Most of the staff could not understand what he was saying. The records had to be kept in English and Carl thought that the ideas they contained had been learned in English. Dr. Agarwal would have struggled with his record keeping in Hindi- his neat narrow columns may have been disturbed by replacing one or two English words with a long winded Hindi phrase or paragraph. But then the record would bear no relationship to the work, or lack of it, going on in the fields. The Hindi job was to go out into the villages, try to promote awareness of family planning by adding a bit to the village lore, and then come back to the office and make sure that the attempt found its way into the circular movement of paper. Incongruously Carl had the Hindi job. However, the Health Ministry was more interested in the English job which revolved around registers and files. Staff would visit selected couples, undertake surveys, and persuade families to adopt family planning. Each directive from the Ministry would be associated with a new bit of book-keeping. The staff interpreted the order through the new book-keeping which would result from it. They would satisfy their superiors by completing the book-keeping rather than the task it was supposed to record.

Carl had a new colleague to work with when the extension educator, Ram Sewak Sinha arrived. Ram Sewak was much more enthusiastic and diligent than Priog Mandel. Loop insertions had been tried and largely dismissed as a tamasha, or show, whilst sterilisations seemed to have an air of coercion about them with the village chief using his authority over poor men to fill up numbers. A touring doctor however thought that condom use might catch on just as tea drinking had. Back during the days of the Second World War hardly anyone drank tea. Then the Tea Board went into the villages giving out free samples. The villagers gradually took to it and now could not start their day without a morning cup. The orders were piling up on Dr. Agarwal's desk to increase condom use, and so Carl and Ram Sewak were able to convince him to support their idea.

Rather than creating a new communications channel, Carl and Ram Sewak would use an existing one. Free condoms would be distributed through schoolteachers. The teachers were under the supervision of Mr. Kumar, whose social circle included those more likely to use the condoms; educated peasants and salaried workers. There was a supply of 600 condoms, but disagreement about how many each man would need in a month. It was agreed that six would be given to each recipient. Therefore 100 men would receive the condoms in the first month. Twenty five teachers would find friends who would use them. The following month they were able to double the supply, and according to Ram Sewak's information 45 teachers were themselves using condoms. By January of 1969 they were giving out over 2,000 condoms and would achieve the government's three year target in six months. Carl would draw on Ram Sewak's farming analogy; without the seed, there would be no crops in the field. The condom was supposed to hold the man's seed.

There was bumper demand for condoms during Holi, but the record keeping could not keep up with the distribution. Dr. Gope in Hazaribagh therefore refused to supply more. He needed a report which detailed how many of the men who had been supplied with the free condoms used them regularly and how many irregularly. Carl argued over the absurdity of the demand. But Dr. Gope was insistent; he suspected that the condoms may be being put to "improper" use. Enough reporting was not being done and so three new columns were added to the reports which would be required for submission. The teachers were now on short rations of condoms. In another block an extension educator had been fined ₹500 for inadequate record keeping. Carl tried to control himself. He did so, for 10 seconds, before blurting out: "It's God damn illegal to do your job in this system!"

***

Sterilisation had been one of the methods of birth control in use since the late 1950s, however the Centre had largely left the matter to the state governments. Maharashtra had been an early adopter of the practice, leading the country in numbers year after year. When the Government of India began setting targets in the mid 1960s, primarily for loop insertions, sterilisations were also made the subject of targets. Whilst 24 million loop insertions were targeted for the Fourth Plan period, the figure of 6 million sterilisations, or 1.2 million per year was also fixed.

Part of the Maharashtra Government's objection to the loop target was that it thought that it was unrealistic. Whilst suitable for young couples who may want to space their births, sterilisation was the preferred method for older couples with three or more children.[ccclxxiv] In July 1967 the Maharashtra Government submitted a proposal to the Centre for compulsory sterilisation of parents with three or more children. Concerns were immediately raised that compulsion might lead to "trouble", but the Health Minister, Sripati Chandrashekhar told the Rajya Sabha that the proposal was under consideration by his ministry.[ccclxxv] The matter led to some sharp exchanges in the Lok Sabha the following month. It was even dubbed a "sarphira" or madcap suggestion by Kanwar Lal Gupta of the Jana Sangh.[ccclxxvi] The Deputy Health Minister, Bayya Suryanarayana Murthy insisted that the proposal was still under consideration- it had been referred to the law ministry- but compulsory sterilisation would never be introduced "unless and until the nation accepts it".

By November the Centre no longer needed to take a decision on the matter as the Maharashtra Government had decided to withdraw its proposal. Nonetheless, by early 1968 it had emerged that more sterilisations had taken place over the previous year than loop insertions: 1.4 million people had been sterilised, actually exceeding the Plan target, whereas only 740,000 women had accepted the loop.[ccclxxvii] Almost one-quarter of these sterilisations had been done in Maharashtra.[ccclxxviii] The state was leading the country, reaching a figure 150% of its targeted number.

The first signs of what might go wrong with a government drive for sterilisation did not come from Maharashtra however, but Haryana. The former Deputy Chief Minister of Haryana, Chand Ram recounted events in Siwan village where poor scheduled caste men, young and old, were being rounded up from tea stalls and bazaars by the local police and forced onto operating tables to undergo sterilisations.[ccclxxix] On 28 December 1969 men from the neighbouring Kheri village were rounded up on the pretext of being given land and then marched to the operating centre. There were some protests and slogan shouting, and some children might have thrown stones. The police arrived in greater numbers in Siwan the following day, fired blanks, then shot one young man dead, dragged him along the ground, stripped the women and beat them with lathis. Even the village children were not spared. The local police had become keen on sterilising scheduled caste men ever since the state government announced the award of a transistor radio to anyone who could claim 20 vasectomy cases. Similar reports of sterilisations of teenage boys and old men in their 70s were coming in from across the country.

Vasectomy numbers had been declining during 1969 and 1970, however the push for sterilisations received a boost during the monsoon of 1971 in Kerala. In July alone 63,418 men had been sterilised at a camp held at the Ernakulam Town Hall.[ccclxxx] The camp was initiated by Shankar Krishnakumar, the district collector, who worked in co-ordination with the district family planning bureau headed by Dr. J.K. Dass. Krishnakumar made personal appeals for community involvement and oversaw a district wide publicity campaign. He personally supervised over 500 committees which undertook promotion and field work both before and after the campaign. Each of the district's 101 village councils, 4 municipalities and its corporation were assigned targets and given specified dates on which to send their men to the camp site which made the provision of transport easier to manage. The camp was marketed as a kind of family planning festival. Field publicity units would tour each village council the day before they were scheduled to send their men to the camp. There were decorated floats and processions and much slogan shouting in support of family planning in and around the camp. The Town Hall was decorated with flags and streamers, lights and pictures, and puppet shows were performed. There were even cultural programmes given by Kerala's eminent literary and musical artists. Those who had undergone a vasectomy were invited to address the crowds and a sign announcing the tally of vasectomies stood outside the hall. The whole operation was run from a central control room. The flow of patients through the operating rooms was smooth and sanitary standards were high. Each acceptor received ₹45 in cash and another ₹55 in kind in the form of food rations, saris and mundus, a free meal at the camp, vitamins and a shopping bag.

The results of the 1971 Census were published in 1972. The Government of India's ambitious target setting, the distribution of the loop, and occasionally aggressive sterilisation drives did have some minimal effect; the birth rate declined from 41 to 39 per 1,000 of the population. However, the death rate also declined to 19 per 1,000. And so the population of India increased by 108 million to 548 million.

The Government of India was encouraged by the success of the Kerala vasectomy camps and more camps were undertaken across the country later in 1971, the most successful of which was in Gujarat. A serious lapse occurred in Gorakhpur in March 1972 however when eight men died after undergoing a vasectomy at a camp and another six were infected with tetanus.[ccclxxxi] District Magistrate Sehgal had to admit that the deaths were due to surgical negligence. He called it "a severe setback". The camps continued throughout 1972, but by early 1973 the reports of malpractice and coercion started to become more frequent. Reports came in from Madhya Pradesh that teachers were being asked by the education department to bring in at least two men for vasectomies.[ccclxxxii] In some states temporary government employees were being asked to bring in vasectomy cases with the lure of permanent employment.[ccclxxxiii] In Maharashtra, always the leader in sterilisations, milkmen in Thane had even gone on strike over alleged coercion for vasectomies and the state government had to announce a probe.[ccclxxxiv] The issue made its way to the Lok Sabha with Jana Sangh members raising the case of intoxicated boys being operated on in vasectomy clinics in Ghaziabad.[ccclxxxv] There was some confusion over the boys' age however. Nonetheless, the Deputy Health Minister Amiya Kumar Kisku thought that in a mass camp approach some abuses were bound to creep in and the media should not make too much of them.[ccclxxxvi] The Government of India was making plans to expand the programme over the following year.

Plans changed however in July 1973 when it became clear that the budget provision for family planning was much lower than expected and that this would lead to the freezing or curtailment of many programmes.[ccclxxxvii] The reduction in funds was attributed to the drought and the need to divert resources to the creation of employment. Construction of rural family planning centres had been halted and the mass vasectomy camps, which were generally held to have been a great success, were stopped. This did not lead to a downward revision in targets for the states however- they were to make do with fewer funds. The provision for family planning had already been halved, from ₹112 crores to ₹54 crores. By September the already halved figure was again reduced by ₹15 crores.[ccclxxxviii] It was into this situation of funding cuts and the curtailment of programmes that a new Union health minister was appointed in November 1973. Karan Singh, the heir apparent of the princely state of Kashmir at the time of its accession to India in 1947, had resigned as civil aviation minister after an Indian Airlines crash in March. His resignation was not accepted. However, after another crash in May, in which the Steel Minister S. Mohan Kumaramangalam died, he refused to resign. He was eventually accommodated with the health ministry in a Cabinet reshuffle.

Karan Singh announced a new "package plan" for health

services, of which family planning was one element, in April 1974. Whilst addressing the media he said that "In the final analysis poverty is the problem, not the people, and fertility control is an integral part of our strategy to fight poverty."[ccclxxxix] Later in the year, in August, addressing the World Population Conference in Bucharest he seemed to reverse this position as he told the world that "development is the best contraceptive". It was thus unclear whether contraceptives would fight poverty, or whether bringing people out of poverty would work as a contraceptive. Nonetheless, over the next 18 months, which included the imposition of the Emergency in June 1975, an announcement was made almost every other month that a bigger announcement was just around the corner.

***

In January 1976 Prime Minister Indira Gandhi intervened and told a conference of doctors that "we must now act decisively and bring the birth rate down speedily. We should not hesitate to take steps which might be described as drastic."[cccxc] She went on to say "Some human rights have to be kept in abeyance for the human right of the nation- the right to live, the right to progress." In February Sanjay Gandhi included family planning in his 4 point programme for India's youth- the other three points were planting trees, promoting literacy and abandoning the practice of dowry. In March he was arguing that economic progress would not be possible without successful family planning: "All our industrial, economic and agricultural progress will be of no use if the population continues to rise at the present rate."[cccxci]

The statements of the prime minister and her son foreshadowed the arrival of a new National Population Policy in April. The Health Ministry had been at work on the policy over the previous year or more, and it did include some striking new features. The legal age of marriage was increased to 18 for girls and 21 for boys in in order encourage later marriages and lower fertility. Representation in the Lok Sabha would be frozen according to the 1971 Census figures to provide a penalty for states with expanding populations. Federal funding for the states would also continue to work off the 1971 Census figures. Most important for the immediate future however was the provision for higher incentives for sterilisations: ₹150 would be offered for sterilisations of a man or woman with two children whilst ₹100 would be offered for those with three or more children. Group incentives would also be introduced for doctors, labour unions, village councils and co-operative societies.

Sanjay Gandhi had been monitoring the results of a few vasectomy camps in Delhi in February and March, however it was only after the announcement of the National Population Policy that a renewed sterilisation drive was launched in the states in June. Until this time the Emergency, which had been declared a year earlier, had not had a big impact on the lives of rural Indians. Many did not even know there was any Emergency. Sanjay's sterilisation drive thus brought the Emergency to the villages. The campaign was most intense in the states closest to New Delhi, or the states in which chief ministers were most dependent on Sanjay's good favour. Even as the sterilisation drive gathered momentum during the monsoon, and then intensified as winter approached, Sanjay appeared, in public at least, far from a family planning demagogue. He did not give fiery speeches citing the urgent national need for Indian men with too many children to be sterilised. He did make mention of family planning and its necessity in the context of economic development, however it was always mentioned in conjunction with the other points in his programme- planting trees, banishing dowry and increasing the literacy rate. In fact, his public pronouncements were quite soothing and reassuring: there would be no coercion and no one would be forced into a vasectomy.[cccxcii]

Soon after Sanjay's 4 point programme had been

announced the Congress Party President, Devakanta Barua directed Party members to implement it despite its lack of official sanction. Sanjay himself was said to harangue visiting Congress chief ministers in New Delhi after which they would return to their state capitals and call for the implementation of the 4 point programme in their speeches.[cccxciii] Sanjay added the eradication of casteism to his programme, and so it became the 5 point programme.

A slew of family planning incentives and disincentives, penalties and rewards were announced, some of which were implemented, others of which never made it through the state secretariats. The Maharashtra Government passed its own legislation for compulsory sterilisation of couples with three or more children. It never received assent from the Centre. Sanjay's influence was however evident in the dramatic increase in sterilisation targets in each of the states. State governments seemed to be competing for publicity and political approval as to which was doing the highest number of sterilisations. The fact that the public was well aware of Sanjay's manic influence behind the scenes, which seemed at variance with his calm public statements, only worked to enhance his myth.

The official sterilisation target for 1976/77 was 4.3 million. However, after states began raising their own targets- Delhi announced an increase from 29,000 to 200,000, and Uttar Pradesh from 400,000 to 1.5 million- the nationwide target was doubled to 8.6 million. These revisions were said to have come at Sanjay's orders. The Ministry of Health and Family Planning was largely bypassed.[cccxciv] State chief secretaries worked closely with the district collectors at the local level. Sterilisations took place in mobile camps which were organised by state health authorities which were notified that specific numbers of sterilisation acceptors would be presented at particular times and places. Meetings were frequent, often daily, telephone calls were made and telegrams sent, and the message was made clear that the meeting of sterilisation targets would influence promotions in the state bureaucracy. The Uttar Pradesh chief secretary even threatened to stop salaries and suspend government officials who did not meet sterilisation targets.[cccxcv] He wanted his officers to galvanise their staff and report back to him and the chief minister's secretary.

In small towns and villages it would be ticketless travellers on the railways who might be excused a fine if they accepted a sterilisation.[cccxcvi] The ticket inspector would thus be able to meet his target. School teachers would also have to meet their targets and visit the homes of their students and persuade fathers to accept monetary incentives and help the cause by being sterilised. If the family was a large one, the child's admission to the school might be dependent upon sterilisation. Often teachers' salaries were dependent upon meeting personal sterilisation targets. Daily wage earners and construction workers would be told by their contractors that they could only get work if they could produce a certificate showing that they were sterilised. The contractor would also have to meet a target provided by the Public Works Department as a condition of their continued association. The sterilisation incentive would be equivalent to 4-6 weeks' pay. The alternative was unemployment. Fathers with large families would have their rations denied at the local Fair Price shops if they did not undergo sterilisations. This was a situation laden with irony, for often men would previously have increased the number of children on their ration card in order to increase their rations. They could not now admit to having fewer children, besides which the ration shop owner would not let go of the opportunity for a sterilisation by accepting that the customer had fewer children than the ration card specified. Meanwhile, vagrants on the fringe of society would be susceptible to being rounded up by the police to meet their sterilisation targets.

Just as had happened in 1969, the situation ran out of control in a village in Haryana. However, in 1976 the village was a Muslim one rather than Hindu scheduled caste. The Uttawar village council had been leading resistance to sterilisations. [cccxcvii] The villagers were woken up at 3 am on 6 November 1976. About 400 adult men were rounded up, taken to the police station, charged with criminal cases, mainly related to the possession of firearms, and then taken away for sterilisation. Just weeks earlier Muzzafarnagar in western Uttar Pradesh had experienced anti-family planning violence. Estimates vary but it is likely that 30 people died and another 70 were injured in rioting in the district.[cccxcviii] Anti-family planning violence also took place in Delhi, just kilometres away from Parliament. Most of the rioting towards the end of 1976 took place in predominantly Muslim areas. Protesters who were fired on, police who had to contain riots, and government officers who were carrying out the drive in an aggressive manner were among the dead. Countless numbers of men, mainly in rural India, spent the winter of 1976 trying ever more creative ways to avoid being rounded up for sterilisation. The Pushkar Mela, the annual camel fair in Rajasthan, saw a record low number of visitors.

***

In the 1950s the Government of India had tried educating its people on the merits of family planning only to find that results did not come quick enough. During the decade between the censuses of 1951 and 1961 the population of India rose by 80 million. Then, in 1965, the government sought a technological solution to the population problem in the form of the intrauterine contraceptive device, or the loop. However, as Carl Pope found out, the loop was an attempt at a technological solution to what was ultimately a social problem. Loops needed to be physically accepted by Indian women, however they also needed to be psychologically accepted. In southern Bihar, in Barhi and Hazaribagh it was evident that the bureaucracy which administered the family planning programme was more concerned with ensuring the smooth flow of paperwork rather than limiting the size of families. Some states were also engaging in their own sterilisation drives, but by the time that the 1971 census was published the Indian population had once again grown over the previous decade, by 108 million.

The demise of the loop in India in the late 1960s was also symbolic of the failure of a two decade long American project to assist in the modernisation of the Indian economy. Carl Pope, a young Peace Corps volunteer, would be among the last of the Quiet Americans in India. By 1969 most bureaucrats in New Delhi, irrespective of their ideological orientation, wanted fewer Americans telling them what to do. When Richard Nixon came to power in January 1969 he also wanted to retreat from the internationalism which had been associated with John Kennedy and his advisers earlier in the decade. And so, there was general agreement between the governments of India and the United States that aid in all its forms would be significantly reduced. This would not be instant, the American presence in India was huge. In 1969, after more than a decade of being paid for shipments of wheat in rupees, the United States owned around 40% of the Indian money supply.[cccxcix] Carl and Judy were not alone in India, there were 1,300 other young American volunteers at work across the country.

The Indo-Soviet Peace Treaty of August 1971 had come about after it was made clear that the United States would not support India in the event of Chinese aggression. When India defied the United States in December 1971 and defeated Pakistan in a war to help create the new state of Bangladesh, American aid was suspended. Rhetoric against American aid became more strident across India over the following year, which coincided with Indira Gandhi's high socialist phase. There was a call from within the Ministry for External Affairs for the withdrawal of all American aid workers within a month in May 1972.^{cd} The Americans did leave, but tried to claim that their withdrawal came about as a result of the success of their long aid effort in the country.^{cdi} The operations of the Peace Corps were wound down. The US AID building in New Delhi was donated to the Government of India.

The Swedish economist Gunnar Myrdal had famously dubbed India a "soft state" in his book *Asian Drama* in 1968. The failure of the Government of India's family planning programme seemed to provide evidence to support the label. The issue was one of state capacity and the Indian state had, since Independence, seemed incapable of delivering development programmes to its people. This was most evident in rural India. During the 1950s the government had tried to deliver development through the Community Development Programme. Yet that effort was largely dependent on the humble village level worker, who would often be frustrated by both the village he worked in, and the bureaucracy he worked for. When the state governments attempted to implement land reform they understood that it could only go so far for fear of antagonising the prosperous farmers on whom they depended for votes. When Jawaharlal Nehru boldly announced that rural India would move to a new era of co-operative farming in 1959, he had to retreat from the idea within a couple of months due to opposition from both farmers and the nascent opposition in Parliament. The pattern was repeated in the family planning programme of the 1960s. Sterilisations would be encouraged until too many excesses occurred and too many people began to protest. The loop would be promoted until too many Indian women complained. By the early 1970s it was clear that the Indian state was incapable of enforcing its will on an unwilling people.

The reason for the unwillingness of the Indian people, particularly rural Indians, to limit the size of their families was discovered by Mahmood Mamdani, a doctoral student at Harvard University, when he went to examine the results of a family planning programme in Ludhiana, Punjab in 1971.[cdii] For the smaller landholders the need to hire farm labour could spell financial ruin, and so the only resort was to use labour within the family. This economic necessity took itself to a logical conclusion for small marginal land holders; they had every incentive to increase the size of their family labour force. The farmers whom Mamdani interviewed expressed the hope that they would have enough children, spaced reasonably close together, so that some might go away and work and accumulate savings which would allow for the purchase of more land, whilst the others stayed back and worked the existing land and so saved on the necessity for hiring farm hands.

If the high cost of labour was an incentive for larger families among small and medium land holders, it was also one for the landless. After all, the more children they had, the more hands for farm labour, and the more land they might work as sharecroppers. This had forced a change in the traditional aversion to girl children; women and girls worked with their husbands and brothers, and so the more children a landless family had, the more land it could take on contract. Although the fact that the daughter would eventually leave the family upon marriage, just at the point of her highest agricultural productivity, meant that the disfavour toward girls never fully faded away. Whether landed or landless, children were the little helpers who lightened the load on both the farmer and his wife. They would bring grass and water for the cattle before going to school in the mornings, help in the fields when they returned in the afternoons, deliver meals to the fields, bring back the utensils, and the young girls could help with the cooking and daily chores.

Besides those who owned land, and those who worked on it, there were in the villages and small towns those who traditionally provided services, both high and low, meeting the needs of society for everything from haircuts and tailoring to teaching and accounting. In the absence of an economy which generated a large amount of employment either in agriculture or in the towns and cities, the traditional service communities, had, like their counterparts on the land, every rational economic incentive towards having more children rather than fewer. The model which Mamdani found perfected was a simple one. Have three or four sons. Each would be able to finish high school by earning doing agricultural work after school. One would be sent to college whilst the others stayed back and earned the money for his fees and boarding. The college going son would return and work through the summer, earning part of his expenses. After graduating his earnings would go towards educating the next in line and he would not marry until the second brother could earn and educate the third. The model only broke down when it encountered the bane of the young across India: educated unemployment. And thus, among the barber and tailor families which Mamdani encountered family planning was rare, and when it did occur in the form of vasectomy it was too late. A man would already have seven children. One educating the next in the hope of a better life for all.

The debate over whether development would bring a reduction in population growth or whether population growth would prevent development had persisted since the 1930s. In his presidential speech before the Congress in 1938 Subhas Bose had warned that India could not have its population rise by 30 million each decade and expect to see the benefits of economic planning. During the 1950s it was the Gandhians who were most influential in the Indian health bureaucracy and so the alternative perspective, that economic development would provide an incentive for smaller families was ascendant. Dr. Sushila Nayyar was an advocate of this reasoning. It does seem however, that her insistence on the precedence of economic development was intended to provide a modern mask to cover the more traditional moral concern over artificial contraception. Nonetheless, by the 1960s the situation had become so urgent that Dr. Nayyar, who had become health minister, put her moral objection aside and advocated the widespread distribution of the loop. In 1973 in Bucharest Karan Singh famously told the world that "development is the best contraceptive". By 1976 Sanjay Gandhi was in charge and he shared Subhas Bose's 1938 concern. Nonetheless, his brief attempt to turn India into a "hard state" ended in failure. In a sense both sides of the argument were right. But in the end, both were wrong.

In India after Independence economic development was so slow and uneven that it could do little to arrest national population growth, which would continue to make the task of raising living standards more difficult. By the time that the Government of India had essentially admitted defeat and rolled back its family planning programme some of the benefits of development were starting to be felt, particularly in the south of the country, and so fertility did begin to slow down in the early 1980s. Yet the population had already doubled in 30 years. And even the 1980s fertility slowdown was slow, and uneven, and so by the time of the fiftieth anniversary of Independence in 1997 the population had tripled and most of India remained mired in poverty. Economic development was too slow and unreliable a contraceptive, whilst the poor of India could never be forced to limit their families in the interests of development. For most Indians, rural and urban, development came through the only assets they could readily produce, children.

Sanjay Gandhi's efforts to impose family planning on an unwilling population only served to create an uprising against his mother's government. Indira Gandhi called for national elections in February 1977, opposition leaders were released from jail and press censorship was lifted. Within weeks opposition forces, divided by ideology, managed to unite in the form of a new Janata, or People's Party. The Party was not really one, but a coalition of four main Parties, led by Indira's old antagonist, Morarji Desai. Stunningly, the disparate Janata Party won the national elections in a landslide. Most of their gains came from northern India where Indira's Congress was almost wiped out. However, the government did not suffer any serious losses in the south of the country. Given that family planning had been most aggressively pursued in northern India over the previous winter, and had barely been implemented in the south, it could be inferred that the electoral verdict was one in protest against male sterilisations. Rural Indians in the south might have been much like their counterparts in the north a year earlier; they may not have even known that there was any Emergency and hence held little ill will against Indira and Sanjay. Prime Minister Morarji Desai's new Janata government immediately changed the name of India's population control programme from "Family Planning" to "Family Welfare" and reverted to the older consensual approach. Moreover, despite their ideological differences- they were variously ex-Congressmen, Hindu Nationalists, Socialists, Trade Unionists, and farmers' leaders- all members of the Janata Party were principled opponents of the economic system which had been built in India since Independence. They would now, in 1977, have their chance to restructure the Indian economy according to their own ideals.

SEVEN

Actually Existing Socialism

When the National Planning Committee convened in 1939, amongst its first divisions was that between the agrarians like Joseph Kumarappa and industrialisers like Jawaharlal Nehru and Subhas Bose. Kumarappa was quite sincere in his conviction that heavy industry need not be discussed by the National Planning Committee. Both Nehru and Bose sought to calm tempers and keep Kumarappa, essentially a representative of Mohandas Gandhi and his followers, in good humour by offering the assurance that cottage industries would not be neglected. They made the point that the two approaches were not mutually exclusive; heavy industries could co-exist with cottage industries, and cottage industries would also be given encouragement. When the National Planning Committee created subcommittees for both cottage and rural industries, and manufacturing industries some confusion arose. The definitions of various types of small industry had not been settled. Modernists like Jawaharlal Nehru and K.T. Shah had their own idea of small-scale industries, which whilst not directly contradictory to the Gandhian idea, was somewhat distant from it. They were interested in small workshops using machinery, whereas Gandhi wanted to encourage traditional village industries which used as little machinery as possible.

The universal appeal of small industries grew from the belief that they would create employment across the length and breadth of the country. No one could imagine how a few big factories could create the employment needed in as vast a land as India. In the years immediately after Independence politicians would call for greater government assistance to small industries, not based on the Gandhian principles of decentralisation and the sanctity of village life, but that it would provide a remedy for the problem of unemployment and underemployment. This idea found even fuller expression when Prasanta Mahalanobis devised his Draft Plan Frame in 1955. Resources were being redirected into heavy industry, which, it was conceded, would not create much employment. Small industries, or "hand industries" as Mahalanobis called them, would be encouraged to produce consumer goods, something which would balance the employment equation and create jobs in smaller towns and villages across the land. The most immediate policies to encourage small industries were enacted in the cotton textiles industry. Production from large cotton mills was subjected to an excise duty, restrictions on production were initiated and smaller spinners and weavers were given the sole right to produce saris and dhotis. India's employment prospects would thus come to depend on the performance of small industries.

The main thrust of Prasanta Mahalanobis's Draft Plan Frame, and India's development model for the ensuing decades of the 20th century, was heavy industry in the public sector. The creation of a large and dominant public sector grew from the first principles of socialism. Heavy industry need not be exploitative, as it was in the capitalist system, as long as its ownership was socialised. Control of industry through the establishment of public sector enterprises would allow for better working conditions and the return of profits to the government treasury for redistribution and reinvestment, rather than the poor working conditions and the disappearance of profit into private hands which prevailed in capitalism. The core of the industrialisation drive was steel. More specifically, public sector steel mills were to drive the programme of import substitution. Steel was the most basic requirement of modern manufacturing and so the government established plants at Bhilai in Madhya Pradesh, Rourkela in Orissa, and Durgapur in West Bengal in the 1950s. The hope was that once India had substantially achieved import substitution and could make its own machines in its own factories from its own steel, it would save valuable foreign exchange and be well on the way to self-generating economic growth.

Self-generating economic growth had been illusive however and by the time of the election of 1977 many had given up hope that it might ever arrive. After Indira Gandhi ended the Emergency the election campaign in February was a short and rushed affair. Opposition leaders barely had time to put together a coalition, the Janata Party, and the discourse on pressing national issues was not well developed. The main theme of Indira's opponents was a return to freedom after the authoritarianism of the Emergency. Yet they could have said just about anything and still been elected, such was the mood against Indira and Sanjay in rural northern India.

The Janata Party came to government with a tally of 345 seats in the Lok Sabha. Most of their gains were in northern and western India and the two biggest beneficiaries were Morarji Desai from Gujarat, at the head of a remnant of the old Congress Party, and Charan Singh from Uttar Pradesh who represented the prosperous farmers of the states closest to Delhi. The Hindu Nationalist Jana Sangh formed a sizable part of the new formation, as did the Socialist Party. The two prime movers in the new government, Morarji Desai and Charan Singh, who would become prime minister and home minister respectively, were critics of the economy which had been built over the previous three decades. Morarji Desai always had to temper his criticism however. Whilst he was partial to village industries, he could never be too strident in his criticism of the public sector; he had been chief minister of Bombay and Union finance minister. Charan Singh was also a former Congressman, he had been the revenue minister in Uttar Pradesh in the 1950s before leaving the Party in the 1960s due to a disillusionment with the Nehruvian economic model. His first doubts had come in the wake of the push towards co-operative farming. He too wanted more emphasis on village industries, but, having been away from the Congress for longer, he could be more strident in his criticism of public sector heavy industries. The Jana Sangh leaders like Atal Behari Vajpayee and Lal Krishna Advani were more motivated by cultural nationalism than economic ideology, yet they were also amenable to the promotion of village industries. The Socialists like Chandra Shekhar, the Young Turk of a decade earlier, and the trade unionist George Fernandes criticised the Nehruvian model for not being socialist enough; they saw themselves as defenders of the public sector.

***

Mohandas Gandhi wrote the resolution on village industries which was passed at the Congress session at Bombay in October 1934. The resolution authorised Joseph Kumarappa to form the All India Village Industries Association. The new Association would work as a part of the Congress to revive or encourage dead or dying village industries for the moral and physical advancement of villages. Gandhi gave his, by 1934, familiar thoughts on the slow death of India's villages, the evils of mechanisation when it made human labour redundant, the menace that mills posed to Indian villagers and also provided some clarity on the precise type of village industries he had in mind.[cdiii] Villagers would work in their own cottages as they had done since time immemorial and they would do so according to village methods. These simple methods could be improved as they had been in the cases of hand ginning, hand carding as well as hand spinning and hand weaving. Some critics had suggested that this was an overly individualistic plan for production, yet Gandhi insisted that he was not opposed to the formation of village co-operatives. Products made by villagers in their cottages could be pooled together and the profits divided. The villagers could work under supervision and according to a plan and the raw materials could be supplied from a common stock. In fact, this type of thing was already being practiced in the All India Spinners' Association.

Gandhi went on to provide the background of some of his thinking on village industries.[cdiv] He had first picked up the idea on his Harijan tour of the Malabar. He saw that the villagers had not really taken to khadi, but they still had leisure time. In this state of voluntary idleness they would never be capable of winning swaraj. They would always be prey for exploiters, whether they be foreigners or Indian city dwellers. The prevailing state of dependence was only making the villagers dull. Instead the villagers could take up the work of their ancestors which had died out. There were many goods for daily use which villagers had made themselves until not so long ago but for which they now depended on supplies from the city. Villagers should be using their time to make useful products and city dwellers should be using those products. Gandhi thought that the goods which could be revived were primarily those of diet and dress. He had spent much time advocating the use of khadi for dress, however it was also clear that the villagers could make most of their own food. Given that flour, rice and sugar were increasingly being processed in mills, the villagers were just becoming suppliers of raw materials for their city based exploiters. Instead they could process these ingredients themselves.

The man tasked with running the All India Village Industries Association, Joseph Kumarappa, wrote a book covering its theory and practice in 1936, *Why the Village Movement?* Towards the end of the work he made the distinction between village industries and cottage industries. Village industries were those which affected the whole country because their products were in universal demand, mainly those connected with the production of food such as rice, oil, flour and sugar processing. There were also industries which could provide farmers with subsidiary occupations such as beekeeping, sericulture and lac cultivation and industries which were usually the vocation of specific communities spread across the country such as tanning, pottery and carpentry. Cottage industries manufactured curios and luxury items. In some cases the demand was not universal, in others goods might be used every day. These could include soap making, printing, dying, art and metal working.

Gandhi's efforts to revive both khadi spinning and village industries grew into a broader, philosophical advocacy of decentralisation. He thought that decentralisation was indispensable to the practice of non-violence, for centralisation required force. Decentralisation was required for full mental and moral growth and he wanted power devolved to India's hundreds of thousands of villages rather than concentrated in Delhi and Calcutta and Bombay.[cdv] Society should approximate an oceanic circle, radiating outward, rather than a pyramid with its apex at the top built on a large base at the bottom.[cdvi]

Joseph Kumarappa also elaborated on the ideal of decentralisation in *Why the Village Movement?* Decentralisation was the obvious solution in a capital scarce country like India in which there was plentiful labour, much of which was unemployed or under employed. Only hand work could produce the diversity and variegation which were at the heart of decentralisation, and only decentralisation could give life to true democracy. Decentralisation would work well when raw material and markets were close to the centres of production. Decentralisation would ensure an even distribution of wealth and make for a more tolerant people. Better distribution of purchasing power would arise from better distribution of production, higher wages would lead to higher effective demand and supply would then follow that new rural demand. Each producer would become a little entrepreneur and exercise initiative and responsibility and practice more business-like methods.

Bringing the market closer to production would mean that there would be no difficulty in selling goods. Avoiding centralisation of wealth and power would mean that peace would not be disturbed on a national scale.

Among Jawaharlal Nehru's first statements to the National Planning Committee was: "there was no inherent conflict between cottage industries and large-scale industries".[cdvii] He thought they need not clash "unless they were developed independently of each other and without any co-ordination." It was at Subhas Bose's behest that Joseph Kumarappa was brought onto the committee but from the start he tried to prevent large-scale industry even being discussed. In seeking to prevent the discussion of industrialisation Kumarappa was essentially asking the committee to disband, yet his fellow committee members went ahead nonetheless. As the meetings continued Nehru maintained his assurances that there was no inherent conflict between cottage industries and large-scale industries, but Kumarappa kept up his principled dissent. Sir Mokshgundam Visvesvaraya was just as adamant about the need for immediate steps for industrialisation. Kumarappa went on to make his argument that in the absence of state control over public enterprises, and given that the Congress was against private enterprises which competed with cottage industries, it would be best to concentrate on cottage industries for the time being. Both he and Sir Visvesvaraya resigned shortly thereafter. Gandhi thought that the National Planning Committee was largely a waste of time.[cdviii]

When the National Planning Committee constituted a Subcommittee on Rural and Cottage Industries its terms of reference were quite clear. It would "survey the conditions of cottage and village industries", look into their issues of marketing and finance and competition from foreign and Indian centralised competitors, examine demand trends and the potential for promotion and revival, taxation issues, ways to standardise and regulate prices, means of protection and conditions of work and wages, and define a cottage industry. The matter of definitions was brought before the chairman of the committee in May 1940. The matter was one of which type of industry would fall under the purview of the Manufacturing Industries Subcommittee and which should fall under the Cottage and Rural Industries Subcommittee. Nehru was eventually able to provide a formulation: cottage industries were those which either used no mechanical power and either hired or did not hire labour and those which used mechanical power but did not hire labour, whilst small-scale industries used mechanical power of low intensity and hired labour, and large-scale industry used mechanical power of high capacity and hired labour.

Much of the work of the subcommittees for cottage and rural industries, and manufacturing industries had already been done by April, and so the distinction between cottage industries and small-scale industries was not sharply drawn in their reports. The Manufacturing Industries Subcommittee made some general recommendations for "mutually beneficial co-operation" between cottage industries and large-scale industries, whilst the Rural and Cottage Industries Subcommittee continued to focus on cottage industries of the Gandhian variety.

The Rural and Cottage Industries Subcommittee submitted a report, based on the draft resolutions formulated by Gulzarilal Nanda, to the National Planning Committee in September. The subcommittee's resolutions were largely accepted. In its final resolutions the committee sought to encourage cottage and rural industries in the context of an economic plan to serve the 90% who were unable to secure their material needs, often living in semi-starvation, economic idleness and insecurity. The committee blamed the decay of India's rural industries on the policies of the British East India Company which had suppressed them in favour of British industry without providing any occupation in exchange. Other means needed to be taken for improving the standard of living, but cottage and rural industries had the potential to create employment in the villagers' own homes, allow them to follow more than one occupation, and increase their purchasing power. Employment would be created for the largest number of people and the drift of villagers into the cities would be prevented. The committee recommended the establishment of a Cottage Industries Board which would provide assistance for finance, supplies, marketing, production techniques and management. The committee also wanted large-scale mechanised industries which competed with rural industries and received state support to be owned or controlled by the state so that there could be proper co-ordination between the two types of industry.

Nehru's distinction between cottage industries and small-scale industries had not initially garnered much attention, however the idea of specifically small-scale industries began to receive encouragement as the Second World War continued. A conference was held in New Delhi in March 1942 which resolved that the large aggregate of demand could not be met from pre-war sources or from large-scale industries and so it was decided to encourage small-scale industries by procuring a large proportion of war requirements from them.[cdix] Arrangements were made to order these goods through the provincial co-operative departments and the local director of supplies. These government departments were also directed to provide supplies, finance, technical guidance and management assistance to small-scale industries. When an Industries Conference was called in December 1947 in New Delhi it devoted some time to the revival of cottage industry and the encouragement of small-scale industry. The departmental committee of the conference thought that each term, cottage industry and small-scale industry, was well understood and so it was not necessary to define them. Like the National Planning Committee, the conference recommended the establishment of a Cottage

Industries Board, but this time it included small-scale industries in its ambit. Small-scale industries were divided into three categories: those which were auxiliary to large-scale industries, those which engaged in supply or repair services, and those which manufactured finished goods. Industries were then further classified according to their supply requirements.

The Industrial Policy Resolution of 1948 stated that cottage and small-scale industries were suited for the better utilisation of local resources and for the achievement of local self-sufficiency for certain types of consumer goods. It was noted that the expansion of cottage and small-scale industries depended on the provision of supplies, cheap power, technical advice, organised marketing, and where necessary protection from competition from large-scale manufacturers. The revival of village and small-scale industries found a place in the Directive Principles of State Policy in the new Constitution of 1950. An International Perspective Planning Team visited India in 1954, jointly sponsored by the Ford Foundation and the Government of India, after which the first institutions for the development of village and small-scale industries were established: the Central Small Industries Organisation, the National Small Industries Corporation, the Khadi and Village Industries Corporation, and later the Small Industry Extension Training Institute.

The Industrial Policy Resolution of 1956 reiterated the government's commitment to cottage and village and small-scale industries. It did so however, in the context of encouraging the "decentralised sector" to become self-supporting and integrate with the large-scale sector. For this the government would focus on improving production techniques in order to avoid technological obsolescence. It was at this time that small industries found their way into Prasanta Mahalanobis's Draft Plan Frame and the Second Five Year Plan as a means of employment generation which would compensate for the redirection of resources towards capital intensive heavy industry. By 1956 the principal features of small-scale industry policy had thus emerged. Some specific measures included the establishment of a network of industrial estates in which work sheds would be equipped with facilities which would be made available to entrepreneurs at subsidised rents. The Industrial Estate programme was initiated in 1957 with the opening of the Okhla Industrial Estate in New Delhi. A number of products would be reserved exclusively for the small-scale sector, starting with dhotis and saris. A list of products would also be purchased by the government exclusively from the small-scale sector. Large and small industries were to be linked through an ancillarisation programme, and machines would be made available to entrepreneurs on a hire purchase basis with easy repayment terms. Technical counselling would be provided to small units to improve their efficiency and viability.

Much of the appeal of cottage and village and small-scale industries came from the idea that they alone could generate employment across the length and breadth of India. This idea that smaller industries would be able to create employment on a scale which larger industries could not was prevalent in the early 1950s in the highest levels of government. Shriman Narayan Agarwal, the author of *The Gandhian Plan of Economic Development for India* had become General Secretary of the All India Congress Committee after Independence. He had spoken with Vinoba Bhave and announced that "If surplus human labour in both villages and cities had to be absorbed in gainful employment, the village and small-scale industries would have to be given the highest priority."[cdx]

The employment dictum was also repeated by government ministers. Depending on their ideological orientation, and their audience, they would variously advocate small-scale industries, or cottage industries, or village industries, or all of them as the solution to India's unemployment problem. The Deputy Minister for

Commerce and Industry, D.P. Karmarkar argued that large-scale industries could not provide adequate employment: "A time may come when India as a whole may be prosperous and the national income may be large yet at the same time there may be a large mass of our countrymen who continue to live under-nourished and unemployed. It is here that the small-scale and medium industries have a role to play."[cdxi] In Bombay the Chief Minister, Morarji Desai repeated the precept: "The real problem before the country is not one of unemployment but one of under-employment; and to tackle the problem we should encourage as many cottage and small-scale industries as possible."[cdxii] The theme was maintained by Prime Minister Jawaharlal Nehru who stated that the level of employment would be a yardstick of progress and it was therefore of the "highest importance" that village industries form part of the economic planning process.[cdxiii] Nehru maintained the same position in 1953 as prime minister that he held in 1939 as the chairman of the National Planning Committee; he did not see any real conflict between village and large-scale industries.

***

The employment generating potential of small-scale industries was held in such high regard in India in the late 1950s that a film was even made on the theme in 1959. *Apna Haath Jagannath*, which loosely translates as *God's Power is in One's Own Hands*, was released in February 1960. The film was directed by Mohan Segal and based on a story by the Marathi writer Gajanan Digambar Madgulkar.

Apna Haath Jagannath begins with Madan Lal Malhotra's dilemma. Before he can start earning he has to study and clear his exams, but before he can do that he has to raise ₹200 in college fees within three days. His mother Lajwanti, praying before an idol of Lord Jagannath, suggests he approach his father for the money, she would accompany him. Madan's father Dhaniram only earns

₹150 a month. He does not know where he would get the money from and like harried fathers everywhere, complains that money does not, in fact, grow on trees. But Lajwanti assures him that after Madan passes his B.A. exams he will get a job as a tehsildar or mamlatdar, a local government officer, and there will be no worries. But Dhaniram is still waiting on his salary. Madan's sister Sheela offers him ₹10 which she had been patiently saving for the sibling festival bhaiya dooj all year.

The film is set in Punjab, and so Madan encounters a turbaned young man on the street. The young Sikh has got a permit for the consumption of alcohol. By 1959 permits and licences had become necessary for seemingly every conceivable act of daily life, something which led Kaifi Azmi to write a ditty on the issue:

Dunia se bada tu dunia basane wale

Tujhse bhi hai unche permit banana wale

Hue paida to permit rahe jinda to permit

Uthe murda to permit

Paida to permit jinda to permit

Murda to permit dekho yeh jamana

Permit Permit Permit permit ke liye mar mit

Permit bina is jahan mein do dinom bhi na jiya jaye

Permit Permit Permit

You are bigger than the world, you created the world

*But even higher than you are the ones
who make the permits*

When born a permit, stay alive a permit

Wake up dead a permit

Born permit, alive permit

Dead permit, look at this era of ours

*Always a headache for a permit permit
permit permit*

*You can't even live for two days in this
world without a permit*

Permit permit permit

Madan cycles up to a Caltex petrol pump. A young woman drives up in her convertible American car, honks for service and Madan rushes out. She wants three gallons of petrol. He fills up six gallons and ends up spraying the petrol all over the young woman's dress. But they have made their acquaintance. There ensue a few comic scenes in which the young lady walks into a cloth store and Madan pretends to be his brother Chagan, and then a flower stall where he pretends to be another brother. They are supposed to be triplets.

It turns out that the young woman has just come to small town Punjab from the big city of Delhi. Her father encourages her to enrol in a B.A. course at the local college, and, in a coincidence, she walks into a class with Madan, of the petrol pump, and cloth store, and flower stall. The teacher introduces Miss Indumati to the class and then insists that she sit next to Madan, still trying to hide his face. Madan is the topper of the last exam and receives praise from the professor. He tells the students that Madan is also a great sportsman. The lecture hall erupts in applause. He is now redeemed in Indumati's eyes. The professor even wants all the students to read Madan's exam paper.

After class Indumati is about to drive off when she sees Madan, asks for his exam paper, and offers him a ride home. The two seem to be getting along well. Madan assures Indumati that his small town is a great place with no shortage of attractions. When it comes time to drop Madan off she suggests they go back to the little working class neighbourhood where they had met the previous day. But then, in a particularly grand comic turn, Madan insists that he does not live in such a place but in a bungalow and so picks one out and gives Indumati directions. The bungalow is Indumati's. She plays along and drops him off and drives away.

When Madan gets home his father informs him that he is considering going into debt to pay his admission fees. Madan drops in on the women of the family singing a hymn to Lord Krishna and has the devious idea of selling the idol of Jagannath. He does so, gets money for it, and goes to the university on the last day before his admission fees are due. Indumati sees him at the counter and their cat and mouse game continues. He wants to excuse himself after the calamity at her house, but she follows him in her car. He explains the previous day's events. Behind the laughter and cheer of the poor there is a lot of pain, and so when a small moment of pleasure came along he wanted it to last as long as possible. So he pretended that he lived in a bungalow rather than a working class neighbourhood. Indumati does not mind. The lengths that Madan went to keep the moment going showed just how much he liked her.

Madan returns home to find his mother beating his little sister Munni for the disappearance of the idol only to tell her that it was in fact him. Madan reasons with his mother that what is happening is a demonstration of what she had always told him; that when devotees are in trouble, God comes to their rescue. Besides which he had not sold the God that resides in her heart. He would buy her idol back from his first earnings. When Dhaniram wants to know how the admission fees were paid for Lajwanti makes up a story about saving bits from the money he gave her for household expenses. Dhaniram accepts the story and is relieved. He even apologises to his son for taking his anger at himself out on him and wishes him well in his exams. Madan takes his mother's blessings and gets to work.

Madan passes his B.A. exams. He is ecstatic. He rushes home, tells his mother and she thanks God. His sisters are excited. He will take his mother on a pilgrimage to Kashi, pay for Sheela's wedding in grand style, and buy dozens of frocks for Munni. Dhaniram walks in. He too is pleased, now Madan can run the household. He is old and tired and just wants to rest. All his pain has been lifted. He cries tears of joy. He feels that it is really he, as a father who has passed. He tells his son to rush to his friend Prem Nath, who is a big officer in the Secretariat who will set him up with a job.

But Prem Nath cannot do anything for Madan. Even if it was his own son there is little he could do. Getting government employment is tough, and even when a vacancy does come up there are thousands of BAs and MAs on the waiting list. All he can suggest is that Madan look beyond government employment. Madan does try his luck at a school, but the headmaster informs him that he needs a teaching degree, whereas all he has is a B.A. Even if he earned a teaching degree the headmaster could not make any assurances. For two vacancies there were five hundred applications. He goes to the transport manager for an office job. There are no office jobs, but does he have any technical skill? He does not. He lines up at the employment exchange and is told that it can't be predicted when his number will arrive. Ninety percent of graduates want an office job, and there just aren't that many available. Madan then has an argument with his

The Licence Raj

father who admonishes him for not finding a job. Madan insists that he had made his rounds of all the offices, but there was just nothing available. His father tells him that there are middle fails and metric passes who are soldiers and officers. Madan tells him that times have changed.

Madan wanders down to the washermen's steps by the river. The washerman Ram Lakhan gives him a speech on the merits of manual labour. Ram Lakhan is happy with his life because he earns his daily bread through the work of his hands. The problem for Madan's type is that he could not do manual labour because his family's honour would be tarnished. But why, after all, did the Lord Jagannath not have hands? Because he had given them to humanity to use for work. A seed of thought is planted in Madan's mind.

Madan then breaks into song and dance with the washermen and washerwomen. The song implores everyone to wash away the stains from their hearts, alluding to the prejudice against manual labour. Madan meets with Indumati who tells him that she has a possible marriage proposal from a labour welfare officer. He earns in the thousands and comes from an affluent family. Madan jokes that he sounds so good he wants to marry him. But Indumati doesn't appreciate the joke. She wants to marry Madan and has even lined up a meeting with her father. Madan then informs her that he has started work as a washerman down at the river. He is not joking. He will learn the trade and then open a unit for washing, dying and printing in the city.

Madan arrives for the meeting with his prospective father-in-law, Dewan Kulwant Rai. Comedy ensues because it was this man that he had bickered with at the washermen's steps the previous day. Kulwant asks him about his plans. Madan tells him that he wants to open a laundry in which there will be washing, dying and printing. Kulwant is not unimpressed but suggests that he will need capital to start the business. He asks Madan what his father does. Madan replies that he is a cashier. Kulwant's mood turns. He now remembers Madan from the argument at the steps and begins to thunder that he will not give his daughter to any washerman. He kicks Madan out and scolds his daughter and takes her to her room. Dewan Kulwant Rai has decided. Indumati's marriage will be with Narender, the labour welfare officer.

Madan's problems are compounded when an old lady turns up at his house with a sack of clothes for washing. She tells his parents that it is better to give washing to people she knows and help them rather than strangers. They insist that there must be some mistake. Dhaniram claims that no one in his family has done such low work for seven generations. But the old lady insists that Madan is a washerman and she wants to drop some clothes for cleaning. Madan arrives and yes, it is true, he is a washerman. Dhaniram goes berserk. Doesn't he care for the family's honour? How will his sister get married? Is this what he has educated Madan for? Madan protests that he is not picking pockets for a living. Besides, he does not have any false sense of pride. Dhaniram announces that Madan is now dead to him. Lajwanti begs Madan to give up such work, but Dhaniram grabs him and throws him across the courtyard.

Madan goes to see Indumati and tells her what happened. He has been kicked out of home by his father. He laments that until a person becomes something in life he is a stranger to his own family. He would go somewhere, he doesn't know where, but it would be far away. Indumati insists that he can only go if he takes her along. Madan protests. She is the daughter of a rich man. She would not be able to withstand the depravations of life with him. She claims that just being with him would be enough. If he left without her she would take some poison and kill herself. Madan relents and agrees to wait for her at 11 in the evening in the grove for their getaway. Later, Indumati has her bags packed but is met at the door by her father who throws her back inside. The rain sets in,

Indumati is stuck at home, whilst Madan waits for her all night in the grove. By morning he gives up, muses on the fickle ways of love, and women, and society, and makes his way out into the world.

News of Dhaniram's death reaches Lajwanti. The diligent and honest cashier had embezzled some funds from the bank in order to pay for his daughter's wedding and so had drowned himself in the river. Madan has started his laundry in Bombay and returns to town. The first person he sees is Ram Lakhan, the washerman whom he addresses as 'gurudev'. He is excited and shares the news that he now has 20 employees and has brought gifts for all. He has even brought cash for his father who should now be happy. He would touch his father's feet and say that he would now take the responsibilities of the house on his shoulders. His father would now rest. Ram Lakhan begins to cry. Madan walks in on his mother who is praying, her eyes closed singing another hymn to Lord Krishna. He places the idol of Lord Jagannath before her and she opens her eyes. Her son has now returned. He is a man who earns. Everything will be fine.

Madan goes to see his sister Sheela at her in-law's home on the occasion of bhaiya dooj. They both know what their father did and they both blame themselves. Sheela says that if she did not exist then father would not have had to take such extreme measures. Madan says that if he had been able to earn and manage the house he would not have done what he did. Sheela tells Madan that she prays for his success. They are sharing a moment when mother-in-law comes down the stairs and says that she will not tolerate any washerman, particularly one from a family of thieves, in her house and kicks Madan out. It is enough that they keep his sister in their home after all that has happened. Madan goes to the bank to return the money which was stolen so that his father up in the heavens will not have any stain attached to his name.

Madan wanders over to Indumati's bungalow only to find

that guests are arriving for her wedding. He will return to Bombay in the evening. Meanwhile Ram Lakhan visits Indumati's house, and as she is being adorned in her wedding finery, informs her that Madan is back in town, and he has made a success of himself. Indumati decides to leave the bungalow and drive after Madan's bus. She would not want him to think of her as unfaithful to his love. But, speeding along, she swerves to avoid a head-on collision and ends up veering off the road. Back in hospital the doctor announces that it is unlikely that she will ever regain the use of her legs. Indumati has fled from the scene of her wedding and so, besides the physical injuries, her father is disgraced. Narender, the labour welfare officer and groom arrives and is sanguine about the situation. If he could have done anything to unite Indumati with Madan he would have. Indumati does not now want to be a burden on Madan. Narender suggests that he and Indumati at least remain friends.

Back at his textile unit Madan has an economic dilemma. The government has stopped the import of foreign dyes which means that the merchants are selling their existing imported stocks at high rates on the black market. He suggests to his customer, a cloth merchant, that he use Indian dyes. The merchant erupts. He has placed an order for cloth with imported dye, so that is what he will get! Madan then gives a little speech about how the country cannot progress if it remains obsessed with foreign goods. He would not buy on the black market as a matter of principle. But the merchant will not relent. He demands all the cloth he has given for dying back by the evening. Madan protests; theirs is a small unit and for the merchant's big order they have rejected a dozen smaller ones. His workers maintain that they are with him. In a quick cut Madan goes to the office of the Joint Director of Industries (Small-Scale Industries). Within seconds he walks out with a spring in his step and the paperwork to ensure the supply of dye.

Madan returns to his sister's in-law's house, this time in a

European suit and tie. Word had spread that Madan had come into some money and so Sheila's mother-in-law comes down the stairs welcoming the young man back. After all, if she had not scolded him that day, he would never have been motivated to become the big success he is now. Madan now has a unit in his hometown and Narender babu, Indumati's former fiancé arrives to inspect the unit in his official capacity as labour welfare officer. He speaks to Madan, mistaking him for a worker, asking him how he is treated. He has no problems. His co-worker echoes this; their only problem is that they don't have any problems! And so Narender babu decides to felicitate Madan for his exemplary behaviour as an employer. In a late twist Dhaniram, who never actually died, comes back to town in the guise of Gopal, takes up work in Madan's dying unit, his identity is eventually revealed, and Madan is reunited with Indumati and they marry. Narender babu announces that Indumati will regain the use of her legs within a week.

***

At the same time that *Apna Haath Jagannath* was being filmed and released Pheroze Medhora and A.P. Murdeshwar from the United Nations Educational Scientific and Cultural Organization undertook a study of small industrial units in Howrah, across the Hooghly river from Calcutta. Their report could be considered the academic, rather than filmi portrayal of small-scale industries in India in 1960.[cdxiv]

There were many iron foundries and engineering works which had come up in the late 19th and early 20th century in Howrah to support the dockyards and roperies and there were also jute mills. Howrah was close to the coal fields and iron and steel works of Bengal, Bihar and Orissa and a was a major rail hub for eastern India. It was home to more than 75% of Calcutta's small engineering units. These were mainly turning shops and petty manufacturing units, many of which served as manufacturing feeders and ancillaries. Blacksmithies also proliferated; a high level of precision was not required in their metal work and there was plenty of scrap available. Both the turning shops and blacksmithies worked on steel, pig iron and brass. For some products like nails and rivets they would compete, but the turning shops produced a wider variety of products and were capable of greater precision. Howrah's small-scale entrepreneurs were usually from working class backgrounds and would act as their own unit manager. Most were of the Mahisya caste, which was thought to be a result of their numbers in the area rather than a special affinity for small-scale industry.

Howrah's small-scale turning shops were dark and grimy and not always made completely of bricks and mortar. The UNESCO researchers noted that the entrance was often the only passage for direct sunlight. Dim electric lights covered one side of the little factory above the machine which made work possible. The floors were uneven, the machines randomly spaced, supplies and finished goods were dumped wherever possible. Physical work conditions were worse than in large-scale industry. Workers lacked job security and earned low and irregular wages. They would float around from shop to shop for work and recruiting was informal; a sign would be put up outside the unit or the owner would just ask an employee to bring in someone whom they knew who could do the job. Most workers were teenagers when they started. There was no trade unionism and not much scope for it given how fluid employment relations were. Small-scale units did not come under the provisions of the Factories Act which required higher standards for the employment of workers in larger factories. Generally, employers and employees were happy with one another. They often came from the same caste and class and there was flexibility in their relationships. Employers could let an employee go when there was no work. Likewise an employee could move on whenever they wanted. Employers would advance their workers wages when they really needed it. They would sometimes dine together after work.

Despite the long history of small-scale manufacturing in Howrah half the units surveyed had been setup during the previous five years. Most entrepreneurs were sole proprietors and the original investment in the turning shops was usually ₹4,000 or less. Half the survey respondents had to borrow to raise this sum. Most of those who borrowed to start their units did so from family members. One factor which kept capital costs low was the use of second-hand machines and self-made machines. Only around one-fifth of the machines in use were new. There was little formal accounting; a professional accountant could not be employed and the owner usually did the job himself. Most said that they priced their products by adding a fixed margin to the cost prices, only a minority accepted the market price.

The family capital used to get started would soon become scarce once operations began. Small units could not avail of formal sources of capital in the market which meant that expansion would have to take place from the unit's own resources. At the point at which the unit might want to expand, it would still be too small to go to the formal capital market. Given that half the units surveyed had been in operation for more than five years, this meant that they had remained small and never grown to become medium sized operations. A major impediment to growth was the lack of formal education among the entrepreneurs. They had often been shop workers themselves and understood the technical aspects of the manufacturing process yet lacked rudimentary business knowledge. Almost all the small units in Howrah were dependent on job-work, or individual orders. They could not therefore produce on assembly lines. The workflow was uneven and operations and the assignment of work within a unit would change frequently. Turning shops rarely worked on a single product all year. Overheads had to be kept low and demand could not be anticipated.

Small units in Howrah also suffered from fission, or the practice of an employee quickly gaining technical skills and then raising a small sum to start his own unit. An employee could start out on his own by simply taking an existing unit or machinery on a lease. Supplies and castings were readily available in neighbourhood shops. Semi-skilled and unskilled labour was also abundant. Middlemen would then create a market, buying from the units which offered the cheapest price. Howrah seemed to resemble one big factory which was artificially divided into a large number of small units. Risks were divided among the competing units however. Units grew in number rather than size. New units could gain orders through lower prices or inferior quality goods which meant that there were minimal profits available for all. Any prospect of earning higher profits would only provide an incentive for an employee to leave and start his own unit. Given that most entrepreneurs were former workers, once they had risen to the status of owner and earnt just enough above their previous wage, they were reasonably satisfied and had little further motivation for expansion.

Part of the problem for small-scale entrepreneurs in marketing their products was that very few had any direct contact with their market. Almost all had to work through middlemen, who included wholesalers, retailers, and larger manufacturers. The larger manufacturers were generally located in Howrah and received contracts from the government and then sub-contracted them to smaller units. The wholesalers and retailers were in the hardware business and generally located across the Hooghly on Clive Street and Canning Street in Calcutta. The wholesalers and retailers would secure their orders from the government and the jute mills and tea gardens and would cross the river and shop around among the small Howrah units with a sample or design or description of the required product. Sometimes the order would be sub-divided among different units. There were many fewer middlemen than small-scale producers, and they maintained close relationships with their buyers. It was thus the middlemen who always held the stronger bargaining position. Nonetheless, they did bring some order to what might otherwise have been a chaotic market.

In addition to dealing with middlemen to sell their products, small entrepreneurs in Howrah also had to go to them for supplies. The government issued permits for industrial components, however only one among the survey's participants had acquired one. Most pointed to the government's tardiness in issuing permits and the need to pay for an entire quota in one instalment in cash. Small entrepreneurs therefore had to buy their supplies from the market at a price which was anywhere between 25% to 100% above the government rate. Most would prefer to pay the higher rate rather than deal with the government. The one respondent who did get the permit found it was insufficient for his requirements. Two government undertakings had been established which might have helped the small-scale producers of Howrah- the Small Industries Services Institute (West Bengal) and the Central Engineering Organisation. Most of the survey participants readily acknowledged the need for government aid and most wanted greater access to finance. However, only two owners had any contact with the government: one who became a member of the Central Engineering Organisation, the other was the one who had obtained the permit.

***

By April of 1960 the Government of India had announced that small-scale units would not have to apply for a licence under the Industries (Development and Regulation) Act. Government ministers, particularly the Gandhians among them, continued to call for a renewal of cottage and village industries. Morarji Desai, by now Union finance minister, repeated the adage that village industries might only be done away with after many decades when everyone had good employment and a decent income, but for the time being they were to be encouraged for their employment generating capacity.[cdxv] The Chief Minister of Bombay, Yashwantrao Balwantrao Chavan noted that the industrialisation push of the Third Five Year Plan would still leave 5 million or 10 million unemployed across the country.[cdxvi] There was a need to plan in a way which prevented manpower from being wasted and afforded relief to the masses at their village door with minimal need for machinery. Prime Minister Jawaharlal Nehru did strike a divergent note however.[cdxvii] He made the point that village industries could only prosper if they began to use more modern techniques.

During the early 1960s an important change in thinking on small industries took place. Rather than advocating the revival of village industries, more and more politicians and bureaucrats began to call for the industrialisation of India's villages. In February 1961 the Union Commerce and Industry Minister, Manubhai Shah stated that rural industrialisation would be "a must" for the first year of the Third Five Year Plan.[cdxviii] He wanted at least three rural industrial estates in each state with at least ten small industries in each estate to start with. These rural industrial estates would help to ease the disparity in development between urban and rural areas and also generate employment in the villages. The following day the All India Small-Scale Industries Board recommended that state governments allocate 50% of the funds which they were receiving for small-scale industries for their development in rural areas.[cdxix] The Government of India accepted the Small-Scale Industries Board's recommendations in September. By 1963 "rural industries", or taking modern industry to rural India, rather than "village industries", or the revival of traditional production techniques in the villages, were considered to be the basis of a "new strategy" for the promotion of small-scale industry.[cdxx] It was thought that taking industry to the villages would promote "balanced development" of the country's backward areas and meet local demand for essential goods. Industrialisation was now considered the only hope for the unemployed in the villages.

The old village industries ideal was falling into further disrepute as stocks of khadi began to pile up. Khadi was the original Gandhian village industry, however by the mid 1960s there were increasing calls for state khadi boards to be scrapped. Opposition members in the Maharashtra Legislative Council wanted their state khadi board to be disbanded.[cdxxi] They argued that it had "utterly failed" in achieving its objectives and public funds were being "wasted" with no noticeable benefits to the poor whom it was supposed to be benefitting. One member suggested using the money for cow dung gas in the villages, whilst another suggested that khadi was just a "fad" amongst those who still talked about it. At the start of the 1960s there was close to ₹8 crores worth of unsold khadi piling up each year.[cdxxii] The All India Khadi and Village Industries Board wanted further government subsidies to bring the sale price down and clear the stockpile.[cdxxiii] However, the Board itself was falling into disrepute in New Delhi.[cdxxiv] It could not even prepare a consolidated profit and loss account or a balance sheet. The Planning Commission began to restrict the Khadi Board's role in forthcoming Plans.

The production of saris and dhotis had initially been reserved for production in the small-scale sector. In May 1967 the Government of India announced that 43 more products would be reserved for small producers, including car radiators, toasters, heaters, buttons, hypodermic needles, lamp shades and spectacle frames. The Development Commissioner for Small Industries, Venkatasubramanier Nanjappa noted that big business people would no longer be able to produce these products, however he largely projected this greatly expanded reservation for small-scale industries as the result of the success of the sector over the previous decade. Small-scale industries were producing products which even larger companies had not yet ventured into. They had been supplying the nation's defence needs during the war with Pakistan and were also contributing to the country's exports.

Shortly after Indira Gandhi submitted her note on economic policy to the All India Congress Committee in July 1969 the Ministry of Industrial Development began work on expanding the list of products reserved for the small-scale sector. By this time reservation for the small-scale sector had taken a deeper ideological colour and was being spoken of in the press as a "big blow to monopolists".[cdxxv] In November 1970 another 43 products were added to the reserved list, which took the total to 98. In February of 1971 73 more items were reserved for the small-scale sector. Some products had been de-reserved, however the total now stood at 128. The newly reserved items included automobile ancilliaries, garage equipment, electrical wires, insulators, pressure die castings, drums and barrels, tins and torch light cases.

Amidst the spate of new reservations for small-scale industries, the slightly older push for rural industrialisation was also receiving support in New Delhi. The Pandey Working Group sought to identify backward areas for industrial development whilst the Wanchoo Committee looked into financial and fiscal incentives for starting industries in these backward parts of the country. Their recommendations led to government subsidies for the establishment of new small-scale industries in officially designated backward areas as well as concessional finance and credit facilities and transport subsidies. These new measures to encourage the spread of small-scale industry to rural areas were trying to alter a persistent pattern. By the end of 1968, of the 125,000 registered small-scale units, 80,000 were in the relatively industrially advanced areas of Madras, Maharashtra, West Bengal, Punjab and Delhi.[cdxxvi] Within these regions small-scale units tended to be concentrated in the cities. Howrah accounted for 66% of all of West Bengal's small-scale units.[cdxxvii] When World Bank economists toured the country in 1972 and asked about the development of small-scale industries in rural areas they were told the same thing by officials everywhere they went: "It is impossible to grow small-scale industry where nothing else grows."[cdxxviii]

***

Khadi had been the original village industry, and as Independence approached Mohandas Gandhi's advocacy did not wane. Provincial elections had been held in 1946 and a Congress government had come to power in Madras. It was in Royapettah in September that Gandhi told a prayer meeting that "mills are injurious of rural India".[cdxxix] The following month the Prime Minister of Madras, Tanguturi Prakasam announced that new cotton mills would not be allowed in the province and existing mills would not be allowed to expand. Madras continued to lead the way in khadi promotion and the restriction on mill production in the years after Independence. Even Rajaji, a Gandhian capitalist, was in favour of these restrictions and took them further when he became chief minister in 1952 by banning Madras mills from producing saris.

At the start of the 1950s the principal means of encouraging cotton spinners and handloom weavers was the imposition of an excise duty on the production of large cotton mills. The Khadi and Other Handloom Industries Development (Additional Excise Duty on Cloth) Act was passed by Parliament in 1953. In March 1956 the excise duty was reduced on coarse dhotis and saris whilst it was maintained on other coarse and medium varieties. Reducing the excise duty on coarse dhotis and saris was intended to benefit the poor. This measure encouraged the mills to manufacture more coarse dhotis and saris and reduce their production of finer quality textiles. Excise rates were increased in 1956 on non-dhoti and sari mill made cloth. Handlooms and powerlooms were exempt from the increase. There was a surcharge on processing and an additional excise duty was imposed on the mills when sales tax was abolished in 1957. However, the increasing excise had impacted the demand for lower quality cloth and so in October 1956 the government had issued an excise rebate for cloth which was produced in excess of the average during the first half of the year. Excises on medium quality cloth were also reduced. After a flood of coarse cloth onto the market, the rebate was withdrawn in January 1958.

The Industries (Development and Regulation) (Amendment) Act was passed in 1956. The Act allowed the government to control production in the textile industry and divide annual output between small and large producers. In addition, the production of textile machinery was also controlled and a ban was placed on the import of foreign machinery. The Second Plan did not allow for increased production by the mill sector for domestic consumption. The mills were only allowed to install new automatic looms as long as production was for export. The mill sector was to produce 350 million yards for export. The restriction on this production was to be enforced by the Cotton Textiles (Control) Order 1956 which made it compulsory for all composite mills, those which both spun and wove cloth, to have their looms registered with the Textile Commissioner.

The decentralised sector was divided among three different types of producers. There were spinners of the Gandhian variety, handloom weavers, and powerloom weavers. In 1956 handlooms were producing 495 million yards of cloth and they were allowed to increase their production to 1 billion yards by the end of the Second Plan period.[cdxxx] Powerlooms, which were producing 275 million yards in 1956, were to raise their output to 475 million.[cdxxxi] The ambar charkha, an improved four spindled spinning wheel, was also supposed to contribute 300 million yards by 1960.[cdxxxii] The latter half of 1956 saw demand outstripping supply. But rather than allow mills to produce more, the government increased the excise on mill made cloth in order to reduce demand. The revenue from excise on the mill sector doubled that year. Mills were the left with unsold stock. The excise was steadily cut during the late 1950s but still remained higher than the 1955 level. During the Second Plan period the mill sector produced around 5 billion yards of cloth each year whilst the handloom and power loom sectors almost doubled their output to 3 billion yards.[cdxxxiii] Mill production was stagnant, whilst handloom production rose only marginally. It was the powerloom sector which experienced a boom in production.

The Planning Commission had estimated that 9.3 billion yards of cloth would be required each year by the end of the Third Plan period.[cdxxxiv] Around one-third of this total was reserved for handlooms and powerlooms. The mills were allowed to install 25,000 new automatic looms and were to expand production to 5.8 billion yards per year, an increase of 800 million.[cdxxxv] The mill sector did not reach its target, falling short by 1 billion yards in 1966.[cdxxxvi] Handlooms and powerlooms almost reached their targets. New production targets were set for the Fourth Plan in April 1969. Domestic demand was predicted to be 8.5 billion metres for cotton and 1.5 billion for rayon and synthetic textiles.[cdxxxvii] It was projected that 850 million metres would be exported, bringing total demand to 10.8 billion metres.[cdxxxviii] Production capacities were allocated on an almost even basis between the mills and the spinners and weavers, but when targets could not be met due to a shortage of cotton the allocation for the mill sector was reduced.

With all the restrictions on mills in the domestic market, and constant government direction towards exporting, it might be expected that the mill owners would have turned to international markets. However, there was the problem of the supply of cotton. The practice of import substitution and protection to Indian cotton growers had induced a reliance on Indian cotton and a restriction on synthetic fibres. The Indian cotton crop was variable and of low and medium quality. India did try to become self-sufficient in long staple cotton, but the crops remained variable and there were frequent shortages. During the 1960s and 1970s cotton production grew by 30%, but government policies led to a decline in imports of long staple cotton, so most Indian mills could only supply course quality cloth.[cdxxxix] Cotton yields in India were growing, but still lagged well behind international competitors, and so the competitiveness of the Indian textile industry steadily eroded. Indian producers also faced rising labour and fuel costs, power disruptions and labour unrest. As a result of static national income and rising prices, during the 1960s and 1970s per capita consumption of cloth was actually decreasing.[cdxl]

Contrary to the Planning Commission's directions, cotton textile exports remained largely stagnant. Indian textiles had not improved in quality, whereas international competitors had invested in new machinery such as automatic screen printers. International buyers wanted flawless cloth which could only be produced on automatic looms. Indian mills had little incentive or capacity to invest in new automatic looms, in many cases due to restrictions on the import of machinery. Indian textile exports thus remained confined to coarse and medium quality cloth. Even India's limited exports to Europe and America declined due to competition from Pakistani and Chinese producers who made better cloth at cheaper prices.

The question of what to do about the handloom weavers could never be adequately resolved. In 1954 the Kanungo Committee wanted to convert handlooms into semi-automatic or powerlooms over a 15-20 year period. The Second Plan largely concurred with this recommendation and allowed for the installation of 35,000 powerlooms, but the conversion only took place in the co-operative societies. Only 11,000 were installed.[cdxli] Most handloom weavers opposed the conversion idea. They were supported by the Karve Committee of 1956. The new committee wanted both powerlooms and mills restricted at their existing numbers. The number of powerlooms did grow rapidly during the 1960s and 1970s but there was little conversion of handlooms. Another government working group made similar recommendations to those of the Kanungo Committee in 1964 but was overturned by the Sivaraman Committee in 1974 which argued that an excise duty should be applied to the production of powerlooms so that they could not prey on the handlooms.

With the rapid growth of powerlooms the dilemma of how to deal with the problem of "unauthorised" powerlooms arose during the 1970s. The mill owners claimed that the powerloom weavers were taking advantage of concessions which were really meant for the handlooms.[cdxlii] Handlooms continued to expand under protection, whilst powerlooms provided the more direct competition to the mills. The powerloom weavers employed similar technology to the mills, just on a smaller scale, and so they benefitted from government policies. They had lower costs and a cheap labour force which had not been unionised. However, the suspicion arose that many of the powerlooms were owned by mill owners and traders trying to circumvent the government's rules. In addition, mills had started subcontracting to powerlooms and then packaged and marketed the products under their own brands. Many of the millhands who went on strike would go and work on sub-contracted powerlooms.

The Government of India introduced the Controlled Cloth Scheme in 1964. The scheme specified that a certain proportion of mill production had to be of coarse cloth and sold below a fixed minimum price. The Controlled Cloth Scheme lasted until 1978. During the life of the scheme 111 mills were closed down and many were nationalised.[cdxliii] Mills which were nationalised were incorporated into the National Textile Corporation. The newly nationalised mills, the ones made sick by the scheme in the first place, were to produce cheap cloth. Those mills which had survived in the private sector were levied with an additional excise duty, to support the nationalised sick mills. By 1984, the Government of India had spent ₹2,200 crores on sick mills which continued to lose ₹400 crores each year.[cdxliv] There were many causes of industrial sickness, but the biggest was that mills had been allowed only a declining share of production for over 30 years.

***

Bringing more industrial activity under government control had always been at the top of every socialist's charter of demands. Socialising the means of production would be the first serious step towards establishing a meaningful socialism in India. The process was slow at first.

In 1947 the All India Congress Committee's Economic Programme Committee spoke of establishing a just social order. All new industries in defence, key and public utility industries as well as those which were large in scale or monopolistic in nature were to be reserved for public ownership. Any private enterprises which fell within this category were to be nationalised within five years. Banking and insurance were to be nationalised.

The Industrial Policy Resolution of 1948 reflected the compromises which had taken place between the socialists and conservatives in the Congress Party. The country was in the midst of an economic crisis, specifically a downturn in investment, and so the intention to nationalise private enterprises was deferred for ten years. Increased production rather than redistribution was the immediate priority, whilst a vast field was left to the private sector. The aim of an economically interventionist state had not been abandoned, however it was recognised that the state did not have the capacity or the resources to be able to involve itself in industry as much as it wanted. The state would expand its activities, and even open units in new sectors, but it would not acquire and manage existing private sector enterprises. Private enterprise had a valuable role to play, for the "meanwhile". Of the industries reserved for the state, arms and ammunition, and railways were already reserved, whilst the third, atomic energy, did not yet exist. In six more sectors- coal, iron and steel, aeronautics, shipbuilding, telephony and minerals, new undertakings were to be left to the state. Existing private enterprises in these fields would be left alone for 10 years. The third category in the Industrial Policy Resolution covered all remaining industries, which were to be left to private enterprise.

Between the adoption of the Industrial Policy Resolution of 1948 and the beginning of the First Five Year Plan in 1951 the government only established three public sector units- Indian Telephone Industries, Indian Rare Earths and the Indian Finance Corporation.[cdxlv] At the time no private company manufactured telephone equipment, whilst Indian Rare Earths was established by the Department of Atomic Energy to process minerals for the production of atomic energy and the Indian Finance Corporation was created to provide easier access to finance for private companies. Another 16 public sector companies were established during the First Plan period.[cdxlvi] Four were development agencies, whilst another eight were in heavy industry: Hindustan Cable, Nahan Foundry, Hindustan Machine Tools, Hindustan Steel, Hindustan Insecticides, Bharat Electronics, Hindustan Antibiotics, and Hindustan Shipyard. Air India and Indian Airlines were the result of the nationalisation India's private international and domestic airlines. The Ashoka Hotel was built for an international conference for which there was no hotel big enough in the capital. Hindustan Housing produced cement for prefabricated construction. During the First Plan period investment in public sector companies was still only half that in private sector companies.[cdxlvii] After the Congress accepted the goal of a "socialistic pattern of society" at Avadi in January 1955 the government nationalised the largest commercial bank in the country, the Imperial Bank of India in May. In January 1956 over 200 private life insurance firms were nationalised to create the Life Insurance Corporation of India.

The Second Five Year Plan started to direct investment into the public sector and a new Industrial Policy Resolution was announced in 1956. The new Resolution reflected the ascent of the socialists and the waning power of the conservatives within the Congress. Amongst its objectives, the Resolution sought to expand the public sector; the state would assume a predominant and direct responsibility for setting up new industrial undertakings and undertake state trading on a larger scale. The state would assume responsibility for industries over a wider area both in industries of basic and strategic importance as well as those industries in which only it had the capacity to provide the necessary investment. Again, the Industrial Policy Resolution provided for three categories. In the first were industries of basic and strategic importance and public utilities which would be the preserve of the state. These included 17 fields of which 4 were to be central government monopolies- railways, aeronautics, arms and ammunition and atomic energy. The other 13 industries were iron and steel, heavy plant and machinery, heavy electricals, coal and ore mining, minerals, metal mining and processing, aircraft manufacture and shipbuilding, telephony and electricity. Existing private sector units in these fields were not precluded from expansion and the state could seek their co-operation in establishing its own new units. The second category was one in which industries would be progressively state owned and the state would "generally take the initiative" in establishing new units. There were 12 industries in this category including aluminium, machine tools, chemicals, pharmaceuticals, fertilisers, rubber, and road and sea transport. The third category, again, included all other industries, which were to be left to private enterprise. The Industrial Policy Resolution of 1956 did not make any declaration on nationalisation.

Between 1956 and 1964 the Government of India started another 41 public sector enterprises.[cdxlviii] Most were small in size and required relatively low levels of investment. Fourteen were developmental agencies. Five operating companies were nationalised: National Newsprint and Paper Mills, Parag Tools, Mazagaon Dock, Garden Reach Workshop and Mogul Lime. The remaining 22 enterprises were either involved in heavy industry or trading operations. Heavy Engineering Corporation, Heavy Electricals and Indian Refineries all operated in the area reserved for new government enterprises. The remaining five- the Fertiliser Corporation of India, Fertilisers and Chemicals Travancore, Indian Drugs and Pharmaceuticals, Shipping Corporation of India and Neyveli Lignite Corporation operated in the second category in which private enterprise was not prohibited. The other five new public sector enterprises competed directly with the private sector: State Trading Corporation, Travancore Minerals, Janpath Hotel, Minerals and Metals Trading Corporation, and Central Road Transport Corporation.

As the Second Five Year Plan was being prepared politicians understood the need to ease the fears of private sector industrialists. In February 1955 the Union Minister for Production, Kyasamballi Chengaluraya Reddy told a committee of the All-India Manufacturers Association that the fears held about discrimination against the private sector were based on the wrong notion that the public sector competed with the private sector.[cdxlix] Reddy suggested that the public sector should be considered a "national sector" which was concerned with the country's welfare and the establishment of a socialistic pattern of society. As long as the private sector did not conflict with the public sector in the attainment of these ideals it would have vast scope in the country's industrial development. The Chief Minister of Bombay,

Morarji Desai insisted that it was wrong to speak about the public and private sectors as two entities working in different directions. They were, after all, an integral part of a whole striving for the progress of the country.[cdl] He wanted the public and private sectors to work together as a team and maintained that controls would be necessary as long as so many people were living in miserable conditions.

The Union Finance Minister, Sir Chintaman Deshmukh spoke of the "artificial" rivalry between the public and private sectors in July.[cdli] He wanted to refute the allegation that the public sector was starving the private sector of capital. He said that both sectors were serving a common purpose- "the public weal". He argued that the success of the private sector in drawing upon public savings would depend on the way in which public sector enterprises were run. Later that month the Bombay Revenue Minister, Bhausaheb Hiray urged that the public and private sectors work as parts of a "single organism" to secure the resources needed for the country's development.[cdlii] He also argued that both sectors had the same aim- the country's national well-being. The Prime Minister, Jawaharlal Nehru had also been expounding on this theme. He did not think that there was any conflict between the public and private sectors; there had to be planning whether for the public or the private sector.[cdliii] The private sector would be given room, but it had to fit in with the Plan. Planning would not be planning after all, if it did not cover both sectors. By June of 1956 he was able to state that there was no conflict between the public and private sectors in the Second Five Year Plan.[cdliv] Rather than being in conflict, the public sector and the private sector were, in fact, complementary to each other.

***

During the height of the American engagement with the Indian economy the World Bank had sent a team of economists to India in 1964 and 1965 under the leadership of Bernard Bell. In addition to Bell's report to the President of the World Bank, George Woods, his team had prepared 14 volumes of analysis on all aspects of the Indian economy. The sixth volume concerned "Manufacturing Industry with Special Reference to Public Sector Enterprise". [cdlv] The volume was the work of the World Bank economists Kenneth Bohr, Jochen Kraske, Frank Lamson-Scribner and Romano Pantanali. Their report came in the wake of the first flush of investment in public sector heavy industries. Most public sector enterprises which had been established in the late 1950s had started production which meant that an assessment of their performance had become possible.

The Third Plan allocated 54% of all investment in industry to the public sector. Most of this spending was on the heavier component industries- steel (92%), electrical machinery (80%), industrial machinery (60%), and chemicals (50%). These four sectors combined accounted for 80% of government spending on the public sector in industry. This meant that the government's industrial efforts were concentrated in a small number of large public sector enterprises. In 1964 there were 29 central government industrial undertakings. But the largest, Hindustan Steel, accounted for 64% of total investment. The four largest together- Hindustan Steel, Heavy Engineering Corporation, Fertiliser Corporation of India and Heavy Electricals (India)- accounted for 85% of investment. This meant that the performance of these four public sector enterprises was essentially the performance of public sector enterprise in India.

Whilst over half of government investment in industry was supposed to go to the public sector at the start of the Third Plan, the actual amount of investment fell short of the original target. By the middle of the Plan it was evident that fewer projects were being executed, at a much higher cost than was originally budgeted for. In addition, the projects were taking longer to execute than had been originally planned. The investment to output ratio was at the staggeringly high level of 11 to 1. Much of this low increase in output was the result of the difficulties in executing public sector projects; cost overruns, design, procurement and construction delays, and the problems of getting output up to target levels once operations had started. However, given that most government investment was going into capital intensive industry, it was to be expected that it would, at least initially, have a high investment to output ratio. Moreover, there was a need in many of these enterprises to adapt to the use of local resources like coal and ore, train a local labour force in new skills and develop effective large-scale organisations. Even into the mid 1960s very little had been produced.

The actual costs often exceeded the estimates. The average cost increase was 65%. Rather than changes to the original projects, in most cases it was due to faulty initial estimates of project cost. This was particularly true of the Nangal Fertiliser Plant and the Neyveli Lignite project. The most common reasons for inadequate cost estimates were simply missing items; fees and costs for consultants and foreign experts, training expenses and import duties, township costs and working capital. The Planning Commission attributed these to a lack of experience, but they could hardly be considered unavoidable. Directly related to the cost increases were delays in project implementation. Most of the delays took place between the time of commitment of resources to the project and the achievement of full production. The average time needed to complete the four stages of project implementation was 10 years. If the approval and planning phase was deducted it was 7 years. This also meant that down the line foreign exchange requirements were greater than originally anticipated and the savings of foreign exchange on imports were also delayed. In some cases the cost increases put the viability of the original project proposals into doubt. In others it was doubtful to start with.

In some public sector enterprises like the Heavy Engineering Corporation the prospect of profits could only be maintained if domestic prices were inflated well above imports. Given that 10% was considered a satisfactory rate of return for public sector enterprises, as of early 1964, only 12 of the 27 public sector industrial enterprises could achieve this rate. All 12 were comparatively small enterprises which accounted for 3% of total government investment in the sector. None of these smaller profitable enterprises were dependent for supplies or markets on other public sector enterprises. None were particularly innovative and none were subjected to price controls. Most of the larger enterprises, which accounted for 97% of the government's investment, were not yet in full production. If they were producing at near capacity, with one exception, Hindustan Machine Tools, they could not return 10%. Management was inexperienced and the one cost advantage, low labour costs, seemed to dissipate due to the tendency to enlarge the workforce.

Projects were generally initiated from a concern for physical requirements and altered before being completed as the originally estimated requirements were changed. Alternatives were rarely examined systematically, and most often not at all. Technical appraisals were often incomplete and the economics of the projects were rarely considered. The locations of projects were influenced more by a desire to spread largesse throughout the states than for economic viability. Approval was often given before a detailed project report had been submitted. The simple existence of a current or future need for a particular good was generally considered evidence of the economic desirability of establishing a production facility. Rarely was the return on investment the deciding criteria for starting operations. Government officials were using input-output matrices, rather than taking the relative cost of the inputs and outputs into account. Export demand or import supply did not figure in the calculations except as an afterthought. Estimates of requirements were formulated by government committees, ministries, and consultative and planning groups of both government and private industry co-ordinated by the Planning Commission. In many cases these groups did not have adequate data about existing industrial capacity in India, let alone the ability to make forecasts about future requirements. Often an ad hoc government committee would state the need for a particular product, and then a consulting group would put together the project proposal.

Fertiliser projects were recommended in locations without ready access to either raw materials or markets. In the Neyveli Lignite case, the project consultants were asked how best to develop resources at Neyveli in Madras. Other locations were not considered. The heavy electrical plant was located in Bhopal due to a desire to reward Madhya Pradesh, rather than finding an economically viable site. Officials had to conform to the government directives that industrially backward areas be favoured and those which were "industrially congested" be avoided. In the case of the Heavy Electrical Plant at Bhopal the extremely poor financial results were actually incorporated into the project report, as was the need to import supplies. The fact that the project was still approved could only indicate that the government was not overly concerned with the financial viability of the project. Something similar happened at Neyveli. The need to reduce dependence on imports was usually sufficient grounds for approval. Final approval needed to be obtained at the Cabinet level in New Delhi.

Often in-principle approvals of new public sector undertakings were given based on preliminary project estimates. It was usually ad hoc committees which gave approval, but the Planning Commission had started to take a more active role as had the Project Co-ordination Division of the Ministry of Finance. The system seemed to be more suited to obtaining consensus among the ministries rather than analysing the economic feasibility of the projects. There were no agreed economic or financial standards against which projects could be judged. The emphasis on physical needs and the secondary concern for costs may have been related to the tendency to consistently under-estimate costs. The need for the government to be an employer, carry industrialisation to backward areas, operate model communities and provide for each of the states tended to militate against the economic efficiency of industrial plants.

Projects were often approved "subject to adequate foreign exchange being available". The need to then arrange finance and foreign exchange led to cost blowouts. It was only at the time of procurement that more realistic estimations of cost became apparent and the means of financing would often change the character of the project itself. The project reports rarely met the standards of foreign lenders and the need for import licences often led to delays. Delays could also occur due to the need to organise a workforce, deliver equipment to the site, problems with local clearances, and complicated procurement procedures. In the case of steel production it was not realised that it took longer to establish mines and quarries and establish serviceable transport links than to establish the steel plant.

There were frequent changes to public sector projects whilst they were under construction. These changes could occur due to deficiencies in the original project report; items were omitted, supplies were found to be inadequate and limitations of the site were underestimated. Material shortages would necessitate a redesign; cement would have to be substituted for steel as occurred at Neyveli. The stages of construction would also sometimes have to be altered. At both Bhopal and Ranchi the original schedules were changed after construction had started. In some cases the product which the plant was to produce would change. This could delay completion of the plant by six months to a year. The capacity of the plant might be changed without any new project report.

Public sector enterprises also faced the problem of procuring supplies, particularly steel and imported components. This was generally a result of the foreign exchange shortage and the measures taken to address it. In some cases the lack of foreign exchange allocation for supplies had cut output of public sector plants by far more than the cost of supplies. Allocations of supplies had to move through the usual government channels. Each enterprise had to submit to its ministry its foreign exchange requirements for the coming six months. This request would then be forwarded to the Ministry of Finance. Sometimes steel could be sourced domestically, but not the particular type required, and not in sufficient quantities. Once the foreign exchange had been allocated the enterprise then bid on supplies and had to apply for an import licence. There may have been problems of availability of particular currencies at particular times. In some instances the time taken for the allocation to be received meant that a new bid had to be made. Estimating foreign exchange requirements was a difficult task given the complexity of new projects; units were going into production at different times, difficulties with equipment could not be anticipated and the need for spares could only be guessed. A blanket foreign exchange allocation could be provided which helped in the case of the Nangal fertiliser plant. Yet the practice of blanket licences was discontinued. Even public sector management could not be trusted not to misuse its foreign exchange allocation.

When an emphasis was placed on industrial development through the public sector in 1955 the only government employees with any experience of industry were in the railway workshops and ordnance factories. Technical training was increased and training schemes undertaken for large public sector projects. Young engineers were sent abroad for training with foreign technical collaborators, whilst training facilities were set up at the plant sites in India. The problem of meeting the requirements for administrators and managers was of a different scale. Yet there was no appreciation that this new task of management of industrial concerns would be very different to that of regular government duties, and so there was no parallel training for government officers at the upper management level in industrial and financial control and cost accounting.

Low salaries were not enough to attract Indian managers from the private sector, whilst there was a reluctance to hire foreigners in managerial rather than technical positions. The task of public sector management thus fell to the state and central and railway civil servants. The persistence of a system of appointing generalist civil servants as managers subject to periodic transfers was an impediment to the development of a healthy public sector. The government had recognised the problem of a shortage of managerial labour and so in 1957 established an Industrial Management Pool. The initial aim was to recruit 200 managers to fill public sector positions. There were 18,000 applicants, of whom 212 were chosen. Only 130 accepted the offer. There were further dropouts which meant that 105 held jobs under the program. There was difficulty placing the 105. The program was not continued after the initial batch of 1959.

Functions were not clearly defined, responsibility not focused where it could be effective, and authority appeared to depend on consensus. Important decisions were made slowly; there was a constant need for rules, regulations and concurrence. Management was diffused throughout a bureaucracy with little technical or managerial capacity. The project design and development were usually handled by the ministry and then lumped onto management complete, rather than involving it in the process from the start. Many later problems could have thus been anticipated and avoided. Approvals for expenditure over small amounts had to go through the financial manager who reported to the ministry, not the manager of the enterprise. Tenders had to be invited for even the smallest requirements. The government audit was another inhibiting factor; auditors looked at the propriety of expenditure, not just that it was made and accounted for, and they were not generally concerned with the overall performance of the undertaking.

***

Ian Little was among the diminishing number of British economists who retained an interest in the Indian economy after Independence. His most famous work, *A Critique of Welfare Economics* supported the efficacy of free market choices in enhancing economic welfare, which made him more amenable to his American peers than his colleagues at Oxford. He joined the Americans on the Bell Mission in 1964 and contributed an appendix to their volume on the public sector in India. He went and visited the new Heavy Electricals plant at Bhopal in Madhya Pradesh.

The heavy electrical industry had been reserved for the public sector in the Industrial Policy Resolution of 1948. A heavy electrical industry was first proposed in the same year. There were initial reports from consultants, but further consideration was deferred until 1950 due to financial issues. The idea was then revived in 1952 and a long argument between the Ministry of Production and the Ministry of Commerce and Industry ensued over the capacity of the private sector and its ability to meet growing demand. Little thought that these conversations were based on "almost ludicrous underestimates of demand."

The general thinking was that if the case for sufficient internal demand was established, then so was the case for building a factory. It was, from the start, recognised that the manufacture of heavy electricals would be unprofitable. There was some concern from the Ministry of Finance and the Ministry of Commerce and Industry, but it was not enough to persuade decision makers that India might allocate scarce resources in other directions. Self-sufficiency was raised as a justification. Yet there was no explicit argument for why India should be self-sufficient in heavy electricals. Little thought that even in war time should supplies be disrupted, heavy electricals would be the last thing that the country would be worried about.

The Iyengar Committee reported on the question of a heavy electrical public enterprise in March 1955. The committee showed that there was enough demand but that the private sector would not manufacture the heavier equipment due to its unprofitability. Committee members drew up an output mix for the proposed factory. Lighter equipment was included in the output mix to add some profitability in the first decade. Given the scarcity of managers it was thought that it would be better to have fewer big units in which they could work. Heavy rotating equipment could also be included in the same factory. The original product mix was initially adhered to and would continue to influence the development of the project. But demand had been underestimated, and so relatively more products were to be manufactured, to create a big enough factory. The lighter products would offset the losses from the heavy ones, and the best managers would come under the one roof. Little noted that demand was actually much greater than anticipated, and there could have been more, smaller units with greater specialisation.

Little thought that the single unit at Bhopal could only be managed by the best managers in the world, provided they were not subject to the fetters which were placed on public sector managers in India. It would have been better to lose some slight economies of scale and break the unit up into more easily manageable factories. The managerial problem was caused by the bill of goods determined by the Committee. To use the capital intensive factory at a high level of efficiency involved bringing together 10,000 parts into a phased series of engineering and assembly operations to merge into a smooth flow of production. Domestic supplies were of uneven quality and could not be relied upon, imports were subject to foreign exchange and licensing restrictions and the labour force was not yet skilled. There were few suppliers anywhere in the world who could supply all the bewildering array of inputs needed. Associated Electrical Industries was chosen but it was not competitive in the required supply lines. Little thought that if the units had been broken up there would have been a better chance of getting more competitive suppliers. The Committee did not insist on any equity participation from the consultants- it might have given them an incentive to design a more economical factory.

The Committee had already decided on what there was demand for, the products it wanted to produce and that it wanted a single factory. Little thought that it may have been better to leave these things to the consultants to report back on, or maybe several specialised consultants would have been better than one. The Government of India decided to move ahead with the project in March 1955 and another committee, the Khera Committee was formed to choose consultants and further examine the scheme. The committee member K.N. Ranga Rao wanted specialised units and consultants but was overruled. Eleven firms were approached and the Electrical Experts Committee was formed to evaluate their replies. Of the seven which offered to collaborate four were eliminated, which left the choice between AEI and Siemens. Khera chose AEI for unconvincing reasons. Little thought that Khera might have been partial to AEI simply because the firm was British. AEI did not have a good reputation as far as costs were concerned. There was little consideration in AEI's report on the operating and selling costs inherent in different sites. No internal rate of return on capital was calculated. AEI was not even asked for any economic calculation.

Little noted that just a glance at the figures could show that even if all expectations were fulfilled the Bhopal plant would be an uneconomic project. He thought that the project as laid out in the project report was unacceptable by any possible economic criterion and should have been rejected. The report was accepted in March 1957. There was an agreed output of ₹12.5 crores worth of goods and the factory would be designed so that this could be achieved on a single shift whilst allowing for eventual double shifts. The single shift idea was shocking to an economist. Eventually a compromise was reached. Little thought that the government may have been better off just purchasing a factory overseas, which would have actually ensured the savings in foreign exchange; there were better ways of spending money in India. The heavy electricals factory at Bhopal was not going to contribute to national income, nor make a profit, nor save foreign exchange and so should have been rejected.

The foreign exchange crisis of 1957 meant that the Bhopal project had to be replanned in three phases as resources became available. Phase 1 was approved in July 1957. Phase 1 was still at an early stage of construction when in early 1959 the original plan for construction was reverted to. At the end of 1957 the decision was taken to double output to ₹25 crores. But then the output mix was changed which increased the output value and factory requirements. Yet there was no new report on the economics of these changes. AEI was asked to prepare a new report. The output value increased even more.

The heavy electricals project proved much more costly than anticipated. The factors which led to the cost overrun were phasing, the change in output mix, delays in completing Block II due to a shortage of steel, higher prices for equipment, lower output, losses on the township, and larger inventories and expenditure in anticipation of Block IV. It could have also just been simple underestimation of capital costs by AEI. Output by the end of 1964 was between ₹6 crores and ₹7 crores. In addition, there had been a month long lockout due to labour troubles. The prices that the factory was charging were close to double those of comparable imported products. The unit was running losses, incurring huge expenses on wages, interest, miscellaneous costs and consultants. The privately owned manufacturer Kirloskar was consistently profitable. The gross value added was small and the net value added still negative. The contribution to national income also remained small. Because the output was sold at a higher price than imports it was not a useful indicator of import savings. A large number of components had to be imported, the foreign consultants had to be paid, and the domestic inputs would have had an import component to them as well. Import savings would not be more than ₹1 crore.

Little's impression of the Heavy Electricals plant at Bhopal was of an excessively expensive setup in which too little was happening. Labour had excessive rights and there was not enough delegation to middle and lower management. The problem was the "civil service spirit"; the managers did not want to risk their careers by moving away from civil service precedents. The rewards were few, the penalties were great, and they were subjected to a triple audit. There were problems with local suppliers and the tendering system which resulted in delays and excess stocks. Little was not an engineer, but the technical questions seemed obvious and mainly related to waste and idle capacity. His impression was of an engineer's dream come true. Any board of directors in an industrialised country would never have allowed the engineers to get away with it. AEI did not have anything so grand itself, nor did any firm in the world. Little thought that it would have been better to build up slowly. There was a feeling of standing in a gothic cathedral rather than a factory.

***

Between 1969 and 1980 134 public sector enterprises

were established. Only 85 had been started over the previous 20 years.[cdlvi] The government was moving into businesses which did not always need huge investments of capital or long gestation periods for profitability, and were not necessary for industrialisation such as medium and light engineering, agricultural products, textiles, trading, construction and consultancy. During 1969 and 1970, the Prime Minister, Indira Gandhi became the country's leading advocate for a strong public sector.

Indira's advocacy grew in the weeks after her clash with the Congress President, S. Nijalingappa in April 1969. When she addressed the delegates to the Indian National Trade Union Congress in Kerala in May she made it clear that she did not think that there was any way that India could progress without enlarging the public sector in order to give it a dominant position.[cdlvii] She made the ritual statement that there was no conflict between the public and private sectors. Yet she gave it a sharper edge. It was only when one sector encroached on another that conflict would arise. Indira thought that the field left open for the private sector in India was vast but was not sure that it had been as fully exploited as it should have been.

Days after nationalising the banks in July, Indira isolated the reason for the public sector's failure so far: the people who managed public sector enterprises had not been committed to the government's ideologies and policies.[cdlviii] Later, in October, when businessmen in Bombay complained of the government's ever shifting position on the private sector, sometimes lauding its role and at other times heaping blame on it, the prime minister suggested they read back over their own speeches running down the public sector.[cdlix] She also reminded them that the private sector enjoyed its position entirely due to the protection provided by the government. In December she insisted that besides financial profits, the public sector also needed to be recognised for the "social profits" that it was making.[cdlx] She felt that the public sector had a prominent position in name but not in fact and that needed to change. Months after the split in the Congress Party, Indira made a more fervent appeal.[cdlxi] She was addressing a convention organised by the Institute for Socialist Education in New Delhi. She told her audience that socialism could only work if the public sector was vigorous. People were attacking the public sector but what they were really attacking was the public sector's larger objective- the establishment of a socialist society.

After the election of 1971 Indira Gandhi's government began a renewed surge of nationalisation. This acquisition of private companies was initially largely the work of one man. S Mohan Kumaramangalam had been one of the Leftist students in Indira Gandhi's social circle in England in the mid 1930s. He subsequently became a member of the Communist Party of India. By the mid 1960s he was pushing a novel line within the Party. He thought that its sometimes doctrinaire opposition, or distance from the Congress was only driving the ruling Party towards greater co-operation with Rightist forces. In order to achieve the aim of non-capitalist development he argued instead for greater co-operation between Communists and the Socialists within the Congress, and the infiltration of the Congress.[cdlxii] His thesis was rejected by his Party in 1964, but then accepted in 1969. In between, as if to lead the way, Kumaramangalam did not renew his membership of the Communist Party and instead joined the Congress. In 1966 he became Advocate-General of Madras under a Congress government and the following year went to the Centre as Chairman of Indian Airlines. From the time of the Congress split in 1969 until elections in 1971 he was a leading strategist of the Congress Left. Indira then appointed him minister for steel and mines in her new Cabinet. By this time there were almost 70 ex-Communists and Socialists in the Congress Parliamentary Party.[cdlxiii]

Whilst bank nationalisation had been a part of the political discourse dating back to Independence, the nationalisation of coal mines had not been on the agenda. Only a month prior to its enactment Kumaramangalam had denied that it would take place; only the amalgamation of smaller mines would be undertaken.[cdlxiv] Coal had been included in Schedule A of the Industrial Policy Resolution of 1956 in which all new enterprises were to be the sole responsibility of the state, but over the ensuing 15 years the government had not moved to nationalise existing private sector mines. However, the government had, in 1957, through the Coal Bearing Areas (Development and Regulation) Act reserved all untouched collieries for development by the public sector. The private sector would be left with its existing collieries which would eventually be exhausted.

Most of the Cabinet was opposed to nationalisation of the coal industry. Yet Kumaramangalam made his case largely devoid of ideology and was, ultimately, persuasive. In October 1971 214 coking coal mines and coke oven plants were taken over through an ordinance and subsequently nationalised in May 1972. Then, in January 1973, 464 non-coking coal mines were taken over under an ordinance and were nationalised in May 1973. And so, the entire coal industry, barring the coal mines attached to private sector steel plants, had come under public ownership. Part of Kumaramangalam's aim was to bring coking coal mines under public ownership in order to better manage India's scarce supply, which he argued the private sector was wasting through slaughter mining in its quest for profits.[cdlxv] The second reason was to expand production in order to meet the needs of the iron and steel industry. Kumaramangalam claimed that the increased production of non-coking coal would be beyond the investment capacity of the private sector. Both he and Indira went on to argue that private coal mines were exploiting workers.

Kumaramangalam also managed to nationalise the copper and refractories industries. There were two refractories companies in the private sector- Asian Refractories

Limited and Assam Sillimanite Company Limited. Refractories are materials which can withstand intense heat in the manufacturing process. The reasoning for nationalising Asian Refactories was quite broad; it was to "meet the requirements of the iron and steel industry".[cdlxvi] The government needed help at its Bokaro steel mill. Asian Refactories had shut down in 1968 and been auctioned off to the Birlas. Their application to takeover the company was still pending before the Monopolies Commission when Kumaramangalam intervened and nationalised it. He thought it was "a good deal"; the equipment was still modern.[cdlxvii] Assam Sillimanite was taken over by the government even before it could be put up for auction in 1972. It was eventually nationalised in 1976. The government was also keen to acquire the Indian Copper Corporation which had a 10,000 tonne capacity. Kumaranagalam justified the acquisition on the grounds that the country urgently needed greater production of copper to save on foreign exchange expenses on imports.[cdlxviii] He wanted to do away with "artificial lines of demarcation" between the private and public sectors in the industry, eliminate monopoly control and better develop the industry. Kumaramangalam admitted that the government had made a mess of its previous venture in the field at Khetri and Indian Copper was thriving in the private sector, but he insisted that it could not expand without government investment.[cdlxix] Being a private sector enterprise it invested only that amount which it thought would generate a profit. The government had no such hesitation.

In July 1972 the government took over the management of the Indian Iron and Steel Company in West Bengal. Kumaramangalam justified the takeover by citing mismanagement by the managing agents. He charged that the neglect of maintenance and modernisation of the plant had brought it down to 60% of total capacity.[cdlxx] It was Kumaramangalam's long held belief that the government had made a great mistake after

Independence in starting its own steel plants rather than just nationalising the existing private sector plants and benefitting from their infrastructure and management expertise.[cdlxxi] Nonetheless, he made no overt appeal to socialist ideology whilst nationalising the Bengal steel plant. K.D. Malaviya, who later became steel minister, referred to it as a penal action rather than an ideological one.[cdlxxii] However, IISCO was already heavily dependent on public sector financial institutions. The government held just under 50% of its shares through public sector banks and insurers. The alternative to nationalisation would have been to let the mill shut down. This would have been as sizable a loss to the government as it would have been to the mill's private sector owners. During the first two years of government control the plant had not been officially nationalised. The government was deciding what to do, but Kumaramangalam stated that the mill would not go back the private sector. It was just a matter of what form the government takeover would take.[cdlxxiii] The government had to consider the matter of preserving the jobs of some 40,000 workers at the mill and its associated mines.

Most of the public sector enterprises acquired or established after 1969 made losses.[cdlxxiv] The public sector, taken as a whole, was already making losses in 1969, however the tendency to nationalise loss making private sector units, as well as to continue starting new units which required a gestation period before which profits could be made, only exacerbated the problem. Whilst the consolidated losses of 74 public sector enterprises in 1969 totalled ₹38 crores the combined losses of 168 public sector enterprises in 1980 came to ₹182 crores. Not a single public sector enterprise was running at full capacity: less than half could run at 75% capacity and one-quarter were running at only 25% as late as 1980. When profits were made they remained low. Before interest and tax the average during the 1970s remained around 10% or 15%. Public sector manufacturing units averaged only 3-5% profits whilst the private sector made 17-23%. Three-quarters of the profits being generated came from units which did not have to deal with competition. They were monopolies which could set prices which consumers would have to accept.

***

Jawaharlal Nehru's enthusiasm for steel almost matched Mohandas Gandhi's passion for khadi. During the 1950s he included a trip to a local steel plant on most of his foreign tours. The steel plants were mainly located in newly socialist and communist countries and were the pride of their workers and governments. Nehru variously visited steel plants in Manchuria, Tblisi, the Urals, Belgrade, Warsaw, Dusseldorf, and Stockholm. He was sure that he wanted to start public sector steel mills in India rather than acquire the existing private sector plants in Bihar and Bengal: "Suppose we want more steel as we do. Instead of acquiring the Tata concern, it is far better for us to put out money on new plants. We want any amount of steel. The more you think of it, the more you realise that all our future development, industrial development, depends on steel."[cdlxxv]

The Tata concern which Jawaharlal Nehru spoke of had a long history. Late in his life, towards the end of the 19th century, Jamsetji Tata began to act on his long held desire to make steel in India. In a quip which has passed into Indian business folklore, when told of Jamsetji's plans the Chief Commissioner of the Indian Railways, Sir Frederick Upcott replied: "Do you mean to say that Tatas propose to make steel rails to British specifications? Why, I will undertake to eat every pound of steel rail they succeed in making."

During his last years Jamsetji kept corresponding with colonial officials in search of government assistance for a steel plant and visited the United States, Britain and Germany to learn more about the industry. He signed an agreement with an American firm to design a factory and began to secure supplies, however he died in 1904 before he could start the project. Jamsetji's heirs continued the quest however, and a site for a mill was found in the jungles of Bihar. The village, Sakchi was later renamed Jamshedpur. The area had adequate water supply, was located not far from iron ore deposits and coal fields and was only 250 kilometres from Calcutta. Work began in 1908 and by 1911 the mill had an annual production capacity of 100,000 tonnes. The first steel ingots were produced in 1912. Capital had been raised in India, however the technical managers were brought from abroad. The mill was managed by an American until the start of the Second World War, by which time its management had been largely Indianised.

At the start of the First World War Tata Steel was producing around 50,000 tonnes of steel a year.[cdlxxvi] India's annual consumption of steel stood at 1.2 million tonnes, which meant that in its infancy the Tata mill was only supplying 4% of the country's annual demand. The first extension of plant capacity came in 1917 when it was raised to 500,000 tonnes.[cdlxxvii] During the 1920s and 1930s capacity was steadily expanded to 1 million tonnes which made the Tata mill the largest in the British Empire.[cdlxxviii] On the eve of the Second World War it had come to supply 75% of annual demand in India. Tata Steel did experience a financial crisis in the early 1920s as a result of cheap imports arriving in the Indian market, however the company was able to draw on debt and benefit from the government's new tariff protection to Indian producers. Tata Steel became profitable again after 1925 and expansion in the late 1920s and early 1930s was financed from accumulated profits rather than debt. During the Great Depression Tata Steel was among the lowest cost producers of pig iron in the world and began exporting. During the Second World War the Tatas went on to make large profits due to buoyant demand, however the plant was starting to deteriorate due to intense capacity utilisation.

The Indian Iron and Steel Company was founded in 1918 by Martin & Company, a Calcutta based partnership between Sir Thomas Martin and Sir Rajen Mookerjee. Their plant at Hirapur produced pig iron for export to Britain and Japan. The Steel Corporation of Bengal, managed by Burn & Company, another old Calcutta based construction firm founded by Alexander Burn in the 18th century, which had been taken over by Martin & Company, established a steel mill next to the pig iron mill with an initial capacity of 270,000 tonnes in 1937. The town, like Jamshedpur, had been renamed after the owners and become Burnpur. By the end of the Second World War the Burnpur plant was producing around 200,000 tonnes of steel a year. Between them, the Tatas and the Burns were able to meet India's annual demand for steel. The Steel Corporation of Bengal was amalgamated with the Indian Iron and Steel Company in 1953. The managers became known as Martin & Burn Company.

The Industrial Policy Resolution of 1948 had stipulated that new steel plants would be reserved for the public sector whilst only giving an assurance that existing private sector plants would not be nationalised for another 10 years. Nonetheless, the Birlas did express interest in getting into the steel business. In 1954 the group entered into an agreement with a British consortium to build an integrated steel mill at Durgapur in West Bengal. The Birlas had only raised about 10% of the required capital, however the government rejected their proposal not on financial grounds, but that it violated the provisions of the Industrial Policy Resolution. New steel mills were reserved for the public sector.

The Second Five Year Plan period was a prosperous one for both the Burns and the Tatas. The government sanctioned an expansion of the capacity of the Tata plant to 2 million tonnes, doubling its pre-Independence capacity. The Burn steel plant's capacity was raised to 1 million tonnes. Tata Steel entered into an agreement with an American firm and only took two years to double its capacity. The Burn steel plant doubled its capacity within four years with help from British consultants. The troubles for both companies started with the coming of the Third Five Year Plan. No provision was made for any expansion of capacity in the private sector. The Tatas had applied for capacity expansion in 1961 but were rejected. The government would reconsider its position when the new public sector steel mills could not produce the required amount, but by that time it was usually too late for the private sector to meet immediate demand and so imports would have to be procured. The Tatas' proposal for capacity expansion was rejected once again in 1963, this time because it included a proposal for a new plant across the river from the existing one in Jamshedpur. Whilst a proposal for expanding an existing plant might at least be entertained, a new plant would be a breach of the Industrial Policy Resolution.

Martin & Burn Company applied for capacity expansion before the Fourth Plan. Martin & Burn wanted to double capacity to 2 million tonnes but were allowed only 1.3 million in the first of a two phase programme. However, even this smaller increase was delayed due to a dispute over earlier government loans provided to the company. The government had been nationalising the company by stealth. Those earlier loans were to be repaid in the expectation that the government would raise the administered price of steel. However, after 1963 the government began to insist that payment be made in the form of equity in the company. The second phase of expansion never took place and so the capacity of the Burn steel plant settled at 1.3 million tonnes. In the 15 years after nationalisation of the Burn mill the government could only produce an average of 564,000 tonnes of steel each year, which was about half the production achieved during the early 1960s under private ownership.[cdlxxix] This figure was even lower than the lowest points of production under private ownership- the

60% capacity which prompted nationalisation.

The Government of India's efforts to enter the steel industry began in December 1953 when it came to an agreement with a German combine, Krupp and Demag, to build a steel plant at Rourkela in Orissa. Another agreement was reached with the Soviet Union in February 1955 to assist in building a second steel plant at Bhilai in Madhya Pradesh. Later in the year the government also took over from the Birlas their initial deal with the British consortium to build a plant at Durgapur in West Bengal. All three plants had become fully operational by the early 1960s and all three came under the control of Hindustan Steel Limited. A fourth steel plant was built at Bokaro in Bihar. The United States government was initially interested in assisting with the project in the early 1960s during the Kennedy administration, however it ran into Congressional opposition to the project primarily due to the fact that the plant would be completely government owned. Eventually the Russians assisted in the establishment of the plant in 1967. Production started in 1972, however the project's first stage was only completed in 1978. Hindustan Steel Limited was replaced by the Steel Authority of India Limited in 1973. By the mid 1970s 75% of Indian steel was being produced in the public sector.[cdlxxx]

Public sector steel plants were loss making enterprises in the 1960s.[cdlxxxi] It was Hindustan Steel Limited's large and consistent losses which contributed to the disrepute of the public sector and stoked the criticism of some Congress leaders in the summer of 1969. By 1967-68 Hindustan Steel Limited's annual loss stood at ₹40 crores, whilst its accumulated losses since its inception in 1954 totalled ₹250 crores. The group made huge losses in eight of the ten years of the 1960s. The profits which the group made in two years were due to the higher prices which it could charge due to the partial decontrol of steel prices. The Steel Authority of India Limited's profits only began to become consistent after 1973 due to the introduction of a dual pricing policy; some higher prices could be set by the steel producers whilst other lower prices were mandated by the government. The Steel Authority was able to show profits in 7 of the 10 years of the 1970s.

The main structural problem for the profitability of public sector steel producers was that whilst price rises were increasingly possibly due to the government's relaxation of controls, there was little effort to reduce production costs through enhancing efficiency and rates of capacity utilisation. Prices would rise and profits would be reported, until they were overtaken by costs and then there would be a return to losses. The high costs of public sector steel mills were generally attributed to the machinery which in some cases was not suited to Indian conditions. The machinery at public sector steel plants produced a high ash content which inhibited higher capacity utilisation. Machinery was most often not maintained properly and allowed to deteriorate over the decades, partially due to bureaucratic delays. In addition, due to political pressures public sector steel plants had to employ many more workers than required, in some cases two or three times the number initially planned for. The workforce of public sector steel plants generally suffered from poor morale. Militant unions, often competing with one another, particularly at the Durgapur plant in West Bengal, ensured many days of lost work time each year. In 1983 the Steel Authority of India Limited had 125,861 employees at work in its plants producing 6.1 million tonnes of steel each year.[cdlxxxii] Kobe Steel of Japan produced the same quantity with 13,069 employees.[cdlxxxiii] As a result, public sector steel plants in India produced steel at the highest cost in the world.

Whilst the public sector steel plant at Bhilai in Madhya Pradesh was considered an exemplar, and the plant at Durgapur in West Bengal was a laggard, none of the Steel Authority of India Limited's operations could match the Tata plant at Jamshedpur for its consistent profitability, high levels of capacity utilisation, improving efficiency and harmonious industrial relations. The Tata employees at Jamshedpur only ever referred to the steel plant as "hamari company" or "our company".[cdlxxxiv] This high morale and employee loyalty and been built over decades and in some cases three generations within a family had worked at Jamshedpur.

As early as 1923, Ratanji Tata stated: "We are not putting up a row of workmen's huts at Jamshedpur. We are building a city."[cdlxxxv] As soon as the plant started manufacturing steel, the Tatas employed the British economists Beatrice and Sidney Webb as consultants. They wrote memorandums on "Cooperative Store, Benefit Funds and Thrift Agencies" and "Medical Services and the Welfare Works at Sakchi".[cdlxxxvi] Sidney Webb then recruited professors from London University to visit Jamshedpur to assist in the planning of the company's welfare services. The company hospital was built in 1931. By the 1980s it was one of the best run hospitals in India with 1,000 beds and 140 doctors providing treatment in most specialisations. There were three additional hospitals for eye care, tuberculosis and cancer. The company's immunisation programme, carried out through mobile vans, had brought the death rate in the town to close to one-third of the national average and infant mortality was less than one-quarter the rate in the rest of India.[cdlxxxvii] The company also provided free education to 27,000 students in 15 primary schools, 9 high schools and 7 colleges. The company was also running an Integrated Rural Development Programme to provide irrigation and better farming practices in the town's surrounding villages. The company provided housing for about half its employees. Jamshedpur, unusually for India at the time, had an underground sewage system. The company provided free electricity and filtered drinking water. The company managed the roads, sanitation and garbage collection. The population of Jamshedpur was thus among the healthiest in India. The aesthetic centrepiece of Jamshedpur was Jubilee Park, set on a 200 acre plot featuring a Mughal garden with multicoloured lights and fountains.

***

Advaita, or non-duality is among the oldest ideas of esoteric Hinduism. The atman, or soul is thought to be the same as brahman, or the highest metaphysical reality. Advaita provides a philosophical aversion to antagonism, division and conflict. There is no need for difference. In reality there are no antagonists, divisions are illusory, and conflict is futile. In the ultimate analysis all is really one. It was this type of thinking which Jawaharlal Nehru had railed against, without naming it, when he wrote *Whither India* in 1933. Yet as chairman of the National Planning Committee, and later prime minister, he became a master of it himself. Advaita was a necessary device for a Congress president constantly having to reconcile opposing views and interests. At the first meetings of the National Planning Committee Nehru had tried to assure Joseph Kumarappa and his fellow Gandhians that there was no inherent conflict between cottage industries and large-scale industries. He maintained this position as prime minister, yet his assurances were less frequent and less convincing. His attention had turned to industrialisation and the construction of a dominant public sector. He now had to calm the nerves of India's capitalists and so turned to Advaita once again. There was no inherent conflict between the public sector and the private sector. Each had its place and each would work towards the greater good. Most of Nehru's colleagues were also non-dualists. Bhausaheb Hiray, the Bombay revenue minister put it best when he said that the public and private sectors were "one organism". Yet, in the material world, all cannot be one. For every product reserved for small-scale industries, larger factories would be prevented from its manufacture. For every industry that the public sector dominated, the growth of the private sector would be stunted.

It is often lamented that Mohandas Gandhi's ideas were largely forgotten in the years after Independence. In the matter of small industries this is only partially true. Gandhi's ideas were not forgotten, yet they were distorted. The problem was initially one of definition. It might have seemed like a minor point, but there was a big difference between the village industries which Mohandas Gandhi and Joseph Kumarappa wanted to pursue and the small-scale industries which Jawaharlal Nehru and K.T. Shah were interested in. When appeasing the Gandhians assurances were initially made that village industries would be encouraged. Yet after Independence it was small-scale industries, mainly urban rather than rural, which received the most government assistance. By the end of the 1950s most Indian cities had "industrial estates", both official and unofficial; Okhla in New Delhi, Ulhasnagar in Bombay and Howrah in Calcutta, which looked like large factories artificially divided into smaller ones. The main beneficiaries, as researchers from UNESCO found out, were the middlemen. By the 1960s the problems of small-scale industries were becoming apparent. The Industrial Policy Resolution of 1948 had stated that small-scale industries would require the provision of supplies, cheap power, technical advice, organised marketing, and where necessary protection from large-scale manufacturers. Yet small-scale industries were largely deprived of supplies, cheap power, technical advice and organised marketing, yet they were increasingly protected from competition from large-scale producers. Had they been provided with the former rather than the latter they would have likely grown organically according to local demand and there would have been little need for government reservations. Meanwhile, village industries of the type that Gandhi envisaged, and village industrialisation of the modern sort, never occurred, whilst the production of khadi fell into financial disarray. The one industry which came close to fulfilling Gandhi's original vision was cotton textiles. He thought that should the day come when the big cotton mills closed down, India would be pulsating with new life. Jayaprakash

Narayan had also written of nationalising the cotton mills in *Why Socialism?* Many cotton mills had either closed down or been nationalised by the 1970s due to policies to protect smaller spinners and weavers, yet the result was not a new dawn but a huge recurring bill for the Government of India.

Jawaharlal Nehru's enduring sense of mission came from his belief that India had to industrialise as quickly as possible. He and Prasanta Mahalanobis believed that industrialisation would largely be the work of the public sector and it was during the Second Plan period that the government began to move into heavy industry on a huge scale. It was not long however before critics of this approach emerged. Nehru's opponents would never tire of pointing out that scarce resources were being allocated to heavy industry at the expense of agriculture and that the public sector returned losses year after year. Public sector enterprises caused a drain on the government treasury rather than replenishing it with profits which could be redistributed. When they did make profits it was often through price gouging, or charging customers higher prices than they should otherwise pay.

The whole public sector enterprise seemed to betray a lack of understanding of economics. As Ian Little pointed out, it could only have been designed by an engineer. The first step in the decision to produce was to discern whether there was demand for a product, rather than whether it could be produced efficiently. The mere act of producing in the public sector made that production legitimate. The public sector steel plants at Bhilai, Durgapur and Rourkela were the icons of the public sector project in India. Twenty five years after beginning to produce steel in the public sector, the Government of India still needed to import steel. By the 1970s the Tata Steel plant at Jamshedpur was the last remaining big steel producer in the private sector. Yet it was the Tata Steel plant which provided a model of both economic efficiency and urban planning. In addition, industrial relations were harmonious; there had been no major industrial dispute for decades. Workers thought of the company as their own. Jamshedpur thus most closely resembled the workers' utopia which Jayaprakash Narayan had read about in Mikhail Ilin's *Moscow Has a Plan* in the 1930s. Ironically, the Tatas' industrial utopia was located in Bihar, young Jayaprakash's home state, and had already begun to take shape by the time that he was writing in 1936.

The question of whether India's planned economy was really socialist has persisted since its inception. Those on the Left, both during the years of economic planning, and in retrospect, have been averse from using the word "socialist" to describe the Indian economy after Independence. The Licence Raj, in their estimation, was a perversion of socialism. Even leaders of the Swatantra Party like Rajaji and Minoo Masani would taunt Jawaharlal Nehru, calling the economic system he created "state capitalism". They were using a rhetorical device to shame him and the Congress Party for having created a system which was actually serving a small coterie of capitalists who could work the bureaucracy rather than one which served the people. Yet, the Licence Raj was specifically socialist, from its inception, in its ideals and its execution. It was, to adapt the Soviet leader Leonid Brezhnev's formulation, India's "actually existing socialism". Indian socialism, by the time it had started to take form in the 1950s was an incongruous combination of Gandhian and Nehruvian thinking, which in itself was a more profound attempt at non-dualism. Small-scale industries co-existed with large-scale public sector heavy industries. As Milton Friedman foresaw in 1955, too little capital was combined with too much labour in small-scale industry and not enough labour was combined with too much capital in heavy industry. Most economic studies point to medium sized businesses as the most dynamic, efficient, and fast growing in terms of employment and profitability. Yet it was precisely these medium sized businesses which were stifled for decades after Independence.

When the Janata Party came to power in March 1977, its members found it difficult to speak in one voice on the issue of the public sector. In April the member for Bombay North-East, Subramanian Swamy called for the elimination of the public sector excepting for some vital segments of the economy.[cdlxxxviii] In May Chandra Shekhar, the President of the Janata Party and veteran socialist stated: "The Janata stands for the public sector. It is firmly of the view that the public sector is vital and essential for the growth of the economy."[cdlxxxix] The Industry Minister, George Fernandes who had led the railway workers' strike in 1974 was constantly raising the spectre of nationalisation and warned that the government would move into the management of private sector firms which were engaging in unfair trade practices.[cdxc] The Finance Minister, Hiralal Patel, a conservative and former officer of the Indian Civil Service made it clear from the start however that the government would not undertake any shift away from the public sector.[cdxci] In fact, over time he came closer to the Socialists' position and began to call for a bigger public sector, one which would increasingly produce consumer goods in addition to its existing presence in heavy industries, something which might enhance its profitability. The Prime Minister, Morarji Desai was not as partial to the public sector and in his last months in office told public sector managers to show profits or "pay the penalty".[cdxcii] When Charan Singh replaced Desai as prime minister he was a little less direct, advising his ministers in charge of key economic portfolios to improve the performance of public sector enterprises under their responsibility.[cdxciii]

Members of the Janata Party were able to reach more ready agreement on the issue of small-scale industries. There was no opposition to the idea within the Party, only varying degrees of support. Morarji Desai and Charan Singh, the two most powerful men in the government, had long been advocates of small-scale industry, specifically village industries and rural industrialisation, whilst the Jana Sangh members had also embraced the idea. The Socialists, although more enthused by heavy industry, were not opposed to small industries. Thus, in December 1977, George Fernandes presented a new industrial policy to the Lok Sabha which included the reservation of 324 new products for small-scale industry. The total number stood at 504, although there was some concern that the list might have been inflated by creating multiple new distinctions within existing product categories.[cdxciv] The number would grow to over 800 in the following months. Yet perhaps more radical was the government's decision to stop issuing licences for establishing factories in towns with a population of more than 500,000. The policy was to come into effect from December 1978 and would have essentially forced the industrialisation of rural India. Yet the Janata government did not last very much longer. The coalition had disintegrated by the monsoon of 1979, and after becoming prime minister for a matter of days in August, Charan Singh's government fell and he acted as a caretaker prime minister until elections could be held in the winter. And so, the Janata Party attempt to fundamentally restructure the Indian economy came to a quick end.

Indian planners had created as closed an economy as they could. The aim was self-sufficiency, or self-reliance as it came to be known. However, the question of what role exports might play in the economy soon arose. India was pursuing a path of import substitution, and provision for exports had not received much attention in Prasanta Mahalanobis's model. The issue became more urgent because, as was discovered during the foreign exchange crisis of 1957, a country which did not earn foreign exchange from exports, could not pay for imports in foreign exchange. As a result, the Government of India quickly became dependent on foreign aid donors to make up the perennial foreign exchange shortfall. Nonetheless, Jawaharlal Nehru did begin to make appeals for an increase in exports and during the 1960s the Government of India initiated a host of export promotion schemes. But could a country which was pursuing import substitution simultaneously promote exports? Indian exporters faced all the problems of a controlled economy; an overpriced rupee, problems with infrastructure, difficulties in procuring imported components, and a lack of incentive to export given the protected domestic market. All of these factors led to a lack of competitiveness in foreign markets. Indian politicians assumed that just by encouraging Indian businesses to export that exports would boom and the foreign exchange crises would be resolved. Yet there had to be demand for India's products abroad. This issue was not just one of production after all, India had to compete with its neighbours who all produced better products at cheaper prices. Nonetheless, India did have one particular product which was in great demand abroad and which had not been factored into the government's calculations.

EIGHT
Indian Exports

Professor Bellikoth Raghunath Shenoy was the only one among 21 invited economists to note his dissent to the Second Five Year Plan in April 1955. His main concern was with deficit financing. He thought that a resort to borrowing by the government, either from the domestic market, or international lenders, would only lead to inflation and further hardship on Indian consumers. The Second Plan started to unravel sooner than he expected, and for a slightly different reason as foreign exchange reserves began to plummet during 1957. Three years after expressing his initial scepticism over the Plan, Shenoy delivered a lecture to the Forum of Free Enterprise in Bombay in March 1958.[cdxcv] A number of explanations for the foreign exchange crisis had been in circulation, the most popular of which was that a liberalisation of import licensing had led to a depletion of foreign currency reserves. Yet Shenoy thought that the principal cause of India's foreign exchange problem was its inability to export. India's industrial and agricultural production had been rising during the 1950s, but exports were actually below the levels maintained prior to the Second World War. Shenoy did try to make a connection between his initial concern over inflation and the low level of exports. Inflation was driving domestic production and consumption at the expense of exports, and the demand for imported components for the manufacture of products for the domestic market was also putting pressure on foreign exchange reserves. Furthermore, Indian exporters were hampered by a rigid exchange rate for the rupee. The result was constant difficulty with the national Balance of Payments and the necessary resort to import restrictions. The remedy for India's foreign exchange problem, according to Shenoy, was not to further restrict imports, but to step up exports.

The need to boost exports was accepted quite quickly in official circles in New Delhi. By the early 1960s the Government of India had established a plethora of schemes and institutions to encourage Indian exporters. Part of the new export drive was stimulated by government fiscal measures, direct and indirect financial transfers to Indian manufacturers seeking out export markets. There were exemptions on sales taxes, refunds of indirect taxes, direct tax relief, direct subsidies and concessions on transportation costs. The State Trading Corporation also joined the export effort, in effect subsidising Indian commodity producers by buying their produce for a higher price than it could sell it abroad. There were Marketing Development Funds and Export Promotion Councils, yet it was the Ministry of Commerce and Industry Development Wing's import entitlement schemes which proved most popular among Indian businesspeople. The list of industries covered by these import entitlement schemes was published in a Red Book. There were Part I schemes and Part II schemes, permissible imports and supplementary entitlements. A principle of "directness" of the imported components into the domestic manufacturing process guided decisions on allocations. A secondary market soon developed in which import allotments sold for a premium. Most often beneficiaries imported more than their specified industry allocation. The intention of all these government measures was for Indian exporters to be given special rights to imports based on their export performance. Yet one Bombay cotton trader saw things in a different way. He put the government's new import entitlement schemes to his own purpose and ended up building one of the greatest business empires of his time.

The Government of India's export promotion measures did have some effect. Exports began to rise in the early

1960s. India's traditional export commodities like jute began to recover after stagnant export performance in the 1950s, whilst newer engineering and chemicals industries began to send their goods abroad. With the devaluation of the rupee in 1966 and the hesitant move towards a more open trading regime it might have been thought that exports would boom. Yet exports again entered a lull in the late 1960s and only exhibited tepid growth in the first years of the 1970s. The old impediments remained; rising labour costs, worker strikes, restricted access to imported components, a captive domestic market which provided little incentive to export, and a still rigid, if less overpriced rupee. In addition, India had to compete with Asian rivals which were increasingly orienting their economies towards a specifically export based model of development. The spike in global oil prices after 1973 could have dealt a crippling blow to an oil importing nation like India. Yet the phenomenon was an equitable one. Whilst the Government of India faced a rising oil bill for the remainder of the decade, oil producing economies needed labour to sustain their national infrastructure expansion programmes. It was workers from India, and even more from Pakistan, who met this demand for labour in the newly oil rich states of the Middle East.

The problem was that exports had not been factored into the first Indian economic plans. Exports were not even a part of Prasanta Mahalanobis's initial equations for self-sustaining economic growth. His vision of industrialisation was one of import substitution. Only those components which were necessary for India's nascent heavy industrial manufacturing units would be allowed to be imported. Yet the inability of bureaucrats to constantly assess and adjust to Indian industry's import needs meant that very often Indian manufacturing units simply had to go without and reduce their production capacity. Prasanta Mahalanobis's approach to international trade has sometimes been dubbed "export pessimism". Yet his Draft Plan Frame only gave expression to a consensus within the Indian elite. India's market had been left open by the British for a century and in that time agricultural commodities had been looted and industries had been left to die. The shared vision of all Indian economic planners of the time was for India to become self-reliant once again.

***

International trade was the only topic on which all the Indian economic planners of the 1940s agreed. This was all the more remarkable due to their ideological diversity. They were variously Congress Party nationalists, Bombay capitalists, Calcutta ex-communists and Gandhians from Wardha.

The National Planning Committee's Subcommittee on Trade was chaired by Kasturbhai Lalbhai, a cotton mill owner from Ahmadabad. In presenting the subcommittee's interim report he maintained that internal trade was of greater importance than foreign trade. This stance was reflected in the final report of the subcommittee which devoted double the amount of space to internal trade, or trade between provinces in India, as it did to trade between India and the world.

The introduction to the trade subcommittee's final report made mention of the Roman historian Pliny the Elder. Pliny had left a record of India's ancient trading prowess. The Roman Empire would annually import more from India than it exported and thus have to pay for its trade deficit in gold and silver. Pliny had dubbed India "the sink of all the world's gold". Nonetheless, the subcommittee members did not think that India's modern trading prospects were very bright. There did not seem to be much scope in tea due to the International Tea Restriction Scheme. As India already had a monopoly on jute, there was little room for expansion. Indian raw cotton was less fine than American and Egyptian varieties and had been facing tariff barriers in recent years. The market for oilseeds was being narrowed as other bidding agents were being developed. Most tobacco was consumed in the domestic market. The trade subcommittee came to the conclusion that besides raw cotton and linseeds it would not be possible to increase total exports.

Kasturbhai Lalbhai and his colleagues thought that it was necessary to accept that tariff protection and the rise of new competitors were a permanent part of the international trade system. The desire in India for a controlled economy would also necessarily restrict the expansion of trade. Exports were not necessarily worth striving for if they were made because goods could not be profitably sold in the home market and because there was no other source of livelihood. Furthermore, there did not seem to be much advantage to be gained from trade treaties. The only possibility of a trade agreement was one with Britain which, the subcommittee thought, should be avoided if India wanted to go down the path of rapid industrialisation. Trade treaties always burdened the less developed countries, as was evident from the Ottawa Agreement of 1932. The subcommittee wanted to encourage exports of semi-manufactured and manufactured goods and saw the need to seek out non-European markets. The subcommittee recognised that imports would be limited by exports. Since exports could not be raised overnight there would need to be restrictions on imports.

The import substitution model outlined in the Bombay Plan sought to develop heavy industries for the production of power and capital goods. The development of these heavy industries in India would lessen the country's dependence on foreign countries for the plant and machinery required for further industrialisation, which in turn would reduce dependence on external finance. Consumption goods would be made in India by cottage producers. The Bombay planners thought that agricultural goods which were dependent on foreign trade like jute, tea, cotton and oil seeds brought uncertainty to economic life. They wanted industries which could process these agricultural commodities within the country to reduce this uncertainty. The goal was for India's agricultural production to feed the population rather than export to foreign markets. A policy of directing agricultural production inward would necessarily mean that the export trade would quickly diminish. Both greater consumption of domestic agricultural production within the country, as well as the development of consumption goods industries would mean that the volume of imports would also decline.

The People's planners mainly discussed trade in the context of agricultural production. They quoted contemporary economic writings which asserted that if manufactured goods were produced for foreign rather than home consumption, or if the bulk of the population was not benefitting from the increase in national income associated with industrialisation, there would be no increase in purchasing power. Production would then be for exports and there would be a decrease in the level of imports of consumer goods. The People's planners maintained that there needed to be an emphasis on the internal economy. Purchasing power needed to be raised through agricultural development in order to avoid the creation of a fascist economy; it was through the expansion of the internal market that the economy would grow. The People's planners were certain that the state would have to exercise monopolistic control over foreign trade and financial transactions with foreign countries. Without these controls the plan may not even be able to be carried out. Burgeoning agricultural production would lead to agricultural surpluses which could be exported and cover the external finance needed for the execution of the plan.

Taking Gandhian economics to its logical conclusion, Shriman Narayan Agarwal thought that the development of more or less self-sufficient economic units would reduce the need for trade to a minimum. In Agarwal's plan an economic unit would have a radius of 5 miles and be largely self-sufficient. The creation of self-sufficient units would avoid exploitation by middlemen and strain in the transport, currency and banking systems. Restricted internal trade would take place according to the needs of village communities and be oriented to the greatest possible local consumption. Only surplus goods would be exported and only goods which could not be produced locally would be imported. With localisation of production and consumption the problem of distribution would be simplified.

Agarwal viewed the aim of planning as the attainment of maximum self-sufficiency so that international trade would be restricted to the surplus production of different countries traded for mutual benefit. Imports would be procured to meet local deficits in production. The present system was based on greed and exploitation setting in play the forces of imperialism and war. India would not exploit or be exploited. India would only import that which could not be manufactured locally and export that which was demanded abroad and only it could produce. Agarwal noted that Gandhi had stressed that it would be pointless to reject imports simply because they were imports. Yet Agarwal thought that to import such goods when they could be made in India would be foolish. He wanted an end to the exploitative trade system. Trade would have to be controlled by the national government rather than be left to private businessmen. Some imports needed to be banned and a high tariff imposed to protect Indian producers. For Agarwal it was clear that free trade was dead.

***

The report of the National Planning Committee's Subcommittee on Trade made mention of Pliny the Elder's reference to India's status as a trading power in the ancient world. Yet there had been a long passage of history in which India had dominated world markets which was much less distant. The cause of the prevailing antipathy towards international trade was India's experience of colonial rule. Yet India had, for a period of around 600 years immediately prior to British rule, been the world's foremost exporter of cotton textiles.

Cotton had been grown for millennia in Punjab in the north-west, in Bengal in the east, Gujarat in the west and on the Deccan plateau and Coromandel coast in the south. The skills to turn the cotton fibre into yarn, the yarn into cloth and then bleach, dye, paint or print materials were highly developed across the country. It was the coastal regions of Gujarat, the Coromandal coast of Tamilkam and coastal Bengal which excelled in the manufacture of cotton textiles. Besides long coastlines, each of these three regions had port facilities and the commercial infrastructure for the manufacture and distribution of cotton textiles in markets across the Indian Ocean region. Gujarat largely supplied markets in eastern Africa and the Gulf, whilst the Coromandel Coast supplied south-east Asia. Bengal was known for its fine muslins and silk and cotton blends. Traders from Punjab took their wares overland into Persia and central Asia.

Gujarati cotton textiles were being traded at Aden at the entrance to the Red Sea as early as the 13th and 14th centuries. In the 15th century they were being brought to Yemen, while in the sixteenth century up to 20 ships carrying Gujarati cotton textiles arrived each year at the northern Red Sea coast of Jidda. Zeila on the southern side of the Gulf of Aden also received ships carrying textiles from Aden and Gujarat, whilst Hormuz in Persia received its own regular supply of Gujarati textiles. By the 16th century Aden had become a hub for the shipment of Gujarati cottons to Cairo and the Mediterranean. At the end of the 16th century the Red Sea area was Gujarat's main export market.

Gujarati cottons had become dominant on the horn of Africa and the Swahili coast. Massawa and Berbera traded in Gujarati cottons and supplied markets in the region. Mogadishu also maintained trade links with Gujarat, and Malandi and Mombasa received direct voyages from Cambay on the Gujarat coast. African merchants from these towns also sent their own ships to Cambay to receive goods. Zanzibar and Mafia received their Gujarati cottons via Mombasa. The ruler of Pate, Mwana Mkuu even constructed his own vessels for trade with Gujarat.[cdxcvi] From these African coastal towns and ports Gujarati cottons were then transported inland to the source of the consumer demand. Swahili merchants took Gujarati cottons into the Zambezi valley and a bumper trade of imports directly from India was carried on in Mozambique. At Sofala at the southern mouth of the Zambezi river in the middle of the 15th century Gujarati cloth was the only item of international trade.[cdxcvii] The local people were not interested in anything but the Gujarati cottons which they were familiar with.

By the middle of the 17th century 250 tonnes of mainly Gujarati cloth entered East Africa each year.[cdxcviii] There were half a million pieces coming into east-central and south-eastern Africa by the middle of the 18th century.[cdxcix] These textiles were used by Gujarati merchants for the purchase of slaves and ivory. There was a market for ivory in India, whilst the slaves were traded forward in the region and the southern Atlantic. Private Indian shipping from Surat expanded as did Indian and European commerce into the western Indian Ocean region. Surat declined as a major port in the 18th century however due to the decay of the Mughal Empire as well as British competition from Bombay.

From the 1740s Gujarati merchants shifted their focus from the Red Sea to East Africa, sourcing their cotton from Jambusar in southern Gujarat, a region which had boomed under Maratha rule. Among the different types of Gujarati cotton in circulation in East Africa were; capotins, blue and white cloth in checks or stripes, ardians, plain dyed cloths in different sizes, dotins which were strong coarse cotton cloths, canequins which were coarse calicoes dyed with indigo in blue or black, chaudheres were plain white calicoes, longuins, long cloth in white but sometimes brown or blue and jorians which were plain white calicoes.[d] Samatares and zuartes were the most expensive cottons and so the most prestigious.[di] From the 1780s it was zuartes which became the most sought after and African caravan leaders would not accept any other variety.[dii] Yet East Africa was far from a captive market. By the 1790s demand for some previously popular Gujarati cottons had collapsed; the locals were not accepting capotins and ardians but only zuartes and some dotins.[diii] In addition, there were regional differences in demand.

The Portuguese understood the reasons for the continuing success of Indian merchants in the market. They provided cabayas which were in fashion, ordering them from Diu with new designs which would be relayed to their partners in Diu during the monsoons.[div] Seeing these new fashions coming in each year it was the Indian merchants rather than their European competitors who the African buyers would seek out. Information about changing consumer preferences would be communicated by the local vashambadzi, or agents.

Gujarati merchants did not always have an easy time in their African trading operations. They had to seek the protection of local rulers and different caste groups would compete amongst themselves for patronage and markets. When a massacre of Gujarati Banias took place in Mocha in the late 17th century many wound up their operations and left, trying to repatriate whatever money they had back to Diu. At another time Gujarati Bhatias from Kutch worked with the ruler of Oman to make business more difficult for the Gujarati Banias. Yet by the 17th century a Gujarati business model for trade on the East African coast had clearly developed. The Gujaratis used family firms, usually partnerships, to expand their merchant networks. Heads of family firms would raise capital and remain in Diu, a Portuguese enclave on the Gujarat coast, from where they would manage the business. Senior family members were sent overseas to manage daily operations and took junior members with them. These junior members, or travelling agents became a presence in Mozambique in the middle of the 18th century. Laxmichand Motichand rose from junior status and spent 40 years in Mozambique amassing a fortune and a reputation for creditworthiness as a merchant.[dv] Those employed from outside the family were fellow Banias. Agents would then branch out and set up their own family firms. They did have to deal with dalals, or brokers, who were not Banias for the supply of cloth from Gujarat. Letters would flow back and forth from Mozambique to Gujarat on commercial happenings as well as the trust standing and creditworthiness of merchants within the network.[dvi] Some Gujarati merchants started to go to the Portuguese courts in the 18th century to adjudicate on their commercial disputes.

The English explorer Antony Jenkinson reached Bukhara in 1557 and found Indian merchants selling textiles in the city.[dvii] They brought with them cottons and linens rather than gold, silver, or spices. Forty years later Darya Khan Multani was bringing Indian artisans to Samarqand where they manufactured cloth from local yarn and wool.[dviii] In the 16th century Multanis dispatched their gumasthas, or agents beyond the Hindu Kush. They expanded from Iran all the way to Moscow. By the middle of the 17th century there were 35,000 Indian merchants across Eurasia.[dix]

Reminiscent of ancient Rome, in Isfahan it was said that Indian merchants carried away the country's silver and gold as payment for their cottons and linens.[dx] Multan was a major textile manufacturing centre situated in an important cotton growing tract in southern Punjab and northern Sind. Local weavers would also weave raw silk imported from Bukhara. The stocks bound for Persia and Central Asia were loaded onto bullock carts or on the back of camels. It was mainly Punjabi cloth, but also Gujarati cloth which was being sent north. Given the tonnage of cloth being exported each year it is clear that India was clothing Persia and Central Asia in the 16th and 17th centuries.[dxi]

Multani merchants in Persia were both Hindus and Muslims. The Hindus were mainly Khatris and Marwaris. Just as amongst the Gujarati traders of East Africa, family and caste firms created the trust required to carry on business in a distant land. Juniors from within the caste were trained in commercial disciplines. They were then advanced capital in cash or in kind, most commonly in cotton textiles which could be sourced at below wholesale prices. Textiles would be transported using Afghan Powinda caravans. Punjabi merchants then lived in their own caravan serais, or settlements once they reached their destination and these serais would soon become Little Indias. Punjabis would spend 7 or 8 years in Central Asia, rationing their stock and getting involved in other commercial activities. When they made a sale they would invest the profit, usually in money lending. Punjabi moneylenders could enforce their debts with the co-operation of local governments which understood their importance to their economies. This did create some resentment from the local people who felt like they had become second class citizens in their own country. When the Punjabis returned home they would settle their accounts.

Indian settlements in Astrakhan started to grow from the 1620s as Punjabi merchants arrived from Persia. From there they went further upstream to Volga. Russians were not enforcing their own trade regulations and so Punjabi merchants arrived in Moscow by the 1680s. The merchants from Astrakhan were marketing cotton and silk. As in Persia, so in Russia, Punjabi merchants contributed to the stream of silver entering India. The Indian business community rapidly declined after 1723 however, and it was wiped out within half a century. Political events within Russia led to an interruption to trade with Persia and India and prohibitions against Indian involvement in the Russian economy. The Safavid empire also collapsed in Persia and with it the security of Indian merchants. Fewer Indian merchants arrived in Astrakhan from Persia. The Mughal empire was also beginning to disintegrate in India.

***

The Portuguese were the first to circulate Indian cotton in Europe, closely followed by the Dutch and the British. European merchants initially moved Indian cottons through Lisbon and Antwerp. In Lisbon as early as 1508 church vestments and accessories were being made with patterned fabrics from Calicut and Cambay.[dxii] Portuguese traders directed Indian cotton back to Portugal, West Africa and Mediterranean markets as well as to the Caribbean and Latin America. Lisbon based merchants carried Indian cotton to northern Spain, coastal France and southern England prior to 1550. Throughout the 1500s European monarchs and aristocrats assembled collections of Asian luxury items including embroidered and painted Indian cottons. Lower quality printed and painted cottons were being prized by common folk. Portuguese pedlars were selling Indian calico in the Basque region. They found a ready market, so much so that local authorities tried to eradicate, or at least limit the calico trade.[dxiii]

The Portuguese took Indian calico to Southampton in 1541. By 1577 even those among the lowest classes of southern England furnished their homes with Indian cottons. Quilts were also imported by the Portuguese into Europe from India. Pillows, counterpanes, coverlets, quilts stuffed with cotton, painted and patterned were all coming from India. Portuguese naval and military motifs intermingled with Hindu mythological figures, beasts, birds, fish, sailing ships, artillery, the flowers of the Indies mixed with European figures.[dxiv] Common floral embroideries subsequently became more popular.

European embroiderers then began to imitate Indian patterns and techniques in the 16th and 17th centuries. Indian textiles were in demand by the Habsburg courts and the court of Henry VIII.[dxv] The Earl of Leicester, Queen Elizabeth and Bess of Hardwick were all patrons of Indian textiles.[dxvi] As early as 1618 Bengal quilts were receiving high prices at auctions, prompting East India Company officials to write back to Bengal for more supply.[dxvii] By the early 18th century Daniel Defoe noted how Indian calicoes had penetrated English homes.[dxviii]

It was during the second half of the 17th century that Indian cottons became personal clothing and fashion in Europe rather than being used for household purposes. Indian cottons had properties which could not be matched by European worsteds and woollens, including permanent colour and washability. The fastness of permanence of colour allowed them to be both exposed to protracted light and be washed. Indian cottons soon began to transform European ideas of cleanliness; both overgarments and undergarments could now be regularly washed. On price cottons were a substitute for low and medium quality worsteds and woollens. As a matter of fashion they could replace silks and new draperies. Lower class folk could mark themselves apart from their peers by wearing calicoes. Even local manufacturers' wives would wear the Indian imports whilst their husbands protested against them.[dxix]

By 1681 Indian calicoes were replacing previously used materials in constructing English garments. By the 17th century there were calico bans across Europe and some attempt at import substitution as European artisans tried to draw and colour and dye Indian cottons. The ban in France lasted from 1689 to 1759. The Indian technique of resist dying was based on the waxing of areas to remain undyed. This was a labour intensive procedure to produce white motifs on blue backgrounds which involved waxing most of the cloth. In an effort to replace imports of Indian cloth European producers began learning the Indian technique of waxing and tepid indigo formation towards the end of the 17th century. By the early 18th century European producers were experimenting with new techniques which were not known in India. Cold vats were used by dissolving indigo in iron sulphate. The process was invented in England in 1734 and replaced the hot fermentation of indigo and was followed by the creation of English Blue and China Blue. English producers in Lancashire were, by the 18th century, producing their own printed textiles which were being exported to France as Indian chintzes. Most often they were accepted by French commercial buyers and consumers because they did not know the difference.

By the 18th century the purchase of Indian cottons started to outstrip consumption of worsteds and woollens, yet a profound change was taking place among European textile producers.[dxx] By the 1760s Europeans had learnt all the techniques for fashioning textiles which they had been unfamiliar with a century earlier like block printing, painting, the use of mordants, reserve and reverse styling.[dxxi] European producers also built and modified these processes to produce new products like copper printed textiles, combining knowledge of dyes and textile printing from Asia with European aesthetics of printing and etching on paper.[dxxii] The cotton textile producers of Lancashire, Catalonia, Orange, Joy en jossa, Mulhouse, Neauchatel, and Prague were developing their own varieties of cotton textiles.[dxxiii] The process of import substitution did not just serve to satisfy demand in European markets but also allowed for exports. European cottons were now being taken to North America, South America and West Africa. British traders opened up the West African market with English textiles woven from Indian raw cotton. A farmer's son from Lancashire, John Kay patented the flying shuttle in 1733 and water and steam powered machines further mechanised textile production in the later years of the 18th century. Within three generations Europe had moved past its dependence on Indian cotton textiles to produce its own high quality cloth.

The Indian domination of the world cotton textile trade over a 600 year period had arisen from a mastery of production processes. By the late 18th century British producers had not only mastered the old Indian techniques of textile production, but moved past them with both the machinery and technical skill to produce more cloth of a higher standard at a cheaper price. This was as great a blow to the British East Company, which had profited from the textile trade with India over the previous two centuries, as it was for the Indian spinners, weavers, dyers and merchants whose livelihoods depended on foreign demand for their products. The East India Company was able to adapt however. After its victory on the battlefield at Plassey in 1757 the merchant adventurers of the Company became the rulers of eastern India. The Company became a government and began to earn its revenue by taxing the Indian peasantry. Diminishing profits from the trade in Indian cotton textiles were partially made up by the export of Indian raw cotton to Britain where it would be manufactured for domestic and international consumption. The Indian traders who had taken Indian cotton abroad also began to fade away. Indian merchant networks in Asia and Africa never disappeared entirely, yet they greatly diminished throughout the 19th century, coming to be confined mainly to finance rather than trade. There were simply fewer Indian products which were prized abroad.

Pliny the Elder's reference to India as the sink of all the world's gold was well known in colonial India. It featured in British history books. Yet the memory of India's more recent domination of the world textile market had, by the 1940s, seemingly vanished. It was as if a century of English education had erased an entire historical experience from the Indian mind. This is all the more incredible in a land in which caste memories stretch back not just centuries, but millennia. It is even more surprising in the case of Mohandas Gandhi. He was a

Gujarati and a Bania, who had travelled to South Africa to work as a lawyer. He took up a brief for a Gujarati Muslim merchant and ended up staying for 21 years. Yet the African milieu which he came into was very different from that of just a century earlier. The majority of Indians in the colony were coolies, or labourers, rather than merchants, and Indians had become a subject people of the British Empire. It is unlikely that, given his way of seeing and feeling, Gandhi would have been particularly inspired by the memory of a Gujarati merchant like Laxmichand Motichand who had spent 40 years trading textiles in Mozambique. Yet, like his peers in the English educated class, he had no consciousness of it. The aversion to trade shared by all members of the Indian elite on the eve of Independence was as much a lapse of memory as of foresight.

***

Between 1947 and 1966 India's share of world exports declined from 2.5% to 0.9%.[dxxiv] There was some respite due to a surge in international prices during the Korean War from 1951 to 1953. However, stagnation in both average prices and export volumes ensued during the Second Five Year plan period. Besides cashew kernals, iron ore and coffee, there was no statistically significant upward trend for any of India's export commodities. Most export commodities showed a dismal rate of growth in earnings as well as a falling share of the world market. In the five major commodities which accounted for over half of India's exports- processed jute, tea, cotton textiles, vegetable oils and oilseeds, and raw tobacco- there was a significant reduction in India's share of world trade.

Export controls, quotas, and duties, inflation and policies to encourage domestic consumption all worked to stifle the growth of exports during the 1950s. Export controls which were started during the Second World War continued on jute until 1958 and cotton textiles until 1953. Controls were continued on tea and raw cotton from 1947 into the 1960s. Controls were also applied to the export of vegetable oils in 1952, and raw wool, coffee, manganese ore and hides and skins in 1953. Prohibitive duties were maintained on India's principal exports for most of the 1950s. In 1951 and 1952 the export duty on hessian, made from jute, reached 1500%. The export duty on tea averaged around 40% and on raw cotton approximately 200%. The Government of India sought to encourage domestic tea consumption by keeping the local excise duty much lower than the export levy throughout the decade. The Coffee Board engaged in its own promotional campaigns to get more Indians drinking coffee.

World trade in jute had been stagnant since before the Second World War and remained so in the 1950s. Price was not the main determinant in stagnant trade, the growth of bulk deliveries and modern packing and storage techniques had made the older jute burlap containers of more limited use. Only significant price reductions in processed jute could maintain trade volumes. However, India's declining share of the world market was primarily due to a failure to maintain competitiveness, particularly with Pakistan. After 1954 Pakistan emerged as a major rival to India in the international processed jute market and began to subsidise its exports at an effective rate of 25%. The Government of India had removed export controls in 1952 and then towards the end of the decade began lowering the export duty, but did not go so far as to subsidise jute exports in the way that Pakistan did.

Tea imports in developed countries had been largely stagnant for the two decades since the Second World War. However, India's falling share of world exports could be attributed to a lack of international marketing compared to Ceylon. Indian teas generally competed with African rather than Ceylonese teas which were of a higher grade, yet the Indian tea industry had largely fallen into an uncompetitive state due to rising labour costs, export levies and quotas. Export quotas were administered to ensure domestic supply and keep domestic prices low. Yet the quantity of exports each year fell short of the allotted quotas. Nonetheless, there was still a premium on export quotas as some exporters wanted to export more than their assigned quotas. Those tea producers who did export had to do so at a higher price than they otherwise would which reduced their competitiveness in the international market.

The decline in India's share of cotton textile exports was relatively small compared to that in processed jute and tea. Both Britain and the United States also experienced falling shares of world exports. The most dynamic exporter of the 1950s was Japan which almost doubled its share of world exports. There was growing demand for synthetic fibres, whilst many previously importing countries were developing their own cotton textile industries. As in other export industries, India experienced rising labour costs and enhanced relative profitability in the domestic market. Yet, the stellar Japanese performance in export markets was attributed to government policies, which were, in effect, the opposite of those pursued by the Government of India. The quality of Japanese exports improved as investments in automatic screen printing were made, whilst the Japanese Government mandated that only washable coloured cloth, or cloth of even higher quality could be exported. The government had restricted the installation of automatic looms in India and handloom weavers were being protected. Indian cotton textile exports thus remained of the coarse and medium varieties which were most easily replicated by import substituting efforts in industrialising countries.

The most complete fall in India's share of world exports occurred in the market for vegetable oils and oilseeds. Prior to the Second World War India's share of world groundnut exports stood at 44.5%. By 1960 it had fallen to 3%. The decline in linseed exports was not quite as dramatic. India accounted for 10.9% of world exports prior to the war which fell to 3.9% by 1960. Government controls, sometimes amounting to bans during the 1950s, were aimed at ensuring domestic availability at moderate prices. The only exception was in 1955 after a bumper crop of groundnut oil which led to an easing of export restrictions. Controls were reimposed the following year. The production of vegetable oil was also constrained by government policies to protect village industries, specifically the rudimentary production techniques of the old village ghanis, or oil pressers. India's share of its fifth principle export, tobacco, declined marginally during the 1950s. The United States was disposing of its surplus stocks of Virginia tobacco on international markets, whilst Rhodesia had entered into long term supply agreements with international customers. Nonetheless, the Government of India did not take any significant measures to boost the export of Indian raw tobacco.

Whilst the Government of India had focused on export controls during the early 1950s in order to ensure domestic supplies at low prices, the experience of the 1957 foreign exchange crisis prompted a host of initiatives to encourage export growth. The new policy of export subsidisation was pursued through both fiscal measures, or direct financial incentives to exporters, and import entitlement schemes which allowed exporters to import valuable commodities and components in proportion to their exports. The fiscal measures included exemptions from sales taxes and refunds of indirect taxes on foreign and domestic inputs, in addition to direct tax concessions, subsidies and concessions on rail transportation costs. India's export performance started to improve during the first three years of the Third Five Year Plan. During 1962, 1963 and 1964 both the value and volume of Indian exports began to rise.

***

An unintended consequence of the Government of India's export promotion drive in the 1960s was the creation of the greatest fortune made in independent India. Dhirubhai Ambani was a young Gujarati Bania who, as if pushed by the forces of history, went to Aden, a British port at the entrance to the Red Sea, in the 1950s.[dxxv] He initially worked for a French firm, A. Besse & Co., overseeing the distribution of petroleum lubricants in the region. He soon started trading on his own account. His great ambition however, was to make his name in India, and so he returned to Bombay and began to trade in the city's cotton markets. Yet during the early 1960s young Dhirubhai was sharp enough to see that he could put the government's new import entitlement schemes to his own use.

The Government of India did not encourage the production of synthetic fibres which meant that there was only one viscose factory, owned by the Birlas, and one nylon plant, owned by the government. Whilst a supply of polyester material was smuggled in from Japan, the legal supply largely came from imports on replenishment licences. Import licences were issued to registered exporters of textiles which allowed them to import material in proportion to their export earnings. Some of these replenishment licences were not officially transferable, and imports had to be made by the "actual user" of the material. Dhirubhai paid higher margins than the other traders and so became the main player in the replenishment licence market. The margins were slim, but he soon exercised effective control over the supply of polyester yarn in India. He imported most of his yarn from Asahi in Japan or Ital Viscosa through Dr. Rossi, an Italian long resident in Bombay.

In 1967 reports began to emerge that actual user licences were being traded and misused. Mr. Ramchandani, the Assistant Collector of Customs in Bombay impounded all consignments of imported artificial fibres arriving in the city. The government then issued an order that the importer of the yarn had to weave it into cloth. The traders in the polyester yarn market then defaulted on the loans they had taken to pay for the imports and the market came to a halt. Dhirubhai fought the Bombay Customs authority on the issue for six months and went to see the Finance Minister, Morarji Desai in New Delhi. There was a quick hearing of the importers' appeal in the Customs Excise and Gold Appellate Court. Justice Oberoi found in favour of the appellants. Dhirubhai was thought to have been the engineer of the judicial settlement, the details of which were not made public.

Tonse Ananth Pai of the Syndicate Bank was Dhirubhai's principal banker during the 1960s. Even after his bank was nationalised in July 1969 Pai continued on the board and was appointed Union commerce minister and later trade minister in Indira Gandhi's governments. The result of this sequence of events was that Dhirubhai had a well-wisher both at a major bank and inside the Cabinet. In 1971 when Dhirubhai persuaded Pai to allow the import of polyester filament yarn against the export of nylon fabric he argued that if he could export nylon, or 'art silks' at ₹4.25 per yard, more than double the price of the old scheme, then he should be rewarded with permission to import polyester filament yarn, a relatively scarce commodity in India. The government initiated a Higher Unit Value Scheme.

The domestic price of polyester filament yarns was seven times the prevailing international price, so even if Dhirubhai's exports of nylon or polyester were sold at a loss, it scarcely mattered given his 600% profit on the import of polyester filament yarns. Dhirubhai's exports did seem to make their way to some rather obscure, or as yet undiscovered international markets, such as Poland and Saudi Arabia. There were rumours that he was buying his own exports in these far flung markets by sending the notional buyers foreign exchange through the hawala route, the traditional Indian system of paperless money transfers. Sometimes the exports would be given away at low prices in duty free ports or even dumped and left behind. Dhirubhai would have to pay a premium on the hawala transaction and then purchase the polyester filament yarn, which he had gained an entitlement to, for import back to India. Even after these expenses the profit would be around 425%.

However, in August 1977 the commerce minister in the Janata government, the one time Young Turk and ardent socialist, Mohan Dharia cancelled the High Unit Value Scheme. Imports of polyester yarn would no longer be dominated by exporters. The premium on licences for polyester filament yarn crashed, so Dhirubhai intervened and started to buy licences at the new low price and took credit for imports totalling ₹5 crore. Then, on 2 September, a commerce ministry official announced another change: the old requirement for exports was restored. Those who had entered into import contracts would be able to import directly but in future importers would have to get their licences from the State Trading Corporation which would control the import of polyester yarn. It was not for another six months that the State Trading Corporation received its first shipments of polyester yarn however. In the meantime, Dhirubhai's Reliance was able to take delivery of all the polyester filament yarn which it had the right to import and again exercise near monopoly power in the Indian market. By the late 1970s about two-thirds of the production of the Reliance polyester plant at Naroda in Gujarat was being diverted to exports in order to continue procuring polyester yarn under the High Unit Value Scheme. Yet as the scheme came to an end Dhirubhai, after a decade of producing polyester in India, started to manufacture for the domestic market. By this time Dhirubhai Ambani was the largest textile producer in the country.

***

Indian exports had been stagnant during the late 1960s, rising in dollar terms by 0.6% a year.[dxxvi] Export performance grew moderately in the early 1970s, yet it was the dramatic rise in the price of oil after 1973 which initiated a burst of construction and development activity across the Middle East which in turn stimulated demand for a new type of Indian export. Qatar had to meet 90% of its demand for labour from guest workers.[dxxvii] Saudi Arabia's First Development Plan required 500,000 foreign teachers, technicians and workers.[dxxviii] During the late 1970s Iraq was building bridges and roads stretching over 5,600 kilometres.[dxxix] During the same period Libya was spending $2.5 billion on infrastructure and required engineers, technicians, and labourers.[dxxx] In 1976 there were just 4,200 Indian workers going to the Middle East. The figure surged to 272,000 in 1981.[dxxxi] Kuwait, Bahrain, Qatar, Oman and the United Arab Emirates imported two-thirds of their labour force as temporary migrants.

The largest group of Indian workers in the Middle East was in the construction industry- housing, docks, roads, airports, offices and industrial plants. They were labourers, carpenters, engineers and managers. Construction work was short term but companies would move their workers between projects. Indians were also employed in industry and services as factory workers, shop assistants, hotel staff, engineers, bankers and clerks. Indian doctors and nurses staffed the region's hospitals. Indian engineers designed highways, communications networks and power plants. Wages were relatively high and there was a reasonable prospect for workers to stay in their host countries for an extended period.

In countries where there were large numbers of Palestinian workers the numbers of South Asians, both Indians and Pakistanis, were lower. Yet due to concerns over political rivalries and the spread of religious ideologies, and the necessity to give fellow Arabs equality of status and pay, the incentive toward employing Indians, who kept their heads down and worked for lower pay remained. Indians were not attracted to job opportunities back home like Westerners were and spoke better English than other Asians.

There were two occasions in the early 1980s when the Government of India stopped the flow of migrants to protest or express solidarity with Indian workers- when a Cypriot construction firm was faced with a strike by Indian workers who were then expelled by the Government of Oman, and when the Government of India banned the migration of single uneducated women from Kerala to Kuwait after reports that they were being mistreated. In both cases it was protests from Indian workers who wanted to go to Oman and Kuwait which forced the Government of India to relent. When Gulf governments moved to restrict migration the Government of India would protest that such moves would adversely impact the Indian economy.

Emigration to the Middle East provided a partial solution to the unemployment problem in Kerala, Karnataka, Goa, Maharashtra, Gujarat and Punjab. Remittances helped families pay debts, purchase land, build houses, send children to better schools, and cover wedding costs. Housing was often provided by employers- barrack style for construction workers. Medical care was also generally provided. Food was served in company canteens and there were enough cheap Indian restaurants. There were few temptations- no bars, no casinos, no brothels. There were great incentives to save- to send larger remittances home, to purchase property, and to insure against the prospect of unemployment upon return. Indian workers in the Middle East generally sent home at least one-third of their income.

The growth of remittance receipts was rapid in the late 1970s. In 1974-75 remittance receipts were 7% of exports. By 1980-81 they were 32%.[dxxxii] Remittances were growing fast enough to allow India to import more without the usual pressures on foreign exchange reserves. These remittances from migrant workers in the Middle East largely mitigated the effect of the rise in oil prices. Remittances from the Middle East made up approximately 75% of total remittances to India by 1980.[dxxxiii] Migration to the West was usually permanent which made the propensity to remit earnings lower, despite the higher capacity to remit. Indian migrants in the West also had higher dependency ratios, that is, they lived with their families, which meant that they had less need to send money back to India.[dxxxiv] Remittances to Kerala were growing at a faster rate than the domestic product of the state. In 1980 remittances formed one-quarter of the state's domestic product.[dxxxv]

The population density in India in the early 1970s was 182 people per square kilometre.[dxxxvi] In Kerala it was 549. Kerala had reached India's 1971 level of population density as far back as 1901. Each resident of Kerala could notionally claim 0.18 hectares, amongst the lowest levels in the world. Only 56% of the population was engaged in agriculture, compared to the national average of 70%. Kerala thus had amongst the highest population density in the world and the population continued increasing at 2.6% each year. At the start of the 1960s there were 58,000 educated unemployed in the state. By the end of the 1970s the figure stood at over 200,000. Unemployment for the scientifically trained was 18.3%, or roughly double the national figure of 9.1%. The number registering on the state's employment exchanges was about 151,000 in 1961. By 1978 it had reach 1 million. In 1971, even prior to the Gulf oil boom Kerala had the highest rate of emigration in India.

Remittances from the Middle East were going to Kerala's most backward districts. It was remittances which brought the consumption levels of the three most backward districts above the state average. However, the inflow of remittances from the Gulf did not seem to spur any sort of self-sustaining development. Most of the money flowing into the state was not being used for productive purposes; there were almost no investments in debentures, shares and financial securities. Instead most of the remittances went into land, buildings and jewellery. Land values in the late 1970s skyrocketed. At the same time construction materials doubled in price. In small villages in the Mallapuram district a cent of land did not rise about ₹125 in the early 1970s. By the end of the decade the price ranged from ₹800 to ₹2,500.[dxxxvii] One survey showed that out of 402 respondents only 1 used their foreign earnings to start a factory.[dxxxviii] Part of the reason for the reluctance of Malayalis to invest in economically productive activity was their state's "restive labour situation".

***

Successive Communist governments in Kerala had undertaken a successful programme of land reform, achieved the highest literacy level in India and maintained an effective and accessible system of healthcare. Yet government regulations and militant trade unions had made industrial development almost impossible. Kerala thus had a relatively healthy and well-educated population recently liberated from bondage on the land, with minimal prospects of decent employment.

Given that Kerala is a relatively small state which had a disproportionately high number of workers in the Middle East, most Malayalis had a family member or friend who was making their living across the sea. *Varavelpu*, or *The Welcoming*, was not the first Malayalam film to address the theme of working in a foreign land. Yet when it was released in April 1989 audiences were immediately drawn to its satire of daily life in Kerala. The film was directed by Sathyan Anthikad and went on to become one of the highest earning Malayalam films of the year.

Varavelpu opens with the family sitting down to take their first breakfast together after seven years. Murali had missed his home food. The air was so hot and dry there. But didn't he have air conditioning? He lets the family in on his secret. Here in Kerala he is a great Gulf worker.

But over there he had been doing manual labour, lifting bricks for the first two years. Where did the question of air conditioning arise? Murali's brothers, Narayanan and Kumaran, tell him to keep the matter in the family. It was a matter of shame. Murali insisted that he had not written about it in his letters because he did not want to hurt or alarm the family. There was nothing much he could say to his Arab bosses, they would send him on the first flight back to India. Rukmini, Narayanan's wife, suggests that if conditions were so harsh he should not have gone in the first place. Murali asks how that could have been. The house had been mortgaged, both his brothers were unemployed, and with the remittance money he sent the family had risen over the past seven years. Shantha, Kumaran's wife gets emotional. Murali had sacrificed everything for them. But then Murali drops a veritable bombshell. He does not want to go back to the Gulf. He wants to stay in Kerala. The brothers and their wives look at each other in shock and puzzlement. Murali moves into the next room to read the paper. They follow him.

Does he mean what he just said? Yes, he is sick of it there. You open your window and all you get is the noise from construction sites and oil tanks. There are no coconut trees, no paddy fields, no pleasant scenery. No palm trees. Kumaran wants to know what the use of palm trees is. Murali insists that the Gulf is not beautiful like Kerala. Yes, but the Gulf has surplus petrol and diesel which is not available in Kerala, Kumaran points out. They are missing Murali's point. He is home sick. Do they celebrate the Vishu festival there? Or Onam? Kumaran still does not get it. He suggests that Murali should take some flowers and fruits from Kerala with him. Narayanan agrees. Murali's mind is made up however. He is not going back. He has some money in his Non-resident Indian account and he will use it to start a business and settle down in Kerala. In any case, his visa has expired.

Kumaran takes Murali to meet his business partners, Sunny Lucas and Tony Pallakad. He boasts that they are great bar contractors and they could make and break state governments- the politicians were scared of them. They had another auction for a contract coming up, and he suggests that Murali join them in their business with the money from his NRI account. It was the only profitable business to which he should put his money. After investing, all he would have to do would be to check the accounts and take his share of the profits.

Murali then goes to Narayanan's restaurant to inform him that he will be investing in Kumaran's business. Narayanan sits Murali down. He is the elder brother, shouldn't he have been consulted? Didn't he give him ₹500 when he left for Dubai? Murali points out that the money only got him to Bombay, not Dubai. Would joining the liquor business be good for the family's reputation? Narayanan lets Murali in on a little secret. Kumaran had been smuggling spirits into Kerala from Tamil Nadu and got caught by the police. He had to spend a huge amount on avoiding a case. Kumaran was just a big smuggler. If Murali joined in his business he would probably end up in jail. Narayanan has a better idea. There is some vacant land nearby. Why not open an air-conditioned restaurant? He would manage it and Murali could just collect his profits at the end of every month. Murali would develop a great name as the owner of an air-conditioned restaurant. He readily agrees and Narayanan sends him home to get his lunch from Rukmini. He warns him to keep a distance from Shantha, who is cunning like her husband Kumaran.

Back at home Murali's maternal uncle has arrived. Ammavan is irritated that he did not know in advance of Murali's arrival, and also that he did not bring any goodies like soap and fragrance. Did he at least bring a bottle of liquor? Ammavan needs it to bribe a local tax officer. Murali explains that Customs had seized his belongings. Ammavan mentions that he had paid for his mother's hospital expenses before her death. Murali tells him about his various business plans. Ammavan beckons Murali outside, away from the competing sisters-in-law. He says he will advise him like a father. In all the years he was sending back money from the Gulf, did his brothers buy any property with his money in his name? No, they had used the money for their own welfare. If he opened the air-conditioned restaurant Narayanan would cheat him. Ammavan has a better idea. Invest in a coconut farm. The price of land keeps increasing, even after just one year he could sell it for double the price. Ammavan knows of a great coconut farm nearby. He is here to help. He would just send the coconut money to Murali every month. Kumaran pulls Murali in the room. What had he gone to the Gulf and worked so hard for, to run some glorified tea shop in Kerala? Murali would get a bad name for running this tea shop. Besides, he had lost face in front of his partners, Sunny and Tony. Murali informs him that he has moved past the air-conditioned restaurant idea. He will now invest in a coconut farm.

The tea and breakfast service from Shantha has slowed down. She had to make it for Kumaran who had to go out early because of the loss of face with his business partners. He had to arrange new finance. Murali can get the tea himself if he wants. So, he goes out with his self-got tea and picks up the morning newspaper from the steps in front of the house. He reads a notice. A bus is for sale. It runs on the Chitikavu temple route and has a stable permit. His friend Hamsa thinks it is a good idea. It would be a great way to come up in life. He could boast about being a bus owner. Besides, before leaving for the Gulf, hadn't he taken a conductor's licence? People were waiting to buy a bus with a route. Hamsa could work as a cleaner. Murali did not want to work as a conductor however. They could appoint someone else to do that job. The bus would probably be old, but the route was the main asset. They could book a new bus later to work the same route.

After going for a test drive in the bus, Murali goes home and announces to his brothers that he has made a decision. He will purchase the bus in a week's time. He tries to sell the idea that the family prestige will be enhanced by having a bus owner in the family. There are a few suggestions on what to name the bus. The sisters-in-law want the bus service named after their husbands, but when those suggestions fail they suggest naming it after their children. Murali announces that the bus will not be named after any one family member. Since the family has come up through his Gulf remittances, it will be named Gulf Motors.

Murali and Hamsa open their little office. People had been approaching Hamsa for the conductor's job. He suggests to Murali that he demand ₹10,000 in security from them. Murali will have none of it. They are poor workers. He is a bus owner now, but was a worker himself until not long ago. He does not want to spoil the employer-conductor relationship by demanding a deposit. It is only workers' dedication which would make a business successful. There are so many unemployed. His aim is to create a business which would employ 50 people. Kumaran arrives in his jeep. He is still sore from being humiliated in front of his partners but he has one favour to ask Murali, after which he will not ask for anything more. Sunny and Tony know a driver and a conductor. Murali should give them a job. Sunny and Tony are looking on smoking cigarettes, dressed in silk and wearing gold chains. Murali has no objections as long as they are qualified. Qualified? Chathukutty is an ex-military driver with 20 years' experience! The conductor, Valsan is also active and honest. Before Kumaran could give a name for the cleaner's job Hamsa intervenes. He has already claimed it.

The problems start when Chathukutty runs into a petty stall at a junction. Murali has to pay ₹8,000 in compensation to the owner. Murali arrives at the bus stall in his Ambassador in a rage. He wants to know where the blind idiot is who caused the accident. Chathukutty is reading the newspaper in the bus. He explodes at Chathukutty who protests that he did not cause the

The Licence Raj

accident deliberately. But Murali grabs the paper from his hands and flings it away making more references to his blindness. He had earned the money for the bus from working hard in the Gulf. If this was the Gulf the authorities would have chopped off his body parts already! He calls Chathukutty a useless fellow and complains that his brother Kumaran had sent him to destroy him. He would leave Chathukutty for now as he was his brother's man, besides which Murali was a worker at heart. But if it happened again, Murali would kill him.

At night two men come to visit. Murali's nephew wakes him up. Maybe they have come for bus concessions? It is Prabhakaran, the K.B.T.U. district secretary. K.B.T.U. stands for the Kerala Bus Transport Workers' Union. Murali might have been in the bourgeoisie Gulf but Prabhakaran is here to tell him how things work in Kerala, the workers' land. He could not just scream and threaten a worker like Chathukutty. The workers would rise up. They have self-respect these days. He is giving Murali a warning. Prabhakaran and his associate storm off. Narayanan arrives and bows low as they leave. He tells Murali to sort the matter out. Even politicians fear Union leaders like Prabhakaran. He knows from experience. He has to restrain his anger with his restaurant workers and handle them gently.

Murali heeds Narayanan's advice and approaches Chathukutty at the bus stand the next day. Chathukutty brother! Namaskaram! What headlines do today's newspaper bring? Murali pats his belly. What did you have for breakfast? How are all the members of your family? How many children do you have? Why not bring them along to work? They could have free bus travel if they wanted. With the labour troubles temporarily sorted out, they start their route only to be hailed down by the Brake Inspector. Murali had not met with the Inspector after buying the bus. He did not know that he had to. There was a new inspector and word had got around that he was strict. Valsad brings the bus log. Murali thinks that the Inspector might show him some respect as the owner of the bus: "I am Muralidharan. Very glad to meet you." He offers his hand. The Inspector ignores it. Where are the RC book and papers? He wants to know when the bus started its route. How many are sitting? How many are standing? Valsan gives a low estimate of the standing passengers. The Inspector says that he would not allow a bus in such poor condition to run. Murali says that he is going to buy a new bus. "I won't allow anybody to violate the rules." He asks Valsan whether he exhibited the time schedule. The parking permit? The bus would not even get a fitness certificate. There has been a major violation of permit conditions. He would not allow it.

The Inspector approaches the bus. The tyre is not in good condition. Is there a first aid box with medicines? Chathukutty suggests to Murali that the Inspector is just checking the first aid box because he wants money. Just give him a bribe and the matter will be over. Murali takes out his wallet. But the first aid box is largely empty and there are cockroaches racing through it. The attempt to bribe the Inspector does not go well. He asks if Murali is trying to degrade an officer of the government. The Inspector then gives his order to Valsan, in English: "This vehicle shall not be used in a public place until the vehicle has been passed as "fit for use" by the authority competent. Ok?" He then instructs him, in Malayalam, to take all the passengers off the bus. He switches back to English: "Take this vehicle to my office at a speed not exceeding 15 kilometres per hour."

Murali goes to see the Inspector at his office. He narrates his story of hardship and apologises for testing a government inspector's honesty. The Inspector thinks that the public perception of government officials is that they are corrupt and he wants to correct it. He does not have to survive on Murali's money. He has a television, a video cassette recorder and a garden, three watchmen, and five Alsatians for which he has to spend ₹150 each month on food. He couldn't even give a charitable donation with the money that Murali was offering him. That is all well and good, but what Murali needs is a fitness certificate, otherwise he would have to keep coming to the office each day. He would pay a fine, change the tyre and keep medicines in the box. The Inspector lets him off this time with a fine. Murali bounds out of the office, "Success. Success!" He gets accosted by Govindan Nair, a travelling repairman who keeps 20 different bus parts with him in his sack and knows exactly what is wrong with the bus- the central bolt is out of alignment. He even offers Murali half price for his services. But Murali just wants to be left alone. He is on his way back to his office and is being accosted by a friend for a job when a bus driver shouts that a girl has slipped from his bus.

When Murali reaches the scene a crowd is beating up Hamsa. Chathukutty and Valsan have fled. The crowd accosts him. He and Hamsa make their way to the hospital. Hamsa blames the accident on Chattukutty who did not stop on his whistle. He asks Murali if he insured the bus. He had not. Hamsa suggests that he will have to pay the girl compensation directly. He doesn't think the injury is serious. So it should not be too much. They ask the nurses. The girl has a small fracture in her leg. An operation would be needed. Hamsa tells Murali that if the police come and file a case he will be finished. The only way to avoid this would be to convince the girl to say that she had fallen down by her own mistake. The onlookers from the bus who had accompanied the girl to the hospital leave her room. Murali and Hamsa make their entrance. The injured girl is the same one he had met on his first morning at his new office. Her name is Rama, she had come asking for a concession but Murali, bowing to advice from Hamsa had denied her one. She had been riding the bus to her printing press where she is an apprentice and been making snide comments about the owner since. Murali is now at her sufferance. Rama will not let the opportunity pass. She has lost her leg. Lost her life. She starts to cry. But then Murali decides to battle her sob story with his own. He also knows what pain is. He makes his proposal. When the police arrive, just tell them that you slipped because of your own mistake. He will take care of her medical and personal and family expenses. He would fall at her feet. But one is fractured.

The bus gets back on the road. Murali narrates his growing financial troubles to Hamsa. He had bought the tyre on credit. He does not think that the cash flow from the ticket collections is enough to keep him going. The upcoming festival has the potential to solve the financial problems however. They could get a permit to run the bus non-stop, raise enough money for repairs, and then purchase a new one. Rama arrives at Murali's house demanding her money. He gives her some and asks for patience. He has not received the festival takings, but once he does he will give her more. And then Chathukutty and Hamsa arrive with more bad news. Valsan has gone missing. He has run off with the festival collections. Hamsa suggests that Murali go to his brothers for financial help but he refuses. He setup the business on his own initiative after all. He will go to a financier. He will raise some money by pledging the bus as security. He visits the financiers, signs the papers, and receives the cash.

Murali has renewed his old conductor's licence, so he will now be the conductor of his own bus. The bus gets going again, only to be hailed down by the Inspector. He is getting angry. Chattukutty had not been obeying his signals during the festival. He starts quoting the rule book. Rule 113/1. The other day he had seen the vehicle replenishing the fuel tank with passengers on board which was in contravention of rule 56/2. Murali protests that he had followed the Inspector's instruction and resoled the tyre and put medicines in the first aid box. He had even become a conductor of his own bus. Is that so? Well, according to Section 96 he could be punished. For not wearing a uniform. He could even cancel his licence. The

Inspector boasts that he could find a hundred flaws in a perfect vehicle! He now wants to know about the wiper. Chathukutty says the wiper does not work. But Murali wants to know when they would use it outside of the rainy season. Murali asks Chattukuthy to get the wiper so that the Inspector could eat it. The Inspector takes this as a personal insult. But the encounter is over for the day.

Prabhakaran, the Union leader re-emerges. He had received a complaint that Murali had become his own conductor after dismissing the previous one. Prabhakaran claims that Murali degraded Valsan's parents at their home. Murali admits that he had done so and that it was reasonable. Prabhakaran waves his finger. He had warned him once. He had created a false story to dismiss Valsan. There was no false story, Murali insists. He had to go into debt because of Valsan! Prabhakaran claims he had seen many owners putting on such performances. He wants salary for Valsan from the point of termination, and if he is not re-appointed to his job, then compensation. Murali would give it to him. If he ever saw him again.

Valsan is spotted in front of a tea stall. Hamsa informs Murali. Murali storms over and grabs Valsan and starts to beat him up but is restrained and he gets away. Prabhakaran gets news of the altercation and again demands that Murali apologise to Valsan and the Union and reinstate him. Murali refuses. And so whilst plying the route the next day a small Union demonstration, replete with flags and slogans, stops the bus. The crowd shouts "Gulf Man, this is Kerala, be careful!" Valsan, with a bandaged hand and an arm in a sling, is at the front of the procession. Into the standoff drives a blue Ambassador. The labour officer of the area, Ramakrishnan arrives and tries to affect a compromise between Prabhakaran and Murali. They meet in his office. Both men almost come to blows and Prabhakaran storms out. Murali decides to go to the police and the courts to break the Union's stoppage of his bus. A police jeep drives in with a court order to break the strike. The police start their lathi charge of the workers so that the bus can proceed. Murali taunts Prabhakaran as the bus drives away- you now have competition from the courts and the police.

Having cleared the Union picket, Inspector is waiting. The Inspector threatens to cancel the fitness certificate and demands the RC book. But Murali has had enough. He grabs the Inspector by the arm. He is not going to resole the tyre, or replace the wiper, or stock the first aid box. Inspector tries to physically stop the bus from starting. Murali throws him in the grass. Later, the Union's thugs come with hammers and axes and begin to destroy the bus. Murali takes on half a dozen thugs single-handedly, but cannot prevent the damage being done to the bus. Windows are broken, tyres are punctured and seats are razed. Prabhakaran arrives, taunts Murali, "you are a great owner", and punches him in the face. He instructs the thugs to break the bus. Murali hits back and the two get into a prolonged fight. Murali eventually fights them all off with his iron rod. But his bus is destroyed.

Murali and Prabhakaran meet at Ramakrishnan's office. The Bus Owners' Association refuses to support Murali's cause. He had not approached them when he bought the bus. Murali claims he is not receiving their support because he is not connected. He is not a member of the Lions Club and does not have a Diners card.
Ramakrishnan begins to take his side. Murali had started the bus with his hard earned money, did not cheat his workers, and was employing three people. He starts to lecture Prabhakaran. What did he achieve by defending a criminal and looting a bus besides ruining employment for three people? Prabhakaran now claims that Murali destroyed his own bus to take revenge on the Union protesters. Murali stands up. If Gulf money did not keep pouring in, thousands of people, like Prabhakaran, would die of hunger. Everyone wants their consumer goods, like video cassette recorders, which they bring back on the cheap from the Gulf. Murali throws more invective at

Prabhakaran and the two almost come to blows again. Ramakrishnan also joins the tirade. Prabhakaran has ruined a man. Anyone who starts a small business became "bourgeoisie" but the Unions would not touch the really big owners. Prabhakaran claims that he has been bribed by Murali to speak on his behalf. This time Murali has to keep Prabhakaran and Ramakrishnan from coming to blows.

Murali sits in his gutted bus. The Inspector drives up. Murali resorts to sarcasm. Everything is in perfect order. If only he can now get a fitness certificate, he would be happy. But the Inspector feels some sense of remorse, and empathy. He did not try to give Murali a hard time deliberately. He was new in the job and was trying to show his power without yet having much experience. But what favour was he expecting? Murali did not want any favours. The Union leaders had finished him off. The Inspector feels guilty. Murali should take it as a lesson. He should try to buy a new bus. He is not speaking as an officer but as a friend.

Murali faces up to his two brothers and his uncle in the front room of the family home. Ammavan says that he is paying for his haughtiness. Narayanan is ashamed to even sit in his restaurant because of the infamy that Murali has brought. Kumaran is fearful that the politicians might turn against him because of all this. Murali needs ₹30,000 to buy a new bus, and so he asks his brothers directly for the money. Ammavan excuses himself from the room. Narayanan tries to leave, but Murali wants an answer. He says that Murali should not have involved himself in such a dangerous business, besides which, he had just put down a deposit for some land the previous day. If he had asked earlier things might have been different. He has two daughters and has to keep some property for their future. Kumaran says that Sunny Lucas is in Bombay, whilst Tony's mother is in hospital. How could he ask his partner in such a condition? His own business is facing great risk. Things have gone down suddenly.

The financiers come for their money. Murali cannot provide it, and the surety, the bus, is gutted. They will take him to court. Govindan Nair, the travelling repairman wants Murali to give him the parts which the financiers would not take with them. Prabhakaran is addressing a Union meeting outside a factory. The police are watching on. Murali wanders up. He grabs Prabhakaran's microphone and starts to speak to the crowd. Ultimately no one wants to start a factory in Kerala and the state is full of unemployed people looking for low paying jobs abroad. He calls for doing away with the Union leaders who stand between the employers and employees. A melee ensues. Murali ends up in jail and Ramakrishnan comes to the police station to bail him out. The police officer tells him that the local member of the state Legislative Assembly has put pressure on him not to grant bail. Ramakrishnan threatens to call a minister. Murali is released.

Rama comes up with a proposal for pledging her house and land to get Murali back in business. But he has decided to go back to Bombay. He knows many people there. It would not be hard to arrange a new visa for Dubai. He promises to write to her. He boards a bus which drives off into the distance.

***

Murali was the ideal Indian export because he did not face the impediments of other Indian exporters. Indian manufacturers were usually reliant on the domestic market for safe profits. Murali faced the prospect of unemployment in Kerala. Exporters suffered from shortages of electricity. Murali just needed his bare hands and the will to work. Exporters faced perennial problems procuring imported supplies. All that Murali needed was a visa, which was quite easy to come by. Exporters had stiff competition from international rivals. Murali and his peers were the best product in their category on the labour market; Indians were cheaper, more hard working and spoke better English than their Asian competitors. Indian economic planning had, from the start, been marked by its sophistry. The bigger and more complex and intricately modelled that an economic plan was, the better it was thought that it would work. Yet the officials of the Planning Commission had never factored the export of Indian labour into their plans. Perhaps the thought of low skilled Indians working abroad, largely fleeing the failures of the planned economy was just too much of an affront to their expertise. Yet after 20 years of trying to boost Indian exports through a plethora of government schemes, remittances from Indian workers in the Middle East had, in just four years in the late 1970s, come to account for almost one-third of India's export earnings.

Indian workers in the Middle East were under no legal obligation to send remittances back to India. Yet it was the primary motivation for going in the first place. The practice of sending money home was rooted in Indian culture and family life, transcending religion and region and language and caste. The universal desire, depicted in the initial dining table conversations between Murali and his family in *Varavelpu*, was not to better oneself as an individual, but to improve the social and economic standing of one's family, both for the present, and for future generations. The remittances sent to Kerala in the 1980s by workers in the Middle East did not spur an economic boom, save for construction and property. Yet they did raise living standards. Malayalis ate better food, wore better clothes, sent their children to better schools, and watched films on video cassette recorders and the latest televisions in larger homes. These migrant remittances were also having an impact at a broader national and macroeconomic level. Indian exports had been stagnant in the early 1980s, but migrant remittances allowed the Government of India first to mitigate the impact of the huge rise in the price of oil, and then indirectly helped to support a new drive for industrialisation and infrastructure investment. Migrant remittances were known as "invisibles" in India's national accounts yet continued to play a significant and steady role in supporting government finances throughout the 1980s.

The Dhirubhai Ambani story contains some particularly intricate patterns of history. Like Gujaratis of centuries past, young Dhirubhai travelled to the Red Sea port of Aden. He was not initially a merchant or trader however. He was a manager for a French firm which handled much of the region's circulation of industrial products. He was, in the 1950s, much like the Indians who would arrive in greater numbers in the Gulf in the 1980s, a semi-skilled worker hoping to earn some money and save enough to return and make his life in India. Dhirubhai had been trading on his own account during his time in Aden and exhibited a much larger appetite for risk than many of his Gujarati colleagues. Yet his more serious trading activities would begin when he returned to Bombay. He became a player in the cotton market but quickly understood the potential of new synthetic fibres, particularly polyester. He had just returned from the Red Sea region where Indian cotton textile merchants had plied their wares for centuries prior to British rule. Dhirubhai was not especially interested in exports, yet the Government of India was trying to encourage Indian manufacturers to export in greater quantities through import replenishment schemes. During the 1960s and 1970s, a time of otherwise quiet for Indian industry, Dhirubhai managed to accumulate the largest and quickest fortune in independent India by building a textiles factory in Naroda, Gujarat which produced enough polyester for export to secure import replenishment licences which would ensure windfall profits by cornering the import of polyester yarn. The exports which he sent out to the world were considered dubious. He may have even been buying them himself through conduits in foreign markets. Yet when the High Value Unit Scheme came to an end in the late 1970s, Dhirubhai had the largest polyester factory in

India and promptly switched his attention to the Indian market. Thus, a Gujarati with no particular interest in exports went to the Middle East, the site of Gujarati enterprise for centuries, only to return home to India to build a factory which sent out notional exports to the world to take advantage of a government scheme which allowed for the import of a scarce commodity, the profits from which would eventually create a factory thriving enough to serve the Indian market. Dhirubhai's polyester may even have clothed many of India's real exports as they left for work in the Gulf in the early 1980s.

India's climate and geography made it an ideal land for the cultivation of cotton. Yet cotton was grown elsewhere in the world during the 600 years that India dominated the global cotton textile trade. The principal reason for India's domination of the world cotton textile market was that its skilled spinners, weavers and dyers held a mastery over the most advanced production technologies of their time. In addition to an ideal climate, skilled workforce, and ready access to technology, India also benefitted from both its governments, which provided a secure environment for trade and built the necessary infrastructure, such as ports and roads, to transport Indian textiles abroad, and its intrepid merchants, who took India's wares as far afield as Java, and Mozambique, and Samarqand, and Moscow. It was when British technology made Indian production obsolete in the mid 18th century that the textile industry, which had sustained Indian prosperity for so many centuries, collapsed within a matter of decades. The British invention of the fly shuttle and the development of superior dying techniques and steam powered cotton mills occurred at the precise time that the British were becoming rulers of India. The policies of the British East India Company, and later the Crown in the 19th century only served, through iniquitous tariff policies, to exacerbate what was a matter of technological obsolescence. The Marathi writer Ramkrishna Vishwanath, had, as early as 1843 seen the obvious potential of Indian cotton mills, with their ready access to a plentiful supply of both cotton and cheap labour, to begin to dominate world markets once again. Whilst Indian mills did proliferate in the late 19th century, they had to compete with mills in Lancashire which enjoyed British Government protection. They then ran into another obstacle. Mohandas Gandhi tried to set the nationalist movement in direct opposition to modern Indian manufacturing, particularly the cotton mills which might compete with homespun khadi. The Government of India's measures to protect hand spinners and handloom weavers in the 1950s only served to preserve production techniques which had been obsolete since 1733.

Of a survey of 402 Malayali migrant workers in the Middle East, only 1 had used their earnings to start a factory in Kerala. Malayalis were not confident that their hard earned money would be safe given both the restive labour situation and maddening regulations prevalent in the state. Part of the reason that remittances did not spark an economic boom in Kerala was well illustrated in *Varavelpu* by Murali's running conflicts with both the Brake Inspector and the Union leader, Prabhakaran. Murali was a small businessman. He wanted to ply a bus between villages. He employed 3 people to start with, but his ambition was to provide work for 50. Yet his bus operation, although small in size, did not benefit from any protection for small-scale industries. He was thus left to face the Unions and the government Brake Inspector on his own. Some of Murali's business troubles might have been of his own making. He had bought a second-hand bus and started running it before properly investing in its renovation or repair or fully understanding all the government's regulatory requirements. When old Govindan Nair approached him with his bag full of spare parts and spotted the bus's engine problem and offered to repair it for a good price, Murali brushed him away. But the bus's technical faults could always have been fixed. They were the least of Murali's worries. He spent much of his time trying to keep the Brake Inspector in good humour so that he did not ground his bus. One of his three employees, Valsan, the conductor, absconded with the festival takings and then turned against him. Yet whilst all the other characters in the film, including the Brake Inspector, were, in the end, afforded their humanity, Prabhakaran was given none. He was so obstinate and egotistical and doctrinaire that he ended up destroying Murali's bus, and his little dream of providing jobs in his local community. Murali was a small businessman, amongst the smallest, and in his conflict with Prabhakaran the larger businessmen of the Bus Owners' Association refused to take his side. He thought it was because he was not part of their club.

NINE

The Bombay Club

During the late 19th century the swadeshi movement led a resurgence of Indian owned enterprises. This revival was most evident in Bengal where Bengalis tried to start their own cotton mills, chemicals laboratories, iron foundries, paper factories, banks, insurance agencies and shipping companies. Most of the swadeshi enterprises being created in Bengal were small however. Big business was still dominated by British capital. The oldest British business houses had their headquarters in Calcutta and were managed by venerable managing agencies on behalf of the owners. The first modern Indian industrialists were the cotton mill magnates of Bombay and Ahmadabad. They were not always held in high regard. In one of India's earliest silent films, *Bismi Sadi*, or *20th Century*, the director Homi Master told the story of a small town street hawker, Devdas who goes to the big city, becomes a cotton mill owner, is knighted by the British and then disowns his humble roots. Devdas's wife and daughter suffer hardship and dishonour and he repents only on his deathbed. The miserable working conditions of mill hands and the debauched lifestyles of the mill owners and their heirs were recurring themes in the silent films of the 1920s and 1930s. Prior to the First World War Indian industry had been dominated by this first generation of cotton mill owners. It was only after the war that younger Indian entrepreneurs set their sights beyond cotton weaving and entered a diverse range of modern industries. Moreover, just as in government, so in business and finance, the British presence began to diminish and Indians entered once British preserves; British shareholdings in Indian businesses declined dramatically between the wars whilst Indian control grew. The new voice of the Indian capitalist class was the Federation of Indian Chambers of Commerce and Industry and its leading spokesman was Ghanshyamdas Birla. The Federation was the representative of Indian rather than British big business interests and although it had to maintain a working relationship with the government, it managed to nurture tacit support for the Congress, which it increasingly viewed as the government in waiting.

The idea of licensing Indian businesses was one which was slightly separate from, but concomitant with the idea of economic planning. The issue of licences for Indian enterprises was supported by many leading Indian businessmen even prior to the Second World War when the government began licensing on a larger scale in order to control production for war purposes. An Industries Bill had begun to be drafted before the establishment of a Planning Commission was agreed to after Independence. The Industries (Development and Regulation) Act was passed by Parliament in October 1951 and its "object and reasons" read:

> *The Bill brings under Central control the development and regulation of a number of important industries the activities of which affect the country as a whole and the development of which must be governed by economic factors of all-India import. The planning of future development on sound and balanced lines is sought to be secured by the licensing of all new undertakings by the Central Government.*

The key phrase in the passage was "sound and balanced lines". The socialist rhetoric of the later 1950s was still some time away. "Sound and balanced" could have meant many things to different people. "Sound and balanced" would not be offensive to capitalists. It might be mildly encouraging to socialists. It did not commit the government to any specific principle which could not later be reversed. Or any policy which might be pursued in the future. It was perfect bureaucratic language. Yet it soon became clear that the government's attempts to administer industrial licensing could not meet even this nebulous standard. When, in the mid 1950s, the Ministry of Commerce liberalised import licences, it was thought to have caused a foreign exchange crisis. Once the government became aware of the crisis, import licensing was restricted to an even greater extent than before the liberalisation. Import replenishment licences were offered to exporters in the early 1960s. These replenishment licences were put to dubious use in cornering imports of scarce commodities and foreign exchange. Domestic licences for industrial expansion seemed to be given on an ad hoc basis, almost always to the country's biggest industrialists. In addition, the bureaucrats in New Delhi were getting buried under piles of their own paperwork.

During the late 1950s the main opposition parties in Parliament were Socialist and Communist and they were concerned that licensing was only working to the advantage of their antagonists, the capitalists. Prime Minister Jawaharlal Nehru decided to appoint his former associate Prasanta Mahalanobis to look into the matter in 1960. It took Mahalanobis four years to produce a report which largely confirmed the concerns about the power of the big business houses and recommended further study. Rabindra Kishen Hazari was one of India's leading research economists and had studied the phenomenon of the concentration of wealth and market power in the 1950s. He was asked by the Planning Commission to present a report in 1965. A later parliamentary enquiry, known as the Dutt Committee, was to look into industrial licensing in even greater detail and report back with recommendations. Out of the Mahalanobis Report had sprung the Monopolies Enquiry Commission which recommended the establishment of a permanent Monopolies Commission to prevent the abuse of market power and the further concentration of wealth. All of these parliamentary and Planning Commission studies had found that it was the Birlas, principally Ghanshyamdas and his brother Braj Mohan, who had received a disproportionate number of licences since the system began.

The Monopolies Enquiry Commission's recommendations were accepted by the government and at the start of the 1970s another, judicial, branch was added to the Licence Raj. In addition to industrial licensing, India's large private companies would have to appear before a Monopolies Commission which would be able to scrutinise their applications for capacity expansion. The aim was to prevent India's biggest businesses growing even further. Yet it soon became clear that the government could not do without them.

***

The number of companies registered in India quadrupled between the First World War and the Second, rising from 2,668 in 1918/19 to 10,657 in 1938/39.[dxxxix] In 1918, the British controlled 72% of these companies, Indians controlled 13%, whilst 15% were under mixed control. Twenty years later British control had dropped to 40%, Indian control had risen to 34%, and companies under mixed control had also risen to 24%. The rise in companies under mixed control suggests a determined Indian attempt to capture control of an increasing number of local companies. Modern Indian industry had sprung from the cotton textile sector. However, after the First World War Indian industrialists began to expand into sugar, paper, starch, shipping, engineering, and air transport. Like young Ghanshyamdas Birla, Indian businessmen were challenging traditional British monopolies in the jute and coal industries. At the end of the First World War Indian investments in these industries were just under one-quarter of the total. By the eve of the Second World War they had risen to just under one-half.

The start of the First World War caused a sudden disruption to imports into India. This proved to be a boon for businesses in India, both British and Indian. Temporary scarcity conditions meant that demand for goods which would otherwise have been imported was met by local businesses. The only major obstacle to greater production and larger profits was machinery. Indian factories imported most of their machinery from Britain, Germany and Japan, and so instead of procuring new machinery existing machinery was put to work on longer shifts, particularly in the cotton and jute mills of Calcutta. The Bombay mills required more power to sustain more intense production and this demand was met by the Tatas who moved into electricity generation and expanded their hydroelectric grid in western India. They launched the Andhra Valley Power Supply Company in 1916 which generated hydroelectric power in the region surrounding Lonavala. The Tata Power Company, founded in 1919, generated power from the water resources of the districts near Poona. By 1920 the Tata hydroelectric system was able to meet the industrial and consumer power needs of the Bombay Presidency.

Tata Steel continued to expand during the war, supplying most of the Government of India's requirements whilst imports remained disrupted. The British Raj would not have been able to do without them, yet the Tatas only grew in stature amongst Indian nationalists as a "national house". This was a period of great expansion for Tata & Sons; just prior to the war the group added a new cotton mill in Bombay, Tata Mills, and also moved into the production of cement. The Tatas' Indian Cement Company in Porbander was not the first, but it would prove to be the most successful Indian venture in the field over the following decades. Sir Dorabji Tata, Jamsetji's successor, opened another cement unit,

Shahabad Cement Company in Bihar. The later years of the war were particularly buoyant for the Tatas as they founded firms in engineering, electrochemicals, construction, sugar, soap, commercial banking and insurance. Not all of these enterprises lasted; some were specifically setup to take advantage of the scarcity conditions of the war. The Tata insurance venture, New India Assurance Company was among the few new companies started during the war which endured.

It was during the First World War that the Marwaris, originally from the region surrounding Jodhpur in south-western Rajasthan, began to move from their traditional businesses in financial services and took up modern industrial enterprise. Some Marwaris had established cotton mills in Bombay, Poona, Nagpur and Indore prior to the war, yet the process of modernisation started in earnest amongst the Marwaris of Calcutta. They dominated the domestic trade in raw jute in eastern India, held a sizable share of the export trade, and acted as banias, or moneylenders to Calcutta's leading British business houses. British firms, known as managing agencies, managed large industrial concerns on behalf of the owners and would offer substantial shareholdings to their managers and business partners. When share prices boomed during the war, these British managers and businessmen with little long term interest in the companies in which they held stock, sold their holdings. The Marwaris, with their windfall profits made from commodity trading during the war, were thus able to buy their way into modern industry, albeit at a premium.

The Birlas were best positioned to take advantage of the surge in jute exports during the war and opened an export office in London in 1917. Ghanshyamdas, who was just 20 years old in 1914, was the family member most responsible for the group's huge growth in net worth during the war years. The sick cotton mill which he acquired in Delhi in 1916 was the first industrial venture in which the Birla family exercised complete management control. In 1918 Ghanshyamdas formed Birla Brothers with his elder brother Rameshwardas, a managing agency which would oversee the family's industrial units. Most boldly, that year, the Birlas progressed from trading in the raw jute market, to producing processed jute, setting up their own mill in Calcutta in an attempt to challenge the monopoly exercised by the expatriate Scottish community.

The Tatas were the leading Indian business house at the end of the First World War. Yet they, like their fellow Indian industrialists, had to survive the recession of the early 1920s. Their cotton businesses prospered during the 1920s, but most of the Tata enterprises started during the First World War had to be wound up, with the exceptions of Tata Oil Mills and Tata (Cotton) Mills. Expanded domestic production and the resumption of imports after the war forced cement prices down which eventually led the Tatas to merge their cement companies into a pan-Indian conglomerate, Associated Cement Companies in 1936. Tata Steel also experienced similar difficulties.

The Tatas decided to expand steel production at the end of the war by investing in more plant equipment only for the recession of the early 1920s to set in. Imports resumed and domestic demand declined. Yet steel was Jamsetji's legacy, and so his heirs would not countenance the prospect of leaving the industry. Sir Dorabji pledged his personal fortune to secure a loan in India, money was raised in London and senior managers lobbied the Government of India for protection for the domestic steel industry. The Tatas, enjoying their reputation as the standard bearer of modern Indian business, were supported by the moderate Indian nationalists who had won election to the new Indian Legislative Assembly in Delhi. High officials of the Raj also remembered their services rendered during the war. A subsidy was given to steel rails in 1924 and then in 1927 levies were placed on imported steel. The government also helped the

Jamshedpur steel mill by placing large orders for its industrial and railways requirements.

Jehangir Ratanji Dadabhoy Tata had come to India in 1924 after a childhood in France. By the early 1930s he was playing an increasingly dominant role in the affairs of the group and was appointed chairman in 1938. It was J.R.D. who led the Tatas into aviation. He was a keen amateur pilot and started Air India as an air mail service between Karachi and Bombay in 1932 but the venture stalled due to the outbreak of the Second World War. Another new project, Tata Chemicals, which was to start a factory at Mithapur on the coast of the princely state of Baroda also had to wait until after the war. By the late 1930s the Tatas had 14 major companies with combined sales of ₹280 crore.[dxl] Most of the Tata companies were in heavy industries which required large investments, technical managerial expertise and long gestation periods for profitability.

Birla Jute Mills faced inevitable opposition from Calcutta's Scottish jute mill owners and Ghanshyamdas Birla had even contemplated selling the mill to Andrew Yule & Company.[dxli] Yet he persisted in the industry and the mill became operational in 1922. The Birlas did not setup another jute mill but seven other Indian owned mills were established in and around Calcutta during the 1920s. There were no major Birla stock market floats for the decade after the start of the Calcutta jute mill, however one more cotton mill was established in Gwalior and another was acquired in Calcutta. The Government of India had started to provide tariff protection to the local sugar industry which encouraged the Birlas to setup five sugar plants in the eastern districts of the United Provinces and the western districts of Bihar between 1931 and 1933. This sudden burst in domestic production led to excess supply however, and so the Birlas started to appeal to nationalist sentiments, marketing their "Pure and Refined Swadeshi Sugar".[dxlii] By the end of the 1930s the Birlas were the third largest producer of sugar in the country.[dxliii]

The Birlas established another cotton mill, this time in the north, Sutlej Cotton Mills in Lahore in 1936. The youngest Birla brother, Braj Mohan led the family's entry into the paper industry in 1936. Much like jute two decades earlier, paper was a British monopoly. Braj Mohan's Orient Paper Mills was the first Indian venture in the industry. The mill was expected to take advantage of new technology which allowed for the manufacture of bamboo pulp into paper, yet it had not started production when the Second World War broke out. The Birlas' other pioneering venture, Textile Machinery Corporation, was to manufacture the machinery for cotton mills in India, yet its operations were taken over by the Government of India during the war. Unlike the Tatas who focused on heavy industry, most Birla ventures were still in consumer goods industries which required relatively low levels of investment and technical management expertise. By the eve of the war the Birlas had 11 companies under their management but the net worth of their group was much smaller than the Tatas.[dxliv] Despite this it was G.D. Birla rather than J.R.D. Tata who emerged in the 1930s as the voice of Indian industry through the Federation of Indian Chambers of Commerce and Industry.

During the last years of the British Raj the Indian businessman with the grandest sense of adventure was Walchand Hirachand Doshi. The Doshis were Jains, originally from Idar, a tiny town halfway between Ahmadabad and Udaipur. Walchand had grown up in a traditional Bania milieu in the small town of Sholapur in the southern part of the Bombay Presidency. Like Ghanshyamdas Birla he decided to branch out from his family's traditional moneylending business and started by supplying fuel to a Sholapur cotton mill. He then moved into railway construction in partnership with Laxman Phatak who had worked for the local railways. Their first project was completed in 1903 and, like many other Indian suppliers, their partnership grew to prosperity during the First World War. Walchand then decided to launch into shipping.

When in 1919 Walchand heard that the Maharajah of Gwalior was putting the *SS Loyalty* up for sale he decided to buy it. He persuaded some of the leaders of the Bombay business community to join him and the Scindia Steam Navigation Company was thus formed. The company's initial share issue was oversubscribed. But Scindia Steam would have to take on the commercial power of the British India Navigation Company which had merged with P&O and held command of the eastern waters. The head of British India Steam Navigation, James Lyle Mackay, the Baron of Inchcape, had been in India since 1874, owned three managing agencies and was influential in government circles. Walchand thus had troubles finding a ship repairer and a shipping agent in London. He tried to capture the India-Europe passage but was unsuccessful and so had to concentrate on coastal services around India. Scindia Steam even had trouble on the India-Burma route as P&O drastically reduced its freight rates and benefitted from government patronage. By 1922 Mackay was trying to persuade Scindia Steam's Board members to sell the company to British India Steam Navigation. Most of Scindia's directors were inclined to sell, yet Walchand thought of their venture as a bearer of Indian nationalism; it was their right to run ships off the coast of their motherland.[dxlv] Mackay eventually persuaded the Scindia Board to restrict its fleet to seven ships and confine its operations to the Indian coastline for 10 years. The agreement was renewed on slightly better terms in 1933, but Walchand continued the fight, helping smaller Indian shipping companies, taking over the management of three more shipping firms and entering the Haj pilgrimage passage in competition with the British companies which dominated the route.

After the end of the First World War Walchand merged his Walchand Phatak & Co with the Tata Construction Company. Walchand only held a minority stake in the new company, however he remained active in its management and eventually became managing director. During the 1920s Tata Construction acquired Marshland Price & Company and a Calcutta cement pipe firm which became the Indian Hume Pipe Company. Two subsidiaries were created- Hindustan Construction Company and the All India Construction Company- which sought tenders for major infrastructure projects. The Tatas eventually sold their stake to Walchand who then renamed the new entity Premier Construction Company. Like the Birlas, Walchand entered the sugar industry in the early 1930s. His Ravalgaon Sugar Farm Limited was located in Nasik district and the sugar growing complex became known as Walchandnagar. Walchand and his brothers, Gulabchand and Lalchand, developed one of the most efficient sugar farms in India and built their own light railway to connect the farm to the main local railway line.

Laxmanrao Kirloskar started as an art student in Bombay and then turned his hand to bicycle repairs and sales in his hometown of Belgaum. He moved into the manufacture of agricultural implements and received assistance in the form of cash and land from a former classmate, Bhawanrao Shriniwasrao Pant Pratinidhi, who had become the ruler of the princely state of Aundh. Prior to the First World War the Kirloskar product line still consisted of two main items however- the improved iron plough and the shaft cutter. The Kirloskars did not make windfall profits during the war; demand for their plough rose, yet so did the cost of production. Kirloskar Brothers, until then a partnership, became a public company in 1920. The drilling machine, windlass, draw pulley, groundnut decorticator and an improved plough became part of their expanded product line in the 1920s. The most innovative additions to their offering were a diesel engine and a centrifugal pump for irrigation. Laxmanrao had taught himself the basics of engineering and designed most of the new products himself. His son Shantanu however studied engineering at the Massachusetts Institute of Technology and came into the business in 1926. He created a superior engine and also developed a new sugarcane crusher. Rural demand was effected by the Great Depression and during the 1930s the company remained solvent by taking its products directly to farmers across the country and offering after sales service. The Kirloskars tried to make nuts and bolts but were undercut by cheaper imports. They also experimented with a wide variety of products including looms, steel furniture, lathes, gas plants and body building materials for commercial vehicles.

Shri Ram's family was one of the original promoters of Delhi Cloth Mills, but its stake was too small to exercise control over the management of the company. Shri Ram's father worked as a salaried company secretary and he also became a joint secretary of the company prior to the First World War. DCM benefited from the army's demand for tents during the First World War, and when civil servants started to move to the new capital from Calcutta, but had to wait for their offices to be completed, Shri Ram spotted his opportunity. He formed a new company in which DCM was given a 50% stake, whilst he shared the other half with a contractor who had government connections. The tent contracts were lucrative and all three shareholders made large profits. From his new earnings Shri Ram and his father were able to increase their shareholding in DCM to 16% and take control of the company.[dxlvi]

Most of India's cotton mills were located in western India, principally Bombay and Ahmadabad. DCM was the only major cotton mill to serve the Delhi & Punjab market. The Delhi mill did well in the 1920s and even survived the depression years by focusing on coarser cloth. Shri Ram provided incentives to sales agents and the company also benefitted from the intermittent calls of the Congress to boycott foreign cloth. DCM also setup another mill in Lyallpur in western Punjab. Like many of his peers in the Indian business community, Shri Ram diversified into sugar. He personally supervised the construction of a factory in Meerut district to the north-east of Delhi and within a year of starting operations, in 1933, almost half of DCM's profits came from sugar.[dxlvii] However DCM's Daurala sugar factory would face the same problem of a glut of production as other local producers.

Shri Ram's old friend from Rawalpindi, Madan Lal Bhagat convinced him to invest in the Bengal Pottery Works, an old swadeshi enterprise, which, after many years, was yet to develop into a sustainable business. Bhagat's father had been a potter and he thought he might be able to turn the company's fortunes around. With Shri Ram's investment the company attracted prominent Bombay investors. Bhagat diversified the company's products away from ceramic insulators which were dependent on government orders towards consumer goods which were popular in the bazaars. He faced competition from cheap imports from Japan, but managed to turn a profit most years, and installed a new plant just before the outbreak of the Second World War. Shri Ram also entered light engineering, acquiring the newly established Jay Engineering Works in Calcutta in 1937. The company's main product was a sewing machine, which had not been selling well, and after the takeover plans were made to diversify the product range. New factories were designed and machinery purchased but the new equipment had to be diverted to the production of wartime supplies for the government.

Newer, smaller entrepreneurs were also entering industry. Juggilal Singhania from Kanpur established a cotton mill in 1921 and his son Kamlapat then started cotton, jute and sugar mills and an engineering firm. Jamnalal Bajaj from Wardha started a sugar mill and a steel rolling mill in the 1930s. Ramkrishna Dalmia, a Marwari who had settled in Rohtak setup his own sugar mills in Bihar and then got into the cement business establishing factories across the country. Karamchand Thapar from Ludhiana joined his relatives in business in Calcutta before founding his own trading firm and entering the sugar, coal and paper industries. The Seshasayee brothers-in-law, trained as engineers, started a road transport company around Trichinopoly in Madras. They moved into the servicing and sale of buses, cars, and motorcycles and then designing, supplying and erecting electrical installations. The brothers formed three public companies between 1924 and 1937 all of which were well subscribed by local investors. C. Rajan Iyer founded the Indian Steel Rolling Mills in Madras in 1934, the first steel rolling plant in southern India.

The Second World War came as a financial relief to the Indian business community. The Great Depression had not been as severe in India as in the United States and Europe, but it had led to falling demand, and for most of the 1930s, a struggle for survival. As during the First World War, the supply of imports into India was disrupted, and so local demand drove a rise in the prices of locally made goods. Once again factories ran at full capacity and manufacturers and distributors both made large profits. The supply of imported equipment was again limited, which meant that there was little scope for reinvesting profits into expanded production capacity. In addition, the Government of India was requisitioning supplies from Indian producers to meet the needs of the war effort, which only led to a further spike in prices and profits. There were artificial shortages of food, coal and steel which led the government to control prices. The British Government also effectively borrowed from the Government of India by paying for its purchases of war supplies in India by crediting the Reserve Bank of India's account at the Bank of England with pounds sterling, which came to be known as "the sterling balances". This then allowed the Reserve Bank to print money in India to provide to the Government of India to make its purchases. The only significant controls on Indian industrialists were an excess profits tax and a compulsory deposit scheme to discourage excessive dividends. Nonetheless, the looming problem for Indian industry was the obsolescence of its machinery. Investment had not been possible during the 1930s due to the Great Depression and then, when profits returned during the war, imports of capital equipment halted and existing machinery was worked on double shifts.

Tata Locomotive and Engineering Company, established in 1945, produced the trucks which became ubiquitous on Indian highways and eventually developed into the largest business in the Tata group. The Birlas founded Hindustan Motors in 1942 which started manufacturing cars in collaboration with Morris Motors in Calcutta in 1950 and went on to produce the Ambassador, the most enduring icon of the Licence Raj. Walchand Doshi, inspired by Sir Visvesvaraya's vision of an industrialised India had tried to start a shipyard in Bombay, and an aircraft production unit in Mysore, as well as Air Services of India, all of which had to wait until the war ended. He joined the Tatas and Birlas in car manufacturing, partnering with Chrysler to form Premier Automobiles in 1947. Premier produced the Padmini, which ranked second only to the Ambassador in icon status on the Indian roads. The Kirloskars also setup a factory in Mysore, and then in 1946 established the Kirloskar Electric Company which manufactured electric motors. In southern India the Seshasayees continued their expansion in infrastructure, expanding their Madras Electric Company, taking over the Mettur Chemical and Industrial Corporation, and launching Fertilizer and Chemicals Travancore Ltd. Still more new businesspeople were coming forth, like the Mahindras, Kailash and Jagdish, brothers from Ludhiana who had been educated in England and joined the civil service only to resign and start their own ventures. Their partnership with Ghulam Mohammad came to an end at Partition, but they continued in business in independent India as Mahindra & Mahindra.

Indian socialists had been particularly dismissive of Indian capitalists, not necessarily for their business practices, but for their proximity to British capital. Indian businessmen were variously dubbed the "junior partners" or stooges or minions of imperial capital. Yet it was clear that just as Britain's traditional laissez faire policies had undergone a dramatic reversal after the First World War and Indian businesses were increasingly protected from foreign competition, Britain's dominance of industry in India was also declining. In the years after the war Indian businessmen were quickly becoming the senior partners in once British companies. The socialists' dismissal of Indian capitalists was not just a matter of doctrine but of feeling. Indian capitalists were held in universal low repute in Indian society in the 1940s. The new Indian capitalist was a modern incarnation of the traditional village moneylender in the minds of most Indians. All the loathing traditionally reserved for the village bania was simply transferred onto the Indian mill owner. Yet the scorn heaped on its businessmen only obscured the fact that India at Independence was endowed with one of the biggest and most dynamic entrepreneurial classes in Asia.

***

The Industrial Policy Resolutions of 1948 and 1956 divided industries into three categories. The first was that in which the government would exercise complete control over production. In the second the government would have a predominant presence and new private enterprises could not be established but existing private enterprises would be allowed to continue. The third category encompassed all other industries, which were to be left to private enterprise. The first two categories were mainly made up of heavy industries. In practice most of the growth of new private enterprises in the 1950s occurred in two ways. The first was the acquisition of British businesses from their departing owners. The second was investment in a burgeoning automotive sector.

The Bangurs, Marwaris who had been active in business and finance in the princely states of Rajputana, began to acquire British owned jute mills in Calcutta after the

Second World War. They continued buying businesses from departing British owners in the 1950s: Kettlewell Bullen, a managing agency, Bengal Coal, the Midnapore zamindar estate, Ganges Manufacturing, and Bengal Paper. The Goenkas, an old Marwari trading family of Calcutta benefited the most from the British exodus from the city. Even at the time of Independence they had been mainly confined to the traditional role of money lending. Their clients, among the city's biggest managing agencies, began to leave, and generally preferred to sell to their creditors whom they had known for many years. The Goenka scion, Keshav Prasad oversaw this spree of acquisitions, beginning with Octavius Steel which controlled sugar mills, power companies and a colliery. The Goenkas also acquired Duncan Brothers which brought them tea gardens and jute mills. In the 1960s Keshav Prasad acquired a group of companies owned by a Jewish family, B.N. Elias. The owners had grown exhausted dealing with labour troubles in West Bengal. The acquisition brought a jute mill, a radio manufacturer and a tobacco company.

Brij Mohan Khaitan initially supplied fertilisers and crates to Assam tea plantations in the 1950s. He was offered a minority equity holding in Williamson Magor, an old British tea plantation which had fallen on hard times. The erstwhile British managers were largely absent, which allowed Brij Mohan to become managing director. He continued buying equity and became the company's chairman. The British owners did not take much persuading to sell their remaining stake. Brij Mohan went on to buy more British tea plantations through the acquisitions of Mcleod Russell and Macneil & Barry. Vithal Mallya, a stocker broker in Calcutta had been acquiring shares in the British owned United Breweries prior to Independence. The brewery was located in Bangalore and Mallya completed the acquisition when the owners left after 1947. Similarly, Mohan Oberoi had begun his acquisition of British owned hotels prior to Independence, buying Calcutta's Grand Hotel. After Independence he acquired India's largest chain of hotels after buying the British owned Associated Hotels group.

Muttaiya Annamalai Chidambaram established Automobile Products of India which was the first Indian company to produce scooters. The Bajajes were also diversifying into two wheel and three wheel scooters. The Mahindras' fortunes rose in 1947 as they secured the India distribution rights for jeeps from the American Willys Overland Company. They began assembling and manufacturing jeeps and grew to dominate the market by the end of the 1950s. The Mahindra brothers also partnered with foreign firms to manufacture elevators, tractors, alloy steel and hydraulic machinery. Hari Prasad Nanda established the Escorts group which initially distributed household electrical appliances and then dealt in second-hand cars before moving into the manufacture of earth moving machinery, tractors and motorcycles with foreign partners. T.V. Sundaram Iyengar founded TVS & Sons and manufactured powered bicycles and automobile parts. S. Anantharamakrishnan developed the Amalgamation Group, manufacturing tractors, diesel engines, and automobile parts. A.M.M Chetty founded the Murugappa Group which initially produced bicycles in Madras, whilst Braj Mohan Munjal also started making bicycles in Punjab in 1956. K.M. Mammen Mapillai began making tyres in 1961 in collaboration with the American Mansfield Tyre & Rubber Company. Bharat Forge was established in 1964 by Neelkanth Kalyani and soon began to manufacture auto components, steel tubes and electronics.

The Congress held an overwhelming majority in the first and second Lok Sabhas. The opposition parties of significance were Socialist and Communist. This status as the only parliamentary opposition gave them the opportunity to voice their concerns and be heard on the national stage in disproportion to their small numbers. Communists had been making suggestions in the Lok Sabha as early as February 1958 for rooting out the "evil" from the economy which they thought sprang from "the power of monopoly capital in the private sector".[dxlviii] In August the Communist members, K.T.K. Tangamani and V.P. Nayar introduced a private member's bill to prevent monopolies and unfair business practices.[dxlix] Days later the Lok Sabha rejected Nayar's call for a parliamentary enquiry into "monopolistic concerns".[dl] A similar resolution moved by R.B. Gour, a Communist member of the Rajya Sabha, was rejected in November.[dli] In both cases the Industry Minister, Manubhai Shah stated that there was no existing concern over monopolies and the government would not allow them to develop in the future. The Communists finally had their demand fulfilled two years later during a discussion of the Third Five Year Plan in the Lok Sabha. The Prime Minister, Jawaharlal Nehru stated that national income and per capita income had risen since the start of economic planning, but he thought it would be desirable to enquire more deeply into exactly where these increases had gone.[dlii] In October the Planning Commission established a probe into the concentration of wealth and means of production. The committee was chaired by Prasanta Mahalanobis.

The Mahalanobis Committee reported in 1964. The committee found that it was big companies which had received most assistance from the Industrial Finance Corporation and the National Industrial Development Corporation. Private companies were borrowing from the government and then investing in other group companies whilst receiving generous tax incentives and holidays. Committee members thought that the antidote to this domination of financial resources was constant scrutiny, regulation and possible nationalisation. There had been a trend to reducing market dominance in some markets as the economy grew yet the more menacing aspect of economic concentration was the concentration in industry generally, rather than just one product or segment. It was control rather than ownership which increasingly mattered.

The Mahalanobis Committee drew on the research of R.K. Hazari who had outlined the way in which controlling interests could be held with little nominal investment and several companies could be controlled as part of one group. Hazari's study had divided group companies into inner circle concerns and outer circle concerns. Twenty leading business groups had been selected for the study which covered the period from 1951 to 1958. Hazari had shown that the shares of capital of the 13 biggest groups had increased through the 1950s and the top 4 showed a still higher degree of concentration. Hazari compared this concentration of wealth and market power to inbreeding. It was easy for the bigger players to gain control over companies with little investment. He thought that this might lead to anti-social consequences. The committee also drew on a report of the Reserve Bank of India on joint stock companies. The Company Law had reformed the managing agency system, but the bigger managing agencies had grown in power and concentration remained in the banking sector. Interlocking directorships were common and the larger groups were better at obtaining foreign capital. It was thought that the concentration of commercial power could be controlled by the expansion of the public sector and encouragement to small-scale industries. The committee recommended further study.

In April 1964 the Government of India appointed a Monopolies Enquiry Commission chaired by Kulada Charan Das Gupta, a retired Supreme Court judge. The Commission submitted its report in October 1965. Palamadai S. Lokanathan, a professor of economics from Madras University who had worked on the Bombay Plan, suggested the establishment of a permanent body to protect against the evils of market concentration. There were mixed reactions from the chambers of commerce; some were in favour, whilst others thought that the existing legislation and regulatory apparatus were adequate. Those in favour conditioned their support on the independence of the proposed body. The Enquiry Commission accepted Lokanathan's suggestion and called for the establishment of a permanent Monopolies Commission and a register of restrictive trade practices. The Director of Investigation would be something like a committing magistrate who could investigate on his own initiative or on complaints from members of the public, the central government, or state governments. The new commission would decide on mergers, acquisitions, directorships and the expansion of big business houses and India's biggest businesses would have to submit annual reports.

The government then responded to the Monopolies Enquiry Commission report with a resolution in September 1966. The proposal to establish a statutory commission was accepted but it was to be limited to restrictive trade practices and advisory powers on the concentration of economic power. The Monopolies and Restrictive Trade Practices Bill was introduced into the Rajya Sabha in August 1967 and was then sent to a joint select committee. The Federation of Indian Chambers of Commerce and Industry presented its criticisms of the Bill to the joint select committee. It was pointed out that the move to discourage the expansion of firms with a value of over ₹1 crore was not in keeping with world trends; even a ₹1 crore company could be considered small.[dliii]

Separate to the ongoing enquiries into monopolies, the Planning Commission had appointed R.K. Hazari to provide a report on industrial licensing. In his report Hazari outlined the practice of big business houses submitting multiple applications for licences for a single product. In some cases they were meant to foreclose licensable capacity. He had found that this was particularly true of Birla applications. The Birlas had a persevering interest in a vast multitude of products, interest which defied several deferments or rejections and which later attained consummation in approvals. The interest sought to overwhelm authorities with multiple proposals the moment the opportunity arose. A large number of Birla licences had not been followed through to the Capital Goods (Import) Control stage. The sheer volume they were putting through generally yielded results for at least two or more applications. If most of the licences did materialise they could be spaced out to suit the group rather than the economy as a whole. If they were rejected, they remained on the waiting list ahead of any future applications. Hazari noted that the fact that every company worth over ₹25 lakhs had to apply for a licence and that they could be rejected on the basis that licensed capacity had already been allocated excluded new entrepreneurs who could offer good quality products at competitive prices. Having foreclosed the market, the Birla management then turned licences into large, quick profits. The Birla companies which appeared among the applicants and received licences generally had little to boast of on their balance sheets. They were usually trading or finance companies.

Hazari showed how licensing was initially a negative policy instrument, but when planning for industry began during the Second Plan it turned into a positive instrument for sanctioning capacity to meet Plan targets. Yet in practice licensing was not concerned with actual fulfilment, the foreign exchange cost, the output resulting from additional capacity, or the cost of additional output. It paid homage to the idea of import substitution regardless of how much foreign exchange was actually being saved simply because of the urge to industrialise. There had been big shortfalls in output in basic industries, limited regionally balanced development, and it was doubtful that licensing had properly channelised investment.

Hazari outlined the recognised defects of the licensing system. Licensing was only the first of the hurdles to be crossed so just procuring a license did not mean there would be installed capacity. An exaggerated picture of capacity might scare away some entrepreneurs who were chronologically late whilst encouraging foreclosure and retaining licences which were unimplemented. Licences were issued for 10% to 25% above the Plan end targets which put pressure on foreign exchange and possible collaborators and suppliers which led to bottlenecks and delays and difficulties planning with business partners. There were considerations and reconsiderations at various levels of government which led to further delays. There was little follow-up to see that the capacity had been implemented. Even the authorities were not always aware of the total investment and foreign exchange commitments of the licences issued at any given time.

Hazari pointed out that the Planning Commission did not set guidelines and there was no pressure for proper feasibility studies. Licensing had proceeded on the assumption that capacity was the only variable in a changing economic environment. The Planning Commission had never been involved in setting priorities for which industries should receive foreign exchange. Nor had it given any guidelines on how conflicting priorities should be reconciled. There was no direction on how lags were affecting the drive for more capacity. Entrepreneurs wanted to be at the head of the que and foreclose as much capacity as possible whilst there was not enough research for the vetting of projects. Licences or letters of intent were often issued liberally with the assumption that the applications would be more thoroughly scrutinised at the Indigenous Clearance or Capital Goods (Import) Control level. Hazari lamented the ad hocism evident in the case of the allocation of foreign exchange against exports. The system of licensing lost sight of the relative importance of individual projects by trying to cover the whole of an industry. Bureaucrats were assailed with hundreds or thousands of applications without clear criteria to make their decisions. The reshuffling of licensing lists was based on historical precedence rather than economic planning. Unutilised capacity was common. And a licence was just the first of many approvals needed before production could begin.

When the Hazari report was tabled in Parliament in April

1967 it proved to be useful material for the Young Turks- the young Congress Socialists, as well as the Communists. Young Chandra Shekhar was particularly strident in claiming that the Birlas had "hoodwinked not only the government but the nation."[dliv] He and his colleagues kept up a demand for a probe into the dealings of the House of Birlas for over two years. Morarji Desai, in his capacity as deputy prime minister used his power to prevent any probe, however after the split in the Congress in August 1969, the Prime Minister, Indira Gandhi finally relented and a comprehensive probe into the Birla group and other business houses was announced. A one man government enquiry led by the former Chief Justice of India, Amal Kumar Sarkar started work in February 1970.

The Hazari Report had also prompted the Government of India to form an Industrial Licensing Policy Enquiry Committee, or the Dutt Committee as it came to be known. The committee submitted its findings to Parliament in July 1969. The Birla practice of submitting multiple applications for a single product had already been documented in the Hazari report, however the Dutt Committee examined a series of other well known anomalies which big business houses used to work the licensing system.

The first anomaly which the Dutt Committee listed was known as "undue advantage". There was considerable discretion in decision making which meant that entrepreneurs had no easy way of knowing how and why a decision had been reached but they could not complain because of the power of the government. The larger industrial houses maintained "stations" in New Delhi to navigate the system. The smaller houses could not afford these stations which put them at a disadvantage. Closely related to "undue advantage" was the practice of "on file decisions" in which licensing decisions would be taken without going through the normal procedures of the Licensing Committee. Furthermore, the Licensing

Committee would often reverse its own decisions without any new facts being provided by the applicants.

There was a problem of "early intimation". Licences were rarely announced in government gazettes which meant that getting news of a new licence was in itself an advantage due to the first-come-first-served method of allocation. The Dutt Committee examined the file relating to the aluminium industry. The first paper in the file was a letter from Ghanshyamdas Birla to the government thanking it for inviting him to establish an aluminium plant at Rihand. Then in October or November of 1957 after discussions with representatives of Birla and R. Venkataswamy Naidu a decision was taken that Birla would develop an aluminium plant at Rihand and Naidu would develop one at Mettur. The applications for licences came at a later stage. Birla's Hindustan Aluminium also practiced another technique which the committee called "misuse of a letter of intent". The company claimed that its negotiations abroad were being hampered by a lack of a licence. The government issued a letter of intent to allow it to continue to negotiate. Later when the terms proposed for the project by the company to the government were found to be unsatisfactory, the plea was made that negotiations with foreign companies and financial institutions had reached such a delicate stage that were a licence to be denied it would only lead to embarrassment and an adverse impact on India's investment climate. This was also an example of what the committee saw as the favour being shown to large business houses, particularly after the foreign exchange crisis of 1957, which were able to raise their own foreign exchange resources abroad. Further, the Birla aluminium plant was an example of conditions attached to licences which were not being enforced. When objections to the issue of a licence were raised, a condition to meet the objection would be attached to the licence. In the case of Hindustan Aluminium, a licence for expansion was provided in 1963 on the condition that increased production from the aluminium smelter would only commence once a captive power plant was installed. This condition was not enforced. Another condition was that if the import of aluminium oxide could not be procured from the plant's own foreign exchange resources then it should be arranged through exports. Neither was this condition met.

Furthermore, the Dutt Committee noted that changes to items on the banned list might come at suitable times for particular applicants. The committee looked into the case of the Birlas' Century Chemicals and its application for a licence to make the fertiliser dichlorodiphenyltrichloroethane, or DDT. At the start of 1966 DDT was on the banned list which meant that licences would not be issued except for substantial expansion of existing factories. The only Indian producer was the government owned Hindustan Insecticides. In April 1966 a minister wrote that whilst Hindustan Insecticides was the only producer in India, the production of DDT was not confined to the public sector and the government was considering proposals from the private sector for its production. In reality no such proposals had yet been received. In June the ministry went against advice from the Directorate General of Technical Development and recommended that DDT be taken off the banned list. In September DDT was put on the merit list. The next month the Birlas' Century Chemicals applied to produce 3,000 tonnes of DDT a year. Century Chemicals was issued a letter of intent in March 1967.

A rule stated that licensing decisions had to be taken within three months, but it was in abeyance. Yet there were cases in which decisions were taken in record time seemingly without due diligence. This was known as "expeditious disposal". The Dutt Committee did not object to expeditious disposal as such, just that prompt disposal was not given to all similar applications but to particular applicants for whose cases special instructions were issued. In addition, some applicants could speed up the disposal process by making informal enquiries about objections or queries which were being made by the licensing authorities and then provide supplementary information. The committee cited the Birla Brothers' application for a licence to produce guar gum in February 1961. It was placed before the Licensing Committee within two weeks before waiting for comments from the Food and Agriculture Ministry or the Textile Commissioner. A representative of the Directorate General of Technical Development was present at meetings of the Licensing Committee, however often the principal technical agency had not been given the chance to study the case in advance and so could not provide its appraisal. Haste usually led to a lack of checking of applications. In the Birla guar gum case, the Birlas' statements about their previously sanctioned capacity were taken to be true which led to much higher further capacity being awarded than they should have been entitled to. This was closely related to the instance of what the committee called "special advantages that proved illusory". In another case the Birlas' Hindustan Motors was given a licence in 1957 to manufacture iron and steel castings and forgings to take advantage of existing unutilised capacity. But the company only ended up producing iron castings and not steel castings. When the government realised this in 1965 the company put in an application to import steel.

The Dutt Committee noted that the application form for licences did not require information about the cost of the product. Estimates of capital costs and foreign exchange requirements were vague and continued to undergo changes both as the application was being scrutinised and after the project commenced. Often the licence holder would return with a request for a small amount of imported capital equipment which it claimed would allow for a large amount of capacity expansion. Most often substantial capacity expansion was found by the Licensing Committee to be more economical than the establishment of a new unit. This resulted in a sense of security for larger business houses; once established in an industry they felt confident of receiving a substantial share of future capacity allocations. The committee labelled all of this "inadequate scrutiny".

The report of the joint select committee on the Monopolies and Restrictive Trade Practices Bill was published in February 1969, and a revised Bill was tabled in the Rajya Sabha in July 1969 and in the Lok Sabha in December 1969. Asoka Mehta of Morarji's Congress, Minoo Masani of the Swatantra Party and K.L. Gupta of the Jana Sangh criticised the Bill for not including public sector monopolies, whilst the Young Turks of the Congress and the Communists felt the bill was "not drastic enough".[dlv] The Bill was eventually passed by the Lok Sabha and was actually more radical than the recommendations suggested by the Monopolies Enquiry Commission. It omitted part of the preamble, reduced the financial ceiling for companies to be brought under the Act, conferred powers on the government rather than the commission, and gave the government the right to refer any company it wanted to the commission. There was a much more elaborate definition of interrelated undertakings, the Act also added serving the "common good" as well as balanced regional development to the commission's objectives, did not set time limits, limited appeals to the Supreme Court, and gave the government the power to request information from any company. In addition, the commission could control company directorships. The Monopolies and Restrictive Trade Practices Act was brought into force on 1 June 1970.

The government's response to the Dutt Committee was announced in February 1970. Licences were to be issued liberally in the ₹1 crore to ₹5 crore investment range to those entrepreneurs who were not from the big houses. In the end there was no free licensing in the middle sector as the committee had recommended. In January 1972 a decision was taken to allow bigger companies to better utilise capacity. And then a new policy was issued in February 1973. Big business houses were to be kept in the core sector. There was some streamlining from October 1973. Diversification was liberalised in 1974. Further rationalisation of installed capacity was allowed in 1975. More liberalisation took place during the Emergency, but the bigger business houses were not included in the new provisions. Businesses which did not come under the Monopolies Act could even modernise equipment if it took them beyond licensed capacity. Amal Kumar Sarkar resigned from his own inquiry into the Birla group in April 1970 just two months after being appointed. The Sarkar enquiry, as it continued to be known, was eventually abandoned in April 1979 after incurring ₹1.64 crore in expenses.[dlvi]

***

Bajaj Auto and Automobile Products of India applied in October 1970 and February 1971 for retrospective expansion of their existing production capacity of two and three wheel scooters.[dlvii] Both applications were referred by the Government of India to the Monopolies Commission in July 1971. In September 10 died in a stampede in Udaipur when 15,000 people arrived to register their names for the allotment of scooters.

The Commission conducted a combined enquiry and presented a common report into the two applications in January 1972. The chairman, A. Alagirisamy, a former judge of the Madras High Court and D. Subramaniam, a director of inspection, income tax and audit, formed a majority which prevailed over the minority consisting of H.K. Paranjape, a member of the Dutt Committee.

API started the production of scooters in India in 1955, followed by Bajaj Auto in 1960. In April 1961, it was decided that there would be no expansion of supply. Then, due to a shortage of supply the decision was reversed in 1965. Both were given licences for 24,000 units. In 1969 the government began looking into the possibility of establishing a public sector scooter plant. Total scooter production increased from 13,000 in 1961 to 60,000 in 1970. Bajaj produced 32,000 and API produced 25,000. Both exceeded their licensed capacity. Bajaj had proposed to expand its capacity to 100,000 units and API to 60,000. The government had already indicated that 48,000 was the capacity which was likely to be approved, so both companies reduced their applications to this lower figure but urged the commission to consider their original higher number.

In its submission to the commission, Bajaj Auto stated that within 10 years of starting production of scooters it had built up an efficient production unit that produced good quality scooters which earned a high degree of consumer satisfaction. The government's controls on scooter prices had reduced the real price but the company had been able to bear it due to economies of scale achieved after expansions of capacity and improvements in efficiency. During the 1960s the import component of the two wheel scooter had been reduced from 74% to 4%. The company had been spending large amounts on research and development and further efforts towards import substitution were being made. The company's emphasis on quality and service was the reason why it was able to change its brand name from Vespa to Bajaj after the end of its foreign collaboration and maintain customer acceptance. Bajaj Auto emphasised that it required an early expansion of capacity due to the increase in pending orders which stood at 229,000 in March 1971. The company would be able to produce 100,000 scooters by better utilisation of its existing facility with little extra investment. Even when production of 48,000 scooters was reached the price of the scooter, which was around ₹2,000, could be reduced by ₹150 due to economies of scale. The company projected that it could produce 60,000 scooters within a year of receiving permission and 100,000 within two and a half years.

The National Council of Applied Economic Research had estimated that demand for scooters would come to 87,000 units in 1973. Bajaj Auto thought that this estimate was low. The company anticipated demand for 120,000 units. The minority report agreed with Bajaj Auto's estimate and forecast demand for 300,000 units by the end of the 1970s. India could become a large producer both to satisfy the huge domestic market and international demand. In 1969 applications for licences had been invited and 23 Letters of Intent had been issued. Of these, by 1972 only Enfield and Escorts had started producing scooters, and each sold only 6,000 units a year. State governments were also planning to start their own smaller scooter plants and so the issue remained of whether capacity of Bajaj and API should be restricted to allow for capacity expansion of the other existing and prospective units. The Minority accepted that Bajaj Auto and API would achieve greater economies of scale with increased capacity and pass cost savings on to consumers. The smaller government plants would charge consumers higher prices. The Minority thus concluded that it would be wrong to prevent Bajaj and API from producing at the optimum level simply to encourage newer smaller entrants to the market. Given the growing demand for scooters, the Minority did not see any reason for maintaining an artificial shortage. The Minority thought that given that production of scooters needed to be maintained at a high level to achieve economies of scale, and this tended towards oligopoly, restricting production capacity only allowed producers to charge higher prices than they would otherwise be able to.

The Minority recognised the need for large producers and also endorsed big scooter makers' applications for capacity expansion but thought that it was important that the control of the expanded scooter units not remain in the hands of those who would use the benefits of higher capacity for purely private profit to the detriment of the public interest. The Minority thus recommended taking steps to reduce or eliminate the Bajaj family control over

Bajaj Auto, and the Chidambarams' control over API. The Minority thought that the fact that both Bajaj Auto and API were ready to finance their expansions from internal resources indicated that they had been allowed too high a rate of profit over the previous decade. The Minority saw this ploughing back of profits for the benefit of shareholders as consumer exploitation, inconsistent with the type of economy which was trying to be built up in the country. A suggested remedy was that the capacity expansion be financed by the issue of new equity to public sector financial institutions. Both Bajaj Auto and API would eventually be turned into joint public-private enterprises.

The majority report did not accept some of the larger projections of demand for scooters and thought that the long waiting list was the result of people putting themselves on the list multiple times. The Majority expressed some scepticism over whether Bajaj Auto could actually produce 100,000 units given that it used the batch process of production. In addition, the Bajaj scooter model was already 10 years old, neither Bajaj nor API had exported many units, and the purchasing power of the middle class was thought to be eroding. Demand for motorcycles and mopeds needed to be taken into account and it was uncertain that ancillary units would be able to supply the spare parts for the larger number of scooters.

The Majority was also reticent to provide a large increase in capacity to Bajaj Auto when the Government of India had invested $2 million in importing machinery from Italy to produce scooters in its own 100,000 unit capacity plant. The Majority wanted to leave some capacity to the state industrial corporations and their scooter projects. The state scooter companies might sell higher priced scooters initially, yet given the excess of demand over supply, they would not have any trouble finding customers. Given that the Government of India had encouraged these smaller public sector scooter projects it would not be fair to have all the existing capacity divided between the two big private sector companies. If this was allowed then all the state corporations' expenditure would be wasted.

Given that the Majority was not going to allow for the higher capacity expansion to 100,000 units, it did not see any reason to alter the management or ownership of Bajaj Auto or API. The Majority went on to praise the Bajaj management for maintaining a constant sale price over the previous five years. The Majority was reluctant to interfere with the management which was responsible for developing technical competence and a high quality, reliable product. The Majority approved capacity expansion up to 48,000 units for both Bajaj Auto and API on the condition that they reduce their sale price by ₹50, absorb any future cost increases up to ₹50, spend 1% of their net sales each year on research and development, and that both companies contribute to a proposed government research organisation.

The government received the Monopolies Commission's reports in January 1972 and conducted a hearing for the applicant companies and interested parties. The industrial corporations of Gujarat and Rajasthan opposed capacity expansion for Bajaj Auto and API entirely. If expansion was allowed then it should not exceed that recommended in the majority report. Bajaj Auto assented to the conditions in the majority report but maintained that it would not require any more funds to expand production up to 100,000 units. The owners did not want to alter the existing shareholding pattern. If this was made a condition for expansion then they would prefer not to expand at all. API only objected to the condition requiring investment in research and development. The government approved capacity expansion for both Bajaj Auto and API up to 48,000 in accordance with the conditions in the majority report and orders were issued in November 1972.

In April of 1973 Bajaj Auto applied to increase production

of three wheel scooters to 15,000, and API put in a similar application in September. Both applications seemed to be indirect means of increasing their two wheeler production given that the original capacity expansion had included both two wheelers and three wheelers. Both companies were allowed separate increases in capacity for three wheeler production. In April 1974 Bajaj put in another application to raise its capacity to 100,000 scooters. The government suggested some conditions: loans for the expansion would be subject to a convertibility clause, if the capital cost was high then more equity in the company should be issued to the public rather than the family, the import of machinery should satisfy government regulations, 2,000 scooters should be exported each year for 5 years starting from 1976 and the company should stagger its loans. Bajaj Auto accepted the conditions on loan convertibility, the import of machinery and the staggering of loans. The company ended up largely assenting on the equity issue and agreed to export 10,000 scooters by 1981 if it received a licence by March 1975. The government then agreed to allow capacity to increase to 80,000 units on two additional conditions: Bajaj Auto would export scooters for seven years and there would be no foreign collaborations. Factories were able to exceed their licensed capacity by 25%. Bajaj Auto could now produce 100,000 units.

By 1977 Bajaj Auto held 56% of the Indian scooter market. The company made another application for capacity expansion in March 1978, this time for 160,000 units. In this instance objections were heard from both the Uttar Pradesh state government's U.P. Scooters and Bajaj Auto's old rival API. U.P. Scooters submitted that whilst it had been issued a licence to produce 24,000 scooters it had not been able to arrange finance to start production since 1973 as the bankers would cite "market limitations". API pointed out that Bajaj Auto was the market's dominant producer and so allowing it to expand would contravene both the government's Industrial Policy and the provisions of the Monopolies and Restrictive Trade Practices Act. In addition, small ancillaries units catered to Bajaj Auto because of its position as the market's biggest buyer. Permitting the expansion of Bajaj Auto which had its factories in Maharashtra would only exacerbate regional disparities in industrial development. API argued that the long waiting list for Bajaj scooters was inflated with speculative registrations. The government noted that according to the Industrial Licensing Policy of 1973 Bajaj, as a large business house should not have been allowed in the scooter industry. Yet an exception had been made due to consumers' preference for Bajaj scooters, its excellent sales and repair service, its role as an exporter, its ability to fund its expansion from its own resources, and the lack of any objection from the public sector Scooters India Limited. The government dismissed U.P. Scooters and API's arguments. It noted that API had started making scooters before Bajaj Auto, yet it was Bajaj which was preferred in the market. U.P. Scooters had closed down production not due to a lack of finance but inappropriate production equipment, and there were doubts over whether it would ever start production through small-scale units as it had suggested. The government stipulated another set of conditions similar to the last, most of which were accepted by Bajaj Auto, as they had previously done. The government approved capacity expansion to 160,000, or, in effect, 200,000 units.

***

During the 1970s the Tatas found it increasingly difficult to get clearances and approvals for new projects and the renovation of existing factories. They were restructuring their group which had come to encompass more than 150 companies, and had to do so in the wake of the abolition of the managing agency system and the passage of the Monopolies and Restrictive Trade Practices Act. By 1977, the Tatas finally had to concede their preeminent position in Indian business to the Birlas. J.R.D. Tata was thought to share a good relationship with Indira Gandhi, whose government had been withholding clearances, yet have a strained one with the new Prime Minister, Morarji Desai. Contrary to expectations Desai promptly issued the requisite clearances. The years of the Janata government were more productive for the Tatas as they constructed a new thermal power plant, invested in a new automotive plant near Pune, and modernised the steel plant at Jamshedpur. They were again ahead of the Birlas by the time Indira Gandhi returned to power in 1980.

The Birlas had been expanding abroad. Aditya, Braj Mohan's son, was considered a whiz kid in the Indian business world in the mid 1960s. It was at this time that the Birlas were being labelled the chief beneficiaries of the Licence Raj, yet young Aditya, having setup a small cotton spinning plant after returning from the Massachusetts Institute of Technology, found regulations and licensing so stifling that he chose to expand his operations in Thailand. The Thapars had their collieries nationalised in 1973, and so also decided to invest in South-east Asia and the Gulf. The Kirloskars also opened export offices abroad, and setup the India-Malaya Engineering Company. The Walchands' construction business in India and the Middle East flourished and Laxmi Mittal went to build a steel plant in Indonesia. Most other prominent Indian business families were content to maintain their existing operations and product lines.

The private realm of family business and entrenched privilege was explored by Shyam Benegal in his 1980 film *Kalyug*, or *The Dark Age*. *Kalyug* was generally understood to be a modern retelling of the old Mahabharata story of cousins going to war to ensure the survival of their own branch of the family and preserve its power and status. Benegal was best known for searing dramas of rural injustice and exploitation, yet *Kalyug* portrayed the other extreme of Indian life- the sheltered world of Bombay industrialists.

Kalyug's warring cousins descend from Puranchand and Khubchand. Savitri is Puranchand's widow. Her eldest son is Dharmraj who is married to Supriya. They have a little boy, Parikshit. Her next son is Balraj. His wife is Kiran. Their son Sunilraj is a young man. Savitri's third son is Bharatraj. He is married to Subhadra. Khubchand is Puranchand's elder brother. He is now in a wheelchair. His wife is Devki. Their eldest son is Dhanraj who is married to Vibha. They have two small daughters, Diya and Keya. Khubchand's younger son is Sandeep who is unmarried. Bhishamchand raised his nephews, Khubchand and Puranchand, but never married. Given Khubchand's paralysis, Bhishamchand now acts as the patriarch of his wing of the family. That leaves Karan Singh, the only character from outside the family and caste. He is a bachelor and senior manager in the Khubchand group.

Kalyug opens with Sanjay of the Khubchand group receiving a fax requesting finalisation of the tender document. Sanjay then drives into the premises of the Khubchands' engineering division. Dhanraj and Karan inspect the plant in their suits and safety masks. Champaign is opened and Karan, Dhanraj and Sanjay toast to the STS project. A Mercedes glides into the leafy grounds of the Puranchand engineering works. Bharat walks into the office and grills his manager, Saxena. He has news that they have lost the STS contract. Was it that costings were too high? Overheads? Machining hour rates? Rejection percentages? Contingency margin? Profit percentage? Saxena maintains that they were all kept to a minimum. Then how the hell could this happen? Balraj walks in. Bharat informs him that this is the fourth time they had lost the contract. He blames the cousins. But where is Bhaisahib? Bhaisahib is their elder brother, Dharmraj who is at the horse races.

The Puranchands have a meeting in their drawing room. Bharat wants to know how the cousins' tender quotation could have come in under theirs. Dharmraj's wife Supriya thinks that Karan Singh is behind it. The Khubchands arrive for Bhishamchand's birthday celebrations. The birthday party scenes are the film's best: there is calmness and gentility, Hindustani classical vocals play faintly in the background. The chaos outside is implied. Diya and Keya sing "Happy Birthday" to Bhishamchand. The elderly women, Savitri and Devki, fuss over Parikshit and mull over whether sending him to boarding school is a good idea. Everyone applauds Diya and Keya. They feed old Bhishamchand sweets. Sandeep and Balraj have to sneak their drinks in a backroom. Devki wheels Khubchand out when he starts coughing too much. A guest recites some Urdu poetry. Kishen Chand asks Dhanraj why he is stoking competition between the two wings of the family. He replies that it is through competition that the nation will progress. Kiran admires Vibha's jewellery. Balraj comes and starts teasing them: whenever women come together, all they talk about is jewellery and fashion. Karan holds Keya. Savitri wants to know if he will be holding other people's children forever.

Bharat of the Puranchands and Karan, the Khubchand manager meet in the living room. Bharat congratulates Karan. What, did you work some magic on the STS project? Karan maintains that he just submitted his tender. Bharat suggests he let the next tender go through to Puranchands' side. He would let Karan manage the contract on a doubled salary. Bharat suggests that they shake on it. Karan ignores the request. Dhanraj, the Khubchand heir is looking on. Bharat teases Karan- do you have some relation with Dhanraj? Karan replies that it is friendship. Dhanraj then wants to know what Karan and Bharat were talking about. He was offering double salary. Dhanraj exclaims, "Bastard!". Bharat then approaches Bhishamchand and complains that they had been stealing projects by underquoting on the tender. What "herapheri", or shenanigans were they engaging in to be able to underquote like that? Bhishamchand lets it slip that it was Karan Singh's doing: they had managed to get three high precision imported machines.

In the car on the way back Bharat explains that the Khubchands received a "special contract" from the government because of Karan Singh's connections in England. To fulfil the contract they needed three imported high precision machines to be cleared by the government. They still had those machines in their possession and had used them to underquote on the previous three tenders. There was not even any question of costings. Bharat tells Dharmraj that they would have to appeal under any circumstances. Dharmraj advises Bharat to keep a cool head.

Karan finds out from Dhanraj that the Puranchands have appealed against the award of the STS contract. The Khubchands have a discussion. Karan suggests that the Puranchands will have raised the objection over the imported machinery. Bhishamchand says that he had warned them of the possibility. Karan says that it was Bhishamchand who signed off on the tenders. Dhanraj says that if the government accepts the Puranchands' argument over the machines then the previous three projects would be halted and they would lose ₹57 crores. But then the matter of the imported machines was quite confidential. How did they know? Dhanraj stares at old Bhishamchand, who then admits that he may have let it slip to Bharat at the birthday party.

Kishan Chand arrives to congratulate Bharat on winning the appeal. The ₹57 crores worth of contracts would now come to him. But Bharat insists that what he really wanted was the machines. Then the fun would begin. Kishen is Dharmraj's wife Supriya's brother and is trying to set his daughter Subhadra up with Bharat. He goes to see the matriarch of the family, Savitri to get her blessings. But she tells him to speak to Bharat directly. Everyone seems to assent but passes the matter along for more permissions. "Is this a government office that you need so many permissions?" The matter is settled and so Bharat and Subhadra go on an evening dinner date. They watch a Kathakali performance and then proceed to dinner at an upmarket restaurant. Karan is having dinner with Saxena, Bharat's manager. Saxena leaves before Subhadra notices Karan across the room. Bharat lets out some abuse in Karan's direction and also informs Subhadra that it was Bhishamchand who had raised Karan.

Dhanraj is discussing business with Bhishamchand. Bhishamchand reminds Dhanraj that despite the government contracts going to the Puranchands, he would ensure that the machinery would stay with them. He thinks that Puranchand's sons would never go against his word. Dhanraj thinks that there is no guarantee of that. Bhishamchand tells him to do what he wants, but first get rid of him. Dhanraj calls Karan into his office. Bhishamchand has refused to head hunt Saxena from the Puranchands. But it is ok, the machinery will not be transferred to them. Karan is not alarmed. After all, they are Dhanraj's cousins. Dhanraj thinks it is time that Karan knew the truth. Puranchand was impotent, so his wife Savitri had to be impregnated by a guru, Swami Premanand. Karan is not interested. Even if Bhishamchand couldn't stop the transfer of machinery, there are other ways of doing it.

The Puranchands and Khubchands come together for Bharat and Subhadra's wedding. After the wedding the family gathers to watch a video of proceedings and the elders, Savitri and Bhishamchand, meet in another room to try and sort out the business conflict. Bhishamchand puts the onus on Savitri to speak with Bharat. She assures Bhishamchand that her son would never go against her word. Swami Premanand arrives as the family is watching the wedding video. In the other room Savitri suddenly turns. The Swami has been invited just to humiliate her. She says that she will not get involved- Dhanraj and Bharat will now have to sort the matter out themselves. Later, Dhanraj puts Bhishamchand out to retirement. He is seen off by the staff at the factory and garlanded on his way out. Dhanraj puts Karan in charge.

At the Puranchand engineering plant it seems that the workers are refusing to work. A small altercation ensues. The Union has rejected the new contract. A worker is threatened with being charge sheeted. A melee ensues on the factory floor. Pandey gets up on a platform and orders all the workers to put down their tools. They will go and meet on the grounds outside. Balraj, the usually relaxed and jovial middle brother, sends for Mhatre the recognised Union leader. Mhatre arrives and tells Balraj not to make the mistake of charge sheeting the workers. Balraj replies with the well worn employer complaint that workers just do what they want and go on strike whenever they want- there is such a thing as discipline. Mhatre says that it is Pandey who is instigating the workers over the bonus issue so that he can take control of the Union. Mhatre tells Balraj not to worry. There will be a meeting at the factory gate and workers will resume after that.

Mhatre addresses the workers at the gate and tells them that it is wrong to raise the bonus issue now. Work had stopped because of their mistake, and so it should be resumed. The management has guaranteed that no worker will be charge sheeted, and no one will be suspended. Pandey rises from among the workers. Everything Mhatre is saying is a lie. They trade barbs. Pandey starts instigating the workers, telling them that the Puranchands have just received a ₹57 crore contract and that they should get a bonus. Mhatre tells the workers that the Puranchands are not even making a profit on the contract, but even still the management is promising a bonus once the contracts are completed. Pandey says that it should put it in writing. Mhatre says that the contracts are important for the nation; they are not just labourers, but also citizens. Pandey claims that this is just a diversion. Pandey takes the workers with him.

Balraj tries to drive into the factory, but by now Pandey is leading the strike. Mhatre is leading his loyalist Puranchand Union. The two Unions clash. It is night. Pandey is cycling away and is attacked by goons. Later, Pandey addresses his followers on the open field, directing invective against Mhatre. But Mhatre has a man in the crowd who throws a projectile and cuts Pandey above the eye. The police move in to break up the crowd. Dhanraj comes back to Karan. Things have worked, there is a lockout. This means that for the time being there is no question of the prized machines going from the Khubchand factory to the Puranchand factory.

Bharat makes his way back to town after his honeymoon with Subhadra and discusses the situation with Balraj in the car on the way from the airport. The lockout has to be lifted at all costs. They have to meet the deadline for the STS project. But Dharamraj will be hard to convince. Pandey arrives for a meeting with Bharat and Balraj. They come to an agreement: management will only recognise Pandey's Union, in which he will make the decisions, but there will be no bonus until the new project is complete. Pandey insists that the workers have to be given the confidence that the matter of the bonus is still being discussed. Bharat agrees.

Karan thinks that the new industrial peace at the Puranchands is nothing to worry about. Pandey won't let go of the bonus issue. He will be like a time bomb. Once the government gets a whiff of scandals at the Puranchand factory they will cancel the contracts and with it the order to transfer the machinery. Besides which the Puranchands' prestige in the markets would plummet. Karan outlines an action plan. There is a consignment of special imported steel due in a few days. But before the trucks can reach the Puranchand factory they will be hijacked. The Puranchands will file the usual police complaint and claim for insurance, but just at that time the police will be informed that those very trucks which were supposed to be hijacked are at the Puranchand factory.

Bharat thinks that the theft of the steel was not to sell on the black market, but to sabotage the STS project. Balraj goes to check the factory in the middle of the night. Just as he is about to drive away, Sandeep, the younger Khubchand son drives by. Balraj spots the car and Sandeep tries to speed away. A car chase ensues. Balraj eventually stops Sandeep's car and drags him out to interrogate him, but Sandeep hyperventilates. Sandeep, who had a physical frailty to start with, is dead on arrival at the hospital. Dhanraj thinks that the Puranchands have murdered his younger brother.

Saxena is praised for his technical samples and told by Dharamraj that he will be given holidays soon. Bharat asks whether he has been contacted by Karan. No. But if he was, he would tell them, wouldn't he? Of course. The next scene is of Karan wining and dining Saxena. Saxena is not sure of how he feels about what he has done. But he wants to go to America for further studies. Karan can help him, he just needs to do a bit more work. Saxena is worried. The contracts come under the Ministry of Defence. The Central Bureau of Investigation means something in India. The technical samples are subsequently rejected. Bharat's suspicions of Saxena are confirmed. They would bring in a foreign expert in Saxena's place.

Bharat thinks that the Puranchands should try and exercise some control over the Khubchand management, using his father-in-law Kishen as a conduit. But Dharmraj thinks that this would only intensify the fight. Bharat doesn't care. So be it. Their name is low in the market, and they are being blamed for Sandeep's death. Balraj comes and confirms the news. Saxena has run off to America. Then Supriya comes with more bad news. There is an income tax raid at their house by a party of 10 or 15 government officers. Bharat is fed up. This was the last thing remaining. One of the tax inspectors inspects Supriya's underwear. She asks him if he has any

The Licence Raj

manners. He asks her if her family earned its black money with manners.

Savitri goes to see Bhishamchand who tells her there may be a way to manage the situation, but she would have to tell Karan the truth. It was because of her father's superstitious beliefs that he had Swami Premanand impregnate her when she was a virgin, which meant that she had to let Karan go after giving birth. Bhishamchand then had her hastily wed to Puranchand, who kept the Swami in their house. Meanwhile, Bharat tells Kishen Chand in the car that he wants to launch a share raid on the Khubchands and buy himself some seats on their board. But for that he will need money. Savitri goes to see Karan. She tells him that she has another son, the eldest of them all. He should ask Bhishamchand who he is. Karan curls up in the foetal position, listening to European classical music. The share buyup is underway and Dhanraj does not like it. Karan argues that their stock price is increasing, but Dhanraj can't bear the thought of Puranchands on his board. They would need money to buy new machinery, but there was no scope for a loan. Karan argues for coming to an understanding. Dhanraj unveils a plot to murder Bharat. He will be eliminated at a meeting scheduled with the Nigerian industries minister. Karan objects and walks out.

Karan has to decide what to do. He rings through to the Puranchands and speaks with Savitri. He does not identify himself but gives her a warning that Bharat's life is in danger. He is about to have an accident. Savitri stops Bharat from attending the meeting, retreats into the home and Bharat sends Sunil, Balraj's son in his place. Savitri then returns and tries to stop Sunil, but it is too late. He has already left. News gets back to the Khubchands from the Puranchands that Sunil has been killed in an accident. Dhanraj is on the phone with his banker, Bhatia, who has heard that Karan is about to resign. Bhatia insists that he should not let it happen- the stock price would fall and the draft facilities would have to be reconsidered. Dhanraj assures Bhatia that he won't let this happen. He then hangs up the phone and turns to Karan and informs him that the company has accepted his resignation. Dhanraj feels that the person he had trusted since childhood has betrayed him. Karan leaves, and Dhanraj takes a handgun from his drawer and puts it in his jacket pocket. Dhanraj is then pictured at home sitting in the dark. Only a small lamp provides light. He is inspecting his weapon. He receives a call from Bhatia. Questions are about to be raised about his three projects in the Lok Sabha. Dhanraj would have to give his personal guarantee if he wants the loan. Karan rings with a plan to save the company. Dhanraj rejects him.

A jeep follows Karan Singh's car. He is going to see Bhishamchand at his retirement bungalow. Karan is contemplating suicide. Bhishamchand advises him against it. He is run over changing a tyre on the road back. Savitri tells her three sons that Karan has been murdered, and that he was also hers. An explosion is heard in Dhanraj's room after he has retired after the family dinner. Bharat is drunk on his bed. His sister-in-law Supriya cradles him and says that she will look after him. His wife Subhadra leaves the room. It will be left to Parikshit, the little boy and sole heir, on his way to boarding school, to take care of the business in the future.

***

By the early 1980s the old Hindi defence, used to insist that one was not so rich- "Hum koi Tata-Birla nahin hain", "We are not Tatas or Birlas", had a new addition. The defence now went "Hum koi Tata-Birla-Ambani nahin hain".

The Tatas persuaded non-resident Indians to invest in the expansion of the Tata Engineering and Locomotive Company. In 1983 a Tata Strategic Plan was agreed upon. Ratan Tata, the heir apparent, wanted to streamline the group and move into high technology. Tata Finlay became Tata Tea, Tata Chemicals expanded, Tata Power added a plant, the engineering and locomotive company produced a new vehicle, Tata Telecom was formed, as was a new watch company. The group also expanded in the cement and power industries. The Birlas expanded in the 1980s but Braj Mohan died in 1982 and Ghanshyamdas died the following year. There were 200 group companies and six subgroups of the family, many of which were interlinked which made a neat division difficult. It took almost four years until a resolution was reached in the middle of 1987. Braj Mohan's son Aditya received around 40% of the group and became the bearer of the Birla legacy, moving into the gas based fertiliser and petrochemicals industries as the decade closed.

In October 1980 Reliance received one of three licences for the production of polyester filament yarn, the condition being that it locate its factory in a backward area, Patalganga in Maharashtra.[dlviii] There were 43 applicants for the licences and Reliance beat some of the older business houses, including the Birlas. The Patalganga plant was licensed to produce 10,000 tonnes a year, whilst the other two licence holders, Orkay Silk and J K Synthetics were each given 6,000 tonnes capacity. Dhirubhai and his eldest son Mukesh had, with the India representative of DuPont Suresh Kothary, been to the DuPont headquarters in Delaware and convinced executives to sell the company's technology, including polymerisation machinery, which had not been transferred to any customer outside the United States. He was integrating backwards from textile processing into the petrochemicals business, an industry with much greater prospects for growth. By now Pranab Mukherjee was the commerce minister. It was his ministry which set tariffs and anti-dumping duties and he could work with the finance ministry to control import licences through the chief controller of imports and exports. Luckily again for Dhirubhai, Mukherjee became finance minister at the start of 1982 and was more directly able to control tax policy. The finance ministry also supervised the Reserve Bank of India, the nationalised banks and controlled regulation of the stock market.

Nitish Sengupta was the most important bureaucrat in the finance ministry as the capital markets were experiencing a renewal in the early 1980s. Sengupta was responsible for administering the rules under which companies could issue shares or bonds and the price which they could charge for their offers. An idea had been floating around for the greater use of convertible debentures, which would initially behave like bonds, paying interest and then at a later point be converted to shares and pay dividends. Companies would pay a lower rate of interest on their initial debt, given that the holder of the debt could convert it into equity later on. Investors could earn interest whilst the company's projects were gestating and then become shareholders once they started.

Reliance had become a public company in October 1977 and was listed on the Bombay and Ahmadabad Stock Exchanges in January 1978. The initial par price was ₹10. There were more rights and bonus issues in the late 1970s and the banks converted 20% of the company's loans into equity in September 1979. Even before the finance ministry's policy changes on convertible debentures, Reliance issued Series I partially convertible debentures in October, raising ₹7 crores. Reliance then issued three more series, one bigger than the last up until April 1982 raising close to ₹100 crore. The Tatas were also using the technique to raise capital, but Dhirubhai managed to gain an unusual clearance for converting the non-convertible parts of each of the four series into equity. This move smoothly converted ₹70 crores worth of debt into just ₹10 crores worth of equity and raised reserves to ₹60 crore. Instead of paying interest of ₹9 crores, Reliance only had to pay dividends of ₹3 crores. The run of good fortune continued into 1984 when the company raised another ₹80 crores through an E series of partially convertible debentures. By 1986, since the time of its initial float back in 1978, Reliance had raised over ₹900 crores, more than half that amount coming from one issue of debentures alone.

The right to import polyester yarn was still, in the early 1980s, restricted to the actual users. Large cotton textile mills did not qualify, despite the trend towards cotton/polyester blends. Only small art silk power looms could be designated actual users by the Customs House in Bombay. As a result, Reliance would give the polyester yarn to small power looms and then take it back for finishing and dying at the Naroda plant in Gujarat. In November 1982, three weeks after the plant at Patalganga started production the Government of India placed an extra ₹15,000 per tonne duty on the import of polyester yarn. Reliance could raise the prices which it charged to India's small power loom weavers, and they would have to accept it.

It was another strange case: Reliance, leading the Synthetic Fibre Association of India, was arguing that foreign producers were flooding the Indian market with cheap imports which was adversely impacting local producers, the biggest of which was, Reliance. The small power loom workers protested against the new duty, claiming that local production had been increasing, although not nearly enough to meet Indian demand. Power loom workers would have to pay more for imported polyester yarn, whilst the more expensive foreign yarn and the ongoing excess of demand for polyester yarn gave Reliance a case for expanding the capacity of its new plant. Patalganga started producing more, doubling India's total output. By 1984 Finance Minister Mukherjee endorse a higher licensing capacity for industry and by 1985 Reliance received its retrospective increase in licensing capacity for the Patalganga plant.

In the early 1980s Reliance was not paying any corporate tax on profits; it was constantly expanding, constantly taking on more debt and so it always had enough cost deductions to offset against its profits. In 1983 Finance Minister Mukherjee announced that companies would have to pay 30% after depreciation but before deductions. Reliance managed to circumvent the new rule by inflating its depreciation. Reliance increased its asset value by capitalising its future interest payable on the loans it had taken for new projects. This increased the depreciation it could claim before profits. The company managed to avoid large sums on excise duties by declaring a section of its production 'wastage'. Bombay Customs allowed the bulk buyers discount which Asahi of Japan gave Reliance whilst other companies might have been investigated for under invoicing.

In 1982 Pranab Mukherjee announced a change in investment rules so that Non-resident Indians could repatriate their earnings on stock market investments in India. Reliance shares had been under attack on the share markets, but suddenly had some mysterious new investors. All the investments from Non-resident Indians into the Indian stock markets were coming into Reliance. All 11 foreign companies were based in Britain and some had names as cheeky as Fiasco Investments and Crocodile Investments. It turned out that these investment companies had been established in the late 1970s, initially with British directors, only to have an influx of Gujarati names onto their boards in the early 1980s. Most directors had the surname Shah. The biggest shareholder was one Krishna Kant Shah, a childhood friend of Dhirubhai's who had settled in Leicester. Krishna Kant held an interest in Leicester city politics, but none in Indian polyester processing.

***

When it was released in 1980 *Kalyug* was considered an engrossing tale of warring business families. The film was directed by Shyam Benegal, a leading light of the parallel cinema movement and provided some relief to educated audiences being bombarded by increasingly crude Hindi films. Yet decades later *Kalyug* can be viewed with some amusement.

The Puranchands and the Khubchands were fighting over three machines for which special import permission was required from the government. The family was not given any specific markers to denote its place of origin. However, it can be inferred that they were north Indian Baniyas. Given the status of the Birlas in the 1970s as the country's leading industrialists and, for the socialists, the country's archetypal capitalists, it could also be reasonably deduced that *Kalyug* is an imagining of the Birla family. There were two prominent Birla brothers in the 1970s, Ghanshyamdas and Braj Mohan.

The Puranchands and Khubchands lived the high life of society soirees, expensive restaurants, discos, horse races and honeymoons in Udaipur. Alcohol is a dominant motif of the film; leading characters popped champagne bottles, snuck drinks in back rooms and nursed glasses in the evening. Yet the trading castes of India, particularly those from Marwar in Rajasthan, were not known for their fast living. They were among the most socially and economically conservative people in the world. They were usually teetotallers and vegetarians who married early and spent their lives steadily increasing their inherited wealth. They got their daughters married off quickly into fellow Marwari families of similar wealth and status. They passed their businesses down to their sons for whom they found brides from fellow Marwari families of similar wealth and status. Their heirs repeated the process. When it came time to divide the family assets the process may have been protracted, but it was usually amicable and either sorted out within the family or left to a trusted arbitrator. They were not known to kill their cousins over a government contract. Or even keep guns in their offices. In one of *Kalyug's* final scenes, Dhanraj, the eldest Khubchand son, sits in a reclining chair under a lamp inspecting his gun. He is pictured in half light as his thoughts turn to the murder of his cousin Bharat in revenge for the death of his brother Sandeep. India's industrialists were made to resemble the Corleones, the mafia dons of *The Godfather* films.

Kalyug is most valuable as a record of the abiding concerns of the Left in India. India's socialists and communists traditionally nurtured as much hostility to Hinduism as capitalism. *Kalyug's* Hindu figure is Swami Premanand. His entrance is accompanied by ominous music. His name is a play on the Sanskrit words for love and bliss. His only purpose is to impregnate women on behalf of their superstitious fathers and impotent husbands. The madness of capitalism is, however, the film's overarching theme. The government is strangely invisible. The only time that its officers appear is for an income tax raid. The labour movement is shown to be corrupt and divided, the workers' cause betrayed by Union leaders who make compromises with owners in pursuit of their own ends. Shyam Benegal allows Karl Marx's conclusion that capitalism contains the seeds of its own destruction to play out in an upper class Bombay on the cusp of the 1980s. Yet in *Kalyug* it is the capitalists, rather than capitalism, who are made to destroy each other.

The first years of economic planning were quiet ones for the Tatas. They retained their position as India's largest business group, yet the growth of their companies was not spectacular. The general perception was that they were not very adept, or at least not very eager in their handling of the bureaucracy in New Delhi. Their self-image, generally shared by the Indian people, was one of probity in business dealings. They were not given to greasing palms or shuffling money into brown envelopes or stuffing it into briefcases. During the 1950s and 1960s it was the Birlas who became the first masters of the Licence Raj. The Birlas quickly mastered just about all the key techniques of industrial licensing in India: on file decisions, multiple applications, expeditious disposal, undue advantage, and foreclosure of licensable capacity.

In addition, the Birla companies benefitted from close relationships with the banks and G.D. Birla's old association with the Congress Party. The Birla owned newspaper *The Hindustan Times* was generally considered to be partial to the Congress. All of this made the Birlas, rather than the Tatas, the object of the socialists and communists' wrath in the 1960s. Much of the government's moves to tighten licensing and pass monopolies legislation was in origin, an attempt to control the growth of this one business house. However, even more adept than the Birlas was Dhirubhai Ambani. He did not have the huge range of industrial interests that the Birlas had, he was initially focussed on polyester, yet his handling of government policies and relationships saw his fortune rise each year during the 1970s. His talent then shifted from import replenishment licences to the equity markets as he sought to raise money for expansion. Friendly government policy changes from successive finance ministers and bureaucrats helped him grow even faster in the early 1980s as he began transforming Reliance Industries into a diversified industrial conglomerate. He seemingly managed to conjure many multiples of the money usually raised by the issue of debentures and avoided paying large amounts of tax in the process. By the 1980s India's most successful businesspeople were all, by necessity, the products of a mature system of crony socialism.

It was one of the most profound perversions of the planned economy. Economic planning was supposed to bring balance to the economy and equilibrate supply and demand so that there would be no shortages or gluts in the market. In addition, wealth was supposed to be redistributed according to a socialistic pattern of society. The public sector was supposed to secure the commanding heights of the economy. The Industrial Policy Resolutions of 1948 and 1956, having exhausted government resources in heavy industry, largely left the rest of the economy to private enterprise. The Industries (Development and Regulation) Act of 1951 was supposed to provide for sound and balanced economic development. Yet, quickly, during the late 1950s and early 1960s licensing became so complex that the only people with the time, knowledge, and resources to navigate the system, India's established industrialists, benefitted and continued to grow their businesses. Licensing was thus largely working to block the entry of new entrepreneurs. By the 1960s a number of government appointed committees had looked into the matters of both industrial licensing and monopoly power. The recommendations of these reports were tentative, noting the failures of the system and some remedial measures which could be taken to reform it. Yet their reports were entering the Indian political milieu of 1968 and 1969; socialists were ascendant in the Congress and a split in the Party loomed. Thus, both the relatively modest recommendations of the Monopolies Commission and the Industrial Licensing Committee took a life of their own and became much more radical once they entered the bureaucracy and took form in new legislation and departmental policies. Industrial licensing changed from year to year but became increasingly personalised around the Prime Minister, Indira Gandhi and her circle of official and unofficial advisers. The Monopolies Commission, when it came to life, was even more powerful than the one which the Enquiry Commission had recommended. In 1969 the remedy for the failure of regulation and licensing was considered to be more regulation and licensing.

The attempt to prevent big businesses from growing was a futile one. The Bajajes were not among India's biggest industrialists, yet given that they made scooters, which were the most accessible form of motorised transport in India in the 1970s, theirs was a household name. They had been manufacturing since the 1960s and made a good product at a reasonable price. They regularly sought permission from the government to expand capacity and were generally granted it. Yet with the arrival of the Monopolies and Restrictive Trade Practices Act in 1970 and the Monopolies Commission in 1971, they would constantly have to appear before what amounted to a Monopolies court during the 1970s. During their first hearing the Majority was not in favour of the capacity expansion which they had requested, yet did not want to disturb their holding in their family business. The Minority was in favour of capacity expansion, yet in order to balance what would amount to increasing dominance of the market, wanted to dilute their shareholding. The Majority was tying the Bajajes' legs up whilst allowing them use of their arms. The Minority thought there was no need to tie up their legs, cutting off their arms would be better. Most years the Bajajes would return to the court for further permission for expansion, it kept being given, just not for the number requested. It was clear that Bajaj Auto was the leading scooter maker in India and coming close to exercising monopoly power. Yet the court could not reject its applications for capacity expansion entirely or even direct the division of the company. There were fundamentals of economics involved. The government had tried to create a plant but could not get it running. Bajaj had a competitor in API, yet it was much smaller. It was the Bajajes who were best placed to produce more scooters, efficiently and at a competitive price and meet the demand of consumers on the waiting list who had largely been forgotten in the court's hearings. It was their expertise and size which alarmed the government. Yet without that size and expertise there was no way of satisfying the market. And so the government continued to make exceptions to its own rules. What ensued was a kind of haggling in which both sides started with their desired number, knowing that it wouldn't be received, knowing the number which would be agreed, but engaging in the play of bargaining so that each party could walk away with its dignity intact.

Business in India was becoming a little less of a club during the early 1980s. In 1970 Indira Gandhi had repealed laws respecting international patent rights, but the full effect was only felt a decade later. Lupin

Laboratories, Paras Pharma, Sun Pharmaceutical Industries and Dishman Pharmaceuticals all grew rapidly. Dr. Reddy's Laboratories, which would become India's largest pharmaceutical company, was launched in 1984. A thriving subsector in indigenous drug manufacturing emerged, led by Ajay Piramal who acquired Nicholas Laboratories from an Australian multinational. New entrepreneurs were emerging in information technology, television, and communications. Tata Consultancy Services, Hindustan Computers, WIPRO, Infosys and Moser Baer all began operations. Entrepreneurs took to assembling Japanese television kits and marketing them under Indian brand names like Onida and Videocon. New firms were making auto parts, batteries and processing diamonds. Chemicals companies, construction and property groups, and alcohol distillers all started to grow. Yet the new environment of the early 1980s in which entrepreneurs, both old and new, were growing their businesses was a precarious one. The old economy was being sustained by new money.

TEN
The World Has Changed

Optimism about the Indian economy abounded in the first years of the 1980s. Indira Gandhi returned to power in 1980. She promised to restore law and order and get the economy moving again. As 1982 began she declared that it would be a Year of Productivity. Yet it could easily have been named the Sanjay Gandhi Memorial Year. He had died in a plane crash in June 1980, but it was just the type of language he would have appreciated. He had played his role during the late 1970s in eroding the commitment to socialism within the family, and this seemed evident in Indira's increasingly conservative rhetoric. Her elder son Rajiv was elected to Parliament in 1981. He had lived a quiet life as a pilot for Air India in the 1970s and bore none of his younger brother's political stigma. In 1982 he oversaw the preparations for the Asian Games in New Delhi. The operation was run with corporate efficiency from control rooms using the latest computers. The import of colour televisions was allowed so that India's middle class could enjoy the spectacle. In 1983 the Seventh Summit of the Non-Aligned Movement was also hosted in New Delhi and Prime Minister Indira Gandhi welcomed leaders from Asia, Africa and the Middle East. The fortunes of both India and the Nehru-Gandhi family seemed ascendant once again. What is more, the economy began to surge with discoveries of oil in the fields of Bombay High. India's credit rating in international markets was strong and visiting bankers would urge the Government of India to borrow more in international financial markets.

By the end of the 1980s India faced an economic

apocalypse. When another Janata coalition came to power at the end of 1989 the Prime Minister, Vishwanath Pratap Singh announced that the coffers were empty. International bankers no longer thought that India was a good credit risk. The Government of India, which had always borrowed conservatively and prided itself on never having defaulted on a debt, was downgraded by international ratings agencies. The reasons cited were both a deteriorating economy and a volatile political situation. Moreover, expatriate Indians, whose deposits of foreign exchange had supported India's reserves for more than a decade, and who were not easily alarmed, also started to withdraw their money. India's pride, its foreign policy of Non-Alignment, was also undermined as a new Prime Minister, Chandra Shekhar had to reluctantly support the American war effort in Iraq in January 1991 in exchange for a loan from the International Monetary Fund. The Reserve Bank of India had to revalue its gold just to inflate the levels of India's foreign exchange reserves. The Reserve Bank took to selling stores of gold seized from smugglers, and then had to offer its own gold reserves as security against the advance of hard currency from the Bank of England. Prime Minister P.V. Narasimha Rao told the nation on 22 June 1991- "There is no time to lose. The government and the country cannot keep living beyond their means and there are no soft options left."[dlix]

The conditions for a crisis of the scale which broke out in 1991 had been forming for over a decade. The government was spending beyond its means and borrowing increasing amounts both within India and abroad. Vast increases in spending on the agricultural sector started in 1979 during the last days of the Janata government. Successive governments also had to absorb losses from the public sector and spend scarce foreign exchange when it could not produce vital industrial materials in sufficient quantities. Production of grain had increased but edible oil had not, which necessitated further expenditure on imports. The government had to provide subsidies to the rural poor in the form of food through the Public Distribution System, and to the rural rich in the form of discounted fertiliser. It even had to subsidise Indian exporters in order to make their products competitive in international markets. Oil production stagnated as the decade went on and so the government had to again import increasing quantities of oil. None of the limited economic reform measures initiated by either Indira or Rajiv concealed the fundamental structural flaws in the Indian economy. Some only worked to reveal them.

Part of the problem of the Indian economy was politics. When the Janata Party came to power in 1977 it ran a particularly chaotic government. Some order seemed to be restored when Indira Gandhi returned to power in 1980. Whilst stability prevailed, a more highly developed form of patronage politics became entrenched at the Centre. The result was ever growing government expenditure. When Rajiv Gandhi assumed power stability seemed to continue. Yet after 1987 his image was irreparably tarnished by an arms deal scandal. Rajiv's Finance Minister, V.P. Singh turned against him and brought many of the surviving remnants of the old Janata Party together. He succeeded in coming to power in 1989 but was himself overthrown by a Janata veteran, Chandra Shekar, who then led a weak minority government. Chandra Shekhar's Finance Minister, Yashwant Sinha was unable to present a Union Budget in 1991. Rajiv withdrew outside support for the government prompting national elections.

***

Until the late 1970s India's cinematic villains were usually rural landlords. During the 1950s the erstwhile zamindars were shown to be either pitiful, a remnant of a bygone era fading away in dilapidated mansions, or devious, plotting with capitalists from the city to swindle land from peasants for the construction of industrial mills. In the 1960s the rural villain became a thakur rather than a zamindar, representing the shift in power on the land to smaller, but more proximate and ferocious landowners. At this time India's politicians were still held in high regard. The leaders of India in both New Delhi and the state capitals were veterans of the Independence movement, revered both for the sacrifices they had made in the struggle against British rule and their personal austerity and high standards of probity in public life. It was only in the 1970s, as the Emergency approached and politics seemed to become dystopic, that politicians began to appear as villains on the cinema screen.

Amongst the first to introduce political villains to Indian audiences was Jabbar Patel, a young director of Marathi films. In 1974 in *Saamna,* or *The Confrontation*, Patel pitted an honest old Gandhian against a corrupt and criminal small town politician. In 1979 he brought the theme to the city in *Sinhasan*, or *The Throne*, a story of a contest for power between the chief minister and finance minister of Maharashtra. The characters were loosely drawn from the contemporary politics of the state and the film was based on the novels of the journalist Arun Sadhu.

Sinhasan begins with the arrival of a journalist, Digambar Tipnis, to watch the proceedings of the Maharashtra State Assembly. The Minister for Food and Civil Supplies, Anandrao Tople addresses the Assembly. In the state government's 709 consumer societies 136,000 litres of kerosene had been distributed, so what is the opposition complaining about? An Opposition member claims that the kerosene had vanished between the government and consumer and demands an enquiry. The Opposition benches roar in support. The speaker tries to bring the discussion to a close, however another Opposition member rises- this is a matter of life and death for the poor, their stoves are not lit, there is no light in their homes. Another claims that kerosene is being found in the open market- the Assembly should be allowed to discuss the issue. The discussion is brought to a close.

The Finance Minister, Vishwasrao Dabhade rises to table the state level distribution report for 1975/76. The Minister of State for Social Welfare, Budhajirao then submits his report to the Assembly. He presents the accounts register of his department- (A)-1231, (P), (C), (K), 327. The Agriculture Minister, Manikrao Patil then rises to table the *Report of the Konkan Agricultural University for 1972/73*. He comes under attack from the opposition benches. He should be ashamed. Was he sleeping all this time? It is an insult to the Assembly. He should be punished.

An Opposition member rises citing rule 102. He informs the Revenue Minister, Dattaji Jadhav that towns across Maharashtra like Dhule, Nasik, Pune, Satara, Sangli and Solapur are experiencing severe drought. Thousands of cattle had died. The public is suffering under water scarcity. There had been two starvation deaths in Vangni Khurd village in Shirud district. He wants to know what the state law and order apparatus has to say, what decisions have been made, and what action would take place. The minister then rises and informs the Assembly that a full enquiry has been undertaken and the Opposition member's claim is wrong and baseless. He had received the news of the starvation deaths and visited Vangni and conducted a personal enquiry. He is gathering momentum when the Chief Minister, Jivajirao Shinde rises and excuses himself. He leaves to take a telephone call. It is an anonymous caller. He issues a warning. There is a big conspiracy being hatched against the chief minister. Shinde asks his assistant Mogre where the call came from. Mogre tells him it was from Delhi. The chief minister knows it was not from Delhi. He returns to the Assembly.

Dattaji Jadhav is explaining his personal enquiry in Vangni. The complaint was that Venkoba Dalpat had died of starvation, but Venkoba was actually a man of some standing; he owned 21 acres of land, half of which was fertile. When the supposed starvation occurred there were

15 or 16 bags of grain stored in his house. Besides which he had died at the age of 71. This should be noted by the Assembly. In addition, according to his wife and children Venkoba had died of old age and diabetes. The minister seems quite pleased with his rebuttal. The Opposition members claim that even if there was no starvation death that did not mean that people were not struggling with drought. In order to wake the stupid system up, did villagers literally have to start dying en masse in their villages? Another Opposition member claims that black fungus was found on sorghum in Athri district in Vidharba. Another wants to talk about the Konkan. Pense rises to state that in Ratnagiri they had started sowing sorghum but the situation is hopeless, and it is worse in Kulaba district where the rice is infected with root worm.

Chief Minister Shinde passes a note to the speaker to excuse himself. He goes home to rest and is checked by a doctor. The doctor tells him that there is nothing to worry about, but he should wear a neck brace for a couple of days. On the way out Mogre wants to know what is happening. The doctor asks him whether he wants to know the truth, or the version for the press bulletin. The truth is that there is nothing wrong with Shinde at all. But he is happy to play along. He isn't sure, but there is probably something going on in politics for the chief minister to have feigned an illness.

The next morning Shinde calls the journalist, Digambar. He had read the morning newspapers which had printed the news of his illness. He invites Digambar over to his bungalow. He wants to know what he thinks of Manikrao Patil. He had heard off the grapevine that Manikrao had a meeting in Aurangabad the previous week and Mavatrao had also gone. Digambar points out that the meeting was in Manikraos's constituency. Shinde maintains that he is not stupid. He knows what is going on and how close the two had become recently. He wants to know if Digambar has any news. He will make his enquiries and let him know. Shinde did not think it was so important that he actually look into the matter, but he did want his paper to try to suppress news of the drought. He had already raised the issue with Digambar's editor at a meeting at the editor's brother-in-law's flat.

Digambar gets a call from Finance Minister Dabhade's daughter-in-law. She passes the phone to her father-in-law. He knows that Digambar was speaking to the chief minister and wants to know what the conversation was about. Not much, just talk of the drought, and the news of his health which had been published that morning. What was the cause of the illness? Digambar thinks he might have eaten something he shouldn't have. Dabhade suggests that it was the nasty phone call alerting him to a conspiracy which might have triggered the mystery illness. Digambar asks what truth there is in the idea of a conspiracy. Dabhade says there is none. He wouldn't have the time for it. Besides, he is happy with his position. Content with whatever God had given him. Why would he take the pains for such a thing?

After a game of badminton Dabhade and his daughter-in-law sit down for tea in the bungalow garden. They plan their next move. Because of the phone call they would have to alert the lobby in Delhi. He wants her to call De Costa, the Union leader. They had not yet met. They would need to meet for a couple of hours, in private. Call him for a meeting at the Golf Club. Shinde is on a call with Raosaheb Tople. He is calling from the office of the chief minister's co-operative bank in Chirungute. Shinde wants him to keep an eye on Satara, Sangli and Solapur districts, the Assembly members from Pune as well as the co-operative banks. Raosaheb says he will work the phones when he gets home. Shinde suggests that they keep in touch on a daily basis. He walks out of a meeting with the Revenue Minister, Dattajirao and finds the Agriculture Minister, Manikrao who had been waiting for him for an hour. They sit down. Dattajirao informs Shinde that he had spoken with the finance secretary in Delhi that morning. Manikrao drifts and starts talking to himself: yes, Dattajirao should keep talking, the chief minister's position is strong, but Manikrao's time will come. He would even avenge the insult of having been kept waiting.

Manikrao and Dabhade meet in the hall of the Assembly. Manikrao is still brooding over the insult of having been kept waiting but Dabhade tells him to be big hearted and forget about it. Manikrao insists that he has 40 Assembly members from Marathwada. At any moment he could get 1 million people together or collect 1 million rupees. And yet still he is being treated like garbage. Dabhade reminds him of the meeting at Usman's house in the evening. Both Digambar and another man loitering in the corridor, Patole see the two of them talking. Patole phones the chief minister's office about the meeting and says that he will keep an eye on both Dabhade and Manikrao.

Raosaheb Tople steps out of the door of his village home. A small villager, Sonya, and his daughter touch his feet. He moves into his office. There are rifles on the wall. His assistants sit on cushions. A call comes in from Wasgherekar. Raosaheb says that he supports the chief minister. They should stand behind him. The leadership issue will be discussed later. The chief minister had called and Raosaheb had promised his support. He agrees that farmers' issues are being ignored, but the real issue is the cess. The industrialists are making the profits. The politicians will put pressure on them. But that is not the immediate point. The immediate concern is for stability. Whatever happens Dabhade should not become chief minister. Shinde is a lion. All their Assembly members should be informed. Raosaheb calls his son Ashok in. He gives him a scolding. He had got him married, he had two children, but still kept flirting around. Sonya was at his door everyday telling him to either take his daughter in his home or get her married. Ashok claims he does not have any relationship with her. Raosaheb does not believe him.

The meeting between Dabhade and De Costa finally takes place in a basement over a game of snooker. After engaging in banter they sit down for tea. What does De Costa think of the chief minister? He is a scoundrel. But what if the two were to stand in competition for the top post? It would be equally hard to choose as they were both scoundrels. De Costa might support Dabhade, but on some conditions. He insists he should be allowed to run the Unions the way he wants. Some factories have lockouts which have to be removed. And cases which had been filed against Union members during previous strikes, besides those for murder, should be withdrawn. That was all fine. But does he have any personal conditions? He is evasive. Those conditions cannot be written down. But if they were not fulfilled he would thrash the new chief minister with sandals outside the Assembly.

Dabhade's daughter-in-law is speaking to the Dalit Assembly member, Budhajirao on the phone. It is late. Papa is next to her. She suggests Budhajirao speak to him as he is in a good mood. Does Budhajirao know why he called? The anonymous call had become a big issue and it is clear that the chief minister would now challenge him to an open contest for the post. He wants to strengthen his camp. What is Budhajirao's opinion? He is non-committal. There is some joking about lunch and how good looking daughter-in-law thinks Budhajirao is. Dabhade says that Manikrao is merging his camp with his. It looks like his side has the numbers and Budhajirao might also want to join him. In that case, Budhajirao tells Dabhade that he is with him and his block of Dalit MLAs will back him. But then he hears some static in the background of the call. He thinks that the phone might be tapped. Dabhade is more concerned about the pledge of support. Budhajirao starts to sweat. There is a closeup of a portrait of Chief Minister Shinde on the wall.

Budhajirao goes to meet Nana Gupte, the speaker of the Legislative Assembly. But then Nana gets a call from the

The World Has Changed

chief minister. He has called him to make a request on the issue of Budhajirao and the fraud of 19 lakhs in the municipality of Dariyapur. The case is with Nana and he wants him to admit it. Nana says he will make an enquiry. What is the need of an enquiry? Shinde knows that Budhajirao is there. He needs to be present in this session of the Legislative Assembly. He is an irregular attendee and Shinde wanted Nana to make him a regular one. But what about the rules? Rules could be bent. Is Nana going to tell Shinde about rules? Nana sits back down with Budhajirao. He drifts into a flashback.

He is a younger man. He walks with his wife on the beach. His wife is scared. Her sister Radha has become a widow and moved in with them. She does not like the way Radha stares at him. It is giving her bad ideas. Nana thinks it is nothing to worry about. She says they will go and sit on their usual rock. Nana tells her to go ahead, he will come after finishing some work. He calls out to her to be careful. He is still on the beach reading through his booklet. But then she gets a migraine and falls in the sea. She calls for help. Nana gets up, runs to the shore, but then stops and just looks as she gets taken in by the surf. He turns back and is stopped by a Dasturji, a Parsi priest, who says to him in English "You didn't save her." "You are a murderer." But then a younger Shinde takes care of the matter. It will be reported as an accidental death. He will make sure that there are no more enquiries. The Dasturji had left for his son who lived America. He would not return to India for at least six months.

Nana now remembers the favour. Nana explains to Buddhajirao exactly what is going on. The chief minister was just on the phone to him wanting the fraud case admitted to the Assembly. It will be introduced by Budhajirao's own cousin Kamble. Budhajirao says Nana is like a father. His reputation is on the line. Nana begins to lecture him. No one can escape their sins. He will definitely admit the case. It is a matter of principle. One thing that Budhaji could do is to fall at the chief minister's feet and beg for forgiveness.

It is Raosaheb Tople's 57th birthday. Drummers march in a procession through the village. Villagers gather to witness Raosaheb and his wife perform a religious rite with a pandit. Sonya and his daughter had been watching the procession, but as he leaves a group of young men grab him and start beating him up. His daughter comes with her child to prevent them. They start beating her up too. The procession passes by. Religious folk songs are then performed for Raosaheb. He is garlanded. Both Sonya and his daughter have been killed. Ashok and his men have done the job. They won't tell Raosaheb. They will need to dispose of the bodies themselves. They will say that they died of starvation. The word gets into the newspapers that Dalits have died of starvation.

The Unions announce a closure of Mumbai (as it always was to Marathi speakers). Chief Minister Shinde wants to get through to Raosaheb Tople. Dabhade is having dinner with Usman. A colleague suggests that Dabhade let the battle begin, they had waited long enough. Usman says that their side would lay down their lives should the need arise. Dabhade just wants them to hand in their resignations. He wants to maintain the appearance that he is not involved in the machinations. Usman owns millions with businesses spread through the Gulf and the far corners of Africa. Dabhade suggests that should he become chief minister, he would surely get a big ministerial portfolio. News comes over the radio that the Mumbai closure has been a total success. There was some isolated stone throwing. The children played cricket on the deserted streets. Finance Minister Dabhade will make an important announcement in the evening.

Dabhade calls a press conference on the lawns of his bungalow. He has decided to resign. He blames it on the corruption prevailing over the previous 10 years. He had borne it for so long with a smile on his face. He has a high personal regard for the chief minister, however there is a drought and the Chirangute starvation deaths had been badly handled. Is there even a certain policy for the industrial sector? There is unrest throughout industry. Is there a single factory in all of Maharashtra which does not have problems? There are problems of the farmers and the Dalits which have been left unresolved. There are unstable policies in education. He cannot bear it any longer and so he will return to his village and tend to his farm. A journalist puts it to him that his resignation would create political instability. Dabhade suggests that such instability could be prevented by the High Command in Delhi changing the leadership of the state Party.

Chief Minister Shinde wants Digambar to arrange a meeting with De Costa. Digambar visits De Costa and convinces him to call the chief minister. Shinde is honoured by his call. He invites him for a meeting. They meet on his terrace. De Costa says that neither of them rule the city. It is the smugglers who rule Mumbai. Shinde does not agree, but if they both worked together they could erase the smugglers. De Costa thinks that is true, but over the previous 10 years smuggling had not been curbed. It had increased. Shinde thinks that there are other more pressing issues- poverty, lack of food, unemployment, villages without roads or electricity, people walking miles for water. He asks De Costa what the two of them could do for the poor. De Costa thinks he is just trying to divert him from the smuggling issue. De Costa states that he is going to call a press conference and name the ten biggest smugglers in Maharashtra. He will issue an official challenge to the government to catch them. The conversation deteriorates. Shinde tells De Costa that he does not understand the difficulties of government. De Costa calls him an insect; the day people like him left politics would be the day the country had some hope. Shinde says that new insects would just move in. They then sit down for tea. Shinde is thinking of changing labour policies at the grassroots level and wants De Costa to carry out the changes as labour minister in the government. He suggests that his Party is not actively backing him on the matter, particularly Dabhade. De Costa recognises that he is being used as a pawn in their chess game for the chief ministership; if he refuses the chief minister might have him arrested on some trumped-up charge. De Costa requests 48 hours to consider the offer.

Two children lie on a bed. A wife is preparing food. Her husband is worshipping a deity. Panitkar sits down to the meal. His wife wants him to come home early. He says he will. She does not believe him. Most nights he comes home at 2 or 3 in the morning. The neighbours envy the money he earns but do not realise how hard he works. She wants to go and visit her mother as a family. But he cannot come. He had not taken leave for three years. He even worked Sundays. Panitkar then leaves for work, wife and children waving goodbye from the second floor. He walks in on his boss having some men beat up his colleague Ramu. The boss, Mehta, is a seth, a Gujarati merchant, dressed in a silk dhoti kurta with a merchant's cap, a gold chain and gold rimmed glasses. He carries a cane. He welcomes Panitkar into the room. Mehta wants Ramu to tell him what really happened. Ramu insists that he threw the keys to the warehouse away in a hurry because of the sudden raid. When Ramu swears on his mother's life that he did not throw the keys away purposely Mehta seems satisfied. The Customs official had been able to reach the warehouse because of the thrown away key, but thankfully there was nothing inside. Mehta invites Panitkar to sit down for tea.

Mehta suggests that Ramu should be kept an eye on. He complains of how hard he works. He works all day and gives the money to his wife who enjoys it. Panitkar suggests they could opt out, go back to their villages, build bungalows, live peaceful lives off their earnings. Mehta calls him a child. Panitkar ask where his duty is for the night. Mehta asks him about De Costa. Were they friends? No, he just knew him from his days in the Union. Mehta warns Panitkar to keep away from him. He is to ask Hasan where his duty for the night will be. Panitkar goes home. His wife tells him to leave the job. He could get another job even if it was for less pay. He says that the children would have to finish their education before he could think of it. His wife insists that other children also go to school. But he is thinking on another level. Their children have to be very successful. They should have "first class careers", whether he would live to see it or not. He does not want his wife to have to ask anyone for anything.

Manikrao is on his swing asking himself whether he will become chief minister. His soul will not rest until he attains the post. He thinks that Dabhade will need his and Dattaji Jadhav's support. But he would only give his support in exchange for the post of chief minister. Raosaheb Tople is talking with his nephew, the Minister for Food and Civil Supplies, Anandrao Tople. Raosaheb wants Chief Minister Shinde to go along with the story that the Dalit deaths occurred over fights over liquor. He reminds Anandrao that he is from the chief minister's camp and has been working day and night for his election. The chief minister had already ordered a secret enquiry. It had come back the same day and reported that Sonya's daughter is pregnant by Raosaheb's son Ashok. Raosaheb then calls Shinde. He wants to meet but he feels that the chief minister is angry with him. Shinde claims he is busy. Tople asks for his forgiveness. Shinde hears him out and even calls him his brother-in-law. Tople invites himself over for dinner. He thinks that the matter is solved. Raosaheb then makes his way back to his village in a blue Ambassador. A truck blocks the way. He is attacked by a group of Dalits. They smear black paint on his face and parade him on a donkey. De Costa calls Digambar to inform him of his press conference. News breaks that De Costa has been attacked on the Thane highway.

Manikrao arrives at Dabhade's farmhouse for a Satyanarayana prayer ceremony. Manikrao goes inside and prostrates before the deity, asking to be made chief minister. They go for a walk in the garden. Dabhade is Anglicised, likely public school educated, and carries on the pretence of upper caste Indian politicians. He maintains that he does not seek any high post for himself, but it is supporters who demand it, and should he be given the responsibility he would humbly serve, not for himself, but for them and for society at large. Manikrao is rustic, of peasant stock and has no such pretensions. They represent the old and new forces of Indian politics. Comedy is created as two men who share a common language but speak in different idioms try to settle some business.

Manikrao wants to know who will be chief minister. Dabhade says that Manikrao should take the post. He is not hungry for it. But. People in his camp are making the suggestion that he be chief minister. Manikrao suggests that whatever is done should be by a common vote, so that there are no differences of opinion. Dabhade says that the Konkan camp supports him. But first they have to get rid of their common enemy. He estimates that he has 66 Assembly members whilst Manikrao would have about 40. But Manikrao insists that he has 68 including 40 from Marathwada. He points out that he has support in Nagar and Vidharbha. Vidharbha is not completely with Dabhade. There is some hard bargaining back and forth. Dabhade suggests Manikrao should check his numbers. He insists he does not need to. Dabhade proffers that Manikrao become home minister. Manikrao suggests that Dadbade create a post of deputy chief minister. Sure, Manikrao can take it. No. Manikrao insists it would be for Dabhade. Once again, Dabhade claims that whilst he would accept it, his block might not. Dattaji Jadhav is on his way. Word has already got back to Shinde of the goings on at the farmhouse.

Mehta is on the phone to Hasan. He gets news of a raid on his Grant Road warehouse. Dabhade, Manikrao and Dattaji are sitting working out their strategy. Shinde is informed that his brother-in-law has been arrested in the smuggling raid. Shinde pops some pills and starts sweating. This time he has a real heart attack. Back at Dadbhade's farmhouse Dattaji states that he has 10 Assembly members. If the main opposition party joins them then they could topple the government. Dattaji has been in contact but they will only provide their support if he is made chief minister, otherwise they would want the chief minister's post for themselves. Manikrao is not amused. Dabhade suggests that they rotate the chief ministership between them. By seniority he would be the first. And then Dattaji, and then Manikrao. Daughter-in-law walks in with news that the chief minister has had a heart attack. Shinde has words with Buddhajirao from bed. He and Anandrao Tople go to see Dattaji. Mehta gives Panitkar instructions to handle a big consignment. But then Ramu turns on Panitkar. Mehta has received orders from above. Panitkar is shot dead.

Chief Minister Shinde announces his cabinet reshuffle. Dabhade will be given the social welfare and sports portfolios. Dabhade receives the news and says he will refuse. He will take the fight to Nagpur. The number of ministers has been increased from 14 to 17. There will be 25 deputy ministers. Digambar, the journalist rubs his eyes and begins to visualise the slums. There is screeching music in the background. The chief minister's allocation of new portfolios plays in the background as the camera moves at ground level, and then switches to an aerial shot of a city slum. There will be a deputy chief minister. Finance will go to Manikrao Patil who will also get the deputy chief minister post. The screeching background score continues as the camera pans upward across the city's new luxury apartment blocks. Dattajirao Jadhav will take the revenue and industries ministries and Anandrao Tople will get labour and irrigation. Buddhajirao will get education and culture. An emaciated child swings, screaming in a hammock. Slightly older children pick through a garbage dump. An urchin lies on a footpath. The chief minister continues his remarks. He highlights the representation for the Konkan in his new Cabinet. Digambar begins to feel nauseous. He leaves the room and walks out onto the street. The screeching gets louder. A beggar approaches. He does not say anything. He just makes strange sounds whilst holding out his empty palm. Digambar responds by making his own strange sounds and weird faces. He holds out his empty palm and points to it. He then pats the beggar on the back and walks off, laughing madly. He walks down the road waving his hands above his head. The newly rewarded ministers embrace the chief minister. They then sit and laugh together. *Sinhasan* closes with the lyrics "Ushakal hota hota, kal ratra jhaali". "Just as we were expecting the sun's dawn, the nightmare arrived."

***

Sinhasan was loosely based on contemporary power struggles within the Congress Party in Maharashtra. An ambitious finance minister wanted to unseat a wily chief minister and they both looked to the Party High Command in New Delhi for support. The state's Cabinet ministers seemed oblivious to the squalor of Mumbai's slums and the suffering of Maharashtra's villages as they schemed to attain higher office. When the Congress system fell apart in New Delhi in February 1977 and a new Janata Party, comprising four main opposition groups came to power, something of the madness of *Sinhasan's* final scenes began to play out on the national stage.

Whilst the Congress suffered its first losses of power in the southern states in the 1950s, it was only in the late 1960s that its power began to wane in the state capitals of the north. A Samyukta Vidhayak Dal, United Legislators' Party took office in Uttar Pradesh, Madhya Pradesh and Bihar after 1967. These SVDs represented agrarian castes- Jats in Haryana and Uttar Pradesh, Kurmis and Koeris in Bihar, and the Lodhs in Madhya Pradesh. SVDs generally brought together coalitions of the Left and Right centred around a faction of disgruntled former Congressmen. The biggest of these was the Bharatiya Kranti Dal, the Indian Revolution Party formed in 1967 by Charan Singh, the former Congress revenue minister of Uttar Pradesh and leader of the state's Jat community. When the Emergency came, it was Charan Singh's Bharatiya Lok Dal, Indian People's Party which was most keen for an alliance of opposition parties. And when the Janata Party went to the polls in February 1977 it did so on the BLD's election symbol of a farmer carrying a plough. The BLD, formed in 1974, comprised Charan Singh's old BKD, some remnants of the Swatantra Party, Raj Narain's Samyukta Socialist Party and other smaller parties. The new Party was based upon an AJGAR caste coalition- Ahirs, Jats, Gujars and Rajputs. They were low, middle and high castes of northern India united by their rising economic power on the land.

Charan Singh's Bharatiya Lok Dal was firmly ensconced in the middle of the Janata Party's contest for power after its victory over Indira Gandhi's Congress. The BLD held 68 seats in the Lok Sabha. Morarji Desai's Congress (O) held 55, and the Socialist Party held 51. The largest Party in the coalition was the Hindu nationalist Jana Sangh which held 90 seats. Jagjivan Ram had only recently left Indira's government and formed the Congress Forum for Democracy and he and some independent former Congressmen together contributed 34 seats. The initial contest was for the prime minister's post. Morarji Desai brought his own support in the form of his Congress (O) members, however despite being a lifelong Congressman he was known for his latent Hindu nationalism and social conservatism, and so could also count on the support of the Jana Sangh. Yet the Socialist Party was naturally opposed to Desai, as were most of the more radical members of the Congress Forum for Democracy, the Young Turks of ten years earlier. The young socialists supported Jagjivan Ram. Charan Singh was in favour of neither man. Jayaprakash Narayan and J.B. Kripalani acted as elders and anointed Morarji prime minister based on his long administrative experience and personal integrity. Morarji's Congress (O) held six Cabinet posts. Charan Singh's BLD held four Cabinet posts, whilst the Jana Sangh and the Socialists received just three ministries each. Jagjivan Ram was appointed defence minister and Charan Singh became home minister. Charan Singh's bid for the deputy prime ministership was rejected. Jagjivan Ram, who had a strong following among the Dalits of northern India, was given the post. Charan Singh thus became Morarji Desai's principal antagonist. Neither did he accept the election of Chandra Shekhar, the former Young Turk as president of the Janata Party.

Charan Singh resigned from the National Executive and the Parliamentary Board of the Janata Party just over a year after forming a government in April 1978. State politics was just as important as politics at the Centre as the Janata Party had also formed governments in the big northern states which provided the core of Charan Singh's support. His Partymen in Haryana, Uttar Pradesh and Bihar were all facing difficulties because of the interference of the Party leadership in New Delhi in state politics. Charan Singh alleged that this interference in state politics was coming from the very top, that is the Party President, Chandra Shekhar. Devi Lal, Chief Minister of Haryana and close associate of Charan Singh, was asked by the Janata Party leadership to seek a vote of confidence. Ram Naresh Yadav, the Chief Minister of Uttar Pradesh and another of Charan Singh's men, was also clashing with Chandra Shekhar. Atal Behari Vajpayee, the Jana Sangh member and external affairs minister sought to mediate and asked Charan Singh to withdraw his resignation. He said that he could not think of the Janata Party without him.[dlx] The Jana Sangh was sharing power in state governments in Punjab, Haryana, Rajasthan, Himachal Pradesh, Uttar Pradesh, Bihar and Madhya Pradesh and had its chief ministers in place in Himachal Pradesh, Rajasthan and Madhya Pradesh. It was the Sangh's first substantive experience of power in the Central government and in the states and so it had the largest interest in preserving the Janata coalition.

Devi Lal was successful in proving his majority in the Haryana assembly, yet this only opened up a schism between the Bharatiya Lok Dal, and the Congress (O) and the Congress Forum for Democracy. The erstwhile Congressmen then sought the remove Ram Naresh Yadav from the chief minister's post in Uttar Pradesh. Yadav proved his majority in June. The BLD and the Jana Sangh were in a de facto coalition to exercise power in Uttar Pradesh and Yadav received the Sangh's support. Both Charan Singh and Raj Narain were making public statements about Morarji Desai and other ex-Congressmen's manipulative politics.[dlxi] Meanwhile, the Jana Sangh was having problems with the socialists in the Madhya Pradesh Assembly. Raj Narain, Charan Singh's closest political associate, was even asking for Chandra Shekhar's resignation.[dlxii] The Congress (O), the Congress Forum for Democracy and the Chandra Shekhar group of socialists then raised the issue of Party discipline.[dlxiii] Morarji asked Raj Narain to either show cause for his indiscipline or resign.[dlxiv] Whilst Morarji had appointed Justice Jayantilal Chhotala Shah to investigate the Emergency, Charan Singh wanted Indira arrested. He started hounding Morarji for the role his son Kanti seemed to be playing peddling influence for big industrialists, including Dhirubhai Ambani. He also abetted the publication of Jagjivan Ram's son in compromising sexual positions. By June 1978 he was lambasting his own government as "a bunch of incompetent people", something which forced Morarji to demand his resignation.[dlxv] On 30 June 1978 Charan Singh resigned from Cabinet.

Upon leaving Cabinet Charan Singh began demanding an inquiry into Kanti Desai's business dealings. He asked his followers to march on Delhi on 17 July. The Janata National Executive persuaded him to withdraw his resignation from Party posts. Both the Jana Sangh and Bharatiya Lok Dal opposed Party elections in July, uncertain as they were of their strength. The Jana Sangh pleaded for Charan Singh's return to Cabinet. Chandra Shekhar supported Morarji Desai's prerogative in the matter. At this time the cleavage in the Janata Party was between ex-Congressmen like Morarji Desai and Chandra Shekhar and the veterans of anti-Congress politics, Charan Singh and the leaders of the Jana Sangh. Yet a change was taking place. The Bharatiya Lok Dal was weakened in the states by Charan Singh's withdrawal from Cabinet. And out of Cabinet an alliance with him was less beneficial to the Jana Sangh. During the monsoon of 1978 the Jana Sangh began moving gradually closer to Morarji Desai's Congress (O), its natural ideological ally.

Both Charan Singh's Bharatiya Lok Dal and the Socialist Party had been putting pressure on Morarji Desai to appoint a Second Backward Classes Commission in order to extend reservations in Central government institutions to shudra, or labouring castes. The first Commission had been formed in 1953. It had identified over 2,000 "Other Backward Classes" but disagreements amongst its members and a note of dissent from its chairman allowed Jawaharlal Nehru to leave the matter to the states. In December 1978 Morarji Desai appointed Bindheshwari Prasad Mandal to the Second Commission, something which sparked off conflict between Charan Singh's Bharatiya Lok Dal which represented the lower castes likely to benefit from any recommendation for reservations and the Jana Sangh, which represented the higher castes which had the most to lose. The two Parties had already been clashing over instances of Hindu-Muslim violence, and the Jana Sangh had already withdrawn support for BLD governments in Bihar, Haryana and Uttar Pradesh.

Rather than bringing Charan Singh back into Cabinet, Morarji Desai was partial to making him Party president. However, a signature campaign was started against any such move. The Jana Sangh was moving closer to Morarji Desai who described Charan Singh's latest proposed farmers' rally as a "political conspiracy".[dlxvi] Madhu Limaye, a Socialist Party member had joined Charan Singh in spreading news of Kanti Desai's fundraising activities. On 22 December Charan Singh spoke to the Lok Sabha on the way he had been eased out over the "Kanti affair".[dlxvii]

The long threatened farmers' rally took place in New Delhi on 23 December 1978.[dlxviii] It was the biggest political rally in the capital, officially called a "kisan sammelan" or farmers' gathering. Hundreds of thousands of farmers from the states closest to Delhi gathered to celebrate Charan Singh's 77th birthday. The chief ministers of Punjab, Haryana, Uttar Pradesh and Bihar were all in attendance.

Charan Singh denied that the rally had been called as a ploy to force his way back into the government. In an hour long speech he focused on the neglect of farmers in the 30 years since Independence. They made up the bulk of the population, yet their problems had not been addressed. Even when leaders of peasant stock ascended to high posts in the government they forgot their roots when exercising power. Back in 1960 incomes of farmers and city dwellers were not very different. Since then city folks had seen their incomes quadruple, whilst farmers' incomes were static. Rural people could not compete with their city counterparts because of the high cost of education. More than 100,000 villages did not have drinking water. Only 14% of civil service officers came from rural backgrounds and agricultural officers did not enjoy the same prestige as officers in other services. Charan Singh lashed out at his own Janata government for wasting money on United Nations meetings in New Delhi and the renovation of government convention centres when the money could have been better spent on irrigation. Only 24% of India's cultivable land was irrigated. The number of people living off agriculture had increased since Independence just as neighbouring Asian nations were achieving prosperity by shifting their economic base from agriculture to industry. If a family had four children only two should work the land, the other two should take up professions; the number of people working in the fields should decline and production should increase. And then, striking an emotional note, Charan Singh told his audience that mothers in the villages could only give their babies milk when they cried. Villagers were taking to bad city habits and drinking more. Relatively prosperous farmers had been dubbed "kulaks" by the intelligentsia, after the wealthy and selfish farmers of pre-Communist Russia, but he pointed out that 15% of farmers in India held between half and one hectare each. Ministers and industrialists had no right to call farmers kulaks. He called for a legal ban on big industries in order to eradicate poverty and lower unemployment. Big industries had hampered the progress of the country; they employed just 11% of the population.

The farmers' rally adopted a 20 point charter of demands.[dlxix] The most significant for India's finances were points 5 and 8. All agricultural inputs- electricity, water, fertilisers, pesticides and seeds- should be provided at low prices by granting subsidies when necessary. And excise duties on crude oil, fertilisers, electricity and other agricultural inputs and outputs should either be removed or greatly reduced.

About six weeks later, after Charan Singh had been inducted into Cabinet as deputy prime minister and finance minister, the chief ministers who had sat on the stage at the farmers' rally, and the chief minister of Rajasthan, paid him a visit.[dlxx] They presented the new finance minister with a joint statement of demands which included the abolition of central taxes on fertilisers and tractors, the abolition of wealth tax and estate duty on agricultural land and implements, national crop insurance, and Central government loans for houses for the landless. Charan Singh asked them if they had anymore demands. They did not. He then asked, "What will you say if I give you even more than you have asked for?" The chief ministers said, "We will be extremely grateful." And they all laughed.

When Charan Singh presented his Budget on 28 February the urban elites in the public gallery sat stunned.[dlxxi] He outlined what came to be known as "soak the rich" tax proposals, drawing cheers from his fellow rural members of parliament. He paid tribute to the energy and toil of millions of Indian farmers and detailed how he would transfer resources on a huge scale to the countryside. The Congress member, and Indira Gandhi loyalist from Maharashtra, Vasant Sathe, sitting on the Opposition benches, tried to inject some wit into proceedings. He called Charan Singh's performance "a taxing speech".

The objections of the urban elite, which were well expressed in the English language newspapers, centred on the higher taxes applied to an array of consumer goods. The surcharge on income tax was also raised. The prices of soap, detergents, cooking oil, toothpaste, kerosene, chocolates and chewing gum, pressure cookers and scooters were all to rise. There were new duties on cosmetics, televisions, stereos, air conditioners and furniture made of steel. Yet despite the new set of corporate and personal and indirect taxes, the Budget of 1979 would run the largest deficit since Independence. The official increase in spending on agriculture was only 3.3% and on irrigation it was only 5.6%.[dlxxii] However, this figure was somewhat deceptive. Due to transfers between plan and non-plan expenditure the rise seemed small, yet in effect it actually came close to 60%. Levies on agricultural inputs were decreased, more was being spent on the rural integrated development programme and plans were being made to subsidise irrigation and storage facilities. The expenditure on the fertiliser subsidy grew by 40%.

Rather than attacks against his son Kanti, Charan Singh and Raj Narain began to target Morarji Desai for his Hindu nationalist leanings, an approach which would also bring the Jana Sangh into a clearer ideological conflict. In December 1978 Desai had introduced a Freedom of Religion Bill which sought to outlaw forced conversions and also removed Marxist influenced history books from educational curriculums. In May 1979 he sought to have the issue of cow slaughter put on the Constitution's concurrent list so that the states would be able to devise their own laws on the subject. However, Charan Singh was trying to have the Jana Sangh ministers expelled from the Cabinet for failing to renounce their membership of the Hindu nationalist Rashtriya Swayamsevak Sangh, or National Volunteers Organisation. This was a new demand, for Charan Singh had defended this right as far back as 1976. The Socialists had opposed "dual membership" all along. Charan Singh's Bharatiya Lok Dal forced a vote on the dual membership issue and Raj Narain managed to gather 47 MPs to form a new Janata Party (Secular).

In July Yashwantrao Balwantrao Chavan of the Congress (U), a breakaway faction of Indira's Congress (I), tabled a no confidence motion in the Lok Sabha. He was not expecting much, but it led to further splitting within the government with more Bharatiya Lok Dal members and Socialists moving to the new Janata Party (Secular). The remaining members of the Janata Party nominated Jagjivan Ram as their parliamentary leader which led the Prime Minister, Morarji Desai to resign. By the end of July Charan Singh was prime minister. As the leader of the Janata Party (Secular) he was given three weeks to prove his majority. Besides support from a motley crew of Socialists, ex-Congressmen, Muslim Leaguers and Communists, he also had to accept the support of Indira Gandhi. Indira wanted the cases against her and Sanjay to be dropped. Charan Singh thus had to decide which of two factions of the old Congress to seek support from- the Congress (U) or the Congress (I). He had already left another two, Morarji's Congress (O) and the Congress Forum for Democracy, behind in the old Janata Party. Rather than giving Jagjivan Ram, the leader of the old

Janata Party, the chance to show his strength on the floor of the Lok Sabha, Charan Singh recommended the dissolution of parliament.

***

National elections were held in January 1980. Formal campaigning started just three weeks prior to the poll dates, however informal campaigning had been taking place since the fall of Charan Singh's short lived government in August. These interim months had seen the proliferation of civic groups in cities demonstrating against sharp rises in the prices of vegetables, sugar, cooking oil, petrol, educational fees and housing. Religious rioting seemed to become more frequent than usual, with even the placid steel town Jamshedpur rocked by riots in September after earlier instances in April. There was also more violence in rural districts as erstwhile landowners tried to take back farms which had been redistributed during the most recent attempt at land reform.

Indira Gandhi started her campaign with the two themes she would maintain as she toured the country: the breakdown of law and order and rising prices under the Janata government. Bringing the two together, she quipped that in an economy of rising prices and scant law and order the only thing which had become cheap was life itself.[dlxxiii] In New Delhi on 14 December she said that even residents of the capital did not feel safe walking the streets as crime had acquired an alarming proportion.[dlxxiv] What was more disturbing was that people were coming to accept the situation. The following day in Unnao she stated that a government which could not ensure security of life for the people had no right to stay in power.[dlxxv] In Mirzapur on the 17th she accused the Janata government of making the country bankrupt in just two and a half years of misrule.[dlxxvi] The next day in Surat she warned her audience that the Janata's bias against big industry and modern technology could jeopardise the nation's self-sufficiency and defence capabilities.[dlxxvii] In an election broadcast on All India Radio, Indira found her campaign slogan: "Elect a government that works."[dlxxviii] She urged voters to support the Congress and return the country to "order, stability, purposeful governance and progress." Indira returned to power with a commanding 374 seats in the Lok Sabha. Charan Singh's Janata Party (Secular) and Chandra Shekhar's Janata Party managed to win just 71 seats between them.

Just as the country was going to the polls an old agitation in Assam against the influx of residents from Bangladesh became more confrontational. The picketing of the state's oil refineries started in earnest in the last week of December 1979. Assam supplied around one-third of India's domestic production of oil. The All Assam Students' Union and the Assam Gana Sangram Parishad, or Assam Peoples' Struggle Council, called for picketing of government owned oil refineries at Digboi, Gauhati and Bongaigon, and for employees of the refineries to stop reporting for duty.[dlxxix] When police tried to clear picketing on 18 January at least six people died, including the technical manager of Oil India who was dragged out of his car and killed by a violent crowd.[dlxxx]

The Home Minister, Zail Singh visited Assam in February and the Prime Minister, Indira Gandhi visited in April. Whilst talks made progress and the agitation would intermittently be suspended, picketing of oil installations continued. The vicinities of oil installations were declared protected areas in March and the army was rushed in to clear pickets in April. The Armed Forces Act was promulgated for most of the state, however this only intensified the picketing. By April it was estimated that the country was losing ₹100 crores a month due to the disruption to the oil supply.[dlxxxi] The government had to import 200,000 tonnes of diesel a month just to keep the agricultural economy functioning during the harvest season. Even when the students and the government came to an understanding during the monsoon, and the movement was in abeyance, the picketing of oil installations continued.

Picketing intensified once again in November and rather than just guarding oil facilities or breaking up pickets the army was called in to man oil pipelines and refineries in order to ensure supply. The local employees of Oil India and the Oil and Natural Gas Commission refused once again to work. Army engineers took their place. By 10 November the army could announce that it controlled all of Assam's oilfields.[dlxxxii] Army engineers had trained at the ONGC oil facilities in Ahmadabad the previous summer and took over production wells, oil installations and pumping stations and launched Operation Indra Vajra, invoking the Vedic God Indra's Divine Weapon. Oil India and ONGC employees returned to work and operations began to normalise from January 1981. The Finance Minister, Ramaswamy Venkataraman estimated that the country had lost ₹1,000 crore in foreign exchange alone over the previous year of agitation in Assam.[dlxxxiii]

India's foreign exchange reserves began to fall in September 1979. The main reason for the decline was the slow growth in exports and large rise in the bill for imports. The international price of crude oil and petroleum products had spiked due to the disruption to supplies from Iran which was in a state of Revolution. There were more imports of industrial components and edible oils, and prices of imported fertilisers and non-ferrous metals had also increased. The situation was not worse because of buoyant remittances from workers in the Gulf. By May of 1980 foreign exchange reserves had fallen by almost 20% in 7 months.[dlxxxiv]

The Government of India's latest foreign exchange crisis came just as dramatic change was taking place in Washington D.C. Upon assuming office in January 1981, one of President Ronald Reagan's first decisions was to issue an order to cut government spending. In February he asked Congress to cut foreign aid to meet only current commitments.[dlxxxv] Foreign aid was not alone, by March it became clear that all forms of government spending, barring defence expenditure, would be severely curtailed. The cuts to foreign aid had an ideological component. Republicans generally associated large flows of foreign aid with the internationalism favoured by Democrats. Moreover, providing American aid money to multilateral organisations was considered just a step away from a New International Economic Order. Secretary of State Alexander Haig, who had tried to preserve as much foreign aid funding as possible, announced to a congressional committee that the Reagan administration would place emphasis on bilateral rather than multilateral foreign aid transfers.[dlxxxvi] This bode ill for India given that around two-thirds of its annual receipts of foreign aid came from multilateral organisations, principally the World Bank and its lending affiliate the International Development Association.[dlxxxvii] The United States was the biggest donor to these multilateral organisations and was also the biggest donor to the Consortium, the group of nations formed in 1958 to assist India's economic development. The Consortium had become institutionalised and met every June in Paris to decide on annual aid flows to India.

By July of 1981 the Government of India had initiated talks with the International Monetary Fund. The government requested a $4 billion loan to finance the balance of payments deficit which was estimated at $3 billion for the financial year 1980/81. The loan would be the biggest in the Fund's history. This was also the first time that the Government of India was seeking a loan under the Extended Facility Arrangement which was thought to be more politically sensitive due to its stringent conditions. The loan was to be made in three yearly instalments. At the end of each year the Fund would review India's compliance with loan conditions and the policies taken to address the balance of payments problems. However, the money for the loan came only partly from the International Monetary Fund's own resources. It was also financed by money which the Fund had borrowed from Saudi Arabia.[dlxxxviii] The interest on the Fund's portion of the loan would be 6.25%. The interest on the Saudi Arabian portion would by 13.25%. Overall interest on the loan would average around 7-8%, which was less than half the cost of borrowing in international commercial markets. The loan would be repayable in five to ten years in twelve equal instalments.

By September the size of the loan had risen to $5.7 billion. Tentative approval had been given by the Fund's officers and research team, however final approval was still required from the board of governors. It was at this time that it became clear that the United States would oppose the loan. The United States Treasury Secretary Donald Regan termed the loan "very large" and "very unusual".[dlxxxix] In the end the American opposition to the loan was symbolic, it merely abstained from voting and India had sufficient support from most of the nations represented on the board of governors to ensure its approval. The conditions of the loan, when they emerged, appeared to be relatively relaxed. The Government of India would have to increase interest rates for loans to the public sector and move to balance budgets by cutting back on subsidies. The most important condition however was a restriction on government borrowing in international commercial markets to $1.8 billion for three years.

The Government of India had, since Independence, followed a conservative approach to borrowing abroad. Most borrowing had been undertaken from governments and official agencies, either directly from the World Bank, indirectly from the Consortium, or bilaterally from foreign governments. Whenever foreign exchange crises arose, as they had in 1957, 1965 and 1973, the Government of India's response would be to replenish foreign exchange reserves by severely restricting imports and seeking aid from friendly foreign governments. Yet when Indira

Gandhi returned to power in January 1980 her government took a new approach. She had vowed on the campaign trail to get the economy moving again and wanted to boost industrial production. Yet much like in the early 1960s, India suffered from shortages of infrastructure and foreign exchange. Instead of the traditional response, the government sought funds not just from the International Monetary Fund, but from international commercial lenders. Even before approaching the International Monetary Fund, in the first six months of 1980, the Government of India had borrowed $880 million in eurocurrency markets, an increase from $61 million the previous year.[dxc] This new, more adventurous approach to international borrowing was summed up by the Finance Minister, R. Venkataraman who told the Rajya Sabha that he preferred to mobilise resources by borrowing rather than "savage taxation".[dxci]

With aid from the United States likely to become more difficult, the Government of India began to seek new sources of funds. In April 1982 the government announced that it intended to borrow from the Asian Development Bank in Manila.[dxcii] India was a founding member of the Bank but had not yet drawn on its resources. It would not draw on concessional loans however, which might restrict lending to other poor developing nations. In May the Indian Mission approached the European Economic Community's European Investment Bank in Brussels to begin lending.[dxciii] It was around this time that European and American bankers began to urge India to diversify its commercial borrowing. Michael von Clemm, Chairman of Credit Suisse First Boston, suggested, whilst on a visit to Bombay, that India could not afford to ignore the Eurobond market. He said that entering the bond market would strengthen India's negotiating position with the banks and "show your face in the market-place and establish your name and creditworthiness should you want to make a big issue, say, ten years from now."[dxciv] Sir Michael Clapham of

Grindlays Bank shared the sentiment. He thought that the Indian economy was remarkably stable, even more stable than the British economy and India was receiving rock bottom rates in international banking circles.[dxcv] Even the United States Treasury Secretary Donald Regan was encouraging India to go to the international commercial markets: "both of these nations (India and China) probably could do a lot more in the public markets than they have, and by public markets I mean in the sense of worldwide markets, private markets. They are credit worthy nations and should be borrowing in the open market."[dxcvi]

India had in fact been borrowing large amounts from international commercial markets in order to fund investment in infrastructure expansion since 1981. These commercial loans were taken by Indian public sector commercial banks for disbursal to Indian businesses and by public sector industrial enterprises for investments in infrastructure development and capacity expansion. A representative of the finance ministry or an economic attaché of the Indian Embassy would be present for the finalisation of contracts in London, Tokyo, Paris or New York. He would sign the documents, providing the Government of India's guarantee for the loan.

The first significant entry into the international money market in 1981 came with the drawing of a $200 million loan for the Oil and Natural Gas Commission and a bigger $680 million dollar loan for the National Aluminium Company.[dxcvii] Other smaller loans were raised, one more by ONGC, another by the Industrial Credit and Investment Corporation of India. In that first year of commercial borrowing India raised more than $1 billion. In 1982 three more large loans were raised; $600 million for the National Thermal Power Corporation, $200 million for Air India, and $110 million for Coal India. Another $1 billion dollars was raised in 1982. Smaller loans were raised by ONGC, ICICI, and the Industrial Development Bank of India. In 1983 the borrowings came to the lower figure of $800 million. ONGC raised $400 million and Vizag Steel $90 million. Smaller loans were raised by the Export Import Bank, ICICI and the Orissa Mining Corporation.

The terms of these commercial loans were considered favourable, partly because of India's good standing in international financial markets. Interest rates were largely dictated by perceptions of country risk. The risk of default by Indian companies, public and private, was considered low. These were commercial loans, and they worked on the simple commercial principle that loan funds needed to be invested and then return a higher rate of profit than the rate of interest before repayments fell due. If the loaned funds were being put to productive and profitable use, then repayment would not be a problem.

As the Government of India was entering the international financial markets to fund its infrastructure expansion programme, two old problems recurred. One of the causes of the foreign exchange crisis of 1981 was the sudden rise in the international price of oil, but another was the continuing poor performance of exporters. Between 1979 and 1985 exports were stagnant.[dxcviii] Exports to developed nations actually fell. Exports of manufactured goods fell until 1982 and the volume of engineering goods exports fell throughout the period. The total earnings from exports also declined because of a decline in international prices. The decline could be attributed to recession conditions in the early 1980s, besides the old structural impediments to exporting from India, including an overpriced rupee. In addition, the Government of India's Budget deficits were rising. After Charan Singh's 1979 Budget, some order was restored in 1980 and 1981 as the government prepared to approach the International Monetary Fund. An announcement that the fertiliser subsidy would be abolished was even made.[dxcix] However, fertilisers were just one among many goods being subsidised by the third and fourth years of the government as pressures from lobby groups and concerns from Congressmen preparing to go the polls caused fiscal discipline to loosen. The fertiliser subsidy, which stood at around ₹600 crore when Indira Gandhi returned to power in 1980, was tripled in 1983 and 1984 to ₹1,800 crore.[dc]

At just the time that oil supplies were being blocked from Assam and the international price of crude oil was surging, the Oil and Natural Gas Commission began the first of a series of discoveries of oil in the fields of Bombay High. Oil had been discovered off the west coast in the 1960s with assistance from a Russian oil exploration team and the first well was sunk in 1974. Oil was struck in April 1980, 120 kilometres south-west of the existing Bombay High oil fields. The new flow of oil was expected to be 17,000 gallons a day.[dci] Oil was struck again in September 1981, 35 kilometres east of Bombay High. The new discovery was even bigger; it would provide for 147,000 gallons a day.[dcii] More oil was found in February 1983 in the Ratnagiri structure of Bombay High. Initially testing estimated a smaller flow of 10,500 gallons a day.[dciii] Oil and gas was also being discovered in the Godavari basin on the Deccan in southern India. In 1982-83 oil production in India surged by 30% from 13.2 million tonnes to 18.2 million tonnes.[dciv] Two-thirds of total production came from Bombay High. Not all of the recently discovered sites had started production and the Oil and Natural Gas Commission's target for 1983-84 was set at 23.3 million tonnes, almost three-quarters of which would come from Bombay High.

The Government of India's experiment with commercial borrowing worked largely due to the miniature oil boom in Bombay High. In 1980 domestic production of oil totalled 10.5 million tonnes, whilst imports totalled 20.6 million tonnes.[dcv] The Government of India thus had to import two-thirds of its annual oil requirement and spend three-quarters of export earnings on oil alone. Both the loan from the International Monetary Fund and commercial loans contracted by the Oil and Natural Gas Commission funded an accelerated programme of extraction from Bombay High. The higher domestic production meant that by 1984 the situation had been reversed as imports of oil had been reduced to 13 million tonnes, or less than one-third of domestic demand, and only one-third of export earnings had to be spent on the import of oil.[dcvi] The Government of India's oil import bill halved during this period, both due to the lower volume of oil imported and lower international oil prices.[dcvii] This was an example of successful import substitution, albeit in a natural resource rather than a manufactured good.

By October of 1984 the Government of India's international finances were in such good order that the Finance Minister, Pranab Mukherjee could announce that the government would forgo the remainder of the International Monetary Fund Extended Fund Facility which was open to it under the terms agreed in 1981. Addressing a chamber of commerce in Bangalore on the 27th he stated, "Our foreign exchange reserves attained an all-time record of over ₹6,200 crore and our credit rating in the international market is among the best."[dcviii] Even after Indira Gandhi was assassinated four days later international bankers retained their confidence in India. A bit of political instability had been factored into Indian lending. Religious rioting was not uncommon in India and the government machinery would soon get things back to normal. "It is business as usual with us."[dcix]

***

When Rajiv Gandhi became prime minister in November 1984 he inherited an economy which had been held together by a surge in the extraction of oil from the fields of Bombay High. Oil was India's biggest recurring foreign exchange expense and the need to import about half the amount of just four years earlier came as a relief to the government treasury. Yet the government continued to maintain large Budget deficits. Most of the government's spending went on just a few items and they were revealing of highly developed flaws in the Indian economy.

The public sector had a problem with capital accumulation. It did not return enough on the investment which the government made each year. In many cases public sector enterprises lost thousands of crores of rupees. The public sector also had difficulty with production. The failure of public sector steel plants to produce enough for India's domestic industrial needs meant that the government had to spend foreign exchange on importing steel. The price for sustaining such a huge public sector and government apparatus also had to be paid; the government had to pay its employees more. And, of course, India is a big country in a dangerous neighbourhood, and so spending on defence kept growing at rapid rates each year. There was also a deficiency in India's food economy. Whilst production of grains had increased, the production of oil seeds and processed edible oil had stagnated. Again, the government was forced to import edible oils each year at great foreign exchange expense. In addition, the government had, since Independence, been subsidising food prices and the expense had only grown with the expansion of the Public Distribution System. Indian farmers had come to expect a subsidy on the price of fertilisers. The government's accumulated budget deficits thus had both a domestic and international component; its expenses were payable in both rupees and dollars.

The new Finance Minister, Vishwanath Pratap Singh, reduced direct taxation substantially in his Union Budget of March 1985. Corporate tax rates were lowered, estate duties were abolished and wealth taxes were drastically cut. Personal tax rates were reduced and the minimum threshold for personal tax was raised. The level of assets needed to bring firms under the scrutiny of the Monopolies and Restrictive Trade Practices Act was raised by five times. There were 25 categories of industry which were delicensed, in addition to bulk drugs and related drug formulations. Even those firms still subject to the monopolies legislation could be exempt from it for licensing purposes in 27 industrial categories. Broadbanding, the use of production facilities for similar products, was allowed in 28 industrial groups. Automatic permission was provided to expand industrial capacity by one-third each year. There were to be no limits on production capacity of non-consumer electronics goods. Liberal permission was provided for imports and foreign technological collaboration. The government began to relax the restrictive trade regime in the first half of 1985 and liberalised the import of capital goods, technology and industrial components. Many categories of industrial machinery were put on the Open General Licence and customs duties were reduced. These customs duties were slashed on capital goods for fertiliser and power projects. A new open door policy was initiated for investments in electronics and liberal imports of computer systems were allowed.

The array of liberal economic measures made a substantial number of Congressmen nervous. On the first day of the All India Congress Committee session in New Delhi in May 1985 Rajiv Gandhi sought to have a resolution passed which stated that "policy instruments relevant at one stage cannot be treated as sacrosanct...nor are they ends in themselves."[dcx] This part of the text did not make it into the resolution passed the following day. Congressmen were fearful that the Party might be drifting towards the Right. In his closing remarks Rajiv thus told committee members that the Congress would not deflect from its chosen path of socialism, "come what may".[dcxi] The single biggest task before the Party was the upliftment of the poor and downtrodden masses.

An attack on the public sector was launched not by Rajiv Gandhi or one of his inner circle but by Vasant Sathe, an old Indira Gandhi loyalist from Maharashtra. He had been appointed energy minister in Rajiv's Cabinet. In October at Pune he spoke before an audience gathered to witness Kirloskar's 10,000th engine being handed over to Coal India Limited. The occasion was symbolic; it marked the transfer of technology from a private Indian engineering company to a large heavy industrial public enterprise. Sathe used the occasion to lash out at the bureaucrats who ran public sector undertakings. He accused them of only being oriented towards the movement of files.[dcxii] He even subjected the Licence Raj to a bit of ridicule. Whilst urging car manufacturers in January 1986 to produce cars at lower prices more suitable to the Indian market he referred indirectly to the Ambassador and the Padmini, the iconic cars of the Indian roads, as "two historical samples".[dcxiii]

In August of 1986 Sathe put his thoughts to paper in a series of three articles for *The Times of India*; "We Can't Go On The Way We Are", "The Millstone of Public Sector", and "What Ought to Be Done". Sathe sought to explain the reasons for the inability to generate productive employment for the majority of the population, the enduring disparities of income and the lack of improvement in living standards. He lamented that economic growth was only confined to a small section of the population, which was symbolised by the skyscrapers and slums of Delhi, Bombay and Calcutta.

Figures of aggregate increases in production were often used to show industrial and agricultural progress, however Sathe wanted to use per capita measures to demonstrate that production in India could not provide for the population. Per capita availability of electricity came to 180 kwh. In developed countries it was 7,000 or even 10,000 kwh. Yet even the figure of 180 kwh was illusory as in rural India the amount was closer to 30 kwh. In India per capita availability of steel was only 18 kg compared to 50 kg in China and over 600 kgs in the industrialised countries. In addition, the production of both steel and electricity was so costly that most of the population could not afford either. Sathe gave the example of the coal industry which had received a hundred fold increase in investment since it was nationalised in 1973. Production had not even doubled. Wages had multiplied by five times, yet the output per manshift in the mines had decreased. In open cast mines it took 600,000 Indian workers to produce less than 30,000 Australian workers could produce. Prices of coal in India did not match the high cost of production which meant that the industry had accumulated losses of ₹1,280 crores since nationalisation. The problem, Sathe maintained, was with the public sector.

Sathe thought that the cause of India's dismal economic performance was "the adoption of a wrong conception of socialism which equates over-employed, top-heavy, inefficient and an unaccountable public sector with socialism." Whilst in socialist countries the public sector was run by an ideologically committed Party, in India it had been left to an ideologically indifferent civil service which was not held accountable for performance and results. In addition, most of the public sector enterprises were made monopolies, shielding them from the basic element of efficiency, competition. Continuity of management was not allowed at the top. Investment in the public sector had fuelled the rise of a nouveau riche class of contractors whose income evaded assessment and formed a huge pool of unaccounted for money. A small segment of the population attained affluence and all production was catered to its needs. What was needed was competition and access to technology from whichever part of the world it came from. Indian production had to become internationally competitive, only then would exports become possible. The solution was to produce more, particularly consumer goods, and augment the purchasing power of rural Indians.

Whilst addressing a meeting of the Congress's parliamentary executive at the end of August Rajiv Gandhi assured parliamentarians that Vasant Sathe's views were his own and did not reflect those of the government.[dcxiv] In affirming the government's commitment to the public sector Rajiv emphasised that it was necessary for public sector enterprises to work efficiently and for public money invested not to go down the drain. The success of the Seventh Five Year Plan would depend on the efficient and satisfactory performance of the public sector.

The public sector's failing was most evident in the steel industry. During the Sixth Plan period, starting in 1980, ₹2,500 crores had been spent on public sector steel plants yet they were unable to produce an extra ingot of steel.[dcxv] The additional capacity created during the period was short of the target by 25% and utilisation was still lower. During 1984 the aggregate production of the five public sector steel plants was less than it had been in 1980. A large increase in the price of steel had converted Steel Authority of India Limited losses into a small profit, but this was still supported by subsidies and explicit write offs. The price of Indian steel was almost double that of German steel. SAIL's production difficulties were attributed to overstaffing, poor labour morale, inter-union rivalries, low labour productivity and technological obsolescence. In the Bhilai steel plant in Madhya Pradesh 33,000 workers had another 30,000 who administered and serviced them. The Bhilai workforce had 25 labour unions. The result was that in 1985 the Government of India had to import 1.5 million tonnes of steel at a cost in foreign exchange of ₹700 crores.

In July 1986 the Fourth Pay Commission recommended increases in pay and allowances for the Government of India's 5.2 million employees.[dcxvi] The Commission recommended an increase of 20% in basic pay, in addition to an improved dearness allowance formula, an increased city compensatory allowance and a more liberal house rent allowance. Dearness allowance, which was compensation for inflation, would be paid twice a year. It had been 13 years since the last pay revision, so when the new pay scales came into force in October the more than 20 million strong community of Central government employees and their families received some relief. The Commission estimated that its recommendations would cost the government an extra ₹1,925 crores a year. In addition, when the Commission submitted the second part of its report on pensions in December, it recommended a similar increase for pensions and a dearness allowance paid twice a year. The pension recommendations would cost the government an extra ₹300 crore a year.

In December of 1986 V.P. Singh, who had been appointed defence minister, announced that the defence budget was likely to be increased by 36% to almost ₹12,000 crores. He said, "I need not elaborate on the compulsions of the geopolitical climate which has made the increase in defence expenditure."[dcxvii] India's defence expenditure as a percentage of Gross National Product increased by 1.5% in just one year to 6%. It appeared that the Government of India was not just spending on defence of India's international borders, but to put down an insurgency in Punjab. In Parliament in March 1987, Rajiv Gandhi rejected calls to cut down on defence spending yet agreed that it should be "streamlined".[dcxviii] He did not rule out more spending on defence but claimed that it would not make any supplementary budgetary demands. Those calling for defence cuts were "anti-national, sabotaging this country's interests."

Indian troops were sent to Sri Lanka as the Indian Peacekeeping Force in July. Initially consisting of a 10,000 strong force of the 54th Infantry Division, the IPKF was supposed to keep the peace between government forces and separatists which had emerged from the Indo-Sri Lankan Peace Accord. The costs of the peacekeeping operation were hidden under pension provisions in the annual defence budget. There were skirmishes with Pakistani forces in Siachen and build-ups on the borders with both Pakistan and China throughout the year. It was defence spending which also initiated Rajiv Gandhi's political demise. The Bofors arms deal scandal dominated the Indian media throughout 1987. The prime minister appeared to have received kickbacks on a major defence deal. His Defence Minister, V.P. Singh, resigned from the government.

The monsoon rains of 1987 were 20% below the average level. The worst drought of the century ensued. Almost two-thirds of crop lands were affected and the livelihoods of 80 million farmers and their families were ruined. Even prior to the drought the food subsidy cost the government ₹2,132 crores.[dcxix] That record high figure was expected to rise with the increase in offtake of grains from the Public Distribution System and provisions for drought relief programmes. The offtake of grains had grown by 20% in the first eight months of 1987 and more grains were being disposed of at concessional prices. The food subsidy consisted of the money provided by the Government of India to its Food Corporation of India. The amount had been rising steadily from ₹1,352 crore in 1984. The Food Corporation had received a soft loan of ₹1,200 crores simply to pay the interest on its loans. Paying the interest on the Food Corporation's borrowing, ₹300 crore in 1986, had become a part of the food subsidy.

Imports of edible oils began in 1976, primarily to meet the requirements of the vanaspati oil industry. Imports rose to almost 1 million tonnes in 1981, to 1.6 million tonnes in 1983, and had settled at 1.2 million tonnes by 1987.[dcxx] The demand for edible oils had been growing both due to a fast rise in the population, and a slower rise in living standards, yet production had stagnated at around 3 million tonnes a year. The average amount spent in foreign exchange each year on edible oil imports totalled over ₹700 crore. In 1988 imports reached a record high of 1.8 million tonnes, costing ₹1,000 crores.[dcxxi] One-third of the imported edible oil was allocated to the vanaspati industry and two-thirds to the state governments for sale through the Public Distribution System. Both the vanaspati industry and the Public

Distribution System were receiving imported edible oils at subsidised rates. Part of the problem of production of edible oils in India was that oilseeds were a rainfed rather than an irrigated crop. Indian scientists had developed improved oilseeds, yet they were only suitable for cultivation under ideal, irrigated conditions. Most farmers, particularly in western India, grew their oil seeds under dry conditions.

At the beginning of 1986 the Government of India raised the price of fertiliser in keeping with rises in the prices of other publicly subsidised goods. The amount spent on the fertiliser subsidy had reached ₹2,000 crore. The price rises were expected to reduce the total subsidy bill by ₹400 crores.[dcxxii] The fertiliser subsidy benefitted a specific segment of India's agricultural sector. One-quarter of the country's districts accounted for three-quarters of total fertiliser consumption.[dcxxiii] These districts were mainly in Punjab and Haryana in the north, and Andhra Pradesh and Tamil Nadu in the south. Domestic fertiliser production had, until 1980, been slow and the Government of India had to rely to a greater extent on imports. However, during the early 1980s domestic production of fertiliser increased. But then demand began to stagnate. Successive poor monsoons meant that farmers required fewer fertilisers and stock began to pile up. The stockpile had reached 3.51 million tonnes by the middle of 1986.[dcxxiv] It might have seemed that imports could be curtailed, yet whilst India had an abundant supply of some types of fertiliser, there were other types which it did not yet produce. Around 30% of India's annual fertiliser requirement still had to be imported as no Indian producer could yet produce potash fertiliser.

One of the main constraints on fertiliser production in India was frequent electricity cuts, which meant that fertiliser plants could only produce at around 80% of their capacity.[dcxxv] By 1988 the imported component of the huge fertiliser subsidy was relatively small- ₹119 crore.[dcxxvi] It was the use of domestic fertilisers which was being subsidised, costing a total of ₹2750 crore. Much as he had professed support for the public sector whilst noting that it had to perform, Rajiv Gandhi stated his commitment to subsidies for farmers, and the fertiliser subsidy specifically, whilst noting the mounting costs to the government treasury. In February 1988 at a meeting of the Bharat Krishak Samaj, or India Farmers' Society, he assured farmers that the government would continue to provide them subsidies. Yet he urged them to ask the question- "Should there not be a proper balance maintained between subsidies and prices?"[dcxxvii]

Whilst V.P. Singh had been appointed defence minister at the end of 1986, Rajiv Gandhi had not yet appointed a new finance minister. He thus presented the Union Budget in February 1987. The Budget deficit was predicted to be ₹5,608 crores.[dcxxviii] The deficit of the previous year was triple that which had been estimated, coming to ₹8,285 crores. The figure might have been even higher had the government not drawn close to ₹3,000 crores from its oil and gas corporations' surpluses. The interest the government had to pay on its loans had increased by 10% to almost ₹10,000 crores. The prime minister's political capital, which had seemed abundant in 1985, had been rapidly diminishing. Amongst the numerous revolts, insurgencies and rebellions that he had to deal with, perhaps the most menacing for his potential electoral fortunes were farmers agitations led by Sharad Joshi in Maharashtra and Mahendra Singh Tikait in Uttar Pradesh.

When Rajiv Gandhi presented the Union Budget for 1987 he included a record allocation for rural development schemes of ₹2,050 crores.[dcxxix] This was an increase of ₹200 crore over the previous year. The National Rural Employment Programme received ₹480 crores and the Rural Landless Employment Guarantee Programme received ₹725 crores. Both schemes aimed to provide a guarantee of 100 days of employment in a year to one member of every rural family. The Government of India was providing allocations from its surplus stock of wheat to the states in order to encourage them to expand these schemes. Similarly the drought prone areas programme received ₹47 crores, the desert development programme ₹39 crores, ₹125 crores was earmarked for the Indira Awas Yojana, or Indira Housing Scheme, which would provide housing for scheduled caste and schedule tribe rural families, and the Integrated Rural Development Programme received ₹310 crores. Rajiv declared that agriculture was the "bedrock of the economy" and that growth in the sector was crucial to the removal of poverty.

By May of 1987 the Planning Commission thought it necessary to put together a Budget deficit control plan for the ensuing two years. In January of 1988 Rajiv repeated the call for greater fiscal discipline. At a breakfast meeting of economists in New Delhi he urged them to "define the country's minimum acceptable development needs and find ways and means of achieving them."[dcxxx]

When the new Finance Minister, Narayan Dutt Tiwari presented the Union Budget in February he estimated a total Budget deficit of ₹7,484 crore.[dcxxxi] As Tiwari delivered his Budget speech he told the Lok Sabha: "our socialism is our own. It is not a foreign transplant." The provisions for spending in rural India continued from the previous year. The 1988 Budget included a 40% increase in outlays on agriculture and irrigation, more credit for farmers at low interest rates and cheaper fertilisers and pesticides.[dcxxxii] A Jaldhara scheme to help marginal farmers in drought prone areas to acquire pump sets at nominal rates, a Kutir Jyoti scheme for electric light connections, a village population improvement programme, a programme for digging a million wells through the employment generation schemes and a national agriculture relief fund were all announced. Public sector banks were directed to lend 17% of their total advances to the agriculture sector. Farmers would also get a 7.5% discount on the already subsidised price of fertiliser.

Rajiv Gandhi went to Faizpur in Uttar Pradesh on 11 March 1988 where his grandfather, Jawaharlal Nehru had tried to introduce the idea of economic planning to the Congress in December 1936. Nehru had spoken of "a great planned system for the whole land and dealing with all these various national activities". Rajiv used the occasion to tell his audience of all the steps that his government was taking to assist farmers.[dcxxxiii] In New Delhi, finance ministry officials were hopeful that a good monsoon would wash the Budget deficit away. When asked what might happen if the monsoon failed again the Finance Secretary, S. Venkitaramanan replied, "We have contingency plans and we shall see."[dcxxxiv]

***

During the first months of 1988 it became evident that the Government of India was facing both an incipient debt crisis and diminishing reserves of foreign exchange. An increasing proportion of new debt, mainly contracted within India from captive public sector banks, was being used to pay interest on the government's existing debts. The total interest bill on government debt had risen from ₹2,604 crores in 1980 to ₹14,100 crores in 1988.[dcxxxv] During April, May and June of 1988 foreign exchange reserves declined by ₹1,905 crores, or over 25%.[dcxxxvi] Most of the rapid depletion of reserves was caused by repayments for the loan taken from the International Monetary Fund in 1981 which had fallen due. During April and May the Government of India repaid $140 million of the $3.9 billion it had borrowed earlier in the decade. A repayment of $665 million was scheduled for later in the year. Another $105 million had to be repaid for a slightly earlier drawing from the IMF trust fund in 1980.

What brought a simple government debt trap and a foreign exchange crisis together was the Government of India's decision to borrow in international commercial markets, not to finance infrastructure projects as it had done earlier, but to finance its current spending. In addition, almost all of the government's foreign exchange reserves were made up of funds which Non-resident Indians had deposited in special foreign currency non-resident accounts. This was considered "hot money" as it could be withdrawn at short notice. The inflow had been primarily into U.S. dollar accounts and had coincided with a recession in the American economy. It was suspected that given that the foreign currency non-resident accounts were earning interest higher than international rates, they were being used to contract further borrowing abroad. However, the American dollar had started appreciating and it was anticipated that American interest rates would also rise. The concern was that these dollar deposits might find higher earning prospects elsewhere. Thus, the government was replicating the strategy of the last foreign exchange crisis, in a more precarious economic environment. The government was once again seeking more commercial loans abroad and also inducing expatriate Indians to deposit their earnings in India, rather than restricting imports and seeking concessional aid from foreign governments. Yet by September of 1988 talk of an approach to the International Monetary Fund had already begun in New Delhi. The irony was that foreign exchange reserves had diminished due to the start of repayments of the last loan from the IMF.

Shankarrao Bhavrao Chavan replaced Narayan Dutt Tiwari as finance minister. He had the task of presenting his government's last Budget before an election in February 1989. Chavan was thought to have struck a fine balance in maintaining the government's spending on rural schemes and subsidies and controlling the ever rising Budget deficit. Although not quite as forceful, his technique was similar to Charan Singh's in 1979; he would tax the rich and middle class through excise duties on consumer goods and luxuries in order to fund spending in rural India. An income tax surcharge of 8% was placed on incomes above ₹50,000.[dcxxxvii] There were new taxes on foreign and domestic air travel, automobiles, televisions, motorcycles and scooters. Chavan maintained rural spending, whilst announcing a new employment guarantee scheme bearing Jawaharlal Nehru's name. He could thus announce a Budget deficit of ₹7,337 crores, some 5% lower than in 1988.

The first negotiations for a loan from the International Monetary Fund began in earnest shortly after the 1989 Budget. Both the outgoing finance secretary S. Vekitaramanan and his replacement Gopi Arora travelled to Washington to discuss a loan of between $3 billion and $5 billion.[dcxxxviii] Foreign exchange reserves had been depleted to the point that they could only pay two and a half months' worth of imports. However, just weeks later S.B. Chavan ruled out the prospect of an IMF loan for the coming financial year. Hinting that the conditions imposed had been too harsh, he stated "As for the next year. We will see the conditions."[dcxxxix] Gopi Arora travelled to Paris in June to seek more assistance from the Consortium and managed to confirm commitments for an extra $400 million.[dcxl]

When Indira Gandhi was assassinated in October 1984 the serving Finance Minister, Pranab Mukherjee was thought to have been too presumptuous in making a bid for the prime minister's post. When Rajiv Gandhi became prime minister he eased Mukherjee out of the Cabinet and promoted V.P. Singh to the finance minister's post. V.P. Singh was a Rajput who had been adopted by the Raja of Manda. He became the Raja of the feudal estate, near Allahabad, as a child prior to Independence. He was elected to the Uttar Pradesh Assembly in 1969 on a Congress ticket and became chief minister of the state in 1980. However, he tendered his resignation after his failure to control the state's dacoits, or bandits. He was then inducted into the Union Cabinet as commerce minister in 1983. With the change of leadership and a new portfolio he found himself in charge of an increasingly liberalising economy.

It was generally thought that Rajiv and his inner circle of advisers were behind the moves to minimise licensing, ease import restrictions, reduce the scope of monopolies legislation and lower taxes. Yet it would be V.P. Singh who would be credited or blamed for the success or failure of these policies. He was both an old time Raja and an old time Congressman and so he was not about to be cast as a friend of India's wealthiest industrialists or become a patron of the unbridled consumerism of the middle class. Rajiv and his coterie had reduced taxes in the conventional classical belief that economic activity would accelerate and simplification of the tax code would encourage tax compliance rather than avoidance. In the end the government would collect more tax. Yet V.P. Singh interpreted the new tax policy in his own way. He thought that the key to raising more tax, given the simplified and lowered taxes, was to enforce the tax code more rigorously. Thus, during 1985 and 1986 he was associated in the public mind not with a liberalising economy, but with a series of tax raids against India's wealthiest people. He enjoyed making aggressive statements against India's monied men. At the All India Congress Committee session in May 1985 he even stated that the only places for black money hoarders and tax evaders were jail or the Arabian Sea.[dcxli] Yet he eventually breached the rules of engagement between India's political and economic elites. He was eased out of the finance ministry and given the defence portfolio.

V.P. Singh was as much of a "Mr. Clean" as Rajiv Gandhi was. Initially they made a formidable team. Yet once the Bofors arms scandal broke in the early months of 1987 he resigned rather than have his own name tainted. He was thus in a perfect position to launch a revolt against the government on the issue of corruption. He gathered together the surviving members of the old Janata Party and formed a new Janata Dal. Much of his rhetoric was reminiscent of Jayaprakash Narayan's campaign against Indira Gandhi. The Janata politicians focused on the corruption of the Congress, now represented in the person of the prime minister. In addition, farmers movements in the states had been agitating for the waiving of loans. The Bharatiya Janata Party took up the demand in New Delhi in March.[dcxlii] In May the Janata Dal promised to write off loans of up to ₹10,000 to small farmers, artisans and agricultural labourers.[dcxliii] It was estimated that fulfilling the promise would oblige the Government of India to transfer ₹14,000 crores to its own nationalised banks, which ran on very slim margins in the first place.[dcxliv]

The Janata Dal came to power at the end of 1989. Yet it did so in a much less emphatic manner than the Janata Party did in 1977. V.P. Singh's government had to rely on outside support from both the Hindu nationalist Bharatiya Janata Party and the Communist Left Front. The new Finance Minister, Madhu Dandavate presented his Union Budget in March and fulfilled the promise to waive loans to small farmers, labourers and artisans. The Budget deficit was expected to be reduced by 20%.[dcxlv] This seemed like a remarkable figure. Yet given that the deficit had risen to a high of ₹14,000 the previous year this still left a staggeringly large figure of ₹9,165 crores. Dandavate had followed the same approach as his predecessor S.B. Chavan who sought to maintain agricultural spending and as many subsidies as possible by increasing taxes on the rich and middle class. Dandavate also increased taxes on refrigerators, cars, washing machines, video cassette recorders and chocolates. However, the sizable increases in revenue would come from taxes on iron, steel, cigarettes, import duties, and, most significantly, crude oil, petrol and diesel. The price of petrol at the pump immediately rose by as much as 40% across the country.[dcxlvi]

Almost as old as the food subsidy was the Government of India's export subsidy. The government had been subsidising exports for almost 30 years, since the early 1960s, and the expense formed a relatively small but significant part of the Budget deficit. There was a slight increase in the level of the export subsidy during Rajiv Gandhi's government. More imports were made available to exporters through replenishment licences, first half and then all of business profits made through exports were made tax deductible, and the interest rate on export credit was reduced. Exporters were given easier access to imports of capital goods by removing selected goods from licensing requirements and abolishing duties. The policies had their intended effect, and when combined with a depreciation in the real rate of exchange of the rupee Indian exports started to surge. Yet, in the closing months of Rajiv's government it had become evident that this was not enough. The trade deficit remained, and it had only grown. Although exports had grown by 28% in 1988, imports had grown by the same amount.[dcxlvii]

At the same time that Government of India had been encouraging exporters it had also been liberalising imports. The two policies were part of a strategy. It was thought that easier access to imported components would make Indian exporters more competitive. Yet a significant share of imports was diverted to what came to be known as the "kit culture". Indian manufacturers of consumer goods, particularly televisions and automobiles, were importing components, principally from Japan, and using them to assemble goods according to kit specifications for the domestic market in India. The media singled out the assembly of colour televisions for sale under Indian brand names as an example, but these television component imports only amounted to ₹275 crores each year.[dcxlviii] The state owned Maruti car company, which had partnered with the Japanese company Suzuki to make the Indian people's car was, with other light commercial vehicle producers, importing ₹8,000 crores worth of auto components each year.[dcxlix]

Given that the Government of India's problems of mounting debts and depleting foreign exchange reserves were evident as early as the first months of 1988, what allowed the economic catastrophe to play out in slow motion was that international oil prices remained relatively low. By late 1988 the Government of India was importing 22 million tonnes of oil a year.[dcl] In 1984 the government imported 10 million tonnes or 33% of domestic demand. The figure had risen closer to 50%. Oil had started to flow from the Cauvery basin and whilst it was of higher quality than Bombay High oil, it was also more difficult to extract, and overall national production had stagnated. Yet in 1988 and 1989, just as the government's finances were faltering the price of oil halved from around $20 a barrel to $10. At this time the greatest pressure on foreign exchange reserves came from repayments to the International Monetary Fund for the 1981 loan. What speeded the economic crisis up was Iraq's invasion of Kuwait in August 1990. The Organization of the Petroleum Exporting Countries had already increased the price to $21 a barrel and it was expected to rise above $30.[dcli] This sudden rise in the price of oil changed the nature of the Government of India's ongoing negotiations with the IMF. The Fund now had to make arrangements for all oil importing developing nations which were being adversely affected by events in the Middle East.

International banks had always been confident of the Government of India's creditworthiness. However, by the start of 1990 foreign bankers had started to make their own discreet enquiries about the soundness of the new National Front government.[dclii] In April each year world financing bodies assessed the economic order of nations and ratings agencies assessed the credit rating of those intending to raise money in international capital markets. India had been trying to get concessional lending from the Asian Development Bank but had been unsuccessful, and there was a limit to lending from the World Bank. Some of the conflicting statements from National Front ministers had confused international bankers. They wanted reassurance and clarity from the Finance Minister, Madhu Dandavate.

It was in October that Moody's Investor Service downgraded both India's long-term and short-term credit rating.[dcliii] This would make borrowing more expensive. India's new long term credit rating of Baa-1 was the second lowest rating which still allowed for borrowing. Moody's justified the downgrade citing India's rising debt over the previous years. India's export capacity was not high enough to meet its foreign exchange obligations, debt was more expensive and so the debt service burden was higher. A large current account deficit prevailed with a high rate of inflation and the credit agency did not have confidence that the National Front government would be able to reduce the Budget deficit. Moody's cited India's "fractious domestic political conditions" which made it difficult for the government to reduce its spending. It also cited "deepening political and social rifts" in Indian society. The Moody's downgrade only heightened fears among expatriate Indians about the safety of their deposits in the country. Some of the hot money had already started to be withdrawn which exacerbated the foreign exchange difficulties.

In a measure of how desperate the situation had become, in the same month as the ratings downgrade from Moody's, the Reserve Bank of India decided to revalue its gold in order to boost India's foreign exchange reserves. The revaluation was a dramatic one- from ₹84 for 10 grams to ₹1,992.[dcliv] The Reserve Bank wanted to present a better picture of the country's foreign exchange reserves before a likely approach to the International Monetary Fund. Overnight it seemed that the Government of India had become richer by ₹6,342 crores. The valuation of the Bank's gold reserves had not changed since 1969. The step had not been taken earlier due to a convention of national accounting which would have classified the increase as a form of deficit financing. With bigger foreign exchange reserves India would be better placed to meet some of the conditions placed on an IMF loan.

Whilst the Government of India had been in negotiations for a loan with the International Monetary Fund for over a year, the situation became more urgent with the surge in oil prices after August 1990. India was joined by other developing nations in persuading the Fund to allow for borrowing from its Compensatory and Contingency Financing Facility. Provision had not been made for borrowing from the Facility to meet foreign exchange obligations for the purchase of oil. The Fund agreed and the Government of India began a new line of negotiations to avail of an emergency loan.[dclv] By December the figure expected to be drawn from the Contingency Fund was $500 million, and the amount to be drawn in the form of standby credit was expected to be $1.2 billion.[dclvi] With international commercial lenders closing their books to the government, the Fund was the lender of last resort. The only alternative was a larger $4-5 billion loan for structural adjustment. The total amounts agreed on between the Government of India and the International Monetary Fund in January 1991 came to just over $1 billion from the Compensatory and Contingency Financing Facility and $770 million in standby credit.[dclvii] The standby credit would be available within two weeks.

Given that just a few months earlier the Compensatory and Contingency Financing Facility had not allowed for borrowing to pay for oil bills the new lines of credit were considered a great triumph for the Government of India. It was only when news of American military aircraft refuelling at Indian airports broke at the end of January that some began to make a connection. The first to do so were India's Unionists. The Indian Federation of Trade Unions asked on 30 January whether there might be any connection between the recent arrival of American aircraft and the $1.8 billion IMF loan.[dclviii] By 3 February both the Communist parties and the Congress were calling for an emergency session of Parliament to discuss the matter. The government claimed that the refuelling was just a result of good relations between India and the United

States and that the decision to allow it had been taken earlier by V.P. Singh's government.[dclix] His government had fallen in November after the Bharatiya Janata Party withdrew support over his decision to arrest its leaders who were campaigning for the construction of a Ram temple in Ayodhya. On 18 February when asked about the refuelling of American military aircraft at Indian airports the new Prime Minister, Chandra Shekhar said "Bandh kar di gayi nahin, Bandh ho gaya." "It has not *been* stopped. But it has stopped."[dclx]

The end, when it eventually came, was swift, and not as difficult as had been imagined. Chandra Shekhar had relied on outside support for his government from Rajiv Gandhi's Congress Party. Rajiv withdrew support in March prompting a national election. The Finance Minister, Yashwant Sinha was thus unable to present a Union Budget. He had already started restricting imports. Non-resident Indians began withdrawing their dollar deposits from Indian banks. Rajiv was assassinated on the campaign trail in Tamil Nadu in May. The Congress was returned to power. P.V. Narasimha Rao, a former chief minister of Andhra Pradesh and veteran of the Union Cabinet was sworn in as prime minister on 21 June 1991.

Narasimha Rao had been handed a file by the Cabinet Secretary, Naresh Chandra on the 19th detailing the parlous state of the economy and the steps needed for reform. Such plans for reform had been circulating, or gathering dust, in the bureaucracy for many years. Ajit Singh, Charan Singh's son, who was industry minister in V.P. Singh's government sought a report on reform of industrial policy from Amar Nath Verma, the industry secretary and Rakesh Mohan, the economic adviser to the ministry upon assuming office.[dclxi] A draft of their report, which provided a framework for the dismantling of the Licence Raj was released on 1 June 1990. No action was taken within the Government of India yet Gopi Arora, the previous finance secretary who had been sent to Washington as an executive director of the International

Monetary Fund, used some initiative and presented the report to the Fund on 13 June as a token of India's willingness to reform.[dclxii] In fact, the bureaucracy, and Gopi Arora in particular, had kept the International Monetary Fund believing that reform of the Indian economy was imminent for over a year. With a new prime minister commanding a workable majority in Parliament it had become possible.

Narasimha Rao did not object to Naresh Chandra's file. He accepted his cabinet secretary's assessment and began to assemble a team which would be able to implement wide ranging reform of the Indian economy. It was not accidental that the finance minister would not be a politician. Rao's first choice for the job was Indraprasad Gordhanbhai Patel, a veteran of the economic bureaucracy who had most recently served as Director of the London School of Economics. I.G. seemed an ideal candidate; he had called for a "bonfire of controls" in a lecture in London in 1986.[dclxiii] Yet he declined the offer. He later claimed that he was keen to live a quiet life in Baroda and not be "seduced" back to Delhi.[dclxiv] The duty fell to Manmohan Singh, a slightly younger but vastly experienced scholar and bureaucrat who had served as Finance Secretary, Deputy Chairman of the Planning Commission and Governor of the Reserve Bank. An economist was required not just for his technical grasp of the complex economic issues which would have to be dealt with over the ensuing months, but because it would be unlikely that any Congressman would be fully committed to the dismantling of Jawaharlal Nehru's planned economy. P. Chidambaram, a young minister from Tamil Nadu, known for his enthusiasm for reform, was appointed minister of state for commerce. Rao had kept the commerce and industry portfolio for himself. He then appointed Amar Nath Verma as his principal secretary and instructed him to work with Rakesh Mohan to create another presentation for reform of the industrial economy.[dclxv] Naresh Chandra continued as cabinet secretary as did Montek Singh Ahluwalia, also known for his support for reform, as commerce secretary. Another young liberaliser, Jairam Ramesh was inducted as officer on special duty.

P.V. Narasimha Rao's team of politicians and bureaucrats set about satisfying the likely conditions for a large loan from the International Monetary Fund, before the Fund could impose them. On 1 July the exchange rate of the rupee against major currencies was devalued by 7-9%.[dclxvi] This initial devaluation had little economic effect, only serving to stir political opposition from the Communist Parties and the Bharatiya Janata Party. Another slightly larger devaluation took place of 3 July bringing the total devaluation of the rupee to 20% in two days.[dclxvii] A cheaper rupee meant that Indian exports would become more competitive, making one of the export subsidies, the Cash Compensatory Scheme redundant. Manmohan Singh directed P. Chidambaram, through Montek Singh Ahluwalia, to abolish the Scheme.[dclxviii]

News had broken on 7 July in *The Indian Express* of a consignment of 47 tonnes of gold which the Reserve Bank of India was sending to the Bank of England as security for the advance of $400 million to pay for essential imports.[dclxix] The Bank had earlier arranged the sale of gold confiscated from smugglers in May, something which had been reported in the press. Yet this latest consignment was not seized gold, but the nation's own treasure. Narasimha Rao was not too worried.[dclxx] He thought that Indians' sympathies would always be with the debtor rather than the creditor. The British would remain the villains. On the same day Rakesh Mohan's old draft for industry policy reform was ready for presentation in a new form. It recommended the abolition of all industrial licences barring a small negative list.[dclxxi] The prime minister leaked the document to the press himself.[dclxxii] On 12 July, Kalyani Shankar published a story in *The Hindustan Times* titled "Industrial Licensing to Go". The note on industrial policy was presented to

Cabinet on 15 July 1991. The policy faced some opposition from Congress veterans Arjun Singh and Makhan Lal Fotedar, yet it was sent back to be recast, rather than reworked. Jairam Ramesh added a preamble honouring the foundational ideas of Jawaharlal Nehru and Indira Gandhi and the Cabinet accepted the note on 23 July.[dclxxiii] Rao tried to convince his fellow Congressmen that he was simply returning to Jawaharlal Nehru's original vision which had been obscured by Indira Gandhi's move to the Left after 1969.[dclxxiv]

The Union Budget was to be presented on 24 July, yet before Manmohan Singh rose to speak, Narasimha Rao, in his capacity as commerce and industry minister had Pallath Joseph Kurien, his minister of state for industry announce the tabling of the new Industrial Policy. The Policy began with the statement: "Industrial licensing will henceforth be abolished for all industries, except those specified, irrespective of levels of investment."[dclxxv] When Manmohan Singh rose to present the Union Budget he began the overhaul of India's trading economy, doing away with import licences, announcing measures for export promotion and reducing tariffs. Capital markets were liberalised and subsidies were reduced on fertilisers, cooking gas and sugar. A $220 million loan had been received from the International Monetary Fund two days earlier. More loans would be arranged in September and November, and January, February and March of 1992.

***

The origins of the economic crisis of 1991 can be traced to 1979 and the demands made on the government treasury by newly assertive interest groups. The biggest interest group of all was that of farmers. Although he projected a rustic image, Charan Singh, the finance minister in 1979, was a man of letters. He had written extensively on the structural problems of the Indian economy, particularly the bias against agriculture and the favour shown to heavy industry and he had his own well developed prognosis for what should be done. He wrote *Joint Farming X-Rayed* in 1959 and *India's Poverty and Its Solution* in 1964. When he published *India's Economic Policy: The Gandhian Blueprint* in 1978 upon coming to power in New Delhi his opinions had changed so little that he could reproduce some passages verbatim from his earlier works. Unusually for a leader of farmers, he thought that there should be fewer farmers. His basic thesis, which he presented to his audience at the farmers' rally in December 1978, was that people should be brought off the land and into small-scale and light industries. In addition, his long held position was that the state should not procure agricultural products. He did not think that the state had the capacity for it, the Indian economy could not afford it, besides which it would be just a step away from Communism. Initially, he was also opposed to the use of chemical fertilisers for the damage that they did to the soil. At most he wanted the government to invest in agricultural infrastructure, particularly irrigation and soil conservation projects and village works. So when Charan Singh delivered a Budget full of largesse for farmers, and increased procurement prices and fertiliser subsidies, it was, in his last days, a negation of almost everything he had stood for throughout his political career. Nonetheless, it was a demonstration to the Indian people of what was possible, and what they should now expect from their politicians in New Delhi.

Related to the expectation of largesse, but slightly apart from it, was a general yearning among the Indian people for prosperity rather than austerity. Indira Gandhi campaigned as the law and order candidate in 1980 and she also sensed that the electorate wanted jobs, consumer goods and more production rather than the customary controls and restrictions on economic life. She clearly aligned herself with big industrial production, whether in the public sector or private industry, in contrast to the Janata leaders' preference for small-scale and rural industries. When she resumed economic planning with the publication of the Sixth Five Year Plan it became clear that, even facing a foreign exchange crisis, her government would not resort to the traditional policy response and restrict imports. Aid flows from the West were decreasing and so the government took to borrowing, both within India, and in international markets, to drive industrial production and infrastructure development. Indira's last government was relatively economically successful because of the fortuitous discoveries of oil at Bombay High. Yet the lesson of Charan Singh's Budget had been learnt by Congressmen. After some relatively restrained Budgets in 1980 and 1981, Budget deficits, driven by spending on subsidies, particularly the fertiliser subsidy, actually grew in 1982, 1983 and 1984. A pattern was established, replicated when Rajiv Gandhi became prime minister. A strong government with a comfortable parliamentary majority would take brave economic policy decisions in its first two years, and then with waning political capital, Congressmen would become nervous and government spending would once again begin to surge, resulting in soaring Budget deficits in the final three years of the government as elections drew near.

The economic crisis of 1991 bore some of the hallmarks of the crises of 1957 and 1980. Just as in 1957 a depletion of foreign exchange reserves was driven by higher volumes of imports combined with relatively slow growth of exports. And just as in 1980 the price of oil spiked, causing a further depletion of reserves. Yet the new element of 1991 was that debt contracted in international markets was being used to pay for current spending rather than infrastructure development. This debt would be repayable in foreign currency, and so a debt crisis morphed into an enlarged and more complex foreign exchange crisis. From 1980 a structurally flawed economy had been artificially stimulated with credit. The structural flaws of the economy constrained production. Indian farmers could not grow enough edible oil. Public sector plants could not produce enough steel. The production of oil for petroleum had slowed. In addition, Indian exporters could not produce goods which could compete in international markets which meant that they too had to be subsidised. When the supply of imports was liberalised it satiated the hunger for consumer goods in India rather than the needs of manufacturers for components for finished goods which could be exported. Rather than undertaking the restructuring required to allow for increased production and greater competitiveness, the government continued to pay the bill in subsidies and write-offs of public sector losses.

Prime Minister P.V. Narasimha Rao accepted the file presented to him by his cabinet secretary. He could have reformed as little as possible, as previous prime ministers had done, and scrounged together enough money to keep the economy solvent and avoid disturbing the economic structure which the Congress Party had built over four decades. Reform might have had to wait for the next economic crisis, which going by the established pattern, would have been due in 1997 or 1998. Yet Narasimha Rao understood how difficult a task that too would have been. Negotiations had been continuing with the International Monetary Fund for over two years by the time he came to power. The Indian concern had always been for the conditions which the Fund might impose on a large loan. When the Gulf War started and the price of oil rose, the Government of India was no longer alone. In addition to its pre-existing economic ailment, India was now among a group of developing oil importing countries which could together approach the Fund for assistance. When assistance was provided in January 1991 it was much larger and more liberal than expected. Just as opposition politicians suspected, the conditions attached to the IMF loan were not economic. Due to the turn of events in Iraq and Kuwait the United States was content to impose military rather than economic conditions. American military aircrafts were allowed refuelling rights at Indian airports, bringing to an end a zealously guarded policy of Non-alignment in international relations. Yet with operations in Iraq coming to an end in February 1991, the United States rekindled its long held desire for the liberalisation of the Indian economy. The Cold War had ended, the Soviet Union and its satellite states had revolted against Communism, and so maintaining equidistance between two great powers and receiving favours from both was no longer possible. Narasimha Rao recognised that that the United States and the International Monetary Fund were the only credible lenders. As Manmohan Singh told reporters upon being appointed finance minister:

> *The world has also changed a great deal in the past few years, with several countries smaller than India and with a much lower resource base going far ahead. We cannot therefore be satisfied with the status quo. We have to take a major jump forward to become an advanced economy taking full advantage of modern science and technology.*[dclxxvi]

Afterword

The laws of economics are not as certain as the laws of physics, but they do come close. When Mahadev Ranade argued against the application of the principles of classical economics in India at the Deccan College, Poona in 1892 it is unlikely that he would have anticipated what was to come. His rejection of classical economics had only led him as far as advocating some state intervention in the economy, primarily the building of infrastructure and the provision of credit to private enterprises on easier terms. His vision was similar to that of his fellow Marathi economic thinkers; he saw the Indian economy being driven by abundant labour applied to modern manufacturing. Nonetheless, the idea that India stood apart, that its situation was unique and that the economic policies which had led to prosperity in the West could not be applied came to be universally held by the Indian elite in the first decades of the 20th century. Mohandas Gandhi thought that the laws of economics were not divinely given and the economic policies which had worked for Britain would only be disastrous in India. Jawaharlal Nehru saw capitalism as a relic of history and socialism as its modern remedy. Both the dominant streams within the Congress thus pitted themselves against the laws of classical economics for 60 years through the middle part of the 20th century. They were both reacting to the laissez faire economic policies of the British Raj which they took to be responsible for the poverty of the land and the destruction of Indian industry. Britain's economic policies in India had led to the impoverishment of the Indian people, yet the policies pursued by the Congress Party in the decades after independence did little to alleviate the pain. In some cases they made things worse. The mismanagement of the Indian economy thus existed in a continuum from the Battle of Plassey in 1757, to the fall of the Licence Raj in 1991.

The problems of the Indian economy after Independence were the result of its foundational ideas. The rejection of classical economics had led Mohandas Gandhi to advocate khadi spinning and village industries as the economic salvation of India. Whilst the process of economic growth in the West had occurred through the use of labour saving machinery, Gandhi sought to revive labour preserving techniques. In cities, towns and villages across India labour was being restricted to the use of rudimentary machines, or confined to small workshops, producing too little at too high a cost at too slow a pace, for subsistence wages. Jawaharlal Nehru's solution to the flaws of classical economics was, like his fellow socialists, to socialise the means of production. Nehru sought to build a public sector which would dominate heavy industry, or the "commanding heights" of the economy. Yet, from the 1950s, public sector enterprises would be established whenever demand for a product arose, without any thought to whether it could be supplied efficiently and profitably. The public sector thus began making high priced, low quality products in insufficient quantities to meet demand. Cotton and steel told the story of the Indian economy after Independence. Cotton mills were restricted from producing to meet all of domestic demand in order to protect hand spinners and handloom weavers. The result was that an industry which India's earliest economic thinkers envisaged would be a world leader, was, by the 1970s, driven to ruin. Vast amounts of human and financial resources were diverted to the production of steel in public sector plants in a quest for self-reliant industrialisation. Yet even after 25 years of trying to produce enough steel to meet domestic demand, the Government of India still had to spend valuable foreign exchange on steel imports year after year.

The swadeshi ideal had, by the 1950s, morphed into a quest for self-reliance. India's spinners and weavers, its big public sector factories and private enterprises were all protected behind high tariff walls. In some cases they benefitted from bans on the import of certain types of consumer and industrial goods. The mechanics of an economy resemble those of a motor car of the time. Yet the car that Jawaharlal Nehru and Prasanta Mahalanobis engineered could never get started. Initially the government adhered to a policy of import substitution and export control. The idea was to develop the capacity to make as much of the heavy machinery and tools needed for modern manufacturing in India, whilst restricting exports so that production would serve the domestic market. Just as air needs to be let in and fuel valves opened at precisely the right time to allow for the fuel to be compressed, so imported components needed to be let into the Indian economy to allow Indian producers to manufacture high quality goods at competitive prices. And then, just as spark plugs have to fire at the height of compression, exports would have to be sent abroad to earn the foreign exchange needed to get the economy moving. When, after India's first foreign exchange crisis in 1957, it was realised that the problem was that India was not earning enough foreign exchange through its exports to cover expenditure on imports, the government belatedly began export promotion schemes. Yet it did so whilst continuing to pursue import substitution. The two policies were, in practice, contradictory. It was not simply enough that Indian manufacturers produce in order to export. They had to compete in international markets and often could not produce goods of sufficient quality at competitive prices because they either had to rely on scarce and expensive Indian supplies or deal with restrictions on the import of the latest foreign technology. It was thought that the car would not start because of a lack of fuel. The Americans provided the fuel, in the form of aid money for ten years after the first foreign exchange crisis. Yet the car refused to start. The problem was not one of fuel in the tank. The problem was with the engine. The ideal of self-reliance, that India could, someday, drive on the technological frontier, producing all that it needed, largely independent of the world, remained elusive until the end.

It is often said that it is easy to be wise after the event. Those who administered the Licence Raj and lived to see its demise usually maintained that the ideas which inspired it were pervasive in development economics in the 1950s; import substitution, export control and the development of heavy industries in the public sector found favour in many governments throughout Asia, Africa, Eastern Europe and South America. Whilst the idea of newly independent nations closing their economies and developing their resources for the benefit of their people was an attractive one, there were those who opposed the model. They explained, at the time, quite cogently, exactly how and why a controlled economy would not work. Professors Shenoy and Friedman, and Rajaji and Minoo Masani were not prophets with a mystical ability to see the future. They did not guess right. Their judgement was based upon a sound understanding of the laws of economics, which in turn are based upon an understanding of universal, that is, human nature. Rajaji had to write a defence of the profit motive; profit was what drove businesspeople to make high quality products for their customers and no government could ever do the job as well. Minoo Masani continually drew attention to the enormous misallocation of resources to the public sector; scarce resources could have been better invested in agriculture and light industries which would have created many more jobs. Milton Friedman told the Government of India, in 1955, that too much labour was being combined with too little capital in small-scale industries, whilst too little labour was being applied to too much capital in heavy industries. Bellikoth Raghunath Shenoy dissented to the Second Five Year Plan. He saw that the government was first drawing up its plan, and then trying to find the resources to fund it, much like a Communist regime. Just as the Licence Raj never worked because it was based on flawed ideas, the predictions of its critics came true because they were based on sound ideas.

The problem with the Licence Raj was not just a lack of understanding of economics, but also a lack of capacity of the Indian state. Weak Indian state capacity was evident when the government started to create public sector enterprises in larger numbers in the 1950s. New public sector units had to be managed by civil servants. They were managed in the ways of the civil service. The plethora of rules and guidelines for decision making, layers of checks and balances, and voluminous paperwork all made civil servants averse to taking risks or even making simple decisions. The result was that public sector enterprises, particularly those which absorbed the largest amounts of investment, constantly ran behind production schedules, made expensive products and accumulated huge losses.

Weak state capacity was evident in the account of Ashok's time as a village level worker for the Community Development Programme somewhere in northern India in November 1954. Ashok got trapped between the social dynamics of his village and the demands of the bureaucracy. He had to deal with his boss making unreasonable demands, tiresome paperwork, and a lack of basic equipment, in addition to the caste divisions of the village he was attempting to develop. Ashok was the last man, the representative of the state, the one who would have to make the Community Development Programme work in the village. Carl Pope documented the end of state capacity in his account of his time working on the family planning programme in Barhi, Bihar in 1968. Again, much depended on the last man, in this case, the extension worker Priog Mandel, whom Pope thought had little interest in the job. Pope saw the scam going on in the supply of contraceptive loops and also noted that officials seemed more concerned that the flow of paperwork remain smooth rather than that family planning actually take place. Pope's condom distribution scheme came to an end because a higher official in a nearby town was not convinced that they were being used "appropriately". Whilst state capacity might have broken down with its last men in the villages, the Government of India's most senior bureaucrats in New Delhi were often equally helpless. When, in the wake of the green revolution and a rise in wheat stocks in the late 1960s big statements were made that imports of wheat would no longer be needed and the domestic wheat trade would be nationalised, the attempt had to be abandoned within a matter of months. The government could simply not undertake the task of procuring wheat from farmers across India at a remunerative price and so had to revert to the middlemen who had traditionally dominated the trade.

The economic crisis of 1991 was not India's first. In fact, since the start of the Licence Raj in 1951, it was the fifth. They were all alike. The recurring problems were with foreign exchange reserves and the balance of payments. But when India experienced its fourth major foreign exchange crisis in 1980 the government decided to employ a new strategy. Rather than restricting imports and depressing the economy, loans would be taken from commercial sources abroad. That borrowing was initially reasonably prudent and worked well due to a surge in oil production from the Bombay High fields in the early 1980s. Yet just as one drink among friends often turns into two or three, and then becomes solitary daytime drinking, the Government of India began borrowing abroad not just to fund specific infrastructure projects but to finance its budget deficits. These budget deficits were the result of uncontrolled spending on food and fertiliser subsidies, defence, steel imports, imports of oil, and government salaries. When the fifth and final crisis came, the government reverted to the strategy it had employed the first three times; non-essential imports were restricted and international creditors- governments, international agencies and commercial banks- were approached for loans. Since 1980 the Government of India had been trying to get the economy moving through credit rather than structural reform. The Americans were giving much less money than they used to and other official sources of aid were declining each year. The government thought that it needed to keep the fuel tank full and so it decided to borrow from international bankers instead. Yet there was always much more demand for imports in India than for its exports. The car came to a halt once again. However, rather than providing yet more fuel, the Americans and the International Monetary Fund insisted on replacing the engine.

In many ways the relationship between India and the United States has come full circle. Although ties began to deteriorate with the election of President Richard Nixon and America's tacit support for Pakistan in the War of 1972, and endured years of listlessness and American disinterest, and then sanctions after Indian nuclear tests in 1998, many of the shared interests and values of the 1950s have brought the two nations back together in the early 21st century. The American foreign policy establishment is, again, as in the late 1950s, concerned with the power of China, now effectively capitalist, and its increasing influence not just in Asia but across the globe. Again, the United States sees India as a strategic counterweight to China. The relationship remains hampered by the question of Pakistan, as it has always been. Since 2001 that question has been complicated by America's military commitments in Afghanistan. Although desirous of a deeper economic relationship with India, American security interests in South Asia continued to prevail over its economic interests. Nonetheless, Americans have begun to accept India as it is, rather than trying to shape it. Successive United States administrations have sought to bring India into the nuclear power club rather than exclude it, and India has been accorded far greater importance by the American foreign policy establishment than the structure of its economy has warranted. American ambassadors have continued to make the case for a more open Indian economy, but they have done so, much like in the 1950s, as a matter of ritual. Presidential visits, once rarities, are now a matter of routine. American officials have also learnt the importance of personal warmth and feeling for the success of relationships in India, and so successive American presidents have played Holi, tried to deliver Hindi film dialogues and even sat and spun some khadi.

The economic reforms of 1991 had a delayed effect on Indian politics. With the dismantling of controls on production and consumption India's middle class began to grow at an explosive pace. Although means of measurement vary, it is likely that in the 20 years after the liberalisation of the economy the number of middle class Indians grew by tenfold, to 300 million. Yet it was not until 2014 that a politician arrived who sought to satisfy the Indian middle class's desire for a better life. Narendra Modi had been Chief Minister of Gujarat since 2001. His image as a Hindu nationalist hardliner in the wake of the religious riots of 2002 had been covered in the Indian mind; he had become a development messiah. Prior to beginning his bid for national power, Chief Minister Modi spoke before the *India Today* Conclave in March 2013. He told an anecdote about the mentality of the old Licence Raj. A couple of hunters went into the jungle to shoot tigers. They thought that the tigers were still some distance away. They parked their car and went for a little walk. They came upon the tigers sooner than they thought. The rifles were back in the car. They showed the tigers their rifle licences. The old mentality had taken a new form; instead of showing a licence, people would now show legislative acts. What he wanted was "less Acts and more action". Modi went on to develop these themes on the campaign trail, speaking of "minimum government and maximum governance" and "sabka ka saath sabka vikaas" or "support for everyone, development for everyone". He had a reputation for being business friendly; factories could come up in Gujarat without the usual hassles, law and order prevailed and bureaucrats could work without the constant fear of being transferred. Loud advertisements played in cinema halls proclaiming that Gujarat was "Number One" by every important measure of development. During his

Independence Day speech from the ramparts of the Red Fort in August 2014, Prime Minister Modi announced the abolition of the venerable Planning Commission.

The intellectual elite in late colonial India had largely forgotten India's history of international trade. It is one which has only been rediscovered by historians in the early 21st century. Economic historians have estimated that India accounted for around 25% of the world's output and income in the 17th century. It could be inferred that India held a similar share of world trade. From the time of Independence, and well into the 21st century, India's share of world trade has hovered around 2%. Could India rise once again as a great trading nation? In the absence of an export oriented industrial sector, India's most prized exports continue to be its people. Indians have, since colonial times, gone out into the world in search of work. The inherent enterprise of the Indian people has been recognised across the globe. Indians of all skill levels continue to go abroad in search of better jobs, yet a noticeable change began to take place in the 1990s. Many of the first generation of high skilled Indian migrants to the United States had become fabulously successful. Some of the first big businesses of the internet economy were engineered by Indians. Citibank, IBM, Vodafone, Pepsi, Microsoft, Google, Deutsche Bank, Deloitte, McKinsey, and Mastercard have all had Indian origin chief executive officers. Businesses in India have only just started to explore international markets, acquiring steel plants in Europe, constructing mines in Australia, and providing telecommunications in Africa. Yet these are just the slightest glimpses of the potential of Indian enterprise to return India to its historical role as a world economic powerhouse. Or, as Mahadev Ranade put it in 1893, "the emporium of all of Asia".

NOTES

Chapter One: A Better and Saner Order

[i] Bimanbehari Majumdar, *History of Political Thought: From Rammohun to Dayananda (1821-1884)* Volume 1 Bengal (Calcutta: University of Calcutta, 1934), 71.

[ii] A Hindoo's Letter IV, *Bombay Gazette*, August 20, 1841, Volume LIII, pp 174-175 cited in J.V. Naik, "Foreunners of Dadabhai Naoroji's Drain Theory", *Economic and Political Weekly*, 36 46/47, (November 24-30 2001): 4428-4432.

[iii] *Bombay Gazette*, July 7 1841, Volume LIII, pp22-23, cited in J.V. Naik, "Foreunners of Dadabhai Naoroji's Drain Theory".

[iv] *Bombay Gazette*, July 18 1841, Volume LIII, pp 62-63 cited in J.V. Naik, "Foreunners of Dadabhai Naoroji's Drain Theory".

[v] A Hindoo's Letter IV, *Bombay Gazette*, cited in J.V. Naik, "Foreunners of Dadabhai Naoroji's Drain Theory".

[vi] J.V. Naik, 'Bhau Mahajan and his Prabhakar, Dhumketu and Dnyan Darshan: A Study of Maharashtrian Response to British Rule', *Indian Historical Review*, Vol XIII, Nos 1 and 2 (July 1986- January 1987) ICHR, New Delhi, 1986-87, 135-152 cited in J.V. Naik, "Foreunners of Dadabhai Naoroji's Drain Theory".

[vii] "Inaugural address at the first Industrial Conference", Poona 1890 in Mahadev Govind Ranade, *Essays on Indian Economics* (Madras: G.A. Natesan & Co, 1906), 195.

[viii] "Indian Political Economy" in Mahadev Govind Ranade, *Essays on Indian Economics*, 1.

[ix] "Present State of Indian Manufactures & Outlook of the Same" in Mahadev Govind Ranade, *Essays on Indian Economics*, 105.

[x] J.N. Gupta, *The Life and Work of Romesh Chunder Dutt* (London: J.M. Dent & Sons, 1911), 440.

[xi] *Technical and Scientific Education in Bengal* (October 1886) cited in Sumit Sarkar, *The Swadeshi Movement in Bengal 1903-1908* (New Delhi: People's Publishing House, 1973), 111.

[xii] Bholanath Chandra, *Mukherjee's Magazine*, Volume II 1873 & Volume V 1876 cited in Bipin Chandra, *The Rise and Growth of Economic Nationalism in India* (New Delhi: Peoples Publishing House, 1960), 125.

[xiii] *Sadharani*, 7 Chaitra 1282 (1876) cited in Sumit Sarkar, *The Swadeshi Movement in Bengal 1903-1908*, 97.

[xiv] Sumit Sarkar, *The Swadeshi Movement in Bengal 1903-1908*, 100.

[xv] Ibid.

[xvi] Ibid.

[xvii] Ibid, 104.

[xviii] Ibid, 107.

[xix] Surendranath Banerjea, *A Nation in Making* (Bombay: Oxford University Press, 1925), 192.

[xx] M.K. Gandhi, "How I discovered the spinning wheel", *Young India*, 20 October 1928 in M.K. Gandhi, *The Economics of Khadi* (Ahmadabad: Navajivan Press, 194), 275.

[xxi] M.K. Gandhi, "Swadeshi" An address delivered before the Missionary Conference Madras on 14 February 1916, in M.K. Gandhi, *The Economics of Khadi*, 3.

[xxii] M.K. Gandhi, "The Swadeshi Spirit" Presidential Address delivered at the first Gujarat Provincial Political Conference, Godhra, October 1917 in M.K. Gandhi, *The Economics of Khadi*, 12.

[xxiii] M.K. Gandhi, "Swadeshi in Swaraj", *Young India*, 10 December 1919 in M.K. Gandhi, *The Economics of Khadi*, 14.

[xxiv] M.K. Gandhi, "Swadeshi", *Young India*, 21 February 1920 in M.K. Gandhi, *The Economics of Khadi*, 18.

[xxv] M.K. Gandhi, "How I discovered the spinning wheel", *Young India*, 20 September 1928, *The Economics of Khadi*, 276.

[xxvi] M.K. Gandhi, "Swadeshi", *Young India*, 18 August 1920 in M.K. Gandhi, *The Economics of Khadi*, 24.

[xxvii] M.K. Gandhi, "Swaraj in Swadeshi", *Young India*, 10 December 1919 in M.K. Gandhi, *The Economics of Khadi*, 16.

[xxviii] M.K. Gandhi, "Swadeshi", *Young India*, 21 April 1920 in M.K. Gandhi, *The Economics of Khadi*, 17.

[xxix] M.K. Gandhi, "Indian Economics", *Young India*, 8 December 1921, in M.K. Gandhi, *The Economics of Khadi*, 66.

[xxx] M.K Gandhi, "A Plea For Mills", *Young India*, 17 July 1924 in M.K. Gandhi, *The Economics of Khadi*, 88.

[xxxi] M.K. Gandhi, "The Hand Loom", *Young India*, 14 May 1925 in M.K. Gandhi, *The Economics of Khadi*, 112.

[xxxii] M.K. Gandhi, "Hand-Loom v. Spinning Wheel", *Young India*, 11 November 1926, in M.K. Gandhi, *The Economics of Khadi*, 194.

[xxxiii] M.K. Gandhi, "Village Industries", *Harijan*, 16 November 1934 in M.K. Gandhi, *The Economics of Khadi*, 24.

[xxxiv] Motilal chided Jawaharlal in 1926 for practicing "false economies" in Switzerland where he had taken Kamala for medical treatment. He thought that his son was not adequately clothing his daughter-in-law for the cool climate which would likely negate the effect of the treatment. Motilal's own resources were dwindling as he spent more time on politics so he had arranged a ₹10,000 legal brief for Jawaharlal from one of his wealthy clients so that they could make the trip. See Katherine Frank, *The Life of Indira Nehru Gandhi* (London: Harper Collins, 2001), 40-41.

[xxxv] Jawaharlal Nehru, *Soviet Russia: Some Random Sketches and Impressions* (Allahabad: Allahabad Law Journal Press, 1928).

[xxxvi] P.L. Lakhanpal, *History of the Congress Socialist Party* (Lahore, National, 1946), 20.
[xxxvii] Ibid, 27.
[xxxviii] Quoted in Claude Markovits, *Indian Business and Nationalist Politics: 1931-1939* (Cambridge: Cambridge University Press, 1985), 109.
[xxxix] Ibid, 110.
[xl] Ibid, 113.
[xli] Quoted in Sankar Ghose, *Socialism and Communism in India*, (Bombay: Allied Publishers, 1971) 186.
[xlii] Quoted in Sankar Ghose, *Socialism and Communism in India*, 187.
[xliii] Jayabrata Sarkar, "Power, Hegemony and Politics: Leadership Struggle in the Congress in the 1930s", *Modern Asian Studies*, 40 2 (2006): 357.
[xliv] Ibid, 363.
[xlv] Ibid.

Chapter Two: A Scientific Approach

[xlvi] Nicolas Bukharin, *The Economics of the Transitional Period*, 1920 cited in Adam Kaufman, "The Origin of 'The Political Economy of Socialism'", *Soviet Studies*, 4 3 (1953): 245.
[xlvii] Memorial from Cotton Supply Association, Manchester, to the East India Court of Directors in 1857 cited in Sabyasachi Bhattacharya, "Laissez Faire in India", *The Indian Economic and Social History Review*, 2 1 (1965): 4.
[xlviii] J. Wilson to Walter Bagehot, 4 July 1860, cited in Sabyasachi Bhattacharya, "Laissez Faire in India", 6.
[xlix] Sabyasachi Bhattacharya, "Laissez Faire in India", 6.
[l] Secretary of State to Government of India, Railway Despatch No. 5, 24 January, 1868, cited in Sabyasachi Bhattacharya, "Laissez Faire in India", 11.
[li] Argyll to Mayo, 12 February, 1869. Mayo Papers, bundle 47. Papers of Earl of Mayo, cited in Sabyasachi Bhattacharya, "Laissez Faire in India", 10.
[lii] Fin. Progs, July 1871, No. 83. Government of India Secy. of. State No. 40, 6 Apr. 1870, cited in Sabyasachi Bhattacharya, "Laissez Faire in India", 13.
[liii] Minute by H. M. Durand, Commander-in-Chief of the Army. 31 Mar. 1870, cited in Sabyasachi Bhattacharya, "Laissez Faire in India", 13.
[liv] Fin. Progs. July 1871, No. 83, Government of India to Secy. of State, No. 40, 6 April 1870, cited in Sabyasachi Bhattacharya, "Laissez Faire in India", 13.
[lv] Secretary of State's Despatch (Separate Revenue) No. 6 15 July 1875 and Despatches (Legislative) 11 November 1875 (No. 51) and 31 May 1876 (No. 25) cited in Bipin Chandra, *The Rise and Growth of Economic Nationalism in India* (New Delhi: People's Publishing House, 1960), 218.
[lvi] Bipin Chandra, *The Rise and Growth of Economic Nationalism in India*, 220.
[lvii] Quoted in Bipin Chandra, *The Rise and Growth of Economic Nationalism in India*, 223.

[lviii] Ibid, 224.
[lix] Ibid, 227.
[lx] Ibid.
[lxi] Ibid.
[lxii] Bholonath Chandra, *Mukherjee's Magazine*, Volume V (January-June 1876) cited in Bipin Chandra, *The Rise and Growth of Economic Nationalism in India*, 22
[lxiii] Bipin Chandra, *The Rise and Growth of Economic Nationalism in India*, 231.
[lxiv] Ibid, 236.
[lxv] B.R. Tomlinson, *The Political Economy of the Raj: 1914-1947*, (London: The Macmillan Press, 1979), 58.
[lxvi] Ibid, 59.
[lxvii] Ibid, p 60.
[lxviii] Ibid, 61.
[lxix] Ibid, 62.
[lxx] Purushottamdas Thakurdas et al, *Memorandum Outlining a Plan of Economic Development for India* Part Two (Harmondsworth: Penguin, 1945), 25.
[lxxi] Dwijendra Tripathi, *The Oxford History of Indian Business* (Oxford: Oxford University Press, 2004), 168.
[lxxii] G.D. Birla, *Indian Prosperity: A Plea for Planning* (Delhi: The Hindustan Times Press, 1934).
[lxxiii] The proceedings of the National Planning Committee held in Bombay on 17 December 1930 in
Jawaharlal Nehru Papers, II, 135, I, p. 2, cited in Ragabhendra Chattopadhyay, *The Idea of Planning in India 1930-1951* (Canberra: Australian National University, 1985), 98.
[lxxiv] Ibid.
[lxxv] 'Minutes of the Proceedings of the NPC', 18 December 1938 in JNP, II, 135, I, cited in Ragabhendra Chattopadhyay, *The Idea of Planning in India 1930-1951*, 99.
[lxxvi] Ragabhendra Chattopadhyay, *The Idea of Planning in India*, 100.
[lxxvii] 'Minutes' 20 December 1938 cited in Ragabhendra Chattopadhyay, *The Idea of Planning in India 1930-1951*, Canberra, Australian National University, 1985, 100.
[lxxviii] Ragabhendra Chattopadhyay, *The Idea of Planning in India*, 101.
[lxxix] Ibid, 104.
[lxxx] 'Note submitted to the Chairmen of the NPC by Mr Ambalal Sarabhai' in File No. II Jawaharlal Nehru Papers cited in Ragabhendra Chattopadhyay, *The Idea of Planning in India*, 108.
[lxxxi] 'Minutes of the Proceedings of the NPC' dated 16 June 1939' in Kumarappa Papers File No.11 cited in Ragabhendra Chattopadhyay, *The Idea of Planning in India*, 109.
[lxxxii] Ragabhendra Chattopadhyay, *The Idea of Planning in India*, 110.
[lxxxiii] Ibid, 115.

[lxxxiv] Ibid, 122.
[lxxxv] Ibid, 119.
[lxxxvi] Government of India Press Note 24 June 1941 cited in Ragabhendra Chattopadhyay, *The Idea of Planning in India*, 141.
[lxxxvii] First Report of the Progress of the R.C.C., Section 11 p. 7 cited in Ragabhendra Chattopadhyay, *The Idea of Planning in India*, 183.
[lxxxviii] J.R.D. Tata to Jawaharlal Nehru 10 August 1939, Jawaharlal Nehru Papers, Correspondence File, Volume 98 cited in Claude Markovits, *Indian Business and Nationalist Politics*, 149.
[lxxxix] Letter from J.R.D. Tata to P. Thakurdas dated 30 November 1942 in Purushottomdas Papers.T.P. 291/1942-44 cited in Ragabhendra Chattopadhyay, *The Idea of Planning in India*, 151.
[xc] J. Matthai Letter to Purushottomdas Thakurdas 8 December 1943 in Purushottamdas Papers cited in Ragabhendra Chattopadhyay, *The Idea of Planning in India,* 156.
[xci] Thakurdas Letter to Matthai 13 December 1943, G.D. Birla Letter to Matthai 3 January 1944, in Purushottamdas Papers 291, cited in Ragabhendra Chattopadhyay, *The Idea of Planning in India,* 156.
[xcii] Amery to Wavell 24 March 1944 document no. 447, p. 852 in N. Mansergh *The Transfer of Power* Volume IV cited in Ragabhendra Chattopadhyay, *The Idea of Planning in India,* 188.

Chapter Three: A Socialistic Picture of Society

[xciii] "India Wishes Pakistan Well" Sardar Patel's Assertion, *The Times of India*, 4 January 1948, 1.
[xciv] Quoted in Francine Frankel, *India's Political Economy* (Princeton: Princeton University Press, 1978), 76.
[xcv] Ibid.
[xcvi] Solomon Trone to Jawarharlal Nehru, 12 September 1949, 4 October 1949, 21 November 1949, P.N. Haksar Papers III, Nehru Memorial Museum & Library, Subject 187 cited in David C. Engerman, *The Price of Aid* (Cambridge: Harvard University Press, 2018), 34.
[xcvii] Ibid.
[xcviii] Quoted in Francine Frankel, *India's Political Economy*, 85.
[xcix] Ibid.
[c] File I/(4)/1/(9)/48, Department of Industrial Policy and Promotion, Industry Ministry cited in Vivek Chibber, *Locked in Place: State Building and Late Industrialization in India* (Oxford: Princeton University Press, 2003), 137.
[ci] "Conversation with Mr G.D. Birla", Despatch #859, 10/3/1949, 845.5151 10-349, RG 5 DSR cited in Vivek Chibber, *Locked in Place*, 140.

[cii] "Comments of Shri B.M. Birla on the Industries (Development and Control) Bill" FICCI Circular File 1063, M.A. Master papers Nehru Memorial Museum & Library cited in Vivek Chibber, *Locked in Place*, 140.
[ciii] Vivek Chibber, *Locked in Place*, 140.
[civ] "Report Regarding the Meeting of the Federation's Representatives with the Select Committee on August 5 1949" File 1065 M.A. Master papers NMML cited in Vivek Chibber, *Locked in Place*, 140.
[cv] Ibid.
[cvi] "Comments of Lal Shri Ram on the Industries (Development and Control) Bill 1949" FICCI Circular 27 August 1949 File 1063 M.A. Master Papers NMML cited in Vivek Chibber, *Locked in Place*, p 141.
[cvii] H.K. Mahtab speech on October 11 1951, Constituent Assembly Debates (Delhi: Government of India: 1951) cited in Vivek Chibber, *Locked in Place*, p 155.
[cviii] Jawaharlal Nehru to Lok Sabha 10 August 1951 quoted in A.H. Hanson, *The Process of Planning: A Study of India's Five Year Plans, 1950-1964* (London: Oxford University Press, 1966), 90.
[cix] A.H. Hanson, *The Process of Planning*, 99.
[cx] Ibid, 100.
[cxi] Ibid, 103.
[cxii] Ibid, 102.
[cxiii] Ibid.
[cxiv] Ibid.
[cxv] Ibid.
[cxvi] Ibid.
[cxvii] Ibid, 104.
[cxviii] Ibid, 106.
[cxix] Ibid, 111.
[cxx] Ibid, 114.
[cxxi] Ibid, 120.
[cxxii] Ibid, 119.
[cxxiii] Quoted in David C. Engerman, *The Price of Aid*, 92.
[cxxiv] Quoted in A.H. Hanson, *The Process of* Planning, 120.
[cxxv] Jawaharlal Nehru, "Socialistic Pattern of Society", 22 January 1955, and "Towards a Socialist Society", 9 November 1954 *Selected Works of Jawaharlal Nehru* Second Series 27, 279-283, 373 cited in David C. Engerman, *The Price of Aid*, 92.
[cxxvi] Quoted in David C. Engerman, *The Price of Aid*, 92.
[cxxvii] P.C. Mahalanobis, *Talks on Planning*, (Calcutta: Asia Publishing House, 1961), 3.
[cxxviii] Prasanta Chandra Mahalanobis to Pitamber Pant, 24 June 1954, Pitamber Pant Papers, Nehru Memorial Museum & Library, cited in David. C. Engerman, *The Price of Aid*, 94.

[cxxix] Prasanta Chandra Mahalanobis to Pitamber Pant, 7 July 1954, Pitamber Pant Papers, Nehru Memorial Museum & Library, cited in David. C. Engerman, *The Price of Aid*, p 96.

[cxxx] M.I. Rubinshtein, "Razvitie sovremennoi tekhniki I ee sotsiyal'nye posledstviia", 2 September 1954, ARAN, 499/1/333/12-13 cited in David. C. Engerman, *The Price of Aid*, 98.

[cxxxi] Ragnar Frisch to Prasanta Chandra Mahalanobis 8 August 1953 in Ragnar Frisch Papers, University of Oslo Department of Economics, cited in David C. Engerman, *The Price of Aid*, 98.

[cxxxii] Ragnar Frisch, "A Short Memorandum on a Technique for Elaborating the New Five Year Plan for India" ISI Studies Relating to Planning for National Development, Working Paper No. 5, 11 December 1954, 3, 7-8 in Planning Commission Records, ISI, Folder 15, cited in David C. Engerman, *The Price of Aid*, 100.

[cxxxiii] Jawaharlal Nehru "The Role of Private Enterprise" Speech delivered at the National Development Council Meeting 9 November 1954 in *Planning and Development: Speeches of Jawaharlal Nehru 1952-1956* (Delhi: The Publications Division, Ministry of Information and Broadcasting, Government of India, 1956), 15.

[cxxxiv] Planning Commission Minutes 1 February 1955 (Lange), 3 February 1955 (Degtiar), March 4-5 (Frisch), Planning Commission Records, ISI Folder 116 cited in David C. Engerman, *The Price of Aid*, 104.

[cxxxv] "Economic Conference at Poona" 7 January 1956 *Economic Weekly* 11-12 cited in David C. Engerman, *The Price of Aid*, 106.

[cxxxvi] "The Fourth NDC Meeting" in Government of India Planning Commission Five Decades 1:57-65 cited in David C. Engerman, *The Price of Aid*, 107.

[cxxxvii] Ed. Parth J.Shah, *Friedman on India*, (New Delhi: Centre for Civil Society, 2000), 1.

[cxxxviii] A.H. Hanson, *The Process of Planning*, 132.

[cxxxix] Ibid.

[cxl] Ibid, 140.

[cxli] Quoted in A.H. Hanson, *The Process of Planning*, 144.

[cxlii] Jawaharlal Nehru to Chief Ministers 17 August 1956, *Letters to Chief Ministers* 4:425-431 cited in David C. Engerman, *The Price of Aid*, 164.

[cxliii] Jawaharlal Nehru, Memorandum to Cabinet Ministers 9 January 1957, *Selected Works of Jawaharlal Nehru Second Series*: 172-173 cited in David C. Engerman, *The Price of Aid*, 164.

[cxliv] A.H. Hanson, *The Process of* Planning, 153.

[cxlv] Prasanta Chandra Mahalanobis to Oskar Lange 27 February 1957 Visitor Files, ISI, Folder Lange cited in David C. Engerman, *The Price of Aid*, 164.

[cxlvi] Jawaharlal Nehru "Stop Indulging in Petty Squabbles" 26 October 1957, *Selected Works of Jawaharlal Nehru* Second Series, 49:44 cited in David C. Engerman, *The Price of Aid*, 164.

[cxlvii] T.T. Krishnamachari to All India Congress Committee 1 September 1957 *Asian Reporter* 3:36 1957 cited in David C. Engerman, *The Price of Aid*, 165.
[cxlviii] "India's Balance of Payments: First Half, 1956/57" Bulletin of the Reserve Bank of India, December 1956, 1238-1245 cited in David C. Engerman, *The Price of Aid*, 165.
[cxlix] Jawaharlal Nehru to C.D. Deshmukh 13 January 1958, Jawaharlal Nehru to V.T. Krishnamachari 14 January 1958 Selected Works of Jawaharlal Nehru Second Series 41:190-194, 194-195, cited in David C. Engerman, *The Price of Aid*, 168.
[cl] Minutes of the 310th meeting of the NSC, 24 January 1957, FR 1955-57 8:29-43 cited in Dennis Merrill, *Bread and the Ballot* (Chapel Hill, University of North Carolina Press, 1990), 140.
[cli] "Summary of the Report of the Interdepartmental Working Group on India" 2 May 1957 Randall Series Subject Subseries Box 6 USCFEP cited in Dennis Merrill, *Bread and the Ballot*, 143.
[clii] B.K. Nehru to Morarji Desai, 14 & 21 May 1958, PMO Records, National Archives of India, 27/437/58- PMS cited in David C. Engerman, *The Price of Aid*, 176.
[cliii] Quoted in David C. Engerman, *The Price of Aid*, 177.
[cliv] Ibid.
[clv] "Current Economic Position of India and Prospects of India" 28 July 1958, "Meeting on Foreign Exchange Situation: Text of Statement by Mr. Eugene R. Black." 25 August 1958 Country Files WBGA Folder 1844595 cited in David C. Engerman, *The Price of Aid*, 181.
[clvi] Quoted in A.H. Hanson, *The Process of* Planning, 176.
[clvii] Rostow to Jackson 29 February 1956, Box 56, Jackson papers DDEL, cited in Dennis Merrill, *Bread and the Ballot*, 155.
[clviii] Millikan "India" 20 February 1959 Box 2 Records of U.S. President's Committee to Study the Military Assistance Programme DDEL cited in Dennis Merrill, *Bread and the Ballot*, 155.
[clix] Ibid.
[clx] Dennis Merrill, *Bread and the Ballot*, 157.
[clxi] Quoted in David C. Engerman, *The Price of Aid*, 186.
[clxii] "Power Crisis", *The Times of India*, 24 May 1962, 8.
[clxiii] "Power Shortage Can't Be Overcome in Near Future", *The Times of India*, 22 May 1962, 1.
[clxiv] "Power Crisis", *The Times of India*, 24 May 1962, 8.
[clxv] "Power Crisis in Calcutta", *The Times of India*, 28 July 1962, 9.
[clxvi] "Calcutta Power Cut Jeopardises 3rd Plan Targets", *The Times of India*, 29 July 1962.
[clxvii] Virendra Agarwala, "The Power Shortage", *The Times of India*, 7 December 1961, 8.
[clxviii] "Accumulation of Stocks at Colliery Pitheads", *The Times of India*, 22 February 1961, 3.

clxix "Speedy Steps Urged to End Wagon Shortage", *The Times of India*, 18 March 1961, 4.
clxx "Accumulation of Stocks at Colliery Pitheads", *The Times of India*, 22 February 1961, 3.
clxxi "Coal Crisis Result 60 Foot High Coal Mound Of Overproduction", *The Times of India*, 27 February 1961, 7.
clxxii Ibid.
clxxiii "Maharashtra Asks Centre for More Cement Quota", *The Times of India*, 31 March 1962, 1.
clxxiv "Metal Shortage", *The Times of India*, 14 September 1962, 6.
clxxv "2,000 Foundries Face Closure", *The Times of India*, 7 September 1963, 8.
clxxvi "Metal Shortage", *The Times of India*, 14 September 1962, 6.
clxxvii "No Immediate Solution to Steel Shortage", *The Times of India*, 28 November 1963, 8.
clxxviii Ibid.
clxxix Virendra Agarwala, "Foreign Exchange Crisis", *The Times of India*, 23 November 1961, 8.
clxxx "Menon Sparks Controversy in the Lok Sabha", *The Times of India*, 23 August 1963, 1.
clxxxi "Food Crisis Will Pass by October-end: Shastri", *The Times of India*, 19 September 1964, 1.
clxxxii Jawaharlal Nehru, "The Role of Private Enterprise", speech delivered to the National Development Council 9 November 1954 in *Planning and Development: Speeches of Jawaharlal Nehru*, 18.

Chapter Four: Tillers of the Soil

clxxxiii Bruno Dorin and Frederic Landy, *Agriculture and Food in India* (New Delhi: Manohar, 2009), 67.
clxxxiv Ibid.
clxxxv V.M Dandekar, *The Indian Economy 1947-1992* Volume I Agriculture (New Delhi: Sage Publications, 1994), 211.
clxxxvi P.S. Appu, *Land Reforms in India*, (New Delhi: Vikas Publishing House, 1996), 50.
clxxxvii Daniel Thorner, *The Agrarian Prospect in India* (Delhi: Delhi University Press, 1956).
clxxxviii Albert Mayer, *The Story of Rural Development in Etawah, Uttar Pradesh: Pilot Project India* (Berkeley: University of California Press, 1959).
clxxxix Chester Bowles, *Ambassador's Report* (London: Victor Gollancz, 1954).
cxc The names of the Community Development workers were concealed in the source text- "The Village Level Worker in Action- A Record of Ten Days' Work" in S.C. Dube, *India's Changing Villages* (London: Routledge & Keagan Paul,

1958). However, names such as "Ashok" and "Om Prakash" have been given here for the purposes of characterisation.
[cxci] Quoted in P.S. Appu, *Land Reforms in India*, 56.
[cxcii] Ibid.
[cxciii] Ibid, 61.
[cxciv] Ibid, 62.
[cxcv] Daniel Thorner, *The Agrarian Prospect in India*, 20.
[cxcvi] Ibid, 50.
[cxcvii] P.S. Appu, *Land Reforms in India*, 154.
[cxcviii] Vinoba Bhave, *Bhoodan Yagna* (Ahmadabad: Navajivan Publishing House, 1957).
[cxcix] Jayaprakash Narayan, "Socialism and Sarvodaya", *Tribune* 10 June 1951 in Jayaprakash Narayan, *Towards Total Revolution* Volume 1 (Bombay: Popular Prakashan, 1978), 142.
[cc] Raghavendra Nath Misra, *Bhoodan Movement in India* (New Delhi: S. Chand & Co, 1972), 185.
[cci] Francine Frankel, *India's Political Economy*, 142.
[ccii] Quoted in Francine Frankel, *India's Political Economy*, 143.
[cciii] Francine Frankel, *India's Political Economy*, 161.
[cciv] Ibid.
[ccv] Ibid, p 163.
[ccvi] Ibid.
[ccvii] Ibid, p 167.
[ccviii] Masani's statement in *Modern Review*, cv, 3 (March 1959), 182 cited in Howard L. Erdman, *The Swatantra Party and Indian Conservatism* (Cambridge: Cambridge University Press, 1967), 68.
[ccix] Howard L. Erdman, *The Swatantra Party and Indian Conservatism*, 69.
[ccx] Ibid, 72.
[ccxi] "The Need for a Centre Party", *The Times of India*, 4 June 1959 cited in Howard L. Erdman, *The Swatantra Party and Indian Conservatism*, 79.
[ccxii] Francine Frankel, *India's Political Economy*, p 169.
[ccxiii] Ibid.
[ccxiv] Daniel Thorner, *Agricultural Co-operatives in India: A Field Report* (London: Asia Publishing House, 1964).
[ccxv] H. Laxminarayan & Kissen Kanango, *Glimpses of Co-operative Farming* (Bombay: Asia Publishing House, 1967).
[ccxvi] Dorris D. Brown, *Agricultural Development in India's Districts* (Cambridge: Harvard University Press, 1971), 59.
[ccxvii] C. Subrahmaniam, *The New Strategy in Indian Agriculture* (New Delhi, Vikas Publishing House, 1979).

Chapter Five: The Big Push

ccxviii C. Rajagopalachari, "Freedom under Socialism", *Satyam Eva Jayate*, 16 August 1958 in C. Rajagopalachari, *Satyam Eva Jayate* Volume 1 (Madras: Bharathan Publications, 1961), 188.
ccxix C. Rajagopalachari, "Violent Socialism", *Swarajya*, 19 January 1959 in C. Rajagopalachari, *Satyam Eva Jayate* Volume 1, 266.
ccxx C. Rajagopalachari, "The Touchstone of Policy", *Swarajya*, 21 March 1959 in C. Rajagopalachari, *Satyam Eva Jayate* Volume 1, 306.
ccxxi C. Rajagopalachari, "The Anti-Profit Slogan", *Swarajya*, 15 October 1960 in C. Rajagopalachari, *Satyam Eva Jayate* Volume 2, 650.
ccxxii C. Rajagopalachari, "The Etiology of Controls", *Swarajya*, 6 May 1961, in C. Rajagopalachari, *Satyam Eva Jayate* Volume 2, 831.
ccxxiii C. Rajagopalachari, "The Distempers of the Congress", *Swarajya*, 10 May 1958 in C. Rajagopalachari, *Satyam Eva Jayate* Volume 1, 153.
ccxxiv C. Rajagopalachari, "Welfare Through Compulsion", *Swarajya*, 24 January 1959 in C. Rajagopalachari, *Satyam Eva Jayate* Volume 1, 270.
ccxxv C. Rajagopalachari, "Feuds Within the Congress", *Swarajya*, 22 October 1960 in C. Rajagopalachari, *Satyam Eva Jayate* Volume 2, 661.
ccxxvi C. Rajagopalachari, "The Evils of Whole Time Politics", *Swarajya*, 31 October 1959, in C. Rajagopalachari, *Satyam Eva Jayate* Volume 1, 439.
ccxxvii C. Rajagopalachari, "Immoral Use of Party Power", Swarajya, 12 December 1959 in C. Rajagopalachari, *Satyam Eva Jayate* Volume 1, 474.
ccxxviii C. Rajagopalachari, "Moral Bankruptcy of the Congress", *Swarajya*, 4 March 1961 in C. Rajagopalachari, *Satyam Eva Jayate* Volume 2, 774.
ccxxix Minocher Masani, "Planning or Astrology?" Speech in the Lok Sabha 21 August 1960 in M.R. Masani, *Congress Misrule and the Swatantra Alternative* (Bombay, Manaktalas: 1966), 12.
ccxxx Minocher Masani, "Time for a Change" Speech in the Lok Sabha 19 August 1963 in M.R. Masani, *Congress Misrule and the Swatantra Alternative*, 17.
ccxxxi Minocher Masani, "Who Are These Planners?" Speech in the Lok Sabha 22 March 1965 in M.R. Masani, *Congress Misrule and the Swatantra Alternative*, 28.
ccxxxii B.R. Shenoy & Patrick M. Boardman, "Social Injustice in India", *The Wall Street Journal*, 16 July 1962.
ccxxxiii B.R. Shenoy, "Anti-Progress Planning", *The Wall Street Journal*, 23 December 1963.
ccxxxiv B.R. Shenoy, "Aid for India", *The Wall Street Journal*, 21 May 1964.
ccxxxv Ram Singh Awana, *Pressure Politics in Congress Party*, (New Delhi: Northern Book Centre, 1988), 20.
ccxxxvi Ibid.
ccxxxvii Ibid, 27.
ccxxxviii Ibid, 25.
ccxxxix Quoted in Francine Frankel, *India's Political Economy*, 250.
ccxl John P. Lewis, Memorandum for the administrator, Subject: Betting on India, 14 January 1965, in *The United States and India: A History Through the Archives*

The Later Years Volume I, Eds. Praveen K Chaudhry & Marta Vanduzer-Snow (New Delhi: Sage, 2010) 138.

[ccxli] American Embassy New Delhi to RUERCR/SECSTATE ASHDC, 11 March 1965, in *The United States and India, 146.*

[ccxlii] R.W. Komer, Memorandum for the President, 22 April 1965 in *The United States and India*, 152.

[ccxliii] *Report to the President of the International Bank for Reconstruction and Development and the International Development Association on India's Development Effort*, Volume 1, Main Report 1 October 1965.

[ccxliv] David C. Engerman, *The Price of Aid*, 249.

[ccxlv] David C. Engerman, *The Price of Aid*, 257.

[ccxlvi] B.R. Bell "Visit of Asoka Mehta" 11 April 1966 Country Files WBGA Folder 1844619 cited in David C. Engerman, *The Price of Aid*, 258.

[ccxlvii] William J. Handley to Dean Rusk, 25 April 1966, USAID Records USNA, RG 286, entry p 409, box 11 cited in David C. Engerman, *The Price of Aid*, 258.

[ccxlviii] Rostow conversation with Asoka Mehta, 28 April 1966, NSF Harold Saunders Files, LBJL Box 13, cited in David C. Engerman, *The Price of Aid*, 258.

[ccxlix] U.S. Department of State to New Delhi, 24 April 1966, USAID Records USNA RG 286 Entry P 409, Box 11 cited in David C. Engerman, *The Price of Aid*, 258.

[ccl] K.S. Sundararajan to Bernard R. Bell, 9 May 1966, Country Files WBGA File 1844620, cited in David C. Engerman, *The Price of Aid*, 258.

[ccli] A.A. Dudley conversation with Asoka Mehta, 7 May 1966, CRO Records UKNA Do 189/501 cited in David C. Engerman, *The Price of Aid*, 258.

[cclii] K.S. Sundararajan to Bernard R. Bell, 9 May 1966, Country Files WBGA 1844620 cited in David C. Engerman, *The Price of Aid*, 258.

[ccliii] David C. Engerman, *The Price of Aid*, 263.

[ccliv] Bernard Bell quote as noted by an American diplomat in the Paris Embassy to the U.S. Department of State 8 November 1966, CFPF USNA RG 59 AID-9 cited in David C. Engerman, *The Price of Aid*, 263.

[cclv] Chairman's report of Proceedings, India Consortium Meeting 7-8 November 1966 in Bernard R. Bell Papers, WBGA Folder 1850873 cited in David C. Engerman, *The Price of Aid*, 263.

[cclvi] Annex X to Chairman's report of proceedings, India Consortium, 4-6 April 1967, Country Files, WBGA folder 1844626 cited in David C. Engerman, *The Price of Aid*, 264.

[cclvii] Chairman's Report of Proceedings, India Consortium, 7-8 September 1967, Country Files WBGA, folder 1844845 cited in David C. Engerman, *The Price of Aid*, 265.

[cclviii] David C. Engerman, *The Price of Aid*, 266.

[cclix] Morarji Desai to Robert S. McNamara, 12 April 1968, Country Files, WBGA folder 1844849 cited in David C. Engerman, *The Price of Aid*, 267.

[cclx] John Prior Lewis and Asoka Mehta quotations as reported in Mary S. Olmstead report on McNamara visit, 13 December 1968, SDR, USNA, RG 59, entry A1 5640, box 6 cited in David C. Engerman, *The Price of Aid*, 266.

[cclxi] R.P. Rao, *The Congress Splits* (Bombay: Lalvani Publishing House, 1971) 45.
[cclxii] Ibid, 49.
[cclxiii] Ibid, 50.
[cclxiv] Quoted in R. P. Rao, *The Congress Splits*, 56.
[cclxv] Ibid, 57.
[cclxvi] Ibid.
[cclxvii] Ibid.
[cclxviii] Quoted in R. P. Rao, *The Congress Splits*, 58.
[cclxix] Ibid, 60.
[cclxx] Quoted in R. P. Rao, *The Congress Splits*, 78.
[cclxxi] Ibid, p 82.
[cclxxii] Ibid.
[cclxxiii] Ibid, 83.
[cclxxiv] Quoted in R. P. Rao, *The Congress Splits*, 85.
[cclxxv] Ibid, 86.
[cclxxvi] Quoted in R. P. Rao, *The Congress Splits*, 88.
[cclxxvii] Quoted in R. P. Rao, *The Congress Splits*, 96.
[cclxxviii] Ibid.
[cclxxix] Ibid, 227.
[cclxxx] Ibid, 103.
[cclxxxi] Quoted in R. P. Rao, *The Congress Splits*, 109.
[cclxxxii] Ibid, 122.
[cclxxxiii] Ibid.
[cclxxxiv] Ibid, 124.
[cclxxxv] Ibid, 130.
[cclxxxvi] Ibid, 131.
[cclxxxvii] Ibid, 135.
[cclxxxviii] Ibid, 136.
[cclxxxix] Ibid, 159.
[ccxc] Ibid, 160.
[ccxci] Ibid.
[ccxcii] Ibid, 209.
[ccxciii] Quoted in R. P. Rao, *The Congress Splits*, 211.
[ccxciv] "PM Hits Out at Alliance During Haryana Tour", *The Times of India*, 14 January 1971, 5.
[ccxcv] "Indira Storms Citadel of Congress (O)", *The Times of India*, 17 January 1971, 1.
[ccxcvi] "Rival Flags and Odd Slogans", *The Times of India*, 18 January 1971, 1.
[ccxcvii] "Fresh Mandate Sought for Ushering in Socialism", *The Times of India*, 10 February 1971, 15.
[ccxcviii] "Unprecedented Crowds Cheer PM in Gujarat", *The Times of India*, 19 February 1971, 11.
[ccxcix] "Huge Crowds at PM's Poll Meeting", *The Times of India*, 14 February 1971, 9.

[ccc] "PM Asks for Support to Non-Violent Revolution", *The Times of India*, 16 February 1971, 11.
[ccci] "Drastic Changes Needed in Planning, Says PM", *The Times of India*, 18 February 1971, 11.
[cccii] John. H. Perkins, *Geopolitics and the Green Revolution* (New York: Oxford University Press, 1997), 245.
[ccciii] Ibid.
[ccciv] Baldev Raj Nayar, *India's Mixed Economy* (Bombay: Popular Prakashan, 1989), 318.
[cccv] Francine Frankel, *India's Political Economy*, 524.
[cccvi] Ibid, 528.
[cccvii] Jayaprakash Narayan, "Direct Action of Youth and People", *Everyman's*, 1 December 1974 and "Why Total Revolution?" *Everyman's* 22 December 1974 in Jayaprakash Narayan, *Total Revolution* Volume 4 (Bombay: Popular Prakashan, 1978), 110.
[cccviii] Francine Frankel, *India's Political Economy*, 536.
[cccix] Jayaprakash Narayan, "Total Revolution: It's Concept", *The Economic Times* 10 May 1975 in Jayaprakash Narayan, *Total Revolution* Volume 4, 152.
[cccx] Uma Vasudevan, *Two Faces of Indira Gandhi*, (New Delhi: Vikas Publishing House, 1977), 193.

Chapter Six: The Right to Live, the Right to Progress

[cccxi] N.S. Phadke, "Birth Control in India", *Birth Control Review*, 8 4 (1924): 107 cited in Barbara M. Ramusack, "Embattled Advocates: The Debate over Birth Control in India, 1920-1940", *Journal of Women's History*, 1 2 Fall 1989, 36.
[cccxii] Aims and Objectives of the Sholapur Eugenics Education Society, Handbill, Sanger Collection, Library of Congress, Container 25, reel 17 cited in Barbara M. Ramusack, "Embattled Advocates", 37.
[cccxiii] N.S. Phadke, *Sex Problems in India* (Bombay: D.B. Taraporevala Sons & Co, 1929) & R.D. Karve, *Morality and Birth Control* (Bombay: R.D. Karve, 1921).
[cccxiv] All India Women's Conference, Proceedings of Sixth Session, Madras, 1 January 1932 p 81 at the Margaret Cousins Library, AIWC Headquarters New Delhi cited in Barbara M. Ramusack, "Embattled Advocates", 41.
[cccxv] AIWC Proceedings of the Seventh Session, Lucknow, 30 December 1932, 94-95 cited in Barbara M. Ramusack, "Embattled Advocates", 43.
[cccxvi] *Indian Social Reformer* 5 September 1936 47 No. 1 9 cited in Barbara M. Ramusack, "Embattled Advocates", 46.
[cccxvii] *Marriage Hygiene*, August 1936, 3 No. 1 2 cited in Barbara M. Ramusack, "Embattled Advocates", 47.
[cccxviii] *Indian Social Reformer* 25 May 1935 609-610 45 39 cited in Barbara M. Ramusack, "Embattled Advocates", 53.
[cccxix] Ibid.

cccxx Ibid.
cccxxi Sanger to Gerder S. Guy, 30 November 1935, Sanger LC C26 R17, cited in Barbara M. Ramusack, "Embattled Advocates", 48.
cccxxii Barbara M. Ramusack, "Embattled Advocates", 49.
cccxxiii Ibid.
cccxxiv Letter No. 3 from Sanger to friends and family, 2 January 1936, Sanger SSC, B88, F894, cited in Barbara M. Ramusack, "Embattled Advocates", 49.
cccxxv Barbara M. Ramusack, "Embattled Advocates", 49.
cccxxvi "Gandhi and Mrs Sanger Debate Birth Control", *Asia Magazine* 1936 in *Reproductive Health in India* ed. Sarah Hodges (New Delhi: Orient Longman, 2006), 235.
cccxxvii Ira Klein, "Population Growth and Mortality in British India: Part II The Demographic Revolution", *The Indian Economic and Social History Review*, 27 1 (1990).
cccxxviii B.L. Raina, *Population Policy*, (Delhi: B.R. Publishing Corporation, 1988), 3.
cccxxix Quoted in B.L. Raina, *Population Policy*, 3.
cccxxx B.L. Raina, *Population Policy*, 4.
cccxxxi Ibid.
cccxxxii Ibid.
cccxxxiii Ibid, 28.
cccxxxiv Ibid.
cccxxxv Ibid, 30.
cccxxxvi Ibid, 35.
cccxxxvii Ibid, 36.
cccxxxviii Ibid.
cccxxxix Ibid, 36.
cccxl V.M. Dandekar, *The Indian Economy 1947-1992* Volume 2 Population, Poverty and Employment (New Delhi: Sage, 1995), 36.
cccxli Matthew Connelly, "Population Control in India: Prologue to the Emergency Period", *Population and Development Review*, 32 (4) (2006): 642.
cccxlii Ibid.
cccxliii Quoted in Matthew Connelly, "Population Control in India", 643.
cccxliv Matthew Connelly, "Population Control in India", 643.
cccxlv Ibid, 645.
cccxlvi Nicholas J. Demerath, *Birth Control and Foreign Policy* (New York: Harper & Row, 1976), 65.
cccxlvii Ibid, 69.
cccxlviii B.G. Verghese, "Unwanted Numbers III- Loop Control", 8 July 1965, *The Times of India*, 8.
cccxlix Ibid.
cccl "Simple, Efficacious IUCD Bound to Become Most Popular- Nayyar", 13 July 1965, *The Times of India*, 8.
cccli "'Crash' Programme to Popularise IUD", 18 July 1965, *The Times of India*, 5.

ccclii "Success Ratio of 99% Dr. Lippe's Comment", 31 May 1966, *The Times of India*, 5.
cccliii Ibid.
cccliv Ibid.
ccclv "Loop Should Be Routine Appliance: Dr. Lippe", 9 June 1966, *The Times of India*, 3.
ccclvi Ibid.
ccclvii "Six Million Loops to be Fitted: Family Planning Targets Set", 28 June 1966, *The Times of India*, 8.
ccclviii "Loop Target Unrealistic, Says Maharashtra", 15 September 1966, *The Times of India*, 3.
ccclix "Women Demand 'Delooping'", 26 September 1966, *The Times of India*, 6.
ccclx "Setback in Loop Insertion Drive in West Bengal", 11 October 1966, *The Times of India*, 8.
ccclxi "IUCD Progress Suffers", 29 December 1966, *The Times of India*, p 8.
ccclxii Ibid.
ccclxiii Ibid.
ccclxiv "U.P. Needs Massive Family Planning Drive", 5 October 1966, *The Times of India*, 8.
ccclxv Ibid.
ccclxvi "Only Fringe of Population Covered in Kashmir: Shortage of Doctors", 17 October 1966, *The Times of India*, 8.
ccclxvii "Family Planning: Mysore Presents Mixed Picture", 10 November 1966, *The Times of India*, 8.
ccclxviii "De-looping on increase", 30 January 1967, *The Times of India*, 4.
ccclxix "The Population Explosion", 6 January 1968, *The Times of India*, 6.
ccclxx "Loop Design to be Changed to Reduce Uneasiness", 27 April 1967, *The Times of India*, 10.
ccclxxi "Closure of Loop Factory Feared", 9 March 1968, *The Times of India*, 11.
ccclxxii "Current Topics: Loop Rejection", 15 May 1969, *The Times of India*, 8.
ccclxxiii "Ten Million Loops?", 15 July 1966, *The Times of India*, 8.
ccclxxiv "Compulsory Sterilisation After Third Child Urged, 21 October 1967, *The Times of India*, 5.
ccclxxv "Government Considering Compulsory Sterilisation Plan", 27 July 1967, *The Times of India*, 11.
ccclxxvi "Uproar over compulsory sterilisation move", 4 August 1967, *The Times of India*, 10.
ccclxxvii "Sterilisation Preferred to Other Methods", 29 February 1968, *The Times of India*, 5.
ccclxxviii "Maharashtra in Forefront: Family Planning", 17 May 1968, *The Times of India*, 7.
ccclxxix "Harijans Forced to Undergo Vasectomy: Leader's Charge", 8 January 1969, *The Times of India*, 15.

ccclxxx Veena Soni, "A Spectacular Family Planning Campaign", 22 August 1971, *The Times of India*, A4.
ccclxxxi "8 Die After Vasectomy", 3 March 1972, *The Times of India*, 9.
ccclxxxii "Questionable Means", 26 January 1973, *The Times of India*, 8.
ccclxxxiii Ibid.
ccclxxxiv "Strike by Milk Project Men: Vasectomy Row", 3 February 1973, *The Times of India*, 5.
ccclxxxv "Probe into Vasectomy", 27 March 1973, *The Times of India*, 9.
ccclxxxvi "Population Policy", 26 April 1976, *The Times of India*, 8.
ccclxxxvii "Low Budget May Hit Family Planning", 19 July 1973, *The Times of India*, 3.
ccclxxxviii "Family Planning Outlay Slashed Further", 21 September 1973, *The Times of India*, 9.
ccclxxxix "Package Plan for Birth Control", 6 April 1974, *The Times of India*, 3.
cccxc "Radical Steps Soon to Cut Birth Rate", 23 January 1976, *The Times of India*, 1.
cccxci "No Progress Likely Sans Birth Control", 25 March 1976, *The Times of India*, 9.
cccxcii "No Consembly, Says Sanjay", 18 November 1976, The Times of India, 1.
cccxciii Davidson R. Gwatkin, "Political Will and Family Planning: The Implications of India's Emergency Experience", *Population and Development Review*, 5 1 (1979): 40.
cccxciv Ibid.
cccxcv Ibid, 41.
cccxcvi Ibid, 44.
cccxcvii Ibid, 45.
cccxcviii Vinod Mehta, *The Sanjay Story*, (Bombay, Jaico, 1978), 128.
cccxcix David C. Engerman, *The Price of Aid*, 318.
cd Ibid, 331.
cdi Ibid, 332.
cdii Mahmood Mamdani, *The Myth of Population Control* (New York, Monthly Review Press, 1972).

Chapter Seven: Actually Existing Socialism

cdiii M.K. Gandhi, "Village Industries", 16 November 1934, *Harijan* in *Cent Percent Swadeshi or the Economics of Village Industries*, Ahmadabad, Navajivan Press, 1938, 21.
cdiv M.K. Gandhi, "A.I.V.I.A. its Meaning and Scope", 7 December 1934, *Harijan*, in *Cent Percent Swadeshi*, 26.
cdv Mohandas Gandhi, 8 January 1942, *Harijan* and *Mahatma Gandhi The Latest Phase* Volume 2 (Ahmadabad; Navajivan, 1958), 614.
cdvi Mohandas Gandhi, 28 July 1946, *Harijan*.

[cdvii] Quoted in Raghabendra Chattopadhyay, *The Idea of Planning in India 1930-1951*, Australian National University 1985, 98.
[cdviii] Letter to Amrit Kaur 29 June 1939 in *Collected Works* Volume 69, p. 384 cited in Raghabendra Chattopadhyay, *The Idea of Planning in India*, 112.
[cdix] *National Planning Committee Series Report of the Sub-Committee Rural and Cottage Industries*, Bombay, Vora & Co, 1948, 262.
[cdx] "Ending Problems of Unemployment: Acharya Bhave's Suggestions", 31 July 1953, *The Times of India*, 8.
[cdxi] "Problem of Unemployment in India: Minister on Solution", 1 August 1952, *The Times of India*, 4.
[cdxii] "Foster Cottage Industries: Mr. M. Desai's Plea", 19 July 1953, *The Times of India*, 4.
[cdxiii] "Solving India's Problem of Unemployment: Mr- Nehru on Vital Role of Cottage Industries", 3 February 1953, *The Times of India*, 5.
[cdxiv] United Nations Educational Scientific and Cultural Organization Research Centre on Social and Economic Development in Southern Asia, *Social Aspects of Small Industries in India* (Delhi, UNESCO, 1962).
[cdxv] "Usefulness of Village Industries", 3 January 1960, *The Times of India*, 4.
[cdxvi] "Need to Revive Village Industries Imperative: Chief Minister's Call at Opening of Exhibition", 18 March 1960, The Times of India, 5
[cdxvii] "Place of Khadi in Our Economy", 20 November 1960, *The Times of India*, 1.
[cdxviii] "Industrialise Rural Areas: Shah's Call to State Governments", 10 February 1961, *The Times of India*, 7.
[cdxix] "Economic Rebirth of Rural Areas: Spread of Small-Scale Industries Called For", 11 February 1961, *The Times of India*, 7.
[cdxx] "Rural Industries: II A New Strategy", 27 July 1963, *The Times of India*, 6.
[cdxxi] "Scrap State Khadi Board and Save Public Money: Opposition MLC's Demand", 9 September 1966, *The Times of India*, 12.
[cdxxii] "Estimates Body Criticises Khadi Commission Scheme", 30 March 1962, *The Times of India*, 5.
[cdxxiii] "Accumulation of Huge Stocks", 14 October 1966, *The Times of India*, 9.
[cdxxiv] "Dismal Record", 10 May 1966, *The Times of India*, 8.
[cdxxv] "Govt. to Reserve 69 Consumer Goods for Small Units PM's Plan Big Blow to Monopolists' Hold", 13 September 1969, The Times of India, 1.
[cdxxvi] International Bank for Reconstruction and Development & International Development Association, *Small Scale Industry in India* Volume 1 The Main Report, 22 May 1972, 21.
[cdxxvii] Ibid.
[cdxxviii] Ibid.
[cdxxix] Quoted in S.R.B. Leadbetter, *The Politics of Textiles* (New Delhi: Sage, 1993), 165.
[cdxxx] Ibid, 178.
[cdxxxi] Ibid, 179.
[cdxxxii] Ibid.

[cdxxxiii] Ibid.
[cdxxxiv] Ibid.
[cdxxxv] Ibid, 181.
[cdxxxvi] Ibid.
[cdxxxvii] Ibid.
[cdxxxviii] Ibid.
[cdxxxix] Ibid, 196.
[cdxl] Ibid, 197.
[cdxli] Ibid, 210.
[cdxlii] Ibid, 213.
[cdxliii] Ibid, 180.
[cdxliv] Ibid, 232.
[cdxlv] Dwijendra Tripathi & Jyothi Jumani, *The Oxford History of Contemporary Indian Business* (New Delhi: Oxford University Press, 2013), 79.
[cdxlvi] Ibid.
[cdxlvii] Ibid.
[cdxlviii] Ibid, 80.
[cdxlix] "Fears of Private Sector Unfounded: Assurance Given to Industry", 17 February 1955, *The Times of India*, 4.
[cdl] "Private Sector Will Never Be Abolished: Mr. Morarji Desai", 24 April 1955, *The Times of India*, 1.
[cdli] "Mr. Deshmukh Says: Private and Public Sector Must Co-exist", 3 July 1955, The Times of India, 9.
[cdlii] "Public and Private Sectors One Organism: Nation's Good is Joint Aim", 18 July 1955, *The Times of India*, 4.
[cdliii] "Nehru's Call to Industrialists for Co-operation: Need to Adjust to Ideal of Socialistic Society", 6 March 1955, *The Times of India*, 5.
[cdliv] "Role of Public and Private Sectors: Mr. Nehru Calls for Co-operation", 1 June 1956, *The Times of India*, 1.
[cdlv] *Report to the President of the International Bank for Reconstruction and Development and the International Development Association Volume VI Manufacturing Industry with Special Reference to Public Sector Enterprise*, 1 October 1965.
[cdlvi] Dwijendra Tripathi & Jyothi Jumani, *The Oxford History of Contemporary Indian Business*, 108.
[cdlvii] "Public Sector Must Have Top Place, Indira Tells INTUC", 19 May 1969, *The Times of India*, 1.
[cdlviii] "Public Sector's Failure: PM Gives Reason", 14 July 1969, *The Times of India*, 9.
[cdlix] "PM Tells Business Not to Snipe at Public Sector", 26 October 1969, *The Times of India*, 1.
[cdlx] "Public Sector Needs to be Geared Up: PM", 14 December 1969, *The Times of India*, 1.
[cdlxi] "Indira Defends Public Sector", 3 May 1970, *The Times of India*, 9.

[cdlxii] Baldev Raj Nayar, *India's Mixed Economy* (Bombay: Popular Prakashan, 1989), 299.
[cdlxiii] Ibid, 301.
[cdlxiv] Ibid, 298.
[cdlxv] Ibid, 302.
[cdlxvi] Quoted in Baldev Raj Nayar, *India's Mixed Economy*, 307.
[cdlxvii] Ibid.
[cdlxviii] Quoted in Baldev Raj Nayar, *India's Mixed Economy*, 308.
[cdlxix] Ibid.
[cdlxx] Ibid, 305.
[cdlxxi] Baldev Raj Nayyar, *The Political Economy of India's Public Sector* (Bombay: Popular Prakashan, 1990), 134.
[cdlxxii] Baldev Raj Nayar, *India's Mixed Economy*, 305.
[cdlxxiii] Ibid, 306.
[cdlxxiv] Dwijendra Tripathi & Jyothi Jumani, *The Oxford History of Contemporary Indian Business*, 110.
[cdlxxv] "Neither Russian Nor U.S. Way Suited to India: Mr. Nehru Clarifies Industrial Policy, Socialised Economy Advocated", 18 December 1954, *The Times of India*, 1.
[cdlxxvi] Baldev Raj Nayyar, *The Political Economy of India's Public Sector*, 128.
[cdlxxvii] Ibid, 129.
[cdlxxviii] Ibid.
[cdlxxix] Ibid, 135.
[cdlxxx] Ibid, 141.
[cdlxxxi] Ibid, 143.
[cdlxxxii] Ibid, 197.
[cdlxxxiii] Ibid.
[cdlxxxiv] Ibid, 174.
[cdlxxxv] Quoted in Baldev Raj Nayyar, *The Political Economy of India's Public Sector*, 171
[cdlxxxvi] Ibid, 172.
[cdlxxxvii] Ibid.
[cdlxxxviii] "Public Sector Must Go", 19 April 1977, *The Times of India*, 7.
[cdlxxxix] "Janata For Public Sector: Shekhar", 4 May 1977, *The Times of India*, 9.
[cdxc] "Government May Intervene If Units Are Mismanaged", 13 December 1977, *The Times of India*, 16.
[cdxci] "No Shift Away From Public Sector: Patel", 3 May 1977, *The Times of India*, 9.
[cdxcii] "Show Results Or Go, PM Tells Govt. Sector Heads", 23 March 1979, The Times of India, 8.
[cdxciii] "Improve Public Sector, PM Asks Colleagues", 24 September 1979, *The Times of India*, 4.
[cdxciv] Swaminathan S. Aiyar, "Enlarged Small Sector List is Deceptive", 20 February 1978, *The Times of India*, 1.

Chapter Eight: Indian Exports

[cdxcv] B.R. Shenoy, *The Foreign Exchange Situation* (Bombay: Forum of Free Enterprise, 1958).
[cdxcvi] Pedro Machado, "Awash in a Sea of Cloth: Gujarat, Africa, and the Western Indian Ocean", in *The Spinning World*, eds. Giorgio Riello & Prasannan Parthasarthi (Oxford: Oxford University Press, 2009), 165.
[cdxcvii] Ibid, 166.
[cdxcviii] Ibid.
[cdxcix] Ibid, 167.
[d] Ibid, 172.
[di] Ibid.
[dii] Ibid, 173.
[diii] Ibid.
[div] Ibid, 174.
[dv] Pedro Machado, *Ocean of Trade* (Cambridge: Cambridge University Press, 2014) 33.
[dvi] Ibid, 48.
[dvii] Stephen Frederic Dale, *Indian merchants and Eurasian Trade, 1600-1750* (Cambridge: Cambridge University Press, 1994), 24.
[dviii] Ibid, 76.
[dix] Scott C. Levy, *Caravans* (Gurgaon: Portfolio, 2015), 54.
[dx] Stephen Frederic Dale, *Indian merchants and Eurasian Trade*, 26.
[dxi] Scott C. Levy, *Caravans*, 98.
[dxii] Beverly Lemire, "Revising the Historical Narrative: India, Europe and the Cotton Trade, c. 1300-1800, in *The Spinning World*, 212.
[dxiii] Ibid, 213.
[dxiv] Ibid, 215.
[dxv] Ibid, 217.
[dxvi] Ibid, 218.
[dxvii] James Orchard Halliwell *(ed.), Ancient Inventories of Furniture, Pictures, Tapestry, Plate, etc.*
Illustrative of the Domestic Manners of the English in the Sixteenth and Seventeenth Centuries...
(London, 1858), 78 cited in Beverly Lemire, "Revising the Historical Narrative", 219.
[dxviii] Daniel Defoe, *Weekly Review,* 31 January 1708, quoted in Lemire, *Fashion's Favourite,* 16 cited in Beverly Lemire, "Revising the Historical Narrative", 221.
[dxix] Andre Morellet, *Reflexionss ur lesa vantagesd e la fibref abrication et de l'usaged est oilesp eintes*

en France;p our servir de reponsea ux diversm emoiresd es ... (Geneva, 1758), 42-3 cited in Giorgio Riello, "The Globalization of Cotton Textiles: Indian Cottons, Europe and the Atlantic World" in *The Spinning World*, 267.

[dxx] Giorgio Riello, "The Globalization of Cotton Textiles", 269.

[dxxi] Ibid, 280.

[dxxii] Ibid.

[dxxiii] Ibid.

[dxxiv] Statistics and government policies for the period are drawn from Jagdish N. Bhagwati & Padma Desai, *India: Planning for Industrialization*, (Bombay: Oxford University Press, 1970), Chapters 18 & 19.

[dxxv] Dhirubhai Ambani's adept handling of government import entitlement schemes is drawn from Hamish McDonald, *The Polyester Prince* (Sydney, Allen & Unwin, 1998).

[dxxvi] Vijay Joshi & I.M.D. Little, *India: Macroeconomics and Political Economy, 1964-1991* (Washington D.C.: World Bank, 1994), 83.

[dxxvii] Myron Weiner, "International Migration and Development: Indians in the Persian Gulf" in Ed. Prakash C. Jain, *Indian Diaspora in West Asia: A Reader* (New Delhi: Manohar, 2007), 129.

[dxxviii] Ibid.

[dxxix] Ibid.

[dxxx] Ibid.

[dxxxi] Deepak Nayyar, "International Labour Migration From India: A Macroeconomic Analysis" in Ed. Rashid Amjad, *To The Gulf and Back*, (New Delhi: United Nations Development Programme, International Labour Organisation, Asian Employment Programme, 1989), 96.

[dxxxii] Ibid, 123.

[dxxxiii] I.S. Gulati & Ashoka Mody, *Remittances of Indian Migrants to the Middle East: An Assessment With Special Reference to Migrants from Kerala State* (Kerala, Centre For Development Studies, 1983), 23.

[dxxxiv] Ibid, 22.

[dxxxv] Ibid, 27.

[dxxxvi] Bombay Chamber of Commerce and Industry, *Inward Remittances: Kerala-A Survey* (Bombay: Commerce Research Bureau, 1978).

[dxxxvii] Ibid.

[dxxxviii] Ibid.

Chapter Nine: The Bombay Club

[dxxxix] Dwijendra Tripathi, *The Oxford History of Indian Business*, 175.

[dxl] Ibid, 179.

[dxli] Ibid, 180.

[dxlii] Ibid, 181.

[dxliii] Ibid.

[dxliv] Ibid, 182.
[dxlv] Ibid, 184.
[dxlvi] Ibid, 187
[dxlvii] Ibid.
[dxlviii] "Suggestions for Rooting Out Evil", 20 February 1958, *The Times of India*, 1.
[dxlix] "Move to Check Monopolies", 23 August 1958, *The Times of India*, 9.
[dl] "No Monopoly Concerns", 31 August 1958, *The Times of India*, 10.
[dli] "Need to Curb Activities of Monopolistic Concerns", 29 November 1958, *The Times of India*, 8.
[dlii] "Distribution of Increase in National Income", 23 August 1960, *The Times of India*, 1.
[dliii] H.K. Paranjape, *"Socialist India" Versus Big Business* (Pune: Manak Paranjape, 2000), 33.
[dliv] "Both Congress and Opposition MPs Attack 'Birla Empire'", 30 May 1967, *The Times of India*, 9.
[dlv] "Mixed Reception for Monopolies Bill in Lok Sabha", 11 December 1969, *The Times of India*, 1.
[dlvi] "Rs. 1.64 Crore Goes Down Drain as Sarkar Panel is Scrapped", 19 April 1979, *The Times of India*, 15.
[dlvii] The Bajajes' experience with the Monopolies Commission is drawn from H.K. Paranjape, *"Socialist India" Versus Big Business*.
[dlviii] Dhirubhai Ambani's adept handling of the Indian financial markets is drawn from Hamish McDonald, *The Polyester Prince* (Sydney, Allen & Unwin, 1998).

Chapter Ten: The World Has Changed

[dlix] Quoted in Vinay Sitapati, *Half Lion: How P.V. Narasimha Rao Transformed India*, (Gurgaon: Penguin, 2016), 53.
[dlx] C.P. Bhambhri, *The Janata Party: A Profile* (New Delhi, National, 1980), 61.
[dlxi] Ibid, 64.
[dlxii] Ibid.
[dlxiii] Ibid, 65.
[dlxiv] Ibid.
[dlxv] Sanjay Ruparelia, *Divide We Govern: Coalition Politics in Modern India* (London, Hurst & Company, 2015), 78.
[dlxvi] Ibid, 75.
[dlxvii] Ibid.
[dlxviii] "Link with Party to be Reviewed: Charan Lashes Out at Janata Govt. Policies", 24 December 1978, *The Times of India*, 1.
[dlxix] "Kisans Present Demands", 24 December 1978, The Times of India, 9.
[dlxx] "Scrap Taxes on Farm Inputs, Demand CMs.", 7 February 1979, *The Times of India*, 5.

dlxxi "Charan Toasted by MPs While the Elite is Stunned", 1 March 1979, *The Times of India*, 1.
dlxxii "Budget to Fleece Urban Taxpayer: Relief to Farmers, Rural Industries", 1 March 1979, *The Times of India*, 1.
dlxxiii "Only Thing Cheap Now is Life: Indira" 11 December 1979, *The Times of India*, 15.
dlxxiv "Battle Royal for Mandate Begins", 15 December 1979, *The Times of India*, 9.
dlxxv "Priority for Law & Order Says Indira", 16 December 1979, *The Times of India*, 9.
dlxxvi "Nation Made Bankrupt, Alleges Indira", 18 December 1979, *The Times of India*, 1.
dlxxvii "Janata Persecuted Her, Says Indira", 19 December 1979, *The Times of India*, 14.
dlxxviii "Elect Govt. That Works: Indira", 22 December 1979, *The Times of India*, 1.
dlxxix "Crude Non-Availability Hits Refineries", 3 January 1980, The Times of India, 13.
dlxxx "Violence Rocks Assam Town: 6 Killed", 19 January 1980, *The Times of India*, 1.
dlxxxi "Refineries: Heavy Loss Due to Stir", 13 April 1980, *The Times of India*, 1.
dlxxxii "Army Now Controls All Oil Fields", 11 November 1980, *The Times of India*, 4.
dlxxxiii "Assam Agitation Costs Rs. 1000 cr.in Exchange Alone", 3 January 1981, *The Times of India*, 1.
dlxxxiv "Bleak Prospect", 6 May 1980, *The Times of India*, 6.
dlxxxv "Reagan Proposes Foreign Aid Cut", 20 February 1981, *The Times of India*, 1.
dlxxxvi "Major Shift in US Aid Policy May Hit India", 21 March 1981, *The Times of India*, 1.
dlxxxvii Ibid.
dlxxxviii "Way Cleared for $4-b IMF Loan", 6 August 1981, *The Times of India*, 1.
dlxxxix "Venkataraman Hopeful of Getting IMF Loan: Foreign News", 2 October 1981, *The Times of India*, 11.
dxc "Talks Begin on IMF Loan of $4 billion" 31 July 1981, *The Times of India*, 1.
dxci "Govt. Prefers Borrowing to Heavy Taxation", 8 May 1981, *The Times of India*, 13.
dxcii "India Not to Seek ADB's Soft Loan", 30 April 1982, *The Times of India*, 1.
dxciii "India Seeks EIB Aid for Projects", 3 July 1982, *The Times of India*, 13.
dxciv "Eurobonds Mooted for India", 6 December 1982, *The Times of India*, 1.
dxcv "'Opportunities in India Good'", 3 March 1983, *The Times of India*, 6.
dxcvi "'India and China Should Borrow in Open Market'", 26 September 1984, *The Times of India*, 9.
dxcvii "India Can Borrow Large Funds", 14 January 1984, *The Times of India*, 8.

[dxcviii] Vijay Joshi & I.M.D. Little, *India: Macroeconomics and Political Economy 1964-1991* (Washingron D.C: World Bank, 1994), 157.
[dxcix] "Leading Economists Hail Budget", 23 June 1980, *The Times of India*, 16.
[dc] Vijay Joshi & I.M.D. Little, *India: Macroeconomics and Political* Economy, 164.
[dci] "Oil Struck Off Bombay High", 30 May 1980, *The Times of India*, 1.
[dcii] "Oil Struck Off Bombay High", 5 September 1981, *The Times of India*, 1.
[dciii] "Oil Struck Off Bombay High", 15 February 1983, *The Times of India*, 9.
[dciv] "Record Output By ONGC", 2 April 1983, *The Times of India*, 7.
[dcv] Vijay Joshi & I.M.D. Little, *India: Macroeconomics and Political* Economy, 156.
[dcvi] Ibid.
[dcvii] Ibid.
[dcviii] "India's Growth Rate Far Ahead: Pranab", 28 October 1984, *The Times of India*, 5.
[dcix] "India's Good Credit Standing", 11 November 1984, *The Times of India*, 1.
[dcx] "A Brush with Indian Reality: Not by Pragmatism and High-Tech", 7 May 1985, *The Times of India*, 8.
[dcxi] "AICC Pledges Itself to Socialism", 6 May 1985, *The Times of India*, 1.
[dcxii] "Sathe Lambasts Public Units", 22 October 1985, *The Times of India*, 12.
[dcxiii] "Car Manufacturers Told to Cut Costs", 6 January 1986, *The Times of India*, 9.
[dcxiv] "PM Disowns Sathe's Views on Public Sector Units", 23 August 1986, *The Times of India*, 1.
[dcxv] "Stagnating Steel Industry: SAIL Makes a New Start", 3 December 1985, *The Times of India*, 8.
[dcxvi] "Handsome Pay Hike for Central Govt. Staff", 1 July 1986, *The Times of India*, 1.
[dcxvii] "India's Defence Spending in '87-88", 28 January 1987, *The Times of India*, 8.
[dcxviii] "PM Justifies Defence Spending", 14 March 1987, *The Times of India*, 1.
[dcxix] "Food Subsidy Spiralling", 21 December 1987, *The Times of India*, 17.
[dcxx] "Need to Tap Edible Oil Resources", 22 February 1987, *The Times of India*, 11.
[dcxxi] "Drastic Cut in Edible Oil Imports Feasible: City Notes", 13 October 1988, *The Times of India*, 11.
[dcxxii] "Wide Variation in Fertiliser Use", 11 March 1986, *The Times of India*, 10.
[dcxxiii] Ibid.
[dcxxiv] "Fertiliser Crisis May End Soon", 15 December 1986, *The Times of India*, 23.
[dcxxv] "Concern Over Growing Fertiliser Stocks", 5 July 1988, *The Times of India*, 10.
[dcxxvi] "Fertiliser Consumption, Production Increase", 3 August 1988, *The Times of India*, 20.
[dcxxvii] "PM Tries to Win Over Farmers", 16 February 1988, *The Times of India*, 1.

dcxxviii "Without Direction", 1 March 1987, *The Times of India*, 1.
dcxxix "Rs. 2,050 crores to fight poverty", 1 March 1987, *The Times of India*, 15.
dcxxx "Rajiv Calls for Fiscal Discipline", 12 January 1988, *The Times of India*, 9.
dcxxxi "Tiwari Presents a Populist Budget", 1 March 1988, *The Times of India*, 1
dcxxxii "Schemes to Boost Rural Economy", 1 March 1988, *The Times of India*, 9.
dcxxxiii "Efforts on to Uplift Farmers", 12 March 1988, *The Times of India*, 9.
dcxxxiv "Rain Will Wash Off Deficit: Govt.", 2 March 1988, *The Times of India*, 1.
dcxxxv "Incipient Debt Crisis", 13 May 1988, *The Times of India*, 8.
dcxxxvi Exchange Drain Points to Debt Trap", 20 July 1988, *The Times of India*, 1.
dcxxxvii "Bold for the Season", 1 March 1989, *The Times of India*, 14.
dcxxxviii "Desperate Govt. Seeks IMF Loan", 19 March 1989, *The Times of India*, 1.
dcxxxix "Chavan Evasive on IMF Loan", 13 April 1989, *The Times of India*, 6.
dcxl "Chill from Paris", 22 June 1989, *The Times of India*, 14.
dcxli "AICC Pledges itself to Socialism", 6 May 1985, *The Times of India*, 1.
dcxlii "BJP Ultimatum on Farmers' Loans", 20 March 1989, *The Times of India*, 8.
dcxliii "JD to Launch Mass Movement", 25 May 1989, *The Times of India*, 10.
dcxliv "Waiver of Rural Loans: Coping with Burden Without Tears", 30 January 1990, *The Times of India*, 14.
dcxlv "Budgetary Capers: The Constraints of Politics", 23 March 1990, *The Times of India*, 10.
dcxlvi "Steep Hike in Petrol Prices", 21 March, *The Times of India*, 1.
dcxlvii "Trade Deficit Up by 25%", 19 April 1989, *The Times of India*, 14.
dcxlviii "Winter of Discontent", 14 June 1991, *The Times of India*, 14.
dcxlix Ibid.
dcl "Bonanza From Oil", 2 January 1989, The Times of India, 12.
dcli "Gulf Situation Will Hit India's Oil Import Bill", 7 August 1990, *The Times of India*, 1990.
dclii "Credit Agencies Assess India" 6 May 1990, *The Times of India*, 10.
dcliii "Moody's Lowers India's Rating", 9 October 1990, *The Times of India*, 17.
dcliv "RBI Gold Holding Revaluation to Fortify Reserves", 28 October 1990, *The Times of India*, 14.
dclv "India to Get IMF Relief Fund", 26 September 1990, *The Times of India*, 14.
dclvi "IMF Conditionality: Development is the Gut Issue", 18 December 1990, *The Times of India*, 12.
dclvii "IMF Loan a Major Success for India", 24 January 1991, *The Times of India*, 16.
dclviii "V.P. Govt. Decided on Refuelling", 30 January 1991, *The Times of India*, 15.
dclix "Mystery Over U.S. Planes' Cargo", 3 February 1991, *The Times of India*, 3.
dclx "Refuelling Not Taking Place Says Shekhar", 19 February 1991, *The Times of India*, 1
dclxi Shankkar Aiyar, *Accidental India: A History of the Nation's Passage Through Crisis and Change*, (New Delhi: Aleph, 2012), 26.
dclxii Ibid.

[dclxiii] Sanjaya Baru, *1991: How P.V. Narasimha Rao Made History*, (New Delhi: Aleph, 2016), 78.
[dclxiv] Ibid, 79.
[dclxv] Vinay Sitapati, *Half Lion*, 61.
[dclxvi] Ibid, 58.
[dclxvii] Ibid, 59.
[dclxviii] Ibid.
[dclxix] Shankkar Aiyar, *Accidental India*, 32.
[dclxx] Sanjaya Baru, *1991*, 90.
[dclxxi] Ibid, 63.
[dclxxii] Ibid.
[dclxxiii] Ibid, 61.
[dclxxiv] Ibid, 62.
[dclxxv] Ibid, 64.
[dclxxvi] "No default on repayment: Manmohan" 24 June 1991, *The Times of India*, 13.

INDEX

Advaita, 435
Agarwal, Shriman Narayan, 114-116, 383, 447-448
Ambani, Dhirubhai, 462-464, 482, 537, 560,
Anthikad, Sathyan 469
All India Village Industries Association, 47, 101, 376-377
Apna Haath Jagannath, 384-393
Arora, Gopi, 588, 595-596
Bajaj scooters, 514-520, 538-539
Banerjea, Surendranath, 36, 40-41, 86, 88
Bell, Bernard, 271-279, 411
Benegal, Shyam, 207, 521, 535-536
Bhave, Vinoba, 220-225, 239, 307, 383
Black, Eugene, 161-162
Birla, Braj Mohan, 129, 489, 494, 531, 535.
Birla, Ghanshyamdas, 78, 94-98, 106, 129, 315, 487-494, 531, 535
Bose, Subhas, 13-14, 72-73, 79, 98-101, 245, 318, 370-371, 373, 379
Bowles, Chester, 187-191, 237, 268-269
Bukharin, Nikolai Ivanovich, 77
Community Development Programme 132, 191-202, 232-233, 236-240, 340, 342, 368, 607
Dalal, Sir Ardeshir, 116-117
Dandavate, Madhu, 3, 590-592
Desai, Morarji, 155, 161-163, 225, 255, 264, 276, 279-290, 298-310, 372, 375, 384, 397, 410, 439-440, 463, 509, 558-565
Deshmukh, Sir Chintaman, 131, 134-136, 146, 151, 154-155, 288, 410
Dharia, Mohan, 264, 282-284, 308, 464
Do Bigha Zameen, 207-216, 238-240
Doshi, Walchand Hirachand, 494-496, 500
Dutt, Romesh, 12, 27- 34, 36, 38, 73-75, 88, 91
Eisenhower, Dwight, 159-161, 166
Elphinstone College, Bombay, 10, 11, 16, 19-20, 23
Federation of Indian Chambers of Commerce and Industry, 78, 95, 106, 121, 124, 127, 129-130, 487, 494
Friedman, Milton, 150-154, 174, 438, 606
Frisch, Ragnar, 137-138, 146
Gandhi, Feroze, 156-157, 174, 277
Gandhi, Indira, 2, 8-9, 48, 228, 243-244, 262, 264, 276-290, 298-310, 316, 362, 368, 371, 375, 400, 423-425, 509, 521, 538, 540, 541, 543, 560, 565-575, 589, 598-599
Gandhi, Mohandas, 7, 9-10, 13, 41-48, 59, 73-74, 80, 95, 98, 104, 176, 220, 224, 315, 324, 329-331, 373, 376-378, 401, 436-437, 458, 484, 603-604
Gandhi, Rajiv, 2-3, 541-543, 575-600
Gandhi, Sanjay, 310-314, 316, 321, 362-366, 371-372, 375, 541, 565
Green, Graeme, 6
Hazari, Rabindra Kishen, 488, 505-509
Holland, Sir Thomas, 89
Ilin, Mikhail, 66, 438.

Industries (Development and Regulation) Act 1951, 124, 128-131, 487, 538
International Monetary Fund, 2, 161-162, 171, 269, 542, 569-575, 586-588, 592-602, 609
Jambhakar, Bal Gangadhar Shastri, 14, 19
Johnson, Lyndon, 269, 277-278
Kalyug, 521-530, 535-536
Kamaraj, Kumaraswami, 264, 281-282, 285,
Kennedy, John, 165-167, 367
Komer, Robert, 269-271
Kripalani, Jivatrao, 71, 138-139, 173, 202-203, 558
Krishnamachari, T.T., 156-160, 175, 234, 256, 269
Krishnamachari, Sir V.T., 131, 155-156, 339
Kumaramangalam, S. Mohan, 303, 361, 424-427
Kumarappa, Joseph, 48, 74, 101-103, 185, 203, 373, 376-379, 435-436
Lewis, John P., 265-268, 270, 280
Lippes, Dr. Jack, 346-350
Little, Ian, 418-422, 437
Mahajan, Bhau, 14, 17
Mahalanobis, Prasanta, 4-5, 103-104, 125, 135-137, 142-146, 150-158, 164, 174-175, 177, 240, 256, 374, 382, 437, 440, 444, 488, 504, 605
Malaviya, Keshav Dev, 262-263, 281-282, 427
Maruti car, 310-311, 591
Marx, Karl, 59, 74, 75, 77, 176, 536
Mathai, John, 103, 106, 135
Mayer, Albert, 182-188, 190, 192, 237
Mehta, Asoka, 256, 264-265, 269, 277, 280, 513
Masani, Minocher, 7, 13, 58, 173, 226-228, 241, 252-257, 302, 438, 513, 606
Millikan, Max, 165-166
Mishra, Shyam Nandan, 156, 261-263, 282, 284
Modi, Narendra, 610-611
Motichand, Laxmichand, 452, 458
Nanda, Gulzarilal, 131, 156, 172, 242, 262, 263, 380
Naoroji, Dadabhai, 10-12, 19-24, 28, 31-32, 38, 73-75, 91
Narasimha Rao, P.V, 4, 542, 595-598, 601-602
Narayan, Jayaprakash, 10, 14, 58-69, 75, 78, 224, 244, 252, 305-310, 314, 437-438, 558, 589
National Planning Committee, 79, 100-104, 117, 120-121, 135, 331-332, 373, 379-384, 435, 445-448
Nayyar, Dr. Sushila, 336-337, 345-347, 370
Nehru, Braj Kumar, 157, 161-163, 167
Nehru, Jawaharlal, 2-10, 13-14, 48-60, 68-74, 79, 91, 98-106, 117, 123-177, 183, 202, 242, 249, 253, 262, 315, 339, 368, 373, 379-381, 384, 398, 410, 428, 435-438, 441, 488, 504, 561, 585, 587, 598, 603-605
Neogy, Kshitish Chandra, 118, 131155-156, 174
Nijalingappa, S., 282-285, 288-290, 423
Pant, Pitambar, 164
Patel, Jabbar, 544
Patel, Vallabhbhai, 71, 123-127, 138-139, 244-245

The Licence Raj

Planning Commission, 4, 7, 124-125, 127, 130-146, 154-158, 163-164, 167, 217-219, 223, 242, 254-256, 264-265, 284, 303, 335, 343, 347-350, 399, 403-404, 412, 414, 481, 488, 489, 504-508, 585, 611.
Pliny The Elder, 445, 448, 457
Pope, Carl, 350-357, 366-367, 607
Pratidwandi, 290-298
Rajagopalachari, Chakravarti, 7, 71, 227, 241, 244-251, 257, 302, 314-315, 401, 438, 606
Ranade, Mahadev, 12, 23-28, 34, 45, 75, 78, 86, 603, 611
Ray, Satyajit, 207, 290
Rostow, Walt, 164-166, 277
Roy, Bimal, 206-207, 216, 240
Roy, Manabendra Nath, 109
Salter, Sir Arthur, 92
Sanger, Margaret, 323, 326, 328-330
Sarvodaya Samaj, 221, 224, 307-308, 314
Sathe, Vasant, 564, 577-579
Schuster, Sir George, 78, 92
Segal, Mohan, 384
Shah, K.T., 101, 104, 118, 373, 436
Shekhar, Chandra, 3, 264, 283-284, 308, 376, 439, 509, 542, 559-561, 595
Shenoy, Bellikoth Raghunath, 146, 148-149, 174, 241, 256-261, 442-443, 606
Shroff, Ardeshir, 70-71, 100, 104, 106, 128
Singh, Charan 556
Singh, Karan, Union Health Minister, 361-362, 370
Singh, Manmohan, 596-598, 602
Singh, Vishwanath Pratap 511
Sinhasan, 544-557
Shastri, Lal Bahadur, 7, 156, 174, 177, 233, 242, 243, 264, 266, 268, 276
Shri Ram, Lala, 100, 106, 128, 497-498
Subramaniam, Chidambaram, 155, 174, 233-236, 290
Swadeshi movement, 10, 12-13, 34-43, 121, 486
Tandon, Purushottamdas, 138-139, 173
Tarkhadkar, Bhaskar, 14-16
Tarkunde, Vithal, 110
Tata, Jamsetji, 105, 428-429, 490, 492
Tata, Jehangir Ratanji Dadabhoy, 79, 105, 492-494, 521
The Quiet American, 6
Thakurdas, Purushottamdas, 95, 100, 102, 104, 106
Thorner, Daniel, 180-181, 229
Trone, Solomon 126-127
Varavelpu, 468-485
Vasudevan, Uma, 311-313
Vishwanath, Ramkrishna, 14, 17, 484
Visvesvaraya, Sir Mokshagundam, 78, 92-94, 97, 100-103, 379, 500
World Bank, 8, 126, 161-162, 166, 167, 177, 265, 269, 271, 277-280, 320, 411, 569-570, 592

www.ingramcontent.com/pod-product-compliance
Lightning Source LLC
Chambersburg PA
CBHW021332230426
43666CB00006B/271